THE BLACKWELL COMPANION TO MAJOR CLASSICAL SOCIAL THEORISTS

BLACKWELL COMPANIONS TO SOCIOLOGY

The *Blackwell Companions to Sociology* provide introductions to emerging topics and theoretical orientations in sociology as well as presenting the scope and quality of the discipline as it is currently configured. Essays in the Companions tackle broad themes or central puzzles within the field and are authored by key scholars who have spent considerable time in research and reflection on the questions and controversies that have activated interest in their area. This authoritative series will interest those studying sociology at advanced undergraduate or graduate level as well as scholars in the social sciences and informed readers in applied disciplines.

The Blackwell Companion to Major Classical Social Theorists

Edited by

George Ritzer

Blackwell Publishing

© 2000, 2003 by Blackwell Publishing Ltd
except for editorial material and organization © 2000, 2003 by George Ritzer

350 Main Street, Malden, MA 02148-5018, USA
108 Cowley Road, Oxford OX4 1JF, UK
550 Swanston Street, Carlton South, Melbourne, Victoria 3053, Australia
Kurfürstendamm 57, 10707 Berlin, Germany

First published 2003 by Blackwell Publishing Ltd

This edition and *The Blackwell Companion to Major Contemporary Social Theorists*
originally published together as *The Blackwell Companion to Major Social Theorists* in 2000
by Blackwell Publishing Ltd

Library of Congress Cataloging-in-Publication Data

ISBN 1-4051-0594-1 (paperback)

A catalogue record for this title is available from the British Library.

Set in 10.5 on 12 pt Sabon
by Kolam Information Services Pvt Ltd, Pondicherry, India
Printed and bound in the United Kingdom
by MPG Books Ltd, Bodmin, Cornwall

For further information on
Blackwell Publishing, visit our website:
http://www.blackwellpublishing.com

Contents

Preface

The publication of this two-volume paperback edition is a welcome event. While many social scientists and libraries added the original hardback, single-volume edition of *The Blackwell Companion to Major Social Theorists* to their collections, its price put it beyond the reach of all but the most well-heeled students. Thus instructors were unable, by and large, to assign it to their classes. The publication of these two volumes in paperback solves that problem by making the books much more affordable. Furthermore, dividing the original volume more-or-less in half allows those who teach classical theory to assign volume I, *The Blackwell Companion to Major Classical Social Theorists*, and those who teach contemporary theory to use volume II, *The Blackwell Companion to Major Contemporary Social Theorists*. In addition, for those who teach general courses in theory, both volumes can be assigned. The books can be used as basic texts, or as supplements to more conventional textbooks in social and sociological theory. Since the essays are original contributions authored by experts on particular theorists, the two volumes should also be useful to scholars looking for up-to-date and authoritative overviews of the work of the major social theorists.

Some minor changes have been made to the text, but in the main the essays are the same as those that appeared in the original hardback edition. One major change is that the original introductory essay has been used as the basis for new introductory essays, each directed at the unique concerns of the volume in which it appears. Thus the volume of the classics opens with an essay by Douglas Goodman entitled, "Narratives, *Geistesgeschichtes*, and the History of Social Theory." Goodman's essay outlines five narrative approaches to the history of sociology, making the case for critical and effective histories of social theory that place classical theoretical perspectives in dialogue with present-day theoretical orientations and challenge the ideal of theoretical progress. The volume on contemporary theory begins with an essay by Todd Stillman, "Metatheorizing Contemporary Social Theorists." Stillman catalogues the forces that contribute to intellectual breakthroughs and develops a systematic approach to the intellectual and social factors that have influenced contemporary social theorists.

Overall, these volumes present essays by leading contemporary social theorists on their classical predecessors and contemporary peers. Having written chapters or essays on many of the people covered here, I have a great appreciation for these essays. In fact, I learned a great deal from each of them and I believe that most, if not all, readers will find these essays edifying.

Beyond the contributors, there are a number of other people to thank. I begin with Susan Rabinowitz, who proposed that I undertake this project and was of great help throughout its creation and development. Ken Provencher at Blackwell helped to put the paperback volumes into print. I could not have done these books without the help of Douglas Goodman, who not only wrote the introductory essay to the classical volume but read and commented on all of the essays and helped with the innumerable details involved in bringing this project to fruition. I also need to thank Todd Stillman, who authored the introduction to the contemporary volume and kept track of the revisions. My undergraduate research assistants Zinnia Cho and Jan Geesin also provided valuable research assistance.

George Ritzer

Contributors

Robert J. Antonio is Professor of Sociology at the University of Kansas. He works in classical, critical, and contemporary social theory. Among his publications are: "Nietzsche's Antisociology: Subjectified Culture and the End of History," *American Journal of Sociology*; "The Normative Foundations of Emancipatory Theory: Evolutionary vs. Pragmatic Perspectives," *American Journal of Sociology*; and "Mapping Postmodern Social Theory," in *What Is Social Theory?*

Douglas J. Goodman completed his dissertation, "The Sociology of Freedom," at the University of Maryland at College Park, and is now an assistant professor at the University of Puget Sound, WA. He has published pieces on Lacan, Luhmann, and Habermas, and has written on the sociology of consumption and postmodernism.

Susan Hoecker-Drysdale is Adjunct Professor of Sociology, Department of Sociology and Anthropology, Concordia University, Montreal, Quebec; Visiting Fellow, School of Advanced Study, University of London, 1997–8. Her publications include: *Harriet Martineau: First Woman Sociologist* (1992); "Harriet Martineau (1802–1876): Kritische Sozialforschung: Theorie und Praxis," in *Frauen in der Soziologie: Neun Porträts* (edited by Claudia Honegger and Theresa Wobbe, 1998); "The Enigma of Harriet Martineau's Letters on Science," *Women's Writings: the Elizabethan to Victorian Period* (1995); "Sociologists in the Vineyard: the Careers of Everett Cherrington Hughes and Helen MacGill Hughes," in *Creative Couples in the Sciences* (edited by Helena Pycior et al., 1996); "Women Sociologists in Canada: the Careers of Helen MacGill Hughes, Aileen Dansken Ross and Jean Robertson Burnet," in *Despite the Odds: Essays on Canadian Women and Science* (edited by Marianne G. Ainley, 1990). Her current research and writing focuses on Harriet Martineau, selected women in the historical emergence of sociology, and the history of feminist sociological theory. She is a founding member of the British Martineau Society and the Harriet Martineau Sociological Society.

Robert Alun Jones is Professor of Religious Studies, History, and Sociology at the University of Illinois in Urbana-Champaign. He also has an appointment with the Graduate School of Library and Information Science and is a member of the Campus Honors Faculty. He was the founder and director of the Advanced Information Technologies Laboratory, and is Senior Research Scientist for the Humanities at the National Center for Supercomputing Applications. His research interests include the French philosopher and social theorist Émile Durkheim and his intellectual context, the methodology of the history of ideas, and the scholarly use of electronic documents and networked information systems. He is the author of *Emile Durkheim: an Introduction to Four Major Works* (1986), *The Development of Durkheim's Social Realism* (1999), several edited volumes, and numerous journal articles on Durkheim. He has been editor of *Études durkheimiennes*, and is also responsible for the Durkheim site on the Internet. He is writing a book on the study of primitive religion between 1865 and 1914.

Stephen Kalberg is Associate Professor of Sociology, Boston University. His major publications include *Max Weber's Comparative-Historical Sociology* (1994), *Max Weber's Sociology of Civilizations* (forthcoming), and, as editor, *Weber and Modernity: Key Readings and Commentary* (forthcoming); his translation of Weber's *The Protestant Ethic and the Spirit of Capitalism* was published in 2002. His research interests include classical and contemporary sociological theory, comparative-historical sociology, political sociology, and comparative political cultures, especially German and American.

Charles Lemert teaches sociology at Wesleyan University. He has written many books and articles on various subjects, most recently *Postmodernism Is Not What You Think* and *Social Things*. He is completing *Dark Thoughts*, a study of the troubles race has caused in social thought and culture over the course of the past century.

Victor Lidz was taught by Talcott Parsons at Harvard, and, after graduation in 1962, entered the Department of Social Relations there as a graduate student to continue studies in sociological theory. From 1963 to 1968, he served as Parsons's research assistant. In the 1970s, he taught seminars on new developments in the theory of social action with Parsons at both the University of Chicago and the University of Pennsylvania. Lidz received his doctorate in sociology from Harvard University in 1976. He is presently Acting Director of the Institute for Addictive Disorders, Department of Psychiatry, MCP Hahnemann University in Philadelphia.

Mary Pickering is an associate professor of history at San Jose State University. She received a DEA from the Institut d'Etudes Politiques in 1984 and a PhD from Harvard in 1988. Cambridge University Press published in 1993 the first volume of her major work, *Auguste Comte: an Intellectual Biography.* Thanks to a NEH fellowship, she has almost completed the second volume.

George Ritzer is Professor of Sociology at the University of Maryland, where he has been a Distinguished Scholar-Teacher and won a Teaching Excellence Award. He has chaired the American Sociological Associations's sections on Theoretical Sociology and Organizations and Occupations. George Ritzer has held a Fulbright-Hays Fellowship, has been a Fellow at the Netherlands Institute for Advanced Study and the Swedish Collegium for Advanced Study in the Social Sciences, and has held the UNESCO Chair in Social Theory at the Russian Academy of Sciences. His major areas of interest are sociological theory and metatheory, as well as the application of theory to the sociology of consumption. In the former, his major publications are *Sociology: a Multiple Paradigm Science* (1975/1980), *Toward an Integrated Sociological Paradigm* (1981) and *Metatheorizing in Sociology* (1991). In the latter, he has written *The McDonaldization of Society* (1993, 1996), *Expressing America: a Critique of the Global Credit Card Society* (1995), *The McDonaldization Thesis: Explorations and Extensions* (1998) and *Enchanting a Disenchanted World: Revolutionizing the Means of Consumption* (1999). His work has been translated into many languages: *The McDonaldization of Society* alone has been, or is being, translated into more than a dozen languages. He is currently co-editing the *Handbook of Social Theory* with Barry Smart.

Mary Rogers is Professor of Sociology at the University of West Florida. Her publications include *Barbie Culture* (1999), *Contemporary Feminist Theory: a Text/Reader* (1998), *Multicultural Experiences, Multicultural Theories: a Text/ Reader* (1996), *Novels, Novelists, and Readers: toward a Phenomenological Sociology of Literature* (1993), and *Sociology, Ethnomethodology, and Experience: a Phenomenological Critique* (1983).

Lawrence A. Scaff is Professor of Political Science and Dean of the College of Liberal Arts at Wayne State University, Detroit. He teaches political and social theory, and he is the author of *Fleeing the Iron Cage: Culture, Politics and Modernity in the Thought of Max Weber.* He has published numerous essays in modern social theory, including recent work on Weber, Simmel, the problem of historicism, and issues in cultural sociology. He has also served on the faculty of the University of Arizona, Pennsylvania State University, and as a Fulbright scholar at the University of Freiburg.

Dmitri Shalin is Professor of Sociology at the University of Nevada, Las Vegas, and received his first PhD from the Institute of Sociology, Russian Academy of Science, and the second from Columbia University. He has published extensively in the areas of sociological theory, the history of sociology, and Russian society. He was the editor of special issues of *Symbolic Interaction*, on "Self in Crisis: Identity and the Postmodern Condition" and "Russian Society in Transition."

Jonathan H. Turner is Distinguished Professor of Sociology at the University of California at Riverside. He is the author of twenty-four books and many articles on sociological theory, ethnic relations, institutional systems, stratification dynamics, and evolutionary processes. His most recent research has been on the biology and sociology of human emotions.

Introduction: Narratives, *Geistesgeschichtes*, and the History of Social Theory

Douglas J. Goodman

One of the purposes of this volume is to contribute to the narrative history of social theories. In other words, to tell stories about theories and theorists. This seems harmless and academic, at least until one realizes that neither theories about society nor stories about theories of society are confined to professional academics. Indeed, social change that is not merely reactive requires theories. Pragmatic agents engaged in changing their society cannot avoid thinking about how their society works and how the society affects the way that individuals think. It is but a short step from there to considering how others have thought a society works and how they were affected by their society. Such considerations only become useful when we have developed a story that connects the way that we think about society to the way that others have thought about society. Thus we move naturally from wanting to change society, to developing a social theory, to studying other social theories, to developing narratives about social theories.

This collection contributes to the narrative history of social theories in at least three ways. First, and most obviously, the chapters themselves are narratives about social theorists. They are biographies related to tales of intellectual disputes set within epic social histories. The stories move from the theorists' social and intellectual context to present-day impacts and assessments. Second, the selection of the twelve classical theorists covered in this volume implies a narrative of social theory because this cast of characters was selected to fit if not a specific plot, then at least a *mise-en-scène*. Finally, and perhaps most importantly, this volume provides a source book for constructing not only new theories, but also new narratives of social theory. Retellings and reinterpretations, such as those in this volume, have always been more than a resource for present controversies. They have been an intrinsic part of most of social theory's paradigmatic shifts. Therefore, although any list of theorists covered in a collection such as this one can be read as an official canon, the editor intends that this book be used as "canon fodder" in an open, contestable process of theory construction and reconstruction.

To say, however, that these are narratives, or that they are meant to contribute to narrative reinterpretations is not to say enough, because there are many ways in which the story of social theory can be told and not all of them fit the intention of this collection. In what follows, I will use Richard Rorty's[1] genres of historiography to analyze four types of narrative histories of social theory represented in these chapters. Focusing on one of Rorty's types, I then employ a typology derived from Donald Levine's work to analyze several of the ways in which sociological narratives connect the past to the present in order to suggest progress and continuity. I will close by making the case for the addition of a fifth type of narrative: critical and effective histories (derived from the work of Michel Foucault).

Richard Rorty discusses four genres of historiography and, although he is dealing with narrative histories of philosophy, his typology can be applied to social theory. Let us begin with the genre that Rorty refers to as "most familiar and dubious," *doxography*. A doxography is an old familiar story or the commonsense version of history. In social theory, this would be an approach that enumerates what various authors traditionally called sociologists have had to say about topics traditionally defined as sociological. This type of narrative takes a list of supposedly timeless sociological issues such as order, control, organization, etc., and cites the exemplary contributions made by an equally timeless list of social theorists. It makes the mistake of taking both central sociological issues and exemplary social theorists as natural rather than contestable constructions. Rorty sees this genre as a degenerate form fit only for the most basic pedagogical purposes.

It would be easy in a collection such as this to accept a timeless list of social theorists and simply offer new interpretations of these people and their contributions. While there are certainly a number of such essays here, there are also essays on thinkers who would traditionally not be covered in such a volume: Martineau, Gilman, and Du Bois. The editor made a conscious effort to extend the net and include thinkers who have not heretofore been considered part of the canon. More importantly, the idea that there can be such a timeless list is rejected. All such lists are provisional and it is my expectation that future collections will offer somewhat different rosters. The list of thinkers dealt with in this book tells us much about the state of social theory at the beginning of the twenty-first century (and undoubtedly about the person doing the selecting), but in a decade or two, the list of authors covered will almost certainly be very different.

The idea that there is a timeless list of social theorists can become a straitjacket. At the very least, it quickly becomes dated, because both the social world and social theory are continually changing. For example, a similar book a few decades ago would probably have not included any women. That this collection does indicates both a change in society and in theoretical thinking. While this particular choice – indeed all choices – is open to debate and disagreement, is indisputable is the fact that lists of our centrally important social theorist open to continual change.

Although it may offend the sacred priests of what Robert Alun Jones[2] calls the "Nacirema Tsigoloicos," the work of no theorist is timeless. Marx, Weber, Durkheim, and a few others have been of great importance for a century or more, but the time will come when they, too, will be relegated to the dustbin of history. At some point in the future, the social world will be so different that even Marx, Weber, and Durkheim will prove to be of little relevance in thinking about it. In fact, were this not to be the case, one would be forced to reconsider the whole enterprise of social theory. Changes in both society and social theory are inevitable and necessary. Doxographies obscure this fact.

Similarly, a belief in a timeless list of sociological problems restricts our vision to a horizon defined by a wish to remain still. It obscures the vistas opened up by unpredictable historical movements. For example, the topics of industrialization and modes of production were among the founding problems of modern sociology, but many have argued that the continued focus on them has led to the neglect of important changes in modes of consumption.[3] A recent sociological theory text organized around subjects begins with rationality because it "has been at the foundation of dominant conceptions of modernity."[4] However, even where the topic appears to be abiding, as rationality certainly has, a closer look reveals that its meaning is not. The Kantian concept of reason that structured the debates around rationality at the end of the eighteenth century bears only a genealogical relation to postmodern contestations. The current controversy around rationality has inherited the name and a faint family resemblance, but it is not at all clear that the previous participants – for example, Durkheim and Kant or Weber and Marx – would recognize their progeny. Furthermore, there are certainly a number of theorists, especially those associated with a postmodern approach, who would argue that it is irrationality rather than rationality that characterizes large portions of contemporary society.

The second genre discussed by Rorty is called *rational reconstructions*. This is a presentist project that treats predecessors as contemporaries with whom one can exchange views. However, since the "founders" of sociology often had little to say about the problems we now regard as fundamental, this approach usually involves imagining what they would have said if only they had understood the importance of these issues. For example, Lemert, in his chapter on Charlotte Perkins Gilman, reconstructs some of her writings as an intervention in the debate around essentialism, even though the ambiguity of Lemert's citations from her work suggest that this was an issue that held little interest for her. It is not that Lemert is arguing that Gilman really meant to assert a position on essentialism, but rather that her approach can provide a resource for a move in this current debate in which Lemert is himself involved. Another example would be Hoecker-Drysdale calling Harriet Martineau's analysis an "immanent critique," thereby locating Martineau's method within the debate over the relative ground of normative criticism, although Martineau clearly had no such intent. But, of course, simply because Martineau's naturalistic assumptions did not require a critique that emerged from the system being examined does not mean that her reasoning cannot contribute to our current discussions.

For the purpose of rational reconstructions, it must be assumed that debates as well as concepts are more or less stable. In order to reconstruct the answers of past theorists, we must assume that they would understand today's questions. Furthermore, engaging in a rational reconstruction often means correcting what appear to us now to be their obvious mistakes; for example, reconstructing Durkheim's sacred/profane dichotomy in light of our present anthropological knowledge (see the discussion in chapter 6). This, of course, assumes that we now know better than they do. While this can often be said in the natural sciences, it is not always so obvious in social theory. The primary difference is that in social theory – Rorty makes this same point with regard to philosophy – the people that we assume we know better than are not just predecessors, but include our colleagues. To reconstruct what Marx would say about capitalist classes now that the proletariat revolution looks less than inevitable is to call not just Marx mistaken but also a number of our colleagues who are still waiting for the proletariat to cast off their chains.

The presentism, and assumptions of stable concepts and of knowing better than our predecessors are all serious problems with this approach, but Rorty argues that they are not fatal as long as we are aware of them. These assumptions contribute to a certain necessary reassurance that there is the possibility of progress because the problems we are working on are part of a tradition and not just trivial ephemera. Also, these rational reconstructions provide what disciplinary structures there are in sociology. Without rational reconstructions there would be no neo-Weberians, neo-Marxists, neofunctionalists, or any of the schools of sociology, since they all derive their vitality from reconstructing their received traditions.

There is one final point to be made regarding rational reconstructions, and this has an impact on the cohesiveness of sociological schools. Rational reconstructions do not necessarily converge. Parsons's rational reconstruction of Weber is radically different from Marcuse's.[5] This means that some neo-Weberians may have more in common with neo-Marxists than with other neo-Weberians. Furthermore, since reconstructions are always to some extent fictions, it is not possible to say that one is wrong and it is even difficult to say that one is better than another.

The third genre is *historical reconstructions*. Here, rather than trying to understand what theorists might have said about our present controversies, the goal is to try to understand what they did say in the context of their contemporary controversies. Theoretical pronouncements are situated in their dialogic context and placed in relation to other texts of the period that address similar issues and use comparable rhetorical strategies. Doing a historical reconstruction usually means bracketing later developments and suspending judgments about what we now know better. Although a historical reconstruction is analytically distinct from a rational reconstruction, they are regularly conjoined in practice. The rational reconstruction of what sociologists would have said usually begins with what they did say and involves an interpretation of our present context based upon their reconstructed historical context.

From the historical reconstructor's viewpoint, exemplary theorists may be most valuable where they seem most strange and alien. In other words, they are most useful when they are most difficult to rationally reconstruct. Such extraordinary ideas expose our "essential" questions and "timeless" issues as contingent socio-historical products. Historical reconstructions help us to recognize that there are other conversations than those we think are important today. Rather than assuring us of our progress, the historical reconstruction contributes to understanding our own socio-historical embeddedness.

One of the leading advocates of this approach in social theory has been Robert Alun Jones, author of the chapter on Durkheim in this volume. As he points out, it is a difficult undertaking, since it requires "a considerable breadth of knowledge of economic, political and social as well as intellectual history; a reading knowledge of relevant foreign languages; and at least some understanding of the principles of the philosophy of social science."[6] It is, as Alan Sica notes, "risky for the most able scholars, foolhardy for many others."[7] Even where successful, it can, as Sica points out, be professionally counterproductive. Mary Pickering, for example, argues in her chapter that our understanding of Comte is much too simplistic. However, the revelation of Comte's ambiguous relation to modernity may simply remove him from the canon, thereby devaluing Pickering's cultural capital. This is why a scholar may prefer to do a rational reconstruction such as Jonathan Turner's chapter on Spencer in order to increase the value of his or her intellectual investment.

Jones's chapter on Durkheim demonstrates that historical reconstructions are far from reductionist. Rather than seeing Durkheim's ideas as determined by social forces that are working behind the back of the theorist, Durkheim is presented as involved in debates with his contemporaries and as pursuing specific and concrete projects. Consequently, Jones is able to argue, for example, that it is absurd to read the *Division of Labor* as a challenge to Marx, since it is unlikely that Durkheim would have thought Marx to be a serious antagonist. The question as to whether we should take it as a challenge to Marx despite Durkheim's intent is not raised in this approach.

Kalberg's chapter on Weber demonstrates how important a historical reconstruction can be for understanding the limits of the theorist's concepts. While Weber is often portrayed as a theorist of a universal process of rationalization, Kalberg's historical reconstruction reveals rationalization to be a concept that Weber developed in order to explain the uniqueness of Western culture rather than as a universal drive. Weber's major works analyze specific and complex developments through a historical-comparative approach. Weber never intended his analysis to be applied to world-historical universals.

Finally, we come to the genre that Rorty champions and which he calls *Geistesgeschichte*. Like a rational reconstruction, it involves the idea of progress, but here progress is not simply assumed; instead it is narrated as an explicit part of the story. In addition, it is a narrative of continuity. Our connection to a set of predecessors gives us hope that our project will be continued by our intellectual descendants. It provides the field with a necessary self-assurance and legitimacy without concealing its constructed nature.

A *Geistesgeschichte* works at the level of paradigms and problematics. It gives plausibility to a certain image of social theory rather than a particular solution of a given sociological problem. It defines which projects are sociological and distinguishes them from, for example, social philosophy. A *Geistesgeschichte* would argue for (rather than simply assume) a list of exemplary contributors to this reinterpreted project and it would narrate a story of progress and continuity in that endeavor.

Parsons's *The Structure of Social Action* includes a *Geistesgeschichte*, even though his professed intent was to provide a rational reconstruction. In the second edition of that book, Parsons insisted that it "was intended to be primarily a contribution to systematic social science and not to history, that is the history of social thought."[8] But in order to legitimate his focus on the problem of social action and to be able to refer to economists, philosophers and, at that time, marginal sociologists, Parsons had to construct a *Geistesgeschichte* which became more influential and enduring than his particular theories. Indeed, the selection of classical theorists for this volume is still indebted to Parsons' *Geistesgeschichte*.

In fact, both rational and historical reconstructors rely upon an assumed *Geistesgeschichte* even when they do not find it necessary to construct one themselves. Rational reconstructors do not really want to bother reconstructing and engaging with minor sociologists. Historical reconstructors would like to reconstruct sociologists who are currently relevant or who, they argue, can be. In both cases, there needs to be a narrative that constructs a connection between what was important and what is important. For example, Pickering is most persuasive when she places her historical reconstruction within a *Geistesgeschichte* that connects Comte's complexity to present sociological problems.

A *Geistesgeschichte* is intrinsically related to canon formation. The fight over who fits into the history of a discipline is connected to controversies over the image of the field. It is not just a question of who is discerning enough or original enough to be an exemplary figure, but more importantly, who is sociological enough. For instance, one of Lemert's chapters convincingly argues that Du Bois's ideas are important, but we could still question whether they are social theory. Even though such debates seem to be about the honor of the designation, they are more prescriptive than is usually acknowledged. It is not about who deserves the honor of belonging to a predefined category, but about what the definition of the category should be. First, what criteria should distinguish a social theorist; second, what are the criteria that mark a classic in that field?

Unlike rational reconstructions, *Geistesgeschichtes* must concern themselves with anachronisms. The question of who belongs in the canon cannot be decided merely by present concerns. And unlike historical reconstructions, they cannot stay within the context of the past. *Geistesgeschichtes* must narrate a bridge to the present. Most importantly, this connection between the past and the present cannot be simply assumed. When that occurs, when the *Geistesgeschichte* no longer appears to be controversial, we have degenerated into doxology.

To the list of drawbacks of living in our present age must be added this one advantage: *Geistesgeschichtes* are less likely to degenerate into doxologies. The narratives, the canon and the image of the field seem, in our current condition, to be incorrigibly unstable. Rorty states the invitation that this book intends to offer to its readers. "He or she should be free to create a new canon, as long as they respect the right of others to create alternative canons.... They should be urged to try it, and to see what sort of historical story they can tell when these people are left out and some unfamiliar people are brought in."[9]

A Typology of *Geistesgeschichtes*

Of the narrative forms that Rorty delineates, *Geistesgeschichtes* are those that explicitly construct a story of progress and continuity that connects the past to the present. Its central trope is a specific image of the field and its illocutionary effect is to create a canon. Since so many of the chapters in this collection offer this type of narrative, it may be useful to refine the typology. We don't intend to use this to pigeonhole these essays, since, like all good stories, they use multiple narrative techniques. Rather, we will use the refined typology as "sensitizing concepts" for the analysis of theoretical narratives.[10]

We see in the essays five different ways in which the past is connected to the present in order to suggest progress and continuity: (a) classical; (b) positivist; (c) pluralist; (d) convergent; and (e) contextualist. Donald Levine's perceptive book, *Visions of the Sociological Tradition*, is the source of some of these labels, if not of the precise formulation given them here.[11]

In a classical approach, past theorists are seen as foundational for the discipline and current theoretical approaches are built upon traditions that can rarely be completely superseded. Progress is recognized in the refinement and development of this foundation. A classic has been defined as "a book to be read partly because it is regarded as having been widely read."[12] Put this way, the status of the classic appears circular, but this in no way diminishes its importance. There *is* a circular relation between the present and the past. What is important in the past is a function of our present questions, but our present questions are, to a significant degree, determined by our past. Such, for example, is our relation with Marx. As Antonio's chapter in this volume makes clear, Marx is still a vital resource for our current theoretical problems. But, just as clearly, Marx's relevance for current controversies has as much to do with his prescience as it does with the fact that he helped to delineate what the controversies are; he defined them and brought them to our attention as social theorists. Just as it has been said that all of philosophy is a series of footnotes on Plato, it could be said that social theory, to date, consists of a series of footnotes on Marx.

Continuity and progress is guaranteed by the founding traditions of our field. According to the classical approach, these traditions will be criticized, but they are difficult to entirely supplant, because the criticism usually ends up taking a form that is profoundly influenced by the tradition that is the target of criticism. For example, Marx's theories are sometimes criticized as reflections of the early industrialized capitalist mode of production of his society, and therefore of less relevance to our current mode of production. A moment's reflection will reveal that this criticism is still within the Marxist model. Whatever its intent, this type of criticism does more to perpetuate Marx's ideas by demonstrating their potential for self-criticism than any so-called orthodox appropriation.

With the second type, the positivist approach, past theories are seen as containing dispersed true empirical knowledge mixed in with virtually useless speculation. Progress is seen in the identification, collection, and systematization of this empirical knowledge. The positivist *Geistesgeschichte* tells the story of social theory's progression from a speculative philosophy through a plurality of theoretical approaches and finally entering, or about to enter, its true phase of rigorously empirical investigations. Classical theories represent either speculative philosophy (Comte, Spencer) or one-sided theoretical viewpoints (Durkheim, Simmel, Weber) that have been absorbed and surpassed by a coherent body of scientifically grounded theoretical conceptions. These previous theorists represent a transitional stage on the way to the subordination of ideas to controlled observation.

Merton (see volume II) is often taken as a model for a positivist approach, especially since he began his much cited work on the classics with a quote from Whitehead that seemed to sum up the positivist view. "A science which hesitates to forget its founders is lost."[13] However, Merton interprets this warning somewhat differently than his positivist followers. In the foreword to the second edition of Coser's *Masters of Sociological Thought*, Merton argues that engagement with the classics must include more than simply distilling verifiable hypothesis: "The direct study of masterworks helps us to acquire intellectual taste and style, a sense for the significant problem and for the form of its solution."[14]

It should come as no surprise that Jonathan Turner, who has championed the positivist cause in sociological theory, should present Herbert Spencer through a positivist narrative. Turner argues that we can ignore Spencer's speculation about social Darwinism and his "organismic analogy" and focus on Spencer's use of cross-cultural data and his testable functionalist predictions.

A third type is the pluralist narrative. This approach views the past as a repository of diverse ideas and theoretical standpoints that can contribute to the manifold theories necessary for analyzing a pluralistic society. Here progress is identified with the growth of multiple perspectives, which are necessary for analyzing something as complex and multilayered as society. Social theory is viewed as a collection of paradigms with differing methodological, philosophical, and political assumptions. Often these paradigms are seen as having intimate and necessary relations with other disciplines, such as psychology, literature, philosophy. In this narrative, exemplary theorists are paradigm builders who provide incisive summaries of alternative approaches. What makes their work classic is its inherent plurality and openness to rereadings.

In this collection, Mary Rogers presents Schutz within a pluralist narrative. Schutz is praised for his transdisciplinary theory, which provides a difficult to categorize alternative for such varied subsequent theoretical approaches as queer theory, feminism, multicultural theory, and ethnomethodology. Schutz is seen as enabling a non-reductive dialogue between a European philosophical tradition and an increasingly scientized American sociology. Indeed, one cannot help wondering if Schutz's own plural influences – not only philosophy and sociology, but also law and banking – led to his theory of irreconcilable multiplicities and overlapping but distinct experiential worlds. Neither in his life nor in his theory did these spheres ever converge. At most, Schutz found only bridging concepts to negotiate the overlapping borders.

Simmel is, in many ways, the pluralist *par excellence*. Consequently, it is only from the pluralist approach that his contribution to sociology can be appreciated. As Scaff notes, Simmel never founded a school or movement and never intended to. Instead he contributed daring, impressionistic perspectives. These are practically useless from the classical viewpoint and contain only the faint possibility of providing positivistic hypotheses, but for a pluralist, "it is precisely these alleged deficiencies that have once again made Simmel an engaging presence" (chapter 7).

Convergence is the fourth type of narrative. From this viewpoint, pluralism represents an early stage of partial attempts that we are now able to see as contributing to a coherent totality. Exemplary early theorists are those who identified problems and offered partial solutions that now converge and are surpassed.

Parsons's convergence thesis is a famous example of this. Parsons saw himself as bringing together and developing the views of Durkheim, Pareto, Weber, and Alfred Marshall, among others. Indeed, he argued in the opening chapter of his *The Structure of Social Action*, that one of the main arguments in favor of his own theory was that it could be found in partial and undeveloped form in these previous thinkers.

Shalin's chapter on Mead shows most clearly the importance of the convergence of acknowledged and unacknowledged influences. Mead explicitly engaged the theories of Kant and Hegel in order to show that they were partial solutions that now converged in a new pragmatist social philosophy. Driving this theoretical convergence, as well as driving the convergence between theory and political reform, was the influence of Mead's religious upbringing. Shalin suggests that Mead's social theories were, in many ways, an attempt to transform a failed religious belief into a partial solution that converged with some of the very ideas (e.g. Darwinism) that originally contradicted it.

A fifth narrative type is a contextual approach that sees the history of theory and the status of classics as primarily due to forces that are external to their intellectual content. Social theories are seen as tightly connected to the social context from which they emerge and which they try to describe. Progress and continuity are guaranteed by society – the subject and context of the theories rather than the theories themselves. In many cases, the contextual approach is not a *Geistesgeschichte;* that is, it is not a progressive, self-assuring story that connects what was important in the past to what is important in the present. Instead it functions as an ideology critique, revealing the way in which the cognitive substance of the social theory is subordinate to its political context, whether that political context is a macro one of industrial rationalism[15] or the micro situation of academic reputation of Harvard.[16]

Nevertheless, there are two ways that a contextualist approach can be used within a *Geistesgeschichte*. First, a contextualist analysis can help to explain historical facts that seem to contradict a progressive and self-assuring story. For instance, although Pickering points out the originality of Comte's sociology, which seems to transcend his sociohistorical position, she invokes the "binary logic of his times," and his fragile mental health to explain his views on women. Second, what was important in the past and what is important now can be connected through their relation to an evolving social context. For example, Scaff argues that Simmel is an important representative of *fin de siècle* Vienna. This would seem to make him of merely historical interest, except that Scaff makes the further argument that the type of intellectual whirl in Vienna that was marginal to Western society a hundred years ago has become central to ours. This typology suggests the variety of forms that a *Geistesgeschichte* can take. They all have in common the themes of self-assurance and progress that Rorty argues is necessary. Natural scientists can look to increased control of the natural environment as evidence of progress and be assured that they participate in an endeavor that is going somewhere. Funding agencies can be similarly assured that they are making a good investment. Disciplines that can cure illness, provide energy, and feed people may have little need of legitimating narratives, but Rorty suggests that social theory does need *Geistesgeschichtes*, so that those who devote their lives to such a suspect pursuit maintain their psychological well-being and continue to receive even the slight institutional support that they have now. This is a persuasive argument until we notice that Rorty's own historical studies cannot be located in his typology. *Philosophy and the Mirror of Nature*, for example, could hardly be called a *Geistesgeschichte*. It pursues no theme of progress and self-assurance. Let us then use the phrase that Mitchel Dean[17] borrows from Foucault to describe a fifth genre of narrative – *effective and critical histories* – to put alongside Rorty's doxologies, rational reconstructions, historical reconstructions, and *Geistesgeschichte*.

EFFECTIVE AND CRITICAL HISTORIES

Instead of a self-assuring narrative of progress, an effective and critical history is problematizing. Furthermore, it is pragmatic, using historical analysis to understand the basis for practical transgressive experiments. Its goal is to discover what ideas, dialogues, and practices are still necessary and what can now be seen as merely contingent. For example, Foucault's *History of Sexuality* (discussed in Barry Smart's chapter in volume II), investigated whether the connection between identity and sexuality was still necessary and what new experimental practices involving bodies and pleasure are now possible. We do not find in Foucault the notion that the new experiments represent progress over the old regime. The aim of his historical analysis is to open up novel possibilities, not to establish advancements.

An effective and critical history of sociology is not simply a response to a more pluralist, more postmodern, or even more cynical social context. It is a project that is internal to sociology, "a strategic reformation of the complex relations between sociology and history that are the conditions of existence of sociology as a discipline."[18] In this narrative, the study of exemplary theorists is used to oppose, undermine, or qualify present directions instead of support them. Theorists will find little assurance here since their own contributions will be similarly opposed, undermined, and qualified. Like the *Geistesgeschichte*, an effective and critical history is related to both historical and rational reconstructions. Historical reconstructions are used to challenge our present concerns while rational reconstructions allow historical reconstructions their greatest impact. It is, after all, not a general history, but a history of the present that is being pursued: a history that traces the tricks, ruses, and reversals that have led to what we now consider to be necessary.

This, for example, is what we see in Lemert's chapter on Gilman. Lemert problematizes our relation to social theory by questioning the division between theory and fiction. He positions Gilman's work – both theory and fiction – as practical transgressions meant to shake "the gendered foundations of modern life." And yet we see in Lemert no description of progress in theoretical understanding. Indeed, it is precisely this belief in progress that Lemert rejects in Gilman's thinking.

In his chapter, Lemert does not suggest novel possibilities, but he does praise the imagination that would open up such possibilities, and perhaps that is all that is proper for the author in such a collection. It is certainly all that is proper for the author of an introduction. The real work must be done by the reader.

Notes

1   Richard Rorty (1984) The Historiography of Philosophy: Four Genres. In R. Rorty, J. Schneewind, and Q. Skinner (eds), *Philosophy in History: Essays on the Historiography of Philosophy*. Cambridge: Cambridge University Press, pp. 49–76.

2   Robert Alun Jones (1980) Myth and Symbol among the Nacirema Tsigoloicos: a Fragment. *American Sociologist*, 15, 207–12.

3   For an excellent overview see Don Slater (1997) *Consumer Culture and Modernity*. Cambridge: Polity Press. For an application see George Ritzer (1999) *Enchanting a Disenchanted World: Revolutionizing the Means of Consumption*. Thousand Oaks, CA: Pine Forge Press.

4   Shane O'Neill (1999) Rationality. In F. Ashe, A. Finlayson, M. Lloyd, I. Mackenzie, J. Martin, and S. O'Neill (eds), *Contemporary Social and Political Theory*. Philadelphia: Open University Press.

5   See the essays by Parsons, Marcuse, and others in O. Stammer (ed.) (1971) *Max Weber and Sociology Today*. New York: Harper & Row.

6   Robert Alun Jones (1983) On Merton's "History" and "Systematics" of Sociological Theory. In L. Graham, W. Lepenies, and P. Weingart (eds), *Functions and Uses of Disciplinary Histories*. Dordrecht: D. Reidel, p. 126.

7   Alan Sica (1997) Acclaiming the Reclaimers: the Trials of Writing Sociology's History. In C. Camic (ed.), *Reclaiming the Sociological Classics: the State of Scholarship*. Malden, MA: Blackwell, p. 296.

8   Talcott Parsons (1969) Preface to Second Edition. In *The Structure of Social Action*. New York: Free Press, pp. xv–xvi.

9   Rorty, (1984), p. 67, n. 2.

10   Herbert Blumer (1969) What is Wrong with Social Theory? In H. Blumer, *Symbolic Interaction: Perspective and Method*. Englewood Cliffs, NJ: Prentice Hall, p. 148.

11   Donald Levine (1995) *Visions of the Sociological Tradition*. Chicago: University of Chicago Press.

12   Michael Levin (1973) What Makes a Classic in Political Theory? *Political Science Quarterly*, 88(3), 469.

13   Robert K. Merton (1967) On the History and Systematics of Sociological Theory. In *On Theoretical Sociology*. New York: Free Press, p. 1.

14   Robert K. Merton (1977) Foreword to L. Coser, *Masters of Sociological Thought: Ideas in Historical and Social Context*. New York: Harcourt Brace Jovanovich, p. viii.

15   Bruce Mazlish (1989) *A New Science: the Breakdown of Connections and the Birth of Sociology*. New York: Oxford University Press.

16   Charles Camic (1992) Reputation and Predecessor Selection. *American Sociological Review*, 57, 421–45.

17   Mitchell Dean (1994) *Critical and Effective Histories: Foucault's Methods and Historical Sociology*. New York: Routledge.

18   Ibid., p. 10.

1

Auguste Comte

MARY PICKERING

Love for the principle and Order for the
base; Progress for the goal.
Auguste Comte, Système de politique
positive

In our postmodern world, where doubts about the inevitability of progress and
the value of rationalism have weakened utopian impulses, Auguste Comte
appears at first glance to be a quaint, outmoded figure. The "founder" of
sociology and positivism seems to evoke a faraway era, when the benefits of
social planning and the validity of knowledge went largely unquestioned. Yet as
Robert Scharff (1995, p. 6) has recently suggested, the theories of this important
nineteenth-century French philosopher have perhaps never been so relevant.
Comte foreshadowed many issues that contemporary thinkers are grappling
with today: the basis of truth, the role of politics in modern society, the root of
moral crises, the significance of memory, and the problem of gender, class, and
racial identities. More complex than is commonly assumed, Comte's contribution to social theory bears renewed examination.

THE THEORY

Comte's reputation rests on his dual achievement of establishing a new discipline, sociology, and closely connecting it to a novel philosophical system, which
he called positivism. In the *Cours de philosophie positive*, published in six
volumes between 1830 and 1842, Comte argued that because theory always
precedes practice, the reconstruction of the post-revolutionary world could be

accomplished only by extending the scientific, or "positive," method to the study of politics and society, the last stronghold of theologians and metaphysical philosophers. To adopt the positive method meant tying scientific laws to the observation of concrete facts, especially by avoiding speculations, which were invariably "metaphysical" in nature. In his *Discours sur l'esprit positif* of 1844, Comte further explained that "the positive" designated the real, the useful, the certain, the precise, the relative, and the constructive (as opposed to the "negative") (Comte, 1963, pp. 126–30). Once the positive science of society was established, positivism, the system embracing scientific knowledge, would be unified and complete because all our ideas would be scientific and thus homogeneous. Moreover, the science of society would unite all knowledge because it would focus people's attention on humanity, which was also the object of study of the natural sciences. As a result, everyone would agree on the most essential intellectual and moral principles. Eliminating the anarchy that had ruled since 1789, the new social consensus would become the basis of a stable industrial order.

The science of society was thus the keystone of positivism. Comte asserted that because it would be based solely on the observation of social facts, without reliance on theological and metaphysical dogmas, it would have the certainty and unquestionable authority of the natural sciences. Following Francis Bacon's precept that knowledge is power, Comte assumed that a firm grasp of the scientific laws of society would lead to greater control over this organism. Like other scientific laws, sociological laws would allow one to predict social phenomena and thus formulate suitable social policies. Comte gave the new science of society a specific mission to provide the principles necessary to end the moral, social, and political turmoil caused by the French Revolution of 1789.

To prove that the coming of the positive study of society was inevitable, Comte invented the classification of the sciences. This schema demonstrated that the order in which the sciences were created depended on the simplicity of their phenomena and the distance of these phenomena from man. Astronomy first became a science because it studied the simplest phenomena, those that were farthest from man. The positive method was then extended to disciplines whose subjects were increasingly complex and closer to man: physics, chemistry, and biology, in that order. Each more complex science depended on knowledge provided by the simpler sciences, which had to become positive first. Comte maintained that now that astronomy, physics, chemistry, and biology were positive sciences, it was time for the positive method to be applied to the study of society, which was the most complex science and focused entirely on man. He rejected the arguments of those who sought to reduce the study of society completely to another science, whether it be mathematics (especially statistics), biology, or political economy. To mark the birth of this new independent science, Comte coined a new term for it in 1839: "sociology" (Comte, 1975, volume 2, p. 88).

In keeping with his skepticism regarding metaphysics, he warned sociologists that they could not discover the source or nature of society; they could explain only the way its phenomena were related in space and time. For this reason, sociology comprised two parts, social statics and social dynamics. Both stressed the interconnectedness of the members of the human species in order to counter the egoism of the modern age.

Social statics was the study of the social order. It focused on what kept society together. One crucial aspect of the social order was the family, which taught the importance of love as the basis of moral self-improvement. This love was transferred later to one's family and finally to humanity as a whole. Thus social statics cultivated a person's feelings of solidarity with other members of society. Although his atheism was unorthodox for the early nineteenth century, Comte's views on the sanctity of the family and other moral issues were conventional – in contrast to those of the Saint-Simonians and Fourierists who questioned social institutions.

Giving people a sense of connection with past and future generations of the human species, social dynamics analyzed social development, which Comte represented as continuous, necessary, orderly, and limited. Each social state grew out of the preceding one and generated the next social configuration. The salient feature of this development was that, through exercise, the unique characteristics of the human species – intelligence and sociability – became more dominant within both the individual and society.

Besides delineating the two divisions of sociology, Comte outlined the methods of this new science: observation, comparison, and experimentation. Because every aspect of society had multiple connections, Comte believed the areas of sociological observation were very diverse. Sociologists should study ordinary events, common customs, diverse types of monuments, languages, and other mundane social phenomena. Comte's insights into the significance of everyday life have been verified by recent social and cultural history.

As for experimentation, the second means of scientific investigation, Comte felt its use was problematic in sociology because of the impossibility of isolating any of the circumstances or consequences of a phenomenon's actions. He maintained that like a biologist, a sociologist must study pathological cases, which were forms of indirect experimentation. Because the pathological was simply a variation of the ordinary, examining periods of chaos, such as a revolution, provided clues to normality. The study of social disorder was an important means of gaining insights into the laws of social harmony and history.

Comparison was sociology's third method of scientific investigation. In sociology, there were three types of comparison. One could compare human and animal societies, different existing states of human society (i.e. savage and civilized peoples), or consecutive social states. The latter involved the historical method, which was related to social dynamics and constituted sociology's chief means of scientific investigation. History gave people a sense of social solidarity and continuity, in short a feeling for humanity in the world and their own role in its evolution.

The principal scientific law of sociology was a historical one: the law of three stages. Comte first "discovered" this law in 1822 and revealed its intricacies in his "fundamental opuscule," the *Plan des travaux scientifiques nécessaires pour réorganiser la société* of 1824 (Comte, 1929, volume 1, p. 1). According to this law, each branch of knowledge (e.g. each science) and the mind itself passed through three modes of thinking: the theological, metaphysical, and positive. Such paradigms arose because all aspects of knowledge were interrelated and the mind naturally sought to make all ideas homogeneous.

Each of the three theoretical systems affected politics and society, for in Comte's view all of society represented an organic being in the process of a development influenced by intellectual progress. Intellectual evolution – especially scientific development – was the most advanced form of progress and served as the stimulus to historical change. In an important passage reflecting his idealism, Comte pointed out "that ideas govern and overturn the world, or in other words, that the entire social mechanism rests ultimately on opinions." Like Hegel, he believed that history was the story of the "emancipation of human reason" (Comte, 1975, volume 1, pp. 38, 379). Moreover, as all aspects of society were interrelated, a change in one feature, such as intellectual life, led to changes in other facets of the social organism. Comte wrote, "In effect... all the classes of social phenomena develop simultaneously and under each other's influence" (Comte, 1929, volume 4, "Appendice," p. 135).

In short, the law of three stages was a global one; it referred not only to intellectual evolution but to social and political developments as well. It depicted the different stages of progress that every civilization had to experience as well as a future positive age of social cooperation that was definitive, but not perfect. (Although society would see an increase in both intelligence and altruism, Comte believed ordinary man's moral and intellectual weaknesses – his natural egoism and mental lethargy – would never completely disappear.) The law of three stages also pertained to the intellectual trajectory of every person as he or she went through life. In addition, Comte recognized that the three stages actually represented three mentalities that could coexist at various times in a person's or civilization's history.

In the theological stage, man untangled the mystery of natural occurrences by relating them to supernatural beings, whose character was like his own. The notion that gods represented the first cause of all happenings and were in complete control of the universe was the theory that the mind needed in its infancy to link its observations. There were three substages in this first era of history: the fetishist, polytheistic, and monotheistic. In the first, gods resided in concrete objects. In the second, the gods became independent of the objects. In the third, a single god became the ruling principle. In a society that embraced the theological mode of explanation, priests and military men ruled. The theory of divine right was the reigning political doctrine.

The metaphysical stage of history, which began in the fourteenth century, was a transitional period. In searching for first and final causes, people started to connect observed facts with personified essences or abstractions, such as Nature, which were neither supernatural nor scientific. In the process, metaphysicians replaced priests as the spiritual power. Military men ceded their role as the temporal power to lawyers, for society began to direct its activities toward production, not simply conquest. The state of politics was embodied in the doctrines of popular sovereignty and natural rights.

In the positive stage of history, no discussion of first causes or origins was allowed because the existence of supernatural beings and essences could not be proved. Instead, intellectual discourse was characterized by scientific laws explaining how, not why, phenomena worked. These descriptive laws expressed the "relations of resemblance and succession that facts have among themselves" (Comte, 1929, volume 4, "Appendice," p. 144). Moreover, because production replaced conquest as the goal of society, social relations were based entirely on industry. Politically, industrialists constituted the temporal leaders of this secular, peaceful society. Positive philosophers held the spiritual power.

Contrary to scholarly opinion, Comte did not argue that there should be a dictatorship of scientists in control of the future positive republic. He feared that if the mind grew too powerful, it would stifle progress, for it needed stimulation from the active life. Though an idealist, Comte never maintained that intellectual progress could be separated from material development. Furthermore, he recognized that practical enterprises would always remain most important in society because most men were drawn to the active life, not the intellectual one. If a minority of intellectuals took over the material realm, they would oppress society, lose all motivation, and wallow in admiration of the society they produced. Borrowing a term from his close friend John Stuart Mill, Comte called a technocratic society governed purely by philosophers or intellectuals a "pedantocracy" (Comte, 1975, volume 2, p. 656).

The rise of such a regime could be prevented only by the separation of powers. The industrialists would control the practical, material activities of society, which were dangerous because the requisite specialization led to pride and egoism. These men would be checked by positive philosophers, who would be in charge of ensuring morality and encouraging the growth of ideas and feelings.

Positive philosophers were not necessarily scientists, whose tendency to specialize made them as uncaring and socially indifferent as industrialists. Comte wanted positive philosophers to be men who had a general knowledge of all the sciences, especially sociology. In this way, they would understand the impact of the natural environment and human nature on society and the application of the positive method to social phenomena. Moreover, Comte assumed that intellectual well-roundedness was linked to "altruism," a word he also coined. Thus, because positive philosophers possessed general knowledge and consequently had the widest views and sympathies, they would have the interests of all of society at heart. The breadth of their knowledge and sympathies gave them the legitimacy to speak for the entire community.

Forbidden to rule directly, they would especially advise the industrialists on how to solve the "social question"; that is, the difficulties faced by the working class. Although critics contend that Comte was an apologist for the status quo, he was in truth extremely critical of capitalism for promoting a selfish and materialistic culture. Like Marx, he argued that the appalling class struggle was not due to the workers but to "the political incapacity, social indifference, and especially blind egoism of the entrepreneurs" (Comte, 1975, volume 2, p. 620). Calling for the "personal liberation of workers," he campaigned to resolve the class question by incorporating the proletariat into society

(Comte, 1929, volume 3, p. 402). The positive philosophers would be their biggest allies.

These philosophers would also take control of the educational system to improve people's intellectual development and to give them common ideas and values. Countering man's natural egoism, which was exacerbated by the specialization of the modern age, they would persuade people to develop their inherent sociability and contribute to the common welfare. In short, positive philosophers would direct ideas, feelings, and images toward the improvement of Humanity, which would replace God and Nature as the object of people's respect. Serving humanity would be an imperative for everyone, from housewives to scholars. The idea of humanity would thus hold society together. Comte wrote that the principal result of history was "the spontaneous convergence of all modern conceptions toward the great notion of humanity" (Comte, 1975, volume 2, p. 785).

Though highly schematic, the law of three stages allowed Comte to pull together the natural and social sciences. Unlike Saint-Simon, he rejected the conventional approach of basing the sciences on a single method or on universal logical principles; to him, scientific knowledge itself had to be regarded as a historical process (Heilbron, 1990, pp. 155, 161). Indeed, Comte was the only philosopher of the sciences who was more concerned with their social and political ramifications than their theoretical success and practical results (Grange, 1996, p. 17). In his view, the most effective way to consider the sciences and their consequences was to place them in a historical perspective.

Together with Comte's classification of the sciences, the law of three stages ultimately demonstrated the triumph of sociology and completion of positivism. By providing a program ensuring intellectual rigor and encouraging social cooperation, positivism would lead to a political and social revolution that would be far more efficacious than a mere change in the form of government in bringing about a new, harmonious order. To Comte, practical, institutional reforms could never launch a new era, for they were ineffective and often premature. They did not take into account the fact that the disorganization of postrevolutionary society was due primarily to intellectual and moral anarchy.

Although Comte believed that a firm grounding in the sciences was essential to proper reasoning, he did not support a purely scientistic interpretation of positivism. Indeed, Comte would never recognize the simplistic version of positivism that exists today as his own formulation. For years, scholars have commonly equated positivism with scientism; that is, a naive faith in science's ability to solve all problems through the use of empirical, experimental, and quantitative methods of research. Jürgen Habermas claimed that "positivism stands and falls with the principle of scientism" (Habermas, 1971, p. 67). Gertrud Lenzer accused positivism of being naively reductionist: "The triumph of the positive spirit consists in the reduction of quality to quantity in all realms of existence – in the realm of society and man as well as in the realm of nature" (Lenzer, 1975, p. xxi).

Yet Comte never displayed an excessive faith in the power of the sciences to modify nature and society in a boundless fashion. Respectful of the environment and of the slow pace and direction of change, he argued against using the sciences to satisfy man's love of power and conquest. As suggested above, he was more of a historicist in his approach to the sciences than an enthusiast of scientism (Grange, 1996, p. 139).

The *Cours* is therefore a paradoxical work. It called for a social philosophy based upon the sciences, but as reflected in his concept of the spiritual power, Comte deeply distrusted the regenerative capabilities of the purely scientific spirit. His disillusionment is evident at the end of the *Cours*, where he condemned "the prejudices and passions of our deplorable scientific regime" (Comte, 1975, volume 2, p. 791). The *Cours*, an apparently scientistic tract, was intended to counter the scientific spirit – that is, the "positivity" – of the modern age, whose specialization, egoism, and social indifference caused immeasurable moral harm.

In his hatred of the hubris of scientists, Comte always maintained that even in the realm of what was understandable, scientific knowledge was deficient. He opposed, for example, the statistical approach to scientific research, which he believed overlooked the complexity of human existence and threatened the autonomy and individuality of each science. To him, the power of reason was limited. He wrote that "it was necessary to recognize that ... our means for conceiving new questions ... [was] much more powerful than our resources for solving them, or in other words the human mind ... [was] far more capable of imagining than of reasoning" (Comte, 1975, volume 1, p. 99).

In fact, Comte did not believe in absolute truth, for he was a relativist: "It is no longer a question of expounding interminably in order to know what is the best government; speaking in an absolute sense, there is nothing good, there is nothing bad; the only absolute is that everything is relative; everything is relative especially when social institutions are concerned" (Comte, 1970, p. 71). His relativism was connected to his belief that "exact reality can never, in any way, be perfectly unveiled" to our weak mind (Comte, 1975, volume 2, pp. 103–4). It was particularly impossible to have a complete grasp of social reality, which was extremely complex and involved men's prejudices.

Comte never lost sight of the fact that the emotions were of utmost importance in human existence. This realization was partly due to his recognition that he suffered from depression and could not work if he had emotional troubles. Since his youth, he had considered the emotions the motor of existence; their dominance was necessary to rouse the intellect from its natural torpor and give it moral direction. Indeed, he maintained that love, not reason, was the basic principle of social existence. In the *Cours*, he wrote that:

> universal love, such as Catholicism conceived it, is certainly far more important than the intellect itself in ... our individual or social existence, because love spontaneously uses even the lowest mental faculties for the profit of everyone, whereas egoism distorts or paralyzes the most eminent dispositions, which consequently are more often disturbing than efficacious in regard to true private or public happiness. (Comte, 1975, volume 2, p. 362)

Realizing that reason could not satisfy all human needs, Comte also emphasized that the imagination was crucial to both the creation and propagation of scientific theories. Although he recommended observation as a method of sociological research, he pointed out that complete empiricism was impossible and sterile, for accumulating discrete observable facts about a reality that could not be fully grasped was unproductive. To him, facts could not be perceived or connected without first formulating an *a priori* theory, which required imaginative work. Revealing an awareness of the mind's limitations, he wrote:

> Man is incapable by his nature not only of combining facts and deducing from them several consequences, but of even simply observing them with attention and retaining them with certainty if he does not attach them immediately to some explanation. He cannot have connected observations without some theory any more than [he can have] a positive theory without regular observations. (Comte, 1929, volume 4, "Appendice," p. 144)

Social facts were the most difficult to observe. Because social scientists lived in society, it was impossible for them to notice the significance of familiar social phenomena and to be impartial. To be creative, scientific investigation of all phenomena, especially social phenomena, had to rest on the use of both induction and deduction, rely on rationalism as well as experimentation, and employ man's imaginative capacities.

Moreover, for laws to be scientific, they had to be predictive; that is, they had to display the capability to go from the present to the future and from the known to the unknown (Laudan, 1971, pp. 37–40). Comte wrote, "from science comes prediction; from prediction comes action" (Comte, 1975, volume 1, p. 45). Facts in themselves with no connection to general laws had no predictive value. They were thus not useful.

Comte advocated the use of provisional hypotheses as convenient, artificial devices to link facts and formulate natural laws. These hypotheses could not be considered scientific theories until they were verified by induction and deduction. Comte's representation of hypotheses as useful and respectable tools that serve a crucial function in scientific discovery was an influential idea. His appreciation of the aesthetic considerations in scientists' construction of hypotheses anticipated the work of Thomas Kuhn.

To free scientists from being slaves to direct evidence, Comte also advocated the use of imagination in creating types of "scientific fiction" – hypothetical cases – to elucidate tentatively different scientific problems until the discovery of better evidence. For example, a biologist could insert "purely fictive organisms" between already known organisms in order to make the biological series more homogeneous, continuous, and regular (Comte, 1975, volume 2, p. 728). As reflected in his approach to hypotheses and scientific fictions, Comte intended to offer imagination the "most vast and fertile" field for discovering, observing, and coordinating facts (Comte, 1975, volume 2, p. 102). To avoid giving reason excessive importance in scientific research, he deliberately refused to offer elaborate, universal, ahistorical rules of scientific procedure; he never produced an organon of proof. To him, purely abstract rationalist rules not only made scientific research less flexible but came dangerously close to metaphysical practices (Scharff, 1995, pp. 7, 65). Indeed, a few months before he died in 1857, Comte wrote, "The present...evolution of positivism...depends on sentiment and imagination, and reasoning will henceforth be secondary" (Comte, 1973–90, volume 8, p. 502). His point was to offer scientists of society the widest possible variety of resources that would allow them to construct theories that did not require them tediously to observe facts to no purpose. They must be allowed to go beyond direct evidence without forgetting that ultimately every positive theory had to refer to real, concrete phenomena. Comte's call to resist relying excessively on rationalism to grasp a "real" world has been recently echoed by Jean Baudrillard, who shows a similar appreciation of the symbolic and the poetic (Gane, 1991, pp. 201–2).

Humanity was the most fundamental component of reality. In a famous passage, Comte wrote: "Considered from the static and dynamic points of view, man properly speaking is at heart a pure abstraction; there is nothing real except humanity, especially in the intellectual and moral order" (Comte, 1975, volume 2, p. 715). Comte reinforced the importance of all people being socialized and educated to work for this "real" phenomenon by constructing the Religion of Humanity, whose roots were evident in his early writings. He discussed this religion and introduced the final science of morality in his four-volume *Système de politique positive*, published between 1851 and 1854. Many scholars have asserted that this book was a repudiation of his previous scientific program. Yet in reality there was no significant break in his intellectual evolution. The Religion of Humanity was foreshadowed in the *Cours*, where Comte referred specifically to the need to create a "Positive Church" (Comte, 1975, volume 2, p. 696). The *Système* merely carried forth the program for the intellectual, moral and political regeneration of society that Comte had formulated in the early 1820s.

Whereas the *Cours* dealt with the systematization of ideas and provided a common belief-system, the *Système* covered the organization of feelings as well as the political restructuring of society that would result from the intellectual and moral revolution he hoped to achieve. He explained that because he had already established "fundamental ideas," he now had to describe their "social application," which would consist of "the systematization of human sentiments, [which was] the necessary consequence of that of ideas and the indispensable basis of that of institutions" (Comte, 1973–90, volume 3, p. 61). In view of the fact that the needs of society were not only intellectual but emotional, its spiritual reorganization had to involve the heart at least as much as the mind. As Donald Levine has written, "Comte's positive philosophy...eliminates theology...but retains religion," thus bridging the gap "between the rational imperatives of modern science and the emotional imperatives of societal order" (Levine, 1995, pp. 163, 165). Convinced that a general doctrine and institutional networks were not sufficient to ensure social cohesion, Comte believed that his religion would provide the moral adhesive necessary to hold society together. Ultimately, human unity rested on the sympathies, for it was clear to him that the "essential principle of modern anarchy" consisted of "raising reason against sentiment" (Comte, 1855, p. 10). The positive philosophy would bring about the intellectual and emotional consensus necessary to end anarchy and build the stable industrial society of the future.

The main task of the Religion of Humanity would be to cultivate altruism; replacing Christianity with "a system of terrestrial morality," it was a secular religion of love (Comte, 1970, p. 40). Defending his choice of names for his moral system, Comte explained in 1849 that he had "dared to join...the name [religion] to the thing [positivism], in order to institute directly an open competition with all the other systems" (Comte, 1973–90, volume 5, p. 22). He wanted a clear-cut doctrinal battle with Catholicism to precipitate the triumph of positivism and the start of a new order.

To challenge Catholicism, Comte invented positivist sacraments for baptism, marriage, and death. He also created a special commemorative calendar, with primarily secular saints (Aristotle, Caesar, and Dante), one of whom was to be glorified each day as a servant of Humanity. Comte's theory anticipated the ideas of the sociologist Maurice Halbwachs, who underscored the importance of collective memory in unifying society. Private and public acts of commemoration in the form of worshipping important figures from one's own past and that of Western civilization (highlighted in the calendar) would create a sense of continuity between past and present generations. Such a system of commemoration would also satisfy people's natural "need for eternity" and stimulate them to contribute to the progress of humanity, especially through "benevolent actions" and "sympathetic emotions" (Comte, 1975, p. 778). As Henri Gouhier pointed out, "The Religion of Humanity is essentially a cult of dead people" (Gouhier, 1965, p. 212).

The *Système* also described rituals that would rejuvenate people's emotional life, bring them back into contact with the concrete, and stimulate the arts. Comte was creating an entirely new religious culture, which he felt was crucial for holding society together. He recognized that political action in the new age would consist of using religion, the arts, and education to form collective sentiments, beliefs, and representations.

In outlining the Religion of Humanity, Comte particularly aspired to revive the concreteness, intense emotional spontaneity, and poetic aptitudes of the earliest stage of religious life, that of fetishism (Pickering, 1998, pp. 57–66). Of all the intellectual systems, fetishism, according to Comte, most encouraged the growth of sociability because it inspired "toward all beings, even inert, dispositions [such as veneration, trust, and adoration] that were eminently proper to cultivating...our best affections" (Comte, 1929, volume 3, p. 108). This growth of the emotions destroyed man's animal instincts and fortified his basic sense of humanity.

Although Comte is known as an apostle of progress, he feared the effects of science and abstract thought, which made people proud and egoistic, and he believed the West needed an injection of primitive religion to continue to advance. He was one of the first thinkers to celebrate fetishism, which he connected with the black race and hoped to incorporate into positivism. To him, "the humble thinkers of central Africa" were more rational about human nature and society than the "superb German doctors," with their "pompous verbiage." Comte maintained "The touching logic of the least negroes is . . . wiser than our academic dryness, which, under the futile pretext of an always imposs-ible impartiality usually strengthens suspicion and fear" (Comte, 1929, volume 3, pp. 99, 121). Unlike modern men, the fetish worshippers admired what was concrete and useful and respected the natural world. Comte tried to replicate this kind of worship by encouraging people to devote themselves to Humanity, the "Great Being." The purpose of his neo-fetishist religion was to stress the import-ance of humility and self-effacement by demonstrating that all peoples were related to each other and to the earth, which at the end of his life he called the "Great Fetish." Positivism had to emulate fetishism by recognizing what was beneficial to others in a concrete sense in this world. In 1855, Comte wrote to a friend to explain the "absorption of fetishism by positivism."

> There exists essentially for us only two *beings*, both of which are eminently composite: the Earth, including the stars as appendices, and Humanity, of which the animals capable of association and even the useful vegetables are auxiliar-ies. . . . These are our two masters, which are closely connected at least to us; one is superior in power, the other in dignity, but both are worthy of our continual respect. (Comte, 1973–90, volume 8, p. 39)

In Comte's mind, the highest stage of civilization represented a return to the beginning. "Human reason" at the height of its "virility" must include a "degree of poetic fetishism" (Comte, 1973–90, volume 3, p. 212). Comte was thus one of the first philosophers to contend that fetishism did not belong exclusively to the primitive age and did not always represent a type of false consciousness or prelogical mindset. Condemning racism and imperialism for dividing humanity instead of uniting it, he challenged racial stereotypes when he asserted that one day a "negro thinker" might study his works and lend him his support (Comte, 1929, volume 3, p. 156).

Comte imagined that the chief auxiliaries of the positive philosophers, who epitomized reason, would be women, who embodied feeling, and workers, who represented activity. These two oppressed groups had interested Comte since he was a young man. Unlike the ruling male bourgeoisie, whom he called "extre-mely gangrenous," women and workers were preserved from the artificial, materialist culture of the day (Comte, 1973–90, volume 6, p. 188). He increas-ingly appealed to them for support, after being rebuffed by scientists and other luminaries of his day.

In the aftermath of the Revolution of 1848, Comte joined the issues of class and gender; he maintained that the liberation of both the proletariat and women was necessary for the advent of positivism. But once he discovered the strength of the proletariat's loyalty to socialism, Comte decided in 1851 that the most "important work of positivism" was to persuade women to join him (Comte, 1973–90, volume 6, p. 188). He was weary of the "depressing regime" of men, who were shallow and narrow-minded (Comte, 1973–90, volume 7, p. 158).

Repelled by the "disorders of male reason" and its futile political machinations, Comte found women to represent the best way to unify an increasingly fragmented society (Comte, 1973–90, volume 6, p. 183).

Scholars frequently accuse Comte of being a "phallocrat" desirous only to preserve the current outlines of the patriarchal society (Kofman, 1978, p. 233). He certainly did not approve of feminism and repeatedly condemned bluestockings and the "liberated woman" as aberrant, sexless creatures. Nevertheless, having read Mary Wollstonecraft's *Vindication of the Rights of Woman* as a young person, he criticized men who employed "the horrible law of the strongest" to lord it over women, whom they regarded as a "domestic animal" or "toy destined for all eternity for the good pleasure and usage of his Majesty *Man*" (Comte, 1973–90, volume 1, p. 56). In the 1840s, he finally recognized that the problem of anarchy would not be resolved "as long as the revolution does not become feminine" (Comte, 1973–90, volume 6, p. 108). He feared his own reform movement would be discredited without female support. He begged women not to misunderstand the gist of his thought:

> The fatal antagonism... between the mind and the heart can be resolved only by the positive regime; no other is capable of subordinating in a dignified fashion, reason to sentiment.... In its vain present supremacy, the mind is ultimately our principal trouble maker.... Better judges than we in moral understanding, women will feel in several regards that the affective superiority of positivism... is even more pronounced than its speculative preeminence, which is henceforth incontestable. They will soon come to this conclusion when they have stopped confusing the new philosophy with its scientific preamble. (Comte, 1929, volume 1, 224)

Trying to take advantage of "the feminine revolution" that he believed was about to begin, and appropriating aspects of the contemporary women's movement for his own purposes, Comte put woman at the center of his schemes for renovation in two of his last works, the *Système de politique positive* and the *Catéchisme positiviste* (Comte, 1973–90, volume 6, p. 109). Whereas in the *Cours* he had declared that women were far from the "ideal type of the race" – the male – he declared in the *Système* the need to establish a "cult of Woman," which would make her into a kind of goddess (Comte, 1929, volume 1, p. 259). The *Catéchisme*, which consisted of a dialogue between a woman and a positivist priest, specifically addressed a female audience. It aimed to develop the alliance between positive philosophers and women that Comte was certain would spur the regenerative process.

Although Comte never supported the notion of the equality of the sexes, he did give women a positive identity; they were not simply harlots or housewives as Pierre Proudhon proclaimed, or permanent invalids as Jules Michelet contended. Comte referred to the "feminine genius" in terms of its important function not solely to propagate but to participate in the public sphere and aid the spiritual power in reorganizing society along moral lines (Comte, 1975, volume 2, p. 300). Experts in the emotions, women made men more sociable, complete human beings. To fulfill this mission, they needed to be able to mold public opinion, preferably in the salons, whose revival he favored. Women also required freedom from economic and sexual exploitation. Comte envisioned the "utopia of women," where they would gain "independence" from men, even in their "physical role," by taking control of their own bodies and having children without any male participation whatsoever (Comte, 1929, volume 4, pp. 66–7, 286). Moreover, because they were endowed with the best human characteristic, that of sociability, women, he insisted, should represent Humanity itself. In the positivist temples, Humanity would be always depicted as a woman accompanied by her son. This daring displacement of God the Father in the positivist system reflects Comte's conviction that women were morally superior and would be "in first place in the normal society" of the future (Comte, 1973–90, volume 7, p. 160). Agents of social unity, women were the key to completing the positive revolution and saving the increasingly fragmented West from complete dissolution. Their role illustrates Comte's goal of placing nurturing and empathy at the center of public life in order to create a new, more compassionate and harmonious society.

In his effort to make feeling of paramount importance, Comte also developed a greater interest in art. In the *Système*, he argued that art's power of idealization encouraged the growth of feeling and social solidarity; because it developed the sympathies, art should have a higher place in society than science, whose work was primarily preparatory. He wrote, "Art corresponds better than science to our most intimate needs. It is both more sympathetic and more synthetic" (Comte, 1929, 51). Ideally, it would be possible to blend the scientific spirit with the aesthetic spirit.

Comte tried to fuse the two in his last work, *Synthèse subjective* (1856), which was devoted to mathematics. Here he argued that the scientific spirit was considered dry because the modern specialization that it engendered hurt moral and aesthetic growth. To him, the "abstract habits of clarity, precision, and consistency, which are normally acquired in the mathematical domain," could be fruitfully applied to religious institutions and art (Comte, 1856, p. xi). To demonstrate his principle, Comte set down rules to ensure that future positive philosophers would be poets celebrating Humanity in verse. The poetic age of his doctrine could then commence. In some respects, Comte's views seem to foreshadow those of Max Weber, who also considered rationalization a global process and lamented the "disenchantment" of the modern world.

In sum, Comte's positivist system was never morally neutral or value-free as some scholars have asserted in equating positivism with a quest for objectivity. From the beginning, Comte embraced social activism and a moral goal, for he was convinced that impartiality was inappropriate and indeed impossible in studying society, whose phenomena were close to us; a viable social theory had to depict a better form of social organization. Comte sought to shape the world of action indirectly by molding people's ideas and opinions. Because he believed that intellectual well-roundedness was linked to altruism, he declared that the adoption of the positivist mental outlook would lead first to a new moral order marked by the bonding together of individuals through sympathy, and then to a political transformation that would launch a new positivist era of social consensus, association, and stability.

THE PERSON

Comte was eager for this new era to begin, for he was profoundly disenchanted with his own period. Throughout his life, he had trouble fitting into the society around him and always felt he was an outsider. He later admitted that he sought in "public life the noble but imperfect compensation of the unhappiness of his private life" (Comte, 1973–90, volume 3, p. 36).

In his youth he experienced the disruptive effects of civil war within both his family and his native city. He was born in 1798 in Montpellier, which was one of the southern centers of the Counter-Revolution, the movement that resisted the reforming zeal of the French Revolution of 1789. Comte's bourgeois parents were Catholic royalists also opposed to the Revolution. His childhood was thus full of bitter memories caused by the ordeals of this tumultuous period. In the "Personal Preface" to the sixth volume of the *Cours*, which included an auto-biographical sketch, he pointed out that the French Revolution made a profound impression on him, especially because it was rejected by his family. Comte did not get along with his father, who was a bureaucrat in the tax collection office. Though he was closer to his mother, he alienated her by his unconventional beliefs and behavior. Like many members of his generation with whom he studied at the new Montepellier *lycée*, established by Napoleon, Comte was eager to display his defiance and rebelliousness – a questioning attitude encouraged by his republican teachers. At thirteen or fourteen he announced that he no longer believed in God or Catholicism. Soon afterward, rejecting his parents' royalism and following the example set by the revolutionaries, he became a republican.

A brilliant student with a phenomenal memory, Comte in 1814 gained admission to the École Polytechnique, the prestigious Parisian engineering school. Taught by the best scientists of the day, he learned the importance of the sciences in improving social conditions. He also imbibed the republican, reform-oriented atmosphere of the school. Yet in April 1816 the new royalist government had him expelled for his republicanism and insubordinate behavior. Despite his abridged stay at the École Polytechnique, he remained forever marked by its scientific mindset.

After his expulsion, Comte took courses in biology at the famous medical school in Montpellier, studied history, and read the works of Condorcet and Montesquieu on the "moral and political sciences" (Comte, 1973–90, volume 1, p. 19). In June 1816, he wrote his first essay, which was never published: "Mes Réflexions: Humanité, verité, justice, liberté patrie. Rapprochements entre le régime de 1793 et celui de 1816, adressés au peuple français." Horrified at the royalists' vengeful series of massacres, he condemned the new Bourbon monarchy as well as other oppressive despotisms, namely those of Robespierre and Napoleon, which had had their own share of atrocities. Like other liberal republicans of this period, Comte called for a government based on the "national will"; that is, popular consent (Comte, 1970, p. 421). In his view, enlightened men, such as philosophers and scientists, should lead the way. From the start, there was a certain tension between his elitist and populist impulses.

A year later, back in Paris, Comte began working for Henri de Saint-Simon, an older social reformer, whose "liberalism was ... well known" (Comte, 1973–90, volume 1, p. 27). The extent of Saint-Simon's influence on Comte is still controversial today. It is undoubtedly true that in his many works published during the Napoleonic Empire, Saint-Simon had shown that the creation of a new unified system of scientific knowledge – a "positive philosophy" – centered on the study of society would lead to a new stage of history, where industrialists and scientists would replace military leaders and the clergy. Yet he scattered such critical seminal ideas haphazardly throughout his various writings, along with other less viable notions, such as the necessity of unifying society by means of a single natural law, Newton's law of gravity, which would replace God as "the sole cause of all physical and moral phenomena" (Saint-Simon, 1966, volume 6, pp. 121n1, 154). When Comte started working for him in 1817, Saint-Simon had grown less interested in establishing the theoretical basis of social reconstruction and was turning toward the practical, industrial reorganization of society. He had dropped his faith in scientists and increasingly praised *industriels* (people involved in productive work) for preparing the new order. Comte, however, took up Saint-Simon's original mission of founding the scientific system – that is, the positive philosophy – together with its keystone, the science of society.

It is evident that Saint-Simon gave Comte's thought a certain direction. Although he later denied Saint-Simon's influence, immediately after their break-up Comte was more forthright: "I certainly owe a great deal intellectually to Saint-Simon, that is to say, he has powerfully contributed to launching me in the philosophical direction that I have clearly created for myself today and that I will follow without hesitation all my life" (Comte, 1973–90, volume 1, p. 90). Gifted with a disciplined, methodical mind, Comte built on the legacy given to him by Saint-Simon and achieved an originality of his own. While Saint-Simon was an incoherent autodidact who constantly revised his concept of the science of humanity, Comte had a talent for system-building and synthesis, which he used to develop sociology as a coherent discipline.

Intellectual differences as well as generational tensions soon led to a rupture. Comte broke with Saint-Simon in 1824 after accusing his mentor of trying to take credit for his seminal essay, the *Plan des travaux scientifiques nécessaires pour réorganiser la société*. In this work, Comte had revealed his latest "discovery" – the law of three stages. This law was in fact indebted to Saint-Simon's view that each science passed through three stages – a conjectural stage, a half-conjectural and half-positive stage, and a positive stage – according to its degree of complexity. Yet unlike Saint-Simon, Comte gave this law a new role as the basis of sociology. It was the key to understanding humanity's development in the past, present, and future. Excited about his findings, Comte felt ready to launch his own career.

Despite this rupture, Comte wrote for *Le Producteur*, the journal founded by Saint-Simon's disciples after the old reformer's death in May 1825. He did not join the Saint-Simonian sect, for he maintained purely literary relations with its members. In the two series of articles that he wrote for the journal in 1825 and early 1826, Comte developed his concept of the spiritual power. He was prescient in claiming that the key to power in modern society lay in controlling opinions and ideas. As soon as natural scientists and social scientists took over the educational system, he believed, they would exert enormous influence over society. They would be especially important in checking the corrupt "administrative despotism" that marked the modern age (Comte, 1929, volume 4, "Appendice," p. 187). Henceforth Comte devoted himself to founding the positivist priesthood.

In early 1826 he offered a course on positive philosophy at his apartment, which was attended by many of the great scientists of the day. Yet after the third lecture, he went mad. A paranoid manic depressive, he spent eight months in an asylum. As a result, he could never completely eliminate the suspicion that he was "crazy" – a term often used by his critics to discredit him. Finally recovering with the help of Caroline Massin, an administrator of a reading room who had married him in 1824, he was henceforth always concerned about preserving his mental well-being. His struggles with mental illness made him distrust skepticism as corrosive and strengthened his conviction that a "normal," sane existence necessitated a certain prescribed harmony and a rigid order.

After his convalescence, Comte worked as a mathematics tutor and journalist. Then in 1832 he procured a subordinate teaching and administrative position at the École Polytechnique. He was a *répétiteur* (teaching assistant) and admissions examiner. This non-taxing work left him time to finish the *Cours de philosophie positive* in 1842. Its purpose was to establish sociology, to stimulate the reorganization of society, and to create the foundation for the reform of the sciences to meet the educational needs of modern civilization. One of the founders of the history of science, Comte analyzed the development of each science and its close relationship to the growth of other sciences. The first three volumes covered the history of mathematics, astronomy, physics, chemistry, and biology. The last three volumes treated his new science of sociology. All in all, the *Cours* set down the basic program of study that he had undergone and that he believed the new spiritual power had to master in order to lead society to a new ethic of cooperation.

When Comte began volume 4 in 1838, he experienced another prolonged period of mental illness, which he ascribed not only to the immense intellectual effort required to introduce sociology but to his wife's infidelity. To improve his mental health, Comte underwent an "aesthetic revolution": he suddenly developed an interest in music and poetry. He hoped to use the arts to cultivate his feelings and thereby enlarge his comprehension of society, the new object of his studies. At the same time, he adopted a regime of "cerebral hygiene." To preserve his ego from attacks from critics and to maintain his sense of originality, he abstained from reading newspapers, books, and journals. He allowed himself only the pleasures of great poetry. Cutting himself off from other scholars, whom he accused of disregarding his work, he increasingly retreated from the world. This tendency toward isolation was strengthened when his wife suddenly left him in 1842 after he neglected her advice not to publish the "Personal Preface" to the sixth volume of the *Cours*, which viciously attacked his colleagues at the

École Polytechnique for slighting him. Her departure almost caused another mental breakdown.

Several years later another woman entered his life. In early 1845 Comte fell in love with Clotilde de Vaux, the sister of one of his students. She was seventeen years younger than Comte. Having been abandoned by her husband, she was an aspiring writer trying to gain independence from her parents, who were struggling to support her. Comte pursued her in a very calculated fashion to develop his feelings, which he worried were stunted due to his poor relations with his family and wife. Now that he was about to write the *Système*, which dealt with the emotional side of human existence, he believed he needed more depth in this arena.

Comte represented Vaux as a perfect lady, an angel who made him more virtuous. Moral improvement, he asserted, was imperative for a philosopher because "no great intellect" could develop "in a suitable manner without a certain amount of universal benevolence," the source of lofty goals (Comte, 1975, volume 2, p. 181). He maintained that his adoration for Vaux made him love all of Humanity.

Although Comte now prided himself on being a model of both intellectual and moral strength, he lusted ironically after her body. Considering him only a close friend, Vaux resisted his advances. Yet she was forced to increase her reliance on his good will and financial resources as she began to lose her battle against tuberculosis. In April 1846, she died. During this period, from mid-1845 to 1846, Comte again almost went mad. To immortalize her name, he decided to dedicate to her his next significant work, the *Système de politique positive* (1851–4).

The extent of Vaux's influence on Comte is controversial. Comte claimed she was responsible for his "second career." Scholars from John Stuart Mill to Raymond Aron have usually agreed that there was indeed a break in his intellectual evolution. Yet they considered what he wrote after her death to be far inferior to the *Cours*. The Religion of Humanity, which he erected in her honor, allegedly discredited his earlier scientistic program. Yet just as Comte's earlier work was not completely scientistic, his later career was not entirely sentimental and illogical. His last work, the *Synthèse subjective* (1856), focused almost entirely on the sciences, especially mathematics; it reinterpreted their role from the perspective of the kind of moral education and logic required during the positive age. All of Comte's works form a consistent whole; from the beginning, his concerns were "spiritual" in that he was trying to create a credible general doctrine that would replace Catholicism and still satisfy the human need for beliefs and values.

Although Vaux did not change the direction of Comte's thought, she did reinforce his growing interest in the feelings, and her struggles to establish herself revived his interest in the "woman question," which his bitter relationship with Massin had squelched. The alliance between women and positive philosophers that he had promoted in the closing volume of the *Cours* now became central to his doctrine, as reflected in the *Catéchisme positiviste*.

When the Revolution of 1848 broke out, Comte became eager to gain greater popularity with the common people. Prompted by the belief that every educated person had a duty to enlighten those who wanted to learn, he had given since

1831 a highly successful public course on astronomy to workers. Now seeking to entice the workers from socialism, especially the "communist" doctrines of Etienne Cabet, he founded the Positivist Society to launch the positivist movement and wrote a manifesto, the *Discours sur l'ensemble du positivisme*. In this work, which later formed the opening section of the *Système*, he argued that although positivism did not seek to abolish private property, it absorbed and strengthened the basic principles of communism, in that it agreed that the community should "intervene to subordinate [property] to the needs of society" (Comte, 1929, volume 1, p. 155). Comte also supported the workers' demands for the right to work and a republic where they would hold the reins of power.

However, he soon feared the revolutionaries were becoming too violent and anarchic, and he ended by preferring the dictatorial regime of Louis Napoleon. In 1855 he wrote *Appel au Conservateurs* to persuade all conservatives, including Catholics, to unite with positivists against the Left. Comte's growing conservatism cost him the support of liberals, such as Emile Littré, a leading scholar who had been his most important French supporter. Nevertheless, Comte still had fifty or so faithful disciples in the Positivist Society, which continued to meet once a week. They supported him financially. Such assistance was especially necessary after Comte lost his last job at the École Polytechnique in 1851. His resentment at not being promoted to mathematics professor had led to friction with his colleagues, who finally dismissed him. He depended on his disciples until his death in 1857.

In the last years of his life, Comte ruled the positivist movement in a dictatorial manner, refusing to allow any dissension, especially in matters pertaining to the Religion of Humanity, whose cult he meticulously organized. He also wrote his *Testament*, which enclosed a "Secret Addition"; it was to be used against his wife if she challenged his will and tried to downplay the importance of this religion. The note accused Massin of having been a prostitute – an allegation that has been generally accepted as true. Yet Comte was falling into the binary logic of his time. If Vaux was an angel, Massin, whom he now hated, had to be the opposite, a demonic force, whose representation in the mid-nineteenth century was a prostitute. When Massin did challenge the will and the case went to court, she was shocked to read the "Secret Addition," whose truth she vigorously denied. Just as Comte succeeded in marrying his name with that of Vaux, he forever sullied the reputation of Massin.

Auguste Comte was a brilliant visionary but a difficult, egoistic person. The certainty that he was right, his intolerance of criticism, and his paranoia led to one rupture after another. He lost many important friends, such as Saint-Simon, François Guizot, Emile Littré, and John Stuart Mill. He broke with his wife and his family. He alienated his colleagues. He had difficulty retaining disciples. It is paradoxical that the man who founded the science that specialized in social relations could not get along with other people. And yet, perhaps because of his manic depressive condition, he imagined himself the savior of the world, the "Great Priest" of Humanity, to which he claimed to be devoted. In a sense, he sought in his social philosophy the stability, harmony, and love that eluded him in his private life.

The Social Context

Generating a series of dramatic transformations, the French Revolution seemed to make dreams of salvation plausible. Comte's aspirations cannot be entirely understood without a proper appreciation of the social context in which he wrote. His sociological theory was a direct response to the upheavals caused by the French and Industrial Revolutions, two turning points in Western history that rendered social conditions uncertain and unstable.

The French Revolution was a cataclysmic event that threw into question the legitimacy of the government and the religion upon which traditional society rested. Henceforth, the basis and ends of power were matters of debate. During the sixty-odd years that Comte lived, France experienced nine different governments and revolutions. In their search for a new government, the French people seemed unsuccessful at avoiding the twin problems of mob rule and dictatorship. The various constitutions setting down the rules of government were discarded one right after another. Different social groups, impelled by the new forces of financial and industrial capitalism, manipulated events to their own advantage and to the detriment of the lower classes, who were trying to adjust to a new machine-based economy that threatened their traditional, artisanal ways of life. Having watched political experimentations wreak havoc in his country, Comte, like many of his countrymen, had little faith in purely political solutions to the anarchy of his time and looked with skepticism on such conventional abstractions as the "rights of man" and "popular sovereignty," which he believed had led to this confusion. Like others, from traditionalists on the Right to republicans on the Left, he craved a moral community.

For him, as for the revolutionaries, the idea of regeneration had to be a global program that touched on politics, the economy, morality, philosophy, and religion. Commending the revolutionaries for presiding over the necessary work of destruction, he looked forward to the day when there would be a new, more profound revolution, a *constructive* one instituting a more virtuous society, not just in France but everywhere. By the mid-nineteenth century, he was well aware that all parts of the world were interconnected. Partaking of the Eurocentrism of his time, he assumed that the other areas of the globe would follow European patterns of development. Deeply affected by the disunity and anarchy surrounding him, he created sociology and positivism to give the world the stability, order, and harmony it needed in an industrial, secular age that he recognized would no longer be dominated by nobles and clergymen.

Eliminating the questionable abstractions of both religion and conventional philosophy, positivism would serve as the basis of a new social consensus. To create a grand philosophical synthesis that would appeal to both the Left and Right and thus transcend party politics, Comte drew from many intellectual traditions. Despite his embrace of "cerebral hygiene," he was also deeply affected by developments going on around him. Comte wanted his system to represent not only the completion of the French Enlightenment but the endpoint of a more wide-ranging, European intellectual evolution as well. To him, this great comprehensiveness made his work even more serious and significant. As a result, his doctrine represents a delicate balancing act.

The Intellectual Context

Comte's approach to epistemology and the scientific method was influenced by Francis Bacon, René Descartes, Immanuel Kant, and David Hume. In scientific investigations, Comte recommended achieving a balance between Bacon's stress on induction and Descartes's emphasis on rationalism (or deduction) in order to come up with useful laws. Such laws were to be limited to describing facts, for they had to be constructed in accordance with Hume's warning to avoid the absurd pursuit of first and final causes. Like Kant, who, Comte believed, had elaborated on the British philosopher's conclusions, Hume had stressed the "fundamental dualism between the spectator and spectacle" and had brought mankind closer to the triumph of relativism and nominalism (Comte, 1929, volume 3, p. 588). By showing that an artificial logic provisionally linked our thoughts, both Hume and Kant had taught Comte that people could never know more than what appeared to them through their senses and categories. They thus contributed to Comte's theory of the subjective synthesis, which maintained that knowledge was not comprehensive or objective but rested on the nature of man.

Comte also took a great interest in biology, a science that was in a crucial era of development during his lifetime. It deeply influenced his conception of sociology, especially his idea that society formed an organism. Comte frequently used biological terms, such as "social illness," "pathological case," and "chronic epidemic," to characterize French society (Comte, 1975, volume 2, pp. 16, 48, 50). Four biologists in particular had a large impact on Comte. François Broussais's theory that the pathological was simply a variation of the normal was the source of Comte's concept of the use of experimentation in social studies. Henri Ducrotay de Blainville interested Comte in the influence of the environment on living bodies and turned his attention to the difference between statics and dynamics. Marie François Xavier Bichat's concept that there were three types of human skills – rational, emotive, and motor – inspired Comte's idea that the spiritual power consisted of philosophers, women, and workers. The phrenological doctrine of Franz Gall offered Comte a materialist replacement for the religious explanation of the world and human existence. Comte enthusiastically embraced Gall's principle that sympathy, or sociability, was an innate disposition in every individual because this theory strengthened the positivist argument that people simply needed to be socialized to become more altruistic. Both Gall and Bichat were considered by Comte to be his main scientific predecessors.

A wide variety of social thinkers and philosophers in France and abroad also influenced Comte's development. Montesquieu, Saint-Simon, Johann Gottfried Herder, and Georg Wilhelm Friedrich Hegel taught him that society ultimately represented an application of ideas, particularly moral principles, because a common world view united people. Once the dominant philosophy changed, so did morality and politics. Montesquieu inspired Comte to look for social laws. Saint-Simon recommended the scientific study of society based on *a priori* and *a posteriori* ideas and the history of progress. Making Comte aware that they were living in an age of transition requiring a radical new approach to reconstruction, Saint-Simon also delineated the new temporal and spiritual elites that would take over the emerging industrial-scientific society and direct it toward working productively for the happiness of man on earth. Herder emphasized the importance of a feeling of humanity, and Hegel reinforced Comte's organicism and deterministic approach to history.

Political economists, such as Adam Smith and J. B. Say, turned Comte's attention to the problems associated with industrialization and made him see both the benefits and disadvantages of the division of labor. Comte recognized that the division of labor was crucial to progress. However, he lamented that specialization, which was one of its components, led to a withering of the spirit and a breakdown of the community.

The Scottish Enlightenment philosophers (Hume, William Robertston, Adam Ferguson, and Adam Smith) and the Idéologues (Condorcet, Pierre-Jean-Georges Cabanis, Antoine-Louis Claude de Destutt de Tracy, and J. B. Say) also were influential because of their respective efforts to launch a scientific study of society. Comte appreciated the Scottish philosophers' attempt to establish moral principles on a secular, empirical basis in order to reinforce the progress of the human species from rudeness to civilization. They stressed the importance of studying how government and society developed gradually from man's inherently social nature, not from a contract between strong individualists. Contradicting social contract theory, this emphasis on man's natural feeling of sympathy for others, which was also found in Gall's phrenological doctrine, had a large impact on the positivist concept of human nature. As a means of combating "egoistic metaphysics" – that is, doctrines of individualism – the Scottish theory of man's natural sociability as the basic unifying force in society contributed to Comte's own doctrine of altruism and to the establishment of morality as a seventh science based on the social psychology of man.

Carrying on the legacy of the Enlightenment in the early nineteenth century, the Idéologues tried to develop a social science that would lead to social stability while remaining faithful to the essence of liberalism, the movement that had been salient during the first stages of the Revolution. They imagined a secular, educated elite leading a republic according to the findings of a rational, all-encompassing science of man, not according to vague, potentially dangerous political principles, such as inalienable natural rights. Comte was most impressed by the philosopher who inspired this movement: Condorcet. He admired Condorcet's attempt to establish the science of society on the basis of history, particularly the law of progress of the mind, which was the source of the improvement of humanity. Moreover, Comte acknowledged that he borrowed Condorcet's concept of humanity as a single people experiencing the various stages of history. He thus considered Condorcet his "essential precursor" (Comte, 1966, p. 32).

Comte regarded Joseph de Maistre as "the only thinker" after Condorcet and Gall to whom he owed "something important" (Comte, 1973–90, volume 6,

p. 325). Maistre was part of the "reactionary" or counter-revolutionary school of social thought, which included Louis de Bonald. In the pursuit of a synthesis that would transcend stale ideological debates and appeal to people tired of party politics, Comte staked his claim to the liberal tradition by linking his philosophy to that of Condorcet and the Idéologues. Recognizing the force of the Catholic revival that occurred in France after the end of the Napoleonic Empire, Comte also felt obliged to appeal to the conservative sector of the population. He frequently acknowledged his great debt to the doctrine of the theocrats. He agreed with their assessment that "moral anarchy" was the "great scourge" of the nineteenth century and stemmed from the absence of a general unifying doctrine. Inspired by the conservative thinkers' romanticization of the Middle Ages and their organicism, he looked back fondly on the dogmas and structured spiritual order that he believed formed the basis of medieval social unity. Though a severe critic of Catholicism, Comte conceded that the decline of religion had destroyed this harmonious society and had led to "the most abject" individualism and social fragmentation (Comte, 1973–90, volume 1, pp. 147, 156). He blamed the Protestant Revolution in particular for this state of affairs. It had embraced individualism, which influenced the Enlightenment thinkers and the French revolutionaries and formed the basis of liberalism. According to Maistre, the concept of the autonomous, free individual endowed with natural rights was alarming because man could not be understood apart from the organic society in which he lived. Comte concurred with Maistre's arguments against liberalism, finding it an anti-social doctrine, one that contributed to the atomization, materialism, and corruption of modern society. Impressed by Maistre's assessment that the stress on the sovereignty of reason had left people suffering in an abnormal state of unbelief, Comte agreed that to fulfill the "spiritual condition for the continued existence of human society," people needed "fixed, positive, and unanimous principles," which had to be firmly established by a strong spiritual authority ruling a hierarchial society (Comte, 1973–90, volume 1, p. 147). Maistre argued in particular that social solidarity rested on the unlimited power of the Pope, the source of all valid authority. Appreciating his demonstration of the importance of an institution to the power of a religion, Comte strongly endorsed Maistre's concept that a powerful spiritual authority had to remain independent of the temporal government to ensure a moral order. In short, Comte's system reflected Maistre's stance that a unifying spiritual doctrine and structure represented the key to social cohesion.

Yet Comte by no means adopted Maistre's system in its entirety, for he did not wish to return to the past as the theocrats did. Comte recognized the benefits of progress and the new needs of the future industrial-scientific society. He was deeply influenced by contemporary movements promoting change. As a young man, he had been influenced by liberalism and belonged to various republican organizations before he lost faith in political solutions to the anarchy of his times. Despite his turn to the Right, he was a critic of the status quo and remained an opponent of traditional religion and a monarchical form of government. As mentioned previously, he was also much affected by the women's movement and socialism.

Moreover, Comte was touched by the contemporary romantic movement, many of whose themes came to him through the Saint-Simonians, whom he closely watched. Like the romantics, he despised the bourgeois commercialism of his age, argued in favor of spontaneity, and revelled in his eccentricity, which he considered a source of creativity. At the same time, he shared the romantics' interest in the spiritual aspect of human nature and participated in their celebration of women and the emotions. Comte believed that although the intellectual faculties would become stronger with the advance of civilization and would exert more influence on the emotions, they would still need the superior power of the affections to rouse them from their habitual torpor, give them direction, and subject them to the control of reality. Finally, like the romantics, he looked favorably on the Middle Ages. For this reason, he was most drawn to Sir Walter Scott and Alexander Manzoni, who idealized the medieval period in historical epics. The two writers seemed to epitomize the power of the poet or artist to enchant and ennoble. Such aesthetic power would be important in the positivist republic.

Impact

With such a rich, all-encompassing doctrine predicting a harmonious future, Comte attracted numerous followers on both the Left and the Right in France, Britain, the United States, and Latin America. Pierre Laffitte, one of Comte's disciples, became head of the international positivist movement after his master's death. The "orthodox" disciples in the movement compelled him to develop the religious strain of positivism that had preoccupied Comte at the end of his life. Yet the "unorthodox" Littré rejected Comte's religious construction and transformed positivism into a powerful scientific manifesto for a new generation of anti-clerical republicans, who sought legitimacy for their materialist beliefs and hoped to remake the world with the help of science. In this guise, the doctrine became very compelling to Latin American republicans, especially in Brazil, whose flag displays Comte's motto "Order and Progress."

In France, positivism became the semi-official doctrine of the Third Republic. It was a significant weapon in the republic's battle against the Catholic Church, especially in the struggle surrounding the control of schools. Both Jules Ferry and Léon Gambetta, who were leaders in the Third Republic, were enthusiasts, as was Emile Zola, the famous writer. However, another devotee of positivism was Charles Maurras, who in 1898 founded the Action Française, a proto-fascist movement that denounced "un-French" elements such as Protestants and Jews and claimed support for its authoritarian nationalism on the basis of a scientific study of the "facts."

In England, John Stuart Mill actively corresponded with Comte from 1841 to 1847 and came close to becoming his disciple. He absorbed the essential aspects of Comte's conception of a social science, including the positive method and the law of history. He also responded to Comte's call for educated men to provide constructive leadership to a society undergoing a period of transition. Mill and

George Henry Lewes helped to popularize the positivist doctrine, as did Harriet Martineau, who wrote an abridged translation of the *Cours* (1853), which Comte preferred to his own book. The effects of his theories can be seen in the novels of George Eliot, Thomas Hardy, and George Gissing. Richard Congreve and Frederic Harrison set up rival centers of worship dedicated to the Religion of Humanity, whose secular, scientific principles and humanism had wide appeal as an alternative to Christianity. The Fabian Socialists Beatrice and Sidney Webb were taken with Comte's scientific approach to the study of society, his notion of altruism, and his stress on the role of enlightened leaders of opinion (Wright, 1986).

Comte's concern for the common good and his elitism also proved tantalizing to many American liberals, who found in positivism a new naturalistic philosophy that could replace religion as the foundation of society. In the midst of the professionalization of society, these educated elites appreciated the large role that Comte's new science of society entrusted to well-rounded intellectuals to correct the social problems caused by the concentration of corporate power. Henry Edger, David Croly, Thaddeus Wakeman, Edward Bellamy, Herbert Croly, and Lester Ward were some of the American reformers of the Gilded Age and Progressive Era who were influenced by Comte. They turned liberal ideology away from its traditional libertarian, *laissez-faire* position and made it far more receptive to the idea that an organic community could be created by an interventionist state managed by a professional elite of experts devoted to serving humanity (Harp, 1995).

Comte's influence extended to the science he created, sociology. His interest in preserving social cohesion and harmony was echoed by Émile Durkheim, who adopted Comte's idea that society itself is a reality with its own laws and should be studied in a scientific manner. As reflected in his concept of "anomie," he too measured social health in terms of social solidarity. Durkheim's functionalist approach in the end triumphed over alternative schools of sociology, such as those of his competitors Gabriel Tarde and René Worms, and thus ensured the further diffusion of Comte's ideas in the social sciences (Levine, 1995, p. 168). Lucien Lévy-Bruhl introduced positivist ideas into anthropology. His studies of the primitive mentality may have been inspired by Comte's interest in fetishism, for Comte was the first European thinker to look favorably upon this religion. Other social scientists influenced by Comte include Alfred Espinas, Thomas Buckle, Herbert Spencer, Hippolyte Taine, Ernest Renan, Charles Booth, Patrick Geddes, Leonard Hobhouse, and Lewis Mumford.

Scientists and philosophers, especially philosophers of science, have been affected by Comte's explanation for the uniqueness of science, especially its difference from metaphysics. Comte's recognition of the importance of hypotheses as useful, convenient devices to be used in scientific research foreshadowed the later work of Hans Vaihinger and Henri Poincaré and may have also influenced Claude Bernard, Marcelin Berthelot, Paul Janet, Ernst Mach, Wilhelm Ostwald, and Pierre Duhem. Indeed, in the early twentieth century, the philosophy of science was almost thoroughly positivist (Manicas, 1987, p. 185).

There was in particular a connection between Comte's positivism and logical positivism; both took a similar approach to the problems of determining meaningfulness, distinguishing scientific from nonscientific knowledge, and using the principle of verifiability to criticize metaphysicians. Both argued that the natural and social sciences share common logical bases and a superiority to other forms of knowledge. The leading logical positivists included A. J. Ayer, Otto Neurath, Rudolf Carnap, Moritz Schlick, and Hans Reichenbach.

In many respects, the influence of positivism has been more widespread than that of either Marxism or Freudianism. A great many people today are unknowingly positivists in that they claim to believe only statements supported by tangible evidence. Yet the name of Comte is not a household word, for he has always been subject to severe criticism.

ASSESSMENT

Comte is easy to ridicule. He was pedantic, dogmatic, and authoritarian. His treatment of others was invariably harsh and egotistical. His writing is dry, austere, and convoluted, which makes reading his work a struggle. As for sociology, many of Comte's ideas are not very scientific and seem to be merely assumptions. For example, there is no basis for his schema that there are three stages of history, each of which is rigidly determined and inevitable everywhere in the world. He supported this law of three stages by carefully selecting only those facts that would demonstrate it. His depiction of the third stage of history, the positive one, seems fanciful and "utopian," a reflection of his love of system-building. His epistemology has been criticized for not providing a formal logic of proof; however, Comte's omission was deliberate, for he did not believe one could adequately or usefully define facts, scientific observation, or rules of verification. His rejection of psychology has also been regarded as unwarranted, although critics again have failed to see that his remarks were directed against the speculations of Victor Cousin (Scharff, 1995, p. 11).

Comte's basic impulse to synthesize seems misguided in many respects. In his embrace of French, English, and German philosophical traditions, he betrayed a certain eclecticism, simplicity, and even superficiality. He appeared anxious to synthesize philosophical movements no matter how different they might be. Like his contemporary François Guizot, Comte was trying to find a *"juste milieu"* which would accommodate all opinions. Positivism, in Comte's eyes, would triumph because it would present a doctrine that was even "more organic" than that espoused by the reactionaries and "more progressive" than that advocated by the revolutionaries (Comte, 1975, volume 2, p. 40). In other words, it would create social harmony by combining the traditionalism of the Right and the rationalism of the Left. Comte believed that the Left would be attracted by his hostility toward the Church and established religions; his republicanism; his faith in reason, relativism, and progress; his emphasis on the importance of freedom of discussion to change the world; his concept of radical social reconstruction in the interest of the working class; and his vision of a new industrial and secular order. The Right would allegedly approve of his promotion of traditional values; his stress on a strong spiritual power, duties, hierarchy, order, and stability; and his opposition to equality, popular sovereignty, and individualism. In the end, his synthesis made him highly vulnerable; because he did not cater to one specific group as Marx did, he had no inherent supporters. The Right attacked his anti-religious, anti-monarchical views and his worship of a secular abstraction, Humanity. The Left criticized his brand of illiberalism, which disregarded the rights of the individual and egalitarian impulses.

As a careful reader of Jean-Jacques Rousseau, Comte made the needs of society paramount. The society that he depicted was a highly regimented one, where people were forced to conform to the Religion of Humanity, an artificial creation that substituted Humanity for God as an object of worship, while keeping most of the ceremonies of Catholicism. Consensus would be achieved through uniformity, not by working out differences of opinion. To a certain extent, Comte sacrificed freedom and pluralism for social control, thus exacerbating the problem of the abuse of power. Yet considering his preoccupation with uniting humanity through the recognition of its manifestations in different singularities (individuals, nations, cultures, and religions), Juliette Grange has argued that Comte was not a proto-totalitarian intent on eliminating individualism; indeed, in an effort to reconcile pluralism and holism, he maintained that humanity developed only through the individual. Humanity was a spiritual or moral community, not an institutionalized political construct demanding blind submission and conformity from each member. The unity of humanity rested on the participation of all its individual members, who were necessarily diverse and specialized (Grange, 1996, pp. 270–6).

Despite the defects in Comte's semi-authoritarian solution to the turmoil of the modern era – defects that reflect the tensions of his own time and his fragile personality – his attempt to cure society of its ills continues to be a central objective of the science of society. Comte's admonitions about the dangers of sociology succumbing to the "positivity" of the scientific age are still highly relevant today, when the model of the physical sciences continues to hold great appeal and some sociologists and other scholars remain attracted to an empirical, jargon-laden discourse, one fearful of grand theories. Sociology has become a fragmented discipline that Comte would never recognize as his own, considering his repeated condemnation of modern specialization. Nor would he approve of the direction that philosophy has taken. As Robert Scharff has shown, the so-called "post-positivists," such as Richard Rorty and Hilary Putnam, err today in fostering a detachment from history in their desire to proclaim the beginning of a new era; they never question the legitimacy of their belief in their own maturity, originality, and correctness. They would benefit from taking a new look at Comte's suggestions about the relativism and tentativeness of knowledge – especially the impossibility of validating epistemological proofs – and his demonstration of the importance of reflecting on prescientific practices and their kinship with positivism. Emphasizing Comte's statement that "no conception can be fully understood without its history" (Comte, 1975, volume 1, p. 21), Robert Scharff has maintained that Comte promoted a "historico-critical reflectiveness" among philosophers that is highly relevant today (Scharff, 1995, p. 16). Put into its historical context in a Comtean fashion, the postmodern world may not be as innovative as it prides itself on being. It may well heed Comte's call for moral commitments to the other members of humanity and to the earth, and his recognition of the power of religion. As Juliette Grange suggests, Auguste Comte may well be *the* sociologist for the twenty-first century (Grange, 1996, p. 15).

Bibliography

Writings of Auguste Comte

Ecrits de jeunesse 1816–1828: Suivis du Mémoire sur la Cosmogonie de Laplace 1835 (ed. Paulo E. de Berrêdo Carneiro and Pierre Arnaud). Paris: Ecole Pratique des Hautes Etudes (1970).

Cours de philosophie positive (ed. Michel Serres, François Dagognet, Allal Sinaceur, and Jean-Paul Enthoven), 2 volumes. 1830–42. Paris: Hermann (1975).

Discours sur l'esprit positif. 1844. Paris: Union Générale d'Editions (1963).

Système de politique positive ou Traité du sociologie instituant la religion de l'Humanité, 4 volumes. 1851–4. 5th edn, Paris: Au Siège de la Société Positiviste (1929).

Catéchisme positiviste, ou Sommaire exposition de la religion universelle en treize entretiens systématiques entre une femme et un prêtre de l'humanité. 1852. Paris: Garnier-Flammarion (1966).

Appel aux Conservateurs. 1855.

Synthèse subjective ou Système universel des conceptions propres à l'état normal de l'humanité, volume 1. 1856.

Testament d'Auguste Comte avec les documents qui s'y rapportent: Pièces justificatives, prières quotidiennes, confessions annuelles, correspondance avec Mme de Vaux. 1884; 2nd edn, 1896.

Correspondance générale et confessions (ed. Paulo E. de Berrêdo Carneiro, Pierre Arnaud, Paul Arbousse-Bastide, and Angèle Kremer-Marietti), 8 volumes. 1973–90. Paris: Ecole des Hautes Etudes en Sciences Sociales.

Further reading

Aron, Raymond (1968) *Main Currents in Sociological Thought,* volume 1, trans. Richard Howard and Helen Weaver. Garden City, NY: Doubleday, Anchor Books.

Gane, Mike (1991) *Baudrillard: Critical and Fatal Theory.* London: Routledge.

Gouhier, Henri (1933–41) *La Jeunesse d'Auguste Comte et la formation du positivisme,* 3 volumes. Paris: J. Vrin.

Gouhier, Henri (1965) *La Vie d'Auguste Comte,* 2nd edn. Paris: J. Vrin.

Grange, Juliette (1996) *La Philosophie d'Auguste Comte: Science, politique, religion.* Paris: Presses Universitaires de France.

Haac, Oscar (ed. and trans.) (1995) *The Correspondence of John Stuart Mill and Auguste Comte.* New Brunswick, NJ: Transaction Publishers.

Habermas, Jürgen (1971) *Knowledge and Human Interests,* trans. Jeremy J. Shapiro. Boston: Beacon Press.

Harp, Gillis J. (1995) *Positivist Republic: Auguste Comte and the Reconstruction of American Liberalism, 1865–1920.* University Park, PA: Penn State University Press.

Heilbron, Johan (1990) Auguste Comte and Modern Epistemology. *Sociological Theory,* 8, 153–62.

Kofman, Sarah (1978) *Aberrations: Le Devenir-Femme d'Auguste Comte.* Paris: Aubier Flammarion.

Kremer-Marietti, Angèle (1982) *Entre le Signe et l'histoire: L'Anthropologie d'Auguste Comte*. Paris: Klincksieck.

Laudan, Larry (1971) Towards a Reassessment of Comte's "Méthode Positive." *Philosophy of Science*, 38, 35–53.

Lenzer, Gertrud (ed.) (1975) *Auguste Comte and Positivism: the Essential Writings*. New York: Harper & Row.

Levine, Donald N. (1995) *Visions of the Sociological Tradition*. Chicago: University of Chicago Press.

Manicas, Peter T. (1987) *A History and Philosophy of the Social Sciences*. Oxford: Basil Blackwell.

Manuel, Frank E. (1962) *The Prophets of Paris*. Cambridge, MA: Harvard University Press.

Petit, Annie (1999) *Le Système positiviste: La Philosophie des sciences d'Auguste Comte et de ses premiers disciples 1820–1900*. Paris: Vrin.

Pickering, Mary (1993) *Auguste Comte: an Intellectual Biography*. Cambridge: Cambridge University Press.

Pickering, Mary (1996) Angels and Demons in the Moral Vision of Auguste Comte. *Journal of Women's History*, 8, 10–40.

Pickering, Mary (1997) Rhetorical Strategies in the Works of Auguste Comte, *Historical Reflections/Réflexions Historiques*, 23, 151–75.

Pickering, Mary (1998) Auguste Comte and the Return to Primitivism. *Revue Internationale de Philosophie*, 52, 51–77.

Saint-Simon, Claude-Henri de (1966) *Oeuvres de Claude-Henri de Saint-Simon*, 6 volumes. Paris: Anthropos.

Scharff, Robert C. (1995) *Comte after Positivism*. Cambridge: Cambridge University Press.

Wright, T. R. (1986) *The Religion of Humanity: the Impact of Comtean Positivism on Victorian Britain*. Cambridge: Cambridge University Press.

2

Harriet Martineau

Susan Hoecker-Drysdale

In the preface to her condensation and translation of August Comte's *Positive Philosophy*, Harriet Martineau states that she was motivated to produce the English edition out of her "deep conviction of our need for this book in my own country." Two years later, in her *Autobiography*, she went so far as to state that among all her writings she considered her translation of Comte's major work, which introduced French positivism into English thought, to be the best reflection of her direction and influence. The point of her self-appraisal, written shortly after mid-century, was not so much to identify herself with a specifically Comtean world view as to profess her commitment to science as the source of new knowledge and to sociology and the "moral" (social) sciences as the basis for social progress and reform.

Harriet Martineau (1802–76) subscribed to a broadly conceived science of society, a science which, in her view, would offer the key to understanding societal change and the "uncertainties of the age." As a sociologist, historian, journalist, and public educator, Martineau had a significant impact during her lifetime on the thinking of the British public, and through her publications, in English and in translation into numerous other languages, she advanced the sociological understanding of her readers in Britain, America, and many countries around the globe. From her first publications at age 19 to her last major writings at age 74, Martineau addressed a wide range of subjects and issues in a variety of genres to diverse audiences, publishing over 70 volumes, dozens of periodical articles, and nearly 2,000 newspaper leaders and letters. Her ideas were not only consonant with, but influential for, those of succeeding social theorists.

THE THEORY

Martineau's achievements fall within a number of theoretical perspectives and levels of social analysis, both macro- and microsociological. The theoretical perspectives and epistemological concerns reflected and developed in her major works can be identified as political economy, historical-comparative analysis, theories of history, feminist theory, social stratification theory (including race, class, and gender theory), metamethodology, and the philosophy of science. Although influenced by certain aspects of sociological positivism as well as by sociological organicism, she drew from them selectively. Her work is most clearly compatible with the historical and comparative perspectives and substantive concerns of Weber, Marx, and Durkheim.

In both her theoretical and empirical work Martineau assumes a critical sociological approach, seen particularly in her "immanent critique" of American society. Her strategy is to focus particularly on societal principles, morals and values in relation to the institutional structures, social relationships, and behavioral patterns in which they are concretized, analyzing the inconsistencies, conflicts, and incongruities. Her empiricism is informed by a critical metamethodology, which takes nothing for granted and sets the foundation for a systematic, informed, and reflexive sociological methodology. In a convergence of theory and method Martineau utilizes typological analysis in an innovative manner to examine and compare types of suicide, religion, marriage and family structures, governments, segments of the economy, and occupations. Finally, in her role as a public educator, she contributes in no small measure to the interpretation and communication of theory in political economy, philosophy, politics, sociology, and science.

Interpreting theory: political economy

Martineau began her career in social science with a project designed to serve the aspirations of society toward progress and improvement, and, in so doing, began to realize her self-defined role as a public educator. It was in fact the endeavor of interpreting political economy which constituted her first major theoretical study in 1832–4, an undertaking which developed her nascent interests in theories about society and was responsible for her entry into the public sphere. Her keen interest in theories of political economy shaped her later original sociological work, which systematically recognized the significance of the economy in the social order. This first major work is important in the sense that it involved the interpretation, rather than creation, of theory.

Having absorbed the ideas of Adam Smith, Thomas Malthus, Dugald Stewart, and Francis Bacon, Martineau wrote reviews of works on political economy in the *Monthly Repository* and then a few "eightpenny stories" in pamphlet form, which dealt, somewhat unintentionally, with such political economy issues as the impact of machinery on wages, the identity of economic interests, and social imperatives in a changing division of labor. In 1831 she conceived the idea of writing a series of stories which would illustrate the principles of political economy for the public, facilitate an understanding of the economic laws at work, and thereby foster social progress. The result was her 25-volume *Illustrations of Political Economy*, a monthly series of tales which illustrated the principles of production, distribution, consumption, and exchange, drawn from James Mill's *Elements of Political Economy* (1821). Convinced that the public would not be attracted to Mill's rather academic and somewhat dull exposition of the science, Martineau skillfully utilized the genre of the novelette to inspire some understanding of the principles. She could thereby dramatize the network of class interests and the increasingly complex interconnections of industrial capitalism and the market economy.

Martineau's purpose was to present didactic stories comprehensible to all classes: "all classes bear an equal relation to the science." In this instance, fiction became a means to interpret theory, to communicate principles of political economy as yet inaccessible to the general reader. Martineau seems to have shared Spencer's view that increasingly complex societies are more vulnerable precisely because of the growing interdependence of a multifarious division of labor. Hence the duty of members of all classes to understand the principles and relationships of this complicated social organism.

> If it concerns rulers that their measures should be wise, if it concerns the wealthy that their property should be secure, the middling classes that their industry should be rewarded, the poor that their hardships should be redressed, it concerns all that Political Economy should be understood. If it concerns all that the advantages of a social state should be preserved and improved, it concerns them likewise that Political Economy should be understood by all. (*Illustrations of Political Economy*, volume 1, p. xvi)

The topics in the tales included: labor as the basis of wealth and capital; the growing division of labor and the effects of machinery; the relation between wages, prices, and profits; the importance of individual initiative and labor and the negative effects of state support; the necessity to limit population growth; the principles of a market economy and free competition; supply and demand; the function and supply of money; the advantages of free trade; the positive and negative roles played by unions; productive and unproductive consumption; the requirement of public expenditure for defense, public order, and social improvement; the importance of just taxation and avoidance of public indebtedness (Hoecker-Drysdale, 1992, pp. 21–48).

The work reflected her nominalist view of society as a collection of individuals who are informed and act in consonance out of their rational understanding and belief in the principles or fundamental laws operating therein. Martineau's illustrative narratives caught the public imagination at the time, although, as often happens with first works, in later years she was quite critical of her early efforts.

Theorizing empiricism: Martineau's metamethodology

Following her *Illustrations of Political Economy* series, Martineau turned toward another challenging and more original project. Partly as relief from two years of intensive work and partly out of burning curiosity, she embarked in 1834 on a trip to America. This was to be a mission on behalf of an improved

British understanding of American society: "If I am spared to come back, this country shall know something more than it does of the principles of American institutions. I am tired of being kept foundering among the details. . . . It is urged upon me . . . that I should go and see for myself." During the six-week sea voyage to America and in anticipation of the research ahead, she wrote a methodological treatise, the earliest explicit treatment of sociological methods and social research. It remains a landmark in the development of the art and science of social investigation. *How to Observe Morals and Manners* (1838) includes discussions of metamethodological considerations, principles of social investigation, research strategies and methods, and a framework for the study of a total society which she applied in the three-volume *Society in America* (1837).

Martineau emphasizes that studies in the science of morals must be based on disciplined observation, impartiality, a theoretical framework, and systematic research methods used consistently and self-consciously. The treatise emphasizes the necessity of tracing the impact of societal phenomena on one another and of developing a critical view, in order to understand, for example, the corruptive elements of the "marital status," or the overreliance on public opinion. *How to Observe Morals and Manners* is organized into three parts: "Requisites for Observation," "What to Observe," and "Mechanical Methods."

Following a discussion of metamethodology, Martineau presents her macro-sociological framework for studying a total society. The institutional areas which must be examined include:

1   Religion (churches, clergy, superstitions, suicide).
2   General moral notions (national character, popular culture, stories, idols, songs, literature, treatment of criminals, the aged and children).
3   The domestic state (topography and geography, economics and occupations, family, marriage and children, health).
4   The idea of liberty (police, law, social classes, servitude, communications, education, public opinion).
5   Progress (cultural, economic and technological change).
6   Discourse.

"Wise inquiry into Morals and Manners [will] begin with the study of *things*, using the *discourse of persons* as a commentary upon them" (*How to Observe Morals and Manners*, p. 63). Facts must be gained from the "records" of a society: "architectural remains, epitaphs, civic registers, national music, or any other of the thousand manifestations of the common mind which may be found among every people" (ibid., p. 64). In a later chapter she elaborates on discourse as the indispensable commentary upon the classes of national facts which are observed; it gives meaning and illustration to the evidence of facts. In the study of discourse the traveller or investigator "must seek intercourse with all classes of the society . . . not only the rich and the poor, but those who may be classes by profession, pursuit, habits of mind, and turn of manners. . . . He must study little ones at their mothers' knees, and flirtations in ballrooms, and dealings in the market-place. . . . Wherever there is speech, he must devote himself to hear."

Martineau felt a real advantage as a woman investigator, for it gave her access to the kitchens, the nurseries, the boudoirs, where much of the "inner life" of a people is revealed. Discourse is important precisely because it exhibits a certain character of its own and expresses the distinct national character and values of a society, from which we can derive *types* of societies. But discourse in itself is limited and can be deceptive, particularly because it may not, and often does not, coincide with the facts, nor does it represent an appropriate sample of views and opinions.

The danger always exists that every observer assumes he or she can understand, apart from all other phenomena, human behavior. Martineau emphasizes the need for the observer to refrain from premature conclusions, to be self-conscious of his or her own biases, to examine all sides and perspectives on issues, situations, and practices, to use a variety of methods in obtaining information, and to immerse oneself, as a true participant observer, enough to know and understand, while maintaining self-checks of distance and objectivity. For these reasons she advocates the use of three specific methodological tools for the corroboration of facts and observations: a diary, to record one's personal reactions; a journal, to record impressions, incidents, anecdotes, descriptions; and a notebook, to record the facts of daily life. These were mechanisms for systematization and self-monitoring.

Martineau utilizes typological analysis, at once a theoretical and methodological approach, in a number of instances in her work to organize historical/empirical data and to analyze their contents theoretically. Particularly effective is her examination of religion and suicide in society. Reflecting the methodological influence of Montesquieu, she develops a typology of religion – Licentious, Ascetic, and Moderate – distinguished by the degrees of ritualism, physical or spiritual self-indulgence, and individual liberty, and emphasis on interpersonal sentiment. While all societies hold religious sentiments of key importance in understanding them, she concludes that despotic governments can only prevail where licentious or ascetic religions are dominant. On the other hand, democratic government is possible only under a moderate form of religion. At the same time, religious freedom is the highest expression of democracy. "Religion is the highest fact in the Rights of Man from its being the most exclusively private and individual, while it is also a universal concern.... Religion is, in its widest sense, the tendency of human nature to the Infinite ... [to] the pursuit of perfection" (*Society in America*, volume 3, p. 224).

Likewise, in her analysis of suicide, she designates types of suicide which are indicative of the character of social relationships and the sentiments of the social order. "Every society has its suicides, and much may be learned from their character and number, both as to the notions on morals which prevail, and the religious sentiment which animates to or controls the act." In an analysis not dissimilar from Durkheim's, which appeared more than a half century later, she derives the following types of suicide: (a) suicide as duty, as with soldiers; (b) suicide out of devotion to others; (c) suicide when hope of honor is gone; (d) suicide to protect the virtue of chastity; (e) martyrdom for truth, ranging from veneration to fanatical self-seeking. Martineau linked the prevalence of suicide to a group or society's view of future life, to enslavement as opposed to freedom, to religious practices such as the Suttee, to imitation within certain groups, and to religious beliefs, suggesting that considerations of purgatory, for example, might discourage the Irish and the French from such acts. Suicide out of devotion to others generally carries cultural approbation and martyrdom (*How to Observe Morals and Manners*). Having analyzed the sociological relevance of religion and suicide, she proceeds to an inquiry into the moral and cultural values of a society.

Martineau was so convinced of the importance of suicide for understanding societal relations that she returned to the subject, not only in her America studies but also in an article which appeared in Charles Dickens's *Household Words* and later in one of her collections (*Health, Husbandry, and Home*), in which she developed a somewhat different typology: suicides based upon shame, complete devotion to others, preservation of honor, and withdrawal from duty and expectations of others. She concluded that suicide was more frequent among men, was linked to intemperance, varied according to occupation, district, and education, was related to weak imagination and strong egoism, and probably had a hereditary component. In these discussions she also advocated enlightened attitudes toward the treatment of mental illness.

Martineau's approach in *How to Observe Morals and Manners* is to insist that, in the study of a society, consideration must be given, as in the work of Montesquieu, to the totality of society, including its geographical, climatic, and economic bases; to civilization, as examined by Condorcet, particularly the degree of freedom and equality of its members, especially women; to class structures and cultures and their consequences, as we see later in Marx; and to morals and values, the culture and consequences of religion, as in Weber and Durkheim, as well as the phenomenon of suicide as perhaps a crisis in values or relationships. This important sociological treatise was overshadowed by her other "America studies" and, unlike her other books, was not reprinted for a century and a half, perhaps because it *was* a metamethodological treatise, actually, if not intentionally, aimed at the researcher and epistemologist. There is little doubt, however, that this remarkable piece was of enormous aid to Martineau herself and to those travellers and students of societies who availed themselves of it.

Theorizing America: Martineau's macrosociology

Martineau's macrosociological investigation of America in the 1830s, including the methodological treatise and her analysis of American society, comprise her most significant sociological work in terms of both empirical investigation and theoretical analysis. The study itself, done in the same decade as de Tocqueville's *Democracy in America*, is equally perspicacious, more clearly rooted in empirical fact, and more self-consciously theoretically ordered. In the analysis a systematic framework for the study of social structures, social institutions and their interrelations, and social dynamics is complemented by attention to the idiographic and the ethnographic. The investigation explores empirically, and analyses theoretically:

1 Politics, parties and government.
2 The morals of politics (political office, newspapers, citizenship, sectional prejudice, citizenship of people of color, the political nonexistence of women).
3 The economy, of various regions, including agriculture, transport, markets, manufactures, commerce.
4 The morals of economy, including the morals of slavery, the morals of manufacture, the morals of commerce.
5 "Civilization," her nomenclature embracing the idea of honor, caste and classes, property and intercourse, women, marriage, occupation, health, children, sufferers, utterance.
6 Religion, the science (principles) of religion, spirit, and administration of religion.

Throughout Martineau's analysis of these institutions in America and their interconnections there are several implicit theoretical foci: (a) the discrepancies between normative structures and social behavior; (b) structural inequalities; (c) conflicts and incongruities of values and value systems; (d) the meaning and motives, and their contradictions, of social actors. These foci are woven into the fabric of the study, accompanied by observations, interviews, narratives, anecdotes, descriptions, and statistical and documentary facts. The following analysis attempts to show these theoretical convergences as well as to provide something of the tenor of her own research narratives.

SETTING AND FRAMEWORK Martineau spent two years (September 19, 1834 to August 1, 1836) exploring American society, travelling close to 10,000 miles throughout the United States, visiting many areas more than once, talking with and interviewing people of all ages, classes, races, religions, and political parties. She interviewed and interacted with a wide range of the population, from the highly placed, including the President of the United States, Andrew Jackson, to ordinary persons. She observed and interviewed slaves, mill girls, Indian tribes, members of experimental communities, abolitionists, farmers, workers, feminists, and many others. She visited prisons, hospitals, mental asylums, literary and scientific institutions, factories, plantations, and farms, and lived in all sorts of dwellings, from stately homes to log cabins. She used all possible means of transportation, walked a great deal as she felt that that was the best means of learning about a people, and studied all aspects of the young society. As de Tocqueville did, she brought with her a companion and research assistant, Louisa Jeffrey, to aid her in observation and collection of material and to serve as a second set of eyes and ears (Martineau being by then quite deaf).

Martineau's particular interest in her investigation of America was in the "theory and practice of society," which in fact was her original title for the book. The theoretical stance of *Society in America* can best be understood as immanent critique; that is, an understanding and assessment of the structures and practices of a society on its own terms, not by external criteria, particularly in the relationship between cultural norms and societal practices. In this context, morals and values become the center point for understanding social behavior. She explained at the outset that her purpose was "to compare the existing state of society in America with the principles on which it was professedly founded; thus testing Institutions, Morals and Manners by an indisputable, instead of an arbitrary standard, and securing to myself the same point of view with my readers of both nations" (*Society in America*, volume 1, p. viii). To compensate for the possibility of omission and misinterpretation and in full recognition of the tentativeness of any interpretation, Martineau used immanent critique to scrutinize social behavior in terms of the principles, beliefs, and values articulated in the society's formal documents: the American Constitution, the Bill of Rights, the Declaration of Independence and other institutionalized creeds. The true test of a nation's success, according to Utilitarian standards to which she at least in part subscribed, is the general happiness of its members. She was concerned, therefore, to assess the extent to which happiness or general well-being could be seen to characterize the lives of people in various social groups. Her analysis and conclusions remain solidly in the tradition of early critical sociology.

Her investigation is descriptive, analytical, and critical. As she conducts her empirical research, her methodological self-consciousness is apparent. She is able to capture the richness and variety, as well as dynamism, of life in a thriving, exciting new society, precisely because she adhered to her own dicta, presented earlier, to "seek intercourse with all classes of society" and to search for the "inner life" of society. At the same time, Martineau integrates her observations into more general theoretical analysis within a historical and comparative perspective.

Martineau observed and analyzed critically the complexities of the plantation as a site of contradictions between the ideology of freedom and the practices of slavery, the New England town hall as a cradle of both democracy and bigotry, the prevalence of political apathy within the world's first modern democracy, the legal freedoms enjoyed but social shackles endured by women, and the disastrous societal consequences of the enslavement of a part of the population by the privileged few.

THE MORALS OF POLITICS The analysis is structured around three general concerns: politics and government, the economy, and culture and social institutions. Observations and analyses of the structures, functions, and norms of each are followed by close examination of the morals of politics and the morals of economy. Here Martineau explores the dynamics of power, conflict, and control which occur in everyday life in these arenas. In examining government and politics, for example, Martineau emphasizes the strengths of the system – its principles – and the potential for genuine democracy. "Politics are morals, all the world over; that is, politics universally implicate the duty and happiness of man" (ibid., p. 6). It is in the arena of politics, she maintains, that the theory and practice of a nation's principles intersect, where material realities and the highest ideals confront one another.

The theory that "the majority are in the right" requires that basic principles be secured and that the citizenry have the liberty to ensure a correspondence between the principles and their institutional forms. Inconsistencies arise out of human fallibility rather than political design. Martineau identifies crucial contradictions within American society, in examining, for example, the dynamics of office-holding (e.g. that holding office means the end of one's moral independence), the role of the press (e.g. that it exercises arbitrary power through control of content and perspective), failure of citizenship (through apathy, fear of opinion, or lack of the franchise), significant class, race, and gender differences in observing the law, and the absence of any political and economic power and participation for negroes and women. The flagrant violations of the law by mobs of "white gentlemen" in the North as well as the South left it to the (disenfranchised) women to take responsibility for seeking peaceful means of resolving these conflicts and contradictions. This meant that women abolitionists were suspect in both regions and were frequently harassed, jailed, or, especially if black, beaten or killed as they challenged the corruptions of society.

Martineau found that this new "nation of equals," based upon Enlightenment ideals and lacking a feudal history, created its own hierarchy and class distinctions, exemplifying the "tenacity of rank." She analyzed the many practices which sustained structured inequalities in American society. Although "the law, in a republic, is the embodiment of the will of the people," she noted that the public, commonly uninformed and indifferent, ignored the horrendous treatment of the abolitionists with rationalizations about the respectability of the anti-abolitionists ("the gentlemen of Boston would do nothing improper") and condemned the meddlesomeness and trouble-making of the abolitionists (ibid., 176). Although the citizenship of all society's members was a legal reality, constitutionally, people of color were badly treated. "They are protected as citizens when the public service requires their security; but not otherwise treated as such" (ibid., 195). She noted that prejudice against color was on the increase. Likewise, the democratic principle that "governments derive their just powers from the consent of the governed" is entirely violated given the "political non-existence of women" (ibid., 199). "Indulgence is given her [every woman] as a substitute for justice" (*Society in America*, volume 3, p. 106). Martineau concluded that the denial to negroes and women of the ability to exercise their rights as free citizens within the society constituted the greatest injustice and contradiction in American society. Nonetheless, there were many instances, she reported, of strong-minded and remarkable women and blacks who overcame all odds to free themselves and others.

THE MORALS OF THE ECONOMY The morals of the economy likewise revealed serious problems in the values and goals of the society. Martineau emphasized the high priority given to mercenary rather than human values. Indeed, the pursuit of wealth as possible for all and the reduction of all values to mercenary ones lay at the heart of America's cultural malady. In her analysis of work and honor, she showed that in regions of slavery and/or systems of rank, labor was regarded as degrading; work was debased. In the North and particularly in the rugged but free and open western regions, work was seen as necessary, honorable, and an exercise of one's freedom. She predicted that in this new nation eventually labor would be honored. "America is in the singular position of being nearly equally divided between a low degree of the ancient barbarism in relation to labor, and a high degree of the modern enlightenment."

The culturally accepted notion that women do not work is utterly untrue, she demonstrated, as married or single women did indeed work, enduring low pay or no pay, while being charged with enormous responsibility in holding the society together. In her discussions of the economics of stratification, including race, gender, and class, she drew attention to the "mean whites" of the South, who worked with their hands, had no prospects and few positive life chances, and took the harshest attitudes toward negroes. (A similar discussion is found eighty years later in Max Weber's discussions of class in America.) By contrast, there were white plantation women who taught the slaves to read, in relationships of respect and friendship.

The morals of slavery revealed the horrendous degradations of negroes and women, particularly black women, the disregard for human rights, and the hypocrisies of mistreatment and exploitation of men, women, and children within a declared system of honor. Contrarily, the morals of manufactory and commerce showed that, in a democratic society, work was of a higher calibre, resulting, for instance, in improvements in manufacture. In that context, there existed a concern, if rather paternalistic, of employers for employees and a spirit of enterprise emerging from a "sordid love of gain," a love of art, and the practice of benevolence and philanthropy. Again, however, practices of specula-tion, greed, and support for the profitable institution of slavery created the problematics of this free and open economy.

CIVILIZATION "The degree of civilisation of any people corresponds with the exaltation of the idea which is the most prevalent among that people" (*Society in America*, volume 3, p. 1). Martineau examined "civilization," which in the old world still corresponded with the low idea that "the generality of men live for wealth, ease and dignity and lofty reputation," rather than with inner values. Although the new world was forged out of the fundamental human values of truth and justice – as expressed in the Revolution and the Declaration of Independence – its members remained captivated by the old world's pursuit of wealth rather than social and political freedoms.

These economic realities and accompanying values resulted in peculiar and perhaps destructive conceptions of social honor. "It is true that it is better to live for honour than for wealth: but how much better, depends upon the idea of honour" (ibid., p. 10). While moralists, scholars, professionals, and even some merchants were dissatisfied with the importance attached to wealth, general lifestyle and consumption practices as well as the American idea of honor seemed solidly based on obvious signs of consumption and leisure and an exaggerated concern with reputation and the opinions of others. Tensions existed, therefore, between the tendency toward maintaining an aristocratic European-derived culture, on the one hand, and an obsession with wealth and the real opportunities of economic freedom and mobility within a republic, on the other. In the absence of an established class system, according to Martineau, patterns of consumption, leisure and accumulation of a most conspicuous and self-conscious nature became crucial social indicators. In that context, women became vehicles of display and consumption (ibid., pp. 37–53). These value incongruities posed significant problems for American society as it attempted to both profess and practice its cultural ideals.

According to Martineau, these contradictions were exhibited in the inter-course and discourse of the members of society: a good-natured, friendly, and hospitable people who nevertheless engaged in duelling; a population generous in time and money in the service of others who held a preoccupation with the practice of flattery; and an enterprising and idealistic society which allowed itself to be dominated by the pressures of public opinion. Martineau included within her analysis an examination of the mechanisms which supported the class system, as, for instance, in her discussions of the rules and distinctions in socializing, anticipating Simmel's concept of sociation, where classes establish their own rules for interaction and inclusion. Rules of imitation paralleled rules of anti-commensality in relations between negroes and whites. The class, and even caste, system challenged the very authenticity of the ideology of equality. Nevertheless, even within the context of materialistic, superficial and anti-democratic behavior, Americans were distinguished in the honor given to the intellect and the intellectual as well as in their desire to be open and to com-municate on a variety of subjects.

RELIGION After exploring the status of women, children and sufferers, and those marginalized by virtue of being criminal, mentally ill, disabled, poor, or alcoholic, she explored the literary life of the society, completing her study of American society with an analysis of religion. With particular sociological finesse, she distinguished the science of religion from its spirit and practice, and dealt specifically with the history, theology, and current status of religion, the spiritual ethic and meaning of religion, and the "administration" or social organization of religion. She emphasized the need to separate the role of theo-logical research ("the science of religion") and the open pursuit of ideas from the function of preaching and administering to the religious needs of the population. Martineau had written considerably about religion early in her writing career; she was well informed on the subject. Examining American society, she was struck by the lack of diversity in religious beliefs in a country exalting freedom of conscience, by religious intolerance, by hypocrisies among the clergy, and by practices of churches as agents of stratification, sometimes helpful but usually ineffectual challengers to the system of slavery. Throughout, the sociological significance of religion was emphasized.

HER CONCLUSIONS Martineau concluded her macrosociological study of America with the suggestion of the tentativeness of her observations, but noted that American society had a smaller amount of crime, poverty, and mutual injury of every kind than any known society. "They have realised many things for which the rest of the world is still struggling" (ibid., p. 298). She held high hopes for this new nation founded upon the principle of equality. Americans were self-governing, she noted, and had avoided an aristocracy, a link between church and state, excessive taxation, and the irresponsibility of any class. Any evils arising out of the legislative or executive branches of government could be remedied by the people themselves. However, her final and most general conclusion was that "the civilisation and the morals of the Americans fall far below their own principles" (ibid., p. 299), that there were severe contradictions between the principles and practices of American social life. Resolution of the two great contradictions of slavery and of women's suppressed condition was required before the republic could realize its true goals and morals. Martineau continued to monitor both issues and analyzed them in periodicals and newspaper leaders until well through the 1860s. The issue of slavery, which she had thought earlier would be resolved, had precipitated a challenge to the very existence of the nation.

A rich ethnography of American society is to be found in the second three-volume work, *Retrospect of Western Travel* (1838), which, though less analytical, contains excursions into the microsociological: occurrences and sites which express something of the quintessence of American social and cultural character.

Interpreting theory: the Comtean system

Martineau declared the rationale for her 1853 translation and condensation of Auguste Comte's *Positive Philosophy* thus: "While our science is split up into arbitrary divisions...and while the researches of the scientific world are presented as mere accretions to a heterogeneous mass of facts, there can be no hope of a scientific progress" (*The Positive Philosophy of Auguste Comte*, volume 1, p. v). The book, she wrote, would be recognized as "one of the chief honours of the century" and must be "rendered accessible to the largest number of intelligent readers." The six volumes of Comte's *Cours de Philosophie Positive*, written and published between 1830 and 1842, were intended to outline the hierarchy of the sciences, to show their development historically and the methods and findings in each as relevant to the whole positive system, and to show that the sciences of observation now needed a new science – social physics or sociology. Undoubtedly, it was Martineau's sense of the urgent need for both a system of the sciences and specifically a science of society which drew her to the task. Human perfectibility and social progress, Enlightenment values fundamental to Martineau's thinking, required knowledge and understanding, not just for the educated few, but for the population as a whole. Martineau believed human beings to be situated in a critical situation in history:

> We find ourselves suddenly living and moving in the midst of the universe, – as a part of it, and not as its aim and object. We find ourselves living, not under capricious and arbitrary conditions, unconnected with the constitution and movements of the whole, but under great, general, invariable laws, which operate on us as a part of the whole. (ibid., p. x)

The six volumes of rather turgid style, repetition, and ennui had to be translated, condensed, and revised into a final version of two volumes. Aware of the obtuseness of Comte's original work, she made clear that hers "is a very free translation." However, she sought the expertise of Professor John Nichol of Glasgow for the sections on mathematics, astronomy, and physics, only the last of which required revision in the form of condensation. As she explored each part of Comte's "rich and diffuse" text, filled as it was with "wearisome epithets," she simultaneously studied the subjects and disciplines discussed in full preparation for the work. She had cultivated a knowledge of science, social science, and philosophy, as seen from her first published essays in the *Monthly Repository*. Her education in languages, classics, philosophy, history, literature, and sciences fully prepared her for the task. Positive philosophy, she was convinced, was the only remedy for the "uncertainties of the age" which haunted and disoriented even the most enlightened and progressive of minds. "The supreme dread of every one who cares for the good of the nation or race is that men should be adrift for want of an anchorage for their convictions...a large proportion of our people are now so adrift" (ibid., p. 5).

Both her interests in science and her indefatigable desire to bring scientific knowledge to the public ("the growth of a scientific taste among the working classes of this country is one of the most striking of the signs of the times") were from her youth integral to her life and work. If society had entered a "critical" period from which regeneration and a new order would emerge, science itself, she believed, would facilitate the "growth of knowledge and the evolution of philosophy." The social sciences, yet to be developed, would be the new basis of "intellectual and moral convictions" not simply for middle-class academics and intellectuals but for the general public – the working classes as well as the bourgeoisie. Her task was to make the public aware of the "great, general, invariable laws" through Positive Philosophy.

Martineau disagreed with Comte's patriarchal, even misogynist, perspective on women, his idea of a hierarchical society with centralized planning and control, and, most certainly, his advocacy of a secular religion with sociologists as high priests and Comte himself as the Pope. While his presentation of a new science of society seemed exactly what was needed, Martineau seems to have regarded the accompanying ideology as regressive, if not reactionary. Nevertheless, she refused to criticize his ideas in the context of the translation, implying in the preface, as in her autobiography written a few years later, that, though she had serious disagreements with Comte, it would be inappropriate to raise them in that context. In fact she did not publish any kind of criticism of Comte's ideas and writings during his lifetime, although some critique appears in later letters (see Arbuckle, 1983, pp. 164–5; Sanders, 1990, p. 233) and in her review of the article "The Religion of Positivism" of 1858 (see *Daily News*, April 9, 1858).

Comte himself was so pleased with Harriet's translation that he informed her that he would replace the original with her version in his *Bibliotheque positiviste du proletaire au dixneuvieme siecle*. He was convinced that Martineau's version should be translated into French, which was ultimately done by C. Avezac-Lavigne in 1871–2. Later, however, Comte was less enthusiastic about Martineau's work when, in his religious phase, he became aware of Martineau's agnosticism.

Other aspects of Martineau's theory

The works just presented remain among Martineau's most salient contributions to sociology in interpreting theory, theorizing empiricism, and analyzing society at the macrosociological level. Nevertheless, her theoretical achievements extend considerably beyond these and include feminist theory, social evolutionary theory, historical sociology, theories of religion, microsociology (socialization, childhood, the sociology of illness and disability, for example), law and citizenship, the sociology of work and occupations, and sociological journalism. Elaboration on these theoretical and empirical works is not possible here. The reader should consult the primary and secondary sources in the accompanying bibliography.

The Person

Harriet Martineau was born on June 12, 1802 in Norwich, England, the sixth of eight children in a Unitarian family of Huguenot descent, significant in shaping the emotional and intellectual lives of Harriet and her siblings. Descendants of the forced migration of Protestants from France in 1686 following the Revocation of the Edict of Nantes, generations of the Martineau family endured minority status as Dissenters but cherished their religious freedoms in the new land, and preserved their French heritage, ensuring that all children were bilingual and educated in the rich historical, philosophical, and literary legacy of England and the Continent. This included most importantly Enlightenment values related to natural rights, respect for the individual, freedom of self-realization, equality of men and women in most matters, and the individual's obligation to serve society. A rather Calvinist posture pervaded this culture.

The primary profession for generations of Martineaus had been medicine, but Thomas Martineau, Harriet's father, became a textile manufacturer. The financial fate of his factory as it endured the consequences of recessions and speculation had serious consequences for the Martineau family, and became, as we shall see, the challenge to which Harriet responded successfully. Her mother, Elizabeth Rankin, was the daughter of a wholesale grocer and sugar-refiner in Newcastle upon Tyne – an intelligent woman of limited education who, in addition to her devotion to the household ("a true nineteenth-century matriarch"; Pichanick, 1980), saw to it that her children were properly educated by tutors at home and in Unitarian schools. She was, nonetheless, stern, with seriously high expectations for the children and sharp reprimands for those who disobeyed. Harriet saw it as "a tyranny of the mind," accompanied by little affection or care for the emotional well-being of her children, particularly Harriet, who became increasingly defiant toward her mother.

The major fact of Harriet's childhood was her poor health. She was passed to a wet-nurse as an infant, was sickly as a child, spent several periods away from the family in "recuperative" situations, and suffered her mother's "cures," which generally exacerbated the problem. Out of fear, physical instability, and emotional deprivation, Harriet responded to family interaction and expectations with trepidation and anxiety. She had been deprived of the senses of taste and smell since childhood and by early adolescence began to suffer from a significant hearing loss. She had largely lost her hearing by the age of twenty and was soon forced to resort to the use of ear trumpets. As the deafness encroached she felt increasingly isolated and unhappy; her family accused her of being stubborn and deliberately difficult. Withdrawal and a sense of unworthiness resulted from negative comments by her mother and other relatives. She prayed in chapel for the angels in heaven to come down to take her away; at one point she contemplated suicide. Harriet's strategy for coping was a turn to religious faith and a precocious study of the Bible. She found sanctuary in books and ideas. Like her siblings, Harriet, an avid reader and learner, studied languages, classics, mathematics, music, literature, biography, history, and religion, and developed a passion to write.

Particularly influential in Harriet's intellectual development were the writings of Shakespeare, Bunyan, and Milton, initially, and later Bacon, Condorcet, Montesquieu, Hegel, Lessing, Smith, Wollstonecraft, Godwin, Wordsworth, Anna Barbauld, and Hannah More. David Hartley, Dugald Stewart, Thomas Malthus, Joseph Priestley, and, by 1830, Saint-Simon, whose work she was introduced to by Gustav D'Eichtal, figured predominantly in the formation of Harriet's interests and ideas in philosophy, political economy, and sociology. She read with enthusiasm the fiction and poetry of such literary figures as Austen, Goethe, Wordsworth, and others. As an adolescent she studied logic, rhetoric, and poetry, extended her learning in Latin, Greek, and Italian, and enjoyed translating Tacitus and Petrarch, and later German and French authors. Harriet nearly married a college friend of her brother James, but the prospective bridegroom became ill and died within a year. She never married, and considered herself to be "the happiest single woman in England."

In 1822 Martineau began her career as a published author in the Unitarian *Monthly Repository*, edited by William J. Fox, with articles on the feminist perspective on religion and on women's education, and by 1832 had published nearly 100 articles, stories and poems in the Unitarian publication. They reveal her literary and analytical skills and her thorough education and breadth of interests, and most importantly anticipate many of her later concerns, as she moved from topics in religion to philosophy, literature, political economy, social issues (slavery, education, women's condition), natural rights, natural theology, science, and the works of Socrates, Godwin, Lessing, Doddridge, and Crombie. Her intellectual and social perspective emerges in, for example, "Essays on the Art of Thinking" (1829) and "Essays on the Proper Use of Retrospective and Prospective Faculty" (1830). In "Theology, Politics and Literature" (1832), she develops a rationale for the moral sciences (the study of Man) and discusses: the importance of positioning knowledge in past, present, and future; induction and analogy as methods of reasoning; and the problems of the ambiguity of terms. In fact, throughout these essays she outlines a scientific epistemology.

Physical science is advancing steadily, and with an accelerating rapidity, under the guidance of philosophical principles. Moral science is lagging behind, blinded, thwarted, led astray by a thousand phantoms of ancient ignorance and error... Let it be ascertained what are the true objects of research, and what is their natural connexion, instead of proposing to split men into parties whose object will be... but to magnify one science at the expense of another... moral and physical science are to [Man] connected in an indissoluble union.

Martineau's first major project was *Illustrations of Political Economy*, discussed above. Criticized for oversimplification and incautiousness in her direct approach, she did not shun controversial and complex issues. The popularity of the tales is attested by extremely high sales (on average 10,000 copies per month), and the fact that, even at moderate royalty rates, Martineau thereby secured not only her financial independence but her reputation as a public educator and interpreter of scientific doctrines.

Harriet's trip to America in 1834–6 resulted in three multi-volume works on American society, as we have seen, and established her as a major social investigator, critic, and travel writer. As after so many such major projects, she sought relief from the hard work of writing and publishing by turning to fiction. In 1839 she published the novel *Deerbrook*, in which the protagonists are a doctor and a governess whose experiences centre on issues of science, work, and occupation.

Martineau endured illnesses throughout her life, which occasionally resulted in a complete withdrawal from daily affairs. In 1839, while on a trip to Italy, she became very ill with gynaecological disorders, returned to England, and spent six years, 1839–44, in Tynemouth as an invalid. Released from the pressures of her regular schedule, she found time and energy to write a historical novel about the Haitian hero Toussaint l'Ouverture (*The Hour and the Man*, 1841), a four-part series of moralistic children's stories (*The Playfellow*, 1841), and a sociological analysis of illness and the patient–caretaker relationship (*Life in the Sickroom*, 1844). In 1844 she was "cured" by mesmerism, of which she wrote in a series *Letters on Mesmerism* (1844), thereby alienating her family and many friends. But Martineau continued to live life as she saw fit, and, upon her recovery, moved to Ambleside in the Lake District, where she designed and built her home, and then left immediately for a seven-month tour of the Middle East. The result of that journey was the three-volume *Eastern Life: Past and Present* (1848), in which she demonstrated the influence of religion on culture and the evolution of religion from magic and superstition to monotheism, from hierarchical godheads to personal belief, from the goal of immortality to a rationalized life of duty and asceticism. Religion had become, for her, a subject for investigation, in which she concluded that an increasingly rational or "intelligent" world had precipitated the growth of rationality in religion within the context of a world-historical evolution of religions.

The 1850s was perhaps the most productive decade of this prolific writer/social investigator, involving the publication, among other works, of a history of England, a book on Ireland, a book on the family and socialization, and her most controversial *Letters on the Laws of Man's Nature and Development* (1851) with Henry George Atkinson. While this exchange between the two was meant to promote the application of scientific method to social life, Martineau was critical of predicating ideas on evidence from the five senses only. She explored other forms of perception, including mesmerism, which she believed united the subjective and intuitive with the rational inductive approach of science. Its materialism and avowed agnosticism, interpreted by many as atheism, made the book her most controversial, and cost her many friendships, including the close relationship with her brother James. The two in fact neither saw nor spoke to one another again.

Soon after becoming a regular contributor of leaders to the London *Daily News* (1852–66), Martineau took up the task of translating and condensing Comte's *Cours de Philosophie Positive* (1853), seeing the potential of Comtean positivism to systematize science and perhaps knowledge in general. In 1855 Martineau became ill again, and this time she was convinced that she was entering the final stage of her life. As someone who had worked diligently throughout her life and who wished to retain control over her own reputation and ideas, she wrote her *Autobiography*, an account of her life, thought, and work, in which she characterized her own intellectual development as having followed the Law of Three Stages: Theology, Metaphysics, and Science. Having had it printed and stored to await her demise, she appointed her American friend Maria Weston Chapman executor of her papers and the *Autobiography*. In releasing the book posthumously Chapman added a volume of *Memorials*, extracts from letters and documents of Martineau and her correspondents. After 1855, however, Martineau once again recovered and entered an extremely busy and productive period of her life. During her last two decades she published compilations of her writings in periodicals and newspapers, as well as major works on India, on Ireland, on health and the military, and on continuing developments in America.

Hers was a life of thinking and writing, but also of investigation, exploration and education. Her journalism allowed her to apply sociological skills to current history in more than 1,600 *Daily News* articles over fourteen years. She continued to publish periodical articles, sustained her voluminous correspondence, and communicated with many individuals and groups regarding major legal and social debates on such women's issues as the Contagious Diseases Act, laws against women, suffrage, and the Salem witchcraft controversy. But she became increasingly weak and by the mid-1870s was ailing considerably. She died on June 27, 1876 at her home, The Knoll, in Ambleside.

The historical and sociological perspective of Harriet Martineau over a lifetime was shaped by and helped to shape the social context. Her life and writings, in fact, reflect the issues, debates, crises, signs of progress, and changing material life in Victorian England. As a known and respected writer and journalist, she played a significant role in influencing social and political change. Yet she recognized her own marginality as a woman, a Dissenter, a disabled person, someone deprived of higher education, a single woman who had to be self-reliant for her livelihood, a woman in the male worlds of writing and science, an agnostic, and a private person who worked in the public sphere. Thus situated, her experiences, education, and precociousness produced an intense sensitivity and astuteness to the public issues, problems, and societal complexities of her age.

THE SOCIAL CONTEXT

The increased rate of change in all spheres, particularly technological and scientific, led to an emerging and substantial Victorian belief in progress. People responded enthusiastically to signs of the modern age: the expansion of railways, the Crystal Palace (emblem of modernity), discoveries in science and medicine, experimentation in many fields, the increasing mechanization of work, new practices in agriculture, and a modern economy of reorganized production which replaced traditional family business practices – some of the many indicators of the promise of progress.

But accompanying these changes were doubts, skepticism, questioned beliefs, and the resistances of patriarchy and empire. Optimism coexisted with anxiety, enthusiasm and adventurousness with anti-intellectualism and dogmatism. The class system was being challenged, while the poor, much discussed in the context of the Poor Laws, were increasing in numbers. Martineau was asked by Lord Brougham to write some Poor Law tales in anticipation of changes by the Poor Law Commission (1834), which in fact established workhouses, much deplored by Dickens, in place of outdoor relief. The state of the workers in terms of housing, literacy, skills, and cultural development became a popular topic of discussion. Wages, hours, and safety in industrial production became issues of polarization, pitting factory owners against unionists speaking for workers' rights and welfare. Women's rights were much discussed, but social, political, and economic freedoms became legal realities only very slowly, especially regarding married women's property, legal rights, sexuality, suffrage, occupation, education, etc. Slavery had been formally abolished in Britain and was widely criticized but survived as a system in the West for two-thirds of the century. The traditional practices of medicine were supplanted in some circles by mesmerism and phrenology.

Agriculture brought both increased production and the disasters of famine. The Malthusian thesis created general concern about the issue of food production in relation to population needs. With her pen Martineau joined those who fought against the Corn Laws, which prohibited imports and kept the prices of corn artificially high and therefore unaffordable to many.

Travel itself as a leisure activity of the middle and upper classes was increasing and becoming redefined. Although the rising middle classes were fascinated with travel to "exotic" cultures, from the Caribbean islands, the Middle East, and African nations to the young American democracy, few popular writers were able to present objective analyses of their journeys. Martineau, however, was able to contribute to new and more sophisticated ethnographical and sociological perspectives on other cultures and to show that travel could serve the sphere of scientific investigation. Issues of colonialism and empire became increasingly interrogated, resulting in serious examinations by some of the consequences of empire for peoples around the globe. In that context, particular attention was directed toward India. Martineau spent considerable journalism and two books questioning the role of the British Empire in India and the country's future.

This was the age of reform: reform in public institutions such as prisons, the military, the factory, agricultural policy, education, health, medicine, and government. Martineau participated in the discourse of reform and influenced courses of action taken. She was keenly interested in prisons and prison reform, visited prisons in America and interviewed men in solitary confinement, wrote a novel (never published) on the life of prison reformer John Howard, and ironically shared a common birthplace with Elizabeth Fry (1780–1845), pioneer in English prison reform. In the areas of military and health reform, Martineau collaborated with her friend Florence Nightingale in convincing the government, politicians, and the public of the need for reform and for the advancement of the profession of nursing. On the issue of factory legislation and in no small degree out of her enthusiasm for new technologies, Martineau often found herself on the side of factory owners, sometimes holding workers responsible for carelessness in the workplace; but she was not beyond publicly criticizing conditions in the workplace and worker exploitation.

Above all, women in all classes were participating to a greater extent in the public sphere, through work, travel, publishing, and reform movements. Martineau was among those bringing women's issues into the public discourse and women's contributions into societal spheres.

THE INTELLECTUAL CONTEXT

As already suggested, Martineau reflects not only the ideas and values of the Enlightenment – natural law, natural rights, liberty, equality, individual self-realization, and societal progress – but also the Victorian frame of mind, embracing the tensions and ambivalences with which Victorians confronted modernity. These perspectives can be best seen, perhaps, in terms of a fundamental tension between the rational and the irrational within the post-Enlightenment milieu. Certainly the clashes between science and religion were significant in the lives of Martineau and her contemporaries. Views on this particular confrontation often determined one's relations with family, friends, colleagues, and the public in general. The Unitarian perspective embraced Enlightenment values while insisting on the importance of religious study and pious self-discipline.

The intellectual world of Martineau's youth was filled with the imposing figures of William Wordsworth, Thomas Carlyle, William J. Fox, and the heady influence of *Pilgrim's Progress* and *Paradise Lost*. In Unitarian circles the works of Newton, Hartley, Priestley, Bacon, Kant, and Stewart were widely read; fascination with the potential of science was prevalent. Among the most attractive and influential intellectual theories were necessarianism, associationism, and later positivism. Necessarianism maintained that natural and unchangeable laws in the universe determine the basis of human action and are beyond the control, if not the understanding, of human beings. This was essentially a theory of causation, but, like a Calvinist version of human conduct, it also carried the message of the "importance of moral habits, the never-failing consequences of moral discipline," as she phrased it in an 1824 article on the study of metaphysics in *The Monthly Repository*. Individual moral responsibility was taken very seriously among the Dissenters, who emphasized particularly one's obligation to serve society, perhaps the Dissenters' first rule of life.

Theories of moral conduct did not suffice, for the inquiring mind, to explain human nature and human behavior *per se*. Hence the turn toward theories of the mind, such as the associationism of David Hartley. Hartley's explanation of the mind, an expansion of Locke's *tabula rasa*, was essentially a process whereby impressions or ideas stimulate related vibrations and associations (Pichanik, 1980). Its limitations prompted many like Martineau to go beyond Hartley to theories of phrenology and mesmerism. Phrenology seemed to provide a more detailed and scientific explanation of the structure and functions of the brain, with little consideration of nonmaterialist or spiritual factors. The influence of materialism grew as Victorians searched for explanations of facts, of the concrete, the verifiable. Phrenology could be translated into practice, into situations of treatment. It led, therefore, into the examination of human nature and the impact of social environment on the individual, of social psychology and sociological questions.

If phrenology broke the barrier toward an understanding of the interconnections between the individual and social influences, mesmerism helped to destroy the other polarity, the mind–body bifurcation. Here materialism is expressed in the context of magnetic force. "Animal-magnetism," expounded by Anton Mesmer (1734–1815), involved the notion that magnetic force could be transmitted from one person to another, with the effect of changing or "curing" certain symptoms. Mesmerists developed the practice of artificial somnambulism, later called hypnosis, a state in which the practitioner could assess the ailment and therefore devise a treatment. Martineau and many of her generation used mesmerism, often quite successfully, to treat symptoms deemed untreatable by medical doctors. Such practices aroused both intrigue and scandal, reflecting Victorians' enormous ambivalence about theories and practices which challenged traditional medicine.

Nevertheless, these theories and practices derived from the intellectual quest for certainty, for proof, for useful facts, for a reconstruction of life based on logical, rational principles. This quest gathered momentum and led to the attraction of positivism for thinkers like Martineau, Mill, Whewell, Comte, and others. Saint-Simon and Comte outlined the sciences, assigned them functions and spheres of study, and showed that science could become the source of social reorganization, mental hygiene, and new knowledge. The controversial nature of these discourses can be seen, for example, in the fact that Martineau and Atkinson's *Letters on the Laws of Man's Nature and Development* (1851), in which they simply reiterated the empirical and materialist discourse and made the case for scientific paradigms, scandalized the British public.

Several intellectual developments and movements in the late eighteenth and early nineteenth centuries significantly shaped the discourse of Martineau's generation. Among the most influential were political economy, the equality and human rights issue, Malthusian theory, and socialism. Here again, ambivalence regarding the merits and costs of industrial capitalism, its effects on population trends, the uncertainties of democratic revolutions, and, finally, the increase of both profits and the proportion of poor in society created theories and opinions which linked, in sometimes peculiar ways, traditional attitudes and institutions with modern goals and practices. This can be seen particularly with regard to issues of political economy and in socialism around such issues as the Poor Laws, Chartism, factory legislation, trade unionism, the class system, and the portrayal of the classes in literature.

IMPACT

In the context of the history of sociological theory and methodology, Harriet Martineau was not only more creative and innovative but also more influential than has previously been assumed. As a member of a generation of Victorian intellectuals, writers, politicians, artists, and professionals attempting to understand and come to terms with the impact of modernity on British society, still imbued with traditionalism, she lent a special voice to the discourse. As a woman situated outside of academic life, as a self-educated and independent scholar, she is not unlike her male contemporaries and predecessors whose education and backgrounds were diverse and, in twentieth-century terms, unorthodox.

By the fact of the popularity of her writings and the breadth of her reputation, however controversial at times, she was a significant author in the Victorian period. With her forays into literature, particularly given her talent for moralistic tales and novels and novelettes of social realism, she inspired her contemporaries: Charlotte Brontë, George Eliot, Matthew Arnold, for example. Her depiction of community dynamics and the culture of social classes in *Deerbrook*, for instance, made an enormous impression on authors and readers alike. Her tales for children, most specifically in *The Playfellow* series, were read to and by British children for many generations. These tales and most of her fictional work were translated into many other languages (German, French, Swedish, Japanese, and Russian, for example) as well, so that she took on a kind of international reputation and presence.

In matters of government legislation regarding the Poor Laws, the Corn Laws, public education, property laws, and individuals' rights and freedoms, Martineau's ideas as expressed in fiction or in periodicals and newspapers exercised considerable influence. The fact that politicians frequently called upon Martineau to help them in proffering a particular political stance on controversial issues offers important commentary on the value placed by the public on her points of view. She effectively used the didactic mode to convince the public of the rectitude of her particular perspective, particularly on the issues of slavery, women, work, and education, as we have seen. But she also exerted considerable authority on issues of the empire, and its impact on colonials and on British society itself. Martineau became recognized as a social critic and authority on American society, India, Ireland, and the Middle East.

In scientific concerns, particularly on the need for the moral or social sciences, Martineau participated in the discourse of science and scientific epistemology and in an examination of the nature and goals of science as a social enterprise. Clearly she was concerned with the practical as well as theoretical and empirical uses of science. She participated in a circle of dialogue and influence which included Charles Darwin, Herbert Spencer, William Whewell, John Stuart Mill, and William G. Sumner. Even in the context of the "scandal" of her book with Atkinson, she brought to the public discourse the idea of a scientific study of the brain and the mind–body problem.

Nowhere was she more influential than in her writings on slavery and on the condition of women. She wrote extensively and over her lifetime on the whole moral question of slavery and demonstrated that societies dependent on that form of domination were bound for failure and crisis. In addition to her novel about l'Ouverture, her extensive analyses of American slavery and the Civil War were read widely and helped to shape the moral positions of many in Europe and America. "A source of much controversy in both Britain and America, it [*Society in America*] played a major role in forming English opinion, particularly among the liberal left of her day" (Lipset, 1981, p. 10). The other instance of her focus on subordination and repression concerned the status of women, in England, Ireland, America, India, and the Middle East, as we have seen. She was the first to sign a petition on behalf of suffrage for women to John Stuart Mill for presentation in the House of Commons. She took up the cause for reform of the Married Women's Property Act, and for women's right to work at decent wages under humane and acceptable conditions. She lectured the British public on the issue of gender equality in education.

Even early in her career, Martineau's reputation as a social analyst was already rather significant, as indicated by the fact that, shortly after returning from America, she was offered by Saunders and Otley Publishers the opportunity to become editor of a proposed new periodical "to treat of philosophical prinicip- les, abstract and applied, of sociology." She would have accepted the invitation enthusiastically but for the intervention of her brother James, who strongly discouraged her formal involvement in such secular scientific work, so Harriet missed an unusual opportunity to move into more academic circles.

Martineau's impact on later sociological theory and sociologists and social scientists has been underexamined and underestimated. Her contributions in many instances have been unacknowledged. But when we examine the intellec- tual backgrounds of leading figures, as well as some of the most innovative and renowned theories and empirical studies, we find the presence of Martineau. Some of these instances have been pointed out above. It can be shown that Martineau was read and appreciated by not only Comte, Spencer, Durkheim, Marx, and Veblen, but also Herkner, Myrdal, Beatrice Webb, Charlotte Gilman, Alice Clark, Edith Abbott, and Annie Besant. Martineau's ideas and original theories, as well as investigatory innovations, converge with their work. The road was not smooth, however. She was criticized and slandered by Karl Marx and Frederic Harrison, and unacknowledged by Émile Durkheim (theories on suicide and on religion), Alexis de Tocqueville (studies of America), Thorstein Veblen, and Gunnar Myrdal.

Evaluation of Martineau's work has been complicated by the scope of her writings and of the issues she engaged with. Like Weber, she is interested in the motivational structures underlying behavior, particularly as they are shaped by cultural and historical contexts and expressed in value systems. Like Durkheim, she understands that the morals and values expressed in religion and translated into politics, for example, lie at the centre of social cohesion, and that the interconnection between the individual and larger social structures is complex and compelling, as studies of suicide reveal. Like Marx, Martineau explored various aspects of work, such as the social organization of work, alienation, and the impact of gender and class on work.

Within the third wave of feminism and, in the last part of the twentieth century, the search for sociology's roots, women's contributions to the emergence of sociology are being recognized, although much remains to be done. Seymour Martin Lipset, in his introduction to the 1961 republication of *Society in America*, stated "Harriet Martineau's *Society in America* is one of the most important of the early efforts to describe and account for these seemingly constant aspects of American society" (Lipset, 1981, p. 9). "Harriet Martineau ... belongs in the annals of those who carved out a niche for a science of society. Moreover, she was one of the first to apply explicitly a sociological approach to comparative analysis" (ibid., p. 37). In the sesquicentennial publication of *How to Observe Morals and Manners*, Michael Hill (1989, p. xxii) asserted that "Martineau undertook pioneering studies – substantive, theoretical, and methodological studies – in what is now called sociology." "In her maturity she was an astute sociological theorist, methodologist, and analyst of the first order" (Hill, 1991, p. 289). Simon Dentith maintained that Martineau was a central figure in the nineteenth-century attempt to "make immediately and practically recognizable principles [political economy] which were widely thought to be abstract and difficult to understand." Deegan stated that Martineau "dared to write her views on society and in support of a daring young discipline: sociology" (Deegan, 1991, p. 14). In *Women Founders of the Social Sciences*, McDonald (1994) shows Martineau's significant contributions to sociology, particularly to methodology. Lengermann and Niebrugge-Brantley (1998, p. 39) have demonstrated that, "Martineau represents in the founding generation both the interpretive paradigm ... and the feminist paradigm."

ASSESSMENT

Undoubtedly, Harriet Martineau merits recognition of her contributions to the field of sociology in terms of her philosophy of science and epistemology, her innovations in methodology and empirical investigation, and her theoretical work, conceptual contributions, and critical analyses. Expressing her vision of a science of society, she engaged in the timely education of both academics and the public regarding the need for such an enterprise. The perspectives she brought to her arguments and analyses were singular in their stance and impact. Singular as well was her ability not only to communicate with the public in her role as public educator, but also to connect sociological knowledge to public issues, to demonstrate the important ways in which knowledge can and must be useful, and to utilize journalism to transmit sociological understandings on local, national, and international subjects. The quality of her work stands well against the standards of the nineteenth century and therefore she clearly can be recognized as the first woman sociologist.

Obviously criticisms can be made of the theoretical sociology of Harriet Martineau. She was creative and original in her theoretical analyses but somewhat incomplete, perhaps a reflection of a proliferation of projects, subjects, and genres in which she worked. Her sociological concepts and typologies are innovative and enlightening, as in the cases of types of religion and suicide, but more elaborate analysis is needed. In the case of her critique of positivism, it is clear that she has a nuanced position but she does not provide us with an explication, which would have been informative and important in the context. Martineau addressed the subject of investigator bias as well as the problem of her own biases (*How to Observe Morals and Manners*); indeed, she frequently indulged in self-criticism and even self-effacement. But her own class origins and personal background influenced her work, often creating serious contradictions, as in her analysis of societal power relations, where she consistently supports the interests of women and slaves but not always of workers or the British poor.

Martineau was an opinionated woman, although a similar male contemporary might have been described as holding "definite and profoundly held views." Webb and others refer to her as dogmatic. She was seen as an apologist for industrial capitalism and bourgeois power, and considered by some to be an "ultra *laissez-faire*" liberal, at least in her early years. In fact, politically she was quite ambivalent, vacillating between the values and goals of liberalism and socialism and reflecting the mixed attitude toward the Enlightenment of her generation's "Victorian frame of mind" (Houghton, 1957).

On the other hand, she was a master of the didactic, which she used effectively to educate and convince. Martineau was an extremely skilled empirical investigator. Her methodological treatise provides a clear guide to maximizing objectivity and clarity in gathering facts, views, attitudes and opinions, and the life experiences of one's subjects. However, she could be extremely moralistic, critical of others' relationships and ethics. Throughout her life she promoted the social usefulness of knowledge, and was not beyond using knowledge for purposes of promoting a particular political agenda.

Perhaps the singular characteristic of Harriet Martineau as a sociologist was her ability to see the interconnections of theory, empiricism, and social policy. Her work flowed easily among these three intellectual functions, because she was keenly aware that a science of society had to operate on the three levels of social knowledge to validate its own *raison d'être* and societal relevance.

Bibliography

Writings of Harriet Martineau

Illustrations of Political Economy, 9 volumes. 1832–4. London: Charles Fox.

Poor Laws and Paupers Illustrated, 4 parts. 1833. London: Charles Fox.

Illustrations of Taxation, 5 parts. 1834. London: Charles Fox.

Miscellanies, 2 volumes. 1836. Boston: Hilliard Grey.

Society in America, 3 volumes. 1837. London: Saunders and Otley (edited by Seymour Martin Lipset, New York: Doubleday; New Brunswick, NJ: Transaction Books, 1981).

How to Observe Morals and Manners. 1838. London: Charles Knight (paperback edition, New Brunswick, NJ: Transaction Publishers, 1989; introduction by Michael R. Hill).

Retrospect of Western Travel, 3 volumes. 1838. London: Saunders and Otley.

Domestic Service. 1838. *London and Westminster Review,* 29, August, 405–32.

The Martyr Age of the United States. 1838. *The London and Westminster Review,* 32, December, 1–59.

The Guide to Service: the Housemaid, the Lady's Maid, the Maid of All Work. 1838, 1839. London: Charles Knight.

Deerbrook, a Novel, 3 volumes. 1839. London: Edward Moxon.

The Martyr Age of the United States. 1839. New York: S. W. Benedict.

The Playfellow: Settlers at Home; The Peasant and the Prince; Feats on the Fjord, 4 volumes. 1841. London: Charles Knight.

The Hour and the Man: an Historical Romance, 3 volumes. 1841. London: Cassell.

Letters on Mesmerism. 1844. London: Edward Moxon.

Life in the Sickroom: Essays by an Invalid. 1844. London: Edward Moxon.

Eastern Life: Past and Present, 3 volumes. 1848. London: Edward Moxon.

The History of England During the Thirty Years' Peace 1816–1846, 2 volumes. 1849. London: Charles Knight.

Household Education. 1849. London: Edward Moxon.

Introduction to the History of the Peace, from 1800 to 1815. 1851. London: Charles Knight.

Letters on the Laws of Man's Nature and Development, with Henry G. Atkinson. 1851. London: John Chapman (Boston: Josiah Mendum, 1889).

Letters from Ireland. 1852. London: John Chapman.

The Positive Philosophy of Auguste Comte (freely translated and condensed by Harriet Martineau), 2 volumes. 1853. London: John Chapman.

Results of the Census of 1851. 1854. *Westminster Review,* 61, April, 323–57.

The Factory Controversy: a Warning Against Meddling Legislation. 1855. Manchester: National Association of Factory Occupiers.

A History of the American Compromises. 1856. London: John Chapman.

British Rule in India: a Historical Sketch. 1857. London: Smith, Elder.

"Manifest Destiny" of the American Union. 1857 *Westminster Review,* 68, July, 1–25.

The "Manifest Destiny" of the American Union. 1857. Boston: American Anti-Slavery Society.

Female Dress in 1857. 1857. *Westminster Review,* 68, October, 315–40.

Suggestions towards the Future Government of India. 1858. London: Smith, Elder.

The Religion of Positivity. 1858. *Westminster Review,* 69, April, 305–50.

The Slave-trade in 1858. 1858. *Edinburgh Review,* 108, October, 276–99.

Endowed Schools of Ireland. 1859. London: Smith, Elder.
England and Her Soldiers. 1859. London: Smith, Elder.
Female Industry. 1859. *Edinburgh Review,* 109, April, 151–73.
Health, Husbandry, and Handicraft. 1861. London: Bradbury and Evans.
Modern Domestic Service. 1862. *Edinburgh Review,* 115, April, 409–39.
Convict System in England and Ireland. 1863. *Edinburgh Review,* 117, January, 241–68.
Middle-class Education in England: Boys. 1864. *Cornhill Magazine,* 10, October, 409–26.
Middle-class Education in England: Girls. 1864. *Cornhill Magazine,* 10, November, 549–68.
Life in the Criminal Class. 1865. *Edinburgh Review,* 122, October, 337–71.
Salem Witchcraft. 1868. *Edinburgh Review,* 128, July, 1–47.
Biographical Sketches. 1869 (new edition, London: Macmillan, 1877).
Harriet Martineau's Autobiography, with Memorials by Maria Weston Chapman, 3 volumes. 1877. London: Smith, Elder.

Further reading

Arbuckle, Elisabeth Sanders (ed.) (1983) *Harriet Martineau's Letters to Fanny Wedgwood.* Stanford, CA: Stanford University Press.
Arbuckle, Elisabeth Sanders (ed.) (1994) *Harriet Martineau in the London Daily News: Selected Contributions, 1852–1866.* New York: Garland.
Blaug, Mark (1958) Political Economy to be Read as Literature. In *Ricardian Economics: a Historical Study.* New Haven, CT: Yale University Press, chapter 7.
Cawelti, John G. (1963) Conformity and Democracy in America: Some Reflections Occasioned by the Republication of Martineau's *Society in America. Ethics,* 73 (April), 208–13.
David, Deirdre (1987). *Intellectual Woman and the Victorian Patriarchy: Harriet Martineau, Elizabeth Barrett Browning, George Eliot.* Ithaca, NY: Cornell University Press.
Deegan, Mary Jo (ed.) (1991) *Women in Sociology: a Bio-bibliographical Sourcebook.* New York: Greenwood Press.
Durkheim, Émile (1951) *Suicide: a Study in Sociology,* trans. by John A. Spaulding and George Simpson. New York: The Free Press.
Durkheim, Émile (1995) *Elementary Forms of Religious Life,* trans. by Karen E. Fields. New York: The Free Press.
Frawley, Maria H. (1992) Harriet Martineau in America: Gender and the Discourse of Sociology. *The Victorian Newsletter,* Spring, 13–20.
Freedgood, Elaine (1995) Banishing Panic: Harriet Martineau and the Popularization of Political Economy. *Victorian Studies,* Autumn, 33–53.
Frost, Cy (1991) Autocracy and the Matrix of Power: Issues of Propriety and Economics in the Work of Mary Wollstonecraft, Jane Austen, and Harriet Martineau. *Tulsa Studies in Women's Literature,* 10 (Fall), 253–71.
Harrison, Frederic (1896) Introduction. In *The Positive Philosophy of Auguste Comte,* trans. and condensed by Harriet Martineau, 3 volumes. London.
Hill, Michael (1989) Empiricism and Reason in Harriet Martineau's Sociology. In Michael Hill (ed.), *How to Observe Morals and Manners.* New Brunswick, NJ: Transaction.
Hill, Michael (1991) Harriet Martineau (1802–1876). In Mary Jo Deegan (ed.), *Women in Sociology: a Bio-bibliographical Sourcebook.* New York: Greenwood Press, pp. 289–97.

Hoecker-Drysdale, Susan (1992) *Harriet Martineau: First Woman Sociologist*. Oxford: Berg.

Hoecker-Drysdale, Susan (1995) The Enigma of Harriet Martineau's Letters on Science. *Women's Writing: the Elizabethan to Victorian Period*, 2, 155–65.

Hoecker-Drysdale, Susan (1998) Harriet Martineau (1802–1876): Kritische Sozial-forschung: Theorie und Praxis. In Claudia Honegger und Theresa Wobbe (eds), *Frauen in der Soziologie: Neun Porträts*. Munich: Verlag C. H. Beck, pp. 28–59.

Houghton, Walter (1957) *The Victorian Frame of Mind, 1830–1870*. New Haven, CT: Yale University Press.

Hunter, Shelagh (1995) *Harriet Martineau: the Poetics of Moralism*. Aldershot: Scolar Press.

Hutcheon, Pat Duffy (1996) *Leaving the Cave: Evolutionary Naturalism in Social-scientific Thought*. Waterloo: Wilfrid Laurier University Press.

Lengermann, Patricia Madoo and Niebrugge-Brantley, Jill (1996) Early Women Socio-logists and Classical Sociological Theory: 1830–1930. In George Ritzer (ed.), *Classical Sociological Theory*, 2nd edn. New York: McGraw-Hill, pp. 294–328.

Lengermann, Patricia Madoo and Niebrugge-Brantley, Jill (1998) *The Women Founders: Sociology and Social Theory, 1830–1930*. Boston: McGraw-Hill.

Lipset, Seymour Martin (1981) Harriet Martineau's America. In *Society in America* by Harriet Martineau, abridged and edited by S. M. Lipset. New York: Doubleday, pp. 5–42.

Logan, Deborah (1997) Harem Life, West and East. *Women's Studies*, 26, 449–74.

McDonald, Lynn (1994) *Women Founders of the Social Sciences*. Ottawa: Carleton University Press.

Marx, Karl (1887) *Capital: a Critical Analysis of Capitalist Production*, the English edition, edited by Frederick Engels, Vol. I. London: S. Sonnenschein, Lowry & Co.

Melman, Billie (1992) *Women's Orients: English Women and the Middle East, 1718–1918*. Ann Arbor: University of Michigan.

Myrdal, Gunnar (1944) *An American Dilemma: the Negro Problem and Modern Democracy*. New York: Harper.

O'Donnell, Margaret G. (1983) Harriet Martineau: a Popular Early Economics Educa-tor. *Journal of Economic Education*, Fall, 59–64.

Peterson, Linda (1990) Harriet Martineau: Masculine Discourse, Female Sage. In Thais E. Morgan (ed.), *Victorian Sages and Cultural Discourse: Renegotiating Gender and Power*. New Brunswick, NJ: Rutgers University Press.

Pichanik, Valerie Kossew (1980) *Harriet Martineau: the Woman and Her Work, 1802–1876*. Ann Arbor: University of Michigan.

Postlethwaite, Diana (1984) New Faiths – the Philosophy of Necessity, "Force," and Mesmerism: Charles Bray and Harriet Martineau. In *Making It Whole: a Victorian Circle and the Shape of Their World*. Columbus: Ohio University Press.

Postlethwaite, Diana (1989) Mothering and Mesmerism in the Life of Harriet Martineau. *Signs: Journal of Women in Culture and Society*, 14, 583–609.

Reinharz, Shulamit (1989) Teaching the History of Women in Sociology: or Dorothy Swaine Thomas, Wasn't She the Woman Married to William I? *The American Socio-logist*, 20 (Spring), 87–94.

Reinharz, Shulamit (1992) *Feminist Methods in Social Research*. New York: Oxford University Press.

Riedesel, Paul L. (1981) Who *Was* Harriet Martineau? *Journal of the History of Socio-logy*, 3 (Spring/Summer), 63–80.

Rivenburg, Narola (1932) Harriet Martineau: an Example of Victorian Conflict. PhD dissertation, Columbia University.

Rivlin, Joseph B. (1947) *Harriet Martineau: a Bibliography of Her Separately Printed Books*. New York: The New York Public Library.

Rossi, Alice (1973) The First Woman Sociologist: Harriet Martineau. In A. Rossi (ed.), *The Feminist Papers: from Adams to de Beauvoir*. New York: Columbia University Press, pp. 117–34.

Sanders, Valerie (1986) *Reason over Passion: Harriet Martineau and the Victorian Novel*. Brighton: Harvester Press.

Sanders, Valerie (ed.) (1990) *Harriet Martineau: Selected Letters*. Oxford: Clarendon Press.

Smith, Sidonie (1987) Harriet Martineau's Autobiography. In *A Poetics of Women's Autobiography: Marginality and the Fictions of Self-representation*. Bloomington: Indiana University Press.

Spender, Dale (1982) Harriet Martineau. In *Women of Ideas and What Men Have Done to Them, from Aphra Behn to Adrienne Rich*. London: Routledge & Kegan Paul, pp. 125–35.

Terry, James L. (1983) Bringing Women in: a Modest Proposal. *Teaching Sociology*, 10, 251–61.

Thomas, Gillian (1985) *Harriet Martineau*. Boston: Twayne Publishers.

Thomson, Dorothy (1973) Harriet Martineau. In *Adam Smith's Daughters*. Hicksville, NY: Exposition.

Tocqueville, Alexis de (1969) *Democracy in America*, trans. by George Lawrence, ed. by J. P. Mayer. New York: Doubleday.

Walters, Margaret (1976) Mary Wollstonecraft, Harriet Martineau and Simone de Beauvoir. In J. Mitchell and A. Oakley (eds), *The Rights and Wrongs of Women*. Harmondsworth: Penguin, pp. 304–78.

Webb, Robert K. (1959) *A Handlist of Contributions to the Daily News by Harriet Martineau, 1852–1866*. Photocopy, published in Elisabeth Sanders Arbuckle (1994) *Harriet Martineau in the London Daily News: Selected Contributions, 1852–1866*. New York: Garland.

Webb, Robert Kiefer (1960) *Harriet Martineau: a Radical Victorian*. New York: Columbia.

Weiner, Gaby Harriet (1983) Martineau: a Reassessment. In Dale Spender (ed.), *Feminist Theorists: Three Centuries of Key Women Thinkers*. New York: Pantheon Books.

Winter, Alison (1995) Harriet Martineau and the Reform of the Invalid in Victorian England. *The Historical Journal*, 38(3), 597–616.

3

Herbert Spencer

JONATHAN H. TURNER

Most introductory sociology texts mention Herbert Spencer, usually as a proponent of such theoretical blunders as organismic analogies, unilinear evolution,
and functional analysis. He is one of those "founding fathers" whose methodological and substantive works are less prominent than those of other founders.
Yet Spencer was far more widely read in his time than either Émile Durkheim or
Max Weber; he rivaled Marx in intellectual influence in the nineteenth century;
and he was one of the most respected scholars of his time. Why, then, do we give
so little thought to this founding father, whose influence in the latter half of the
nineteenth century extended far beyond the narrow confines of academia?

Part of the answer is ideological. Spencer's phrase "survival of the fittest" as it
inspired Social Darwinists and his staunch support for what would today be
viewed as a "right-wing" and "libertarian" moral and political philosophy make
him highly suspect in a field whose ideological sympathies are more collectivis-
tic. Another part of the answer is that, though he had died a decade earlier, his
works still represented the most prominent evolutionary scheme at the time
when evolutionary thought in general fell into disfavor for its ethnocentricism
and racism. Yet another part of the answer is that Spencer thought "big" and
across disciplines at a time when science was beginning to specialize and parti-
tion itself. Still another part of the answer is that one of sociology's emerging
icons, Émile Durkheim, was able to portray Spencer as a crude utilitarian and
individualist (Perrin, 1975) – an unfair assessment of Spencer's sociology which,
surprisingly, continental and American sociology have tended to accept uncritic-
ally. And so when Talcott Parsons (1937) asked "who now reads Spencer?" the
answer was clear: very few.

The goal of this chapter, then, is to indicate why Spencer should be given
another reading as an important sociological theorist.[1] We will begin with his
methodological statements and arrangement of data; then, we will turn to the

theory that he developed and so copiously illustrated with the data that he had arrayed; finally, we will turn to Spencer the person and the context of his time in order to get a better understanding of why he produced his theory and why this theory continues to be relevant to contemporary sociology.

THE METHODOLOGY

The Study of Sociology

Between 1872 and 1873, Spencer published the serialized essays that would become his *The Study of Sociology* (1873). In this book, Spencer makes a strong case for developing a science of human organization. Spencer opens *The Study of Sociology* with two important observations. First, people in general and policy-makers in particular implicitly assume that there are generic forces operating in the universe; otherwise, they could not so confidently proclaim that this or that policy would eliminate a particular social problem. Such proclamations, Spencer argued, reveal an implicit view that the social universe operates in a law-like manner. What lay persons implicitly assume, and what scientific sociologists must pursue, are the laws of human organization. For, if "no effect can be counted upon – everything is chaotic," and so "it behooves us to use all diligence in ascertaining what the forces are, what are their laws, and what are the ways in which they cooperate" (Spencer, 1873, pp. 45, 47). However, and this is the second introductory observation in *The Study of Sociology*, those who argue that the laws of sociology cannot be like those of the "exact sciences" fail to recognize that many of the insights in these sciences are not stated mathematically but, instead, qualitatively; and this fact does not make such laws any less scientific. When scientists must work with natural systems, the precise values of variables and their interactions pose problems of exact measurement and easy quantification. Indeed, as Spencer stressed, there are "factors so numerous and so hard to measure, that to develop our knowledge of their relations into the quantitative form will be extremely difficult, if not impossible" (ibid., p. 45).

The bulk of *The Study of Sociology* is devoted to the methodological problems involved in collecting and analyzing sociological data. Spencer argues that data should be collected and observations made primarily with respect to generic forces rather than to time-bound, particular, and contextual events. Making such observations is, however, difficult for a number of reasons (ibid., pp. 74–92): (a) research problems are often selected for their currency as dictated by public and political moods; (b) research problems are often defined by those who finance research, and these benefactors always have their own self-serving agenda; (c) particular research techniques often come to dominate and skew the nature of the research questions asked and the data collected; (d) research problems can be distorted by commitments to research paradigms and to particular ideologies; and (e) research problems are often biased by the position of investigators in social structures (inside and outside of academia).

These problems are compounded by biases inherent in data gathering and analysis: (a) scholars rarely wish to see their "cherished hypothesis" disproved, so they skew data collection and analysis in conformity with their hypothesis; (b) scholars will rarely accept observations and conclusions that go against their ideological commitments; (c) scholars will often have difficulty in understanding the "meaning" of situations among those they study and will, therefore, miss important dynamics; and (d) scholars rarely collect data longitudinally, and, as a consequence, data and conclusions are often based upon cross-sections of processes at one point in time.

For Spencer, an awareness of these problems and a "mental discipline" can militate against them (ibid., pp. 314–15). Moreover, and this is an extremely important point for contemporary sociology, a division of labor between theory and research can help to overcome these biases. For "men [and women also, one presumes] who have aptitudes for accumulating observations are rarely men given to generalization; while men given to generalizing are men who mostly [use] the facts of others" (ibid., p. 315). There must exist a "kindred antagonism" between theory and research, each working to militate against sources of bias in the other. For as researchers test theories and as theorists call into question the relevance and significance of data, a natural corrective is built into the cumulation of knowledge.

Descriptive Sociology

When reading Spencer's *The Principles of Sociology* (1874–96), one is struck by the immense amount of descriptive detail from historical and ethnographic sources. In fact, *The Principles of Sociology* is such a long work, numbering some 2,200 pages, because it is filled with data. So we should ask: where did Spencer get these data?

In 1873, Spencer published the first volume of his *Descriptive Sociology* (1873–1934).[2] In this and the subsequent volumes Spencer hired professional scholars to array historical and ethnographic data into common categories. The goal was to record the features of past and present societies in ways that facilitated comparisons, and toward this end, each oversized volume contains tabular presentations of data in addition to more discursive summaries. Volumes on societies with a written history record data into the categories from different historical epochs, whereas those on preliterates group societies by geographical region and record the available data for each society into the categories (see Turner, 1985; Turner and Maryanski, 1988; Turner et al., 1998, for reviews of the exact categories used to organize presentation of data).

This project was initiated in 1867 and ended long after Spencer's death in 1934 (Spencer had left money in his will for completion and updating of the descriptions recorded under each category and subcategory). Thus, by 1873, Spencer had introduced his own "human relations area files," some sixty years before the idea was resurrected by George P. Murdock (1953, 1965), who, no doubt, got the inspiration from his teacher, Albert G. Keller, who had been well acquainted with Spencer's *Descriptive Sociology* (because he and William Graham Sumner used the data of *Descriptive Sociology* in their four volume *The Science of Society* (1927), as had Sumner in his *Folkways* (1907)). But by the time that Murdock had begun to assemble ethnographic data in the late 1920s into the Human Relations Area Files (HRAF), most of these preliterate societies had been dramatically transformed by Western exploration and colonial expansion. Moreover, the ethnographies were often specialized, focusing on one theme or topic and, hence, failing to record crucial information.

The great loss in this chain of events is that, as Spencer's star declined in the late 1880s and 1890s, his category system, which is almost equal to that of HRAF today, was lost, with the result that the chance to record critical information on fast-disappearing preliterate societies was gone forever (Turner and Maryanski, 1988). Hence, both sociology and anthropology today suffer from an inadequate database for assessing general theoretical principles; and this inadequacy, along with a growing anti-science movement, has led to a disillusionment with the comparative method in anthropology. Surprisingly, the revival of evolutionary thinking in sociology during the 1960s (e.g. Lenski, 1966; Parsons, 1966, 1971) and again in the 1990s (e.g. Sanderson, 1996; Turner, 1996) has increased interest in societal comparisons, and the fact that Spencer's early lead was never pursued systematically only makes this interest in comparative sociology more difficult to realize. The data are gone, forever; and if Spencer's categories had been used as a basic system for recording ethnographic information on preliterates, comparative sociology would stand on a much firmer empirical base.

In terms of methodology, then, Spencer recognized that systematic comparisons among data assembled from very different types of societies were essential to developing inductively, and assessing deductively, abstract theoretical principles. In the end, Spencer recognized that a science is only as good as its theoretical principles, assessed against a broad spectrum of data.

The Theory

The general systems approach

Long before Spencer turned to sociological analysis in the 1870s, he had written treatises on biology and psychology. Along with his sociological works, these treatises were part of what today we might term a "general systems" approach, where the goal is to articulate a few abstract principles from which the scientific laws of various domains of the universe can be deduced. Thus, the laws of biology, psychology, sociology, and, in Spencer's eye, ethics could be deduced from a few "first principles." In 1862, Spencer wrote these principles down in a book titled *First Principles*, which represented his effort to adopt ideas from Newtonian physics to the analysis of social and ethical phenomena. Indeed, much of the strange vocabulary of Spencer's law of evolution as "an integration of matter and concomitant dissipation of motion, during which the matter passes from an indefinite and incoherent homogeneity to a definite heterogeneity, and during which the retained motion undergoes a parallel transformation," must be seen in this light. For Spencer really believed that he had found the basic principles that guide all domains of the universe – physical, organic, social, and ethical. The details of this analysis are less important than the vision that he had: to unify the sciences with a few fundamental principles, a goal that contemporary general systems theorists still seek to accomplish (e.g. Bailey, 1994).

The basic "general systems" principles in Spencer's grand scheme revolve around a vision of the social world as involving aggregation of individuals, differentiation of their activities into specialized roles and structures, integration of these differentiated roles and structures, and, potentially, disintegration of the social mass when bases of integration prove inviable. The core of Spencerian sociology thus represents an effort to develop general sociological laws on aggregation, differentiation, integration of increased complexity, and pressures for dissolution or disintegration.

The sociological laws of evolution

Spencer is the founder of functional sociology. True, Auguste Comte had employed organismic analogies where the function of a part for the larger "body social" was to be discovered, but it was Spencer who converted Comte's vague analogies into a rigorous sociology. Thus, as Spencer sought to develop the laws of sociology, he couched them in an evolutionary and functionalist framework. The evolutionary portion of this framework emphasized aggregation, growth, differentiation, integration, and disintegration, whereas the functionalist portion stressed the need to examine differentiating social structures in terms of their consequences for meeting the fundamental needs of the social whole.

The functional part of Spencer's scheme begins with his famous organismic analogy, where he compares the properties of organisms to super-organic structures involving relations among organisms. Both organic and super-organic reveal, Spencer (1874–96, volume 1, p. 448) argued, a "parallelism of principle in the arrangement of components" along several lines: both differentiate structure as they grow, both differentiate functions to sustain the life of the whole, both achieve integration through mutual dependence of parts, both are composed of more elementary forms of life, and both can live on for a while after destruction of the systemic whole. If this were all Spencer had to offer sociology, there would be little reason to consider his work important; yet, unfortunately, it is this organismic analogy that still guides contemporary understandings of Spencer.

Far more important than this simple analogy are the functional and evolutionary ideas developed by Spencer. The functional approach pursued by Spencer was analytical: what basic needs or imperatives must all super-organic systems meet if they are to remain viable in their environments? Although Spencer's vocabulary varies somewhat, the substance of his answer to this question remained constant: all systems must regulate their relations with the environment in terms of protection from enemies and from the vicissitudes of the nature; all systems must secure and transform resources necessary to sustain life forms; all systems must reproduce their constituent members and the structural forms and symbols necessary to sustain individuals and the structural units of the larger super-organic whole; all systems must regulate and coordinate activities of constituent parts of the system; and all systems must be able to distribute resources, information, and individuals throughout the systemic whole. Hence, as social systems grow and differentiate, they develop distinctive structures to meet basic functions (ibid., pp. 498–519). This kind of functional analysis anticipates, of course, the functional schemes that became so prominent at the midpoint of the twentieth century, but Spencer did not stop here. Rather, he used this functional scheme to articulate abstract laws about the dynamics of differentiating social systems as they evolve from simple to more complex forms. Indeed, the functionalism soon recedes into the background as an implicit analytic framework for guiding the development of true scientific principles. Yet, for better or worse, we must give Spencer credit for founding functional analysis in sociology; for all who followed him – Durkheim, A. R. Radcliffe-Brown, Bronislaw Malinowski, Parsons, and others who are identified with functionalism – built upon the foundations laid by Spencer (Turner and Maryanski, 1979).

To convert his analytical functionalism into a true theory, Spencer turned to the analysis of evolution. Spencer analyzed evolution in two ways: (a) as a description of stages as societies become ever more complex (Spencer, 1874–96, volume 1, pp. 549–87); and (b) as a set of models and principles about the dynamics of population growth and social system differentiation (ibid., pp. 463–597). It is this second sense of evolution that we will explore here.

Let us begin by discursively summarizing Spencer's argument; then, we can convert this review into more formal principles in table 3.1. For Spencer, the key driving force of human evolution, or the building up of social structure, is population growth, which, in turn, increases with (a) escalated birth rates, (b) conquest or annexation of other populations, and (c) immigration. As a population grows from any or all of these sources, segmentation or the creation of additional social structures like those already in place will increase, but eventually, segmentation and proliferation of older structural forms can no longer accommodate the increased social mass. The reason for this is that logistical loads for sustaining, regulating, and coordinating activities increase to the point where new kinds of social structures will have to be created, or the population will disintegrate.

Table 3.1 The abstract laws of Spencer's theory

The Law of Differentiation

As a population grows, and the greater the rate of this growth, the greater will be the logistical loads facing this population and the greater will be the selection pressures for differentiation and elaboration of productive, reproductive, regulatory, and distributive structures and associated cultural symbols.

The Law of Production

The differentiation and elaboration of productive structures are a multiplicative function of:

A   The size and rate of growth of a population

B   The level of technology available to productive units
C   The skill of labor or human capital
D   The availability of natural resources
E   The differentiation of distributive structures
F   The differentiation of centers of political-legal authority and moderate levels of regulation

The Law of Reproduction

The differentiation and elaboration of reproductive structures are a multiplicative function of:

A   The size and rate of growth of a population
B   The differentiation of productive, regulatory, and distributive structures and associated cultural symbols

The Laws of Regulation

The differentiation and elaboration of regulatory structures (consolidation and concentration of power) are an additive function of:

A   The size and rate of growth of a population
B   The level of material surplus generated by productive forces
C   The volume and velocity of exchange transactions
D   The level of inequality and associated internal threat
E   The level of external threat from surrounding populations

The intensity of selection pressures for centralization of power and its use in regulation of internal activities are an additive function of:

A   The level of internal and external threat
B   The duration and extent to which differentiation of operative and distributive processes have remained unregulated by political authority
C   The intensity of conservative ideological mobilization for increased social control by political authority

The intensity of selection pressures for decentralization of power and its less restrictive use are:

A   An inverse function of the level of internal threat stemming from inequalities
B   An inverse function of the level of external threat from other populations
C   A cumulative function of the duration and extent of restrictive regulation by political authority
D   A positive function of the intensity of liberal ideological mobilization for lessened social control by political authority

The Law of Distribution

The differentiation and elaboration of distributive infrastructures and market structures are:

A   A positive function of the level of production
B   A positive curvilinear function of the level of regulatory authority
C   A positive function of liberal ideological mobilization

At this point in Spencer's argument, an implicit idea contained in all types of functional analysis is introduced: the notion of "selection," but selection of a very special type. Unlike natural selection, which occurs when there is a high level of niche density and a corresponding increase in competition among members of a population for resources, Spencer argues that there is another kind of selection pressure to create new kinds of social structures in order to overcome mounting logistical loads. Such selection can occur alongside more Darwinian selection processes, but this kind of selection does not come from density, *per se*, but from the absence of necessary structures to meet escalating problems of generating sufficient production, reproduction, regulation, distribution, and other key functions that a population must meet if it is to remain viable in its environment. Spencer emphasized that selection processes among human organisms in super-organic systems differ from natural selection, because in human social systems, individuals and the social structures in which they are organized can "think," "plan," and "experiment" with new social forms that can reduce logistical loads; and in deference to Spencer, we might term this "Spencerian selection" to distinguish it from "Darwinian selection." For in Spencer's view, what distinguishes human super-organic structures is their potential flexibility and their capacity to change in order to meet new challenges; and for Spencer, the most fundamental challenges come from the pressures of escalating logistical loads.

Under conditions of escalated logistical loads, both Spencerian and Darwinian selection may be operating; and if a population is to avoid dissolution or disintegration, then differentiation along three axes must occur (ibid., pp. 498–548): (a) production–reproduction, (b) regulation, and (c) distribution. Spencer did not assume that mounting logistical loads and selection pressures would inevitably lead to their resolution; indeed, populations often dissolve and disintegrate when faced with increased selection pressure. He only argued that, if the population is to remain viable in its environment, it will differentiate structures along these three axes.

As selection increases the level of production, it becomes possible to support a larger population. To do so, however, requires differentiation of roles and structures, which, in turn, resolves one set of logistical loads for gathering resources and converting them into usable goods and commodities, while creating new kinds of logistical loads for coordinating the differentiated units. These latter loads increase Spencerian selection for market exchange and interdependence among productive units, and, as we will see shortly, for expanded regulatory authority as well. Differentiation of production creates new logistical loads for reproduction, as older forms of socialization and cultural production prove inadequate for preparing individuals and placing them in the specialized roles of differentiated social structures. Thus, Spencerian selection works to differentiate new forms of reproduction, such as school systems, religious and communal systems, laws and customs, and family systems.

Increased production leads to the expansion of regulatory authority, or the consolidation and concentration of power to coordinate social activity, via two routes. First, increased production generates a larger material surplus that can be usurped through taxation and used to support political decision-makers. Second, increased production generates logistical loads for coordination and control that cannot be met solely by exchange and interdependence. If expanded and concentrated power does not emerge, then evolution is arrested, and, potentially, the population will dissolve under rising logistical loads for coordination and control. Once concentrated power exists, however, it tends to be used to consolidate ever more power and to extract even more of the productive surplus of a society. As a result, inequalities increase, and as inequality grows, the stratification system creates internal threats which force polity to concentrate additional power to suppress dissent and conflict – a tactic which only escalates inequality and internal threat. As a consequence, a society may dissolve under the pressures of this escalating cycle of internal threat, political consolidation and repression, increased inequality, and further escalation of internal threat.

This cycle becomes interrelated with another cycle between what Spencer (1874–96, volume 2, pp. 568–643) termed "militant" societies, relying on concentrated power to coordinate and control activities, and "industrial" societies, employing less concentrated power and a reliance on exchange to control and coordinate activities. Much as Vilfredo Pareto was later to argue, Spencer (1874–96, volume 1, pp. 549–81; volume 2, pp. 568–643) saw societies as fluctuating between concentrated and less concentrated forms of political regulation. As resentments build against concentrated power, then rates of internal conflict, waves of ideological mobilization, and organized social movements become more prevalent and work to reduce the concentration of power and the degree of regulation, thereby transforming a militant system to an industrial one. Yet, as militant control is relaxed, the reduced level of political regulation and the increased reliance on exchange and interdependence as mechanisms of integration eventually begin to generate problems of ineffective coordination and to increase disintegrative pressures, thereby creating selection pressures for a more centralized political system to regain control. For Spencer, all political systems fluctuate back and forth between these two profiles; and so, in Spencer's eye, power reveals a dialectical quality, with its more concentrated and less concentrated forms generating pressures for transformation to their respective opposites.

Geopolitics also plays an important part in power dynamics. Spencer argued that war had been a great force of human evolution, for the simple reason that more organized societies usually win wars and, as a result, the outcome of war selects out less organized populations and ratchets up the level of human organization as the conquered are absorbed into the new, more organized social system. This kind of argument was Darwinian, but a Darwinian analysis that emphasizes the unit of selection as the group or social structure rather than the phenotype of the individual. Yet war also tends to concentrate power in order to mobilize and coordinate resources for the pursuit of the conflict, thereby setting off the disintegrative and dialectical dynamics outlined above. Moreover, success at war tends to expand territories and increase both the size and diversity of a population in these territories, which, in turn, escalates logistical loads for coordination and control as well as for expanded production and for new reproductive structures (if only to integrate the conquered into a society). If these logistical loads cannot be resolved, then internal threats increase, thereby setting polity off on the self-destructive cycle of concentrating more power, increasing inequality, and raising the level of internal threat.

Thus, growth in a population initially leads to differentiation along two axes: production–reproduction (what Spencer sometimes termed "operation" or "operative" processes) and consolidation and concentration of power (what Spencer often termed "regulation" or "regulatory" processes). Lagging somewhat behind differentiation of operative and regulatory processes is the third axis of differentiation under escalated logistical loads and increased Spencerian selection pressure: distribution. For Spencer, distribution operates on two levels. First, there is a distributive infrastructure, such as roads, ports, canals, communication facilities, and the like, for moving people, information, and resources about a territory. If a population grows, especially if its territory expands via war, conquest, and annexation, then infrastructural needs expand, setting into motion Spencerian selection for their development. Such development can only occur with productive surplus and some degree of encouragement from political authority. Second, there is exchange distribution, in which goods and commodities are transferred through market process. Such market forces depend upon a certain degree of development of distributive infrastructure as well as political regulation via a legal system, but as the population grows and differentiates, exchange distribution becomes an ever more prominent feature of the social system. In fact, Spencer went so far as to argue that in the modern era exchange processes had become so well developed that they could reduce the need for governmental regulation. And in some very modern-sounding passages, he argued against the pursuit of war and conflict by polity because such pursuit creates a military establishment and political system that undermine the dynamic forces of a market economy (Spencer, 1874–96, volume 1, pp. 519–48; volume 2, pp. 603–43). In fact, Spencer argued against British colonialism because it would generate, he felt, an ever more "militant" society in which the concentration of coercive power would limit individual freedom, suppress economic innovation, hinder market dynamics, and distort political decision-making toward military rather than diplomatic solutions.

In table 3.1, Spencer's ideas on evolution are stated as abstract theoretical principles – a mode of representation that is consistent with the title of his major theoretical work in sociology (Turner, 1981, 1984a, 1985). The propositions introduce several additional elements to Spencer's theoretical argument, and thus we should pause to review these. The law of differentiation emphasizes that cultural symbols are an important part of differentiation and elaboration of social structures. Unlike Durkheim's inaccurate portrayal of Spencer as a crude utilitarian, Spencer did stress in all of his work the importance of cultural symbols; and, like Durkheim, he saw such symbols as connected to material structural arrangements. Moreover, he recognized that the differentiation and elaboration of cultural symbols add an additional layer and dimension to structural differentiation; and it is this elaboration of cultural symbols that often imposes additional problems of integration and, most particularly, reproduction of members into the increased diversity of not only structural positions but also new systems of symbols.

The law of production lists forces normally considered to be part of production – population size, technology, natural resources, human capital – but this law also communicates some important feedback effects of regulatory and distributive structures. On the one hand, production increases the likelihood that regulatory and distributive structures will differentiate and elaborate, but on the other hand, once in place, these latter structures will have reverse causal effects on production. Thus, as distributive infrastructures and dynamic markets emerge, they feed back and encourage expanded production. Similarly, the existence of moderate degrees of political authority provides the legal framework and regulatory capacities for expanded production and distribution.

The law of reproduction stresses that as populations grow and differentiate new structures and systems of cultural symbols, the processes of reproduction become more complex. At first, kinship systems become more elaborate, but eventually new kinds of reproductive structures must emerge to impart the skills, dispositions, and knowledge necessary for assuring that individuals and collective units can sustain themselves. Spencer's (1860) work on education indicates his interest in reproductive structures, but equally importantly, he stressed that reproduction is a more inclusive process, involving knowledge of the arts, religious dogmas, tenets of law, and other cultural systems. As systems become more complex, the diversity of these cultural systems increases, and it becomes necessary for reproductive structures to be capable of imparting at least some of this broader cultural content.

The laws of regulation summarize Spencer's view that several forces influence the level of political centralization. External and internal threat will generate highly centralized power, and, to a lesser degree, so will prolonged periods of deregulation during which problems of coordination and control accumulate. When these conditions do not prevail, however, a less centralized system of political regulation will be more likely. Production and distribution are critical to the differentiation of political authority, in that each generates the resources necessary to support polity while also increasing logistical loads for some degree of political intervention into productive and exchange processes. Indeed, as production and exchange velocity accelerate, problems of coordination and control generate selection pressures for bodies of law backed by the authority of government; and as a result of these pressures, the polity inevitably grows (even though Spencer was, in his more purely ideological statements, suspicious of all government).

The law of distribution adds a related refinement. For Spencer, the development of a distributive infrastructure and dynamic markets depends upon the level of production, but it also requires some degree of political–legal regulation. Thus, in the proposition in table 3.1, the relation between polity and distribution is curvilinear: some degree of political authority encourages distributive processes, whereas high degrees of regulation will inhibit distributive dynamics and, in turn, production as well.

The laws of institutional evolution

The passages from which we can glean the general theory of evolution summarized in table 3.1 constitute a relatively small portion of *The Principles of Sociology* (roughly, pp. 463–558 of volume 1). In contrast, nearly two-thirds of *The Principles* is devoted to the analysis of social institutions. As noted earlier, Spencer had assembled a vast amount of data on other societies in the present and past; and he used these data to make generalizations about the dynamics of social institutions. Most of his analysis concerns why an institution emerged in the first place, as well as how it differentiated and elaborated its structure during social evolution, but these more descriptive tasks were always accompanied by more abstract theoretical principles.

Spencer's analysis is always functional – that is, what are the consequences of an institution for the larger social whole – but this functionalism is simply a shorthand way to make a selectionist argument. Social institutions emerge and evolve under selection pressures generated by persistent problems facing a population, and as populations grow, these problems become more intense and require elaboration of distinctive institutional systems. Indeed, his selectionist argument is highly sophisticated, far exceeding any other scholar of the nineteenth century.

Spencer's (1874–96, volume 1, pp. 603–776) analysis of "domestic institutions" or kinship systems illustrates this sophistication. He begins with the question of why this institution would evolve. His answer is selection pressures to assure a stable environment for reproduction, to avoid conflicts among males over access to females, and to reduce promiscuity; and then, he turns to the question of why kinship elaborated beyond the nuclear structures typical of hunter-gathering bands. Again, his analysis invokes a selectionist argument: as populations grow, there are pressures to organize larger numbers of individuals, and kinship is the easiest structure to elaborate toward this end, at least initially in human evolution. Kinship can provide a system for sustaining cohesion among larger numbers of individuals; it can provide a basis for political organization through the descent rule; and it can offer a structural unit within which solidarity-producing religious rituals can be practiced. Those growing populations, then, that could elaborate kinship systems would have selective advantages because they could provide for systematic reproduction of new members, organize members politically, organize worship, and, thereby, generate a sense of loyalty and cohesion. And if such populations found themselves in conflict with other populations, the kinship system could become centralized around male authority, although Spencer argued that such centralization would subordinate women. (As an important footnote: Spencer had, by far, the most progressive views on gender issues of any of sociology's founding figures; see Beeghley (1983) for documentation of this point.) Table 3.2 summarizes some of the most interesting theoretical ideas emerging from Spencer's analysis of kinship systems.

After describing the evolution and dynamics of humans' first institution – kinship – Spencer turned to what he termed "ceremonial institutions" in

Table 3.2 Spencer's generalizations on kinship

1 In the absence of alternative ways of organizing societal activities, kinship will become the major organizing principle in a society.
2 The greater the size of a society without alternative ways to organize societal activity, the more elaborate the structure of kinship and the more it will reveal explicit rules of endogamy/exogamy, marriage, and descent.
3 All other things being equal, the greater the conflict, or potential for conflict, the more elaborate the structure of kinship and the more it will reveal explicit rules of exogamy/endogamy, marriage, and descent.
4 All other things being equal, societies in conflict will reveal a strong tendency to be patriarchal (and patrilineal).
5 The more patriarchal a kinship system and the more it exists in a state of conflict, the less is the equality between the sexes, and the more likely are women to be defined and treated as property.

Table 3.3 Spencer's generalizations on ceremony and ritual

1 The greater is the level of political centralization in a system, the greater is the level of inequality and the greater is the concern for ceremonial activities demarking ranks.
2 The greater is the concern over ceremonial activities demarking ranks in a system of inequality:
   (a) the more likely are people in different ranks to reveal distinctive objects and titles to mark their respective ranks;
   (b) the more are interactions among people in different ranks to be ritualized by standardized forms of address and stereotypical patterns of deference and demeanor.
3 The less is the level of political centralization, the less is the level of inequality; and, therefore, the less is the concern with ceremonial activities demarking ranks and regulating interaction among people in different ranks.

volume 2 of *Principles of Sociology* (pp. 3–228). Spencer saw ceremonies as subinstitutional; and he viewed them as a major micro-level force of social control and regulation because they signify the mutual respect of individuals toward each other and, thereby, contribute to the maintenance of social relations. In passages that are reminiscent of Erving Goffman's (1967) analysis of interaction ritual, Spencer analyzed the components of rituals: trophies symbolizing relations, mutilations of body to signify position and self-presentation, exchanges of gifts, visits, forms of address, titles, fashion, and deference-demeanor. In particular, he was concerned with the effects of inequalities in power and authority on ceremonial activity, arguing that the greater the power differentials among individuals the greater will be individuals' attention to all components of ceremonies. Some of the more interesting propositions from his analysis are summarized in table 3.3.

Despite Spencer's reputation as a *laissez-faire*, anti-government ideologue, he developed a sophisticated theory of politics (Spencer, 1874–96, volume 1, pp. 519–48; volume 2, pp. 229–643). Arguing much as current rational choice theorists, he emphasized that government exists to provide utilities not possible by tit-for-tat bargaining or market exchange alone, especially highly valued utilities such as mobilizing for conflict and defense. He viewed government as always revealing a tripart structure, consisting of a head, leaders, and followers, but he also stressed that this structure cannot exist without legitimating ideologies lodged in tradition. Even then, he argued, government generates a number of inherent tensions that can delegitimate political authority and lead to its collapse. Among these tensions are: the tendency of political systems engaged in conquest to overreach their capacity to control expanded territories and diverse populations; the dilemma that all traditional polities face in trying to balance staffing positions with the most qualified against the demands of elites for patronage and for inherited privilege; the tension between preserving the status quo and the need to change under new circumstances; the tendency of government to use its taxation powers to expand polity and thereby burden the society with unnecessary and resource-draining administrative overhead; and the creation of privileged and less privileged social classes, with inequalities generating internal threats and potential class conflict. For simple societies, Spencer argued, kinship, ceremony, and tradition are sufficient to regulate a population, but as a population grows, and especially if it engages in conflict with other populations, polity emerges as a differentiated institutional system, consisting of the tripart structure of head, leaders, and followers. As this structure elaborates, the bureaucracy of government expands; and as the scale of political bureaucracy expands, new systems for generating revenue emerge. At some point, pressures for more representative political bodies mount, especially as individuals become subject to revenue collection systems, and these pressures are most likely to be successful under certain conditions: the lack of war; a decline of strict adherence to religious beliefs; the dispersion of a population geographically; the existence of well organized subgroups; resentments associated with prolonged oppression; the expansion of markets; and the emergence of liberal ideologies. Much of Spencer's analysis provides detail to his more general theoretical statements on the differentiation of regulatory structures, as is evident in table 3.4, where some of the more interesting generalizations from Spencer's discussion are summarized.

At the beginning of *The Principles of Sociology* (volume 1, pp. 145–442), Spencer analyzed primitive religions, or the elementary forms of religion. Some ten years later, in volume 3 of *The Principles*, he examined the evolution of religion from simple to more complex forms and, then, to monotheism (pp. 3–178). For Spencer, all religions reveal three basic elements: beliefs in supernatural beings and forces, organized groupings who share these beliefs, and explicit activities directed toward supernatural forces. The emergence of religion was the result of selection for structures and cultural symbols to reinforce cultural values and patterns of social relations, especially those revolving around power. Spencer believed that religion emerged from dreams about ancestors, evolving into ancestor worship, which, in turn, supported the integrity of the kinship system. As societies became more complex, however, polytheistic religions emerged in response to this complexity; and as political authority became

Table 3.4 Spencer's generalizations on polity and power

Intrasocietal Processes

1 The degree of stability in government is a positive and additive function of its capacity to balance:
   (a) the needs for efficiency and stable succession;
   (b) the creation of privileged classes and potential class antagonisms;
   (c) the expansion of governmental overhead and nongovernmental productivity.
2 The degree of political centralization in a society is a positive function of its level and length of conflict with other societies.
3 The degree of differentiation of subsystems in the government of a society is a positive and additive function of that society's:
   (a) size;
   (b) volume of internal transactions;
   (c) volume of external transactions.
4 The level of inequality and class formation in a society is a positive function of the degree of centralization of political power.

Intersocietal Processes

5 The degree of political centralization among a population of societies in a region is a positive function of the overall rate of conflict among these societies.
6 The degree of political unification among a population of societies in a region is a positive and additive function of:
   (a) the capacity of one society to coerce others;
   (b) the degree of structural similarity and cultural homogeneity among societies;
   (c) the need for a common defense among societies.

   It is a negative and additive function of:
   (d) the size of the territory that a population of societies encompasses;
   (e) the extent to which barriers in the natural habitat reduce transportation, communication, and migration.
7 The extent to which political unification among a population of societies reveals a highly centralized, bureaucratic profile is a positive function of the length and intensity of the conflicts that unified them politically.
8 The extent to which political unification among a population of societies reveals a less centralized and more colonial profile is a positive and additive function of:
   (a) the size of the territory to be governed;
   (b) the size of the population to be governed;
   (c) the level of structural and cultural heterogeneity among the people to be governed.

---

consolidated, the pantheon of supernatural forces became hierarchically ordered to reflect inequality and hierarchical social relations in society. Once the principle of hierarchy was established and built into bureaucratized ecclesiastic structures, a trend toward monotheism was initiated, since, in Spencer's view, monotheism simplified the hierarchy and made legitimation of centralized power more efficient. Yet, despite the symbiotic relationship between the state and religion, tension between the two inevitably increases, for several reasons: the claims of

Table 3.5 Spencer's generalizations on religion

1   The complexity of religious beliefs and ecclesiastical structures is a function of the complexity of social structures, particularly regulatory structures.
2   When kinship is the organizational basis of a population, ancestor worship will be the dominant form of religion, mediated by rituals directed at totems.
    (a) Early religious specialization in systems of ancestor worship involves a medicine man (who drives away evil ghosts) and priests (who make appeals to supernatural forces).
    (b) Subsequent institutional differentiation removes the medicine man and reinstitutionalizes this function in a new medical institutional system.
3   When regulation is increasingly transferred from kinship to polity, religion becomes hierarchical in both its pantheon of supernatural beings and its bureaucratized ecclesiastical structure.
4   Monotheism becomes possible once the principle of hierarchy is established and is used to legitimate the growing regulatory authority of the state.
5   Elites in the state and church eventually come into conflict over their respective capacities to control and regulate taxation, property, privilege, appeals to the supernatural, and rights to control legitimation of regulatory authority, with the state winning out when:
    (a) markets and trade are dynamic;
    (b) production is high and provides adequate resources to support the state;
    (c) law and courts provide alternative bases of legitimation for the state.

religious elites to exclusive rights to legitimate centers of political power; the contention of priests and others in the ecclesiastic system as being the only conduit to the supernatural; the assertion of the priestly class as the center of culture, knowledge, literacy, and art; and efforts of the church to create an independent tax system and claim on economic surplus. For these reasons, the church becomes a self-serving bureaucracy which increasingly comes into conflict with a self-serving state bureaucracy. At various points in history, the state seeks to control the power and privilege of religion; and it is aided in this process by the expansion of markets and by the development of law and other alternative structures that can legitimate the state. These ideas were well developed in the 1880s, and they represent important insights for the time. Table 3.5 summarizes some of the interesting generalizations emerging from Spencer's analysis of religion.

The last section in *The Principles of Sociology* (volume 3, pp. 327–608) is on "industrial institutions," or the economy. Spencer had intended to write on other social phenomena that revealed an institutional quality – linguistics, intellectual activity, morals, and aesthetics – but age and health made this the end of his purely sociological work. This is perhaps the most ideologically biased of the sections in *The Principles*, for it contains many of Spencer's diatribes against unions and guilds. Still, as table 3.6 delineates, a number of interesting generalizations can be culled from these flawed pages. Most of these provide some elaboration on his more general statements on productive processes. Spencer saw a basic feedback relation between primary and secondary production, with the emergence of a service sector generating new forms of production and marketing but also facilitating the operation of primary productive processes and distributive structures in ways increasing the overall level of production. Another feedback relation is the division of labor, which, once specialized, accelerates production because of the efficiencies that it introduces; and Spencer, like Max Weber after him, argued that a complex division of labor is only possible with a labor market unrestricted by kinship, community, guilds, and other forces that limit labor's willingness to sell itself in a market. Again, Spencer returned to a theme present throughout his work: the negative effects of war on a dynamic economy and market system. For while war had been an important force in the evolution of more complex societies, conflicts in the modern era deplete capital for private investment, remove human capital from the labor market, bias technological innovation toward military ends, dampen wants and needs that might translate into market demand for domestic goods and services, and undermine the feedback effects of markets on production. Another theme pursued in Spencer's analysis of industrial institutions is the effects of money and credit in market systems, for without a stable medium of exchange and without the ability to secure credit, capital formation is difficult, market exchanges are restricted, and free labor cannot exert its positive effects on production. Moreover, the use of money allows for the pooling of capital beyond any one individual or kin unit, thereby greatly expanding the capacity to form capital in a wide variety of pursuits. These and other interesting insights are summarized in table 3.6.

Table 3.6 Spencer's generalizations on economy

---

1   As productive structures are differentiated and elaborated:
    (a) the relationship between work and products is severed as the division of labor forces specialization of work activities;
    (b) the production of services increases as a proportion of total productivity;
    (c) the scale and velocity of market dynamics increase.
2   The processes delineated in (1) above are reciprocal and self-escalating, but only under conditions of relative peace with other societies, since the pursuit of war depletes capital, suppresses wants and needs for domestic products, mobilizes human capital for nonproductive activities, stagnates technological innovation or biases it for only military ends, and reduces the dynamic feedback between markets and production.
3   Relative peace will also increase population size which, in turn, will create selection pressures for expanded production and distribution.
4   Until market exchanges can create a stable medium of value for establishing equivalences, distributive processes will be limited, as will the productive processes stimulated by distribution.
    (a) The more media for establishing equivalences are, themselves, not valuable but instead only valuable for the equivalences that they symbolize, the more dynamic will market processes become.
    (b) The more stable and trustworthy a medium of exchange, the more it will stimulate market dynamics.
5   When credit systems can be created as a natural extension of stable monetary systems, the dynamism of markets is increased dramatically.
6   Until the evolution of money, capital formation was limited and inflexible, but with the development of money and instruments of credit, it becomes possible to invest in diverse and flexible forms of production.

Table 3.6   (*Contd.*)

7   The more money can be pooled from diverse sources, the greater is the level of capital formation, the more flexible is the use of capital, and, hence, the greater are its effects on production.
8   The more labor is freed from kinship, community, guilds, unions, and other restrictive forms, the more able is labor to sell itself in a labor market and the more flexible will be the division of labor.

THE PERSON

If one wandered through Spencer's study after his death, there would be few books on shelves, and the atmosphere would appear spartan, if not bleak. How could the library of a man who wrote treatises on ethics, science, sociology, psychology, and biology be so barren? The answer to this question takes us to Spencer's background and how it shaped the development of a very unusual – indeed, rather odd – man (Turner, 1985, pp. 9–15).

Spencer was born in Derby, England, in 1820. Until the age of thirteen he was given private instruction by his father at home, and then he moved to his uncle's home in Bath, where the private tutelage continued. Thus, Spencer never went to school as a young man, and when it came time to go to college, he felt himself unfit because of his lack of formal education. His father and uncles had, however, taught him mathematics and science; so Spencer was far from ignorant. After working as an engineer in the construction of a railroad, he began to write articles for what were then considered radical presses; and after a few years on the fringes of radical politics and journalism, he landed a position in 1848 on the London *Economist*. In 1850, he published *Social Statics*, which championed the cause of *laissez-faire* and the need for restrictions on the power of government. And it is here that his most famous phrase – "survival of the fittest" – reached a wide audience.

In 1853, Spencer's uncle died and left him sufficient money to pursue a career as a private scholar. Soon, major works began to flow from Spencer's pen: *Principles of Psychology* (1855), *First Principles* (1862), *Principles of Biology* (1864–7), *The Study of Sociology* (1873), *The Principles of Sociology* (1874–96), and *Principles of Ethics* (1892–8). In all, Spencer sold more than 400,000 copies of his books, which, then, was an astounding figure; and when one considers that most of Spencer's works were first serialized in popular magazines and periodicals before being bound into books, the scale and scope of his readership was truly enormous.

Spencer was not, however, a traditional scholar. He did not hold an academic position, and so he was not bound by its standards of scholarship. Instead, he frequented London clubs where he associated with the brightest and most famous scientists and intellectuals of his time; and in these associations, he simply absorbed knowledge which would eventually find its way into his works. And when he needed data, as was the case for his *Descriptive Sociology* (1873–1934), he simply hired academics to produce it.

Outside of his club circles, Spencer was an intensely private and neurotic person. It is unclear if he ever consummated sex, although he was a long time friend of George Eliot (a female novelist writing under a male name). He lived alone with housekeepers, wrote for a portion of the day, visited his clubs or consulted with his research assistants; but he did so under enormous psychic strain, for he was often sick, or at least thought that he was, and he was frequently unable to sleep. Thus, when Spencer died, he did so virtually alone in his spartan living space; and because his ideas were beginning to lose their currency, he died a somewhat bitter and sad man.

THE SOCIAL CONTEXT

England at the time that Spencer was writing was the most prosperous nation on earth. Indeed, England seemed to confirm Adam Smith's faith in free markets and competition as the best way to organize society. As the first nation to industrialize and, then, use its colonial empire to further trade and commerce, it was difficult not to be impressed with the power of free trade in markets. Karl Marx and Frederick Engels, of course, saw the downside of this kind of economic system in England and elsewhere in Europe: the ruthless exploitation of workers and the abject misery of the masses. Yet Spencer, like so many of his time, saw the upside: the capacity of capitalism to generate wealth and prosperity for many. Moreover, he firmly believed that unbridled competition in markets unencumbered by excessive government intervention and, more generally, in all arenas of life would indeed promote the fitness of individuals and society.

Spencer also existed in a narrower social context of the lone intellectual writing science and philosophy outside confines of academia but within the broader intellectual circles of London – circles that were soon to die out. He was one of the last such private thinkers, for the intellectual world and especially the scientific wing of this world was fast moving into academia, where specialization and partitioning of intellectual activity would be encouraged. Spencer never was a part of this ivory tower world; he was a general intellectual and philosopher, writing for the literate lay public and the broader community of scientists as well.

He was by the time of his death one of the last of his breed. In the end, the growing compartmentalization of thought was to work against Spencer, along several fronts: he was to have no students to carry on his work; he was not sufficiently scholastic in terms of references and footnotes and, as a consequence, academics were soon to turn on him; he was a generalist in a world rapidly specializing not only between the major sciences but within them as well; and he held no academic credentials at a time when such credentials were increasingly seen as the sign of expertise. So, when Spencer died, his legacy appeared to die with him, only to be rediscovered generations later as scholars grappled with the same problems that had stimulated Spencer.

THE INTELLECTUAL CONTEXT

Spencer walked in elite circles, dining and debating with the leading biologists, physical scientists, and philosophers of his day. From these dialogues he absorbed an enormous amount of knowledge, which, as noted earlier, filtered into his work. This kind of intellectual context is now gone, for can we imagine in the contemporary era leading scientists from many diverse fields gathering informally to discuss and debate their discoveries and ideas?

Aside from this day-to-day interaction with the great thinkers in England, Spencer's theories were influenced by a number of distinct traditions. One was his engineering background, from where comes the basic idea that an increase in size requires an exponential increase in structure to support the larger mass. This idea was developed in *Principles of Biology* and, then, imported into Spencer's sociology in the form of arguments about population size and sociocultural differentiation to support the larger mass.

Spencer borrowed from biology the view that competition among individuals and collective units is critical to formation of social forms, an idea that he initially saw in Thomas Malthus (who obviously was not a biologist) and later in Darwin (who obviously was). He also took from Harvey's embryological studies and Von Baer's physiology the idea that evolution and development involve movement from undifferentiated to differentiated structures marked by interrelated functions. And he took from Darwin the view that differences among individuals and social systems are the result of having to adapt to different environmental conditions.

Spencer drew from the physical sciences the substance of his first principles and the view of science as developing abstract laws. Isaac Newton had shown the power of elegant principles to explain the dynamics of solar systems, and Spencer like so many in this post-Newtonian era felt that the same could be done for all the other sciences, including sociology, where the law of size-differentiation was seen as like Newton's law of gravitation. Moreover, Spencer borrowed the vocabulary of Newtonian physics, and his general law of evolution is couched in the language of physics: matter, motion, force, and the like.

Finally, we need to mention the relation between Auguste Comte and Spencer. Spencer (1864) went to great pains to claim that he was not just following Comte, and he appears to "protest too much" on their relation. But his most intimate intellectual companions, George Elliot and George Lewes, were well versed in Comte's philosophy, so it can be reasonably assumed that he took the idea of the organismic analogy and functionalism from Comte's writings, although he made them far more sophisticated.

Thus, while we can discern some fairly straightforward lines of influence, we must return again to the most unique characteristic of Spencer the lone intellectual: he was an intellectual sponge who absorbed all ideas in which he came into contact; so his sociology reflects a constant engagement with virtually all lines of scientific thought in the second half of the nineteenth century.

THE IMPACT OF SPENCER'S IDEAS

Spencer had an enormous impact on the broader arena of social thought and philosophy in the late nineteenth and early twentieth centuries, along a number of fronts. First, his moral philosophy continued to resonate with the dynamics of free-market capitalism; and, in America, Spencer was hailed as the most important philosopher by early industrialists such as Andrew Carnegie. Second, his famous phrase – "survival of the fittest" – and the underlying argument against government welfare became the rallying cry to Social Darwinism, an unfortunate event in our retrospective evaluation of Spencer. And doubly tragic, his ideas were used by well known geneticists (e.g. Fisher, 1930) to make arguments in favor of eugenics.

Within narrower circles of sociology proper, Spencer influenced Durkheim's analysis in *The Division of Labor*. For Durkheim's basic model is borrowed from Spencer, and to the degree that Durkheim's analysis remains influential, so must Spencer's, since, despite Durkheim's criticisms of Spencer, he took many of the key ideas in *The Division of Labor* from Spencer (Turner, 1984a). For example, the notion in Durkheim's work that population growth increases population density and, hence, the competition leading to a division of labor comes right out of Spencer's *The Principles of Biology* and *The Principles of Sociology*. In addition to influencing Durkheim, Spencer's ideas and methodology exerted considerable influence on William Graham Sumner and Albert Keller in America. Both borrowed from Spencer's data in *Descriptive Sociology* and from his analysis of social evolution of societies from simple to complex forms. In the case of Sumner, Spencer's moral philosophy was borrowed as well.

When we move to the more contemporary era, the impact of Spencer's ideas becomes more difficult to discern. The Human Relations Area Files developed by George P. Murdock (1953, 1965) represent a straightforward adaptation of Spencer's *Descriptive Sociology*, although Spencer is hardly given much credit for the basic idea. The general model of stage evolution is also lost, even as evolutionary thinking has enjoyed a revival (e.g. Lenski, 1966; Turner, 1984b, 1996; Sanderson, 1996). Spencer's model of the evolutionary stages of society is equal to contemporary formulations; so it is a double tragedy that his ideas are ignored by contemporary evolutionary thinkers (exceptions include Carneiro, 1970; Turner, 1996). Spencer's most important ideas on size, differentiation, and modes of integration have been rediscovered in a number of important fields, especially the study of complex organizations, but it is not so clear that thinkers on organizational size and administrative intensity recognize that they are employing Spencerian principles. Spencer's views on selection processes exerted considerable influence on Chicago School urban ecology, and this tradition continues to use Spencerian ideas but few within this tradition realize that they are working with Spencerian theory. Other theorists working within a more purely biological framework, however, have recently recognized the genius of Spencer's work on selection processes and have incorporated his ideas into their theories (e.g. Turner, 1996). Even the impact of Spencer's functionalism remains obscured, despite the fact that Malinowski's (1964) and Parsons's (Parsons et al., 1953) functional imperatives are virtually the same as Spencer's.

Thus, we are left with a curious legacy: everywhere one can see Spencerian ideas in sociology, but in only a few instances are the authors of these ideas aware that they have rediscovered Spencer's sociology. Thus, Spencer's direct impact or, at least, acknowledged impact on modern sociology has been minimal, with a few exceptions.

AN ASSESSMENT OF SPENCER'S WORK

Spencer's work was brilliant for its time. Spencer was the first to see the relationship between system size and differentiation; he was the first to develop a sophisticated functionalism that saw systems as differentiating along production, reproduction, regulation, and distribution; he was the first to develop a sophisticated selectionist argument, in both the Darwinian sense and the sense of decision-making in the face of escalated logistical loads; he was the first to develop a multidimensional theory of power in terms of dialectical cycles, geopolitics, and internal threats; he was the first to enumerate modern-sounding generalizations describing the dynamics of fundamental human institutions; he was the first to array and use a large body of comparative data on societies; he was the first to enumerate in detail the methodological problems facing the social sciences; and he was the first to fully recognize the importance of distributive dynamics on production and to develop theoretical generalizations about these dynamics.

Spencer was, therefore, the pioneer of many important ideas and approaches in sociology. But Spencer's sociology offers more; it continues to be relevant to contemporary sociologists. His methodological analysis of the forms of bias in sociology still ranks among the best statements on this topic ever written; his understanding that the social universe involves many selection processes can continue to inform ecological and functional analysis; his recognition of the relationship among size, competition, selection, and differentiation is relevant for many meso-level and macro-level analyses of social systems; his view that many of the sciences can perhaps be unified, at least to some degree, with an evolutionary–ecological framework is clearly an idea that should not be abandoned; his descriptions of the stages of evolutionary development can inform similar stage models in present-day sociology; and his institutional analysis of religion, kinship, and polity contains many ideas that offer new ideas to specialists in these areas of institutional analysis. Thus, it is clear not only that Spencer was an important theorist in his own time, but that he continues to be an important theorist at the close of the twentieth century.

Notes

1 Fortunately, Robert Perrin (1993) has compiled the most exhaustive primary and secondary bibliography on Spencer. The reader is advised to consult this work for Spencer's complete works and for important secondary works on Spencer.

2 Like all of Spencer's work, *The Principles of Sociology* is a compilation of work issued serially, from 1874 to 1896. Rather than cite the exact years of specific sections of *The Principles*, it is better to cite the entire work, 1874–96, with the volume and page numbers following.

Bibliography

Writings of Herbert Spencer

Social Statics. 1850. New York: D. Appleton (1892).

The Principles of Psychology, two volumes. 1855. New York: Appleton (1898).

Education: Intellectual, Moral, and Physical. 1860. New York: D. Appleton (1888).

First Principles. New York, 1862. New York: A. L. Burt (1880).

Reasons for Dissenting from the Philosophy of M. Comte and Other Essays. 1864. Berkeley, CA: Glendessary Press (1968).

The Principles of Biology, 2 volumes. 1864–7. New York: D. Appleton (1887).

The Study of Sociology. 1873. London: Kegan Paul.

Descriptive Sociology, or Groups of Sociological Facts. 1873–1934. Published with Spencer's personal funds by various publishers.

The Principles of Sociology, three volumes. 1874–96. New York: D. Appleton (1898).

Principles of Ethics. 1892–8. New York: D. Appleton.

Further reading

Bailey, K. D. (1994) *Sociology and the New Systems Theory*. New York: SUNY Press.

Beeghley, L. (1983) Spencer's Analysis of the Evolution of the Family and the Status of Women: Some Neglected Considerations. *Sociological Perspectives*, 26, 299–313.

Carneiro, R. L. (1970) A Theory of the Origin of the State. *Science*, 169, 733–8.

Comte, A. (1896) *The Positive Philosophy of Auguste Comte*, translated and condensed by H. Martineau. London: George Bell.

Fisher, R. A. (1930) *The Genetical Theory of Natural Selection*. Oxford: Clarendon Press.

Goffman, E. (1967) *Interaction Ritual*. Garden City, NY: Anchor Books.

Lenski, G. (1966) *Power and Privilege: a Theory of Stratification*. New York: McGraw-Hill.

Malinowski, B. (1964) *A Scientific Theory of Culture and Other Essays*. London: Oxford University Press.

Murdock, G. P. (1953) Social Structure. In S. Tax, L. Eiseley, I. Rouse, and C. Voegelin (eds), *An Appraisal of Anthropology Today*. Chicago: University of Chicago Press.

Murdock, G. P. (1965) *Culture and Society*. Pittsburgh, PA: University of Pittsburgh Press.

Parsons, T. (1937) *The Structure of Social Action*. New York: McGraw-Hill.

Parsons, T. (1966) *Societies: Evolutionary and Comparative Perspectives*. Englewood Cliffs, NJ: Prentice Hall.

Parsons, T. (1971) *The System of Modern Societies*. Englewood Cliffs, NJ: Prentice Hall.

Parsons, T., Bales, R. F., and Shils, E. A. (1953) *Working Papers in the Theory of Action*. New York: Free Press.

Perrin, R. G. (1975) Durkheim's Misrepresentation of Spencer: a Reply to Jones' "Durkheim's Response to Spencer." *Sociological Quarterly*, 16, 544–50.

Perrin, R. G. (1993) *Herbert Spencer: a Primary and Secondary Bibliography*. New York: Garland.

Sanderson, S. K. (1996) *Social Transformations*. Oxford: Blackwell.

Sumner, W. G. (1907) *Folkways*. New York: Ginn and Co.

Sumner, W. G. and Keller, A. G. (1927) *The Science of Society*, 4 volumes. New Haven, CT: Yale University Press.

Turner, J. H. (1981) The Forgotten Giant: Herbert Spencer's Models and Principles. *Revue Europeene Des Sciences Sociales*, 19, 79–98.

Turner, J. H. (1984a) Durkheim's and Spencer's Principles of Social Organization. *Sociological Perspectives*, 27, 21–32.

Turner, J. H. (1984b) *Societal Stratification: a Theoretical Analysis*. New York: Columbia University Press.

Turner, J. H. (1985) *Herbert Spencer: a Renewed Appreciation*. Newbury Park, CA: Sage.

Turner, J. H. (1996) *Macrodynamics: toward a Theory on the Organization of Human Populations*. New Brunswick, NJ: Rutgers University Press.

Turner, J. H., Beeghley, L. and Powers, C. (1998) *The Emergence of Sociological Theory*. Belmont, CA: Wadsworth.

Turner, J. H. and Maryanski, A. (1979) *Functionalism*. Menlo Park, CA: Benjamin-Cummings.

Turner, J. H. and Maryanski, A. (1988) Sociology's Lost Human Relations Area Files. *Sociological Perspectives*, 31, 19–34.

4

Karl Marx

ROBERT J. ANTONIO

Perhaps no social theorist has generated more intense feelings among more widely dispersed audiences than Karl Marx. His name is identified with some of the twentieth century's major emancipatory struggles and worst forms of repression. As capitalism spread throughout the world from its original centers in Europe and North America, his ideas were appropriated in nearly every corner of the globe, and were revised, blended with other traditions, and applied in heterodox ways. Different Marxisms bear the imprints of highly divergent cultures, times, and sociopolitical aims. The importance of Marx's thought for labor movements and other forms of resistance and insurgency, as well as for various socialist and communist parties and regimes, has made it a topic of intense debate on the left and right. However, his mature work is as analytical and sociological as it is political. For this reason, his ideas have generated diverse lines of social research and social theory. Also, like Nietzsche, Marx provided alternative presuppositions and concepts to other modern social theories, stimulating numerous attempts to refute or dismiss his ideas. Thus, he has been an oppositional reference point for very diverse types of theory (e.g. from functionalism to postmodernism). Although pronounced dead on many occasions, he always seems to rise again from the ashes. Even after the late twentieth century, neoliberal revival, and the politics of 1989, his ideas still pose poignant questions about fundamental issues. Arguably, they may have increased force, free of the weight of communism, in a world where capitalism has triumphed. Because the matters of class, property, exploitation, ideology, alienation, and capitalism are as important as ever, Marx retains his place as one of the main founders of the sociological tradition.

Marx's Life and Contexts

Young Marx: Hegelianism and method

In 1815, three years before Marx was born, his Rhineland birthplace of Trier was ceded back to Prussia. Previously, the town had been annexed by France; Napoleon's regime opposed semi-feudal institutions and extended individual and constitutional rights. Because many townspeople supported the French Revolution, reimposition of conservative Prussian rule generated tensions. Erosion of the economy and increased poverty made matters worse. Consequently, the region was politically active and the utopian socialists Saint-Simon and Fourier drew followers there during the revolutionary years of 1830 and 1848. Marx was born into a comfortable middle-class household, the oldest male of six surviving children. His father, a successful lawyer, embraced Enlightenment ideals and liberal democratic politics. Both sides of Marx's family had Jewish origins and rabbis as recent ancestors. Facing prejudicial restrictions, his parents converted to Protestantism. Jewish ancestry, however, still made them outsiders to some degree, and it would have been a major impediment had Marx attempted to pursue an academic career in Germany (McLellan, 1973, pp. 1–8; Seigel, 1993, pp. 38–44).

In high school, Marx received a mostly liberal humanist or Enlightenment-oriented education. The liberal headmaster and two other teachers were threatened by police authorities for their progressive views. Although several teachers were excellent, the students were mediocre. Even among this group, Marx was hardly an exceptional student, graduating eighth in a class of thirty-two. Ironically, he did poorly in history. Although he was a playful and energetic child, well liked by many of his fellow students, he was also feared by the targets of his sarcastic wit (his lifelong talent for cleverly skewering opponents earned him enemies). At school, Marx embraced Enlightenment ideals and social views, which were nurtured further by his tie to the progressive Baron Ludwig von Westphalen, his future father-in-law. Taking a liking to the young Marx, the Baron helped to stir his interests in romanticism and socialism (McLellan, 1973, pp. 9–16).

In 1835, Marx became a student at the University of Bonn. Although supposedly studying law, he specialized in "drinking and dueling," overspending, and writing poetry. Unhappy with these activities, his father forced him to transfer to the University of Berlin the following year. In a much more serious intellectual environment, Marx soon became a highly committed scholar. His extremely intense study habits probably contributed to his contracting a respiratory disorder so serious that he was released from military obligations. Maintaining very strenuous work habits as an adult, he suffered recurrent bouts of illness. Marx joined the left-Hegelian "Berlin Doctors' Club," engaging ideas that shaped his later intellectual path. He completed a doctoral dissertation on the philosophies of Epicurus and Democritus in 1841, submitting it successfully at Jena. Marx gave up work on a second thesis, required for entry into German academe, when

Bruno Bauer, his associate and leading left-Hegelian, lost his academic position for political reasons (McLellan, 1973, pp. 16–40; Seigel, 1993, pp. 65–75). Engels (1842, p. 336) portrayed, in rhyme, the young-Hegelian Marx:

> A swarthy chap of Trier, a marked monstrosity,
> He neither hops nor skips, but moves in leaps and bounds,
> Raving aloud. As if to seize and then pull down
> To Earth the spacious tent of heaven up on high,
> He opens wide his arms and reaches for the sky.
> He shakes his wicked fist, raves with a frantic air,
> As if ten thousand devils had him by the hair.

Marx became a journalist and soon editor at the progressive *Rheinische Zeitung* in Cologne. A sharp social critic, he focused on political abuses and socio-economic inequality. Attacking new laws that forbade peasants from gathering wood, Marx decried the monopolization of property by the rich and declared the poor as "the elemental class of human society" (Marx, 1842, pp. 234–5). Also, he began to criticize Hegelian political theory, which portrayed the state as a neutral mediator and rational manifestation of the general will (a position that divided right- and left-Hegelians). Marx turned Hegel's "idea" of the state against the "reality" of Prussian bureaucracy, attacking the official's crass pursuit of self-interest and slavish service to aristocratic and bourgeois interests. He also lambasted state censorship and authoritarianism, defending the free press and nascent public sphere and inveighing against the chilling effect of the police state's dragging vocal citizens into court for alleged "excesses" or "insolence" to officials. Favoring a free society that allows open discussion, he held that citizens often know more about sociopolitical problems than officials and should be encouraged to speak up about them, including official corruption. He saw authoritarian bureaucracy producing "passive uninformed citizens who are the object of administration" (Marx, 1843a, pp. 343–51). Marx's early views about free speech, local knowledge, and active citizens anticipated later ideas of "discursive democracy" (e.g. by Dewey, Habermas, Giddens). The circulation of *Rheinische Zeitung* expanded substantially under Marx's leadership. A skilled editor and writer, he continued journalistic endeavors, on a part-time basis, throughout much of his life. However, in 1843, the Prussian government shut down his newspaper, in part because of his sharp attacks on the monarchy and bureaucracy. That same year he married Jenny von Westphalen, and took another editorial position in Paris. There Marx was exposed to the working class and to socialist and communist ideas (McLellan, 1973, pp. 62–6; Seigel, 1993, pp. 65–75).

In *On the Jewish Question* (1843), Marx criticized Bauer's argument to deny Jews political rights, but his own ambiguous and even negative comments about them indicate that he had not come to terms with this aspect of his identity. Overall, however, he moved in a radical direction, away from his earlier progressive liberalism. Opposing the capitalist celebration of "egoistic" or "abstract" persons and the free pursuit of "self-interest" by "isolated monads,"

Marx held that bourgeois "freedom" dissolves feudal ties and extends formal rights, but neither sustains community nor provides adequate opportunities for those below the middle class. Propertyless peasants, artisans, and workers are left without means to activate their new rights. In his view, political freedom, although not meaningless, falls far short of "human" or "social emancipation." Looking for a sweeping transformation of civil society far beyond liberal reform, Marx called for "ruthless criticism of all that exists", "practical struggles," and "communism." Revolutionary rhetoric aside, he distinguished between substantive freedom and formal freedom, arguing that radical democratic or "true" liberty requires socio-economic equality as well as legal rights. This fundamental issue of genuine inclusion remains a most pressing problem for current democracies (Marx, 1843c, pp. 141–5; 1843d, pp. 162–74).

In the *Critique of Hegel's Philosophy of Law*, Marx attacked Hegel's equation of the actuality of the Prussian state with its democratic constitution, arguing that he justified the repressive monarchy by attributing a more abstract "logic" to an already abstract document that had little to do with political reality. In his view, Hegel sanctified the real as rational (Marx, 1843b). In the *Economic and Philosophical Manuscripts* of 1844, Marx accused Hegelians of not starting with "real corporeal" people in their actual "social" relations, but with "abstract nature" and "thought entities." He held that their "idealism" confuses legitimations with reality, and, thereby, encourages passive acceptance of existing political conditions. Marx implied that all bourgeois thought is prone to this fatal error. Stressing consciousness and its appearances, Hegel addressed human development in the idiom of "spirit." By contrast, left-Hegelians followed Ludwig Feuerbach's "inversion" of Hegel, or shift to materialist explanations of theology and philosophy. This reversal of the primacy of spirit was aimed to avert the alienation that Hegel himself decried. After initially embracing this view, Marx broke with Feuerbach, arguing that he was too philosophical, dwelled too much on the critique of religion, viewed the material realm too inertly, and focused too exclusively on generic "man" or the human "essence" (Marx, 1845). Overall, Marx believed that the Hegelians' abstract philosophical approach, even in materialist form, was ahistorical and, thus, ignored truly important human problems.

Earlier, Marx said, in a letter to his father, announcing his conversion to Hegelianism: "I arrived at the point of seeking the idea in reality itself. If previously the gods had dwelt above the earth, now they became its center" (Marx, 1837, p. 18). This statement expresses a Hegelian methodological theme that Marx retained long after his "break" with the Hegelians. He saw Hegelian "historicism" as a bridge between the "is" and "ought," which were split in Western religion and philosophy. For Hegel, normative ends, which guide and give meaning to action, originate entirely within historical experience. Rejecting transcendental views of values and the related epistemological dualism between "subject" and "object," Hegel argued that we are the authors of our world; as historical beings, we negate existing conditions, create new ones, and make ourselves in the process. However, he held that our self-creation is estranged, because we see our own objectifications as alien objects and, thus, lose our agency. Yet, in the long run, he argued, we gradually overcome this alienation by mediating contradictory facets of experience through heightened self-consciousness, struggle, and labor. In this regard, his argument about masters and slaves was especially important for Marx. Hegel held that masters seek self-recognition by dominating slaves, but languish in the contradiction that coerced recognition is worthless. By contrast to the master's falsity and inactivity, Hegel contended, struggles and labor cause slaves to grow wiser and stronger and to ultimately triumph. In his view, through the same striving, humanity eventually will discover its authorship of the world, creating a state where each person's particularity is recognized by all others, and achieving the condition of "Absolute Spirit," or total freedom and rationality (Hegel, 1807).

Focusing on capitalism and wage workers' "estranged labor," Marx broke with Hegel's "abstract" emphasis on consciousness and equation of objectification with alienation. However, Hegel's idea of self-constitutive labor remained at the center of Marx's thought. At the very moment of his "break" with Hegelianism, he argued that socialist humanity and world history are "nothing but the creation of man through human labor" (Marx, 1844, pp. 305, 332–3). He also called for "determinate negation" of capitalism's contradictions, hoping to preserve its progressive facets, yet create a new socialist world that moves toward a terminus of freedom and rationality. Marx pitted what he considered to be the progressive facets of capitalist production against its backward features, and universalistic aspects of modern democratic ideology against bourgeois repression and inequality. Reframing Hegel's method of "immanent critique," he sought to anchor his theory in specific historical bases rather than philosophical historicism. This move began the broader tradition of "critical theory," which roots theory and critique in concrete historical contradictions, actual social movements, and nascent developmental directions. Although shifting from speculative philosophy to materialism, Marx's theory contained a strong Hegelian residue that animated its emancipatory themes, linkage of theory and practice, and most fruitful empirical questions. But this core aspect of his lineage is also the ultimate source of the distinct tensions between the sociological and political facets of his thought.

The move to materialism: capitalism and modernity

In the middle and late 1840s, Marx framed the historical and analytical foci of his mature theoretical program. Responding to growing class tensions, inhering in rapid industrialization and proletarianization, fellow young-Hegelians Moses Hess and Frederick Engels addressed political economy critically and became communists. Marx followed their path, and Engels became his lifelong collaborator. Although Engels understated his role in the partnership, he contributed very substantially to Marx's thought and their common project through his editorial capacities and critiques and his own ideas and works. Also, he financially supported the spendthrift Marx and his family. With the help of Engels, Marx broke with Hegelian philosophy and developed his materialist approach to history and sociology. Although political upheavals were an immediate stimulus to Marx's work during this period, accelerating capitalist development became more and more his chief concern. Marx's most decisive context was the Second Industrial Revolution, or the appearance of the complex of mechanized industry, mass labor organizations, interventionist state, modern urbanism, and world market, and profound alteration of almost all traditional modes of association, thought, and everyday life, which he inscribed together under the sign of "modernity."

In the *1844 Manuscripts*, Marx began to transform Hegel's idea of estranged objectification into a historically explicit materialist theory of social development and of the rise of the capitalist "mode of production." In this unfinished text, clear signs exist of his later views about class struggle, proletarian revolution, and abolition of private property. Implying a fundamental contradiction in the heart of capitalism, he portrayed the division of labor as a fusion of repressive class hierarchy with progressive socio-technology. In his view, capitalist development "fetters" progress in the same stroke that it advances it. He also held that we are *social beings* and that modernity's "economic" transformation has a "*social* character"; even monadic, atomized, liberal individualist humanity arises from capitalism's social matrix (Marx, 1844, pp. 298–9, 317–22).

After expulsion from turbulent Paris in 1845, Marx made his decisive break from philosophy in an unfinished collaborative effort with Engels, *The German Ideology*. They turned the Hegelian primacy of ideas and passive view of the material domain "right-side up." This text articulated much more explicitly the bases for their later views of materialism, capitalism, and revolution. Marx considered the work the start of their mature program (Marx and Engels, 1845–6; Seigel, 1993, pp. 177, 181). Marx and Engels described how "large-scale industry" was overturning the premodern world and creating a new global order. They saw hypermodern factories, markets, and capitalist class relations supplanting traditional forms of production, social ties, and hierarchies and replacing local autonomy and particularity with centralized interdependence and homogeneity. In their view, the Second Industrial Revolution was creating "world history for the first time, insofar as it made all civilized nations and every individual member of them dependent for their satisfaction of their wants on the whole world, thus destroying the former natural exclusiveness of separate nations" (Marx and Engels, 1845–6, p. 73). Engaging political economy even more directly, Marx's *Poverty of Philosophy* (1847) provided an early published version of this nascent materialist point of view.

Marx's and Engels's publicly important political pamphlet *The Communist Manifesto* (1848) probed similar themes more dramatically and eloquently. Originally the party platform of the German "Communist League," the essay became a political catechism for later communist movements. Writing in the revolutionary climate sweeping across Europe, Marx and Engels hoped that the capitalist class would soon smash the remains of the old order and elites, attain complete political power, and create global capitalism and liberal democracy, which they saw as the stage for proletarian revolution. They expressed their materialism lucidly and succinctly, applied it to capitalism, and located it *vis-à-vis* other socialist and anticapitalist approaches. In their immanent critique, they detected nascent crises, revolutionary tendencies, and seeds of postcapitalism. Holding that they were amplifying historical tendencies that favor the determinate negation of capitalism, they argued that competition drives the bourgeoisie to constantly revolutionize the productive forces and radically and untiringly transform society and culture. Marx and Engels asserted that the entirety of premodernity's "fixed, fast-frozen relations, with their train of ancient and venerable prejudices" were being "swept away" and "all new-formed ones" were becoming "antiquated before they can ossify." Regardless of unparalleled material progress, they saw capitalism to be "like the sorcerer, who is no longer able to control the powers of the nether world...called up by his spells." They were optimistic, however, that after "all that is solid melts into air," people will come to their "sober senses," see things clearly, take self-conscious collective agency, and shape history rationally in an emancipatory direction (Marx and Engels, 1845, pp. 487–9).

The mature project: irrational surface and rational depth

Marx was expelled from Belgium in 1848, was invited back to France, and then went to Germany as editor of the radical *Neue Rheinsiche Zeitung*. When politics shifted rightward in 1849, he was expelled from Germany with a passport good only for Paris. Because the new, reactionary French regime restricted him to Brittany, he fled to London. Living the rest of his life in the belly of the beast, the great anticapitalist theorist experienced directly advanced modernity in the seat of liberal individualism and the first nation to undergo the Second Industrial Revolution. Marx was often active in working-class movements (leading the First International 1864–72), but, at other times, withdrew from politics. Although continuing journalism, he and his family depended on regular, generous financial support from Engels. Marx fathered eight children; four died before reaching adolescence. He and the family maid had a son who was given to foster parents and kept secret. But Marx was generally an attentive and loving father, very supportive of his three daughters' intellectual and cultural development. The Marx family apparently was closely knit and warm. Residing first in a poor neighborhood of London, they later moved to a middle-class section and lifestyle. But Marx suffered from his children's deaths, and from recurrent, painful, and probably work-related health problems (concerning his eyes, stomach, liver, lungs, inflammations, headaches, and boils). Although Marx left an enormous corpus of collected works, he was tormented by his inability to finish projects, especially his magnum opus, *Capital*. Finally, he regretted his constant trouble with creditors and financial dependency, and their impact on his family. In a letter to Engels, he lamented that, at 50 years old, he was "still a pauper," recalling his mother's earlier admonition that he should have "made capital" instead of merely writing about it (Marx, 1868, p. 25; McLellan, 1973, pp. 189–225; Seigel, 1993, pp. 195–9, 253–89, 375–87).

Although reactionary forces held sway by mid-century, Marx, at first, remained optimistic that bourgeois revolution would succeed on the Continent and that England's liberal democracy and advanced bourgeoisie and working class had swept away all the precapitalist detritus or main blocks to proletarian revolution. In 1850, Marx and Engels declared that a "new revolution can no longer be very far away." Yet Marx's *Class Struggles in France* (1850) departed from the *Manifesto's* linear scenario, reporting counter-revolutionary paralysis and internecine class and subclass conflict (Marx, 1850, pp. 71–145; Marx and Engels, 1850b, p. 377). His *Eighteenth Brumaire* (1852) was much more pessimistic. At the start of this scalding report on the rise of the second Napoleonic dictatorship, Marx recalled Hegel's point that major historical "facts and personages" happen twice, asserting that he "forgot to add: the first time as tragedy, the second time as farce." The work's opening paragraphs, among the most beautifully written and circumspect in all of Marx's corpus, state disappointedly that we do not make our history just as we please. Rather,

> The tradition of all the dead generations weighs like a nightmare on the brain of the living. And just when they seemed engaged in revolutionizing themselves and things, in creating something that never yet existed, precisely in these times of revolutionary crisis they anxiously conjure up the spirits of the past to their service and borrow from them names, battles-cries and costumes in order to present the new scene of world history in this time-honored disguise and this borrowed language.

After the "revolution," Marx held, the French state returned "to its oldest form," based on "the shamelessly simple domination of the sabre and the cowl" (Marx, 1852a, pp. 103–4, 106).

In the *Brumaire*, Marx reported how Louis Bonaparte became dictator, aided by the Parisian lumpenproletariat, or underclass mob of easily bribed riffraff. In his view, the new regime echoed previous absolutism, but concentrated power much more totally, sweeping both bourgeoisie and proletariat from center stage. Anticipating Weber, Marx held that the earlier parliamentary democracy's modernized, centralized, rationalized bureaucracy was an ideal means for carrying out a *coup d'état* and asserting total power. He blamed the bourgeoisie for creating the conditions of their own demise; their manifestly selfish, one-sided pursuit of short-term, material interest created a Frankenstein's monster, or total state, that appeared to be "completely independent" of the material base and leading classes. Arguing that "state power" could not really be "suspended in mid air," Marx stated that the dictatorship represented the class interests of "small-holding peasantry." He considered this stratum to be the most backward in French society, living in what he considered to be "stupefied seclusion," isolated by their proto-feudal productive forces, lack of cooperative and communicative links to modern classes, and backward lifestyle, culture, and interests. Although still claiming that proletarianization and commodification of rural life would eventually undermine the new regime, the *Brumaire* illustrated dramatically that capitalism's rationalizing locomotive could lead to nightmare fusions of modernity and tradition (portending fascism and Nazism) as well as to socialism's promised land (Marx, 1852a, pp. 147–51, 181–97).

During the same period, Engels provided an even more pessimistic report about the complete failure of the bourgeois revolution in Germany, which he attributed to its backward and complexly split class structure. He argued that the bourgeoisie were more soundly defeated there than anywhere else in Europe and that the dissolution of the provincial and national assemblies and restoration of aristocratic power constituted the death of political liberalism in that nation. Rather than decisive bourgeois hegemony and liberal democracy on the Continent, the revolutions of 1848 stirred counter-revolution and fresh fusions of aristocratic and capitalist power. Moreover, Marx observed that Britain's prosperity was creating "political indifference," neutralizing the progressive possibilities of its highly developed bourgeois institutions and advanced working class and generating a conservative drift away from progressive democracy (Engels, 1851–2, pp. 5–13, 91–6; Marx, 1852b, c).

Although Marx stuck to his materialist agenda, he was no longer optimistic about capitalist modernization bringing us to our senses and making capitalism transparent at the surface level of simple empirical observation. In the *Brumaire*, he spoke about the Napoleonic regime's "superficial appearance" (i.e. state autonomy) as a veil covering the underlying logic of capitalism. This idea of the blinding, fettering effects of ideological illusion can be found in his earlier work, but he now held that immanent critique must dig much more deeply and theoretically to grasp the factors that shape capitalism's highly distorted sociopolitical surface. Marx implied that these conditions stalled completely emancipatory possibilities, which seemed to be at hand a few years before (Marx, 1852a, pp. 127–8). As Seigel argues, the reversals of the 1850s caused Marx to doubt his former belief that "empirical experience" provided direct access to the "real truth" (Seigel, 1993, p. 362; also see pp. 193–216).

In the early 1850s, Marx started to amass a great deal of "economic" information, but it was not until 1857, spurred by an international economic crisis and rekindled revolutionary hopes, that he began to refine his mature theory of capitalism in the *Grundrisse* (1857–8) and in *Contribution to the Critique of Political Economy* (1859). Stressing relations of surface and depth, Marx held that everyday appearances and understandings of capital circulation are characterized by fundamental "mystification"; money and commodities are treated as an independent realm of "things" rather than "a social relation." Although "monetary crises" draw out "immanent" contradictions of capitalism, Marx argued, the money form's illusory independence "shrouds" the tensions at the same time that it manifests them. He said that "in the process of exchange, as it emerges on the surface of bourgeois society, each gives only while taking, and takes only while giving," yet both roles depend on "having" or ownership. In his view, basic property and class inequalities are seen as external to circulation's "free" and "equal" exchange. Marx saw the unequal exchange between workers and capitalists (i.e. wages for labor power) to be capitalism's most profoundly mystified and pivotal social relation. His counterfactual theory of value explained capitalism's surface by transposing the apparent relation between things into an unequal relation between persons. Overall, however, Marx held that the "semblance of simplicity disappears in more advanced relations of production" (Marx, 1859a, pp. 275–6, 289; 1859b, pp. 433, 462).

The first volume of *Capital* (1867) appeared about a decade after Marx began his major effort to theorize capitalist political economy. He planned originally to complete six books of his magnum opus. Although filling many notebooks for the broader study, he never finished it. After Marx's death in 1883, Engels edited and assembled the two unfinished core volumes, completing them in 1885 and 1894. Karl Kautsky later edited the three volumes of *Theories of Surplus Value* (1905–10), or Marx's critical history of economic theory. Engels held that Marx's various illnesses and political activism slowed the project, but the fact that his theoretical work often had to be left to the dim light of the night was also a factor (his daytime hours were occupied with journalistic, polemical, and letter writing and with family affairs). Seigel raises other possible factors: unresolved tensions between Marx's Hegelian residue and his materialism, reservations about core aspects of his theory, and psychological problems originating from his childhood experiences (Engels, 1885, pp. 1–5; Seigel, 1993, pp. 329–92).

Stressing the deadly serious, dogged pursuit of an enormous project, Engels described Marx's "unparalleled conscientiousness and strict self-criticism," leading to constant broadening of the scope of issues, searching for ever more historical support, and doing "incessant study" (Engels, 1885, p. 2). In this light, the effort to fully develop his theory was perhaps more important to him than publication. This normative orientation and tendency to leave major corpora of unfinished work to be published posthumously characterized certain other first-generation modern social theorists (e.g. Max Weber and George Herbert Mead). The material and cultural climate of later twentieth-century, professionally specialized, intellectual spheres is an entirely different terrain. Here, unpublished work is considered stillborn or a dead letter. Although earlier modern theorists' sunny ideas of "science" and "truth" are now seen as passé or misguided, their practices should be read in the context of the different ethical and social meaning that "doing theory" had in their time. Reflection on the matter might provide insight into some of the weaknesses as well as strengths of contemporary social theory.

MARX'S SOCIAL THEORY

Contra liberal individualism: discovery of the social

Adam Smith's liberal individualism provides an excellent departure point for moving to explicit consideration of Marx's social theory (Smith, 1776, pp. 3–5, 13–17, 423). Opening the *Wealth of Nations*, Smith illustrated his core concept of the "division of labor" with his famous pinmaker example: a single worker, carrying out all steps of production alone, would be hard pressed to make twenty pins, or possibly even one pin, a day, while ten specialized producers, working together, could produce 48,000 a day or about 4,800 each. Smith suggested that the division of labor increases productivity geometrically, but he saw the market as the ultimate source of progress, rather than labor's complex cooperation. He held that the division of labor originates unintentionally from individual human nature or the universal "propensity to truck, barter, and exchange one thing for another" and the "natural" inclination to pursue individual interests. In his view, capitalist markets unleash heretofore repressed free choice and self-interest, generating an ever more dynamic, efficient, abundant division of labor and, overall, a freer, more rational society. Smith contended that competitive individualism and spontaneous association, based on fleeting contractual relations and consumer choices, produce social harmony, and that the magic of the market's "invisible hand" would be destroyed by socio-political regulation and planning.

Paralleling Smith, Marx held that twelve cooperating masons accomplish much more than one mason working alone for the same number of hours. But he argued that this difference manifests "the creation of a new power, namely, the collective power of the masses." Describing the cooperating masons to be "omnipresent" and to have "hands and eyes before and behind," Marx implied *sui generis* social capacities that inhere in cooperative activity, but do not exist at the individual level per se. He stated that:

> Just as the offensive power of a squadron of cavalry . . . is essentially different from the sum of the offensive . . . powers of the individual cavalry . . . taken separately, so the sum total of the mechanical forces exerted by isolated workmen differs from the social force that is developed when many hands take part simultaneously by one and the same undivided operation. (Marx, 1867, pp. 325–6)

Whereas Smith stressed individual powers released by capitalist markets and bourgeois individualism, Marx emphasized social capacities already present in the "simple cooperation" of premodern or primal humanity. In his view, "different but connected [cooperative] processes," such as joint hunts or harvests, exist everywhere, along with individual activity and independent production. Marx held that even "mere social contact" and consequent "emulation" and "stimulation" enhance existent individual powers and generate new ones, while active cooperation overcomes the "fetters of . . . individuality" and harnesses the "capabilities of the species" (Marx, 1867, pp. 325–9).

Although he agrees that market growth stimulates expansion of the division of labor, Marx's view of the process differs sharply from Smith's position. Marx saw modern industry's spectacular productive advances as deriving from its quantitative extension and qualitative transformation of *sui generis* social powers, especially tacit knowledge flowing through complex cooperative networks and becoming overt in technology and planning. But he held that the capitalist system, which brings the new ultra-powerful "combined organism" into being, also tears producers from their communities, imposes Darwinian competitive struggles among capitalists, and destroys sociocultural regulation. By contrast to premodern cooperation and communal property, Marx held, capitalism separates individual producers from their means of production (i.e. productive forces), concentrates them in the hands of capitalists, and fuses cooperative activity fully with coercion. In his view, unrestrained pursuit of self-interest generates a profound tension between individual activity and complex cooperation, rather than the spontaneous harmony predicted by Smith. As

Engels said, this "contradiction" appears as the "antagonism" between bourgeoisie and proletariat (Engels, 1892, p. 311; Marx, 1867, pp. 325–35, 355–61).

Marx's presuppositions about human nature reverse Smith's vision of the self-interested individual as prior to society. Marx held that the human being is "at all events a social animal" or an "ensemble of the social relations" (Marx, 1845, p. 4; 1867, p. 326). He saw individuality to be an emergent property of "definite" social relationships within historical communities; it is constituted by our patterns of association, cooperation, and language (Marx, 1845, pp. 43–5). Marx argued that claims about an "inherent" split between the individual and society universalize possessive individualism and hypostatize capitalism's primary contradiction between private productive property and complex social cooperation. However, he also saw capitalism as the matrix for a richer, freer social individuality aware of its ties and responsibilities to others and both product and agent of the emergent highly differentiated, reflexive sociocultural order. By contrast to Smith, Marx saw publicly planned production and distribution as enhancing rather than impeding progress. In his view, self-conscious collective agency arises from complex cooperation, and provides seeds of an emancipated post-capitalist order.

Marx's theory of history: historical materialism

The aim of specifying and qualifying earlier Enlightenment conceptions of science and knowledge and of forging new sciences, designed to capture differentiated forms of life in their particularity, connect Marx and certain other first-generation modern social theorists with Darwin. Engels held that, "Just as Darwin discovered the law of development of organic nature, so Marx discovered the law of development of human history" (Engels, 1883, p. 467). Marx called for a "historical" or "social" materialism to go beyond early modern ideas of a general and abstract "science of Man." He embraced Hegel's idea of human historicity, but rejected his "abstract" emphasis on spirit (which he believed retained taints of religion and metaphysics and stopped short of a new understanding of history). Although crediting classical economists for bringing material matters into view, Marx attacked their "abstract," individualistic idea of human nature. His materialism was an attempt to transcend dialectically these points of view, retaining key features, yet ultimately breaking with them and creating a new framework.

In an early statement of the materialist conception of history, Marx and Engels (1845–6, p. 37) held that "It is not consciousness that determines life, but life that determines consciousness." Responding to critics and rigid interpreters, Engels asserted, after Marx's death, that "the *ultimately* determining element in history is the production and reproduction of real life. More than this neither Marx nor I ever asserted" (Engels, 1890, pp. 397–8). Like Darwin, they stressed the centrality of material activities and struggles. In particular, they held that human development must be seen in light of the species' uniquely creative, powerful, and diverse ways of producing for its basic animal needs and how the exercise of these capacities generates distinctly new human needs and human history. Friends and foes, alike, have often interpreted this position in narrow ways, even though Marx and Engels stressed that their "standpoint" is "human society, or social humanity." They saw the "historical life-process" as "twofold," or as both "natural" and "social"; our relationship to nature is mediated by social processes (e.g. cooperation, language, ideas, and customs) that "fetter" productive powers in certain ways, but that also enhance them progressively and make possible eventual emancipation from our original subservience to nature, including our "second nature" or human domination (Marx and Engels, 1845–6, pp. 31–2, 36–7, 41–5; Marx, 1845, p. 5).

Marx stressed "real, active," or "definite individuals," entering "definite social and political relations," producing themselves in specific ways, and, thus, acting as agents of their own history. As stated above, however, he argued that we do not create ourselves of our own accord; instead, people operate under "definite material limits, presuppositions, and conditions independent of their will" (Marx and Engels, 1845–6, pp. 35–6; Marx, 1852b, p. 103). We are born into ready-made, hierarchical sociocultural worlds, which track our ideas and actions in innumerable ways. Stressing the most pervasive source of this systematic social constraint, Marx saw class as an aggregate of people sharing a wide range of limits and possibilities, flowing from their common location *vis-à-vis* societal property relations. He contended that class has an "independent existence against . . . individuals" or that it frames the conditions under which we make ourselves regardless of our consciousness, identity, will, or striving (Marx and Engels, 1845–6, pp. 77–9). For example, feudal class relations (i.e. peasant producers tied to plots and hegemonic lords that controlled landed wealth by military means) reproduced, generation after generation, distinct types of superordinate and subordinate lives, which neither lords nor serfs freely chose. This view of class as a *sui generis* entity gives Marx's thought its distinctive "structural" thrust.

Marx held that as soon as productive powers are advanced to a level where surpluses are large enough to free a significant portion of the adult populace from labor, a fundamental class split arises between "ruling classes" (e.g. feudal lords), who govern politically and culturally and exert effective control over productive forces, and subordinate "direct producers" (feudal serfs), who operate the productive forces and create basic goods and services. He saw these two deeply contradictory class locations as all-important sites of structural advantage and disadvantage and "class struggle." Marx stressed that "class conscious," politically organized class struggle sometimes forges new class structures and reshapes social life *in toto*, but he was also aware that it is usually haphazard, local, and disconnected from overt class identity and conscious collective agency. He saw classes and subclasses engaging in internecine conflict, obscured by complex splits between opposed fragments in single classes and by cross-class alliances between different legal "orders" and status groups. Thus, class struggles are often refracted through ethnic, racial, gender, religious, and other forms of sociocultural conflict. Marx frequently portrayed extremely fragmented class relations. His admission that, in advanced capitalist societies, "middle and intermediate strata . . . obliterate lines of demarcation everywhere" and deflect class consciousness belies his linear hopes about a final showdown between the bourgeoisie and proletariat (Marx, 1894, p. 885). Thus, his declaration that "The history of all hitherto existing society is the history of class struggles" does not mean that they are readily visible or must move history forward (Marx and Engels, 1845, p. 484).

In long-term human history, Marx contended, productive forces, despite many temporary setbacks, advance progressively so that the level of "surplus product" (i.e. exceeding bare subsistence) increases relative to "necessary product" (i.e. required for subsistence). The consequent availability of growing levels of "surplus labor," devoted to overall social development, generates enhanced powers of production, higher standards of subsistence, more differentiated sociocultural orders, and more varied and distinctive human needs. As implied above, however, Marx held that this materially driven civilizing process has been mediated by class and, thus, has operated in a highly unequal way. For example, spectacular built environments and elaborate symbolic cultures of the "great civilizations" were based on a huge divide between "mental" and "physical" labor and relentless extraction of the surplus labor and product of peasants and slaves by ruling political, military, and religious elites. In Marx's view, material and social progress has been and continues to be thoroughly entwined with class domination.

According to Marx's materialist "guiding principle," knowledge about production is necessary to understand the fates of individuals as well as the development of social orders (Marx, 1859a, pp. 262–4). In particular, he stressed the need to study how ruling classes appropriate surplus, seeing this as the most important and veiled social process. Marx considered the historically specific way "in which unpaid surplus labor is pumped out of direct-producers" to be the "hidden basis of the entire social structure" (Marx, 1894, p. 791). He argued that ruling classes and their allied intermediate strata (e.g. priests, scribes, politicians) create ideologies that mystify exploitation as "divinely sanctioned," "natural," "inevitable," and "just," or conceal it completely. For Marx, ideology is the unintended result of parochial class situations as well as an outcome of conscious, strategic political efforts to distort reality. Overall, Marx saw his materialism as a counterhegemonic method that strips away ideology, laying bare the "real bases" of society and posing critical questions about its dynamics and reproduction, which are otherwise systematically suppressed.

Marx saw societies as "social formations," having interrelated parts, governed by systematic internal relations. The most central concept in his materialist framework is *mode* of production, which includes "productive forces" (i.e. natural resources, tools, labor power, technology/science, modes of cooperation), or those factors that contribute directly to the creation of necessary and surplus product, and "property relations," or class-based social relationships that determine who has effective control over the productive forces and the disposition of product and who must engage in productive labor. Marx considered the mode of production as the "base," or ultimate determinant, of social formations. However, as explained above, he held that the "material factor" included sociocultural facets; even the simplest productive forces (e.g.

prehistorical stone tools) require application of rudimentary technical ideas and social cooperation. Arguably, Marx's own materialist analyses stress most centrally class struggles over the forms of property. Overall, his materialism focuses more on social relationships oriented to material factors than on material conditions *per se*.

In Marx's framework, *superstructure* entails nonproductive "modes of intercourse" and "ideology" that help to reproduce the social conditions necessary to maintain the mode of production. Marx saw the state's coercive powers and other control mechanisms as the most vital means of perpetuating productive forces and property relations. He considered the legal, administrative, military, and ideological arms of complex states to be overtowering sources of class power. But he also argued that other organizations and associations (e.g. families or voluntary groups) help to control, socialize, indoctrinate, or otherwise fashion people to fit into or comply with the existing system of production. Marx contended that "ruling ideas" contribute centrally to this process. Although he did not clarify the exact scope of ideology, he usually implied delimited areas rather than culture *per se*. He knew that, in liberal societies, even counter-hegemonic ideas, like his own, could find their way into public life. Marx saw all social life as bearing the imprints of material conditions. Yet he held that certain facets of culture play a very direct role in the reproduction of the mode of production, while others have little to do with the process.

Marx's materialism points to likely structuring and transforming conditions. It holds that productive forces are usually the "ultimate causal agent" of major change, but treats class struggle as its immediate "motor." Referring to conditions that either muffle or intensify class struggle, Marx spoke of relations of "correspondence" and "contradiction," which occur within the mode of production or between it and superstructure. For example, he held that early capitalist labor organization, technology, and markets "contradicted" the feudal manor's and medieval guild's forms of production and property relations and their related complex of laws, economic ethics, and customs. In his view, the "fettering" of nascent capitalism's superior productive forces by exhausted feudal remnants opened the way for political class conflict between the bourgeoisie and feudal strata. The victorious capitalists eventually captured the state, creating "corresponding" political, legal, and sociocultural forms that fit the emergent mode of production.

The issue of the "primacy" of the material factor, or its status as the "ultimate determining" force, has been one of the most enduring and intense topics of Marxist debate. However, Marx himself was somewhat ambiguous about the topic. Following Adam Smith and other early economists, his "soft" position implied that overall sociocultural development depends on the level of material production and types of appropriation. For example, today's mass culture could not be grasped without reference to the advanced capitalist mode of production. But the fact that it determines the overall sophistication, quantity, and diversity of goods and complexity of culture tells us relatively little about any specific commodity or facet of culture. Treating material forces as a matrix that sets broad limits, this soft position provides sociocultural phenomena relative autonomy. In this regard, Marx's view that epochal social transitions must be rooted in qualitative transformations of production is now repeated by many non-Marxist anthropologists and comparative sociologists, theorizing shifts between hunting and gathering, horticultural, agricultural, and industrial societies.

However, Marx also suggested, at times, a "hard" type of material determination. For example, asserting that "social relations are very closely bound to productive forces," he held that technological transformations "change all" our "social relations" ("The hand-mill gives you society with the feudal lord; the steam-mill, society with the industrial capitalist"). He also asserted that a social formation is never "destroyed before all the productive forces for which it is sufficient have been developed, and new superior relations of production never replace older ones before the material conditions for their existence have matured within the framework of the old society" (Marx, 1847, p. 166; 1859a, p. 263). Hard determinism also appears in his claims about the "inevitability" of certain tendencies of capitalist development or of proletarian victory and socialism. Such points imply that politics and culture are epiphenomenal "reflections" of material dynamics. Hard determinism and counterclaims about the relative autonomy of political and cultural factors have constituted a major boundary separating "scientific," "mechanical," or "orthodox" Marxism from "critical," "Western," or "revisionist" Marxism. Anti-Marxist and post-Marxist critics, stressing a more sweeping or even complete autonomy of politics and culture, usually see Marx as a hard materialist, and, on that basis, reject his ideas *in toto*.

Although hard determinist passages exist in Marx's texts, he suggested much more often a complex, historically contingent materialism, which ought not to be reduced to "technological determinism" (i.e. social change arises from technical change) or to "reflection theory" (i.e. ideas are mere emanations of material reality). He frequently pointed to changes arising from diverse sources (e.g. ideological and political as well as material), which deflect class struggles and blur their outcomes. After Marx's death, Engels criticized the hard determinism of younger Marxists. Although admitting that heated debates with opponents led Marx and him to sometimes rhetorically overstate "the economic side," he insisted that their intent was to create "above all a guide to study, not a lever for construction after the manner of the Hegelian." Embracing a softer view of material primacy, he held that the various facets of culture and society exert their own effects. Engels insisted that Marx and he always believed that "history must be studied afresh," that different societies must be "examined individually," and that the relations between the various structural facets are contingent and cannot be deduced in advance (Engels, 1890a, p. 396; 1890b).

The later split over determinism has been primarily between views that treat materialism as a strict or total ontology giving warrants about "inevitable" patterns of change or indubitable historical truths and approaches that employ it as a heuristic principle pointing to likely sources of tension, conflict, and change and to distinctive types of questions about contingent historical processes. Engels argued unequivocally that he and Marx intended the second or more open-ended, undogmatic form of materialism. Although sometimes making hard ontological claims, Marx employed materialism primarily as a heuristic device. His ideas about the shaping force of the material realm were bound up with emergent capitalism's unparalleled materialist powers and agendas, which led even Weber to speak of their "inexorable" determining force. The rationalizing power of later capitalism, especially that of today's neoliberal structure of accumulation, has produced more narrowly tracked, exactly calculated, and global forms of material determination than even Marx could have imagined. Overall, however, he was prescient about materialist trends that his contemporaries did not see. Yet he still implied mainly an open *historical* materialism posing foci, problems, and issues for a distinctly Marxian sociology.

Even in highly complex, premodern civilizations, productive forces tended to develop incrementally over hundreds or even thousands of years and to diffuse slowly between different regions. By contrast, modern capitalism generated, with lightning speed, a nascent "world market," a "global division of labor," and a greater variety of powerful productive forces than all preceding civilizations put together. Marx's materialism bore the marks of this peculiar time, and, perhaps, is best understood as an effort to come to terms with its unique, new capitalist world, rather than with history *in toto*. The primacy that he gave to material factors arose from his experience of the radical changes wrought by the revolution in productive forces, which, as at no previous time, advanced sweepingly and altered everyday life profoundly.

Marx's theory of capitalism: labor, value, and extraction

Marx's main contribution to social theory derives from his effort to explain capitalism and overall social modernity through the lens of his materialism. He held that the dynamic of all previous class societies was ongoing; capitalism's developmental tendencies are still shaped by the appropriation of unremunerated labor and product and patterns of resistance to this extractive process. He considered the relationship between the historically specific ruling class and subaltern class of direct producers as the most fundamental social site and center of his inquiry. Rather than entrepreneurship, supply and demand, and consumer choices, Marx saw capitalism's most basic facet to be its complex fusion of advanced technical means of production with highly rationalized means of extraction, which, he held, generate the aforementioned radical disturbance and transformation of social life – "modernity." Thus, he also pointed to conditions that distinguish capitalism from all earlier modes of production.

Marx held that the primary modern class relation, between capitalists and workers, lacks the transparency of precapitalist ties between ruling classes and direct producers. In the simpler orders, he argued, goods are generally produced and consumed locally and productive relations are mostly with one's family and neighbors. Patriarchal domination of women and children and aristocratic exploitation of slaves, serfs, and free peasants employ direct forms of personal dependence, unfreedom, and extraction, which contrast starkly with uncoerced cooperation and production. Holding that "every serf knows" that the lords extract "a definite quantity of his own personal labor power," Marx contended that precapitalist modes of appropriation are visible and understandable to producers (Marx, 1867, p. 77).

By contrast, Marx held that capitalist modes of cooperation and exploitation are obscured by a highly complex and gravely distorted sociocultural surface. He argued that "the specific social character of each producer's labor does not show itself except in the act of exchange" (Marx, 1867, p. 73). In his view, the exceptionally extensive, impersonal productive and extractive networks are "invisible" to average people. Competitive market relations occlude further capitalism's cooperative side, while ruling ideas, equating wage labor and formal-legal equality with substantive freedom and equality, veil its extractive processes. Marx saw the bourgeois interpretation of the capital–labor relation (i.e. a voluntary contract and commensurable exchange between equals) to be a gross distortion. He thought that wealth and ready access to political, police, and cultural means of control provided capitalists with an enormous advantage over single unaffiliated workers. Also, he held that mechanization and deskilling rob workers of the market leverage formerly held by artisans. While the capitalist's livelihood does not ride on the contract with any single worker, semiskilled operatives usually lack the savings to sustain them in a strike or long search for a "good job," and are easily replaced by individuals from the "reserve army" of unemployed. Overall, Marx saw the contractual view of wage labor (i.e. "free labor") as a central means of ideological domination, shoring up and reducing the costs of the coercive power relation between capitalists and workers.

Marx held that prices, wages, profits, and other capitalist "economic" factors are profoundly "mystified"; they are treated as if they have a life of their own detached from socially organized production and the all-important extractive relation between capitalists and workers. Historicizing Hegel's idea of alienated objectification, Marx referred to the "fetishism of commodities," whereby they are transformed into "independent beings" with their own extrahuman, inherent motions, impacts, and interrelations. In this regard, "a definite social relation... assumes...the fantastic form of a relation between things." Marx argued that economists conceal the role of capitalist property relations and appropriation by analyzing prices and wages as manifestations of subjective choice and supply and demand. He compared this view to that of idealist medieval historians, who equate "the middle-ages with spirituality" and, thus, hide the "secret history ...of its landed property." While the young Marx saw capitalist dynamics to be transparent or immediately given, he now treated them as distorted refractions of forces operating below the surface. Probing the depths, the mature Marx fashioned a counterfactual social theory aiming to "discover" underlying, shaping "conditions and relations of a definite, historically determined mode-of-production" (Marx, 1867, pp. 72–3, 76, 80–3).

Revising earlier ideas of Smith and Ricardo, Marx framed his "labor theory of value" to explain commodity production and capital accumulation. By contrast to his concepts of class and ideology, his view of value is sometimes treated as "economic theory" and, therefore, separate from his sociology. However, his main point is precisely that economic phenomena are not mere emanations of an independent realm of technical conditions or of an individual psychology

of self-interest. Rather, they are "social relations." Marx challenged the bourgeois view of capital as a "mysterious and self-creating source of interest," which
he considered to be an "automatic fetish." He wanted to expose such ideas as
reifications, arising from the matrix of capitalism's sweeping commodification of
sociocultural life (Marx, 1894, p. 392). He intended his labor theory of value to
identify the very heart or engine of commodification and, especially, to shed light
on the central, yet highly mystified, historically specific form of unpaid labor and
related mechanisms of class control.

Marx saw the "immense accumulation of commodities" to be capitalism's
most distinctive surface feature, arguing that only recently have people become
so dependent on commodity production that "growth," or ever-expanding markets and money-making, is now experienced as a "end in itself" and purpose of
social life (Marx, 1867, pp. 35, 151–2). He defined the "commodity" as any
object that has "use value" (i.e. provides for some want or need) and "exchange
value" (i.e. trades systematically against other goods). While individual preferences are central for use values, Marx held, exchange value is a crystallization of
"social substance," or the "labor time" that it took to find, mine, refine, or make
the object. In his view, bourgeois economists mystify capitalism by reifying its
surface phenomena, or treating the proportions at which various commodities
exchange against each other as happenstance outcomes of subjective consumer
choices. By contrast, he argued that prices are "simply the form under which
certain social relations manifest themselves," and that, as all commodity forms,
they are "the material envelope of the human labor spent upon it." Thus, for
Marx, the "definite," capitalist social process of appropriating labor time operates beneath the flux of market prices and, ultimately, determines their overall
pattern (Marx, 1867, pp. 35–70, 91–2).

Marx qualified his theory of value in a number of ways. Rather than labor
time *per se*, he stipulated that the exchange value of commodities reflect
"socially necessary" labor time, or the average intensity of labor reflecting an
industry's level of development. From this vantage point, a subsection of producers, employing very inefficient or backward processes, do not shape overall
exchange values in an industry. Also, Marx held that subjective preferences and
supply and demand have substantial effects on the "market prices" of individual
commodities. For example, when particular goods are in great oversupply or
have gone out of style, they can be priced at far less than their labor values or be
worthless. The converse occurs when a highly desired or essential commodity is
in short supply. Marx saw use value to be highly historically variable and, thus,
to exert powerful multicausal effects on market prices. Although conceding that
bourgeois economists provide reasonably effective tools for analyzing these
"accidental" price movements, Marx believed that their theories fail to grasp
the causes of systematic or overall price patterns. Finally, Marx's theory of value
itself presumed conditions approximating the free market. He held that monopoly and other bureaucratic manipulations can distort value relations. Depending on the situation, monopoly prices may be set far below or far above their
labor values. Surface fluctuations aside, Marx argued, aggregate prices in an
entire capitalist industry or economy gravitate toward an average price set by

socially necessary labor time or labor value (Marx, 1867, pp. 35–70, 270; 1885, p. 292; 1894, pp. 190–9, 437–8). Most importantly, however, Marx's main aim was not to predict price formations, but to lay bare the "social" or extractive process underlying them.

Seeing the commodification of labor or rise of wage labor as the heart of developing capitalism, Marx stressed labor power's unique characteristics as a commodity. He held that the value of "labor power," as other commodities, is set by the labor time needed to reproduce it; in this case, "the means of subsistence necessary for the maintenance of the laborer" (Marx, 1867, pp. 167–76). Although class struggles between capital and labor determine just how close wages are to subsistence, Marx argued, workers usually produce much more value than is returned to them in wages. Accordingly, by contrast to all other commodities, labor power produces systematically more value than it commands in exchange. This "surplus labor time" is crystallized in the objects produced by workers and realized in the money-form when capitalists sell the items as commodities. Marx contended that overall capitalist profitability depends on the unequal wage exchange, deriving ultimately from systematic appropriation of surplus labor time and consequent "surplus value." Thus, accumulation depends on proletarianization and rationalization of labor processes. The fate of individual capitalists rides on their capacity to maintain high "rates of exploitation" or to minimize paid labor time and maximize surplus value. Darwinian economic competition requires them to employ strategies such as increasing labor discipline, reducing real wages, extending work hours without added compensation, finding new pools of workers accustomed to lower levels of subsistence, and engineering the work process and overall factory regime to maximize the speed and intensity of labor per time unit. In this fashion, Marx attempted to theorize capitalism's specific form of unpaid labor and most basic site of ideological distortion and class conflict.

Expressing contradictory facets of capitalism, Marx posed binary oppositions, related to the commodity's "two-sidedness" (i.e. use value and exchange value). He pitted "concrete labor," or specialized activities that produce use values, against "abstract labor," or the "homogeneous human labor" crystallized in exchange value, and, especially, *real wealth*, or the various use values created by concrete labor, against *abstract wealth*, or the profits and accumulated capital based on surplus value or expropriated labor. Marx used these polar ideas to draw out the tensions between capitalism's distorted surface and depth determinants and between its exploitative facets (i.e. modes of appropriation) and its progressive aspects (i.e. revolutionary capacities for producing use values). Most importantly, he held that bourgeois ideology conflates creation of abstract wealth, or capitalist accumulation, with production of real wealth. In Marx's view, the claim that investors or entrepreneurs "create wealth" *per se* is a gross lie that equates private fortune with the overall social wealth that provides for basic human needs. Although conceding that these contradictory sides of economic growth are entwined inextricably under capitalism, Marx held that the two dimensions have fundamentally different qualities and, thus, should be decoupled analytically. He also thought that the two could be decoupled socially in a future postcapitalist order. Marx hoped that his labor theory of value enhanced the historical possibility for separating abstract wealth from real wealth and for creating a society where use value is the primary or even exclusive goal of production and surplus labor is deployed for communal purposes, rather than for private appropriation.

Manufacture to modern industry: "science" enters production

Countering Smith's scenario of a "diligent, intelligent, and ... frugal elite" organizing "lazy rascals" into a responsible workforce (i.e. "primitive accumulation"), Marx contended that capitalism emerged from the dissolution of feudal society and, especially, from expropriation of serf and guild producers, who were "robbed" of their means of production and forced to live by the sale of their labor (Marx, 1867, pp. 713–15). Bringing the complete demise of the old regime, Marx argued, two phases of industrial transformation instituted full capitalist domination and modernity: an initial proletarianization or expansion of *manufacture* (i.e. factory production with limited specialization and simple technologies) and a later move to hyperspecialized and hypertechnical *modern industry*. Marx held that mechanization and, especially, automation magnify greatly the tensions, or contradictory relations, between use value and exchange value and initiate a social decoupling of the production of real wealth from capitalist accumulation. Because "science" replaces "living labor" as the key source of use value and real wealth, Marx argued, modern industry provides the material basis for an ephocal transcendence of capitalism and all earlier class-based social orders dependent on the appropriation of unpaid labor.

According to Marx, manufacture arose gradually from the mid-sixteenth through the late eighteenth centuries in highly developed parts of Europe, especially England. Many propertyless peasant and craft producers were re-employed in small factories. Although seeing manufacture to be anchored in handicraft, Marx held that the beginnings of specialized cooperation advanced "productive power" substantially. Most importantly, separating workers from their means of production, removing labor from the household and family, and employing it within a factory regime of impersonal authority forged a distinct, specialized, "economic" social space for "work" of unparalleled intensity and systematic appropriation of surplus labor time. Money compensation per time unit, or wage labor, provided capitalists with a precise system for calculating rates of extraction. Never before had labor been subjected to such rational appropriation. Marx also argued that increased linkages to wider, more fully monetarized markets intensified competition among capitalists, pressing them into untiring efforts to increase labor coordination, continuity, and discipline. The escalating pace of rationalization centered on maximizing rates of exploitation or surplus-value extraction by increasing the efficiency of production and accelerating the intensity of labor. Because technological change was limited and craft labor was still central, manufacture generated hierarchies based on the relative complexity of functions and a major split between skilled and unskilled labor (Marx, 1867, pp. 336–68).

Marx stressed emphatically that the most important facet of manufacture is the "complete separation" of direct producers from their means of production (Marx, 1867, pp. 714–15). He saw capitalist development "continually" extending and absolutizing this split, stripping workers of their intelligence as well as their property. Marx contended that manufacture initiates the transferal of the individual worker's "knowledge," "judgment," "will," and "cunning" (e.g. formerly basic for hunters and gatherers, peasants, and artisans) to the "workshop as a whole." He argued that modern industry radicalizes this displacement by eliminating remaining pockets of craft workers to overcome bottlenecks and advance rationalization. While manufacture imposes partial, uneven deskilling, Marx held, modern industry's hyperspecialization and mechanization level workers into a homogeneous deskilled mass, or "mere appendage," to the machine. Believing that the industrial operative degenerates into a broken "monstrosity," Marx decried the insouciant bourgeois view of worker stupefaction and marginalization as acceptable costs of "progress" (Marx, 1867, pp. 360–5). Marx held that modern industrial workers suffer terrible work conditions, minimal subsistence, and extreme expendability and that the "reserve army" of unemployed multiplies. Although he noted the appearance of a "superior class" of technical workers (e.g. "engineers" and "mechanics"), he thought that their numbers would remain "unimportant," compared to the massive expansion of proletarian and subproletarian ranks (Marx, 1867, p. 420). However, rejecting utopian ideas of a return to agrarian or artisan production, Marx treated modern industry's mechanization and overall technical rationalization as progressive events. Yet he wanted workers to reap the benefits of the collective intelligence that inheres in the new type of complexly associated labor.

Marx held that modern capitalism's "war of all-against-all" maximizes workshop "despotism" and threatens to "turn all society into one immense factory" (Marx, 1867, pp. 270, 356). Yet he also contended that mass homogenization would stir growing class consciousness and political class struggles, already visible in increased union membership and sociopolitical reform (e.g. the "ten-hour day"). However, he was highly critical of the modest nature of labor's "gains," in a context where human drudgery, misery, and poverty grew explosively and unparalleled productive powers served private fortunes. Marx held that extreme class polarization will eventually generate proletarian revolution. He was aware that such collective agency depends on historically contingent political struggles, but he thought that emancipatory possibilities inhere in capitalism's structural contradiction between rapidly mounting technical capacities for the production of use value, or real wealth, and the fettering force of the ever more frenzied capitalist drive for expanded exchange value. Marx argued that applied science, by reducing reliance on "living labor," diminishes the source of abstract wealth in the same stroke that it revolutionizes the means to produce real wealth. He claimed that mechanization erodes the very basis of capitalist profitability and creates material grounds for socialism.

In Marx's core argument about the "general law of capitalist accumulation," he contended that modern industry produces a trend toward automation among the largest, most advanced producers, increasing sharply the "organic composition of capital" (Marx, 1867, pp. 612–712). In other words, the proportion of "fixed capital," or machines, tools, and other purely technical aspects of production, rises, and the proportion represented by living labor shrinks. Seeing "exchange value" to derive only from the unequal wage labor relation or specifically the unpaid portion of living labor, Marx argued that the popular idea, articulated by classical economists, that "profit" derives from fixed capital or technology obscures "the entire secret of capitalist production" (Marx, 1885, p. 199). Marx saw machinery as a form of "crystallized labor" that cannot create surplus value, even though it greatly speeds up the transfer of value from labor to commodities and contributes even more fundamentally to the creation of use value or real wealth. Marx acknowledged that mechanization can raise profits sharply for individual producers, increasing productivity and market-leverage. Gaining competitive advantages and barriers to entry (i.e. massive fixed capital costs keep out all but the richest competitors), modern industrial firms, using advanced technology, can attain monopoly or oligopoly control of their markets and windfall profits from bureaucratic manipulation of prices. According to Marx, however, such producers employ a perverted form of social power and social planning that goes beyond capitalist accumulation (which is predicated on competition) (Marx, 1894, p. 880).

Marx deduced his "law" of the falling rate of profits from his overall theory of capitalist accumulation and labor theory of value (Marx, 1894, pp. 211–66). Although mechanization initially increases the absolute numbers of factory workers and overall mass of surplus value, Marx held, proportionally less living labor is employed in the productive process and is crystallized in commodities. Thus, he believed that the rate of surplus value and, ultimately, profits must fall. However, he pointed out capitalist strategies that counter the process, e.g. intensifying labor, sinking wages below subsistence, and seeking surplus profits by moving production to "backward" regions with much lower living standards and wages. Marx saw profitability crises to be a major impetus of uneven capitalist globalization. Referring to Western colonialism, he warned of a "new international division of labor" refashioning the globe according "to the requirements of the chief centers of modern industry," and, thus, retarding or instituting one-sided development in peripheral regions (Marx, 1867, p. 451). Marx knew that verifying empirically his law of falling profits would be extremely difficult, or impossible, because of "counteracting influences," partial and unreliable data on profits, and myriad technical problems in computing overall rates of profit. However, he pointed to what he believed to be observable social effects of the process, and, on the basis of his theory, predicted trends toward "overpopulation" of "disposable," or "unemployed," workers, vastly concentrated capital, huge centralized firms, great imbalances of wealth and poverty, overaccumulation and underconsumption of capital, and financial speculation spurring deeper, ever more socially disruptive, cyclical economic crises.

Marx first hinted at this gloomy scenario in his youthful metaphor about capitalism being a "sorcerer" that weds vast productive power to equally vast destructive power and that conjures up enormously powerful, uncontrollable forces (Marx and Engels, 1845, p. 489). However, Marx's optimistic side was not limited to his ideas about proletarian revolution. He also argued that the beginnings of progressive sociopolitical transformation were already visible in advanced capitalism, interpreting trends that appeared with modern industry (i.e. monopoly, managerial control, and state interference) as constituting "the abolition of the capitalist mode-of-production within the capitalist mode-of-production itself" (Marx, 1894, p. 438). Anticipating Berle's and Means's progressive-liberal vision of corporate capitalism's socializing tendencies, Marx contended that emergent corporate planning, separation of management from ownership, employment of knowledge-based technologies, interfirm cooperation, and increased government regulation were "transitional forms" to an emergent postcapitalist order. His vision of late capitalism as "a self-dissolving contradiction" implies the possibility of a peaceful socialist transition (Marx, 1894, pp. 266, 436–41).

Marx suggested that his capitalist "laws of motion" were rooted ultimately in labor-intensive manufacture and age-old class dynamics. Like all previous class systems, early capitalism was still centered on the appropriation of unpaid labor. For this reason, Marx claimed that capitalism, at least in a figurative sense, replays human "prehistory." But he also detected something entirely new or the seeds of a fundamentally different historical dynamic. In *Capital*, he stated that "modern industry... makes science a productive force distinct from labor and presses it into the service of capital" (Marx, 1867, p. 361). His 1857–8 notebooks (*Grundrisse*) for his *magnum opus* traced the long evolution away from independent production to a future state of fully developed capital, where "the creation of real wealth becomes less dependent on labor time and the quantity of labor employed," and "depends, rather, upon the general development of science and the progress of technology or application of science in production." Marx believed that, here, the combined powers of "general scientific work" and an intricate system of cooperation begin an active dissolution of capital (Marx, 1871, pp. 86, 90–1). He held that, in this late stage, capitalist accumulation would be based on a profoundly contradictory, vestigial property relation, while use value or real wealth would depend primarily on the ascendent science/technology form. In this climate, Marx argued, efforts to perpetuate capitalism and wage labor will produce increasingly extreme irrationalities, especially as the biggest industries approach automation and monopoly. At this point, Marx held that the system, even if monopolies continued to dominate, would not operate in accord with the logic of capital.

According to Marx, a fusion of collective intelligence and exploitation inheres in advanced capitalist societies. However, the gradual separation of mental and physical labor and later application of science to production increases the contradictory tendencies. Although driven by capitalist competition, scientific and technological development becomes an increasingly autonomous force, undermining the class relations that originally conjured it up. Marx thought that modern industry refined and suffused, more widely than ever before, the tacit knowledge of associated producers. Moreover, in his view, applied science rationalizes this knowledge, making it more reflective and deliberate. He believed, however, that only a complete severing of the ties with capitalism could control science's destructive tendencies and, finally, decouple production from extraction, coercion, and domination. Pointing to a future moment when "production based upon exchange value collapses," Marx stated:

> Free development of individualities, and hence not the reduction of necessary labor time in order to posit surplus labor, but in general the reduction of necessary labor of society to a minimum, to which corresponds the artistic, scientific, etc., development of individuals made possible by the time thus set free and the means produced for all of them. (Marx, 1871, p. 92)

According to Marx, science domesticated by communal democratic ends would be deployed to help guide an epochal, emancipatory, sociocultural rupture with all pre-existing modes of production.

After capitalism: how soon democracy?

Marx's theories of materialism and capitalism constitute his core legacy in social theory. His enormous public significance, however, derives mainly from his impact on politics, i.e. communist, socialist, and social democratic movements, parties, and regimes, left-leaning labor movements, anticolonial or nationalist insurgencies, liberation struggles, and revolutionary regimes, and even certain "post-Marxist" movements. Marx advocated the unity of theory and praxis, but his political thought is fragmentary and less developed than his other social theory. Although normatively embracing communism, he never elaborated a detailed theory of postcapitalism. According to his historicist method of imman- ent critique, the prospects for revolution depend on the ability to assess and respond to constraints and resources of specific historical situations and levels of development. Thus, divergent social contexts require different types of agency and forbid a comprehensive, general blueprint of postcapitalism in advance. This emphasis on "local knowledge" has been ignored by later twentieth-century critics.

However, images of postcapitalism can still be gleaned from Marx's polemics, programmatic political points, and theoretical asides about communism. In his view, the new order will be "a spontaneous product of a long, painful process of development" and of very advanced material conditions. He asserted that "freely associated" producers will "consciously" regulate their activity according to "a settled plan" in this demystified, postcapitalist world. He contended that capit- alist investment and profits would be eliminated, that communities would decide collectively what needs and wants must be provided for and plan ways to meet them, and that depoliticized public administration will perform the key func- tions formerly provided by capitalist states, firms, and markets. Treating labor and its products as "social" entities, Marx argued, communist planning would return part of the surplus to producers and retain the rest for public purposes (Marx, 1867, pp. 78–80). Engels held that "systematic, definite organization" would end the anarchy of production and war of all-against-all, raising society above "mere animal conditions of existence into really human ones" (Engels,

1892, p. 323). Weber and neoclassical economists demurred, arguing that social-ist planning is doomed to bureaucratic inefficiency and that only competitive markets could effectively process vastly complicated information about produc-tion and consumption and mesh supply and demand. These critics were prescient about Soviet-style, total-planning regimes, but they failed to anticipate the successes of twentieth-century mixed regimes. Marx implied that a science of planning will arise in the new postcapitalist orders, but he did not attempt to confront the broad range of complex technical and political issues concerning socialist planning.

At the start, Marx argued, a new communist society would "in every respect, economically, morally, and intellectually, [be] still stamped with the birth-marks of the old society from whose womb it emerges" (Marx, 1875, p. 85). He contended that sweeping planning capacities cannot be created *de novo*, but must draw on resources of the pre-existing regime. Planners would have to appropriate methods employed by capitalist states and firms, especially their uses of science and technology in production, distribution, crisis management, and overall administration. As explained above, Marx thought that these facets were capitalism's richest, most socialized resources and that their utility would be greatly enhanced after capitalists were expropriated and productive property was socialized. But he argued that communism would still face the hard task of remaking science and technology incrementally and experimentally to fit the emergent conditions.

Marx scolded the German Social-Democrats for exaggerating the immediate benefits to workers from a possible communist takeover (Marx, 1875, pp. 83–8). Arguing that effusive promises would be deflated and cause political failure, Marx's realist stance followed directly from his historicism and materialism. For example, he argued that a major portion of communist workers' surplus product would have to be held back to maintain productive forces, deal with crises, and pay for improved administration, schools, welfare, and other public services. Also, he contended that a new communist regime, attempting to create a mater-ial base for social progress, would reinvest much surplus in technical develop-ment and expanded production. Thus, he felt that the new regime's increased costs would forbid an immediate radical transformation of the conditions of labor and that work would still be remunerated unequally to address unequal effort, skills, and needs. Although implying that the old system's worst abuses would be altered relatively quickly, he stressed that the new society would retain many capitalist facets and problems of life.

In a coldly realistic tone, Marx held that the "first phase of communist society" would carry the "defects" of capitalism's limited "economic" and "cul-tural development." Wanting to avert counter-revolution, he contended that "the first step in the revolution . . . is to raise the proletariat to the position of ruling-class to win the battle for democracy." In his view, the state's coercive apparatus must, at first, remain intact or even be rationalized. He argued that in this phase of "revolutionary transformation . . . the state can be nothing but *the revolution-ary dictatorship of the proletariat*" (Marx, 1875, pp. 87, 95; Marx and Engels, 1845, pp. 504–6). Marx held that the proletariat's politically organized wing would expropriate the bourgeoisie and centralize primary means of production and infrastructure (e.g. banking, communication, transport). They would also "increase the total productive forces as rapidly as possible," and create "industrial armies" in agriculture. Although suggesting some progressive reform (e.g. free education), Marx implied a near total centralization of power by a much enlarged state, which would employ "despotic" force, when necessary, to implement its modernization plan. Speaking of the need for the "strictest centralization," Marx and Engels held that communist state authorities would need to monopolize power and ignore calls for "freedom for the communities" or "self-government." The main aim would be to create productive and sociocultural infrastructure for a later, more complete break with bourgeois society (Marx and Engels, 1845, pp. 504–6; 1850a, pp. 284–5).

Marx also spoke in a utopian manner about a "higher phase" of communism, which would stress "all-round development of the individual" and the ideal of "From each according to his abilities, to each according to their needs." He held that the old "bourgeois society, with its classes and class antagonisms," will be replaced by "association, in which the free development of each is the condition for the free development of all." In the new communal order, Marx contended, people will be freed from labor, and "public power" will "lose its political character" (i.e. the state, as we know it, will fade away). Expressing the same point, Engels stated that "the government of persons is replaced by the administration of things....The State is not abolished. *It dies out*" (Engels, 1892, p. 321). Marx thought that full communism requires a radical rupture with capitalism and an ephocal transformation of institutions, culture, and selves. All this presumes a much higher level of material and sociocultural development, requiring a very, very long period of gestation.

Marx never articulated all-important political constraints on the proposed proletarian "dictatorship." Moreover, his mature scathing views about the repressiveness of bourgeois states and rights suggest a dismissive attitude to liberal institutions, and his passages about the need for bureaucratic centralism, *carte blanche* power, and productivist reorganization, during the transition to communism, imply a possible authoritarian regime or broad suspension of democracy and individual rights in the name of the future communist utopia. Although few and brief, Marx's unqualified passages about proletarian dictatorship were later used to justify forced modernization, stultifying bureaucracy, and overall repression under actually existing communism.

However, Marx's report on the Paris Commune, *The Civil War in France*, offered an opposing scenario (Marx, 1871, pp. 328–43). Embracing enthusiastically the radical democratic, two-month insurgency, he celebrated the Commune's decentralized, participatory features, which proletarian dictatorship seemed to rule out. He held that the Communard working class did not expect "miracles" and that their greatest achievement was the regime's "working existence," which was forged pragmatically by average people employing participatory means, rather than by a political vanguard and scientific-planning elite asserting total power. Marx described how the Commune reduced economic inequality, dismantled capitalist and clerical power, instituted short terms of office, extended suffrage, governed by participatory assembly, and even created "cheap government" by disbanding the army and debureaucratizing administration. Contradicting his idea that radical democracy requires a long gestation, he portrayed "plain" working people, who lacked experience in governance, rising to the occasion quickly, harmonizing prudence with ideals, and undergoing personal transformation in the process. He implied that they became committed to their duties, motivated by social ends, rather than private interests. Marx reported similar tendencies among "all the healthy" elements of other classes and functionaries. Finally, he described graphically the "self-sacrificing heroism" of "men, women, and children," defending their new democracy against the national army and paying with "heaps of corpses" (Marx, 1857–8, pp. 348–55). Leaving aside questions of historical accuracy, Marx's comments about the Commune express a side of his mature political thought (appearing in scattered places in his later work) that expands his youthful view of democracy and clashes with his passages on dictatorship. The Paris Commune essay raises basic theoretical questions. Was the Commune initiating an immediate leap to the "higher stage" of communism? Could radical democracy have been sustained? Regrettably, the Commune was too short lived to address these questions, being crushed brutally by the army.

In the second preface to the *Manifesto*, written shortly after the Commune, Marx and Engels (1872, pp. 174–5) stated that new historical conditions (i.e. "gigantic strides" in industry and working-class party organization) led them to question the work's programmatic section on the transition to communism. They said that they would have reworded it, had they decided to revise the document. However, they did not retract the idea of proletarian dictatorship. Overall, their idea of a postrevolutionary centralization of power has a basis in their broader thought, following, in part, from their stress on "determinate negations." Accordingly, revolution must build on elements of earlier conditions and create new institutions incrementally. Moreover, Marx did not see capitalism providing distinct sociopolitical resources for democratic reconstruction. In his view, the modern state and civil society were perverted totally by bourgeois power and culture, and modern industry and capital evaporated all former bases of communal identity and association. As exemplified by his view of Judaism, he welcomed capitalist leveling of traditional groups as a necessary step in bourgeois rationalization and political consolidation, paving the way for proletarian solidarity, revolution, and ultimate "total emancipation" (Marx, 1843c). Treating the bourgeois revolution as a clearing mechanism, Marx located resources for revolutionary change mostly in economic organization and closely related aspects of science/technology and associated labor. His view of communist transition inhering in and accentuating late-capitalist rationalization does not articulate determinate bases for wider democratic association and culture. It is unclear how such a centralized regime and leveled populace could forge the types of citizenship, groups, values, and selves needed for Marx's ultimate goal of a self-regulating, emancipated society of "associated producers," which he saw, however briefly, emergent in the Paris Commune. In this light, his "higher stage" of communism would, at some point, have to be created *de novo*.

Regardless of the shortcomings, Marx's political theorizing was prescient in ways that many critics ignore. First, twentieth-century labor movements, especially in northern Europe, achieved substantial class solidarity and refashioned capitalism. However, post-Second World War era advances in social rights, substantive equality, and living standards, ironically, weakened the impetus of labor's struggle for socialism. Similar taming of labor's political goals occurred in many advanced capitalist societies (Przeworski, 1985). Reconfigured capitalist workplaces and complexly segmented labor forces, as well as communism's dismal repression and inefficiency, also eroded socialist aspirations and class-based movements. The late twentieth-century neoliberal revival ended the post-war trend toward more robust social states and decreased class inequality, but recommodification began to generate new class-based conflicts. Marx, himself, saw class struggle and dynamics as episodic affairs. Overall, however, working-class movements have had an enormous political impact on twentieth-century capitalism, as Marx predicted. Second, Marx held that state administration could be depoliticized, and even detected this trend in the Paris Commune. Rather than quiescence, he implied that, after the class issue is defused, conflicts over decommodified public goods would shift from challenges about their overall legitimacy to value questions about the relative importance of different issues and to instrumental matters of cost, efficiency, and patterns of public resource allocation. Although recently challenged by global neoliberalism, social democracy, at its postwar height, decommodified many public goods and generated widespread belief in their legitimacy.

Polar political scenarios in Marx's work (i.e. dictatorship versus radical democracy) foreshadowed fundamental splits in the twentieth-century left and contrary directions in Marxist theory. Alvin Gouldner (1980) identified "two Marxisms": determinist positions that legitimate party discipline and state administration versus voluntaristic approaches that affirm spontaneous, radical, or revolutionary actions. The dynamics of twentieth-century Marxism, socialism, and communism were shaped largely by the interplay of these two chief traditions. By the end of the century, however, decline, dilution, or failure of communist regimes and parties, as well as of "wars of national liberation," once again brought forward the problematical issue of democracy and made postwar political agendas seem moribund. By contrast, global neoliberalism, growing inequality, and failing social welfare programs made Marx's core theoretical arguments about socio-economic issues seem relevant again (Cassidy, 1997).

Four areas of tension in Marx's social theory

Of course, like any major theoretical effort, Marx's thought has been criticized on many different fronts. I will not attempt a comprehensive summary of these highly varied critiques, but will point to four important areas of tension in his thought.

THE POLITICAL DEFICIT Smashing Hegel's claims about state neutrality, Marx's early work stressed bureaucracy's gross materialism, toadyism, careerism, formalism, pseudo-meritocracy, and rigid hierarchy. Later, in the *Brumaire*, he anticipated a new form of total power, independent of the leading capitalist class. But he never used these rich insights to theorize a possible dark side to communism. Although celebrating, at times, radical democracy, Marx affirmed late-capitalist industrialism, seeing its complex cooperation and technology as *the* primary social resources of modernity. Even putting aside his comments about proletarian dictatorship, Marx did not attend adequately to the huge problems entailed in state appropriation of productive forces and highly centralized administration. Overall, he implied that expropriation of the bourgeoisie insured that democracy and administrative neutrality would eventually be realized in a very advanced stage of postcapitalism. As Marx predicted, twentieth-century communism suffered the privations of an early social state. However, adding greatly to the anticipated problems of planning, management, and distribution, communist officials became primarily a self-interested privileged stratum, and intransigent political interests and power struggles produced arbitrariness, clientalism, and authoritarianism. Regardless of recent neoliberal trends, the possibilities for socialism or mixed regimes are still an open historical question, likely to arise again in the next serious capitalist crisis. But Marx provides few resources for resolving the complex political and technical problems of such regimes.

THE MISSING EMANCIPATORY SUBJECT Marx's claims about the revolutionary proletariat and inevitability of the conditions that will bring them to power are another deeply problematical theme of his political thought. His hopes about the proletariat bear the imprint of the early phase of the Second Industrial Revolution, when workers were being deskilled and homogenized to fit emergent, Fordist mass production. Shortly after Marx's death, labor began to be segmented much more complexly than he ever imagined; various levels and types of managerial and wage labor positions were differentiated according to divergent educational grades and by gender, race, ethnicity, and other ascriptive criteria. Many writers have analyzed the consequent splits that blocked the type of proletarian solidarity that Marx hoped for. Later twentieth-century restructuring transformed workplaces even more radically, and forged far more complex, globally dispersed segmentation and disjunctive, cross-cutting class, subclass, and status group hierarchies. Thus, Marxian ideas about the revolutionary proletariat or even an alternative unified emancipatory subject appeared moribund. However, in the United States, highly paid technical, financial, and "infotainment" positions increased, while low-wage, part-time service work expanded much more rapidly. Late-century growth polarized jobs, income, and wealth. The professional middle class flourished and the stock market soared, but lower middle and lower segments of the American workforce suffered stagnating wages, increasing insecurity, and eroding health care and benefits. Poverty grew rapidly among female-headed families, minorities, and poorly paid workers. In Europe, "jobless growth" resulted in postwar highs in unemployment. Polarization of income and wealth grew on a global basis, reflecting neoliberal free market and free trade policies and recommodification of public goods. Industrial expansion in "the developing countries" was reminiscent of nineteenth-century capitalism, with wages sometimes below subsistence levels, terrible work conditions, state repression, and a new "labor movement . . . struggling to be born" (Greider, 1997, p. 34). Although unionized, blue-collar, labor declined in many rich countries, restructuring, globalization, and polarization generated class compression and new forms of homogeneity of material fate among many workers. Although Marx's theory of the revolutionary proletariat does not hold under current conditions, his broader ideas about class consciousness and political class struggle are still open questions that may soon be tested again.

OBJECTIONABLE TOTALITIES The idea of "totality" has been a much debated topic in the history of Marxism (e.g. Jay, 1984). Marx created a basis for a historically specific materialist sociology that puts aside wistful illusions, but it is entwined with an impassioned emancipatory ideal that has had divergent directions and impacts. Although Marx's normative project inspired his effort to unify theory and praxis and much of his best sociological work, it has also been the source of totalizing claims about inevitable progress and about how materialism offers *the* explanation of history, *the* correct understanding of the contemporary situation, and *the* single route to emancipation. As many critics have argued, the presumption of grasping history in a total indubitable way has affinity for centralized authority, elite decision-making, and top-down planning. Marxist academic and party politics have often been plagued by this rigidity, taking on the quality of dogmatic religious belief or even an authoritarian catechism. But the counter themes to this rigidity dominate in Marx's overall corpus. Today, new cultural theorists often express a reverse type of dogmatism, universalizing "local knowledge" and conflating totalities with "broad" historical discourses or theories (Fraser, 1989, p. 13n2). Putting the totalizing tendencies aside, Marx's type of broad historical theory is needed more than ever to grasp the global system.

TARNISHED FAITH IN SCIENCE AND MODERNIZATION Marx did not live to experience the application of science to the means of mass destruction or recent threats of overdevelopment, chemical contamination, and global warming. Many theorists' optimistic hopes about science and rationality were shattered or, at least, sobered greatly by the First World War. Moreover, the Second World War era's advanced military technologies, propaganda machines, and fascism, Nazism, Stalinism, the Holocaust, and Hiroshima appeared to be industrial modernization gone mad. The postwar economic expansion once again fueled high hopes about science and technology, but vapid mass consumption, high-tech wars, mass surveillance, major environmental crises and risks, planning failures, and numerous other problems, relating to private and public sector applications of technical knowledge, stimulated strong challenges to the legitimacy of science and modernization. Reminiscent of the Frankfurt School's mid-century "dialectic-of-Enlightenment" critique, new challenges to rational culture reappeared in the form of postmodernism and cultural theory. The

Enlightenment project was reinscribed with the domination of nature, restless instrumentalism, environmental degradation, colonialism, racism, sexism, and even the Holocaust. The cultural left often saw Marx as the prototypical representative of Enlightenment hubris and error. And diverse thinkers heralded a new era, where concern for "risk" and "local knowledge" makes obsolescent deployment of science and planning to solve big public problems and seek socio-economic justice. Is the era of such intervention over? Will the problems be left to fester? Could planning be pacified, or must the old defects always reappear? If planning is exhausted, what options remain? What threats arise from re-enchantment and aestheticized tribal politics? Although Marx's view of science must be rethought, he framed the idea that grossly uneven, unjust, uncontrolled, and unsustainable development arises from a distinctive fusion of science *and capitalism*, rather than from science or rationality *per se*. This question remains a pressing one. In this regard, antimodern critics are amnesiac about the irrationalist and mythic side of fascism. Science and rational culture are major resources of modernity, and will likely be crucial areas of contestation and struggle in the new millennium.

Marx's Place in Modern Social Theory

Crisis of Marxism? Post-Marxism and postmodernism

In the late twentieth century, especially after the 1989 collapse of Eastern European communism and the erosion of Chinese communism from official corruption, the repression in Tiananmen Square, and economic liberalization, many thinkers once again pronounced an end to socialism and the death of Marx. Riding the wave of the politics of 1989, Francis Fukuyama held that Hegel's argument that the liberal state would resolve the contradiction between liberty and equality and end history had been vindicated by "the monumental failure of Marxism as a basis for real-world societies" and by global neoliberal hegemony. Fukuyama held that it is Marx, rather than Hegel, that should be stood "right-side up" (Fukuyama, 1992, pp. 64–5). His neoconservative celebration of ascendent minimalist, free-market democracy and the triumphant defeat of postwar trends toward increased regulation and redistribution was widely covered in the US press. However, many progressive theorists, such as Anthony Giddens, also held that class politics are dead, or have been replaced by the postmaterialist new social movements and "life politics." Taking a more centrist position, "beyond left and right," they were open to engaging liberal views of the market, civil society, and planning. In this context, Giddens stated: "The Promethean outlook which so influenced Marx should be more or less abandoned in the face of the insuperable complexity of society and nature. A drawing back from the ambitions of the Enlightenment is surely necessary" (Giddens 1994, p. 79; Aronson 1995; Boynton 1997).

Even prior to 1989, Marxist and socialist thinkers began to suggest that their tradition was losing vitality. For example, Perry Anderson (1983) held that "Western Marxist" social theory was at an "end"; Martin Jay (1984) chronicled the decline in detail the following year; Ernesto Laclau and Chantal Mouffe (1985) held that materialism and class politics were exhausted, calling for a "post-Marxist" shift to "discursive democracy" and plural new social movement politics; and the Marxist Ellen Meiksins Wood (1986) countered their move vigorously, yet still implied that the new cultural politics were ascendent and had gravely weakened left politics and theory. In the 1990s, many Marxists and former Marxists spoke in pessimistic tones. For example, Habermas (Habermas and Michnik, 1994, p. 11) argued that the left has given up criticizing capitalism at the very moment when economic problems have mounted enormously. He contended that the current situation cries out for increased action from the state, but that political and sociocultural conditions forbid such a move. Similarly, Claus Offe (1996) asserted that the socialist ideal has been emptied of content and that European welfare states are rapidly losing legitimacy. He held that the very idea of progressive modernization, central to Marx's Enlightenment project, is now moribund. Ironically, Offe's claims about "zero options" and "no alternatives" converge unhappily with Fukuyama's cheery view of neoliberal dominance.

A century ago, Georg Simmel (1900, p. 484) spoke about the rise of tragic cultural sensibilities, pointing to a "secret restlessness" and "helpless urgency" that drive people "from socialism to Nietzsche, from Böcklin to impressionism, from Hegel to Schopenhauer and back again." In mid-century, Max Horkheimer and Theodore Adorno held that mass consumption and propaganda neutralized the cultural bases of immanent critique and emancipatory social movements. They held that a new approach was needed to address the nearly complete foreclosure of critical thought by "total administration" and "one-dimensional" culture. Breaking with left-historicism, they shifted from Marxism to a quasi-Nietzschean critique of Western culture. Following Henri Lefebvre's (1962, p. 206) Nietzschean declaration of the exhaustion of Marxism, later thinkers, such as Foucault, Derrida, Lyotard, and Baudrillard, fashioned a postmodern turn. Many late twentieth-century, left-leaning theorists, saw a growing futility in the Marxian program of theory and praxis, and refocused both accordingly. In this regard, recent North American theorists, such as Linda Nicholson and Donna Haraway, or Europeans, such as Anthony Giddens, Alberto Mellucci, Ulrich Beck, and Zygmunt Bauman, applaud many of the same tendencies that Marxists bemoan (Antonio, 1998). They see their breaks from Marxism and fresh theoretical paths as rescuing critical thought and politics from cultural exhaustion. In a sense, they follow Marx's historicist method, which calls for change in response to new conditions, especially when the emancipatory prospects appear bleak or new progressive forces appear on stage. But the recent trends that lead many theorists to the new cultural politics lead others back to political economy and Marx. Paradoxically, revivals of Marxian theory spring from the same climate; fresh critiques, in light of new conditions and exhaustion of older ideas, produce new fusions and possible renewal of the tradition. This "critical" side of the Enlightenment and Marxism gives them multiple lives.

Perhaps the wake of the movements of 1989 will decouple the association of Marx with authoritarian, Soviet-style regimes. Moreover, the antitotalizing themes of recent cultural theories could have a beneficial impact on Marxist theory. Indeed, these sensibilities can already be detected in the plural undogmatic formats of the best Marxist journals (e.g. *New Left Review*). In the same text in which Perry Anderson (1983, pp. 20–7) declared that Western Marxist grand theory was exhausted, he noted the growing body of Marxian empirical-historical work by scholars such as Harry Braverman, Guglielmo Carchedi, Robert Brenner, Immanuel Wallerstein, James O'Connor, and Erik Olin Wright. At the end of the twentieth century, this type of research flourished among Marxian scholars. For example, Erik Olin Wright's (1997) cross-national class project illustrates the period's Marxist sociology, combining comprehensive empirical inquiry with conceptual innovation. In the 1990s, Marxist theorists, such as Ellen Meiksins Wood (1995) and Moishe Postone (1993), produced major interpretive studies, rereading Marx's mature project in a contemporary fashion. Other Marxist scholars, such as David Harvey (1989), Fredric Jameson (1991), and Terry Eagleton (1996), engaged cultural issues and postmodernism. Senior scholars, such as Eric Hobsbawm (1996), Göran Therborn (1995), Jürgen Habermas (1996), and Immanuel Wallerstein (1991), produced major new works. There were also signs of a Marx revival within cultural theory (e.g. Derrida, 1994). Other thinkers produced important Marxian influenced public issue books (e.g. Harrison and Bluestone, 1990; Davis, 1992; Harrison, 1994; Gordon, 1996).

Marx's enduring contribution to social theory

To many thinkers, Marx's view of the capitalist locomotive flattening traditional structures is a troublesome and, perhaps, naive idea. Marx himself had doubts about the scenario near the end of his life, restricting it to Western Europe (Marx, 1881, p. 370). Yet a case could be made that later twentieth-century globalization manifests some of his main expectations about capitalist leveling. Trends toward global markets, an international division of labor, and substantially increased class inequalities correspond to what Marx implied would be imminent toward the end of the nineteenth century. Although his political thought should not be discounted entirely, his critique of capitalism has most relevance for the current scene. The more capitalism triumphs globally, especially in its current highly unregulated and unequal neoliberal form, the more likely Marx's theory will have renewed critical value. Countering this trend, his theory poses basic questions about loosening restrictions on property rights, disembedding economic affairs from political and sociocultural regulation, and recommodifying public goods. Treated as a heuristic tool, his materialist approach need not preclude attention to or diminish the importance of cultural theory, domination, and movements.

Numerous contemporary critics of Marx have argued that "multicausal" theories are superior to his materialism. In their frameworks, capitalism and class inequality are, at best, segmented parts of a multifaceted sociocultural complex and plural field of diverse problems and competing interests. In particular, the cultural left, attacking Marxian totality and economism, oppose what they see as an improper "privileging" of class. Although the new cultural theories have had definite critical value (i.e. raising cultural questions and pointing to sites of domination that were ignored by the postwar left), their emphatic emphases on difference, locality, and multiplicity lose a bit of their edge in a world where the dominant ideology stresses decentered plurality and niche markets. An argument could be made that these views have a strong affinity for the reigning type of liberalism. In this regard, Richard Rorty (1998, p. B5) holds that the cultural left has been largely silent about economic polarization and misery and has no reply to neoliberal claims that the current form of capitalism is the "only alternative." Similarly, Terry Eagleton (1996, p. 23) says that:

> The power of capital is now so drearily familiar, so sublimely omnipotent and omnipresent, that even large sections of the left have succeeded in naturalizing it, taking it for granted as such an unbudgeable structure that it is as though they hardly have the heart to speak of it....With Darwinian conformity, much of the cultural left has taken on the colour of its historical environs: if we live in an epoch in which capitalism cannot be successfully challenged then...it does not exist.

The power of Marx's theory is the compelling case that it makes for the view that capitalism is the most fateful and decisive force in the modern world. It swims against the current tide.

Max Weber argued that "one-sided" theory programs can have great heuristic value if they isolate factors that have decisive impact and are not reified as the single explanation of history. Such theories raise unambiguous questions about vital public matters, generating wide-ranging discussion and oppositional arguments and inquiries. Because theoretical advances and innovations often arise from engagements between contrasting positions, both Marxism and cultural theory could benefit from a climate where they stand beside one another. Marx spelled out the assumptions and provided a systematic rationale for an integrated program of social theory, empirical-historical inquiry, and normative sociopolitical critique. Along with Nietzsche, he remains one of the primary poles of social theory today, as is illustrated by the frequent references to him in the intense battles over modernism and postmodernism and over the value of rational culture and science. While Nietzsche began the current cultural turn, Marx initiated the effort to theorize global, deregulated, unequal capitalism, countering tendencies that render it invisible by treating it as a benign entity, an overwhelmingly affirmative force, or a behemoth beyond change.

In particular, Marx's emphasis on the tension between "abstract" and "real wealth" has renewed pertinence in the current climate of polarization of material and sociocultural life chances, deregulation and disembedding, and expansion of the inequality, power, and privileges of propertied wealth. His core argument that the vast benefits of real wealth, generated by capitalism's scientifically mediated powers of production, should be extended in a much wider and more just fashion poses sharp critical questions about the current tendency to treat as tolerable and even inevitable the increasing misery, drudgery, and insecurity of less advantaged people, while private wealth grows explosively for the fewer fortunate ones in an increasingly "gated" world. During the late 1990s, some thinkers began to question whether the trend toward a "shareholders' society" ought to be shifted in the direction of the "stakeholder" or citizenry. In this climate, Marx's specter becomes visible again. His social theory remains a vital departure point for an alternative way of seeing, thinking, and inquiring in these "postmodern" times.

Bibliography

Unless otherwise indicated, references to works by Marx and/or Engels are to *Karl Marx Frederick Engels: Collected Works*, 50 volumes, published by International Publishers, New York, from 1975 on.

Writings of Karl Marx

Letter from Marx to His Father: in Trier. 1837. In *Collected Works, volume 1*, pp. 10–21.

Proceedings of the Sixth Rhine Province Assembly. 1842. In *Collected Works, volume 1*, pp. 224–63.

Justification of the Correspondent from Mosel. 1843a. In *Collected Works, volume 1*, pp. 332–58.

Letters from the Deutsche–Französische Jahrbücher. 1843b. In *Collected Works, volume 3*, pp. 133–45.

On the Jewish Question. 1843c. In *Collected Works, volume 3*, pp. 146–74.

Contribution to the Critique of Hegel's Philosophy of Law. 1843d. In *Collected Works, volume 3*, pp. 3–129.

Economic and Philosophical Manuscripts of 1844. In *Collected Works, volume 3*, pp. 229–346.

Theses on Feuerbach. 1845. In *Collected Works, volume 5*, pp. 3–5.

The Poverty of Philosophy. 1847. In *Collected Works, volume 6*, pp. 105–212.

The Class Struggles in France: 1848–1850. 1850. In *Collected Works, volume 10*, pp. 43–145.

The Eighteenth Brumaire of Louis Bonaparte. 1852a. In *Collected Works, volume 11*, pp. 99–197.

Political Consequences of the Commercial Excitement. 1852b. In *Collected Works, volume 11*, pp. 364–8.

Political Parties and Prospects. 1852c. In *Collected Works, volume 11*, pp. 369–72.

Outlines of the Critique of Political Economy (Rough Draft of 1857–58) [First Installment]. In *Collected Works, volume 28*, pp. 3–537.

Outlines of the Critique of Political Economy (Rough Draft of 1857–58) [Second Installment]. In *Collected Works, volume 29a*, pp. 307–55.

A Contribution to the Critique of Political Economy. 1859a. In *Collected Works, volume 29b*, pp. 257–429.

The Original Text of the Second and the Beginning of the Third Chapter of *A Contribution to the Critique of Political Economy.* 1859b. In *Collected Works, volume 29b*, pp. 430–507.

Capital: a Critique of Political Economy. Volume 1, The Process of Capitalist Production, ed. Frederick Engels. 1867. New York: International Publishers (1967a).

Letter from Marx to Engels: in Manchester. 1868. In *Collected Works, volume 43*, pp. 20–5.

The Civil War in France: Address of the General Council of the International Working Men's Association. 1841. In *Collected Works, volume 22*, pp. 3–537.

Critique of the Gotha Program. 1875. In *Collected Works, volume 24*, pp. 75–99.

Letter to Vera Zasulich. 1881. In *Collected Works, volume 24*, pp. 370–1.

Capital: a Critique of Political Economy. Volume 2, The Process of Circulation of Capital, ed. Frederick Engels. 1885. New York: International Publishers (1967).

Capital: a Critique of Political Economy. Volume 3, The Process of Capitalist Production as a Whole, ed. Frederick Engels. 1894. New York: International Publishers (1967).

Theories of Surplus Value, 3 volumes, ed. Karl Kautsky. 1905–10. Moscow: Progress Publishers (1963–71).

Writings of Karl Marx and Frederick Engels

The German Ideology. 1845–6. In *Collected Works, volume 5*, pp. 19–608.

Manifesto of the Communist Party. 1845. In *Collected Works, volume 6*, pp. 477–519.

Address of the Central Authority to the League: March 1850. 1850a. In *Collected Works, volume 10*, pp. 277–87.

Address of the Central Authority to the League: June 1850. 1850b. In *Collected Works, volume 10*, pp. 371–7.

Preface to the 1872 German Edition of the Manifesto of the Communist Party. In *Collected Works, volume 23*, pp. 174–5.

Further reading

Anderson, Perry (1983) *In The Tracks of Historical Materialism.* London: Verso.

Antonio, J. Robert (1998) Mapping Postmodern Social Theory. In *What Is Social Theory? The Philosophical Debates.* Oxford and Cambridge, MA: Blackwell.

Aronson, Ronald (1995) *After Marxism.* New York and London: The Guilford Press.

Boynton, Robert S. (1997) The Two Tonys: Why Is the Prime Minister So Interested in What Anthony Giddens Thinks? *The New Yorker,* October 6, 66–74.

Cassidy, John (1997) The Return of Karl Marx. *The New Yorker,* October 20 and 27, 248–52, 254–6, 259.

Davis, Mike (1992) *City of Quartz: Excavating the Future in Los Angeles.* New York: Vintage Books.

Derrida, Jacques (1994) *Specters of Marx: the State of Debt, the Work of Mourning and the New International.* New York and London: Routledge.

Eagleton, Terry (1996) *The Illusions of Postmodernism.* Oxford and Cambridge, MA: Blackwell.

Engels, Frederick (1842) The Insolently Threatened yet Miraculously Rescued Bible or: the Triumph of Faith. In *Collected Works, volume 2*, pp. 313–51.

Engels, Frederick (1851–2) *Revolution and Counter-revolution in Germany.* In *Collected Works, volume 11*, pp. 3–96.

Engels, Frederick (1883) Karl Marx's Funeral. In *Collected Works, volume 24*, pp. 467–71.

Engels, Frederick (1885) Preface. In *Capital: A Critique of Political Economy. Volume 2, The Process of Circulation of Capital.* New York: International Publishers (1967), pp. 1–19.

Engels, Frederick (1890a) Engels to Conrad Schmidt. In Lewis S. Feuer (ed.), *Marx and Engels: Basic Writings on Politics and Philosophy.* Garden City, NY: Anchor Books (1959a), pp. 395–7.

Engels, Frederick (1890b) Engels to Joseph Bloch. In Lewis S. Feuer (ed.), *Marx and Engels: Basic Writings on Politics and Philosophy*. Garden City, NY: Anchor Books (1959b), pp. 397–400.

Engels, Frederick (1892) *Socialism: Scientific and Utopian*. In *Collected Works, volume 24*, pp. 281–325.

Fraser, Nancy (1989) *Unruly Practices: Power, Discourse, and Gender in Contemporary Social Theory*. Minneapolis: University of Minnisota Press, 1989.

Fukuyama, Francis (1992) *The End of History and the Last Man*. London and New York: Penguin Books.

Giddens, Anthony (1994) *Beyond Left and Right: the Future of Radical Politics*. Stanford, CA: Stanford University Press.

Gordon, David M. (1996) *Fat and Mean: the Corporate Squeeze of Working Americans and the Myth of Managerial "Downsizing"*. New York: The Free Press.

Gouldner, Alvin W. (1980) *The Two Marxisms: Contradictions and Anomalies in the Development of Theory*. New York and Toronto: Oxford University Press.

Greider, William (1997) Why the Global Economy Needs Worker Rights. *Working USA*, May/June, 32–44.

Habermas, Jürgen (1996) *Between Facts and Norms: Contributions to a Discourse Theory of Law and Democracy*. Cambridge, MA and London: MIT Press.

Habermas, Jürgen and Michnik, Adam (1994) Overcoming the Past. *New Left Review*, 103, 3–16.

Harrison, Bennett (1994) *Lean and Mean: the Changing Landscape of Corporate Power in the Age of Flexibility*. New York: Basic Books.

Harrison, Bennett and Bluestone, Barry (1990) The *Great U-turn: Corporate Restructuring and the Polarizing of America*. New York: Basic Books.

Harvey, David (1989) *The Condition of Postmodernity: an Inquiry into the Origins of Cultural Change*. Oxford and Cambridge, MA: Blackwell.

Hegel, G. W. F (1807) *The Phenomenology of Mind*. New York: Harper & Row (1967).

Hobsbawm, Eric (1996) *The Age of Extremes: a History of the World, 1914–1991*. New York: Vintage.

Jameson, Fredric (1991) *Postmodernism, or, The Cultural Logic of Late Capitalism*. Durham, NC: Duke University Press.

Jay, Martin (1984) *Marxism and Totality: the Adventures of a Concept from Lukács to Habermas*. Berkeley and Los Angeles, University of California Press.

Laclau, Ernesto and Mouffe, Chantal (1985) *Hegemony and Socialist Strategy: towards a Radical Democratic Politics*. London and New York: Verso.

Lefebvre, Henri (1962) *Introduction to Modernity: Twelve Preludes September 1959–May 1961*. London and New York: Verso (1995).

McLellan, David (1973) *Karl Marx: His Life and Thought*. New York: Harper & Row.

Offe, Claus (1996) *Modernity and the State: East, West*. Cambridge, MA: MIT Press.

Postone, Moishe (1993) *Time, Labor, and Social Domination: a Reinterpretation of Marx's Critical Theory*. Cambridge and New York: Cambridge University Press.

Przeworski, Adam (1985) *Capitalism and Social Democracy*. Cambridge and New York: Cambridge University Press.

Rorty, Richard (1998) The Dark Side of the Academic Left. *Chronicle of Higher Education*, April 3, B4–B6.

Seigel, Jerrold (1993) *Marx's Fate: the Shape of a Life*. University Park: Pennsylvania State University Press.

Simmel, Georg (1900) *The Philosophy of Money*. London and Boston: Routledge & Kegan Paul (1978).

Smith, Adam (1776) *An Inquiry into the Nature and Causes of the Wealth of Nations.* New York: Modern Library (1937).

Therborn, Göran (1995) *European Modernity and Beyond: the Trajectory of European Societies 1945–2000.* London and Thousand Oaks, CA: Sage.

Wallerstein, Immanuel (1991) *Unthinking Social Science: the Limits of Nineteenth-century Paradigms.* Cambridge: Polity Press.

Wood, Ellen Meiksins (1986) *The Retreat from Class: a New "True" Socialism.* London and New York: Verso.

Wood, Ellen Meiksins (1995) *Democracy against Capitalism: Renewing Historical Materialism.* Cambridge and New York: Cambridge University Press.

Wright, Erik Olin (1997) *Class Counts: Comparative Studies in Class Analysis.* Cambridge and New York: Cambridge University Press.

5

Max Weber

STEPHEN KALBERG

> Simple intellectual integrity [involves giving
> account to oneself] of the final meaning of
> one's own actions.
>
> *Max Weber*

Widely recognized as one of the major founding fathers of sociology, Max Weber
(1864–1920) is perhaps today best known for his attempts to define the uniqueness of the modern West and to provide causal explanations for its specific
historical development. However, far from offering a justification for industrial
societies, his sociological and political writings both evidence a profound
ambivalence toward them; although impressed by their capacity to sustain
high standards of living, Weber feared that many of their foundational elements
opposed the further unfolding of human compassion, ethical action, and individual autonomy. At the dawning of the twentieth century, he asked "where are
we headed" and "how shall we live with dignity in this new age?" He worried
that it might become an "iron cage" of impersonal, manipulative, and harsh
relationships lacking binding values and noble ideals.

His search for answers to these burning questions drove Weber to pursue, even
by the ambitious standards of scholarship in his day, an extraordinarily broad
and deep comparative agenda. Standing near the end of a long line of distinguished German scholars who undertook "universal-historical" investigations
and convinced that the uniqueness of any particular society could be isolated
only through rigorous comparisons, Weber's quest led to a series of massive
studies. Remarkably, his empirical research spanned the civilizations of the
ancient world, China, and India; they moved as well, with full sovereignty,
across each century of the West's 2,600-year development. Along the way he

explored, in detailed studies, for example, Old Testament prophecy and the Bible, the medieval origins of Western music, the salvation doctrines of Buddhism, Hinduism, ancient Judaism, early Christianity, medieval Catholicism, and ascetic Protestantism, the decline of the Roman Empire, the accounting practices of medieval trading companies, the possibilities for democracy in Russia, the rise of the caste system in India, Confucianism in China, and mono- theism in ancient Israel, and the many methodological questions at the founda- tion of the social sciences.

Weber's approach to these investigations proved unique. He abjured on the one hand a focus upon single factors – such as economic, political, or religious forces – and sought to offer multidimensional analyses that evaluated the causal weight of both "ideas" and "interests." He attempted on the other hand to *understand* the ways in which persons in various civilizations, in light of varieties of demarcated contextual and indigenous social configurations, attributed meaning on a regular basis to certain "types of action" and not to others. How do persons in different civilizational settings create *meaning* in their lives? Weber sought to investigate this question impartially even though the action of persons across the globe at times appeared to him, from the point of view of his own values, as odd and even bizarre.

THE PERSON

Max Weber was born in Erfurt, Germany, into a distinguished and cosmopolitan family of entrepreneurs, scholars, politicians, and strong women. Most of his younger years were spent in Berlin, where he attended an excellent school that required a strenuous regimen of study. Recognized early on as an exceptional student, he developed a precocious love of learning and a particular fondness for philosophy, literature, and ancient and medieval history. His teenage letters comment upon, among many others, the merits of Goethe, Kant, Hegel, Spinoza, and Schopenhauer. They also demonstrate, as the eldest child, a concern for his overworked, devout mother. Although influenced strongly by his work-obsessed father, a central figure in the city government of Berlin and the state govern- ment of Prussia, he deplored his patriarchal ways and insensitive treatment of his wife.

Weber studied economic history, law, and philosophy at the universities of Heidelberg, Berlin, and Goettingen. His letters indicate a keen awareness of the varying quality of instruction in his lectures and seminars, as well as an inability to curtail rather free-wheeling spending habits. He became the protégé in Berlin of the legal historian Goldschmidt and the Roman historian Mommsen. In 1893 he was appointed to a chair in commercial law at the Humboldt University in Berlin at an unusually young age, and in 1894 he accepted a chair in economics and finance in Freiburg. At the age of thirty-three, having recently married a distant cousin, Marianne Schnitger, Weber evicted from their home his father, who had mistreated his mother. The father's death soon afterwards served as the catalyst for a paralyzing mental illness that endured for more than five years.

During much of this time Weber passively pondered the fate of persons living in the new world of secularism, urbanism, and capitalism.

A trip to the United States in 1904 played a part in his recovery. Journeying across much of the East, South, and Midwest, he gained an appreciation for America's dynamism, energy, and uniqueness, as well as for the self-reliance and distrust of authority widespread in the United States. His most famous work, *The Protestant Ethic and the Spirit of Capitalism* (PE), was completed soon after his return to Germany. Although unable to teach until 1918, Weber began once again to publish on a broad array of topics.

His interest in the "ascetic Protestantism" of the American Quaker, Methodist, Presbyterian, Calvinist, Baptist, and Congregationalist churches derived in part from the religiosity of his mother, Helene, and her sister, Ida Baumgarten. As Christian social activists and admirers of mid-century American Unitarianism, the pious sisters transmitted to the young Weber a heightened sensitivity to moral questions, an appreciation of the ways in which the life of dignity and meaning must be guided by ethical standards, and a respect for the worth and uniqueness of every person. Marianne reaffirmed these values, although they opposed the lessons taught by Max's father: the necessity to avoid "naive idealism," to confront the ways of the world in a pragmatic, even amoral fashion, and to avoid personal sacrifice.

Nonetheless, Weber waged impassioned battles throughout his life on behalf of ethical positions and scolded relentlessly all who lacked a rigorous sense of justice and social responsibility. As his student Paul Honigsheim reports, Weber became a man possessed whenever threats to the autonomy of the individual were discussed (see Honigsheim, 1968, pp. 6, 43) – whether to mothers seeking custody of their children, women students at German universities, or bohemian social outcasts and political rebels. Not surprisingly, his concerns for the fate of the German nation, and for the future of Western Civilization, led him perpetually into the arena of politics. Vigorously opposed to the definition of this realm as one of *Realpolitik*, "sober realism," or wheeling and dealing, he called out vehemently for politicians to act by reference to a stern moral code: an "ethic of responsibility" (*Verantwortungsethik*).[1]

THE INTELLECTUAL CONTEXT

Long before Weber formulated his sociology, many seventeenth- and eighteenth-century thinkers in the West had sought to discover, through the systematic investigation of the natural and social worlds, proof of the existence of an all-powerful supernatural Being. If the centipede's 100 legs moved in a coordinated fashion, this extraordinary achievement must itself indicate the intelligence of a superior Being as its creator (Weber, 1946d, p. 142). The "hand of God" must be at work, it was believed, as in the social world's "natural laws." Once proven, God's existence implied the necessity for "His children" to follow His Commandments. Hence, the investigation of the natural and social worlds held out the promise of embattled Christianity's renascence. The "divine order" would appear on earth and the triumph of Christian compassion and universal love would then banish the danger of a Hobbesian "war of all against all."

Although the nineteenth century brought these hopeful and optimistic investigations to a close, social thinkers in the West only grudgingly set aside an idea prominent in all salvation religions: all history and all activities of the human species possess a higher meaning and direction. Even as openly theological explanations for the purpose of life and history waned, the notion that a component more majestic than mundane everyday activity is bestowed upon human life remained. Whether Utilitarians in England at the beginning of the century or Spencerian Social Darwinists at its end; whether Hegelians or Marxists in Germany; whether followers of Saint-Simon or Comte in France: all these schools of thought, although otherwise so different, articulated the idea that history moved in a lawful manner and in an evolutionary direction. It thus contained a meaning all its own. In his expansive historical studies, the distinguished mid-century historian Ranke discovered the values of Christian Humanism at work through the ages, and the idealist philosopher Hegel charted the history of the West as a progressive realization of the idea of freedom. Even thoroughly secularized German intellectuals at the end of the century – the philosopher Heinrich Rickert, for example – argued that history offered evidence for a firm hierarchy of true values, indeed ones capable of guiding our lives today. The economic historian Gustav Schmoller sought to discover, through historical research, the underlying moral justification for the development of modern capitalism.

History retained a teleology and an "objective meaning" for all these thinkers. Conformity with its unified value system would ensure progress, as well as, in the end, the just ordering of society. Throughout the nineteenth century, and despite the turning by Marx of ethereal Hegelian thought "on its head," a rearguard reluctance to abandon the notion of a transcendental guiding force – now in a sublimated and impersonal form rather than understood as the direct Will of a monotheistic God – prevailed. Even Marx's "scientific socialism" formulated "dialectical laws of history"; the present, he argued, must be understood as only one of many historical stages, all of which lead along a predestined route toward more advanced societies. Protestant Christianity's optimistic view regarding man's capacity to master his sinful human nature and to improve earthly existence constituted the facilitating cultural background for a flourishing of the secular ideas of Progress, Reason, and Freedom, as well as for all ideals of natural justice and all value hierarchies.

Max Weber's works stand directly antagonistic to these ideas of the seventeenth, eighteenth, and nineteenth centuries. With his sociology a new *position* for the human species crystallized, one steadfastly opposed to the notion that history possessed an independent meaning: *persons* now existed as the unequivocal makers of their destinies and as the center and cause of their activities. At the dawning of the twentieth century, Weber insisted that meaning could arise only out of their struggles to mold "meaningful lives" and the choices they made on this behalf: "Every single important activity and ultimately life as a whole, if it is not to be permitted to run on as an event in nature but is instead to be consciously guided, is a series of ultimate decisions through which the soul . . . *chooses* its own destiny; i.e., the meaning of its activity and existence" (Weber, 1949, p. 18 translation altered, original emphasis; see also p. 81; 1946d, pp. 148, 151–2). Several currents of thought that placed the individual in the forefront came here to a synthesis: the Enlightenment's individual endowed with Reason and Rationality, the creative and introspective individual of the German Romantics (mainly Goethe and Schiller), and ascetic Protestantism's activity-oriented individual.[2]

The same antagonism to the notion that the flow of history contained a transcendental meaning accounts as well for Weber's principled opposition to the grounding of knowledge and activity beyond the empirical realm. With the prominent exception of Nietzsche, he saw more acutely than his contemporaries that, once the axial turn from theocentrism and quasi-theocentrism to anthropocentrism had been taken, a unifying set of religious values, the "course of history," or the Idea of Progress could no longer offer the ultimate foundation for the social sciences. The study of the meaning-seeking person must now be firmly rooted in reality: "The type of social science in which we are interested is an *empirical science of concrete reality*" (*Wirklichkeitswissenschaft*) (Weber, 1949, p. 72, original emphasis).

Although the secular and industrial character of turn-of-the-century Germany directly influenced the formation of this central tenet of Weber's sociology, as he himself acknowledged, it must not be concluded that his works are empowered to investigate only those few epochs and civilizations in which individualism had come to the fore and unified constellations of values had vanished. On the contrary, a radically comparative and historical reach characterizes his research. He knew well that subjective meaning may be created in a *vast* variety of ways; indeed, his research revealed that for millennia the overriding beacon of light and guiding force for persons had originated from diverse orientations to the supernatural realm (see Weber, 1946d, p. 149). Even though subjective meaning stands at the core of Weber's sociology, and hence the individualism dominant in his own epoch's "value ideas" (*Wertideen*) is manifest in its fundamental axioms, Weber's methodology emphatically leaves open – to be studied empirically – the extent to which the formation of subjective meaning is influenced by the mundane world or the supernatural realm.

This monumental shift to a radically empirical sociology rooted in subjective meaning must be acknowledged as foundational to Weber's entire sociology. Cognizance of this turn allows its central features to become more easily comprehensible.

The rejection of the search for true values, general laws, and objective facts

Weber's rejection of values rooted in religions and quasi-supernatural ideas as the basis for his sociology, and his focus upon empirical reality and subjective meaning, led him to oppose unequivocally the many attempts at the end of the nineteenth century to define the aim of science as the creation of new constellations of values appropriate to the industrial society. His distinguished colleagues Rickert, Dilthey, Schmoller, Roscher, and Knies had all agreed that investigations of social life must be carried out *in order to* substantiate ideals and norms – indeed, even in the name of science. They feared that secular, capitalist, and industrial societies would be devoid of values, and this abhorrent vacuum must be filled by values discovered by science. Their nightmare vision would otherwise soon become reality: persons would become mere drifting "atoms" devoid of reflectivity, a sense of deep obligation to others, and – not least – a sense of true community (*Gemeinschaft*). As religion declined, a new source for desperately needed values must be found. Science offered new hope.

The notion that science should be viewed as the legitimate source of personal values was more than Weber could bear. He saw in such proposals yet another clandestine intrusion of quasi-religious legacies – now into a domain appropriately defined as exclusively involving empirical investigation. Moreover, he denied the possibility that science could serve as the source of values, for an "objective science" *cannot* exist. Even the hope for such a science is a deception, one rooted ultimately in a bygone world of unified values. It has now become clear, Weber asserts, that *each* epoch – perhaps even every generation or decade – calls forth its *own* "culturally significant value-ideas." Invariably, he insists, our observations of empirical reality take place *in reference to these*. The empirical ground upon which science is based "changes" continually (see Weber, 1949, pp. 72–8).

This unavoidable "value-relevance" (*Wertbeziehung*) of our observations always renders certain events and occurrences visible to us and occludes others. Only *some* "realities" are thrown into relief by the culturally significant values of any specific age: those today, for example, are embodied by terms such as equality for all, freedom, individual rights, equal opportunity, globalization, etc., and dichotomies such as capitalism/socialism and First World/Third World. The specific vantage points dominant in any era *allow* its inhabitants to see only a selected slice of the past and present. Consequently, our search today for knowledge cannot take the same form – as a search for concealed *absolutes* – as in the seventeenth and eighteenth centuries, for the ultimate precondition for such a quest no longer exists: a widespread belief in a set of unified values. For the same reason, our knowledge can no longer be anchored in the quasi-supernatural ideas of the nineteenth century. Furthermore, owing to the invariably perspectival character of our knowledge, we can hope neither to find "general laws" in history nor to write history as Ranke proposed: "as it actually occurred." Thus, in the famous "debate over methods" (*Methodenstreit*), Weber opposed both the "nomothetic" position held by Menger – the formulation of general laws must be the task of the social sciences – and the "ideographic" position held by Schmoller's "historical school of economics": to offer exact and full descriptions of specific cases must be the goal.[3]

Weber admonished vehemently and repeatedly that all attempts to create values through science must now be seen as illusions. All such deceptions must be cast aside in the new post-religion and post quasi-religion epoch:

> The fate of a cultural epoch which has eaten from the tree of knowledge is that it must know that, however completely we may investigate history, we cannot learn its real *meaning* from the results of our research. Rather, we must be able to create

this meaning ourselves. Moreover, we must acknowledge that "Weltanschauungen" never can be the product of the advance of empirically based knowledge. Finally, we must recognize that the highest ideals – and those which move us most deeply – become effective influences upon us only as a consequence of their struggle with other ideals. These ideals are just as sacred to others as ours are to us. (Weber, 1949, p. 57; translation altered, original emphasis; see also p. 18)

We know of no ideals that can be demonstrated scientifically. Undoubtedly, the task of pulling them out of one's own breast is all the more difficult in an epoch in which culture has otherwise become so subjective. But we simply have no fool's paradise and no streets paved with gold to promise, either in this world or the next, either in thought or in action. It is the stigma of our human dignity that the peace of our souls can never be as great as the peace of those who dream of such a paradise. (Weber, 1909, p. 420)

The embrace of multicausality

The search for a single "guiding hand," whether that of a monotheistic God, Adam Smith's "laws of the market," or Karl Marx's class conflict as the "engine of history," remained anathema to Weber. He perceived all such overarching forces as residuals of now-antiquated world views characterized by religious and quasi-religious ideas. Indeed, Weber's adamant refusal to define the "general laws of social life" (Menger), the "stages of historical development" (Buecher, Marx), or Evolution[4] as the central point of departure for his causal explanations[5] paved the way for a focus upon empirical reality and subjective meaning; as importantly, it also provided the underlying precondition for his embrace of radically *multicausal* modes of explanation. Having abandoned reference to all forms of "necessity" as history's moving force, the innumerable actions and beliefs of persons rose to the fore in Weber's sociology as the causal forces that determine the contours of past and present.

His empirical research convinced him that historical change required on the one hand great charismatic figures and on the other hand "carrier" strata and organizations. Moreover, these carriers were, for example, at times political and rulership organizations, at other times status groups or economic organizations, and at still other times religious organizations. His investigations across a vast palette of themes, epochs, and civilizations yielded in this respect a clear conclusion: rather than a causal "resting point," he found only continuous movement across, above all, political, economic, religious, legal, social strata, and familial groupings (see, for example, Weber, 1968, p. 341). Without powerful carriers, even Hegel's "spirit" or Ranke's Christian Humanism could not move history; nor could ideas, world views, or the problem of unjust suffering.

From Eurocentrism to a comparative sociology of subjective meaning

However weakened by secularization, capitalism, and urbanization, the West's overarching set of values remained viable in the nineteenth century and formed a measuring rod against which European social scientists evaluated societies around the globe with respect to their relative "evolution" and "rationality." Had they experienced the same degree of "advancement" as the modern West? Weber's rejection of the twentieth century's quasi-religious value constellations implied both a skepticism regarding the widespread belief in "progress" and an awareness of its contingency. It also laid the foundation for his sociology's radically comparative character and its break from Eurocentric ideas.

The shift to a fully anthropocentric sociology of subjective meaning and empirical reality had the effect of delegitimizing all Western-centric value configurations. As the underlying justification for a social science oriented exclusively to the "ideas of the West" disappeared, firm standards in terms of which other cultures could be observed and evaluated vanished as well. While his colleagues viewed this development with extreme trepidation and correctly perceived Weber's methodology as threatening at its core the "superiority of the West," as well as the very essence of their being, Weber noted an overriding advantage for research: social scientists were now set free to investigate "the other" on its *own* terms. This liberation from a fixed point of orientation meant to him that unconstrained empirical explorations of *subjective meanings* in Eastern and Western, ancient and modern, civilizations could now be conducted.

However, Weber advocated such a radical swing of the pendulum not only owing to advantages he saw for a social science methodology. Rather, an even larger dynamic induced him to bestow an unqualified legitimacy upon decentered, intercivilizational research. "Unconstrained" comparative studies were now urgently *needed* in order effectively to address immediate questions in his own civilization: in what precise ways can the modern West be said to be unique, what are the *parameters* of possible social change in the West, and how does the orientation of actions to values and the *formation* of subjective meaning as such take place? Whereas these same questions deeply troubled his colleagues as well, Weber alone comprehended the potential achievements of a sociology that, through rigorous comparative-historical studies, would be capable of isolating the boundaries of cases and developments, defining significant causal forces, and drawing conclusions regarding the circumstances under which social change occurs, action becomes oriented to values, and subjective meaning is formed. Such a sociology would cast a sharp beam of light upon the modern West's unique dilemmas and crises – and persons would then be more able to make independent, *informed* decisions and to take clear *ethical* positions (see Weber, 1946d, pp. 151–2; Kalberg, forthcoming). The massiveness and extreme thoroughness of his comparative studies cannot be understood without cognizance of this burning motivating concern.[6]

Conflict and ethical action

Weber's mode of research was decentered in a further manner. In breaking unequivocally from all schools of thought that stressed unifying constellations of values, transcendentally anchored value hierarchies, and – through Progress and Evolution – humanity's common and peaceful future, his sociology banished an array of presuppositions that tended to place obstacles against the empirical analysis of reality. Importantly, having done so, his research could better assess the extent to which mundane conflict appears, as well as its contours and causes. For him, the "struggle for existence" did not take place on the grand stage of "human evolution" and in response to a "survival of the fittest" law, as for Social Darwinists, but exclusively as a result of the hard choices that accompany every-day activity. History unfolded out of these decisions, yet not in a unilinear or directed fashion. Paradox, irony, and unforeseen consequences, Weber insists, were manifest perpetually,[7] as well as restless, undirected conflict. The various domains of life that uniquely constitute the modern world (the economic, polit-ical, rulership, and legal), he argues, rather than congealing into a synthesis to drive Progress or to propel a Parsonsian "value-generalization" process, follow their *own* laws of development and very often stand in relations of irreconcilable conflict to one another (see Weber, 1946d, pp. 147–54, 323–59; 1949, p. 18).

In formulating "an empirical science of concrete reality" and emphasizing that persons rather than God, natural laws, or Evolution endow history with mean-ing, several pivotal questions unavoidably confront Weber's sociology. How will our action be oriented? How do we act responsibly? How is ethical action grounded? The liberation from religion-based world views and their legacies led naturally to a degree of freedom, yet just this development called forth the question of how individuals, in industrialized, bureaucratized, and capitalist societies, make choices. Weber's rejection of all schools that defined the modern person's freedom as simply the "philistine freedom of private convenience" (Löwith, 1970, p. 122) rendered these queries all the more urgent, as did his opposition to Nietzsche's answers: his insistence that activity occurs embedded within contexts prevented Weber from placing faith in prophets and great "supermen" (Weber, 1946d, p. 155). Moreover, he argued that secularism, industrialism, and the Enlightenment had already empowered "the people" with rights to such an extent that Nietzsche's call for authoritarian heroes went too far; they would inevitably circumscribe the open, public space now so indispensable for ethically based choices by individuals.

Weber knew well that the social science he proposed failed to offer ethical guidance to individuals. He remained acutely aware that this position disap-pointed in particular the younger generation of his time (see Weber, 1946d, pp. 141–55). Would the elevation of subjective meaning and "concrete empirical reality" to the forefront work out in the end? Or would the modern individual, cast adrift from all directing and obligatory values and traditions, and now forced to locate meaning by reference to his own "demons," become either an opportunistic actor or psychologically paralyzed? Weber rejected the loud calls for "a romantic irrational heroism which sacrifices itself amidst the delirium of self-decomposition" (Salomon, 1935b, p. 384), and scorned, as utopian, all hopes that a politicized proletariat would usher in a more just society. Would configurations of *binding* values capable of anchoring ethical decisions remain? Would the person oriented to and *unified* by values survive? These crucial questions can best be addressed by turning first to Weber's sociology and then to the social context in which he wrote.

The Theory

Some interpreters view Weber as a "theorist of ideas," yet others see him as a "theorist of interests." While the former focus upon *PE* and emphasize the strong role in his sociology of values, religion, and culture, the latter take his analytic opus, *Economy and Society* (*E&S*), as their main source and assert that Weber offers a non-Marxist conflict theory rooted in domination, power, conflict, and individual interests. Still others understand him mainly as a gifted taxonomist engaged in the creation of a vast armament of "ideal types" intended to establish the discipline of sociology on a secure conceptual foundation. In fact, each of these interpretations flows legitimately from the rich vein of his sociological writings (see Kalberg, 1998, pp. 208–14).

However, these commentaries all run astray both by denying the plausibility of opposing interpretations and by casting their focus too narrowly. The broader themes that overcome the seeming fragmentation of Weber's sociology and offer a degree of unity are too often neglected: the ways in which he links ideas and interests, his concern to define the uniqueness of the modern West and to provide a causal explanation of its origins, his search to understand which constellations of social forces give rise to widespread notions of compassion, ethical action, and individual autonomy, his attempt to analyze how action becomes oriented to values, and his focus upon the manner in which persons, in different social settings, create meaning for their lives.

This discussion of Weber's sociology seeks to articulate these central themes while calling attention to the forceful ways in which values, culture, and religion come to the fore in his sociology; domination, power, individual interests, and conflict remain central; and "clear concepts" serve as indispensable foundational cornerstones. This large task can best be pursued by a brief scrutiny of his three major works: *PE*, *E&S*, and *The Economic Ethics of the World Religions* (*EEWR*). Before we do so, a turn to central aspects of the methodology underlying his sociology is indispensable.

Weber's methodology

Weber's sociology departs from a critique of all approaches that view societies as quasi-organic, holistic units and their separate "parts" as components fully integrated into a larger "system" of objective structures. All organic schools of thought understand the larger collectivity within which the individual acts as a delimited structure, and social action and interaction as merely particularistic expressions of this "whole." German romantic and conservative thought at the beginning of the nineteenth century, as well as Comte and Durkheim in France, fall within this tradition.

Organic theories generally postulate a degree of societal integration questionable to Weber. He never viewed societies as clearly formed and closed entities with delineated boundaries. Seeing the likelihood for fragmentation, tension, open conflict, and the use of power, Weber rejects the notion that societies can be best understood as unified. Moreover, according to him, if organic theories are utilized *other than* as a means of facilitating preliminary conceptualization, a high risk of "reification" arises: "society" and the "organic whole" may become viewed as the fundamental unit of analysis rather than the individual (Weber, 1968, pp. 14–15). This may occur to such an extent that persons are incorrectly understood as simply the "socialized products" of societal forces. Weber argues, to the contrary, that persons are capable of *interpreting* their social realities, bestowing "subjective meaning" upon certain aspects of it, and initiating independent action: "[We are] *cultural* beings endowed with the capacity and will to take a deliberate stand toward the world and to lend it *meaning (Sinn)*" (Weber, 1949, p. 81; translation altered, original emphasis). There *is*, to Weber, a realm of freedom and choice.

Many of the pivotal axioms of his methodology remain central to sociology even today. Only a few of its foundational components can be examined: interpretive understanding, the four types of social action, subjective meaning, value-neutrality, and ideal types. Finally, the aim of Weber's sociology will be discussed.

INTERPRETIVE UNDERSTANDING AND SUBJECTIVE MEANING At the core of Weber's sociology stands the attempt by sociologists to "understand interpretively" (*verstehen*) the ways in which persons view their own "social action." This subjectively meaningful action constitutes the social scientist's concern rather than merely reactive or imitative behavior (as occurs, for example, when persons in a crowd expect rain and simultaneously open their umbrellas). Social action, he insists, involves *both* a "meaningful orientation of behavior to that of others" *and* the individual's interpretive, or reflective, aspect (Weber, 1968, pp. 22–4). Persons are social, but not only social. They are endowed with the ability to actively interpret situations, interactions, and relationships by reference to values, beliefs, interests, emotions, power, authority, law, customs, conventions, habits, ideas, etc.

> Sociology...is a science that offers an interpretive understanding of social action and, in doing so, provides a causal explanation of its course and its effects. We shall speak of "action" insofar as the acting individual attaches a subjective *meaning* to his behavior – be it overt or covert, omission or acquiescence. Action is "social" insofar as its subjective meaning takes account of the behavior *of others* and is thereby oriented in its course. (Weber, 1968, p. 4; translation altered, original emphasis)[8]

This central position of meaningful action separates Weber's sociology fundamentally from all behaviorist, structuralist, and positivist schools.

Sociologists can understand the meaningfulness of others' action either through "rational understanding," which involves an intellectual grasp of the meaning actors attribute to their actions, or through "intuitive," or "empathic," understanding, which refers to the comprehension of "the emotional context in which the action [takes] place" (Weber, 1968, p. 5). Thus, for example, the motivation behind the orientation of civil servants to impersonal statutes and laws can be understood by the sociologist, as can the motivation behind the orientation of good friends to one another. To the extent that this occurs, a *causal* explanation of action, Weber argues, is provided. Because it attends alone to external activity, stimulus/response behaviorism neglects the issues foremost to Weber: the *diverse* possible motives behind an observable activity, the manner in which the subjective meaningfulness of the act varies accordingly, and the significant differences that follow in respect to action.

THE FOUR TYPES OF SOCIAL ACTION AND SUBJECTIVE MEANING Social action can be best conceptualized as involving one of "four types of meaningful action": means–end rational, value-rational, affectual, or traditional action. Each type refers to the ideal typical (see below) motivational orientations of actors.

Weber defines action as *means–end* rational (*zweckrational*) "when the end, the means, and the secondary results are all rationally taken into account and weighed. This involves a rational consideration of alternative means to the end, of the relations of the end to the secondary consequences, and finally of the relative importance of different possible ends." Similarly, persons possess the capacity to act *value-rationally*, even though this type of action has appeared empirically in its pure form only rarely. It exists when social action is "determined by a conscious belief in the value for its own sake of some ethical, aesthetic, religious, or other form of behavior, independently of its prospects of success. . . . Value-rational action always involves 'commands' or 'demands' which, in the actor's opinion, are binding (*verbindlich*) on him." Notions of honor involve values, as do salvation doctrines. In addition, "determined by the actor's specific affects and feeling states," *affectual* action, which involves an emotional attachment, must be distinguished clearly from value-rational and means–end rational action. *Traditional* action, "determined by ingrained habituation" and age-old customs, and often merely a routine reaction to common stimuli, stands on the borderline of subjectively meaningful action. Taken together, these constructs – the "types of social action" – establish an analytic base that assists conceptualization of diffuse action-orientations. Rational action in reference to interests constitutes, to Weber, only one possible way of orienting action (see Weber, 1968, pp. 24–6).[9]

Each type of meaningful action can be found in all epochs and all civilizations. The social action of even "primitive" peoples may be means–end rational and value-rational (see, for example, Weber, 1968, pp. 400, 422–6), and modern man is not endowed with a greater inherent capacity for either type of action than his ancestors. However, as a result of identifiable social forces, some epochs may tend predominantly to call forth a particular type of action. Weber is convinced that, by utilizing the types of social action typology, sociologists can understand – and hence explain causally – even the ways in which the social action of persons living in radically different cultures is subjectively meaningful. Assuming that, as a result of intensive study, researchers have succeeded in becoming thoroughly familiar with a particular social context and thus capable of imagining themselves "into" it, an assessment can be made of the extent to which actions approximate one of the types of social action. The subjective meaningfulness of the motives for these actions – whether means–end rational, value-rational, traditional, or affectual – then becomes *understandable*.[10] Weber's "interpretive sociology" in this manner seeks to help sociologists to comprehend social action in terms of the actor's *own* intentions.[11]

This foundational emphasis upon a pluralism of motives distinguishes Weber's sociology unequivocally from all schools of behaviorism, all approaches that place social structures at the forefront (for example, those rooted in Durkheim's "social facts" or Marx's classes), and all positivist approaches that endow norms, roles, and rules with a determining power over persons. Even when social action seems tightly bonded to a social structure, a heterogeneity of motives must be recognized. A great array of motives within a single "external form" is, Weber argues, both analytically and empirically possible *and* sociologically significant. The subjective meaningfulness of action varies even within the firm organizational structure of the political or religious sect. Yet just this reasoning leads Weber to a conundrum: for what subjective reasons do persons orient their social action *in common*, such that demarcated groupings are formulated? This question assumes a great urgency, for he is convinced that the absence of such orientations – toward, for example, the state, bureaucratic organizations, traditions, and values – means that "structures" cease to exist. The state, for example, in the end is *nothing more* than the patterned action-orientations of its politicians, judges, police, civil servants, etc.[12]

Far from formal methodological postulates only, these foundational distinctions directly anchor Weber's empirical studies, as will become apparent. The investigation of the subjective meaning of action stood at the very center, for example, of his famous "Protestant ethic thesis." Yet Weber engaged in a massive empirical effort to understand the subjective meaning of "the other" on its own terms throughout his comparative-historical sociology, whether, for example, that of the Confucian scholar, the Buddhist monk, the Hindu Brahmin, the prophets of the Old Testament, feudal rulers, monarchs and kings, or functionaries in bureaucracies. For what subjective reasons do people render obedience to authority? Weber wished to understand the diverse ways in which persons subjectively "make sense" of their activities. He argued that sociologists should attempt to do so even when the subjective "meaning-complexes" they discover seem strange or odd to them.

VALUE-FREEDOM AND VALUE-RELEVANCE Hence, Weber's sociology does not seek to discover "an objectively 'correct' meaning or one which is 'true' in some metaphysical sense" (Weber, 1968, p. 4).[13] Moreover, neither empathy toward nor hostility against the actors under investigation is central here. Researchers are obligated, with respect to the research process, to set aside their ideological preferences, personal values, likes, and dislikes (of ascetic Protestants, for example, or the bureaucracy's functionaries) as much as humanly possible and to make every effort to remain fair and impartial. Clear standards of inquiry as well as an unbiased observation, measurement, comparison, and evaluation of the sources must be the prescriptive ideal of social scientists. Even if the habits, values, and practices of the groups under investigation are discovered to be repulsive, researchers must strive to uphold this ideal.

To maintain such an "objective" and "value-free" (*Wertfreiheit*) posture with respect to the gathering and evaluation of data, Weber knew, is not an easy task. We are all "cultural beings," and hence values remain inextricably intertwined with our thinking and action; a thin line separates "facts" from "values," and values intrude even into our modes of observation. Indeed, modern Western science itself *arose* as a consequence of a series of specific historical and cultural developments. Nonetheless, the social scientist must make a concerted effort to distinguish empirically based arguments and conclusions from normative – or value-based – arguments and conclusions. The latter should be minimized.

However, with regard to a foundational aspect of the research process, values remain appropriately central, Weber insists: the *selection* of topics. Far from "objective" in some metaphysical or predetermined sense, our choice – unavoidably so, for him – is directly related to our values (*Wertbezogenheit*) and our interests. A sociologist, for example, who strongly believes that persons of different ethnic groupings should be treated equally, may well decide – as a result of this *value* – to study how civil rights movements have assisted heretofore excluded groupings to acquire basic rights.

Yet, with respect to the overall task of the social sciences, Weber again argues that researchers must strive to exclude values: all value-judgments that pronounce, in the name of science, a particular activity or way of life as noble or base, ultimately rational or irrational, provincial or cosmopolitan, must be avoided. The social sciences will not – and should not – assist us to decide with certainty which values are superior. Those of the Sermon on the Mount cannot be proven scientifically to be "better" than those of the Rig Vedas. Nor can social scientists argue that specific values *should* guide our lives. Science provides knowledge and insight, and informs us regarding the various effects of utilizing a certain means to reach a specified goal, yet it must never be allowed to take responsibility for our decisions (Weber, 1946d, 1949).

Weber pronounced such an ethos of "value-neutrality" as indispensable to the definition of sociology – if it wished to be a social science rather than a political endeavor: "Science today is a 'vocation' organized in special disciplines in the service of self-clarification and knowledge of interrelated facts. It is not the gift of grace of seers and prophets dispensing sacred values and revelations, nor does it partake of the contemplation of sages and philosophers about the meaning of the universe" (Weber, 1946d, p. 152). How does the sociologist best proceed to ascertain subjective meaning in the groups under investigation, and to do so in an unbiased fashion? An answer to this question requires a brief discussion of Weber's *ideal typical* mode of analysis.

IDEAL TYPES Although Weber takes the meaningful action of individuals as his basic unit of analysis, his interpretive sociology never views social life as an "endless drift" of solitary and unconnected action-orientations. The diverse ways in which persons act *in concert* in groupings captures his attention, rather than the social action of the isolated individual. Indeed, he defines the sociological enterprise as oriented to the investigation of the subjective meaning of persons in delimited groups and the identification of *regularities of action*: "There can be observed, within the realm of social action, actual empirical regularities; that is, courses of action that are repeated by the actor or (possibly also: simultaneously) occur among numerous actors because the subjective *meaning* is typically *meant* to be the same. Sociological investigation is concerned with these *typical* modes of action" (Weber, 1968, p. 29, translation altered, original emphasis). Such patterned action can result, he argues, from an orientation not only to values, but also to affectual, traditional, and even means–end rational action. The various ways in which merely imitative and reactive behaviors are *uprooted* from their random flow and transformed into *meaning*-based regularities anchored in one of the four types of social action constitute one of his sociology's fundamental themes.

Weber's major heuristic concept – the ideal type – "documents" these regularities of meaningful action. Each of these *research tools* charts the action-orientations of individuals – and nothing more. Weber's ideal type "the Puritan," for example, identifies the regular action of these believers (for example, an orientation toward methodical work and an ascetic style of life). Hence, in seeking to capture patterned action through the formation of ideal types, his sociology steers away from a focus upon isolated action on the one hand and society, societal evolution, social differentiation, and "the question of social order" on the other hand. This level of analysis prevails throughout Weber's texts rather than detailed historical narrative or global concepts. How are ideal types formed?

Not simply a summarization or classification of social action is involved. Instead, and although construction of the ideal type is rooted thoroughly in empirical reality and depends upon the immersion of sociologists in the particular case under investigation, it is formulated, first, through a conscious exaggeration of the *essential* features of a pattern of action of interest to the sociologist, and, second, through a synthesis of these characteristic action-orientations into an internally unified and logically rigorous concept: "An ideal type is formed by the one-sided *accentuation of one or more* points of view and by the synthesis of a great many diffuse, discrete, more or less present and occasionally absent *concrete individual* phenomena, which are arranged according to those one-sidedly emphasized viewpoints into a unified *analytical* construct. In its conceptual purity, this construct cannot be found empirically anywhere in reality" (Weber, 1949, p. 90, original emphasis). While inductive procedures from empirical observations are first followed, deductive procedures then guide the logical ordering of the separate patterns of action into a unified and precise *construct*. Nonetheless, the anchoring of ideal types empirically precludes their understanding as "abstract" or "reified" concepts (see Weber, 1949, pp. 92–107).

Above all, according to Weber, ideal types serve *to assist* empirical, cause-oriented inquiry rather than to "replicate" and directly comprehend the external world (an impossible task, owing to the unending flow of events as well as the infinite diversity and complexity of even a particular social phenomenon) or to articulate an ideal, hoped-for development. Thus, the "Puritan" portrays accurately the subjective meaning of neither a particular Puritan nor all Puritans (Weber, 1968, pp. 19–22). The same holds for ideal types of bureaucracies, brothels, prophets, intellectuals, or charismatic leaders. As he notes, "Concepts are primarily analytical instruments for the intellectual mastery of the empirically given and can be only that" (Weber, 1949, p. 106, translation altered).

Once formed as clear concepts that capture regular action-orientations, ideal types anchor Weber's entire causal sociology in a fundamental fashion: they enable the precise definition of empirical action-orientations. As a logical construct that documents patterned social action, the ideal type establishes clear points of reference – or standards – against which regularities of subjective meaning *in a particular case* can be compared and "measured." The uniqueness of cases can be defined clearly through an assessment of their approximation to or deviation from the theoretically constructed type. "Ideal types such as Christianity... are of great value for research and of high systematic value for expository purposes when they are used as conceptual instruments for *comparison* and the *measurement* of reality. They are indispensable for this purpose" (Weber, 1949, p. 97; original emphasis; see also pp. 43, 90–3).[14]

THE AIM OF WEBER'S SOCIOLOGY Commentaries upon Weber's works have frequently failed to note that he orients his research to discrete problems and the causal analysis of specific cases and developments. He proposes that the causal explanation of this "historical individual" should serve as sociology's primary aim: "We wish to understand the reality that surrounds our lives, in which we are placed, *in its characteristic uniqueness*. We wish to understand on the one hand its context (*Zusammenhang*) and the cultural *significance* of its particular manifestations in their contemporary form, and on the other the causes of it becoming historically so and not otherwise" (Weber, 1949, p. 72; translation altered, original emphasis; see also p. 69; 1968, p. 10).

Hence, Weber opposed strongly the numerous positivist schools of thought in his day that sought, following the method offered by the natural sciences, to define a set of general laws of history and social change and then to explain all specific cases and developments by deduction. He rejected forcefully the position that the social sciences should aim "to construct a closed system of concepts which can encompass and classify reality in some definitive manner and from which it can be deduced again" (Weber, 1949, p. 84), and expressed his clear opposition to the view that laws themselves comprise causal explanations. Because concrete realities, individual cases and developments, and subjective meaning cannot be deduced from them, laws are incapable of providing the knowledge of reality that would offer causal explanations. To Weber, individual cases can be explained causally only by "other equally individual configurations" (Weber, 1949, pp. 75–6; see Kalberg, 1994b, pp. 81–4).[15]

These pivotal components of Weber's methodology will be better understood after a consideration of his major sociological investigations: *PE*, *EEWR*, and *E&S*.

The Protestant Ethic and the Spirit of Capitalism

Weber wrote much of *PE* (1904–5) after returning from a three-month trip to the United States. Its thesis regarding the important role played by values in the development of modern capitalism set off an intense debate that has continued to this day. A genuine classic, *PE* is both his best known and most accessible work. Although Weber comes prominently to the fore in this study as a theorist who attends alone to values and ideas, its methodology exemplifies a variety of foundational procedures utilized throughout his sociology (see Kalberg, 1996, 2002). *PE* also offers a profound commentary upon American society, both past and present. Finally, this study constitutes Weber's first attempt to isolate the uniqueness of the modern West and to define its causal origins.

THE BACKGROUND A number of historians and economists in Weber's time emphasized the importance for economic development of technological innovations, the influx of precious metals, and population increases. Others were convinced that the greed, economic interests, and "desire for riches" of all – but especially of great "economic supermen" (the Carnegies, Rockefellers, and Vanderbilts) and the bourgeoisie in general – pushed economic development past the agrarian and feudal stages to mercantilism and modern capitalism. Disagreeing with all these explanations, evolutionists argued that the expansion of production, trade, banking, and commerce could best be understood as the clear manifestation of a general, societal-wide unfolding of "progress."

None of these forces could offer, Weber insisted, an explanation for that which distinguished *modern* capitalism from capitalism as it had existed throughout the ages: relatively free market exchange, separation of the business from the household, sophisticated bookkeeping, formally free labor, *and* a specific "economic ethos." This ethos stood behind the rigorous organization of work, the methodical approach to labor, and the systematic pursuit of profit typical of this form of capitalism. It was constituted from an "idea of the *duty* of the individual to increase his wealth, which is assumed to be a self-defined interest in itself" (Weber, 2002b, p. 16, original emphasis); the notion that "labor [must be performed] as if it were an absolute end in itself" (ibid., p. 24); "the earning of more and more money, combined with the strict avoidance of all spontaneous enjoyment of it" (ibid., p. 17); the view that the "acquisition of money...is...the result and the expression of competence and proficiency in a calling" (ibid., p. 18); and "the frame of mind that...strives systematically and rationally *in a calling* for legitimate profit" (ibid., p. 26, original emphasis). Embodied in these ideas was a *spirit* of capitalism, and Weber argues vehemently that a full understanding of the origins of modern capitalism requires an identification of the sources of this "modern economic ethos"(ibid., pp. 18, 49–50).

Hence, an investigation of the specific ancestry of this spirit, rather than the sources in general of either modern capitalism or capitalism, was the comparatively modest project of *PE* (See ibid., pp. 16, 19, 34–5, 37, 49–50). After citing numerous passages from Benjamin Franklin, whose values represent to

Weber the spirit of capitalism in a pure form (see ibid., pp. 14–15), he asserts that he has here discovered an *ethos*, "the violation of [which] is treated not as foolishness but as forgetfulness of *duty*" (ibid., p. 16, original emphasis).[16] However, in seeking to unravel the "causal origins" of this new *set of values* and "organization of life," this "positive critique of historical materialism" rejects the view that capitalism's dominant class gave birth to this spirit (see 2002a, p. 160; 2002b, pp. 18–35; Kalberg, 1996, p. 56). It opposes as well the argument that social structures – status groups, or churches and sects themselves – stand at its origin (see Weber, 2002b, pp. 34–5, 55–102; 1946e, p. 292). Instead, Weber wanted to explore, against strong opponents, the "idealist side" (see, for example, Weber, 2002b, p. 125).

THE ARGUMENT[17] After observing various ways in which Protestants seemed attracted to business-oriented occupations and organized their daily lives in an especially rigorous fashion, Weber began to explore Protestant doctrine. He discovered a "world-oriented ethos" typically represented in the Westminster Confession (1647) and the sermons of a seventeenth-century Puritan successor of John Calvin, Richard Baxter (1615–91). For Weber, Baxter's revisions of Calvin's teachings sought above all to banish the bleak conclusions rationally implied by his "Doctrine of Predestination": if the question of salvation constituted *the* burning question to believers (see Weber, 2002b, p. 65), if the "salvation status" of the faithful was predestined from the very beginning, and if God had selected only a tiny minority to be saved, massive fatalism, despair, loneliness, and anxiety among the devout logically followed (ibid., pp. 55–7, 60–3, 202n). Recognizing that the harshness of this decree precluded its continued endorsement by most believers (ibid., p. 65), among other reasons, Baxter undertook doctrinal alterations that, according to Weber, launched the Protestant ethic.

Along with Calvin, Baxter acknowledged that the mortal and weak devout cannot know God's judgment, for the motives of this majestic, distant, and all-mighty Deity of the Old Testament remain incomprehensible to lowly terrestrial inhabitants (ibid., pp. 57–9). However, Baxter emphasized that "the world exists to serve the glorification of God" and that God wishes His Kingdom to be one of wealth, equality, and prosperity, for abundance among "His children" would surely serve to praise His goodness and justice (see ibid., pp. 62–3, 104–5, 114–15, 230–1n). Understood as a means toward the creation of God's community on earth, regular and dedicated work – or work in a "calling" – now acquired a *religious* significance among the devout. Believers comprehended their worldly economic activity as in service to a demanding God, and they could view themselves as noble instruments – or tools (ibid., p. 77) – of His Commandments and His Divine Plan: "Work in the service of all impersonal, societal usefulness [promotes] the glory of God – and hence [is] to be recognized as desired by Him" (ibid., p. 61; see also pp. 106–9, 121, 230n, 243–4n). Indeed, those believers capable of systematic work on behalf of God's Plan could convince themselves that their strength to do so emanated from the favoring Hand of an omnipotent God – *and*, the faithful could further conclude, God would favor only those he had chosen to be among the predestined (see ibid., pp. 116–17).

Moreover, continuous and systematic work possessed an undeniable virtue for the good Christian, according to Baxter: it *tames* the creaturely and base side of human nature and thereby facilitates the concentration of the mind upon God and the "uplifting of the soul" (ibid., pp. 105–6). Finally, "intense worldly activity" also effectively counteracts the penetrating doubt, anxiety, and sense of unworthiness induced by the Predestination Doctrine and instills the self-confidence that allows believers to consider themselves among the chosen (see ibid., pp. 65–6). In this manner systematic work, and as well the "systematic rational formation of the believer's ethical life" (ibid., p. 78), became hallowed or "providential."

However, the singular power of the Protestant ethic to upset the "traditional economic ethic" that had existed from time immemorial originated, Weber argues, not simply in these ways, especially if one wishes to understand the "constant self-control" and "methodical rationalization of life" of Calvinist entrepreneurs (ibid,, pp. 78–80). A further adjustment by Baxter proved significant as well. According to the Predestination Doctrine, believers could never *know* their salvation status; however, in light of God's desire to see the creation of an earthly Kingdom of abundance to serve His glory, they could logically conclude that the production of great wealth for a community by an individual could be viewed as a *sign* that God favored this individual. In effect, personal wealth itself became to the faithful actual *evidence* of their salvation status. Omnipotent and omniscient, God surely would never allow one of the condemned to praise His Glory: "the acquisition of wealth, when it was the *fruit* of work in a vocational calling, [was viewed] as God's blessing" (ibid., p. 116, original emphasis). In His universe, nothing happened by chance.

Thus, and although the devout could never be absolutely certain of their membership among the elect, more business-oriented believers could seek to *produce* the evidence – literally, wealth and profit (see ibid., p. 109) – that enabled them to convince themselves of their salvation status. In view of the unbearable anxiety provoked by the central religious question – "am I among the saved?" – in sixteenth- and seventeenth-century England, a psychological certainty of a favorable salvation status was the crucial issue, Weber emphasizes. Baxter's revisions allowed the faithful to understand their successful accumulation of wealth, and its successful reinvestment for the betterment of God's community, as tangible proof of their chosen status (see ibid., pp. 120, 243n). Uniquely, riches now acquired among believers a *religious* significance: they constituted signs that indicated one's membership among the elect, thereby losing their traditionally suspect character and becoming endowed with a positive "psychological reward." Methodical work became viewed as the most adequate means toward great wealth.

In this manner, a set of work-oriented values heretofore scorned (see ibid., pp. 20, 34) became of utmost centrality in the lives of the devout. Not the desire for riches alone nor the efficient adaptation to economic forces, but only work motivated "from within" by an "internally binding" set of religious values was empowered to introduce, Weber argues, a "systematization of ... life organized around ethical principles" (ibid., p. 76) and a "planned regulation of one's own life" on behalf of work and the pursuit of wealth (ibid., p. 79; see also pp. 77–80).

Only this ethically[18] *ordered way of life rooted in values* was endowed with the methodicalness and intensity requisite for an uprooting and banishing of the traditional economic ethic.

A "Protestant ethic" originated in this manner. Carried by ascetic Protestant sects and churches (mainly, the Presbyterians, Methodists, Baptists, and Quakers), this ethic spread throughout several New England, Dutch, and English communities in the sixteenth and seventeenth centuries. Both the disciplined, hard labor in a calling and the wealth that followed from a steadfast adherence to its religious values marked a person as "chosen." One century later, by the time of Benjamin Franklin's more secularized America, the Protestant ethic had spread beyond churches and sects and into entire communities. As it did so, however, its specifically religious component became weakened and transformed into a "utilitarian-colored ethos" (ibid., pp. 16, 119–21, 123), namely a *spirit* of capitalism.[19] Rather than believed to be among the "chosen elect," adherents of this ethos, such as Franklin, were viewed simply as upright, respectable, community-oriented citizens of good moral character.

PE investigates the "causal origins" of the spirit of capitalism in this way. The subjective meaning of believers, as captured through religious sources and values rather than by reference to social structural factors, rational choices, economic interests, domination and power, specific classes, or evolutionary progress, remains central throughout. The spirit of capitalism gave a decisive – although in the end imprecise – push to the development of modern capitalism. Nonetheless, when Weber turns briefly to our present era in the conclusion to *PE*, he calls attention to an altogether different dynamic. Once the spirit of capitalism has assisted the growth of modern capitalism and this "economic form" has become firmly entrenched amidst massive industrialism, modern capitalism sustains itself, he argues, on the basis alone of *means–end* rational action carried out in reference to external and pragmatic necessities. If present at all, "the idea of an 'obligation to search for and then accept a vocational calling' now wanders around in our lives as the ghost of beliefs no longer anchored in the substance of religion" (ibid., p. 124; see pp. 119–21, 123). The Puritan *"wanted* to be a person with a vocational calling; today we *are forced* to be" (ibid., p. 123, original emphasis).

This case study of the spirit of capitalism's origins stands as a powerful demonstration of the ways in which social action may be influenced by non-economic forces. Sociological analysis must not focus exclusively upon material interests, power, structural forces, and "economic forms" to the neglect of cultural forces and "economic ethics," Weber insists. Yet sociologists must also reject a focus alone upon "ideal" forces. "*Both* sides" must be given their due and a "single formula" must always be avoided: "It is not, of course, the intention here to set a one-sided spiritualistic analysis of the causes of culture and history in place of an equally one-sided 'materialistic' analysis. *Both are equally possible.* Historical truth, however, is served equally little if either of these analyses claims to be the conclusion of an investigation rather than its preparatory stage" (ibid., p. 125; original emphasis).

Hence, and although *PE* demonstrates the ways in which values influence the playing out of economic interests and provide the "content" for social structures,

Weber recognized that a series of broad-ranging *multicausal and comparative* investigations would be necessary for a full understanding of the origins of modern capitalism. "Ideas" *and* "interests" must be scrutinized. If the spirit of capitalism is to have an impact upon the development of modern capitalism, constellations of political, economic, stratification, legal, and other factors must congeal, he was convinced, to formulate a conducive context (see ibid., pp. 125, 240n; Marshall, 1980). *PE* comprised simply the first step in Weber's grand scheme to investigate the causal origins of modern capitalism. *EEWR* took up this theme[20] and, indeed, broadened it to the question of the origins of "modern Western rationalism."

The other major work of his mature sociology – a systematic treatise that lays out the conceptual tools and research procedures for his wide-ranging comparative-historical sociology, *E&S* – provided the theoretical framework for the *EEWR* studies. This analytic opus must first be addressed. In both works, Weber renounced any search for a single, encompassing causal equation: "This sort of construction is better left to that type of dilettante who believes in the 'unity' of the 'social psyche' and its reducibility to *one* formula" (ibid., p. 247n; original emphasis).

Economy and Society

Incomplete and published posthumously by his wife, *E&S* addresses, as does *EEWR*, the ways in which the West must be understood as unique. Frequently, by reference to configurations of both "ideal" and "material" patterns of action, it also explores the causal origins of the West's specific developmental pathway. However, unlike *EEWR* and *PE*, *E&S* seeks mainly to provide a systematic grounding for the discipline of sociology as distinguished from the fields of history and economics. This three-volume work constitutes the analytic treatise for Weber's comparative-historical, interpretive sociology.

Written over a period of eleven years (1909–20), *E&S* ranges across an astonishingly broad comparative palette. Weber examines, for example, status groups, the state, classes, ethnic groups, the family, the clan, and political organizations on the one hand, and a vast array of types of economies, cities, salvation religions, and rulership and legal organizations on the other hand – and does so not by reference to the twentieth century or a single society, but in a sweeping universal perspective. His strokes are at times broad and encompass developmental trends and patterns over centuries, even millennia, in a variety of civilizations, yet thorough historical research anchors his analysis throughout. Perhaps herein lies its claim to be one of the twentieth century's most remarkable contributions to the social sciences: while "a sociologist's world history... [that] raises some of the big questions [regarding] the modern world" (Roth, 1968, p. xxix), it also rigorously attends to details. Weber is engaged in a breathtaking project: a *systematization* of his vast knowledge of the ancient, medieval, and modern epochs in China, India, and the West, as well as of the ancient Middle Eastern civilizations, into a theoretical treatise that will serve to guide the practice of his comparative-historical, interpretive sociology. He wishes to do so, however, without moving to an abstract level of analysis devoid of a solid empirical foundation.

This attention to detail, combined with the continuous formulation of analytic generalizations, renders *E&S* a difficult, even tortuous, work. Models heuristically useful to researchers are created again and again, yet only after a painstaking examination of numerous historical cases. Some ideal types are of more limited scope and pertain to a specific period, others range broadly and even universally; some are more static, and serve as conceptual yardsticks to assist the definition of empirical cases; others are more dynamic and include sets of hypotheses; still others are "developmental models" comprised of many stages. While the shorter part I (written later) emphasizes model building, and indeed often appears as simply a compendium of concepts, the longer part II focuses more upon historical cases, as well as upon brief (and incomplete) causal analyses of particular developments, before formulating models. The sheer dryness of the definitions in part I and the disjointed, back and forth movement between the historical evidence and the construction of ideal types in part II repeatedly tests the patience of even the most enamored reader. Unfortunately, Weber never provides a summary statement of his aims, themes, or procedures.

Not surprisingly, interpreters of this opus have generally examined only those discussions that have become classic statements and *de rigueur* reading for both theorists and sociologists engaged in specialized research: the chapters on law, status groups, prophets, religion, charisma, rulership in general, the bureaucracy, and the city. Although these sections deserve careful scrutiny (see below), a focus upon them alone fails to reveal the true originality and enduring usefulness of this treatise. An exploration of the five axes that dominate this labyrinthine work will articulate its underlying trajectories. In the process, the major modes of analysis and research procedures of Weber's comparative-historical, interpretive sociology will be delineated. A brief perusal of each must suffice.

"LOCATING" SOCIAL ACTION: SOCIETAL DOMAINS AND IDEAL TYPES

Convinced that the crystallization of social action into patterns is not random, yet also not to be grasped by reference to a "social system," "cultural order," "social fact," or "generalized other," Weber aims throughout *E&S* to specify *where* such regularities are likely to arise. The foundation for his entire agenda has been laid to the extent that he succeeds in *locating*, analytically, meaningful action. Indeed, this task must be undertaken if his interpretive sociology – the understanding by the sociologist of the subjective meaning persons in diverse groups attribute to their action – is to constitute more than an empty, formalistic enterprise.

Based on massive comparative historical research, Weber argues in *E&S* that social action – largely though not exclusively – congeals in a number of "societal domains" (*gesellschaftliche Ordnungen*): the economy, rulership, religion, law, status groups, and universal organizations (family, clan, and traditional neighborhood) domains.[21] To him, persons are "placed into various societal domains, each of which is governed by different laws" (Weber, 1946a, p. 123). *E&S* undertakes the huge task of delimiting the major domains within which social action significantly crystallizes. It then identifies the themes, dilemmas, or sets of questions indigenous to each domain. For example, a focus upon explanations for suffering, misfortune, and misery distinguishes the domain of religion, while the domain of rulership is concerned with the reasons why persons attribute legitimacy to commands and their motives for rendering obedience. The status groups domain involves social honor and defined ways of leading a life (*Lebens-führung*). In this manner, analytic boundaries for each domain become established.

With a significant likelihood, action in these domains becomes uprooted from its random, reactive flow and becomes characterized by a directedness. Weber argues that a good probability exists for this action to become *social* action, and most *E&S* chapters discuss the particular features of domain-specific social action. For example, with respect to economic activity, action becomes social action "if it takes account of the behavior of someone else...[and] in so far as the actor assumes that others will respect his actual control over economic goods" (Weber, 1968, p. 22; see also p. 341); and action oriented to status becomes social action wherever a specific way of leading a life is acknowledged and restrictions on social intercourse become effective (ibid., p. 932). *Here* we find, with societal domains, a major heuristic tool for the research of the interpretive sociologist. In Weber's terminology, each domain is a domain of subjective meaning (*Sinnbereich*) within which social action and social group-ings are likely to arise.

Nonetheless, and however conceptually pivotal to his entire interpretive agenda, Weber concludes that domains remain too global to anchor his empir-ically based sociology. With respect to this *E&S* task – locating social action – they constitute only a beginning. Patterned orientations of subjectively mean-ingful action can be far more rigorously conceptualized, he argues, by reference to *ideal types*. These constructs capture social action with great precision. As an analytic treatise, *E&S* takes the formulation of ideal types as one of its main tasks.

When Weber forms an ideal type of, for example, the prophet, the functionary in a bureaucracy, the market or natural economy, the feudal aristocrat, the peasant, or the intellectual, he is in each case conceptualizing regular orientations of social action. Thus, the "bureaucratic functionary" identifies patterned orien-tations toward the disciplined organization of work, punctuality, reliability, specialized tasks, and a hierarchical chain of command; and the "charismatic leader" outlines orientations toward persons viewed as extraordinary and a willingness to follow them even if a violation of convention and custom is necessary. Each ideal type signifies an uprooting of action from its amorphous flow and a demarcation of constellations of social action. In the case of most ideal types formulated in *E&S*, Weber sees a likelihood for the congealing of such meaningful action: regular orientations of action with a degree of endurance and firmness – a continuity – are implied. Furthermore, the action-orientations delineated by ideal types imply the possibility that an indigenous causal thrust and staying power may exist empirically. Each ideal type – the patterned action-orientations it implies – retains the potential, depending upon the push and pull of the context of further action-orientations within which it exists, to assert an autonomous (*eigengesetzliche*) influence. Thus, on a broad scale, the ideal types of this wide-ranging treatise locate patterned social action in a far more specific manner than do its societal domains.

The location of meaningful action in *E&S* by reference to ideal types and societal domains fulfills the important task of conceptualizing empirical meaningful action. However, it performs a further crucial service in Weber's interpretive sociology. On a wide-ranging, comparative historical scale, *E&S* assists sociologists *to understand* how a vast variety of social action *can become* subjectively meaningful to persons. In other words, it facilitates the understanding of social action *contextually* – on its own terms, or "from within." In doing so, this analytic opus accomplishes for Weber's *verstehende* project another pivotal task: it opposes all tendencies for sociologists engaged in research to explore meaningful social action solely from the vantage point of their *own* accustomed (and perhaps unexamined) presuppositions. Whenever this occurs, a greater likelihood exists that social scientists will, Weber is convinced, see "unusual action" as odd, irrational, and incomprehensible rather than as subjectively meaningful.

Hence, in locating subjective meaning with the assistance of numerous ideal types and societal domains, *E&S* facilitates comprehension of how values, interests, emotions, and traditions in many empirical settings provide meaning to persons and thereby formulate the foundation for social groupings (see Kalberg, 1994b, pp. 30–46). By enabling an understanding of the putatively "irrational" actions of others as indeed meaningful, it *expands* the imagination of sociologists. For example, the ideal type "missionary prophet" assists "we moderns" to comprehend the ways in which this charismatic figure, who views the cosmos as internally unified by God's Commandments and intentions (Weber, 1968, pp. 450–1), attributes meaning to his actions – however "irrational" they may appear from the point of view of today's scientific and secularized presuppositions. Under some circumstances, action-orientations may "line up" in a concerted fashion and form the foundation for internally consistent and even methodically organized lives. Several of Weber's ideal types chart just such systematically directed action.[22]

IDEAL TYPES AS "STANDARDS" As noted, the ideal types of *E&S*, as conceptual tools, "document" patterned social action and demarcate its "location." In addition, when utilized as "standards" against which the patterns of action under investigation can be compared and "measured," they enable the clear definition of this action. A vast diversity of ideal types of varying scope are formulated in this analytic treatise (for example, feudalism, patriarchalism, missionary prophecy, priests, the Oriental city, natural law, canon law, asceticism, warriors). Perhaps most influential in sociology have been two of Weber's ideal types: "types of rulership"[23] and "status groups."[24]

Rather than a "social fact," an expression of natural laws, or an inevitable culmination of historical evolutionary forces, *rulership* implies for Weber nothing more than the probability that a definable group of individuals (as a result of various motives) will orient their social action to giving commands, that another definable group will direct their social action to obedience (as a result of various motives), and that commands are in fact, to a sociologically relevant degree, carried out.[25] In his famous formulation, rulership refers "to the probability that a command with a given specific content will be obeyed by a given group of persons" (ibid., p. 53). It may be ascribed to diverse individuals, such as judges, civil servants, bankers, craftsmen, and tribal chiefs. All exercise rulership wherever obedience is claimed and in fact called forth (ibid., pp. 941, 948).

Weber's major concern focuses upon *legitimate* rulership, or the situation in which a degree of legitimacy is attributed to the rulership relationship. For this reason, obedience, importantly, acquires a voluntary element. Whether anchored in unreflective habit or custom, an emotional attachment to the ruler or fear of him, values or ideals, or purely material interests and a calculation of advantage, a necessary minimum of compliance, unlike sheer *power*, always exists in the case of legitimate rulership (ibid., p. 212).

To Weber, the establishment of a rulership relationship's legitimacy through material interests alone is likely to be relatively unstable. On the other hand, purely value-rational and affectual motives can be decisive only in "extraordinary" circumstances. A mixture of custom and a means–end rational calculation of material interest generally provides the "motive for compliance" in everyday situations (ibid., pp. 213–14, 943). Yet, in his analysis, these motives alone never form a reliable and enduring foundation for rulership. A further element – at least a minimum belief on the part of the ruled in the legitimacy of the rulership – is crucial: "In general, it should be kept clearly in mind that the basis of every rulership, and correspondingly of every kind of willingness to obey, is a *belief*, a belief by virtue of which persons exercising rulership are lent prestige" (ibid., p. 263).[26]

In essence, rulers seek to convince themselves of their *right* to exercise rulership and attempt to implant the notion among the ruled that this right is deserved. If they succeed, a willingness to obey arises that secures their rule far more effectively than does force or power. The character of the typical belief, or claim to legitimacy, provides Weber with the criteria he utilizes to classify the major *types* of legitimate rulership into ideal-typical models (see ibid., p. 953). Why do people obey authority? From the vantage point of his broad-ranging comparative and historical studies, Weber argues that all ruling powers, "profane or religious, political as well as unpolitical," can be understood as appealing to *rational-legal*, *traditional*, or *charismatic* principles of legitimation. What typical beliefs establish the "validity" of these three "pure types" of legitimate rulership?

1   Rational grounds – resting on a belief in the legality of enacted rules and the right of those elevated to rulership under such rules to issue commands (legal rulership).
2   Traditional grounds – resting on an established belief in the sanctity of immemorial traditions and the legitimacy of those exercising rulership under them (traditional rulership).

3   Charismatic grounds – resting on devotion to the exceptional sanctity, heroism, or exemplary character of an individual person, and of the orders revealed or ordained by him (charismatic rulership) (ibid., p. 215). Under the motto, "it is written – but I say unto you," this mission opposes all existing values, customs, laws, rules, and traditions (ibid., pp. 1115–17).[27]

These issues define the "rulership" domain and distinguish action oriented to it from action in the other domains.

Weber's widely discussed model of "rational-legal" rulership is manifest in the bureaucratic organization. In industrial societies, he argues, this type of rulership becomes all-pervasive. It is legitimated by a belief in properly enacted rules and "objective" modes of procedure, rather than by persons or reference to the legitimacy of traditions established in the past. Thus, bureaucratic administration stands in radical opposition to both charismatic rulership and all types of traditional rulership (patriarchalism, feudalism, patrimonialism). The subsumption of diverse social action under stable prescriptions, regulations, and rules accounts for its *comparative* technical superiority *vis-à-vis* traditional and charismatic rulership. Rights and duties are defined and, by virtue of a position in a hierarchy, empower "a superior" to issue commands and expect obedience: "Orders are given in the name of an impersonal norm rather than in the name of a personal authority; and even the giving of a command constitutes obedience toward a norm rather than an arbitrary freedom, favor, or privilege" (Weber, 1946e, pp. 294–5; see also 1968, pp. 229, 945, 1012).

Moreover, in a systematic fashion, bureaucracies orient labor toward general rules and regulations. Work occurs in offices, on a full-time basis, and involves the formulation of written records and their preservation; employees are appointed and rewarded with a regular salary as well as the prospect for advancement. And work procedures maximize calculation: through an assessment of single cases in reference to a set of abstract rules or a weighing of means and ends, decisions can be rendered in a predictable and expedient manner. Compared to the traditional forms of rulership, such decisions occur with less equivocation: arenas of jurisdiction, task specialization, competence, and responsibility for each employee are delimited on the one hand by administrative regulations and on the other hand by technical training. This technical training can be most effectively utilized not only when realms of competence are defined, but also if an unquestioned hierarchy of command reigns in which "each lower office is under the control and supervision of a higher one." Rulership, including a superior's access to coercive means, is distributed in a stable manner and articulated by regulations (Weber, 1968, pp. 223, 975).

Weber's model emphasizes that a "formal rationality" reigns in bureaucracies: problems are solved and decisions made by the systematic and continuous means–end rational orientation of action to abstract rules, which are enacted through discursively analyzable procedures and applied universally. Because decision-making and the giving of commands takes place in direct reference to these rules, bureaucracies typically imply – compared to the traditional and charismatic types of rulership – the reduction of affectual and traditional action.

He repeatedly calls attention to the extremely impersonal character of bureaucratic rulership. For example, "Bureaucracy develops the more perfectly the more it is 'dehumanized,' the more completely it succeeds in eliminating from official business love, hatred, and all purely personal, irrational, and emotional elements which escape calculation" (ibid., p. 975).

This "pure model," Weber argues, can be utilized as a standard against which the particular empirical case under investigation – the American, English, or German bureaucracy, for example, or the state bureaucracy *vis-à-vis* the bureaucracy in private industry – can be compared. Through an assessment of deviation from this heuristic tool, the main features of the particular case will then become defined and its distinctiveness precisely demarcated.[28] His other widely discussed ideal type, "status group," serves the same purpose.

Weber contends that *status groups* – and not only classes, as for Marx – constitute an independent foundation for social stratification. Viewed through a comparative historical lens, the dominant mode of stratification varies across civilizations and epochs. In the modern West, for example, "*class* situation" has become a more central organizing principle than "*status* situation" (see Weber, 1946e, p. 301). Stratification by status is favored, he insists, whenever relationships of production and distribution are stable, and naked class situation becomes prominent in eras of great technological and economic change. When the tempo of such transformations recedes, a reinvigoration of status structures occurs, as well as an enhancement of the salience of social honor (Weber, 1968, p. 938). How does Weber define "status group" and how does this ideal type, as a conceptual yardstick, assist research?

"Status situation" implies "every typical component of the life of men that is determined by a specific, positive or negative, social estimation of honor" (ibid., p. 932). Thus, social esteem – claims to it and acknowledgment of it – orient social action in this domain. A person's way of leading a life, which in turn rests upon discrete socialization processes and hereditary and occupational prestige, comes here to the fore (ibid., pp. 305–6; see also Weber, 1946e, p. 300).

A status group (*Stand*) appears when persons share a style of life, consumption patterns, common conventions, specific notions of honor, and, conceivably, economic and particular status monopolies. For Weber, status situations, due to an implied evaluation of one's own situation relative to that of others as well as a subjective awareness of common conventions, values, and styles of life, may often lead to the formation of groups. This remains the case even if such groups are at times amorphous (Weber, 1968, p. 932). Status differences become apparent whenever social interaction is restricted or lacking. Stratification by status always implies the "monopolization of ideal and material goods or opportunities," as well as social distance and exclusiveness (ibid., pp. 935, 927; Weber, 1946e, p. 300).

Weber emphasizes that a subjective sense of social honor and esteem may have a significant impact. "Stratification by status" stands in opposition to and may restrict *even* action oriented to classes, material interests, the development of the free market, class conflicts, and hard bargaining. Guilds in the Middle Ages, for example, now and then struggled more fervently over questions of precedence in

festival processions than over economic issues. Distinguished families throughout the world permit courtship of their daughters only by status peers, and
members of "old families" have frequently cultivated a variety of techniques of
exclusiveness, as have the descendants of the Pilgrim fathers, Pocahontas, and
the First Families of Virginia (Weber, 1958, pp. 34, 125; 1968, pp. 933, 937).
Court nobles and humanist literati influenced greatly the character of education
in the seventeenth century, and various "carrier strata" have prominently placed
their imprint upon the formation of religious doctrines and ethical teachings (see
below). This has occurred to such an extent that belief systems undergo profound alterations whenever they acquire a new carrier stratum (see Weber,
1946c, pp. 267–9, 279–85; 1968, pp. 490–2, 1180–1). A single status group
might occasionally set its stamp upon the entire development of a civilization, as
did intellectuals in China, the samurai warriors in Japan, the Brahmin priests in
India, and the business class in the United States.

As ideal types, status groups can be employed as standards against which the
particular case under investigation can be "measured." Its uniqueness can be
defined in this manner. Without these constructs to assist conceptualization, it is
not possible, Weber argues, to conduct the comparative "mental experiments"
(*Gedankenbild*) central for the rigorous isolation of significant causal patterns of
action.

These yardstick ideal types – status groups and the types of rulership – from
E&S, as well as many others that could be addressed, place Weber in direct
opposition to Marx: material interests do not *alone* constitute the single
"engine" of change. On the contrary, Weber's sociology repeatedly contends
that a variety of causal forces are effective in history and that social change
occurs in a non-linear, complex fashion (see below).

IDEAL TYPES AS HYPOTHESIS-FORMING MODELS Many of Weber's ideal
types not only facilitate the clear conceptualization of specific cases or developments, but also delineate hypotheses that can be tested against specific cases and
developments – indeed, in such a manner that discrete and significant causal
regularities of social action can be isolated. Ideal types are employed in *E&S* as
hypothesis-forming models in four major ways.

Their *dynamic* character is the focus of Weber's first type of model. Rather
than being static, ideal types are constituted from an array of regular action-
orientations. Relationships – delimited, empirically testable hypotheses – among
these action-orientations are implied. Second, *contextual* models that articulate
hypotheses regarding the impact of specific social contexts upon patterned
action are constructed in *E&S*. Third, when examined in reference to one
another, ideal types may articulate *logical interactions* of patterned, meaningful action. Hypotheses regarding "elective affinity" and "antagonism" relationships across ideal types abound in *E&S*. Fourth, Weber utilizes ideal types to
chart analytic *developments*. Each model hypothesizes a *course* of regular
action, or a "developmental path."

By erecting a delineated theoretical framework, every model facilitates a
conceptual grasp upon otherwise diffuse realities and formulates causal

hypotheses regarding patterned action-orientations. In doing so, each model assists attainment of the overall goal of Weber's sociology: the causal explanation of cases and developments. A strongly theoretical dimension is also injected by each model into the very core of Weber's comparative historical sociology. Only a few of his elective affinity, antagonism, and developmental models can be noted here.[29]

Weber informs us explicitly that he is concerned in *E&S* with the ideal typical relationships between the economy and "society" – that is, the interactions between the economy and "the general structural *forms* (Struktur*formen*) of human groups" (1968, p. 356)[30] in the major societal domains. In great detail and on a vast scale, he charts out, through constellations of ideal types, the diverse ways in which the various stages in the development of the economy (the agricultural and industrial organization of work; the natural, money, planned, market, and capitalist types of economies) relate to – and influence – the various major stages in these domains: for example, the traditional, natural, and logical-formal types of law; the paths to salvation in the religion domain (through a savior, an institution, ritual, good works, mysticism, and asceticism; see Kalberg, 1990); the charismatic, patriarchal, feudal, patrimonial, and bureaucratic types of rulership; the family, clan, and traditional neighborhood; and an array of major status groups (such as intellectuals, civil servants, and feudal nobles).

Nonetheless, this attention to the interactions between the economy and the other domains never implies its elevation to a position of causal dominance. On the contrary, in distinguishing a *series* of realms, Weber wishes, against Marx, to argue that questions of causality cannot be addressed by reference primarily to economic forces, material interests, or *any* single domain. As he notes, "The connections between the economy and the societal domains are dealt with more fully than is usually the case. This is done deliberately so that the autonomy (*Eigengesetzlichkeit*) of these domains *vis-à-vis* the economy is made manifest" (Weber, 1914, p. vii). Each domain, Weber contends, as manifest through its ideal types, implies the possibility of empirically significant patterns of action. Many passages in *E&S* are devoted to demonstrations of how this takes place in reference to the indigenous themes, dilemmas, or sets of questions specific to each domain. The elevation of a particular realm to a position of general causal priority, Weber insists, must not occur.

Moreover, and despite an orientation to the economy domain, *E&S* charts much more than the relationships between the various groupings in this realm and the various groupings in the other domains. This opus cannot accurately be depicted as addressing only the manner in which diverse groups influence – and are influenced by – the economy. Instead, Weber examines thoroughly the ideal typical relationships, for example, between clan and religious groupings, legal and rulership organizations, groupings in the domain of religion and organizations in the domain of law, the family and rulership organizations, and religious groups and rulership organizations. More specifically, he scrutinizes the relation of logical-formal law to bureaucratic rulership, the family to various salvation paths, and the "ethics" of various status groups to the major salvation paths on the one hand and the types of law and rulership on the other hand. How, then, do the various domains relate analytically to one another? *E&S* proclaims that they do so in patterned ways.

Two concepts in this treatise capture cross-domain relationships: relations of "elective affinity" and "relations of antagonism." While elective affinity relationships imply a compatible intermingling – a non-deterministic though typical and reciprocal interaction of regular social action – of two or more ideal types that share internal features, antagonistic relationships indicate hypotheses of "inadequacy" and a clash, a hindering, even an excluding of the patterned action-orientations implied by each ideal type.

These "logical interactions" of regular action constitute, to Weber, hypothesis-forming models. For example, the intensely personal character of relationships in the family and clan are viewed as *antagonistic* to the impersonal relationships characteristic of the marketplace (an orientation of meaningful action to the "laws of the market" over persons) and bureaucratic rulership (an orientation to statutes, regulations, and laws over persons). Similarly, the relationships of compassion and brotherhood typically cultivated by the great salvation religions are seen as opposing the formal rationality that appears in the later developmental stages of the economy (capitalism), rulership (bureaucracy), and law (logical-formal) domains. And charismatic rulership stands in a relationship of antagonism to all routine economic action: "From the point of view of rational economic activity, charismatic want satisfaction is a typical anti-economic force" (Weber, 1968, p. 245; see Kalberg, 1994b, pp. 102–17).

On the other hand, innumerable cross-domain *affinity* relationships abound as well in *E&S*. For example, and despite wide diversity, Weber detected a series of elective affinities between the status ethic of intellectuals and certain salvation paths. Due to their typical tendency to ponder the world passively, to search for a comprehensive meaning to life, and to deplore the meaninglessness of empirical reality, rather than to undertake "tasks" and act regularly *in* the world as "doers," intellectuals are generally predisposed to formulate notions of salvation "more remote from life, more theoretical and more systematic than salvation from external need, the quest for which is characteristic of non-privileged strata" (Weber, 1968, p. 506; translation altered). Weber also sees logical interactions of elective affinity as typically occurring between the universal organizations and both magic-based and salvation-based religions. Magical religions simply appropriated the general virtues practiced in the family, kin group, and traditional neighborhood (such as fraternity, truthfulness, loyalty to the sibling, respect for older generations, and reciprocal assistance), and salvation religions typically bestowed distinctly positive premiums upon the brotherhood ethic. In all cases, personal relations and person-oriented values predominated. Similarly, Weber discovered elective affinity relations between traditional types of law and patriarchal rulership, as well as bureaucratic rulership and logical-formal law (see Kalberg, 1994b, pp. 108–16).

In this manner, *E&S* articulates a series of cross-domain analytic relationships, all of which are formulated as hypotheses.[31] Indeed, this opus constructs a broad-ranging analytic – one that can be utilized as a theoretical framework to facilitate the clear conceptualization of empirical relationships, as well as their analytical location.[32] One further type of hypothesis-forming model central in *E&S* must be examined: the developmental model.

Weber's *E&S developmental models* hypothesize a *course* of patterned action. In doing so, they (a) facilitate the clear conceptualization of the particular development under investigation, as well as its significant causal forces, and (b) postulate delineated, empirically testable developmental courses of patterned action. In effect, as "technical aids" constructed with a "rational consistency . . . rarely found in reality" (Weber, 1946c, p. 323), each model charts paths that will be taken if certain "irrational" empirical disturbances do not intervene (Weber, 1949, pp. 101–3). "Even developments," according to Weber, "can be constructed as ideal types, and these constructs may have quite considerable heuristic value" (ibid., p. 101).

In formulating these models, Weber repeatedly notes their basically "unhistorical" character. As ideal typical constructions, each captures the *essence* of a development, presenting it in a manner more internally consistent and systematically unified than ever occurred empirically. Hence, because the stages of his developmental models should never be viewed either as accurate renderings of the course of history or as themselves constituting "effective forces," *E&S* diverges distinctly from all evolutionary schools of thought in search of either society's "scientific laws" or history's "invariable stages" – thereby placing Weber in opposition to social theorists as diverse as Comte, Marx, and Spencer. His models serve a more modest task: they aim to provide the researcher with a clear and practical "means of orientation" on the one hand and an array of hypotheses regarding the course of history with respect to a particular theme on the other hand. Whether the analytic path of development laid out by a specific model is followed always remains an issue for detailed empirical investigation by specialists (ibid., p. 103). Thus, these developmental models again testify to the centrality of model-building and hypothesis-formation procedures in Weber's comparative-historical sociology. Only one example can be offered here: the "routinization of charisma" model.

Charismatic rulership is exercised by a person over disciples and followers who believe that he possesses supernatural powers of divine origin. This leader, who arises in emergency situations, may be, for example, a prophet, a war hero, a politician, a leader of the hunt, a demagogue, an oracle-giver, or a magician. In all cases, the rulership attributed to him derives from a recognition of extraordinary qualities, ones not accessible to the ordinary person. Once its genuineness is acknowledged, disciples and followers feel duty-bound to devote themselves completely to the charismatic leader, and he demands a strict obedience. They obey his commands as a result of an immense affection and the conviction that a genuinely personal relationship exists. Indeed, Weber sees an "emotional conviction" as central to the belief of disciples and followers in the charismatic leader's right to rule, one that "internally" revolutionizes their entire personalities: "Charisma . . . manifests its revolutionary power from within, from a central *metanoia* [change] of its followers' attitudes" (Weber, 1968, p. 1117; see also pp. 241–4, 1112–17).

The highly personal character of charismatic rule, as well as its lack of concern for everyday routine, leads it to reject all "external order." The "objective" law received by the possessor of charisma as a gift of God bestows upon him a unique and new mission. For this reason, Weber sees charisma as standing in fundamental and revolutionary opposition to all means–end rational action as well as to all existing and stable forces of daily life (see ibid., pp. 291, 1112–20).

He also stresses, however, the fragility of charismatic rulership. As a consequence of its location strictly in the "supernatural qualities" of great leaders and the necessity for the "superhuman" personality repeatedly to demonstrate unusual powers and a "right to rule," "charismatic authority is naturally unstable" (ibid., pp. 1112–14). Even the greatest intensity of personal devotion to the charismatic leader cannot guarantee the perpetuation of the extraordinary figure's teachings in their pure form. Instead, Weber's "routinization" model proclaims that charisma follows a developmental path characterized by its weakening; it becomes repeatedly absorbed into the permanent institutions of everyday life. Such a transformation of charisma has always been sought by followers in the hope that, in the process, a *permanent* protection against sickness, disease, and natural catastrophe will be acquired (see, for example, ibid., pp. 1131–3, 1146–9, 1156).

The material and power interests of the charismatic community of followers and disciples constitute, in Weber's routinization of charisma construct, an important driving force in institutionalizing the "transitory gift of grace . . . into a permanent possession of everyday life."[33] Preserved by followers in depersonalized (*versachlichte*) form, a weakened charisma becomes attached to the community of disciples and plays, his model hypothesizes, an indispensable role in attracting new followers, in establishing the legitimacy of new status groups, forms of rulership, and religious doctrines, and in facilitating ascent to positions of dominance in status, rulership, and religious hierarchies. Now as a part of everyday life and capable, often through ceremonies involving magic, of being transmitted to family members, offices or institutions, "hereditary," "institutionalized," and "office" charisma serves to legitimize "acquired rights." Altered into these impersonal and routinized forms, charisma, according to this model, is upheld in all these stages in particular by persons with an economic interest in doing so, as well by all those in possession of power and property who see their position of advantage as legitimated by its authority – for example, court officials, priests, parliamentary monarchs, high dignitaries, and party leaders[34] (ibid., pp. 251, 1122–7, 1139–41, 1146–8; Weber, 1946e, p. 297).

Weber's yardstick, affinity, antagonism, and developmental models appear throughout *E&S* and contribute decisively to its rigor, analytic power, and uniqueness. As "constructed schemes," all models alone "serve the purpose of offering an ideal-typical means of *orientation*" (Weber, 1946c, p. 323, original emphasis). With respect to antagonisms across domains, for example, "the theoretically constructed types of conflicting 'societal domains' are merely intended to show that at certain points such and such internal conflicts are *possible* and 'adequate'" (ibid., original emphasis). Yet, in performing this modest task, each model provides a purchase upon ceaselessly flowing realities, thereby facilitating clear conceptualization of the particular patterned social action under investigation. Each hypothesized interaction can then be tested through in-depth investigation. Because viewed alone as mechanisms to facilitate causal analysis, Weber fully expects these "logical constructs" to be "dislocated" when confronted by complex empirical realities. Concrete circumstances and contexts will invariably strengthen or weaken particular analytic relationships. Nonetheless, he emphasizes that sociology, unlike history, *must* include a rigorous theoretical framing – through models – of the problem under investigation.

This remains the case if only because models constitute for Weber the indispensable first step toward his all-important goal of causal analysis. He insists that the typical immersion of sociologists deeply in empirical realities *requires* such constructs if significant causal action-orientations are to be identified, all the more owing to the fundamental character of empirical reality – for him, an unending flow of events and happenings – and the continuous danger that all causal inquiry all too easily becomes mired in an endless description-based regression. By constructing arrays of models in *E&S* that conceptualize patterned, meaningful action, Weber aims to draw sociology *away* from an exclusive focus upon delineated social problems on the one hand and historical narrative on the other hand. Nonetheless, he steadfastly avoids the other side of the spectrum; grounded empirically, his models never move to the level of broad, diffuse generalizations. Rather, these research tools offer limited hypotheses that can be tested against specific cases and developments. To Weber, unique to the sociological enterprise is always a back and forth movement between conceptualization – the formulation of models and theoretical frameworks – and the detailed investigation of empirical cases and developments. If the goal of offering causal explanations of the "historical individual" is to be realized, *both* the empirically particular and conceptual generalization are indispensable.

DRIVING FORCES: THE MULTICAUSALITY OF *E&S* AND POWER Although *E&S* gives priority to the task of model building over causal analysis, Weber's unequivocal embrace of multicausal modes of procedure is apparent. Throughout this treatise, as noted, he focuses upon the patterned social action within the status group, universal organizations, religion, law, rulership, and economy domains. An array of ideal types is connected analytically to each domain, and each indicates the empirical possibility of *regular* action-orientations with a degree of endurance. Thus, each ideal type implies an indigenous causal thrust and staying power or, to Weber, an *autonomous* aspect. Nonetheless, and even though the meaningful action of individuals anchors his sociology, the question "within what *carrier* grouping action occurs" remains fundamental to him. Social action becomes sociologically significant action *only* in demarcated groupings of individuals.

In every society, only *certain* traditional, affectual, value-rational, and means–end rational patterns of meaningful action acquire strong exponents and become important aspects of the social fabric. For Weber, status groups, classes, and organizations serve as the most prominent bearers of action. Each "carries" a configuration of delineated action-orientations. He calls attention, for example, to the ideal typical "status ethic" of functionaries in bureaucracies (duty, punctuality, the orderly performance of tasks, disciplined work habits, etc.; Weber, 1968, pp. 956–1003), the ethos of the neighborhood organization (mutual assistance and a "sombre economic 'brotherhood' practised in case of need"; ibid., pp. 363), and the class ethos of the bourgeoisie (opposition to privileges based upon birth and status, a favoring of formal legal equality; ibid., pp. 477–80; see Kalberg, 1985). Attention to such carriers is characteristic of Weber's sociology.

As he notes, "Unless the concept 'autonomy' is to lack all precision, its definition presupposes the existence of a bounded group of persons which, though membership may fluctuate, is determinable" (Weber, 1968, p. 699; translation altered). In introducing his chapters on traditional and charismatic rulership in *E&S*, for example, Weber summarizes his aims as involving not only an evaluation of the extent to which the "developmental chances" of the major "structural principles" of each rulership type can be said to be subject to "economic, political or any other external determinants," but also an assessment of the degree to which the developmental chances of the types of rulership instead follow "an 'autonomous' logic inherent in their technical structure" (ibid., p. 1002). He insists that this "logic" must be *conceptualized as capable* of exerting an independent effect even upon economic factors (ibid., pp. 578, 1002, 654–5), and discovers – whenever a "bounded group" crystallizes as its social carrier – many empirical cases when it does. Weber is especially aware of the extent to which the attribution of legitimacy to rulership sets an independent driving force into motion. Hence, even while remaining cognizant of the frequent centrality of economic factors, he emphasizes the necessity for multicausal approaches (see ibid., pp. 341, 935). In arguing on behalf of the autonomous potential of action-orientations in the economy, law, rulership, religion, status groups, and universal organizations domains, Weber aims in *E&S* to conceptualize economic action within a broad theoretical framework and to treat "both sides" of the causal nexus (see Kalberg, 1994b, pp. 50–78).

The "level of analysis" in *E&S* – an array of societal domains, constellations of domain-specific ideal types, and social carriers – itself further demonstrates his broad multicausality. It is clear as well by Weber's frequent reference to the importance of a further variety of causal forces: historical events, technological innovations, and geographical forces. Moreover, conflict and competition, as well as interests generally and economic interests in particular, constitute, to him, effective causal forces – as does, not least, power. In his classical formulation, Weber defines power thus: "Within a social relationship, power means any chance (no matter whereon this chance is based) to carry through one's (individual *or* collective) own will (*even* against resistance)" (Weber, 1968, p. 53).[35]

New action-orientations frequently fade or become the victims of suppression by opposing coalitions if power is lacking and alliances fail to take place. Rulers are particularly adept, he insists repeatedly, at forming alliances with the sole purpose of maintaining and aggrandizing power. They seek to balance classes, status groups, and organizations against one another as a matter of course. Power plays a central role in Weber's multicausal analyses of how new patterns of social action arise, spread, and set historical developments into motion, as well as in his investigations of how action-orientations become circumscribed and rendered less influential. Finally, *E&S* also endows *ideas* with a causal efficacy. *Religious* ideas, especially those that address the conundrum of frequent and seemingly random human suffering, might cast an influence across centuries and even millennia. Just the attempts to explain misery and injustice, Weber argues, played a significant role in the development of religions from ones anchored in magic to ones rooted in notions of salvation, ethical action, and an "other-world." Ideas regarding the stubborn persistence of misfortune, as articulated by prophets, priests, monks, and theologians, pushed this development, rather than economic and practical interests alone. Repeatedly, ideas were formulated that clarified the relationship of believers to the transcendent realm – and these ideas implied modes of new meaningful action "pleasing to the gods." Eventually, doctrines were formulated that offered broad-ranging views of the universe, explained suffering in a comprehensive sense, and defined action that promised to bring an end to suffering (see ibid., pp. 349–50, 399–439, 577–9; Weber, 1946a, pp. 122–3; 1946c, p. 324; 1946e, pp. 269–76, 280–5; Kalberg, 1990, 2001).

In sum, attention to a diversity of causal forces characterizes *E&S*, as does Weber's unwillingness to elevate particular forces to positions of general causal priority.[36]

THE INTERWEAVING OF PAST AND PRESENT Weber's attempts to define and explain the uniqueness of a particular present always acknowledge the many ways in which the past perpetually interweaves with the present. This remains the case despite the heroic capacity he sees in charismatic leaders: to sever, given constellations of facilitating conditions, abruptly past and present. Even drastic metamorphoses and the abrupt advent of "the new" never fully ruptures ties to the past (see Weber, 1968, pp. 29, 577), and "that which has been handed down from the past becomes everywhere the immediate precursor of that taken in the present as valid" (ibid., translation altered). Even the monumental structural transformations called forth by industrialization fail to sweep away the past. Viable legacies live on.

Weber's orientation in *E&S* to societal domains and ideal types stands at the foundation not only of its multicausality, but also of its capacity to analyze the multiple and subtle ways in which the past interlocks with the present. As noted, to him, the various societal domains are endowed with an independent, or autonomous, capacity rooted in indigenous questions and problems – and they develop in a non-parallel manner and at their own pace. And each ideal type, in "documenting" patterns of meaningful action, implies the possibility of an autonomous sustaining power. Moreover, Weber endows further forces – historical events, geographical constellations, power, social carriers, conflict, competition, and technology – with an unequivocal causal capacity. The patterned social action of persons in groupings is conceptualized as having many and diverse origins.

Thus, *E&S* offers a "view of society" as constituted from an array of moving, even dynamically interacting, "parts." All "general axiom" schools of sociological analysis that depart from encompassing dichotomies (*Gemeinschaft/Gesellschaft*, tradition/modernity, particularism/universalism), broad themes (the question of social order), or assumptions regarding the "organic unity" and "lawfulness of society" stand radically in opposition to Weber's "open" theoretical framework rooted in ideal types and societal domains. These fundamental features of *E&S* allow conceptualization across an entire spectrum of empirical cases, ranging from those characterized more by flux, competition, conflict, tension, and disintegration, to others characterized more by internal unity and harmony. Furthermore, the familiar concepts at the center of many sociological theories – "class," "the state," "society," for example – are never elevated in *E&S* to a position of special status. Even the dichotomy frequently interpreted by commentators as capturing Weber's "view of history" – his contrast of the stable and routine character of tradition to the revolutionary character of charisma – fails to render the complex relationship in his sociology between past and present.

The wide variety of causal forces articulated in *E&S*, their "open" interaction, and their variable degree of closure enables Weber forcefully to demonstrate that the past and present intimately interweave in many ways. Regularities of social action in some groupings can be recognized as becoming firm and acquiring powerful carriers, even to the extent of developing in terms of their indigenous problematics and penetrating deeply into subsequent epochs; others fail to do so and prove fleeting; still others cast their imprint vigorously and then fade away. The "view of society" that flows out of this systematic opus – as constructed from numerous causally effective, competing, and reciprocally interacting patterns of social action captured in ideal types – easily takes cognizance of the "survival" of some patterns of action from the past and their significant influence, as legacies, upon patterns of action in the present.

Weber often charts legacies, for example, from the religion domain. In the United States, central values from Protestant asceticism – disciplined and routine work in a profession, the regular giving to charity organizations, the perpetual formation by persons of goals, the orientation to the future and the attempt to "master" the world's challenges (*Weltbeherrschung*), an optimism regarding the capacity to shape personal destinies, and a strong intolerance of "evil" – remain integral in American life today, despite the fact that most who act in reference to these values have no awareness of them as linked intimately to a religious heritage (Weber, 1968, p. 1187).[37] Moreover, the "direct democratic administration" by the congregation, as it took place in the Protestant sects in the United States, left a legacy crucial for the establishment of democratic forms of government, as did the unwillingness of sect members to bestow a halo of reverence upon secular authority. The Quakers in particular, in advocating freedom of conscience for others as well as for themselves, paved the way for political tolerance today (see ibid., pp. 1204–10; Kalberg, 1997).

The interweaving of past and present constitutes a major organizational axis in *E&S*. All present-oriented, functionalist modes of analysis stand in strict opposition to Weber's sociology. To him, the past always penetrates deeply into the present, even molding its core contours. He is especially convinced that an identification of the modern West's uniqueness and its possible course of further development *requires* investigations of its historical development.[38]

These five axes remain central throughout *E&S*, the analytic treatise for Weber's comparative-historical, interpretive sociology. In this opus, as well as in his methodological writings, his modes of analysis and research strategies are demarcated, albeit in a poorly organized fashion. Owing to its explicit attention to "both sides of the causal equation" – ideas and interests – *The Economic Ethics of the World Religions* offers a better example of these modes of analysis and research strategies than *PE*. This massive study can be discussed only briefly.

The Economic Ethics of the World Religions

Weber's broadranging studies on China (1951), India (1958), and ancient Israel (1952) expand upon a theme first explored in *PE* in 1904: the relationship between the "economic ethics" of religions and the rise of modern capitalism.[39] Through a series of rigorous comparisons to these civilizations, he sought after 1910 to define the uniqueness of modern capitalism and the modern West more generally, and to offer a causal explanation for its particular path of development.

Moreover, whereas *PE*, in tracing the origins of a spirit of capitalism back to ascetic Protestantism, examined only "one side" of the causal equation, the *EEWR* volumes forcefully articulate a *multicausal* methodology. In exploring the question of why modern capitalism failed to develop before the twentieth century in non-Western civilizations, they investigate "ideas *and* interests." In a central passage in the *EEWR* introduction, Weber notes the complex ways in which "both sides" are intertwined:

> Every attempt at explanation, recognizing the fundamental significance of economic factors, must above all take account of these factors. Nevertheless, the opposite line of causation should not be neglected if only because the origin of economic rationalization depends not only on an advanced development of technology and law but also on the capacity and disposition of persons to organize their lives in a practical-rational manner. Wherever magical and religious forces have inhibited the unfolding of this organized life, the development of an organized life oriented systematically toward *economic* activity has confronted broadranging internal resistance. Magical and religious powers, and the ethical notions of duty based on them, have been in the past among the most formative influences upon the way life has been organized. (Weber, 2002a, p. 160; original emphasis; see also 1968, p. 341)

In this pivotal statement Weber calls attention to a number of causal forces important to him. He emphatically rejects, for example, both greed and a material interest in becoming wealthy; these forces have been universal, yet modern capitalism developed only in a few specific regions and during a particular historical epoch. The putative "general evolutionary sweep of history" is omitted, for Weber insists on focusing upon empirical factors. Although acknowledging unequivocally the importance of the economy and classes, he rejects all explanations that view belief systems alone as the "superstructure" of economic interests. Similarly, a class of formally trained jurists should not be understood as crystallizing simply from capitalistic interests, for then the question arises of why such interests did not lead to the same development in China or India (Weber, 2002a, p. 159). Furthermore, organizations – and even extremely tightly knit sects – do not, he contends, uniformly lead to the same values: "Structurally identical religious sects . . . existed in Hinduism as well as in Christianity, yet their sacred values pointed [the social action of believers] in radically different directions" (Weber, 1946e, p. 292).

Weber's complex multicausality also leads him away from the conclusion that modern capitalism failed to develop first in Asia owing to an absence of innerworldly asceticism. Although his concern, when he examines Confucianism, Taoism, Hinduism, Buddhism, Jainism, and ancient Judaism, remains focused upon an assessment of whether devoutness bestowed "religious rewards" upon methodical economic activity, he insists that single factors never determine historical development. Rather, *constellations* of forces are always central, as well as the manner in which they interact conjuncturally in delineated contexts and thereby formulate unique configurations.[40] By "applying" the domains-based, *multi*causal theoretical framework developed in *E&S*, Weber identifies vastly different constellations of action-orientations related to rulership, religion, the economy, social honor, the family, and the law in each civilization.[41] The many clusters of social action conducive to the unfolding of modern capitalism in China, India, and ancient Israel were, he found, in the end outweighed by a series of opposing patterns of action.

For example, he notes a variety of nonreligious obstacles to economic development in China, such as extremely strong sibling ties and an absence of "a formally guaranteed law and a rational administration and judiciary" (Weber, 1951, p. 85; see also pp. 91, 99–100), and in India, such as constraints placed upon migration, the recruitment of labor, and credit by the caste system (Weber, 1958, pp. 52–3, 102–6, 111–17). He discovers as well, however, an entire host of conducive material forces that nonetheless failed to bring about modern capitalism – such as, in China, freedom of trade, population growth, occupational mobility, an increase in precious metals, and the presence of a money economy (Weber, 1951, pp. 12, 54–5, 99–100, 243).

Weber was quite convinced that modern capitalism could be *adopted* by – and would flourish in – a number of Eastern civilizations. Indeed, he identified the forces that would allow this to occur (on Japan, see Weber, 1958, p. 275). Yet adoption, he insisted, involved different processes than his concern: the *origin* in a specific region of a *new* economic ethos and a *new* type of economy. Furthermore, Weber's analysis identifies great variation across civilizations in the extent to which significant regularities of social action with strong carriers tended to line up and "complement" one another or, conversely, stand in opposition to one another. Pluralistic conflict between relatively independently developing domains arose in the latter case, as well as a societal openness that facilitated regular social change. This "model," Weber argues, significantly distinguishes the Western developmental path (Weber, 1968, pp. 1192–3; see Kalberg, forth-coming).

However, these volumes provide not only a complex causal explanation for modern capitalism's appearance first in the West; Weber also attempts to demarcate the uniqueness of *each* of the *EEWR* civilizations. He defines "Chinese rationalism," "Indian rationalism," and the "rationalism of ancient Israel." He then seeks, first, to offer comparisons and contrasts to "Western rationalism" and, second, to provide explanations for the particular routes of development followed by each great civilization. In doing so, his investigations allowed delineation of a number of further ways in which the West proved unique: it called forth a systematic science based upon the experimental method and carried out by trained and specialized personnel; a more wide-ranging societal significance was assumed by organized and trained civil servants and managers than elsewhere; and a state based upon a "rationally enacted 'constitution' and rationally enacted laws, and administered by civil servants possessing *specialized* arenas of competence and oriented to rules and 'laws'" (Weber, 2000a, p. 152).

Hence, through his *EEWR* studies Weber acquired essential insight, clarity, and knowledge regarding the specific "tracks" within which a number of major civilizations had developed (see Weber, 1946e, p. 280). These tracks called forth in the West in the twentieth century, he argued, the dominance of formal rationality in the domains of law, rulership, and the economy, and theoretical rationality in the domain of science (see below). Great ramifications followed, he insisted repeatedly, regarding the "type of person" (*Menschentyp*) that *could* live under "modern Western rationalism." Yet these volumes also assisted Weber to answer three further burning questions, all of which originated from his skepticism regarding Western civilization's "progress." First, given its distinct features, what is the nature of the social change that *can* take place in the modern West? Second, how do persons in different social contexts – and in different civilizations – formulate meaning in their lives? Finally, what patterned orientations of social action – means–end rational, value-rational, and traditional – have become meaningful in each of the major civilizations, and how did this occur? Because he viewed compassion, ethical action, and a reflective individualism as now endangered in the West, answers to these queries became especially urgent. Would *values* continue to orient social action? The immediacy of these questions itself served to call forth the Herculean motivation required to conduct the *EEWR* investigations.

Although innumerable scholars over the past decades have examined in depth Weber's intense political activities, his volcanic personality, the intellectual origins of his ideas, and his relationships with his many colleagues, we read Weber today owing to the rigor of his sociological writings. Yet *PE*, *E&S*, *EEWR*, and the methodological writings are complex and often extremely difficult to comprehend. Each interpreter of Weber seems to discover a different "Weber" (see Kalberg, 1998, pp. 208–12).

Perhaps this problem is to some extent inevitable in light of the immense scope and complexity of Weber's project. He sought to investigate entire civilizations through interpretive, empirical, multicausal, and context-sensitive procedures, to trace out the unique developmental paths each followed to the present, and to understand the ways in which persons living in diverse epochs and circumstances create meaning in their lives. However, he attempted to fulfill a further daunting task: he wished to define the heuristic tools, modes of analysis, and research procedures for a comparative-historical, interpretive sociology. Indeed, he sought to offer concepts and strategies that could be utilized alike by *verstehende* sociologists engaged in intercivilizational research and others investigating more specialized topics.

As already apparent, Weber's sociology arose in reference to a specific histor-ical background. A turn now to a sketch of the social context in which he lived and wrote will further assist comprehension of its purposes, procedures, and boundaries.

The Social Context

Very rapid industrialization was occurring in Max Weber's Germany. Moreover, compared to the United States, England, and Holland, industrialization began very late, and hence was accompanied by a sense of urgency. Yet Germans were convinced that, if the powers of the state were harnessed comprehensively, their nation would soon surpass its competitors.

However, this "industrialization from above" tended to place in motion a number of forces that curtailed the unfolding of a democratic political culture on German soil. It implied above all that Germany's business elites would be more closely aligned with the state than was the case in most other industrializing nations. A strong and independent class capable of standing against state power – as a countervailing force to open a public arena of participation and the free exchange of views – failed to arise. Economic development occurred more under the hegemony of a caste of government functionaries than occurred elsewhere.

Three further features of German society characterized this "German model." Although it was largely a secularized country by the middle of the nineteenth century, legacies of Luther's political ideas, now in the form of commonly accepted conventions and values rather than explicitly religious belief, endured. They took the form of a deep respect for authority in general and for the state in particular, even to such a degree that, in many regions, the state, its laws, and its functionaries acquired a "halo" of trust and legitimacy. In addition, the par-ticular character of feudalism in much of Germany – innumerable small princip-alities and kingdoms – rendered the authoritarian rulership of the feudal master so direct and immediate that notions of self-rule, individual rights, and repres-entative government never found fertile ground. Finally, and as a result of all these forces, the German working class remained politically weak. Unlike the French, the Germans failed in their attempt to introduce modern forms of egalitarianism and democratic self-governance. Prussian troops crushed the Revolution of 1848.

All these features of its political culture erected significant obstacles to the monumental tasks Germany confronted at the turn of the century. Whereas a stable democracy existed in the United States *before* the onset of industrialization, Germany faced the burdensome task of cultivating and extending region-based democratic traditions *in the midst of* industrialization. In many important ways, these two nations were located at opposite ends of the "modernization" spectrum (see Kalberg, 1987).

Although Chancellor Bismarck had molded a variety of small German principalities and feudal kingdoms into a unified nation in 1871, a "modernizing ideology" – an embrace of democracy and political rights – never accompanied his nation-building. Furthermore, Bismarck's rulership precluded an assertive and independent role for the German parliament, as well as for the population as a whole. In the face of an overwhelming centralization of power, an active, participatory citizenry could scarcely arise. Politics was dominated by the Chancellor, his functionaries, and an antiquated class of agrarian petty aristocrats motivated exclusively by narrow class interests. While successful at calling forth rapid industrialization, as well as a notion of social trust grounded in respect for the state and its laws on the one hand and hierarchical, quasi-feudal social conventions on the other, the German model stood against all developments in the direction of a democratic political culture.

Public sphere ideals that could be nourished failed to appear on a widespread basis. By the turn of the century, massive segments of the population had either turned to introspective endeavors (scholarship, education, art, music, philosophy)[42] or simply withdrawn into private sphere relationships. Others condemned unequivocally the modern, "impersonal and harsh" *Gesellschaft* and sought a return to the putatively stable and compassionate *Gemeinschaft* of the pre-industrial epoch. Varieties of Romanticist movements oriented to the past arose. Still others found refuge in fulfillment of the old Lutheran notion of "vocation": the reliable and dutiful performance of one's workday obligations provided dignity and self-worth. Industrialization rapidly occurred, rooted in part in just this diligent Lutheran work ethic, yet it took place devoid of an internal dynamism or an optimism regarding the future. Compared to most other industrializing nations and despite traditions of parliamentary government and local citizen activism in a number of regions, a severely restricted civic sphere in Germany prevented the widespread development of social egalitarianism and representative democracy.

Not surprisingly, "cultural pessimism" became widespread in the 1890s. Despair, doubt, and a sense of crisis extended throughout much of German society (see Mosse, 1964; Ringer, 1969). Many asked repeatedly, what standards can guide persons in the industrial society? How do we live in this new era? *Who* will live in the modern world? How can ethical and compassionate action survive? "Where are to be found," Dilthey asked, "the instruments for surmounting the spiritual chaos which threatens to engulf us?" (see Salomon, 1934, p. 164).

These questions were also Weber's questions. However, unlike many intellectuals of the time, he refused to withdraw from political activism; nor did he become a resigned cultural pessimist.[43] A tireless actor and lifelong player on the stage of German politics, Weber proved an indefatigable critic – marshalling his relentless and piercing ammunition in innumerable speeches and newspaper articles, directing it alike against nearly all major classes and groupings. He condemned Bismarck for crushing all independent leadership; the German monarchy for blatant incompetence and dilettantism; the bourgeoisie for its weak class consciousness and unwillingness to struggle for political power against the state bureaucracy; the agrarian aristocrats for their militarism, authoritarianism, attempts to deny citizenship rights to the working class, and inability to place the nation's interests above their own concerns for material gain; and the German civil servants for their slavish conformity, obsessive adherence to rules and regulations, meekness, and general unwillingness to take responsibility for their decisions. Weber seemed to admire only the German workers, yet he criticized them as well: while appreciating their competence and notion of duty, he lamented their general passivity in the face of authority (especially compared to their counterparts in France).

Major components of his political and social commentary can only be understood as a complex, even convoluted, attempt to address glaring internal weaknesses in the German political culture and to offer sober and realistic mechanisms to overcome them. He wished to retain high standards of living and efficient modes of organizing work and producing goods – and capitalism, he was convinced, offered the best opportunity for the realization of these aims. Yet the many dehumanizing components of this economic system were apparent to him. Weber's thoroughly sociological analysis of his epoch, and the ways in which he responded to its dilemmas with strategies for action, must be examined briefly.

Weber's analysis

Formal rationality appeared in a nearly omnipresent manner, Weber argued, in the bureaucracies of the industrial society. In its major domains – law, the economy, and the state – decision-making occurs "without regard to persons" and by reference to sets of universally applied rules, laws, statutes, and regulations. Favoritism is precluded as well in hiring, promotion, and certification; an adherence to the dictates of abstract procedures holds sway over all concerns for distinctions in respect to status or personality. The "logical-formal" law of our day is implemented by trained jurists who insure that "only unambiguous general characteristics of the case are taken into account in terms of purely processual and legal factors" (Weber, 1968, pp. 656–7), and formal rationality increases in the economy domain to the degree that all technically possible calculations within the "laws of the market" are carried out. Those who would seek to acquire a mortage are treated by a bank's specialists in reference alone to impersonal criteria: credit reports, savings, monthly income, etc. (see ibid., pp. 346, 585, 600, 1186; Weber, 1946c, p. 331).[44]

Weber sees a different type of rationality as dominant in daily life in the industrial epoch: *practical* rationality. The individual's egoistic interests and merely adaptive capacities come here to the fore, and pragmatic, calculating – means–end rational – strategies are typically employed in order to deal with the common obstacles of everyday life in the most expedient manner. As a consequence of their normal activities, all business-oriented strata in particular exhibit a strong tendency to order their ways of life in a self-interested, practical rational manner (see Weber, 2002b, p. 36; 1946e, pp. 279, 284, 293).

Finally, Weber understands modern societies as pervaded by *theoretical* rationality; in fact, their new "world view" – science – cultivates this type of rationality. An abstract confrontation with reality comes here to the fore, and rigorous experiments, precise concepts, and logical deduction and induction become the tools to address and master reality. Whereas theologians and priests in an earlier age adjusted and refined inconsistencies in religious doctrines through theoretical rationalization processes, the same systematic, cognitive search for explanations takes place today – yet now alone in reference to an *empirical* reality. In both cases, reality is mastered through systematic thought and conceptual schemes. Because it requires a step beyond that which can be observed – "a leap of faith" – religion becomes, to the same degree that a scientific world view ascends to a dominating position, defined as "irrational" (Weber, 1946c, pp. 350, 352; 1946d, p. 154; see Kalberg 2002b).[45]

Formal, practical, and theoretical rationality invariably play central roles in industrial societies, Weber argues, forcefully pushing aside arrays of values as well as traditions from the past. However, none is capable of calling forth and giving sustenance to new sets of *noble* values, he contends. The modern-day functionary in bureaucracies orients his action alone to duty, caution, security, conformity, order, reliability, and punctuality. Laws and regulations must be implemented according to procedures of formal correctness and precedent rather than by reference to higher substantive issues: justice, freedom, and equality. Calculations of interests and advantage dominate the practical rationality of daily life. And the scientist of today is engaged in an enterprise that calls to the fore, as the locus of "truth," empirical observation, description, and abstract synthesizing. Knowledge, insight, clarity, and the "tools and the training for thought" result from satisfactory scientific work, rather than values (see Weber, 1946d, pp. 150–1). What domains of modern life "carry" and cultivate compassion, a brotherhood ethic, binding values, ethical responsibility, and charity? Weber searches, but finds none. On the contrary, now unconstrained by constellations of values such as those in the doctrines of the great salvation religions, formal, practical, and theoretical rationality develop more and more freely and unhindered.

To Weber, cold, impersonal, non-binding, and merely conventional relationships more and more rise to the forefront in this "cosmos." While once firmly anchored and given direction by a "devotion to a cause" – a calling – rooted ultimately in coherent and meaningful configurations of values, social relationships are now largely adrift, blowing back and forth according to momentary interests, strategic calculations, cognitive processes, power, rulership orientations, and interpretations of statutes and laws. An uninterrupted flow of activity more and more holds sway, and the life methodically *directed* toward a set of ideals becomes less and less possible. Whereas the motivation to join an ascetic Protestant church or sect could once be explained by reference to sincere belief, the external benefits of membership – acquisition of an entire community's trust and hence its business – often now become central (1946b, pp. 304–5).

In this historically unique epoch in which "material goods have acquired an increasing and, in the end, inescapable power over people" (Weber, 2002b, p. 124), the "interests of daily life" are becoming empowered even to such an extent that they consistently manipulate and exploit values, Weber proclaims. A clear *disjunction* between firm values and ideals held dear on the one hand and the empirical flow of life on the other hand is lessening. Without such standards, the "pragmatic approach to life" more and more reigns, not only pushing aside ethical ideals and all notions of responsibility, but also the autonomous and integrated – or "unified" – personality "directed from within" on the basis of beliefs and values (Weber, 1949, p. 18; 1946c). Massive conformity will result and individual autonomy will disappear. Ideals, ethical action, and noble values must not become, Weber insists, simply dead legacies from the past, for in the end means–end rational calculations will neither offer *dignity* to persons as unique individuals nor prevent the rule of force. *Who* will live in this "steel-hard casing" of "mechanized ossification"?[46] Will only "narrow specialists without mind" and "pleasure-seekers without heart" inhabit the new cosmos (Weber, 2002b, p. 124)? As Albert Salomon, in his classic interpretation of Weber, asks: "Can man – ... conceived as molded by the passions and tensions of a lofty human soul – still find a place for himself in the modern world" (Salomon, 1934, p. 153)?

In what ways did Weber's sociology offer a response to this "crisis of Western Civilization"? What strategies of action remained available to confront these fundamental dangers and dilemmas?

Weber's response

Weber wished to see a constellation of values and ideals in place that would both effectively orient action and offer dignity to individuals. As a self-conscious defender of Western traditions, these were the values of individual autonomy, responsibility, the unified personality, ethical action, brotherhood, compassion, charity, and a sense of honor. Yet his sweeping comparative studies had convinced him that values die out whenever denied their means of sustenance: strong social carriers *and* vigorous competition with other values. As persons develop loyalties and defend their chosen values against others, values become viable and strong. They then more and more guide action and persons formulate, on the basis of them, a sense of dignity and honor. They also provide a firm grounding for initiative-taking and leadership. However, only particular societies nourish values to the point where they become binding upon persons, even at times despite opposing material interests: namely, *dynamic and open* societies in which pluralistic values struggle against one another. In these societies, persons become "responsible" in reference to a set of values and increasingly able to become ethical beings.

Owing to ubiquitous bureaucratization in industrial societies and the rise of formal, practical, and theoretical types of rationality, Weber feared that the contending arenas indispensable for a flourishing of competing values and a realm of freedom were losing their distinct boundaries and collapsing. As this occurred, society would become closed and leaders – defending values – would fade from the social landscape. Societal ossification, driven by the managerial rule of technical efficiency and not unlike the extreme stagnation that had long ago afflicted Egypt and China, more and more appeared to be the fate of "advanced" societies. Indeed, Weber saw an ominous "passion for bureaucratization" that would lead only to "a parcelling out of the soul" (Weber, 1909, p. 414) and a societal-wide passivity in which people are "led like sheep" (Weber, 1978, p. 282). How would it be possible "to save *any remnants* of 'individual' freedom of movement" (Weber, 1968, p. 1403, original emphasis)? "We 'individualists' and partisans of 'democratic' institutions," he proclaimed, "are swimming 'against the tide' of materialist constellations" (Weber, 1978, p. 282, translation altered), and "everywhere the *house of bondage* is already in place" (ibid., p. 281, translation altered, original emphasis; see also pp. 281–2; 1968, pp. 1402–3). Only an outline of the elaborate and complex strategies he proposed can be offered here.[47]

STRONG PARLIAMENTS Weber argued vehemently that modern societies need institutions capable of cultivating leadership qualities on a regular basis. This could occur in parliaments, for here the aggressive articulation of political positions and the hard competition of political parties are accepted as the normal course of affairs. In the process of open debate and conflict over values and interests, yet also negotiation and compromise, leaders with the "three preeminent qualities" for politicians would emerge: passion, responsibility, and a sense of proportion (Weber, 1946a, p. 115–16). Perhaps even leaders with "inner charismatic qualities" would appear (ibid., p. 113), though also leaders with the sense of detachment that allows judgment. Thus, this institution cultivates leadership characterized by an "ethic of responsibility" and a "passionate devotion to a cause" (ibid., p. 115), and prepares leaders to undertake an indispensable task: on the basis of their values and policies, they are empowered to stand against the formal rationality of functionaries, managers, and technocrats. In doing so, they contribute to the expansion of a societal "free space" within which citizens can debate, make responsible decisions, exercise political rights, and defend values. However, for parliaments to serve as such viable "training grounds" for leaders, this institution must stand strong against other branches of government. Weak parliaments, dominated on the one hand by the state's civil servants and on the other hand by authoritarian politicians, such as Bismarck, will not attract persons capable of becoming leaders.

THE SUPPORT FOR DEMOCRACY Parliamentary democracies, Weber believed, far more than other forms of governing, are capable of calling forth the societal dynamism indispensable for the creation of a viable public sphere within which decisions can be rendered in reference to values. Moreover, like strong parliaments, strong democracies would assist the development of strong leaders, as would democracy's ideals: freedom of speech, individual rights, the rule of law, and the right of assembly. "It is a gross self-deception," Weber argued, "to believe that without the achievements of the age of the Rights of Man any one of us, including the most conservative, can go on living" (Weber,

1968, p. 1403). The contesting of power and rulership monopolies, he is convinced, occurs more effectively in democracies.[48]

THE SUPPORT FOR CAPITALISM Ambivalence characterizes Weber's attitude to capitalism. On the one hand he laments repeatedly the ways in which the "laws of the open market" introduce a merciless struggle, formal rationality, and merely functional relationships that cannot realistically be influenced by a brotherhood ethic or ideals of compassion and charity (see Weber, 1946c, pp. 331–3; 1968, pp. 584–5, 635–40). The introduction of such humanitarian concerns into economic relationships taking place in competitive markets almost always leads to economic inefficiencies and economic ruin – "and this would not be helpful in any way" (Weber, 1968, pp. 1186–7). On the other hand, capitalism's open competition and private enterprise call forth energetic entrepreneurs and vigorous risk-takers; these heroic actors, just as does the sheer irregularity and unpredictability of market forces, introduce societal dynamism (ibid., pp. 1403–4). Socialism not only fails to do so, but also implies a further large step in the direction of a closed and stagnant society. It calls forth, to manage the economy, yet another "caste" of functionaries and administrators.

THE NECESSARY CONSTRICTION OF SCIENCE If defined as an endeavor empowered to prescribe values, Weber believed, science posed a threat to the individual's autonomy and, ultimately, to ethical action. Wherever understood as offering "objectively valid" conclusions and wherever a "caste of experts" becomes perceived, in the name of science, as legitimately erecting norms for conduct, science becomes capable of elevating decision-making even out of that domain where it rightfully belongs: the individual's conscience, values, and "demons." Science cannot – and *must* not – inform us how we *should* live (Weber, 1949, p. 58). Notions of ethical responsibility, honor, dignity, and devotion to a cause can be developed, Weber argues, only when persons are starkly aware of their own values – and this takes place alone when individuals are confronted repeatedly with the necessity of making decisions *for themselves*. Moreover, if a science – understood as prescribed norms – becomes broadly institutionalized, decision-making by "specialists" poses a threat to a society's dynamism and capacity for pluralistic conflict.

Hence, the domain of science must be circumscribed by firm boundaries. Its tasks must remain limited to "methods of thinking, the tools and the training for thought," and clarity: assessment of the suitability of the means to reach the given end (including an ethical ideal) and the unintended consequences of action in reference to particular ideals (see Weber, 1946d, pp. 150–1). By fulfilling even these delimited tasks, science can promote self-awareness and enhance a sense of self-responsibility with respect to a set of values:

> *If* you take such and such a stand, then, according to scientific experience, you have to use such and such a *means* in order to carry out your conviction practically....
> Does the end "justify" the means?...Figuratively speaking, you serve this god and you offend the other god when you decide to adhere to [a particular]

position.... Thus, if we [as social scientists] are competent in our pursuit... we can force individuals, or at least we can help [them], to give [themselves] an *account of the ultimate meaning of [their] own conduct*.... I am tempted to say of teachers who succeed in this: [they] stand in the service of "moral" forces; [they] fulfill the duty of bringing about self-clarification and a sense of responsibility. (Weber, 1946d, pp. 151–2; original emphasis)

Accordingly, Weber insists that professors in university classrooms must not offer to students value judgments, personal views, and political opinions. "So long as [they wish] to remain teacher[s] and not to become demagogue[s]" (ibid., p. 151), they must refrain from discussing the conclusions of their research as "truth."[49] Owing to their high prestige *vis-à-vis* students, doing so presents a great danger: an excessive influence upon them might occur and hence a constriction of their autonomous decision-making powers. In turn, students should not expect leadership and guidance from their professors, for science, unlike politics, excludes the activity – the clash of values – on the basis of which leaders arise.

The support for a strong national state

Weber is well known as a proponent of a strong nation. Some interpreters view him as an unreconstructed nationalist who favored the power of the German state for its own sake.

This interpretation evidences little understanding of Weber's sociology, his appreciation of the underlying dilemmas confronted by industrial societies, and his own ultimate ideals and values.[50] As noted, Weber perceived Western values as threatened by a specter of societal stagnation and ossification. Yet he was convinced that neither the smaller states of Europe, nor England or the United States, were capable of defending them. He saw a crass materialism and an exploitative commercialism in these nations as having whittled away Western values, particularly the notion of an autonomous individual. These nations, he argued, remained incapable of mobilizing internally to resist threatening forces effectively. In addition, Weber saw the West as under attack from the East: Russian authoritarianism, civil servant rulership, and economic underdevelopment had failed to call forth either the values of the Enlightenment on the one hand – Reason and Rationality – or those of the "Rights of Man" of the French and American Revolutions on the other.

In this crisis situation, Weber and the vast majority of his colleagues perceived the German state as a bulwark against the loss of the Western tradition's noble values. A *strong* state would be best equipped to make a stand in defense of action on behalf of these values: individual autonomy, self-responsibility, the unified personality, ethical action, brotherhood, compassion, charity, and a sense of honor. Furthermore, according to him, the German state would not, if it acted alone on behalf of German nationalism, fulfill its "responsibility before history." Rather, Germany now must undertake a far more monumental task: to defend Western values for *all* Western countries. The advance of formal, practical, and theoretical rationality, as well as the functionary's caution, conformity, and striving for security, he argued, was occurring in all industrializing countries, even in the United States.[51]

Weber hoped that strong parliaments, a dynamic democracy, a vigorous capitalism, a modern science lacking a legitimacy to pronounce "correct" values for persons, and a strong national German state would forestall the advance of bureaucratization on the one hand and formal, practical, and theoretical types of rationality on the other. To the extent that this occurred, a series of forces would crystallize to oppose societal ossification and to construct the dynamic *civic* arena so woefully lacking in Germany. As this took place, the fundamental precondition for the nourishing of values would come to the fore: a societal openness that allowed – even fostered – perpetual conflicts over values (*Wertkämpfe*).

Wherever noble values became empowered to orient action, all those aspects of the West Weber held dear, he was convinced, would be defended. The random push and pull of daily life interests and mundane concerns, and the mere "sterile excitation" they give rise to, would then be counterbalanced. Life could become *directed* on behalf of ethical ideals and a passion for "causes" would be awakened: "For nothing is worthy of man as man unless he can pursue it with passionate devotion" (Weber, 1946d, p. 135). And individuals would then practice an "ethic of responsibility" and become accountable for their own actions. Finally, and of pivotal significance to Weber, the ethical ideal itself places a thrust toward community into motion: "The ethical norm and its 'universal validity' create a community, or at least in so far as an individual might reject the act of another on moral grounds and yet still face it and participate in the common life. Knowing his own creaturely weakness, the individual places himself under the common norm" (Weber, 1946c, p. 342).

Yet Weber remains alternately pessimistic about the future and unwilling to predict its contours: "No one yet knows who will live in this steel-hard casing and whether entirely new prophets or a mighty rebirth of ancient ideas and ideals will stand at the end of this prodigious development. *Or*, however, if neither, whether a mechanized ossification, embellished with a sort of rigidly compelled sense of self-importance, will arise" (Weber, 2002b, p. 124).[52] Nonetheless, precisely these overarching concerns drove his scholarly research far and wide. Only comparative investigations could assist Weber to define clearly the ways in which the economies, laws, rulership forms, and religions of the West were unique, to assess possibilities regarding social change, and to understand better the social constellations that assisted an anchoring of meaningful action in values and ethical ideals.

WEBER'S IMPACT

Weber has been acclaimed universally as a sociologist of sweeping range, insight, and conceptual powers, and his works have had a significant impact upon sociology.[53] Remarkably, his influence has resulted more from several of his pivotal essays than from a wide-ranging acceptance of his sociology (see Kalberg, 1996; 1998, pp. 209–14).

Although best known as an "idealist," or an advocate of the power in history of ideas and values, he firmly rejected this position. This odd turn resulted in part from the search by American critics of Karl Marx in the 1940s and 1950s for a strong advocate for their cause, in part from the misleading interpretation by Weber's earliest proponent, Talcott Parsons, and in part from the early translation of *PE* (1930) and the late translation of *E&S* (1968). Weber's "idealism" could be seen throughout the 1940s and 1950s in the works of innumerable "modernization" theorists, all of whom had noted his emphasis upon the importance of a set of values for the rise of the spirit of capitalism and expanded upon it. These theorists argued on behalf of the central significance of values for the unfolding of modern democracies and economies.[54]

Yet Weber's impact expanded far beyond the modernization theorists. As early as the 1930s *PE* had begun to influence empirical research in the sociology of religion, especially with regard to comparisons between Protestants and Catholics. In the 1940s and 1950s his essay on the bureaucracy became hotly debated by students of modern organizations,[55] and in the 1950s and 1960s "Class, Status, Party" (Weber, 1968, pp. 926–40) became widely viewed as offering a necessary correction to Marxian stratification theory. During this same period his writings on the sociology of law and urban sociology became acknowledged as core contributions to these subdisciplines (see Weber, 1968, pp. 641–900, 1212–372). As a consequence of his emphasis upon power and rulership, Weber became understood in the 1960s and 1970s as a major contributor to "conflict theory" and to political sociology. In the 1970s his attention to the ways in which the state may develop autonomously played a role in the rise of "state-centered theory," and his essay on charismatic leadership and its routinization stimulated research in the area of social movements. In the 1970s and 1980s *E&S* indirectly influenced the new field of comparative-historical sociology. Weber's notion that the social sciences must practice an ethos of value neutrality, although articulated by many others as well, gained full acceptance in the 1950s and has remained to this day a central cornerstone in American sociology. The impact of his work has been a sustained one and a variety of subdisciplines have claimed him as their founder.

Nonetheless, a coherent school of disciples has failed to crystallize – a fact explained only partly by the unavailability, until recently, of major segments of Weber's works in English or by the great complexity and breadth of his writings. Rather, foundational tenets of his sociology stand in opposition to the predominantly Durkheimian orientation of macrosociology in the United States and powerful barriers resist a *Weberian sociology*: the central place of organic holism, social structure, institutions, "society," and functional explanations conflicts with his attention to subjective meaning, ideal types, societal domains, power, conflict, an intimate interlocking of past and present, and a radical multi-causality that stresses *both* "ideas and interests"; the aim in American sociology to formulate general laws opposes Weber's value-relevance axiom and his goal to offer causal explanations of unique cases. Furthermore, the widespread focus among sociologists in the USA upon the "question of social order" in specific societies stands against the intercivilizational and outward-looking thrust of his works; the advocacy in America of a "naturalistic" understanding of concepts – as fully capturing reality – opposes the value-relevance axiom and Weber's anchoring of sociology in ideal types; the broad orientation of sociologists in the USA to social roles remains incompatible with his stress upon subjective meaning, organizations, status groups, and societal domains; and the frequent emphasis in the USA upon evolution and unilinear progress conflicts with Weber's cognizance of paradox, historical accident, unforeseen consequences, and the routinization of charisma, as well as his insistence upon the contextual embeddedness of action and the ubiquitous penetration of the past into the present.

To Weber, the present can be comprehended only by reference to an array of historical backdrop forces, yet the forward-looking orientation of American sociology downplays just such influences. In the United States, sociology has only rarely formulated theories capable of conceptualizing the many ways in which cultural forces, for example, stand behind and influence the contours of interest- and power-based struggles and, conversely, power and interests stand behind value-based conflicts – indeed, to such a degree that a dynamism rooted in the tensions between these contending forces frequently characterizes social life. Moreover, Weber's forceful acknowledgment of the significance, for causal explanations, of the manner in which *configurations* of forces crystallize in unique ways places his sociology firmly in opposition to all diffusion theories and all analyses rooted in historical analogies (see Kalberg, 1994a, 1994b, pp. 168–92, 1999, 2001).

These major tenets of his sociology lead Weber frequently to a "perspectival" mode of procedure in which related ideal types are compared and contrasted in respect to the subjective meaning each implies (such as asceticism–mysticism, Confucianism–Puritanism, feudalism–patrimonialism). However, his mode of analysis, rooted in ideal types, places his sociology strictly against all schools that utilize *global* dichotomies (such as tradition–modernity and particularism–universalism), as well as all evolutionary, Social Darwinist, and "universal stage" theories. Thus, it is not surprising that major recent currents in American sociology have opposed Weber: largely rooted in survey research methods, comparative sociology today lacks a notion of subjective meaning and an acknowledgment of the importance of historical forces; state-centered theory and world systems theory both downplay cultural forces, as well as subjective meaning; neofunctionalism opposes Weber's insistence upon the omnipresence of power, rulership, and conflict; and rational choice theory utilizes only one of Weber's four "types of social action" and abjures all situating of individual action within contexts of traditions and values (see Kalberg, 1996).

AN ASSESSMENT

Large questions about the modern world drove Weber's sociology. What is the fate of ethical action, the unique individual, the personality unified by reference to a constellation of noble values, and compassion in the industrial society?

What does the rise of modern capitalism imply for the "type of person" who will live within this new cosmos? What defines the particularity of the West? How have we arrived at our present situation? How do persons in different social contexts formulate subjective meaning in their lives? What sets of social forces lead persons to attach meaning to specific activities? How can we understand the subjectively meaningful action of persons in other civilizations and epochs on their own terms rather than by reference to a hierarchy of Western values? What are the parameters for social change in the West?

Sociologists today only rarely ask questions of this magnitude. Very delimited themes guide research and broad queries are confined to the misty, non-scientific realms of social philosophy. As Weber himself noted, the social sciences require specialized skills and involve specialized research questions. Moreover, if he had not "translated" these wide-ranging questions in his own investigations into rigorous concepts, research strategies, modes of analysis, and methodological axioms, his writings would be understood today as simply a set of commentaries upon the rapidly changing era in which he lived – and only intellectual historians would study them. A *Weberian sociology* would not exist.

Weber created a rigorous and distinct approach that combined concrete, empirical description with theoretical generalization. Distinguished by its staggering comparative and historical breadth, his sociology investigates the social action of persons by reference to values, traditions, interests, and emotions. It seeks to offer causal analyses of unique cases and proceeds by reference to ideal types, societal domains, social contexts, and the exploration of subjective meaning. His studies emphasize that the past is ineluctably intertwined with the present and assert that the orientation of social action to religious, economic, rulership, legal, familial, and status group factors *all* must be acknowledged as causally significant; geographical forces, power, social carriers, historical events, competition, conflict, and technology must also be recognized as viable causal forces. While Weber remains fully cognizant that some societies may become, in certain epochs and as a result of multiple identifiable action-orientations, more closed or even ossified, he scorns organic holism and takes omnipresent conflict and power for granted. However, he also sees that regularities of action – continuities and patterns – arise ubiquitously on the basis of values, traditions, interests, and even emotions.

Moreover, he is convinced that persons repeatedly view rulership as legitimate and render obedience, yet they also from time to time overthrow established ruling groups – only then to erect further authorities. Social change is inevitable, even though it never follows an evolutionary or lawful pathway. Yet it cannot be comprehended by reference *alone* to "material" or "ideal" factors, and least of all to transcendent forces, mysterious causes, or "ultimate" determinants. And while material interests possess a strong grip upon everyday activities, persons are also capable of orienting their action to values, conventions, customs, habits, and emotions, even when doing so flies in the face of their economic well-being. Meaning is formulated in a vast variety of ways, though internally consistent sets of values that address ultimate questions – world views – have congealed in the major civilizations to set the "tracks" within which meaningful action becomes defined (see Kalberg, forthcoming). In studying relationships, groups, organizations, epochs, and civilizations of interest to them, sociologists take as their task the interpretive understanding of meaningful action. However, they also seek to understand the social dynamics that give birth to specific meaningful patterns of action and sustain them, and the further social forces that lead to their alteration.

Although impressive in many ways, Weber's ambitious approach is not without weaknesses. Its sheer complexity and frequent lack of clarity have led often to the charge of inconsistency. For example, while subjective meaning stands at the center of his methodological writings, the language Weber utilizes in his comparative-historical works frequently leaves the impression that structural forces constitute his concern.[56] The translations have constituted a longstanding problem in just this respect, and many Anglo-Saxon readers have accused Weber of becoming, in violation of his own methodological premises, a structural sociologist. Other interpreters have found the concept at the foundation of Weber's approach troublesome: the ideal type. Guidelines for its formation and application, it is argued, have remained imprecise and insufficient. These same opponents have generally rejected Weber's view that sociological generalization is appropriately limited to the conceptual level only.

Further common criticisms have cut to the core of Weber's sociology. Many have faulted his orientation to subjective meaning as such, questioning the viability of an approach that takes motives as pivotal. A number of more recent sociologists insist that interaction, creativity, identity formation, and narrative accounts must constitute the fundamental level of analysis. Moreover, while subjective meaning rooted in means–end rational action may be identifiable, critics contend further that value-based subjective meaning will always remain amorphous and problematic. Indeed, some have questioned whether an analytic armament that includes traditions and values is at all necessary for sociologists: persons act, they argue, by reference on the one hand to pragmatic interests and on the other hand to external constraints and power.

Not surprisingly, organic holists have attacked Weber's elevation of ideal types and subjective meaning to the center of his methodology and lamented the absence of their major explanatory concepts – "society" and "institutions" – as well as Weber's indifference to "the problem of social order." Many of these same commentators have viewed his definition of sociology's aim – to offer causal explanations of unique cases – as exceedingly modest. In rejecting Weber's view of theory as an endeavor in the service of heuristic ends only and hence as always provisional, and his value-relevance axiom, they seek to establish a sociology empowered to articulate the general "laws of social life," to offer predictions about the future, and, in the name of science, to assist policy-makers and confront injustice. Remarkably, Marxists and neo-Marxists have on these points agreed with the organic holism tradition: the principled incapacity of Weber's sociology to formulate clear-cut mechanisms for social change, let alone avenues of emancipation from modern capitalism, renders his works, they contend, in the end too beholden to the status quo. Weber's critics from the Left argue as well that this "bourgeois" character of his sociology is apparent in its putative "idealism," its failure to elevate material interests to the level of a preeminent causal force, and its unwillingness to recognize the "laws of history."

The strengths and weaknesses of Weber's rich sociology will undoubtedly be debated for many years to come. Even as an array of his essays continues to be widely discussed, the opposition by many schools to the core features of his approach will endure. Nonetheless, as the microchip and globalization revolutions reach into the twenty-first century and continue to bring diverse peoples into direct contact, a place remains for a comparative-historical sociology oriented to the investigation and understanding – on its own terms – of the subjective meaning of persons near and far.

Acknowledgment

I would like to thank Abdullah Al-Wagdani, Robert J. Antonio, Mathias Bös, Lewis A Coser, Guenther Roth, Konstanze Senge, and Kurt H. Wolff for very helpful criticisms and suggestions.

Notes

1 A number of studies examine Weber's life. See Gerth and Mills (1946, pp. 3–44), Loewenstein (1966, pp. 91–104), Honigsheim (1968), Coser (1971, pp. 234–43), Marianne Weber (1975), Kaesler (1988, pp. 1–23) and Roth (1997).

2 That these major currents of thought remained otherwise so difficult to render into a unity laid the foundation for tensions that run throughout Weber's sociology, as will become apparent.

3 His rejection of these positions led him to adopt the ideal type as his major research tool. This construct cut through the middle of the *Methodenstreit* and addressed several of its seemingly irreconcilable conflicts: (a) although "general" and "synthetic," it constitutes only a heuristic tool rather than a historical law; and (b) although formulated in reference to the researcher's interests and values rather than an "objective" reality, the knowledge it provides is verifiable.

4 The frequent translation of Weber's term *Entwicklung* (development) as "evolution" has caused a great deal of confusion.

5 Although nowhere discussed, Weber surely saw Durkheim's elevation of "social facts" to the core of his sociology in the same manner: as a manifestation of a mode of thought still penetrated by the secularized legacies of Western religions.

6 It is also inconceivable that Weber's sociology would have acquired one of its major strengths without having taken this epistemological turn away from a Eurocentric social science, as well as from all quasi-religious and organicist schools: its relentless "perspectivalism," or its capacity to "rotate" factors. This procedure holds a single ideal type (e.g. asceticism) "up to the light" from the perspective of a radically varying ideal type (e.g. mysticism), and then systematically examines the differences with respect to the influence of each upon social action. The "angle of vision" (*Gesichtspunkt*) remains central; "actual reality" – all absolutism – is omitted. Weber is especially fond of noting that a particular phenomenon (e.g. the mystic's withdrawal from the world) is fully "irrational" from the point of view of a second phenomenon (e.g. the "inner-worldly" ascetic's orientation to worldly activity). See Weber (1946c, p. 326), Jaspers (1946, pp. 37–8).

7   "It is . . . a fundamental fact of all history that the ultimate result of political activity often – no, actually regularly – stands in a completely inadequate and often even paradoxical relation to its original meaning" (Weber, 1946a, p. 117).

8   Following Weber, I will be using the terms "meaningful action" and "social action" synonymously. Despite his emphasis upon the *capacity* of the human species to bestow subjective meaning upon action, Weber nonetheless argues that this often does not occur: "In the great majority of cases *actual* action goes on in a state of inarticulate half-consciousness or actual unconsciousness of its 'subjective meaning.' Actors are more likely to 'feel' this meaning in a vague sense than to 'know' it or explicitly to 'make themselves' aware of it. In most cases action is governed by impulse or habit; the subjective meaning of the action (whether rational or irrational) is only occasionally elevated into consciousness. This occurs in the uniform action of large numbers only in the case of a few individuals. Meaningful action that is actually effective – that is, when the meaning is fully conscious and apparent – is in empirical reality a marginal case. Every sociological or historical investigation that analyzes empirical reality must acknowledge this situation. However, sociology should not, for this reason, hesitate to construct its *concepts* through a classification of possible 'subjective meanings'; in other words, as if action consciously oriented to meaning actually occurs" (Weber, 1968, pp. 21–2; translation altered, original emphasis). For this reason, as well as his stress upon *four* types of action (see below), Weber cannot be understood simply as a "rationalist" thinker, as many critics have asserted (see, for example, Eder, 1999, pp. 202–3).

9   He points out that his classification does not seek to exhaust all possibilities, "but only to formulate in conceptually pure form certain sociologically important types to which actual action is more or less closely approximated" (Weber, 1968, p. 26). Weber does not expect to discover *empirical* cases in which social action is oriented *only* to one of these types of action. See the section below on ideal types.

10 Motives for Weber are causes of action: "A motive is a complex of subjective meaning which seems to the actor himself or to the observer an adequate ground for the conduct in question" (Weber, 1968, p. 11).

11 Of the four types of social action, Weber found means–end rational action to be the most easily understandable by the sociologist (see Weber, 1968, p. 5). In all cases, the interpretation of subjective meaning by the researcher must be based upon empirical evidence and rigorous procedures. Nonetheless, it may be quite difficult, Weber acknowledges, for the social scientist to understand certain action as subjectively meaningful. He notes that values "often cannot be understood completely" (ibid.). Yet this problem does not prevent him from formulating an ideal toward which researchers should strive. And, again, in-depth exploration of the contexts within which action occurs will, he argues, assist understanding. Finally, Weber notes: "The more we ourselves are capable of such emotional reactions as anxiety, anger, ambition, envy, jealousy, love, enthusiasm, pride, vengefulness, loyalty, devotion, and appetites of all sorts, and of the 'irrational' reactions which grow out of them, the more readily can we empathize with them. Even when such emotions are found in a degree of intensity of which the observer himself is completely incapable, he can still have a significant degree of emotional understanding of their meaning and can interpret intellectually their influence on the direction of action and the selection of means" (ibid., p. 6, translation altered).

12 "For the subjective interpretation of action in sociological work these collectivities must be treated as *solely* the resultants and modes of organization of the particular

acts of individual persons, since these alone can be treated as agents in a course of subjectively understandable action" (Weber, 1968, p. 13).

13   This distinguishes the "empirical sciences of action," according to Weber, from jurisprudence, logic, ethics, and aesthetics, all of which aim to ascertain "true" and "valid" meanings (Weber, 1968, p. 4).

14   Weber makes this general point further in the chapter on rulership (*Herrschaft*) in part I of *E&S*: "Hence, the kind of terminology and classification set forth above has in no sense the aim – indeed, it could not have it – to be exhaustive or to confine the whole of historical reality in a rigid scheme. Its usefulness is derived from the fact that in a given case it is possible to distinguish what aspects of a given organized group can legitimately be identified as falling under or approximating one or another of these categories" (Weber, 1968, pp. 263–4; Kalberg, 1994b, pp. 84–91).

15   "The existence of a connection between two historical occurrences cannot be captured abstractly, but only by presenting an internally consistent view of the way in which it was concretely formed" (Weber, 1968, p. 2).

16   Weber makes this point even more vividly in a later essay: "The origin of economic rationalism [of the type which, since the sixteenth and seventeenth centuries, has come to dominate the West] depends not only on an advanced development of technology and law but also on the capacity and disposition of persons to *organize their lives* in a practical-rational manner" (Weber, 2002a, p. 160; original emphasis; see also 1946e, p. 293).

17   Only an abbreviated version can be offered here (see Kalberg, 1996, e.g. pp. 58–63; 2002).

18   Weber defines an "ethical" standard as "a specific type of value-rational *belief* among individuals which, as a consequence of this belief, imposes a normative element upon human action that claims the quality of the 'morally good' in the same way that action which claims the status of the 'beautiful' is measured against aesthetic standards" (Weber, 1968, p. 36, translation altered, original emphasis). Social action, Weber contends, can be influenced by an ethical standard even if "external" support for it is lacking and even, at times, despite opposing "external" forces.

19   Rather than a "determinative" relationship, Weber sees an "elective affinity" (*Wahlverwandtschaft*) between the Protestant ethic and the spirit of capitalism. (The earlier translation by Parsons of *Wahlverwandtschaft* as "correlation" is inadequate.) This "weak causal" manner of stating the relationship results in part from Weber's position that the sources of the spirit of capitalism are many and that religious sources constitute *only one* – however significant and not to be neglected – possible source (see Weber, 2002b, p. 49; 1927, pp. 352–67): "It should here be ascertained only whether and to what extent religious influences *co*-participated in the qualitative formation and the quantitative expansion of [the spirit of capitalism] over the world" (Weber, 2002b, p. 49; original emphasis). He notes: "One of the constitutive components of the modern capitalist spirit . . . was the rational organization of life on the basis of the *idea of the calling*. It was born out of the spirit of *Christian asceticism*" (ibid., p. 122; original emphasis).

20   This theme is also prominent in a massive, more historical work by Weber; see *General Economic History* (1927).

21   For this reason, *E&S* is organized around these domains. The unfortunate title of this opus, which stems from Weber's wife, leaves the impression that his sociology is organized around a notion of "society." The title Weber gave to *E&S*'s major section – "The Economy and the Societal Domains and Powers" – points to the centrality of societal domains.

22   Weber saw a particular "methodical rational organization of life" as having a significant impact upon the development of the modern West: the ascetic Protestant.

23   *Herrschaft* is normally translated as either "authority" or "domination." Neither of these terms captures *Herrschaft*'s *combination* of both authority and domination, and hence I am using Benjamin Nelson's translation: "rulership."

24   On this usage of the ideal type, see generally Kalberg (1994b, pp. 87–91).

25   Weber emphasizes explicitly the character of rulership as nothing more than meaningful action-orientations: "Rulership does not mean that a superior elementary force asserts itself in one way or another; it refers to a meaningful interrelationship between those giving orders and those obeying, to the effect that the expectations toward which action is oriented on both sides can be reckoned upon" (Weber, 1968, p. 1378).

26   And: "Experience shows that in no instance does rulership voluntarily limit itself to the appeal to material or affectual or ideal motives as a basis for its continuance. In addition, every such system attempts to establish and to cultivate the belief in its legitimacy" (Weber, 1968, p. 213).

27   For Weber's earlier formulations in Part II, see p. 954; more generally, see pp. 262–3, 953–4, 947. In empirical reality, of course, rulership always appears in some mixture of these pure types. These three models do not represent an attempt by Weber to capture an "evolutionary" drift of history up to the contemporary era (see below).

28   Charismatic rulership is examined below. With regard to traditional rulership, Weber emphasizes: "The validity of a social order by virtue of the sacredness of tradition is the oldest and most universal type of legitimacy" (Weber, 1968, p. 37). On traditional rulership generally, see Weber (1946e, p. 296; 1968, pp. 1041, 958, 1006–7, 216, 226–7).

29   On Weber's dynamic models, see Kalberg (1994b, pp. 95–8); on his contextual models, see ibid. (pp. 39–46, 98–102).

30   As opposed to "culture" (literature, art, science, etc.).

31   For further examples, see Kalberg (1994b, pp. 102–17). These pages also include a discussion of *intra*-domain relationships of antagonism (e.g. the antagonism of charismatic rulership to traditional and bureaucratic rulership).

32   *E&S* also constructs numerous models of antagonism *within* domains. For a discussion of these models, see Kalberg (1994b, pp. 106–8).

33   To Weber, the purity of charisma can be preserved against everyday interests only by the "common danger of military life or a love ethos of an unworldly discipleship" (Weber, 1968, p. 1120).

34   Weber's attention in this model to the role played by pragmatic interests reveals the "sober realism" side of his sociology neglected in the reception of his works influenced by Parsons. Weber also formulates developmental models that chart the closure of social relationships and the monopolization of resources in the economy, rulership, and religion domains (see Kalberg, 1994b, pp. 120–4). Further developmental models outline the rise of formal rationality in regard to the free market and the state, and a "theoretical" rationalization process in the domain of religion (see ibid., pp. 128–40). Qualitatively different "rationalization processes" – in the sense of increasing systemization of social action – are charted, as developmental models, in the rulership, law, religion, and economy societal domains. In investigating the economy in relation to the rulership, religion, and law domains, as well as these spheres of life in relationship to one another, *E&S* formulates a vast *rationalization of action theoretical framework*. These developmental models arrange ideal types along an analytic *course* of increasingly rationalized social action.

35 This is the translation given by Walliman et al. (1980).

36 I have discussed Weber's multicausality, as well as his "conjunctural" mode of establishing causality, in detail in Kalberg (1994b, pp. 32–5, 50–77, 143–92).

37 See also Weber (1927, pp. 368–9; 2002b, pp. 32, 123–4, 243–4n119) and Kalberg (1996, pp. 52–4, 62).

38 On the exceedingly complex relationship between past and present in Weber's sociology, see further Kalberg (1994b, pp. 158–67; 1996, pp. 57–64; 1998, pp. 233–5).

39 *EEWR* also includes two synoptic essays ("Religious Rejections of the World" [1946c] and "The Social Psychology of the World Religions"[1946e]). The major themes in *EEWR* can be only hinted at here. Weber's analyses, for example, of the origins of salvation religions (see Kalberg, 1990, 2002b) and the location of ideas and values in social contexts (see Kalberg, 1994b, pp. 39–46, 98–102; 2002), as well as his analyses of the rise of monotheism (see Kalberg, 1994a), the caste system (see Kalberg, 1994b), and Confucianism (see Kalberg, 1999), must be fully omitted. Weber's masterful analysis of the major tensions in modern Western societies is examined in the "Social Context" section below.

40 Even great charismatic figures, such as prophets, are not viewed by Weber a-contextually. Their influence requires a pre-existing "certain minimum of intellectual discourse" (see Weber, 1968, pp. 486–7).

41 Hence, the common understanding of *EEWR* as a study that utilizes experimental design procedures to isolate the centrality of a particular economic ethic for the development of modern capitalism in the West does not correspond to the methodology Weber actually utilizes in these volumes. On his context-based mode of establishing causality, see Kalberg (1994b, pp. 98–102, 143–92).

42 Although many engaged in these endeavors viewed their activities as ultimately "political" in a broader sense; they sought to prepare Germans to become citizens (see Jenkins, 1996).

43 Many commentators have attended to the famous phrases that conclude some of his books or stand at the center of his political writings and then painted Weber as a bleak and despairing cultural pessimist. These interpretors have focused upon Weber's most prominent image of the future: as an "iron cage" and "house of bondage." Indeed, he remains unequivocally pessimistic in a famous passage in "Politics as a Vocation": "Not summer's bloom lies ahead of us, but rather a polar night of icy darkness and hardness, no matter which group may triumph eternally now" (Weber, 1946a, p. 128). While Weber surely was not an optimistic believer in the unending progress of civilization, as were many American and English social thinkers of his generation, he also cannot be characterized as a dour pessimist. Nor was he a seeker after an idealized past, as his frequently used phrase – "disenchantment (*Entzauberung*) of the world" – has implied to many; his sociological analyses convinced him that this route remained closed. If truly a cultural pessimist or romantic, Weber would have withdrawn into fatalism and passivity, and perhaps even into one of Germany's many "cults of irrationality." Instead, he scorned such cults, mocked the romantics as delusional, and remained an endlessly combative political commentator and actor. The values acquired from his stern Protestant mother precluded any other course.

44 Weber is here formulating ideal types. He is well aware of the many ways in which rule-bound efficiency can be diminished by "red tape."

45 I have addressed these "types of rationality" in greater detail (see Kalberg, 1980).

46   The centrality of individualism (however differently understood) in three schools of
     thought – the French Enlightenment, German Romanticism, and ascetic Protestant-
     ism – again becomes apparent in Weber's analysis.
47   I am here focusing upon his sociological thinking rather than, as is often the case,
     Weber's own political activity. In this regard, Weber was a peripatetic defender of
     individual rights (see Coser, 1971, pp. 242–3, 254–6; Beetham, 1974).
48   Several commentators have argued that Weber's commitment to democracy was not
     one in principle, but was rooted in his view that modern industrial societies con-
     fronted a great danger of societal ossification. It is apparent that Weber, in distrust-
     ing the citizenship skills of the Germans, did not break from the tenor of his times in
     Germany (see Jenkins, 1996). A long period of tutelege in the practices of demo-
     cracy would be necessary, he believed.
49   Weber continues: "Whether, under such conditions, science is a worthwhile 'voca-
     tion' for somebody, and whether science itself has an objectively valuable 'vocation',
     are again value judgments about which nothing can be said in the lecture-room"
     (Weber, 1946d, p. 152).
50   The extreme cosmopolitanism of his own family (see Roth, 1997) also speaks
     against the interpretation that sees Weber as a virulent nationalist.
51   Albeit, in light of an array of forces, at a slower pace than in the European societies
     (Weber, 1946a, pp. 106–14).
52   Weber nearly always, in his sociological writings, qualifies his statements regarding
     the future by the use of terms such as "might," "perhaps," and "potentiality."
53   This section discusses Weber's impact upon American sociology. For an examination
     of his influence upon British sociology, see Albrow (1989).
54   Many proponents of this school misunderstood Weber. In asserting that moderniza-
     tion took place only if certain "functional prerequisites" were fulfilled, Parsons, for
     example, sought to formulate "laws" and a "general theory of society" – thereby
     violating Weber's axiom of value-relevance. Other modernization theorists, arguing
     that economic development would occur only in those countries where a "functional
     equivalent" of the Protestant ethic existed, viewed their research as under the direct
     influence of Weber – all the while neglecting the fundamental *multi*causal, contex-
     tual, and case study orientation of his sociology (see Eisenstadt, 1968, *passim*).
55   However, rather than as an ideal type useful as a "standard" against which empirical
     cases could be compared, Weber's bureaucracy was understood as a depiction of the
     actual workings of this type of organization – and hence criticized as inaccurate
     (mainly for omitting the influence of informal groupings).
56   For example, on behalf of clarity, he should use phrases such as "action oriented to
     feudalism" or "action oriented to Calvinist doctrine." Abjuring such awkward
     phraseology, Weber generally prefers simply "feudalism" and "Calvinism."

Bibliography

Writings of Max Weber

Die Römische Agrargeschichte in Ihrer Bedeutung für das Staats-und Privatrecht [*The
   Significance of Roman Agrarian History for Civil and Private Law*]. 1899. Amster-
   dam: Verlag P. Schippers (1966).
The Prospects for Liberal Democracy in Tsarist Russia. 1906. In W. G. Runciman (ed.),
   Weber: Selections in Translation. Cambridge: Cambridge University Press (1978),
   pp. 269–84.

Debattenreden auf der Tagung des Vereins fuer Sozialpolitik [Debates from the Conference of the Association for Social Policy]. 1909. In Marianne Weber (ed.), *Gesammelte Aufsaetze zur Soziologie und Sozialpolitik*. Tübingen: Mohr, pp. 412–23.

Vorwort [Introduction]. 1914. In K. Buecher, J. Schumpeter, and Fr. Freiherr von Wieser (eds), *Grundriss der Sozialoekonomik, 1. Abt. Wirtschaft und Wirtschaftswissenschaft*. Tübingen: Mohr, pp. vii–ix.

General Economic History. 1927. New York: Free Press.

Politics as a Vocation. 1946a. In H. H. Gerth and C. Wright Mills (eds and trans.), *From Max Weber: Essays in Sociology*. New York: Oxford, pp. 77–128.

The Protestant Sects and the Spirit of Capitalism. 1946b. In *From Max Weber*, pp. 302–22.

Religious Rejections of the World. 1946c. In *From Max Weber*, pp. 323–59.

Science as a Vocation. 1946d. In *From Max Weber*, pp. 129–56.

The Social Psychology of the World Religions. 1946e. In *From Max Weber*, pp. 267–301.

The Methodology of the Social Sciences (edited and translated by Edward A. Shils and Henry A. Finch). 1949. New York: Free Press.

The Religion of China (edited and translated by Hans H. Gerth). 1951. New York: The Free Press.

Ancient Judaism (edited and translated by Hans H. Gerth and Don Martindale). 1952. New York: Free Press.

The Religion of India (edited and translated by Hans H. Gerth and Don Martindale). 1958. New York: Free Press.

Economy and Society (edited by Guenther Roth and Claus Wittich). 1968. New York: Bedminster Press.

Prefatory Remarks. 2002a. In Max Weber, *The Protestant Ethic and the Spirit of Capitalism* (translated by Stephen Kalberg). Los Angeles: Roxbury Publishing, pp. 149–64.

The Protestant Ethic and the Spirit of Capitalism (translated by Stephen Kalberg). 2002b. Los Angeles: Roxbury Publishing.

Further reading

Albrow, Martin (1989) Die Rezeption Max Webers in der britischen Soziologie [The Reception of Max Weber in British Sociology]. In Johannes Weiss (ed.), *Max Weber Heute*. Frankfurt: Suhrkamp, pp. 165–86.

Beetham, D. (1974) *Max Weber and the Theory of Modern Politics*. London: George Allen & Unwin.

Coser, Lewis A. (1971) *Masters of Sociological Thought*. New York: Harcourt Brace Jovanovich.

Eder, K. (1999) Societies Learn and yet the World Is Hard to Change. *European Journal of Social Theory*, 2, 195–216.

Eisenstadt, S. N. (ed.) (1968) *The Protestant Ethic and Modernization*. New York: Basic Books.

Gerth, Hans H. and Wright Mills, C. (1946) Introduction. In *From Max Weber*. New York: Oxford University Press, pp. 3–74.

Honigsheim, Paul (1968) *On Max Weber*. New York: The Free Press.

Jaspers, Karl (1946) *Max Weber: Politiker, Forscher, Philosoph* [*Max Weber: Politician, Researcher, and Philosopher*]. Bremen: Johs. Storm Verlag.

Jenkins, J. (1996) The Kitsch Collections and *The Spirit in the Furniture*: Cultural Reform and National Culture in Germany. *Social History*, 21, 123–41.

Kaesler, Dirk (1988) *Max Weber: an Introduction to His Life and Work*. Chicago: University of Chicago Press.

Kalberg, Stephen (1980) Max Weber's Types of Rationality: Cornerstones for the Analysis of Rationalization Processes in History. *American Journal of Sociology*, 85(3), 1145–79.

Kalberg, Stephen (1985) The Role of Ideal Interests in Max Weber's Comparative Historical Sociology. In Robert J. Antonio and Ronald M. Glassman (eds), *A Weber–Marx Dialogue*, Lawrence, KS: University Press of Kansas, pp. 46–67.

Kalberg, Stephen (1987) The Origins and Expansion of *Kulturpessimismus*: the Relationship Between Public and Private Spheres in Early Twentieth Century Germany. *Sociological Theory*, 5(2), 150–64.

Kalberg, Stephen (1990) The Rationalization of Action in Max Weber's Sociology of Religion. *Sociological Theory*, 8(1), 58–84.

Kalberg, Stephen (1994a) Max Weber's Analysis of the Rise of Monotheism: a Reconstruction. *British Journal of Sociology*, 45(4), 563–83.

Kalberg, Stephen (1994b) *Max Weber's Comparative-Historical Sociology*. Chicago: University of Chicago Press.

Kalberg, Stephen (1996) On the Neglect of Weber's *Protestant Ethic* as a Theoretical Treatise: Demarcating the Parameters of Post-war American Sociological Theory. *Sociological Theory*, 14(1), 49–70.

Kalberg, Stephen (1997) Tocqueville and Weber on the Sociological Origins of Citizenship: the Political Culture of American Democracy. *Citizenship Studies*, 1 (July), 199–222.

Kalberg, Stephen (1998) Max Weber's Sociology: Research Strategies and Modes of Analysis. In Charles Camic (ed.), *Reclaiming the Argument of the Founders*. Cambridge, MA: Blackwell, pp. 208–41.

Kalberg, Stephen (1999) Max Weber's Critique of Recent Comparative-Historical Sociology and a Reconstruction of His Analysis of the Rise of Confucianism in China. In J. M. Lehmann (ed.), *Current Perspectives in Social Theory*. Stamford, CT: JAI Press, pp. 207–46.

Kalberg, Stephen (2001) Should the "Dynamic Autonomy" of Ideas Matter to Sociologists? Max Weber on the Origin of Other-Worldly Salvation Religions and the Constitution of Groups in American Society Today. *Journal of Classical Sociology*, 1(3), 291–327.

Kalberg, Stephen (2002) Introduction to *The Protestant Ethic*. In *Max Weber: the Protestant Ethic and the Spirit of Capitalism*. Los Angeles: Roxbury Publishing Co.

Kalberg, Stephen (forthcoming) *Max Weber's Sociology of Civilizations*.

Loewenstein, K. (1966) *Max Weber's Political Ideas in the Perspective of Our Time*. Amherst: University of Massachusetts Press.

Loewith, Karl (1970) Weber's Interpretation of the Bourgeois-capitalistic World in Terms of the Guiding Principle of "Rationalization." In Dennis Wrong (ed.), *Max Weber*. Englewood Cliffs, NJ: Prentice Hall, pp. 101–23.

Marshall, Gordon (1980) *Presbyteries and Profits: Calvinism and the Development of Capitalism in Scotland, 1560–1707*. Oxford: Clarendon Press.

Mitzman, Arthur (1970) *The Iron Cage*. New York: Knopf.

Mosse, George (1964) *The Crisis of German Ideology*. New York: Grosset & Dunlap.

Ringer, Fritz (1969) *The Decline of the German Mandarins*. Cambridge, MA: Harvard University Press.

Roth, Guenther (1968) Introduction. In Guenther Roth and Claus Wittich (eds and trans.), Max Weber, *Economy and Society*. New York: Bedminster Press, pp. xxvii–ciii.

Roth, Guenther (1997) The Young Max Weber: Anglo-American Religious Influences and Protestant Social Reform in Germany. *International Journal of Politics, Culture and Society*, 10, 659–71.

Salomon, Albert (1934) Max Weber's Methodology. *Social Research*, 1 (May), 147–68.

Salomon, Albert (1935a) Max Weber's Sociology. *Social Research*, 2 (February), 60–73.

Salomon, Albert (1935b) Max Weber's Political Ideas. *Social Research*, 2 (February), 369–84.

Walliman, Isidor, Rosenbaum, Howard, Tatsis, Nicholas, and Zito, George (1980) Misreading Weber: the Concept of "Macht." *Sociology*, 14(2), 261–75.

Weber, Marianne (1975) *Max Weber*, translated by Harry Zohn. New York: Wiley.

6

Émile Durkheim

Robert Alun Jones

The Theory

It is useful to think of social theories as "languages" or "vocabularies" – i.e. ways of thinking or speaking about social phenomena – that are cobbled together by theorists to serve their own, quite concrete interests and purposes. Sociologists whose interest is in the explanation, prediction, and control of human behavior, for example, typically prefer vocabularies containing "thin," abstract, statistical, and mathematical terms. By contrast, those who want to praise or condemn certain behaviors or institutions, establish relations with other cultures or sub-cultures, understand different languages, or grasp the nature of others' suffering will quite naturally prefer "thicker" descriptions, and more interpretive or hermeneutic vocabularies. Sociologists of the first kind tend to view themselves as "discovering facts" about the nature of societies, thus carrying on the tradition of Plato, Kant, Enlightenment rationalism, and modern science. Sociologists of the second type see their allies in Hegel, the Romantics, Nietzsche, Heidegger, James, and Dewey, and are more likely to describe themselves as "constructing narratives" like those of a writer or poet.

Durkheim was clearly a theorist of the first type, i.e. he saw himself as a scientist, "discovering" causal and functional explanations for social facts, which he viewed as a part of nature. But Durkheim's preference for this "scientific" vocabulary, by contrast with its more "literary" counterpart, was still a consequence of his own interests and purposes. The specific nature of these interests and purposes is most obvious in Durkheim's writings on the history and theory of education, and this is where my account of his socio-logical theory will begin. From there, I will move on to a discussion of his sociological method, i.e. the "tool" he used in the effort to realize these interests and purposes. Finally, I will discuss the substantive application of this tool to the study of social facts, including the division of labor, suicide, religion, knowledge, and science itself.

The history and theory of moral education

Shortly after assuming his position at the Sorbonne in 1902, Durkheim began offering a lecture course on the history of educational theory, later published as *The Evolution of Educational Thought* (1938; translated 1977). Throughout history, he observed, the principal aim of education had never been to provide children with "pieces of knowledge," but rather to imbue them with "some deep and internal state of mind, a kind of orientation of the soul which points it in a definite direction, not only during childhood but throughout life" (Durkheim, 1977, p. 30). The Scholastics, for example, evinced an almost superstitious respect toward books, not because they believed these books contained demonstrable truths, but rather because they contained resources useful in *dialectic*, i.e. in scholastic debate. During the Renaissance, this "cult of the book" gave way to a preoccupation with elegance and style, and a form of aesthetic education that Durkheim loathed. But in the seventeenth and eighteenth centuries, this concern for style was in turn replaced by the "pre-eminence of things" – the modern, scientific study of concrete natural phenomena, in all their diversity and complexity. Necessarily secular, Durkheim observed, this modern education must still acknowledge our moral and spiritual needs and, in particular, help us to understand our place in nature, and the extent of our dependence upon it (Durkheim, 1977, pp. 337–8).

A second lecture course on education, published posthumously as *Moral Education* (1925; translated 1961), described the nature of this modern form of education in greater detail. Opposing the Enlightenment notion that there is a single, constant "human nature," Durkheim began by insisting that a society's ideal conception of a person – the kind of moral agent its educational system strives to produce – is relative to each historical period. Educational ideals thus express not the proclivities of individual human nature, but the real needs of real societies; and far from eliciting hidden potentialities within each of us, education actually creates within each of us a new person. Although an ardent supporter of the Third Republic's policies of laicizing the primary and secondary schools, therefore, Durkheim insisted that the historic process of secularizing education could not be simply negative: "It is not enough to cut out," he argued, "we must replace" (Durkheim, 1961, p. 11).

But what kind of person does modern society require? Durkheim's answer comprised three elements. Convinced that the decline of religious authority had left society without any rule or order, Durkheim insisted that the first element of moral education was the "spirit of discipline," i.e. an authoritative constraint existing outside of us, to which our wills and inclinations are subject. This in itself was hardly original, for "discipline" already held an important place in the moral philosophies of Kant and the utilitarians, where it identified and then directed the behavior required by either the categorical imperative or the law of utility. Discipline, in this sense, was necessary to thwart and constrain an otherwise recalcitrant human nature. The distinctive feature of Durkheim's argument – reflecting his more mature understanding of Rousseau – was that discipline was good *intrinsically*, that it was *natural* to human beings because the constraints *themselves* were a part of nature (Durkheim, 1961, pp. 50–1).

Turning to the content of moral education, Durkheim reminded his students that no "egoistic act" – i.e. behavior directed only to the self-interest of the person performing it – had ever been considered moral by any society. But again, Durkheim's point wasn't simply that "moral" acts, by definition, look to the interest of others; on the contrary, a morality elevating the interest of others above those of the self would be self-contradictory, for no person could then accept the other's self-denial. By definition, moral acts must be common and accessible to all, yet at the same time addressed to a living, sentient being outside the self. The only empirically observable entity fitting this definition was the being created by individuals through their association. In this way, Durkheim smoothly folded a major part of the traditional morality of the Church – good works done for others, but ultimately for God – within the secular morality of the Republic, and "the attachment to social groups" thus became the second element of moral education.

As we shall see, this distinction between the "spirit of discipline" and the "attachment to groups" was analogous to a more famous discussion in *Suicide* (1897) – between "regulation" and "integration" – as well as to the more traditional philosophic opposition of "duty" and the "good." But in more traditional usage, Durkheim observed, there is a tension between them: Kantians and rationalists habitually deduce the good from the imperative nature of moral commands, while utilitarians and empiricists frequently derive the sense of duty of the desirability of the consequences of morally obligatory acts. With his typical enthusiasm for the resolution of antinomies, Durkheim insisted that his conception of society as the sole, necessary, and sufficient object of moral conduct contained the means to resolve this contradiction. "Duty" and the "good" are simply two equally appropriate ways of speaking of the same concrete reality: society. There is no genuinely moral act that is not guided by both (Durkheim, 1961, p. 99).

To these two elements of morality, Durkheim then added a third – the autonomy of the individual. For Kant, such autonomy had been the product of the will, guided by a law of pure, transcendent reason (the categorical imperative), imposing itself on the more sensual, inferior aspects of our nature. But our experience of the moral law, Durkheim argued, suggests that it dominates not just our senses, but our reason as well – indeed, our whole nature. Moreover, if the autonomy which Kant would grant us is *logically* possible, it has nothing to do with *reality*, for as creatures both rational and sensual, we would be at war with ourselves.

Instead of a logical autonomy, therefore, Durkheim demanded an effective, progressive autonomy assured only by the study and practice of science. In so far as we *understand* the laws of things – why things are the way they are – we no longer conform out of external constraint, but voluntarily, because it is good to do so, and because we have no more rational alternative. "Conforming to the order of things because one is sure that it is everything it ought to be," Durkheim observed, "is not submitting to a constraint. It is freely desiring this order, assenting through an understanding of the cause" (Durkheim, 1961, p. 115). But the "science" that yields an understanding of these laws is not the product of *individual* reason, any more than *individual* reason created the laws which science understands; rather, science is the *collective* activity dreamed of by Bacon, in which one aspect of nature (society) progressively comprehends another (the physical world).

Durkheim's vocabulary was an attempt to extend this "collective activity" to the understanding of the laws of society. By investigating the degree to which the moral order is founded on the nature of things, he felt that we could learn the extent to which it is as it ought to be, i.e. "normal" rather than "pathological" (see below); and in so far as it is normal, we "freely" (i.e. knowledgeably and consciously) conform. So, henceforth, morality had to be taught by explaining the reasons for things, the causes underlying the particular duties of individuals and groups, and the specific ideals which emerged at certain stages of social evolution. The original element in this argument was not his insistence that this could be done, but his insistence that it could be done without diminishing the dignity and authority of moral rules. As an element of morality itself, the rational comprehension of the reasons for moral rules and ideals became a condition of moral agency itself. For Durkheim, therefore, the study of science – including social science – was itself morally edifying. To produce generations of students capable of such edification was the function not of the Church, but of the School, and, more particularly, of the nascent but rapidly growing discipline of sociology.

Social facts

For Durkheim, sociology was thus an instrument to a larger purpose – the creation of the "new man" of the Republic, to be achieved by confronting generations of French schoolchildren with a moral power greater than them-selves, and thus worthy of their respect and dedication. In *The Rules of Sociological Method* (1895; translated 1982), therefore, Durkheim described sociology as the study of a reality *sui generis*, a group of phenomena different from those studied by any other science. For these phenomena, Durkheim reserved the term *social facts*: "manners of acting, thinking, and feeling external to the individual, which are invested with a coercive power by virtue of which they exercise control over him" (Durkheim, 1982, p. 52). Since these facts consisted of actions, thoughts, and feelings, they could not be confused with biological phenomena; but neither were they the province of psychology, for they existed outside the individual *conscience*.

In addition to defining the subject matter of sociology, *The Rules* was explicit on how social facts were to be recognized and observed. Because the essential trait of social facts is their external coercive power, for example, they could be recognized by the existence of some predetermined legal sanction or, in the case of moral and religious beliefs, by their reaction to forms of individual belief and action perceived as threatening; and where the exercise of social constraint was less direct, as in those forms of economic organization which give rise to anomie (see below), their presence was more easily ascertained by their "generality combined with objectivity," i.e. by how widespread they are within the group, while also existing independently of any particular forms they might assume. Like Francis Bacon, Durkheim also warned us of the quite natural tendency to take our *ideas* of things – what Bacon called *notiones vulgares, praenotiones*, or "idols" – for the *things themselves*. So the most basic rule of all sociological method is *to treat social facts as things*. Other rules followed. As we will see in the discussion of *Suicide* (1897) and *The Elementary Forms of the Religious Life* (1912), for example, the subject matter of research was to include a group of phenomena defined beforehand by certain common external characteristics, and all phenomena corresponding to this definition had to be included; and Durkheim also insisted that sociologists consider social facts from a perspective independent of their individual manifestations.

Normal and pathological

It is by following such rules, as we have seen, that the sociologist can learn the degree to which the moral order is founded on the nature of things, and thus the extent to which it is as it ought to be. This meant that the sociologist must be able to distinguish between the "normal" and "pathological" forms of social facts. "Normal" social facts are simply those found in many, if not all, cases, most of the time, while social facts are "pathological" if they are encountered only in a minority of cases, and for brief periods.

Despite centuries of effort at its annihilation, for example, crime has increased with the growth of civilization. A certain rate of crime, Durkheim thus argued, is a normal social fact, intimately bound up with the conditions of social life. Durkheim wasn't simply saying that crime is a necessary evil. On the contrary, he was arguing that crime is both *necessary* and *useful*. If we consider "crime" as Durkheim did – i.e. as an action that offends strong, well defined collective feelings – then such actions could be eliminated in a society only by a dramatic increase in the strength of these feelings; but if this occurred, those weaker states of collective sentiment, whose milder reactions previously acknowledged mere "breaches of convention," would also be strengthened, and what was merely "unconventional" would automatically become criminal. Moreover, for sentiments to change, they can be only moderately intense, while the only condition under which crime could cease – as we have just seen – must be one in which collective sentiments had attained an unprecedented intensity. The criminal thus becomes the price we pay for the idealist and the reformer.

By contrast with the "normality" of crime, Durkheim described the "forced" and "anomic" forms of the division of labor, as well as the extraordinarily high rates of "egoistic" and "anomic" suicide, as pathological. Consistent with his notion that the sociologist was a kind of physician, he then called for "therapeutic treatment," which – as Durkheim despaired of the modern state to perform such a regulative function – meant an increased role for occupational groups in the supervision of insurance, welfare, and pensions, the settling of contractual disputes, the regulation of working conditions, but above all exercising moral authority over the aspirations of upwardly mobile citizens of the Republic (Durkheim, 1893, translated 1984, pp. 291–328; 1897, translated 1951, pp. 378–84).

Causal and functional explanation

Durkheim was careful to avoid any "teleological" confusion of the *function* of a social fact (the role it plays with regard to individual or social needs) with its *cause* (the fact which brought it into existence). For once we recognize that social facts are real things, external to and coercive upon human beings, it becomes clear that no human need or desire, however imperious, could be sufficient to such an effect. Needs and desires might intervene to hasten or retard social development, but they cannot themselves create any social fact. The association of individual human beings creates a social reality of a new kind, and it is in the facts of that association rather than the needs and interests of the associated elements that the explanation for social facts is to be found.

This led Durkheim to some rules of sociological explanation. When the sociologist attempts to explain a social phenomenon, for example, the efficient cause which produces it and the function it fulfills must be investigated separately. Second, the determining cause of a social fact must he sought among the antecedent social facts, and not among the states of the individual consciousness. Durkheim went so far as to insist that "every time a social phenomenon is directly explained by a psychological phenomenon, we may rest assured that the explanation is false" (Durkheim, 1982, p. 129). Finally, while Durkheim did not deny that a social fact may serve individual needs and interests, sociologists should still seek its function in its socially useful effects (Durkheim, 1982, pp. 134–5).

To demonstrate that one phenomenon is the cause of another, we can only compare those cases where both are simultaneously present (or absent), and ask whether the variations they display in these different circumstances suggest that one depends upon the other. Where the two phenomena are produced artificially by the observer, we call this method *experimentation*; and where the artificial production of phenomena is impossible, we compare them as they have been produced naturally, a procedure called *indirect experimentation*, or the *comparative method*. Here Durkheim embraced J. S. Mill's theory of "concomitant variation" – the notion that phenomena that vary together are connected through some fact of causation. For the manner in which a phenomenon develops reveals its internal nature, and where two phenomena develop in the same way, there must thus be some internal connection between the natures thus revealed.

The function of the division of labor

Durkheim's purpose in *The Division of Labor in Society* (1893, translated 1984) was to show that the increasing rate of occupational specialization in Western societies is a social fact which can be explained, both causally and functionally, by following the principles just described. Beginning with the functional explanation, Durkheim pointed out that, while we like those who resemble us, we are also drawn toward those who are different. But if difference is thus as much a source of mutual attraction as likeness, only *certain kinds* of differences attract, i.e. where we seek in others what we lack in ourselves. Associations are formed wherever there is such a true exchange of services – in short, wherever there is a division of labor. Durkheim thus argued that the economic services rendered by the division of labor are trivial by comparison with its *moral* effect. The true function of the division of labor is that feeling of solidarity in two or more persons which it creates, rendering possible societies which, without it, would not exist.

To determine the extent to which modern societies depend upon this kind of solidarity, Durkheim classified different types of law according to the sanctions associated with them: *repressive* sanctions (characteristic of criminal law) consist of some loss or suffering inflicted on the agent; *restitutive* sanctions (characteristic of civil, commercial, procedural, administrative, and constitutional law) consist only of "the re-establishment of troubled relations to their normal state" (Durkheim, 1984, p. 69). Durkheim was thus able to define two types of solidarity. The first was *mechanical solidarity*, that type of solidarity characterized by the repressive sanctions imposed upon crimes. Since all crimes have one element in common – i.e. they shock sentiments which, "for a given social system, are found in all healthy consciences" – Durkheim was led directly to his important concept of the *conscience collective*: "the totality of beliefs and sentiments common to the average citizens of the same society" (Durkheim, 1984, p. 79). Durkheim endowed the *conscience collective* with quite distinctive characteristics: it forms a determinate system with its own life; it is "diffuse" in each society and lacks a "specific organ"; it is independent of the particular conditions in which individuals find themselves; it is the same in different locations, classes, and occupations; it connects successive generations rather than changing from one to another; and it is different from individual *consciences*, despite the fact that it can be realized only through them.

Durkheim thus introduced an idea which would assume increasing importance in his later work – the duality of human nature. Briefly, in each of us there are two *consciences*: one containing states personal to each of us, representing and constituting our individual personality; the other containing states common to all, representing society, and without which society would not exist. When our conduct is determined by the first, we act out of self-interest; but when it is determined by the second, we act morally, in the interest of society. Thus the individual, by virtue of his resemblance to other individuals, is linked to the social order. This is mechanical solidarity, which, as we have seen, is manifested through repressive law; and the greater the number of repressive laws, the greater the number of social relations regulated by this type of solidarity. The nature of *restitutive* sanctions, however, indicates that there is a different type of social solidarity which corresponds to civil law; for the restitutive sanction is not punitive, vengeful, or expiatory at all, but consists only of a return of things to their previous, normal state. This is the type of solidarity that Durkheim called *organic*, i.e. where mechanical solidarity presumes that individuals resemble one another, organic solidarity presumes their difference; again, where mechanical solidarity is possible only in so far as the individual personality is submerged in the collectivity, organic solidarity becomes possible only in so far as each individual has a sphere of action peculiar to him. For organic solidarity to emerge, therefore, the *conscience collective* must leave untouched a part of the individual *conscience*, so that special functions, which the *conscience collective* itself cannot tolerate, may be established there; and the more this region of the individual *conscience* is extended, the stronger is the cohesion which results from this particular kind of solidarity.

Durkheim thus postulated two distinct types of social solidarity (mechanical and organic), each with its distinctive form of juridical rules (repressive and restitutive). To determine their relative importance in any given societal type, he simply compared the respective extent of the two kinds of rules. The preponderance of repressive rules over their restitutive counterparts, for example, should be just as great as the preponderance of the *conscience collective* over the division of labor; inversely, in so far as the individual personality and the specialization of tasks is developed, the relative proportion of the two types of law ought to be reversed. On the basis of these comparisons, Durkheim was then able to argue that primitive societies are held together primarily by the *conscience collective*, while more advanced societies enjoy that type of solidarity associated with the division of labor.

As we have seen, Durkheim always distinguished the causes of a social fact from its functions. So the causes of the division of labor could not possibly consist in some anticipation of its moral effects, for, as we have seen, those effects could hardly be foreseen. Instead, Durkheim's explanation referred to something he called *dynamic* or *moral density*. First, the real, material distance between members of a society is gradually reduced both spatially (e.g. the growth of cities) and technologically (e.g. advances in communications and transportation); second, this effect is reinforced by the sheer "social volume" of a society (the total number of its members). Durkheim thus claimed to have discovered a law of human societies, i.e. the division of labor varies in direct ratio to the dynamic or moral density of society, which is itself an effect of both material density and social volume.

Defining suicide

Durkheim defined "suicide" as any death which is the immediate or eventual result of a positive or negative act accomplished by the victim himself, when the victim *knows* that death will be the result of his act (regardless of whether or not death is his goal). This definition was subject to two immediate objections. The first was that such foreknowledge is a matter of degree, varying considerably from one person or situation to another. At what point, for example, does the death of a professional daredevil or that of a man neglectful of his health cease to be an "accident" and start to become "suicide"? But for Durkheim, to ask this question was less to raise an objection to his definition than to correctly identify its greatest advantage: that it indicates the place of suicide within moral life as a whole. Suicides, according to Durkheim, do not constitute a wholly distinctive group of "monstrous phenomena" unrelated to other forms of behavior; on the contrary, they are related to other acts, both courageous and imprudent, by an unbroken series of intermediate cases. Suicides, in short, are simply an exaggerated form of common practices. The second objection was that such practices are individual practices, with individual causes and consequences, which are thus the proper subject matter of psychology rather than sociology. In fact, Durkheim never denied that suicide could be studied by the methods of psychology, but he did insist that suicide could also be studied independent of its individual manifestations, as a social fact *sui generis*. Each society, Durkheim argued, has a "definite aptitude" for suicide, the relative intensity of which can be measured by the proportion of suicides per total population, or what Durkheim called "the rate of mortality through suicide, characteristic of the society under consideration" (Durkheim, 1977, p. 48). This rate was both *permanent* (the rate for any individual society was less variable than that of most other leading demographic data, including the general mortality rate) and *variable* (the rate for each society was sufficiently peculiar to that society as to be more characteristic of it than its general mortality rate). Each society, Durkheim thus concluded, is predisposed to contribute a definite quota of suicides; and it was this predisposition which Durkheim studied sociologically.

The four types of suicide

Durkheim acknowledged that there were two kinds of extrasocial causes sufficiently general to have a possible effect on the social suicide rate: *individual-psychological* factors (race, heredity, insanity, neurasthenia, alcoholism, etc.) which, varying from country to country, might explain variations in the suicide rates for those societies; and those aspects of the *external physical environment* (climate, temperature, etc.) which might have the same effect. When neither psychology nor the environment seemed to explain much of the social suicide rate, Durkheim turned to "states of the various social environments" – religious confessions, familial and political society, occupational groups, etc. – across which the variations in suicide rates occurred, and within which their causes might be found. If we look at a map of Western Europe, for example, we see that where Protestants are most numerous the suicide rate is highest, that where Catholics predominate it is much lower, and that the aptitude of Jews for suicide is lower still, though to a lesser degree, than that of Catholics. How are these data to be explained? Again Durkheim considered various causes (minority status, the religious doctrine, the Protestant "spirit of free inquiry," etc.), ultimately concluding that the lack of a common, collective *credo* among Protestants – the more limited extent of their social integration – explains their greater proclivity for suicide.

But if religion thus preserves men from suicide because it is a society, Durkheim reasoned, other "societies" (e.g. the family and political society) ought to have the same effect; and, in fact, Durkheim showed that, while marriage alone has a preservative effect against suicide, this is limited and benefits only men, while the addition of children provides an immunity which husband and wife share. When one marital partner dies, the survivor loses a degree of suicidal immunity, while the immunity to suicide increases with the size of the family, a fact Durkheim attributed to the greater number and intensity of collective sentiments produced and repeatedly reinforced by the larger group. Similarly, the examination of political societies showed that suicide, quite rare in a society's early stages, increases as that society matures and disintegrates. During social disturbances or great popular wars, by contrast, the suicide rate declines, because these disturbances arouse collective sentiments. Suicide thus varies inversely with the degree of integration of the religious, domestic, and political groups of which the individual forms a part; in short, as a society weakens or "disintegrates," the individual depends less on the group, depends more upon himself, and recognizes no rules of conduct beyond those based upon private interests. Durkheim called this state of "excessive individualism" *egoism*, and the type of self-inflicted death it produces *egoistic suicide*.

But if excessive individualism (insufficient integration) thus leads to suicide, so does excessive integration. In primitive societies, religious groups, and the military, we find several kinds of suicide – men on the threshold of old age, women upon the deaths of their husbands, martyrs to religious persecution, servants upon the deaths of their chiefs, soldiers in the heat of battle – in which the person kills himself *because it is his duty*. Such a sacrifice, Durkheim argued, is imposed by society for social purposes; and for society to be able to do this, the individual personality must have little value, a state Durkheim called *altruism*, and whose corresponding mode of self-inflicted death was called *obligatory altruistic suicide*. Altruistic suicide thus reflects that crude morality which disregards the individual, while its egoistic counterpart elevates the human personality beyond collective constraints; and their differences thus correspond to those between primitive and advanced societies.

Egoistic and altruistic suicide are thus the respective consequences of the individual's insufficient or excessive integration within the society to which he belongs. But quite aside from integrating its members, a society must control and regulate beliefs and behavior as well; and Durkheim insisted that there is a relation between a society's suicide rate and the way it performs this important regulative function. Where such constraints are excessive, for example, the individual becomes vulnerable to a type of suicide that Durkheim called *fatalistic*, although he considered it of little contemporary significance, and devoted only a footnote to its discussion. Far more interesting were those instances in which economic prosperity – and thus a weakening of social constraints – was accompanied by dramatic increases in the suicide rate.

How can something generally understood to improve a person's life, Durkheim asked, serve to detach him from it? The answer – which reveals how much he had learned from Rousseau (see below) – was that no living being can be happy unless its needs are sufficiently proportioned to its means; for if needs surpass the capacity to satisfy them, the result can only be a weakening of the impulse to live. In Rousseau's state of nature, of course, the desired equilibrium between needs and means is established and maintained by the laws of nature, e.g. an animal cannot imagine ends other than those implicit within its own physiology, and these are ordinarily satisfied by its purely material environment. Among human beings in more advanced societies, however, "a more awakened reflection" suggests better conditions and more desirable ends; and the aspirations implied by such reflections are inherently unlimited, and thus insatiable. "To pursue a goal which is by definition unattainable," Durkheim concluded, "is to condemn oneself to a state of perpetual unhappiness" (Durkheim, 1951, pp. 247–8). For human beings to be happy, therefore, their individual needs and aspirations must be constrained; and this regulatory function must thus be performed by an external, moral agency superior to the individual – in other words, by society. Durkheim used the term anomie to describe this temporary condition of social deregulation, and anomic suicide to describe the resulting type of self-inflicted death. In the sphere of trade and industry, Durkheim insisted that anomie is less a temporary disruption than a chronic condition. "From top to bottom of the ladder," Durkheim argued, "greed is aroused without knowing where to find ultimate foothold. Nothing can calm it, since its goal is far beyond all it can attain" (Durkheim, 1951, p. 256). Like Rousseau, therefore, Durkheim presents us with a devastating picture of the ambitious, indefatigable bourgeois.

Collective representations

The terms that Durkheim employed in making this argument – "collective tendencies," "collective passions," etc. – were not mere metaphors for average individual psychological states; on the contrary, they were "things," *sui generis* forces which dominate the consciousnesses of individuals. Such an argument, Durkheim admitted, suggests that collective thoughts are of a different nature from individual thoughts, and that the former have characteristics which the latter do not. Individual human beings, by associating with one another, form a psychical existence of a new species, which has its own manner of thinking and feeling. Social life, Durkheim thus admitted, is essentially made up of *representations*; but *collective* representations are quite different from their individual counterparts. In fact, these three currents of opinion – that the individual has a certain personality (egoism), that this personality should be sacrificed if the community required it (altruism), and that the individual is sensitive to ideas of social progress (anomie) – coexist in all societies, turning individual inclinations in three different and opposed directions. Where these currents offset one another, the individual enjoys a state of equilibrium which protects him from suicide; but where one current exceeds a certain strength relative to others, it becomes a cause of self-inflicted death.

Totemism as the most elementary form of religion

Durkheim's primary purpose in *The Elementary Forms* was to describe and explain the most primitive religion known to man, not for its own sake, but in order to better understand "the religious nature of man" (Durkheim, 1915, p. 13). As he had in *Suicide*, Durkheim began *The Elementary Forms* with the problem of defining his subject matter, including a rejection of earlier attempts to define religion as a belief in the "mysterious," "unknowable," "supernatural," "spiritual beings," etc. The difficulty with all such attempts, Durkheim observed, is that these ideas are frequently absent not only in primitive religions, but even in their more advanced counterparts. Emphasizing that religion is less an indivisible whole than a complex system of parts, and that magic – though similar to religion in certain respects – lacks a "church," Durkheim arrived at his own definition: "A religion is a unified system of beliefs and practices relative to sacred things, that is to say, things set apart and forbidden – beliefs and practices which unite into one single moral community called a Church, all those who adhere to them" (Durkheim, 1915, p. 62).

If this is "religion," what is religion's most elementary form? Some writers, like E. B. Tylor and Herbert Spencer, had argued that the earliest form of religion was animism: the worship of the souls of dead ancestors, whose existence was inferred from primitive dream experience. Others, including Max Müller, insisted that the earliest objects of religious belief were the phenomena of nature. But if the animistic hypothesis is true, Durkheim objected, it would mean not only that religious symbols provide an inexact expression of the realities on which they are based (something Durkheim believed), but also that religious symbols are products of the vague, ill-conceived hallucinations of dream-experience – and thus have no foundation in reality at all (something Durkheim most certainly did *not* believe). The naturistic hypothesis seemed to avoid this objection, by basing primitive religious ideas on the *real* forces of nature. But religion itself begins, Durkheim objected, only when these natural forces are transformed into personal spirits or gods, to whom the "cult of nature" might then be addressed. These forces and the reflections upon them could hardly be the source of religious ideas, for such ideas would provide a misleading conception of those natural forces upon which people depend for their very survival. Any course of practical activity based upon them would be unsuccessful, and this would surely undermine faith in the ideas themselves. In effect, Durkheim's objection to both hypotheses was the same – the importance of religious ideas throughout history and in all societies is evidence that they must correspond to some reality.

Durkheim thus considered totemism – the worship of animals and plants – as the most elementary form of religion. The members of totemic clans consider themselves bound together by a special kind of kinship, based not on blood, but on the mere fact that they share the same name. This name is taken from a determined species of material objects (an animal, less frequently a plant, and in rare cases an inanimate object) with which the clan members are assumed to enjoy the same relations of kinship. But this "totem" is not simply a name; it is also an emblem, which is carved, engraved, or drawn upon other objects belonging to the clan, and even upon the bodies of the clan members themselves. These designs seem to render otherwise common objects "sacred," and their inscription upon the bodies of clan members indicates the approach of the most important religious ceremonies. Since the same religious sentiments aroused by these designs are aroused by the members of the totemic species themselves, clan members are forbidden to kill or eat the totemic animal or plant except at certain mystical feasts, and the violation of this interdiction is assumed to produce death instantaneously.

The explanation of totemic beliefs

Durkheim explained these beliefs by appealing to the Melanesian belief in *mana* – a diffused, impersonal "force" that could be invested in certain objects, rendering them sacred. To explain totemism was thus to explain the belief in this impersonal religious principle. How could such a belief be explained? Obviously not from sensations aroused by the totemic objects themselves, for these objects – the caterpillar, the ant, the frog, etc. – are hardly of a kind to inspire powerful religious emotions; on the contrary, these objects appear to be the symbols or material expressions of something else. Of what, then, are they the symbols? Durkheim's answer was that the totemic animal symbolized the clan itself, and that god is nothing more than society apotheosized (Durkheim, 1915, p. 236). In support of this extraordinary claim, Durkheim insisted that society, whether primitive or advanced, has everything necessary to arouse the idea of the divine, e.g. it is both physically and morally superior to individuals, and thus individuals both fear its power and respect its authority. Like the gods, society cannot exist except in and through the individual *conscience*, and thus it both demands our sacrifices and periodically strengthens and elevates the divine "principle" within each of us – especially during periods of collective enthusiasm. It is during such extremely rare gatherings of the entire Australian clan, for example, that the religious idea itself seems to have been born, a fact which explained why its most important religious ceremonies continue to be observed only periodically, when the clan as a whole is assembled. It is this succession of intense periods of "collective effervescence" with much longer periods of dispersed, individualistic economic activity, Durkheim suggested, which gives rise to the belief that there are two worlds – the sacred and the profane – both within us and within nature itself. Most important, the sense thus inspired is not an illusion, but is based on reality; for however misunderstood, there actually is a *real* moral power – society – to which these beliefs correspond, and from which the worshipper derives strength.

The sociology of knowledge

The secondary purpose of *The Elementary Forms* was by far the most ambitious of Durkheim's attempts to provide sociological answers to philosophical questions. At the base of all our judgments there are a certain number of ideas which philosophers since Aristotle have called "the categories of the understanding": time, space, class, number, cause, substance, personality, and so on. When primitive religious beliefs are analyzed, Durkheim observed, these "categories" are found, suggesting that they are the product of religious thought; but as we have seen, religious thought itself is composed of collective representations, the products of real social groups.

These observations suggested to Durkheim that the "problem of knowledge" might be posed in new, sociological terms. Previous efforts to solve this problem had taken one of two philosophical positions: the *empiricist* doctrine that the categories are constructed out of human experience, and that the individual is the artisan of this construction; and the *a priorist* doctrine that the categories are logically prior to experience, and are inherent in the nature of the human intellect itself. The difficulty for the *empirical* thesis, according to Durkheim, was that it deprives the categories of their most distinctive properties: *universality* (they are the most general concepts we have, are applicable to all that is real, and are independent of every particular object) and *necessity* (we literally cannot think without them). For it is in the very nature of empirical data that they be both particular and contingent. The *a priorist* thesis, by contrast, has more respect for these properties of universality and necessity; but by asserting that the categories simply "inhere" in the nature of the intellect, it begs the question of where these categories come from. In sum, if reason is simply a variety of individual experience, it no longer exists; but if its distinctive properties are recognized but not explained, it is set beyond the bounds of nature and thus of scientific investigation.

If we admit the social origin of the categories, Durkheim argued, these problems go away. First, the basic proposition of the *a priorist* thesis is that knowledge is composed of two elements – perceptions mediated by our senses, and the categories of the understanding – neither of which can be reduced to the other. By viewing the first as *individual* representations and the second as their *collective* counterparts, this proposition is left intact (Durkheim, 1915, p. 28). Second, this hypothesis is equally consistent with the duality of human nature – just as our moral ideals are irreducible to our utilitarian motives, so our reason is irreducible to our experience. In so far as we belong to society, therefore, we transcend our individual nature both when we *act* and when we *think*. Finally, this distinction explains both the *universality* and the *necessity* of the categories: they are universal because man has always and everywhere lived in society, which is their origin; and they are necessary because, without them, all contact between individual minds would be impossible, and social life would be destroyed altogether (Durkheim, 1915, p. 30). One might still object that, since the categories are now mere representations of social realities, there is no guarantee of their correspondence to any of the realities of nature. Durkheim's rationalist and rather metaphysical reply was that society itself is a part of nature, and "it is impossible that nature should differ radically from itself" (Durkheim, 1915, p. 31).

Religion and science

Religion reflects on nature, man, and society, attempts to classify things, relates them to one another, and explains them; and as we have just seen, even the most essential categories of scientific thought are religious in origin. Scientific thought, in short, is but a more perfect form of religious thought; and Durkheim thus felt that the latter would gradually give way before the inexorable advances of the former, including those advances in the social sciences extending to the scientific study of religion itself. But religion is also a form of *action* – the religious believer is not just someone who sees new truths, but one who is more joyful, peaceful, and/or strong for being with his god. Durkheim thus agreed with William James, who, in *The Varieties of Religious Experience* (1902), had argued that religious beliefs rest upon real experiences whose demonstrative value, though different, is in no way inferior to that of scientific experiments. As with such experiments, Durkheim added, it does not follow that the reality which gives rise to these experiences precisely corresponds to the ideas that believers (or scientists) form of it; but it is a reality just the same, and for Durkheim, the reality was society. Durkheim also felt that all societies need such periodic reaffirmations of their collective sentiments, and that there is thus something "eternal" in religion, destined to outlive the particular symbols – totemic, Christian, or otherwise – in which it had been previously embodied.

Like Kant, therefore, Durkheim denied any conflict between science, on the one hand, and morality and religion, on the other; for, also like Kant, he felt that both were directed toward universal principles, and that both thus implied that, in thought as in action, man can lift himself above the limitations of his private, individual nature to live a rational, impersonal life. What Kant could not explain (indeed, he refused to do so) is the cause of this dual existence that we are forced to lead, torn between the sensible and intelligible worlds which, even as they seem to contradict each other, seem to presume and even require each other as well. But to Durkheim the explanation was clear: we lead an existence which is simultaneously both individual and social, and as individuals we can live without society no more than society can live without us.

The Person

David Émile Durkheim was born on April 15, 1858 in Epinal, in Lorraine, France. His mother was a merchant's daughter, and his father had been rabbi of Epinal since the 1830s. Part of his early education was thus spent in a rabbinical school; and while his later religious beliefs are best described as agnostic, he remained the product of a close-knit, orthodox Jewish family, as well as that long-established Jewish community of Alsace-Lorraine that had been occupied by Prussian troops in 1870, and suffered the resulting antisemitism of the French citizenry. An outstanding student at the Collège d'Epinal, Durkheim skipped two years, obtaining his *baccalauréats* in letters (1874) and sciences (1875) and distinguishing himself in the *Concours Général*. Intent on becoming a teacher, he left Epinal for Paris to prepare for admission to the prestigious École Normale Supérieure. Installed at a *pension* for non-resident students, however, he became utterly miserable: his father's illness left him anxious over his family's financial security; he was an utter *provincial* alone in Paris; and his intellectual predilections, already scientific rather than literary, were ill-fitted to the study of Latin and rhetoric essential for admission to the École. After failing in his first two attempts at the entrance examination (in 1877 and 1878), Durkheim was at last admitted near the end of 1879.

Despite constant fears of failure, which plagued him throughout his life, Durkheim became an active participant in the high-minded political and philosophical debates that characterized the École. He was soon a staunch advocate of the republican cause, with special admiration for Léon Gambetta, the brilliant orator and "spiritual embodiment" of the Third Republic, and the more moderate Jules Ferry, whose anticlerical educational reforms would soon lead to a national system of free, compulsory, secular education. Though ill through much of 1881 and 1882, Durkheim successfully passed his *agrégation* (the competitive examination required for admission to the teaching staff of state secondary schools, or *lycées*), and began teaching philosophy in 1882; and though his thesis preparation gradually focused on the relationship of the individual and society, it is clear that – until his fateful trip to Germany – he still thought like a philosopher rather than a sociologist.

Responding to intellectuals who blamed the humiliations of the Franco-Prussian War (1870–1) on the superiority of German education, the Ministry of Public Education in France had long made a point of awarding scholarships to the brightest young *agrégés* to visit Germany and become acquainted with recent scientific achievements. With this support, Durkheim was able to visit the universities of Marburg, Berlin, and Leipzig in 1885–6, and returned to publish two articles expressing his admiration for German philosophy and social science. In particular, he praised the "socialists of the chair" for their insistence on the social context of economic phenomena; the Germans' "organic" conception of the relationship between the individual and society, the generally Kantian philosophy and, above all, the scientific study of morality, particularly as pursued in the psychological laboratory of Wilhelm Wundt. For Wundt, according to Durkheim, had simultaneously recognized both the importance of independent social causes and the triviality of individual premeditation. The introduction of such a science of morality into the *lycées*, Durkheim thought, would create precisely that liberal, secular, republican ideology essential to the preservation of the Third Republic.

Fortuitously, an instrument for this purpose already existed. In 1882, the Faculty of Letters at Bordeaux had established France's first course in pedagogy for prospective school teachers, and in 1884 the state had begun to support it as part of its drive for a new system of secular, republican education. The course was first taught by Alfred Espinas, whose *Les Sociétés animales* (1877) Durkheim greatly admired, but who had soon been elevated to Dean of the Faculty. But Durkheim's articles on German philosophy and social science had caught the attention of Louis Liard, the Director of Higher Education in France. A devoted republican, Liard both resented the German pre-eminence in social science and was intrigued by Durkheim's suggestions for the reconstruction of a secular, scientific French morality. At the instigation of Espinas and Liard, therefore, Durkheim was appointed in 1887 as "Chargé d'un Cours de Science Sociale et de Pédagogie" at Bordeaux.

Throughout his years at Bordeaux (1887–1902), Durkheim's primary responsibility was to lecture on the theory, history, and practice of education. Each Saturday morning, however, he also taught a public lecture course on "social science," devoted to "specialized studies of particular social phenomena." It was in these public courses, some repeated several times in both Bordeaux and Paris, that Durkheim's major sociological ideas received their earliest expression, and also changed as he assimilated new ideas and intellectual influences. Durkheim's early approach to the study of social phenomena, for example, was largely evolutionary, historical, and comparative, and focused on law and custom as the best indices of change in social structure; gradually, he came to recognize the importance of ethnographic data, a trend epitomized in his focus on the "crucial experiment" of Australian aboriginal religion in *The Elementary Forms of the Religious Life* (1912). Again, Durkheim's early work exhibited a naive evolutionary optimism common to many Victorian social scientists, suggesting that advanced industrial societies (after a brief period of "pathological" disorganization) would be almost mechanically self-regulating; later, in part under the delayed influence of Albert Schaeffle's *Die Quintessenz des Sozialismus* (1875), he pointed to the need for external regulation by occupational groups, and would embrace socialism, not so much for its economic or political advantages, but because of its "morally regenerative" possibilities. And again, Durkheim's early discussion of the *conscience collective* suggested that shared ideas and beliefs are derivative features of forms of social organization; later, the concept itself virtually disappeared from Durkheim's writing, to be replaced by collective *représentations*, more complex, differentiated states of a society's consciousness, which were also granted increased autonomy and independent explanatory power.

The results of this shift became immediately evident in one of Durkheim's most important achievements: the founding of *l'Année sociologique* (1898–1913), the first social science journal in France. Supported by a brilliant group of young scholars, the *Année* was to provide an annual survey of the strictly sociological literature, to provide additional information on studies in other specialized fields (history of law, history of religion, ethnography, social statistics, economics, etc.), and to publish original monographs in sociology. And while he encouraged his contributors and collaborators simply to work within the general, impersonal framework established in his *Rules of Sociological Method* (1895), there is no doubt that Durkheim, whose own inclination was anti-eclectic if not dogmatic, and who revised virtually all copy and even supervised proofs, imposed his own, powerful personality on the publication.

In general, Durkheim was reluctant to enter the realm of politics, the two notable exceptions being the Dreyfus Affair and the First World War. A Dreyfusard from an early date, Durkheim considered the Affair "un moment de la conscience humaine." He was an active member of the Ligue pour la Défense des Droits de l'Homme, a Dreyfusard group, and when Ferdinand Brunetière, a staunch anti-Dreyfusard, published a defense of the army and the Church against the anarchistic "individualism" of French intellectuals, Durkheim responded with "Individualism and the Intellectuals" (1898), an important, sociologically based argument that modern individualism, unlike that of Rousseau and Kant, was a product of society, a secular "religion" that derived from Christianity, sanctified liberalism, and pointed in the direction of socialism. In 1902, when the successful resolution of the Dreyfus Affair had left both sociology and socialism with a more respectable public image, Durkheim was appointed *chargé d'un cours* in science and education at the Sorbonne. Four years later, he was made *professeur* by a unanimous vote, and in 1913 assumed the prestigious chair of "Science of Education and Sociology."

Durkheim arrived in Paris with a reputation as a powerful intellect pursuing an aggressively scientific approach to all problems (everything else was mysticism, dilettantism, and irrationalism). His "science of morality" offended philosophers, his "science of religion" offended Catholics, and his appointment to the Sorbonne (which, in the wake of the Dreyfus Affair, appeared not above political considerations) offended those on the Right. The appointment also gave Durkheim enormous power. His lecture courses were the only required courses at the Sorbonne, obligatory for all students seeking degrees in philosophy, history, literature, and languages; in addition, he was responsible for the education of successive generations of French schoolteachers, on whom he impressed his sociological theory of secular ethics. The sociology of morality had been an interest as early as his visit to Germany; and though his earliest conception of moral rules emphasized their external, obligatory character, this gradually shifted to an emphasis on the desirable, "eudaemonic" quality of moral actions. The development and deepening of this interest can be traced in both *The Division of Labor* (1893) and *Suicide* (1897); but Durkheim planned to recast these earlier views on morality in a major work entitled *La Morale*. Unfortunately, this went no further than a theoretical introduction, written in the last weeks of Durkheim's life and published three years later; but a sense of its projected content, which relies on a Kantian, "dualistic" conception of human nature, can be gathered from "The Determination of Moral Facts" (1906), "Value Judgments of and Judgments of Reality" (1911), and the discussion of morality in *The Elementary Forms of the Religious Life* (1912).

Of all Durkheim's works, none has afforded such sheer intellectual excitement as *The Elementary Forms*. This is all the more remarkable in light of the fact that, as Durkheim himself later admitted, his earlier treatment of religion was relatively mechanical and unimaginative. The significant change seems to have occurred as a consequence of a lecture course on religion given at Bordeaux in 1894–5, during which Durkheim became familiar with the work of Robertson Smith and James Frazer. Durkheim attempted a provisional statement of these new insights in "Concerning the Definition of Religious Phenomena" (1899); but he had not yet had the opportunity fully to digest the growing body of ethnography on primitive religions, and especially the important accounts of Australian aborigines published by Baldwin Spencer and F. J. Gillen in 1899 and 1904. When these data were combined with the seminal ideas of Robertson Smith's *Religion of the Semites* (1889) and Durkheim's own Kantian and neo-Kantian preconceptions, the result was *The Elementary Forms* – a work which, by any standard, remains a "classic" in the history of sociological thought.

The last course of lectures Durkheim offered before the war also stemmed from a question raised, but not answered, in *The Elementary Forms*: if, as Durkheim at least seemed to imply, all religions are "true in their own fashion," is truth itself "relative" to human interests and purposes? This question acquired a particular urgency in light of the affirmative answer given to it by William James, the increasing interest in James's pragmatism in France, and the use of James's works as a philosophical rationale for what Durkheim considered the anti-intellectualism of the time. Durkheim thus presented a series of lectures in 1913–14 which dealt not only with James but with the elaboration of James's ideas by the Oxford philosopher F. C. S. Schiller, their refinement by John Dewey (whom Durkheim greatly admired), and their extension in the works of Durkheim's life-long rival, Bergson.

With the outbreak of the First World War in August 1914 – despite poor health already induced by overwork – Durkheim devoted himself to the cause of national defense. But when his son, André, a gifted linguist and among the most promising of the younger *Année* circle, died in action, Durkheim withdrew into a "ferocious silence," eventually suffering a stroke. On November 15, 1917, he died at the age of 59.

THE SOCIAL CONTEXT

"When a people has achieved a state of equilibrium and maturity," Durkheim observed in his seventh lecture on moral education, "then the preference for rule and order is naturally preponderant." But "in times of flux and change," the spirit of discipline "cannot preserve its moral vigor since the prevailing system of rules is shaken, at least in some of its parts. At such times, it is inevitable that we feel less keenly the authority of a discipline that is, in fact, attenuated." Durkheim had no illusions about the type of society or historical period he was living in: "We are going through precisely one of these critical phases," he emphasized. "Indeed, history records no crisis as serious as that in which European societies have been involved for more than a century" (Durkheim, 1961, p. 101).

The crisis was in part the consequence of demographic changes. As the birth rate steadily declined and the death rate remained stable, the traditional, fertile, Roman Catholic family confronted its modern, Malthusian counterpart. Parents, concerned to rise socially and to provide a good future for their children, calculated and looked ahead, reflecting the aspirations of individualism and egalitarianism – a movement which particularly affected the lower middle class (Mayeur and Rebérioux, 1984, p. 43). In 1897, Durkheim insisted that both the decrease in births and the increase in suicides were the consequence of a decline in domestic feelings, an increase in migration from the country to the towns, the break-up of the traditional family, and the "cold wind of egoism" which had ensued (Durkheim, 1951, pp. 198–202). Yet economic growth, rapid before 1860 and steady if unspectacular for the twenty years thereafter, slowed dramatically after 1880, a consequence of the decreasing per capita productivity of the labor force and the declining rate of urbanization. Once the second largest industrial power in the world, France quickly slipped to fourth (Mayeur and Rebérioux, 1984, p. 46). With a stable currency and no income tax, however, an urban bourgeois with an annual income of 20,000 francs paid as little as 2 percent in taxes; thus a doctor, lawyer, or engineer who had been prudent under the prosperity of the Second Empire could retire in his fifties with no decline in his standard of living, a prospect which gave rise to the unregulated aspirations symptomatic of Durkheim's "economic anomie." "Conservatives of the time," Mayeur and Rebérioux warn us, "like to assert that the individualism bred by the Revolution had undermined the family, but in fact family feeling had changed rather than weakened. The bourgeois family looked inward, concentrating on the child and his future. It was a family of limited births, anxious to rise in the world through birth control and saving" (Mayeur and Rebérioux, 1984, p. 71). The working class was primarily agricultural, and remained so until the end of the century; but the living conditions, manners, and mentality of the peasants had changed. Railways, especially the little cross-country lines, and improvements in local roads, went far to break down provincial isolation. The town was easier to reach, and its culture was felt through the schools, compulsory military service, mail-order catalogues, and cheap newspapers. If not for themselves, the agricultural working class could at least anticipate an easier, less trying life for their children.

In short, from the early days of the Third Republic until the end of the century, French society was to change very little, and least of all in its traditional social and economic inequalities. Durkheim's consistently uniformitarian view that revolutions were as rare as unicorns thus reflected not only his deeply conservative nature, but a keen perception of the realities of his own society. In fact, those who made the Republican victory possible – the peasantry and the rising middle class – expected no profound transformation of social relations. What they did expect was the end of the political influence of the traditional aristocracy, as well as the Roman Catholic Church, for this would provide them with the opportunity to rise socially.

These expectations would be intimately bound to the precarious future of the Third French Republic. But historically, the French – and especially the peasantry – had held strong reservations about republicanism. Suspected of bellicosity abroad and instability at home, of opposition to the Church, and of egalitarian and even socialist tendencies, republicans won only 200 seats in the National Assembly elected after the fall of the Paris Commune. "So now we have a republic?" observed Zola's peasant-hero Jean Macquart, in La Débâcle (1892, p. 403). "Oh well, all to the good if it helps us beat the Prussians"; but then Macquart shook his head, "for he had always been led to fear a republic when he worked on the land. And besides, in the face of the enemy he didn't think it was a good thing not to be all of one mind." Ironically, the Assembly's ruthless suppression of the Commune – 38,000 were taken prisoner, 20,000 executed, 13,450 sentenced to various prison terms, 7,500 deported to New Caledonia – gave the Third French Republic one of its few reasons for optimism. The proscription and exile of so many "extremists" provided the nascent and extremely precarious Republic an opportunity to evolve in a more peaceful, orderly fashion, and even to attain a degree of constitutional legitimacy; and the absence (or at least quiescence) of these same elements helped to remove the long-held association of Republicanism with violence, instability, and disorder – something essential if the Republic were to win the allegiance of its hard-working, law-abiding, and largely provincial citizenry.

Within the context of the larger European community, such moderation was essential, for in just fifteen years, the position of France had declined precipitously. At the conclusion of the Crimean War (1854–6), Great Britain was an ally, Russia had been firmly defeated, Italy and Germany were simply "geographical expressions," and France was incontestably the foremost power in continental Europe. By the spring of 1871, Britain was no longer an ally, for France had no allies; Russia had gained a modification of the Black Sea clauses of the Treaty of Paris; without any *quid pro quo*, France had been forced to withdraw her troops from Italy, allowing the Italian government to occupy Rome, complete the unification of Italy, imprison Pius IX in the Vatican, and end the temporal power of the papacy; and Germany, whose population already outnumbered France's by more than four million people, had achieved national unity, declared itself an Empire, and would soon become the greatest industrial power on the Continent.

For the French, the natural consequences of this situation included a revulsion for war, a powerful desire for peace and order, the constant affirmation and reaffirmation of patriotism, the elevation of the "sacred" French army to a status beyond political argument altogether, and an utter indifference to the restoration of the temporal power of the Pope. Henceforth, public opinion would favor those like Durkheim, whose republican zeal was tempered by opposition to insurrection and revolution. Even Gambetta became more moderate, acknowledging the imminent rise of what he called "a new social stratum" – *petits bourgeois*, shopkeepers, clerks, and artisans – the class which had profited from the prosperity of the Second Empire, swelled the ranks of investors in the provisional Republic, and thus accelerated the work of postwar reconstruction; and now, given the appropriate education and opportunity, this class would surely support the Republic and strengthen its institutions. Gambetta thus became what he himself described as an "Opportunist" – a name which would characterize the moderate Left to the end of the century. Doctrinaire tenets were shelved in the interest of practical ends, and the electorate was increasingly reassured that, if Gambetta remained a Republican and an anticlerical, he was no revolutionary.

Those who insist on reading *De la division du travail social* as a "dialogue" with Marx's ghost should thus be reminded that revolutionary socialism was virtually non-existent at the parliamentary level of French politics during the period in which that work was conceived. The first series of Jules Guesde's *L'Égalité* appeared only in November 1877, and the second in January 1880. Between the two, the Socialist Workers' Congress of France was held at Marseilles (October 1879), denouncing Gambetta's followers and adopting a Marxist program. But the actual texts of Marx and Engels were almost unknown, and only in 1885 did Guesde's Parti ouvrier publish a complete translation of the *Communist Manifesto*. France, as we have seen, was still a country of peasants rather than urban–industrial workers, and those Paris revolutionaries who had survived the suppression of the Commune were either in prison or in exile, not to be pardoned until 1879.

This helps to explain the central place of laicization within the Republican agenda. To the Opportunists, the Church seemed a growing and increasingly threatening presence. In the syllabus of 1864 which accompanied the encyclical *Quanta Cura*, Pius IX startled the modern world by condemning propositions that seemed self-evident to reasonable people, including the suggestion that the Roman pontiff should reconcile himself to "progress, liberalism and modern civilization." On July 18, 1870, the bishops assembled in St Peter's voted the constitution *Pater aeternus*, declaring the Pope preserved from error when he speaks *ex cathedra* in matters of faith and morals. However ambiguous the Syllabus, and however limited the definition in *Pater aeternus*, in the eyes of other Christians as well as unbelievers, the Church seemed "irretrievably set on the path of absolutism in ecclesiastical government and, by analogy and from the experience of the present pontificate, of reaction in matters social and political" (McManners, 1972, p. 1).

Despite this reactionary posture, the Church enjoyed at least an ephemeral rise in popularity as a consequence of the Franco-Prussian War. Official statistics of the 1870s list 35,000,000 people as Catholics, by contrast to 600,000 Protestants, 50,000 Jews, and only 80,000 "free-thinkers" (McManners, 1972, p. 5). In addition to the sheer numbers of Catholics and the strength of their clergy, a variety of social services were almost entirely in Church hands. But it was in education that the power of the Roman Catholic Church in France seemed to be at its height. Despite the anticlericalism which survived the First Empire and continued into the 1830s and 1840s, the Church had repeatedly tried to improve its position by undermining the university monopoly of higher and secondary education. By 1870, almost 40 percent of the nation's children were educated in Church schools (McManners, 1972, p. 21–2). "Au point de vue sociologique," Durkheim would say in 1905, "l'Église est un monstre" (Durkheim, 1905, p. 369). If so, in 1870 it was a very large *monstre* indeed, and one which threatened to grow still further.

Still, the Catholic Church in France was a deeply troubled institution. Not least among its difficulties, for example, was its lack of a central organization or a distinctive French voice, which made the Church in France dependent on the Vatican, leading to calls – most of which fell upon deaf republican ears – for the "liberation" of the Pope. A second difficulty was that French clergy themselves varied in the degree of their support for Rome. The parish clergy came consistently from the less-educated classes, while the bishops typically possessed literary and classical educations, and were utter strangers to the parochial ministry. Enjoying a salary twenty times that of a *curé*, a bishop inevitably appeared to those below as an aloof, superior figure. By contrast, only one secular priest in ten enjoyed security of tenure; the others could be moved by the bishop at will and, if accused of offences, disciplined without due process.

The aristocracy and bourgeoisie were still interested in the religious orders for their daughters, but nine out of ten candidates for the ministry came from the families of peasants and artisans. As the intellectual foundations of Christian belief came under increasing attack from biblical criticism, natural science, and the comparative study of religion, it is understandable that a ministry thus recruited would be found wanting; and to compound the problem, the educational program of the seminaries was limited to meditation, pious exercises, and the rehearsal of antiquated dogma. McManners finds only two diocesan prelates who, in the 1870s and 1880s, had any first-hand knowledge of the new German biblical criticism that had already inspired Robertson Smith and, largely through Smith, would influence Durkheim.

To this, one must add the indifferent knowledge of an urban, working-class world possessed by a clergy of rural origins, whose language, values, and morals were largely those of an earlier age. The city, Mayeur and Rebérioux (1984, p. 104) emphasize, "a modern Babylon which the Church distrusted, was the citadel of religious indifference," and comparisons of the new districts in Paris with "heathen lands afar" were not uncommon (McManners, 1972, p. 7). The Church was no more apt to appeal to the middle classes. The old, "Voltairean" bourgeoisie of the provinces had largely been reconciled to a vague kind of faith; but Gambetta's "new stratum" was utterly indifferent if not hostile. As for the peasantry, thanks to the invention of the rotary press, post-free railway distribution, and the mass appeal of advertising, the penny newspaper easily reached the countryside (Mayeur and Rebérioux, 1984, p. 116). To this was added the local weekly or bi-weekly newspapers, and the illustrated magazines and catalogues from major Parisian stores. Quite aside from manifestly anticlerical publications, these carriers of a new, popular, Parisian culture, together with military service and improvements in transportation, broadened the horizons of the French people and undermined local, traditional values.

Nor was Roman Catholicism the only religious confession in late nineteenth-century France. There were 580,000 Protestants in France in 1872, and their economic standing and intellectual significance far transcended their numbers (Bury, 1985, p. 156). After the synod of 1872, a division in the Reformed Church produced a liberal Protestant minority which practiced ecclesiastical democracy, rejected theological dogma, reduced religion to a rational morality, encouraged freedom of inquiry, and thus became another component of the secular, republican idea. Protestants like Ferdinand Buisson (whom Durkheim replaced at the Sorbonne in 1902), Félix Pécaut, J. Steeg, and Elie Rabier played important roles in Ferry's educational reforms, and the neo-Kantian philosopher Charles Renouvier, whom Durkheim called "mon educateur," encouraged republicans to become Protestants (Mayeur and Rebérioux, 1984, pp. 107–8). The Jewish minority comprised 50,000 by 1870, most of them living in Paris (McManners, 1972, p. 5). While those who had recently immigrated from Eastern Europe remained isolated by their language and retained their religious traditions, Jews of Alsatian origin (like Durkheim) were largely assimilated. Granted citizenship and the right to vote in the Civil Constitution of the Clergy (1790), these assimilated Jews remained attached to the tradition of the French Revolution, and consistently supported the progressive, secular Republic. Finally, the majority of the brilliant young men trained at the École Normale Supérieure after 1848, as well as the majority of the Republican leaders, were simply agnostics, for whom "the cult of the Great Revolution had become almost a religion, and, in so far as it affected their political thinking, intensified the political offensive of the Left against the Church" (Bury, 1985, p. 156).

French anticlericalism, of course, can be traced back to the literate sensibilities of the Enlightenment, the jest books of the Renaissance, and even the sullen resentments of the Middle Ages. But the "new anticlericalism" that emerged after 1870 bore ironic similarities to Catholicism. In each case, a determined core of "true believers" was outnumbered by a wider circle of occasional conformists and nominal adherents. Moreover, the spheres of nominal Catholicism and ambiguous anticlericalism overlapped, as those Catholics who resented clerical domination and right-wing politics mingled with anticlericals (like Durkheim) whose hatred for priests was not unmixed with a respect and even nostalgia for the moral uniformity of the medieval community. It was in this context that the possibility of a purely lay morality, based on a "science of ethics," was first conceived; and it is the belief in this possibility, as well as the quasi-religious belief in science and progress generally, which distinguishes this anticlericalism from that of earlier ages. "Many of the opponents of the Church," McManners reminds us, "had a reluctant admiration for the system of moral influence they were proposing to destroy, and a vision of a faith to replace it. It was not *écrasez l'Infâme*, but a different sort of bitterness, compounded of attraction and repulsion, a love-hate relationship" (McManners, 1972, p. 17). The Opportunists who came to power in 1879 thus confronted a Church afflicted with serious internal and external difficulties, whose values were largely if not unambiguously discordant with the middle-class, quasi-religious belief in positivism and social progress, and whose political candidates they had repeatedly (and now decisively) defeated at the polls; but it was also a Church which had the respect and even affection of the majority of the population, one whose moral authority the Opportunists envied and longed to replace with their own, equally fervent brand of secular ethics.

Republican administrators thus turned quite naturally to the Church's educational establishments – "the surest guarantee of its continued influence" – as the focal point for their reforms. In such establishments, McManners (1972, p. 45) emphasizes, "so many young minds were imprinted with a permanent allegiance to religion, or a subconscious residual respect for its practices." Such establishments also bore the weight of accumulated resentments: they were patronized by the upper classes, administered corporal punishment, taught children to admire unrevolutionary mendicant saints, and emphasized impractical subjects to the children of a class with rising social aspirations. "A frontal attack on religion," McManners emphasizes, "on the ceremonies by which wives set so much store, the consolations available in the hour of death, the *curé* and all his supporters," would surely have failed. But a "flank attack" on clerical education, which left the Church undisturbed in the private sphere of the family, would surely receive political support. Laicization was also seen as the means to repair the negative consequences of an elitist, humanist, and increasingly impractical form of education, to eradicate differences of geographic region and social class, and to unite the French people and restore their sense of national pride (McManners, 1972, p. 47). Secularism, in short, became synonymous with patriotism, and the removal of clerical control over French education became less a neutral political posture than a "civil religion" of its own.

The laicizing movement grew rapidly. The Ligue de l'enseignement, founded in 1866 by Jean Macé, served as an umbrella for a variety of disparate groups unified in defining free, compulsory, secular education as the overriding national necessity. From 1870 to 1877, it grew from 18,000 to 60,000 members. Similarly, the Société pour l'étude des questions de enseignement supérieur, founded in 1879, sought to influence sympathetic ministers to reform higher education on the model of Protestant Germany; and the *Revue internationale de l'enseignement*, which began to appear in 1881, presented a series of studies of both German and French education – including the important products of Durkheim's 1885–6 visit to Berlin, Marburg, and Leipzig – which created the theoretical foundations for public policy.

On February 4, 1879, the Waddington ministry was formed, with Jules Ferry as Minister of Education. During the period of remarkable political stability which followed, Ferry would be Minister of Education for five years and Prime Minister for three; and it was during this period, undisturbed by opposition from both left and right, that the governing Republicans constructed their system of free, compulsory, secular education. Not surprisingly, Ferry's primary intellectual inspiration came from Condorcet and Comte, whose belief in science, progress, and the power of education he embraced without reservation. But much like Durkheim, Ferry also held a deep respect for the medieval Church, whose schools unified society, mitigated inequalities, taught morality, and thus provided the ethical foundations for an entire social order.

Laicization, in short, was the reform that contained all other reforms. It became the obligation of the state to provide for the education of every child in France. The decisive measure was a law of March 28, 1882, which made education compulsory from six to thirteen years, and eliminated religious instruction from the timetable. The teacher, insisted Buisson, "confines himself to inculcating in his pupils the fundamental ideas which recur in all religious denominations and even outside them." With the appearance of the "Goblet law" of October 30, 1886, members of the religious orders were explicitly denied further recruitment into the state's primary schools, and their replacement with exclusively lay personnel was required within the next five years. In secondary education, the timetable was reformed in 1880 to reduce the role, so prominent in Jesuit pedagogical method, of memorization, composition, and Latin recitation. The classical humanistic subjects retained their primacy, but science and modern languages were given a larger place, and an underlying philosophy of educational realism became perceptible: "The observation of things," Ferry emphasized, "is the basis of everything" (Mayeur and Rebérioux, 1984, p. 88).

THE INTELLECTUAL CONTEXT

At the École Normale, one of the first great minds Durkheim encountered was the French historian Numa Denis Fustel de Coulanges (1830–89). Fustel's classic study of the religious foundations of ancient Rome, *La Cité antique* (1864), was literally awash with ideas that a later generation would automatically recognize as "Durkheimian," e.g. a Cartesian emphasis on doubting preconceptions, the comparative method, a preoccupation with the family as the most elementary form of society, the dismissal of explanations appealing to individual reason or will, the discovery of the origin of religion in a primitive form of sacrificial communion with a god, a rejection of the concern for religious doctrine combined with an emphasis on the stability of ritual practices, the religious origins of institutions like private property, law, and the state, and the identification of "religion" with "society" itself. *La Cité antique* enjoyed an almost instantaneous celebrity, inspiring new interest in the history of institutions among Fustel's followers, including Camille Jullian, who was Durkheim's classmate and edited Fustel's manuscripts. During the time Durkheim was at the École Normale, Fustel was at work on the six volumes of his *Histoire des institutions politiques de l'ancienne France* (1874–93), which included a detailed articulation and defense of the comparative method he had followed in writing *La Cité antique*. "From his time at the Ecole normale," Jullian later recalled, Durkheim "was profoundly affected by the influence of La Cité antique, and by the lectures and examples of its author. He himself has recognized this, and proclaims it openly" (Lukes, 1972, p. 60). Durkheim even dedicated his Latin thesis on Montesquieu to Fustel; but the historian's influence on Durkheim's work seems to have been delayed at least until the mid-1890s, when Durkheim achieved a new understanding of religious phenomena through the study of James Frazer and William Robertson Smith.

The second important influence at the École Normale was the philosopher Émile Boutroux (1845–1921), a disciple of the neo-spiritualist philosopher Jules Lachelier (1832–1918). Boutroux's first major work was *De la Contingence des lois de la nature* (1874), an attack on determinism in its relation to physical and psychological science that ultimately proved to be his *magnum opus*. A devout Roman Catholic, Boutroux argued that phenomenal existence comprises "several worlds, forming, as it were, stages superposed on one another," each studied by a science irreducible to that preceding it (Boutroux, 1916, pp. 151–2). Durkheim dedicated *The Division of Labor* to Boutroux, and in 1907, explaining the origin of his important distinction between sociology and psychology, tried to make his debt clear:

> I owe [this distinction] first to my master, Boutroux, who, at the École normale supérieure, repeated frequently to us that each science must, as Aristotle says, explain [its own phenomena] by "its own principles" – e.g. psychology by psychological principles, biology by biological principles. Most impressed by this idea, I applied it to sociology. (Durkheim, 1907, pp. 612–13)

But if the influence is undeniable, it is not unambiguous. For Durkheim's claims for sociology went far beyond anything Boutroux would have accepted, including a defense of necessary laws of social behavior. Hearing that Durkheim's thesis had been dedicated to him, Boutroux grimaced and then attacked Durkheim's mechanical, necessitarian mode of explanation in *De l'idée de loi naturelle dans la science et la philosophie contemporaines* (1895, translated 1914, p. 198; see Lukes, 1972, pp. 297–8).

Another philosopher Durkheim was reading during these years was the French neo-Kantian Charles Renouvier (1815–1903). Educated at the École Polytechnique, where he specialized in mathematics and natural science, Renouvier had studied under Comte, who was then an instructor in higher mathematics. Influenced by Saint-Simon in the early 1830s, he became a socialist propagandist until, in 1851, the *coup d'état* of Louis-Napoleon destroyed Renouvier's political ambitions. Renouvier became a private scholar, and never held an academic position; but the views expressed in his books and journal articles – uncompromising rationalism, the central concern with ethics and the determination to study it "scientifically," the compatibility of determinism in nature with the freedom presupposed by moral action, concern for the dignity and autonomy of the individual, preference for justice over utility, advocacy of associations independent of the state and public, secular education – exerted a powerful influence on intellectuals of the Third Republic. "If you wish to mature your thought," Durkheim later said to René Maublanc, "devote yourself to the study of a great master; take a system apart, laying bare its innermost secretes. That is what I did and my educator was Renouvier" (Lukes, 1972, pp. 54–5).

Near the end of his studies at the École Normale, Durkheim began to read the works of Auguste Comte (1798–1857), although lecture notes from his philosophy course at the Lycée de Sens suggest that, as late as 1883, he was still not a social realist or even particularly interested in Comte or sociology. It was as he was working on the first draft of *The Division of Labor* between 1884 and 1886, therefore, that he came to see that the solution to his problem might be found in "a new science: sociology" (Lukes, 1972, pp. 66–7). By the time he wrote the introduction to the Latin thesis on Montesquieu (1892), Durkheim could complain that "we have forgotten that this science started up in our own country," for "it was Comte who established it on a sound basis, described its different elements and gave it its own – if somewhat barbarous – name of sociology" (Durkheim, 1997, p. 7e). In particular, Durkheim praised Comte for insisting that social phenomena are natural things and thus subject to natural laws, for his emphasis on careful observation, his resistance to the reduction of sociological explanations to psychological causes, his recognition that the division of labor is a source of solidarity, and his emphasis on the interrelatedness of social phenomena (Lukes, 1972, pp. 67–9, 80–1). Despite Comte's implicit social realism, however, Durkheim found his application of it wanting. "It is ideas which he too takes as the object of his study," Durkheim complained. "Comte has taken his own notion of [social reality], which is one that does not differ greatly from that commonly held... if one proceeds down this path," Durkheim concluded, "one not only remains in the realm of ideology, but assigns to sociology as its object a concept which has nothing peculiarly sociological about it" (1982, pp. 63–4).

At approximately the same time, Durkheim was reading Herbert Spencer (1820–1903), who – despite his methodological individualism – provided Durkheim's social realism with a "treasure of insights and hypotheses" based on analogies between social institutions and biological organisms. By contrast with Comte's sweeping "law of the three stages," Spencer applied these analogies to different social types, themselves classified into genera and species, and subjected them to powerful functional explanations (Lukes, 1972, pp. 82–4). But if Spencer thus discarded Comte's abstract concept, he simply replaced it "with another which is none the less formed in the same way. He makes societies, and not humanity, the object of his study, but immediately gives to societies a definition which causes the thing of which he speaks to disappear and puts in its place the preconception he has of them. . . . What is defined in this way," Durkheim again complained, "is not society but Spencer's idea of it. If he feels no scruples in proceeding in this fashion it is because for him also society is only, and can be only, the realisation of an idea, namely that very idea of cooperation by which he defines society" (Durkheim, 1982, pp. 64–5).

The resources Durkheim needed to construct his social realist vocabulary, therefore, had to be sought in German writers. Durkheim wrote favorable notices of the first volume of Albert Schaeffle's *Bau und Leben des sozialen Körpers* (1885), for example, as well as his *Die Quintessenz der Sozialismus* (1886). In the first paragraph of his review of Ludwig Gumplowicz's *Grundriss der Soziologie* (1885), Durkheim added that this work was further evidence of the German effort to advance sociological studies in every possible direction. "How regrettable it is," he added, that "this interesting movement is so little known and so little followed in France. So it is that sociology, French in origin, becomes more and more a German science" (Durkheim, 1885, p. 627). In 1885 and 1886, Durkheim visited the German universities of Berlin, Marburg, and Leipzig, praising them for their sense of community and corporate life, in sharp contrast to the French taste for "individual distinction and originality"; and he admired still more the German emphasis on the "positive science of ethics," which he wanted to transplant to the French universities so it might then be disseminated through the *lycées*. The so-called "socialists of the chair" – Adolf Wagner (1835–1917) and Gustav Schmoller (1838–1917) – were praised for their social realism, their connection of economics to ethics, and their critique of the Manchester School, which ignored the social context of economic behavior; the leading representatives of the German "historical school of jurisprudence" – Rudolf von Ihering (1818–92) and Albert-Hermann Post (1839–95) – were lauded for relating the study positive law and ethics to customs (Durkheim, 1887, p. 58); and proponents of the German *Völkerpsychologie* – Theodor Waitz (1821–64), Heymann Steinthal (1823–99), and Moritz Lazarus (1824–1903) – were praised for their study of phenomena which, though psychological in nature, "do not have their source in individual psychology, since they infinitely transcend the individual" (Durkheim, 1888, p. 63).

By far the most important German influence, however, was the philosopher and psychologist Wilhelm Wundt (1832–1920). Despite the attractions of the University of Berlin, Durkheim recalled in 1887, "it is always Leipzig that is preferred by foreigners who come to Germany to complete their philosophical education. It is to Wundt and his teachings that this persistent vogue is due. It is this same cause," he added, "which led us to Leipzig, and kept us there longer than anywhere else" (Durkheim, 1887, pp. 313–14). Durkheim described the experiments conducted in Wundt's Psychologische Institut in endless detail, adding that "nothing is more capable of raising in young minds the love of scientific precision, to divest them of vague generalizations and metaphysical possibilities, and finally to make them understand how complex are psychological facts and the laws which govern them" (Durkheim, 1887, p. 433) – an early hint of his notion that the study of science could be morally edifying (see above). Most important, Wundt's great *Ethik* (1886) had offered a genuinely scientific alternative to the French approach to the study of ethics. According to the French tradition, Durkheim complained, moral laws are universally valid in all times and places, the method of ethics is deduction from axiomatic first principles, the individual is an autonomous whole, society is formed by the establishment of relations between these autonomous wills, and the purpose of morality is the perfecting of these individuals. Against this tradition, Wundt and his colleagues argued that moral "laws" are relative to particular times and places, the method is inductive generalization, the "autonomous individual" is an abstraction unknown to science, society penetrates the individual "in every part," and "morality has, as its consequence, to make society possible" (Durkheim, 1887, pp. 336–8, 138).

These issues were foremost in Durkheim's mind as he prepared his Latin thesis on Montesquieu (1892). In a sense, *De l'esprit des lois* became the perfect forge in which Durkheim would shape the tools to be applied in *The Division of Labor* and later works. For Montesquieu (1689–1755), no less than Durkheim, had been troubled by the legacy of Cartesian metaphysics and, no less than Durkheim, sought to temper its emphasis on "clear and distinct ideas" with a language more responsive to the concrete complexity of things. So Durkheim used his Latin thesis on Montesquieu as a way of exploring his own ambivalence about the Cartesian tradition, while also praising Montesquieu's recognition of the real, concrete diversity of societal types, his refusal to deduce "rules valid for all peoples" from artificial first principles, and – anticipating *The Division of Labor* – his explanation of the *esprit* of each societal type as the natural consequence of its structural features. At least equal praise was given to Montesquieu's refusal – so unusual among his Enlightenment contemporaries – to reduce explanations of civil and political law to the principles of human nature, or to some putative, original contract or covenant. Durkheim lamented the extent to which Montesquieu was still bound by the legacy of Aristotle and by the traditions of natural law, not to mention the disturbing element of contingency which leavened the causal explanations of *De l'esprit des lois*. But, recognizing that Montesquieu's "greatest achievement" – the extension of the idea of law to the realm of social phenomena – reflected an undeniable, continuing attachment to the rationalist belief in a determinate order of nature, Durkheim still emphasized how "unique" it was for an eighteenth-century social philosopher to insist that these laws were neither fixed nor immutable. Finally, the notion that "social volume" affects the structures of law and society, which plays so large a role in *The Division of Labor*, was found in Montesquieu's discussion of the conditions of republican government.

It was shortly after the publication of *The Division of Labor* that Durkheim confronted his most formidable intellectual adversary, the French sociologist and philosopher Gabriel Tarde (1843–1904). In his best-known work, *Les lois de l'imitation* (1890), Tarde had advanced a more psychologically based sociology that explained social phenomena as the consequence of the imitation of individual beliefs and desires. Tarde's otherwise generous and respectful review of *The Division of Labor* criticized Durkheim for ignoring the function of the division of labor "in multiplying the objects of [intellectual and moral community] and singularly facilitating their diffusion" – in effect, for ignoring imitation. Durkheim responded in *The Rules of Sociological Method*, insisting that social facts become generalized and diffused because they are obligatory – not the reverse; and in "Les deux éléments de la sociologie" (1894), Tarde responded still more aggressively, denouncing the entire foundation of Durkheim's social realism in Boutroux's distinction between successive, irreducible phenomenal "worlds." In the most fundamental way, Tarde had attacked the very heart of Durkheim's social theory. But by the time Durkheim responded, in the third book of *Suicide*, he had a new weapon – a deeper and more sophisticated understanding of the figure to whom his sociology would owe more than anyone else, Jean-Jacques Rousseau (1712–78).

Rousseau had figured in Durkheim's work from the start, of course, typically as a thinker with an asocial concept of human beings and an artificial concept of society. Undeniably provoked by Tarde, however, Durkheim took another, longer look, giving a lecture course on *Le Contrat social* at Bordeaux after 1896, and another course on *Emile* at Paris after 1902. Transcripts of both sets of lectures have been published, and they reveal a breadth of reading well beyond the two works in question, and a depth of understanding that clearly transformed Durkheim's social theory. Most importantly, these lectures quite literally set out new philosophical foundations for Durkheim's social realism. The dependence on *things*, Durkheim paraphrased Rousseau, is no obstacle to freedom; but "the dependence on *other human beings* – willful, unstable, avaricious, deceitful, etc. – produces the mutual corruption and depravity of master and slave." And then Durkheim confronted the passage in *Emile* that must surely have stopped him cold:

> If there is any means of remedying this ill in society, it is to substitute law for man and to arm the general will with a real strength superior to the action of every particular will. If the laws of nations could, like those of nature, have an inflexibility that no human force could ever conquer, dependence on men would then become dependence on things again; in the republic all of the advantages of the natural state would be united with those of the civil state, and freedom which keeps

man exempt from vices would be joined to morality which raises him to virtue. (Durkheim, 1979, p. 85)

To paraphrase in more Durkheimian terms, if the laws of society could become like those of nature, dependence on individual human wills would again become dependence on things. This new understanding of Rousseau was immediately reflected in Durkheim's discussion of anomic suicide, i.e. the pathological symptom of individual human willfulness, whose only solution was the regulation and constraint provided by society.

As we have already seen, Durkheim himself acknowledged that his early treatment of religion was relatively mechanical and unimaginative. The pivotal influence here seems to have been William Robertson Smith (1846–94), whose works Durkheim encountered while teaching a lecture course on religion at Bordeaux in 1894–5:

> it was not until 1895 that I achieved a clear view of the essential role played by religion in social life. It was in that year that, for the first time, I found the means of tackling the study of religion sociologically. This was a revelation to me. That course of 1895 marked a dividing line in the development of my thought, to such an extent that all my previous researches had to be taken up afresh in order to be made to harmonize with these new insights.... [This reorientation] was entirely due to the studies of religious history which I had just undertaken, and notably to the reading of the works of Robertson Smith and his school. (Durkheim, 1911, pp. 402–3).

There is no doubt that Smith's fascinating *Religion of the Semites* (2nd edn, 1894) – with its comparative approach to the "unconscious religious tradition" preceding and surrounding that of the Old Testament Hebrews, insistence on the temporal priority of ritual over myth, strong distinction between religion and magic, emphasis on the ideas of taboo and sacredness, suggestion that totemism was the earliest form of religion, and that the earliest religious act was one of sacramental communion in which the god and worshippers jointly participated – contained much that would interest the author of *The Elementary Forms of the Religious Life*. But neither is there any evidence, in the years immediately after 1895, that Durkheim knew quite what to do with these ideas – by contrast, for example, with those of Smith's *protégé*, Sir James Frazer (1854–1941), whose *Golden Bough* (1890), with its powerful myth of the "man-god" sacrificed so that his spirit might be passed on unimpaired to his successor, plays a large role in Durkheim's account of altruistic suicide. Even Durkheim's 1899 essay "Concerning the Definition of Religious Phenomena," which defines religion as "obligatory beliefs, connected with clearly defined practices which are related to given objects of those beliefs," has been aptly described by Steven Lukes as "a first, rather groping attempt" (Lukes, 1972, p. 240).

What really caught Durkheim's attention was the publication of Baldwin Spencer and F. J. Gillen's *Native Tribes of Central Australia* (1899) – which would become the primary source of ethnographic data for *The Elementary Forms* – and its almost immediate Frazerian, economic, and utilitarian interpretation.

In fact, Frazer had been corresponding with Baldwin Spencer for several years, and his essay on "The Origin of Totemism" (1899) appeared almost simultaneously with *Native Tribes*. First, Frazer denied the universality of totemism and its long-undisputed connection with exogamy (Durkheim had firmly committed himself to both just a year earlier, in his *Année sociologique* essay on incest). Second, Frazer suggested that some of society's most powerful interdictions had been rationally and purposefully constructed following an earlier period of permissiveness. That the origin of such interdictions lay in the collective unconscious, and that primitive societies could hardly be characterized as "permissive," had been among Durkheim's arguments in *The Division of Labor*. Third, and most alarmingly, Frazer had suggested that the essential function of totemism was to provide for economic needs, and that this was also its sufficient explanation. The fifth chapter of *The Rules of Sociological Method* had been written to oppose such "teleological" confusions of the function of a social fact with its cause, and to insist that needs and desires, while they might hasten or retard social development, cannot themselves *create* social facts at all. Durkheim responded powerfully in "On Totemism" (1902), where Smith proved as useful against Spencer, just as Rousseau had proved so useful against Tarde; and by the time of his lecture course on "La Religion: Origines" at the Sorbonne (1906–7), a rudimentary outline of *The Elementary Forms* had begun to emerge.

Finally, no account of the major intellectual influences on Durkheim would be complete without mentioning the pragmatists. James's *A Pluralistic Universe* had appeared in French in 1910, to be followed by translations of his *Pragmatism* (1911) and *The Meaning of Truth* (1913), at least one with a preface by Bergson; and as we have seen, Durkheim's discussion of science and religion in the conclusion of *The Elementary Forms* had embraced at least one of the ideas in *The Varieties of Religious Experience*. In 1913–14, therefore, Durkheim offered a new course on "Pragmatism and Sociology," and in his first lecture gave two reasons for having chosen this topic. First, pragmatism was "almost the only current theory of truth, and is of topical interest"; second, pragmatism had "in common with sociology, a sense of life and action" (Durkheim, 1983, p. 1). From this point on, however, Durkheim made it abundantly clear that he disagreed with virtually all of the pragmatists' specific arguments (see Lukes, 1972, pp. 485–96). For all of his tampering with the old Cartesian vocabulary, in the end Durkheim fell back on the language of rationalism, realism, natural law, necessary relations of cause and effect, and the correspondence theory of truth.

IMPACT

Durkheim's impact on modern sociological thought has been so great that, to paraphrase one recent commentator, the reiteration of his importance has become something of a ritual performance. The sociological vocabulary he constructed – e.g. social facts as "things," the comparative method, the normal versus the pathological, sacred versus profane, mechanical versus organic solidarity, egoism, altruism, and anomie, the *conscience collective*, collective representations, collective effervescence – is adopted almost unconsciously whenever social theorists talk about what is most important and distinctive in their discipline.

Durkheim's most immediate disciple was his nephew, Marcel Mauss (1872–1950), with whom he collaborated on "Some Primitive Forms of Classification" (1903), on the statistical tables for *Suicide* (1897), and on numerous reviews published in *l'Année sociologique*. In their collaboration, Mauss seems to have had the better sense for concrete social facts, while Durkheim provided the more general theoretical interpretation. Working with Henri Hubert (1872–1927), Mauss published important studies of sacrifice (1899) and magic (1904), but his masterpiece was *The Gift* (1925), a study of systems of exchange as "total social phenomena," including their religious, legal, moral, economic, and aesthetic expressions. In general, however, the Durkheim School suffered a decline after the First World War, reviving significantly only in the early 1970s with the emergence of the Groupe d'études durkheimiennes and a series of articles in the *Revue française de sociologie*, edited by Philippe Besnard. In Britain, the identification of Durkheim with a conservative, functionalist view of society delayed his influence for a comparable period; but Steven Lukes's *Durkheim* (1972) stimulated renewed interest, and the Institute for Social and Cultural Anthropology at Oxford University is currently the home of the Centre for Durkheimian Studies. Even in the United States, Durkheim (like Marx and Weber) was less interesting to sociologists than Comte, Spencer, and Simmel, at least until Talcott Parsons's *Structure of Social Action* (1937) introduced American social science to Durkheim, Weber, and Pareto. Parsons's structural functionalism later made great use of Durkheimian concepts like *conscience collective* and collective representations; and in *Social Theory and Social Structure* (1949), Parsons's student, Robert Merton, made equally significant use of the concept of anomie.

In the 1960s, structural functionalism came under a withering attack, from conflict theorists like Alvin Gouldner and social behaviorists like George Homans, neither of whom was particularly attracted to the Durkheimian vocabulary. But if structural functionalism was the midwife that brought Durkheim to the attention of American sociology, it was by no means the only theoretical perspective that found Durkheim's ideas useful. In *The Social Construction of Reality* (1967), for example, Peter Berger and Thomas Luckmann extended the concerns of phenomenological social theory to structural issues, thus integrating the individual and societal levels. In the same year, Berger's *The Sacred Canopy* provided a brilliant synthesis of Durkheim and Weber's approaches to the sociology of religion, particularly emphasizing what Berger called the *choseité* (literally, "thingness") of external, coercive social facts, including language, collective beliefs, and ritual actions.

Several years later, in his Presidential Address before the American Sociological Association, Lewis Coser attacked many of his colleagues for succumbing to "a veritable orgy of subjectivism" in their adoption of theories like phenomenology and ethnomethodology. Coser's address thus marked the beginning of what George Ritzer has called "the rebirth of interest in structural theory – that is, a return to the roots of sociology in Emile Durkheim's concept of social facts" (Ritzer, 1992, p. 523). Coser urged sociologists not to give in to "the subjectivists," and to return instead to the study of large-scale social structures as the ultimate determinants of other aspects of social reality. Sociologists responding to Coser's call have included Robert Merton, William Goode, Seymour Martin Lipset, and – most important – Peter Blau, whose deterministic brand of structural sociology eliminated values and norms as explanatory variables altogether.

Despite Claude Lévi-Strauss's observation, in *Tristes Tropiques* (1955), that he early arrived at "a state of open revolt against Durkheim and against any attempt to use sociology for metaphysical purposes," one must also agree with his claim (in the same work) that he has been "more faithful than anyone else to the Durkheimian tradition" (Lévi-Strauss, 1973, p. 52). Structuralist anthropology thus owes a large debt to Durkheim, although not to Durkheim's notion of the externality of social facts, but to the later work of Durkheim and Mauss as well as *The Elementary Forms*. Lévi-Strauss's actors are constrained, of course, but by the structures of the human mind rather than by external social things. Similarly, one of the foundational hypotheses of Pierre Bourdieu's sociology has been the insistence that there is a "correspondence between social structures and mental structures, between the objective divisions of the social world...and the principles of vision and division that agents apply to it" (Bourdieu, 1989, p. 7). Loïc Wacquant has characterized this as a reformulation and generalization of Durkheim and Mauss's argument that the cognitive systems operative in primitive societies are derivations of their social systems. Bourdieu extends this thesis into advanced societies, emphasizing the role of the school; providing a causal mechanism for the social determination of classification with his notion of "genetic links"; revealing how such symbolic systems function, not just as instruments of knowledge, but politically, as instruments of domination; and showing how systems of classification constitute a "stake in the struggles" that oppose individuals and groups (Bourdieu and Wacquant, 1992, pp. 12–14).

While Durkheim has been criticized (see below) for neglecting some aspects of social conflict, theorists like Randall Collins have argued that the Durkheimian tradition provides a kind of infrastructure to conflict theory. On the microlevel of interaction, Collins insists, Durkheim provides an explanatory theory of the varieties of class cultures, then building out of these interactions a stratified network that constitutes the macrostructure of domination and power in the society as a whole. "The conflict tradition," Collins concludes, "can be permeated with the deeper explanatory mechanisms revealed by the Durkheimians" (Collins, 1985, p. 173).

Durkheim's sociology of law and crime has received considerable attention. In *Wayward Puritans* (1966), for example, taking up Durkheim's functional theory of crime, Kai Erikson further developed the theory that societies actually create deviance at those times when they are undergoing a boundary-maintaining crisis. As we have seen, Durkheim argued that even a society of saints would create its own "deviants" by magnifying small faults into significant transgressions. Erickson applied this notion to a real society of "visible saints" – i.e. the Puritan settlers of New England – showing how colonial society as a whole (not the "witches," "heretics," and "deviants" within it) created periodic waves of crisis, thus reaffirming social and cultural boundaries. Similarly, in *The Behavior of Law* (1976), Donald Black has extended Durkheim's theory of crime into a more general theory of social control, showing how public complaints about "crime in the streets" and police violence are part of a larger process of the ritual imposition of social order.

Social theories of religious phenomena have depended heavily on Durkheim's ideas. In books like *Purity and Danger* (1966) and *Natural Symbols* (1973), for example, Mary Douglas – like Lukes, a student of Evans-Pritchard – has explored the way symbols maintain group boundaries and social control. In a classic article, "Civil Religion in America" (1967), Robert Bellah explained the beliefs and ceremonies that unite Americans in their devotion to their country, as celebrated in great public rituals like presidential inaugurations and Thanksgiving. While Bellah acknowledged that there is less unanimity on the location of the "sacred" in modern societies than among Australian aborigines, he effectively demonstrates how such a "civil religion" functions at the national level, where the modern state presents its mission and purpose in sacred, transcendent terms. Again, in *The Birth of the Gods* (1960), Guy Swanson developed the controversial view that belief in a high god or monotheistic deity only tends to occur in those societies containing three or more different types of hierarchically ordered sovereign groups. According to Swanson, such complex hierarchies of temporal authority, with one group dominating the others, establish the social conditions that a high god represents or expresses.

Durkheim's view that the fundamental categories of human reason are collective representations has also had a powerful impact on the sociology of knowledge and science. In a famous article published in 1982, for example, David Bloor has attempted to defend a relativist interpretation of Durkheim and Mauss's essay on primitive classification; and other representatives of the so-called "Strong Programme" in the sociology of scientific knowledge have drawn antirealist implications from that essay and *The Elementary Forms*. This has in turn provoked a realist response, most recently articulated by Warren Schmaus: "Although he believed that there are sociological explanations for the very concepts scientists use," Schmaus emphasizes, Durkheim "thought that the social origins of such concepts in no way undermine the reality of that which scientists describe with them" (Schmaus, 1994, p. 256).

Feminist theory has recently been enriched by Durkheim, primarily through a series of articles and a book, *Durkheim and Women* (1994), written by Jennifer Lehmann. Durkheim's views on women are scattered through a surprisingly small number of his works, and Lehmann's reconstruction of a coherent, consistent, and systematic sociological theory of women from these fragmentary remains has been a significant contribution. Durkheim clearly considered women (by contrast with men) more in touch with nature, and less in touch with society, and he used this to account for the differential immunity to suicide enjoyed by men and women under marriage and divorce. Durkheim also considered sexual anomie (suffered more by men) a far greater threat than fatalism (suffered more by women), and this reflects his patriarchal attitudes as well as his policy recommendations.

Finally, it would be a mistake to ignore Durkheim's powerful influence outside of sociology altogether. In the first number of *l'Année sociologique* (1898), for example, Durkheim was outspoken in his disdain for that kind of historiography that focused on individual political figures or military heroes, or on chronological sequences of dynasties, wars, and elections. By 1929, the historians Marc Bloch and Lucien Febvre had founded the journal *Annales: Economies, sociétés, civilisations*, thereby establishing the famous Annales School of French historiography. The School's most distinguished representative, Fernand Braudel, later praised the "completely new sociology" that "rose like a sun" with Durkheim and *l'Année sociologique*, the latter providing "a favourite reading matter for an entire generation of young historians" (see Thompson, 1982, p. 18). Braudel's *The Mediterranean and the Mediterranean World in the Age of Philip II* (1949) – by many lights the single greatest work of history in the twentieth century – is deeply Durkheimian, systematically embracing long-term changes in agriculture, demography, economy, and society that constitute the infrastructure of more short-term political and military events.

ASSESSMENT

Recalling that social theories are vocabularies contrived to serve specific interests and purposes, we should not expect that Durkheim's language would appeal equally to all. Despite his undeniable impact on the development of sociology, therefore, his ideas have been subject to a number of criticisms. The concept of the "social fact" itself must be described as extraordinarily capacious if not downright indiscriminate, incorporating the full range of potentially explanatory social phenomena – population size and distribution, social norms and rules, collective beliefs and practices, currents of opinion – from material to immaterial, and from infrastructural to superstructural levels; and as Durkheim's willingness to focus on the latter rather than the former increased over the course of his career, *The Rules* appeared to straddle an equivocal, intermediate stage (Jones, 1986, p. 78).

It might be argued, of course, that these ambiguities are somewhat relieved by Durkheim's insistence that social facts may be distinguished from their biological and psychological counterparts by their "externality" and powers of "constraint"; but here similar difficulties persist. The suggestion that social facts are external to any particular individual, for example, raises few objections, though a concern for balanced statement might add (as Durkheim increasingly did) that they are also internal to particular individuals; but the suggestion that social facts are external to all individuals can be justified only in the limited sense that they have a prior temporal existence, and any extension beyond these limits is subject (as Durkheim frequently was) to charges of hypostatizing some metaphysical "group mind" (Lukes, 1972, pp. 3–4). The term "constraint" seems to have enjoyed a still greater elasticity, for Durkheim used it variously to refer to the authority of laws as manifested through repressive sanctions; the need to follow certain rules in order to successfully perform certain tasks; the influence of the structural features of a society on its cultural norms and rules; the psychological pressures of a crowd on its members; and the effect of socialization and acculturation on the individual. The first of these usages, Lukes has observed, seems more felicitous than the second (which is perhaps better described as a "means–end" relation), and the last three seem something else altogether: far from being cases of "constraint" or "coercion," they describe how people are led to think and feel in a certain way, to know and value certain things, and to act accordingly (Lukes, 1972, p. 4). It was these latter usages, moreover, which Durkheim increasingly adopted as his interests shifted from the structural emphases of *The Division of Labor* to the focus on collective representations characteristic of *The Elementary Forms*; as he did so, "constraint" became less an "essential characteristic" than a "perceptible sign," and, eventually, disappeared altogether.

Like his definition of social facts, Durkheim's rules for their explanation represent the effort to establish sociology as a science independent of psychology. But here again, "psychology" seems to have meant several different things to Durkheim: explanation in terms of "organico-psychic" factors like race and/or heredity; explanation by "individual and particular" rather than "social and general" conditions; and, most frequently, explanation in terms of "individual mental states or dispositions." In each instance, Durkheim discovered logical or empirical shortcomings; but if social facts thus cannot be *completely* explained by psychological facts, it is at least equally true that even the most determinedly "sociological" explanations necessarily rely upon certain assumptions, explicit or otherwise, about how individual human beings think, feel, and act in particular circumstances. Durkheim's insistence that social facts can be explained only by other social facts was thus both excessive and naive (Jones, 1986, p. 79).

Durkheim's effort to find objective criteria by which "normal" might be distinguished from "pathological" social facts was a rather transparent attempt to grant scientific status to the social and political preferences we identified in the discussion of social context (above). In addition to the logical difficulties of inferring "social health" from the "generality" of a phenomenon, Durkheim himself recognized the practical obstacles to drawing such inferences in "transition periods" like his own; but since economic anarchy, anomie, and rapidly rising suicide rates were all "general" features of "organized" societies, Durkheim's second criterion – that this generality be related to the general conditions of the social type in question – could render them "pathological" only by reference to some future, integrated society which Durkheim somehow considered "latent" in the present. Durkheim, in short, tended to idealize future societies, while dismissing present realities and, like many rationalists, thus appears to have been oblivious to the sheer historical contingency of all social arrangements (Lukes, 1972, p. 29).

The example chosen to illustrate these criteria – the "normality" of crime – reflects the same preconceptions. Even if we accept the argument that the punishment elicited by crime reaffirms that solidarity based on shared beliefs and sentiments, for example, we must still ask a series of more specific questions. Which beliefs and sentiments? Shared by whom? What degree of punishment?

Which "criminal" offenses? Committed by whom? For in the absence of specific answers to such questions (Durkheim's treatment of these issues is unrelievedly abstract), the claim that crime is functional to social integration could be used to justify *any* favored set of beliefs and practices, and *any* type or degree of punishment, simply by arguing that the failure to punish would be followed inevitably by social disintegration. Durkheim's additional claim – that crime is functional to social change – was a simple extension of the view discussed earlier, that law is the direct reflection of the *conscience collective*. But as Tarde was quick to point out, there is no *necessary* connection between the violation of these laws constituting crimes and the sources of moral and social innovation (Lukes and Scull, 1983, pp. 15–19).

As we have seen, Durkheim was a social realist and rationalist: he believed that society is a reality independent of individual minds, and that the methodical elimination of our subjective preconceptions will enable us to know it as it is. As we have also seen, this vocabulary had the advantage of providing young people of the Third Republic with a moral authority worthy of their submission (the "spirit of discipline") and an ideal to which they might commit themselves (the "attachment to groups"); but it is equally true that social facts are themselves constituted by the meanings given to them by those agents whose acts, thoughts, and feelings they are, and that such subjective interpretations are thus a part of the reality to be "known." The question of what religion *is*, for example, is hardly one which can be settled aside from the meanings attached to it by those whose "religion" is under investigation; and any effort to study it independent of such meanings runs the risk not merely of abstracting some "essentialist" definition of religion bearing no relation to the beliefs and practices in question, but also of unconsciously imposing one's own subjective interpretation under the guise of detached, scientific observation (Jones, 1986, pp. 80–1).

Politically, Durkheim maintained that scholars make poor activists, abstained from participation in socialist circles, and generally presented himself as a sociological expert advising his contemporaries on their "true" societal interests; but it is difficult to see how theories which so consistently and emphatically endorsed the secular democratic, egalitarian, antiroyalist, and antirevolutionary values of the Third Republic could reasonably be regarded as devoid of political interests and objectives. The point here is not simply that these theories served political ends, or even that these ends were Durkheim's own; it is rather that here the distinction between social thought and social action becomes elusive to the point of non-existence; for Durkheim's entire social science, including choice and formulation of problems, definition of terms, classification of social types, explanatory hypotheses, methods of proof – indeed, even the denial of all philosophical and political commitments itself – was deeply political (Lukes, 1982, pp. 22–3).

In *The Division of Labor*, Durkheim's early suggestion that social solidarity is an exclusively "moral" phenomenon, of which law is the "externally visible symbol," ignores the frequent conflict of some moral principles with others, some laws with other laws, and morality with legality generally. Durkheim did not deny the existence of such conflict, of course, but he did suggest that it was "pathological," not a part of the "normal" functioning of society, and thus placed it beyond the central focus of his sociological vision. Similarly, Durkheim implied that the state is merely an instrument whose authority reflects the disposition of the *conscience collective*, an implication which excludes most of the concerns so brilliantly explored by Max Weber: the means by which one group in a society achieves asymmetrical control over another; the personal, subjective standards by which the first judges the behavior of the second and renders it consequential; and so on. The point here is not simply that Durkheim did not choose to discuss these issues; rather, the point is that he *could* not, given the reasons why he chose to study law in the first place – as an "external index" of the more fundamental moral conditions of the social order (Lukes and Scull, 1983, pp. 5–8).

Durkheim clearly overstated the role of repressive law relative to the institutions of interdependence and reciprocity (kinship, religious ritual, economic and political alliance, etc.) in primitive societies. Malinowski's *Argonauts of the Western Pacific* (1922), for example, has provided ample evidence of the significance and complexity of relations of exchange among the Trobriand Islanders. In part, this may be attributed to Durkheim's ignorance of the ethnographic literature on primitive peoples, for his pronouncements on "primitive" legal systems in *The Division of Labor* are largely based on inferences drawn from the Hebrew Torah, the Twelve Tables of the ancient Romans, and the laws of early Christian Europe; but he seems to have got these wrong as well. The religious and moral exhortations of the Torah, for example, are largely devoid of "penal" sanctions, and coexisted with a predominantly secular legal system maintained by their "restitutive" counterparts; the sanctions attached to the Twelve Tables were almost equally restitutive; and the gradual emergence of the state as the pre-emptive legal institution of early modern Europe witnessed an *increase* in the relative proportion of repressive laws. Indeed, Durkheim understated the role of repressive law even in advanced industrial societies, in part because he ignored the fact that the nineteenth-century system of penal incarceration replaced the custom of compensating the victims of some crimes financially, and in part because he disregarded the punitive, stigmatizing aspect of many civil laws (Lukes and Scull, 1983, pp. 10–15).

It is also difficult to share Durkheim's confidence in the self-regulating quality of organic solidarity. Durkheim's account of the "anomic" division of labor alone, for example, exposed all the evils of unregulated capitalism: commercial and industrial crises, class conflict, meaningless, alienated labor, etc. (Lukes, 1972, p. 174). But his analysis of these evils was notoriously uncritical: because organic solidarity has evolved more slowly than its mechanical counterpart has passed away, the Third Republic endures a "pathological, disintegrative void"; an analysis which simultaneously implies that these evils are not endemic to modern societies (and thus eviscerates any criticism of them), and conveniently locates the conditions for the successful functioning of "organized" societies in some unspecified, Utopian future. As his work developed, however, Durkheim gradually relinquished the evolutionary optimism which underlay this mechanical, self-regulating, conception of the division of labor, became increasingly attracted to socialism and the potentially regulatory function of occupational groups, and granted greater emphasis to the independent role of collective beliefs in social life.

As the first systematic application of the methodological principles set out in 1895, *Suicide* reveals their limitations as well as their advantages, and thus provides an occasion for considering a number of difficulties – argument by elimination, *petitio principii*, an inappropriate and distortive language, etc. – which, though typical of Durkheim's work as a whole, are perhaps most clearly seen here. Durkheim's characteristic "argument by elimination," for example, pervades both *The Division of Labor* and *The Elementary Forms*, but there is no better example of its power to both persuade and mislead than Durkheim's discussion of "extrasocial causes" in Book One of *Suicide*. Briefly, the argument consists of the systematic rejection of alternative definitions or explanations of a social fact, in a manner clearly intended to lend credibility to the sole remaining candidate – which is Durkheim's own. Durkheim's use of this technique, of course, does not imply that his candidate does not deserve to be elected, but as a rhetorical device, argument by elimination runs at least two serious risks: first, that the alternative definitions and/or explanations might not be jointly exhaustive (other alternatives may exist); and, more seriously, that the alternative definitions and/or explanations might not be mutually exclusive (the conditions and causes they postulate separately might be conjoined to form perfectly adequate definitions and/or explanations other than Durkheim's "sole remaining" candidates). Durkheim's persistent use of this strategy can be attributed to his ineradicable belief, clearly stated in *The Rules*, that a given effect must always have a single cause, and that this cause must be of the same nature as the effect (Lukes, 1972, pp. 31–3).

Petitio principii – the logical fallacy in which the premise of an argument presumes the very conclusion yet to be argued – is, again, a feature of Durkheim's work as a whole. In *The Elementary Forms*, for example, Durkheim first defined religion as a body of beliefs and practices uniting followers in a single community, and later he concluded that this is one of religion's major functions. But there is no clearer instance of this style of argument than Durkheim's "etiological" classification of the types of suicide, which of course presupposes the validity of the causal explanations eventually proposed for them. The point, again, is not that this automatically destroys Durkheim's argument; but it does make it impossible to entertain alternative causes and typologies, and thus to evaluate Durkheim's frequently ambitious claims (Lukes, 1972, p. 31).

Durkheim's repeated insistence that sociology is a science with its own, irreducible "reality" to study also led him to adopt a language that was both highly metaphorical and systematically misleading. This is first evident in *The Division of Labor*, where abundant biological metaphors continuously suggest that society is "like" an organism in a variety of unspecified and unqualified ways; and it is still more pernicious in *The Elementary Forms*, where the real themes of the work – the social origin of religious beliefs and rituals, their symbolic meanings, etc. – are frequently disguised beneath the obfuscatory language of "electrical currents" and "physical forces." *Suicide* combines elements of both; and in particular, this language made it difficult if not impossible for Durkheim to speak intelligibly about the way in which individual human beings perceive, interpret, and respond to "suicido-genic" social conditions (Lukes, 1972, pp. 34–6).

Finally, it might be argued that Durkheim's central explanatory hypothesis – that when social conditions fail to provide people with the necessary social goals and/or rules at the appropriate levels of intensity their socio-psychological health is impaired, and the most vulnerable among them commit suicide – raises far more questions than it answers. Aren't there different kinds of "social goals and rules," for example, and aren't some of these disharmonious? What is socio-psychological "health"? Isn't it socially determined, and thus relative to the particular society or historical period in question? Why are disintegrative, egoistic appetites always described as individual, psychological, and even organic in origin? Aren't some of our most disruptive drives socially generated? And if they are, aren't they also culturally relative? Why are some individuals rather than others "impaired"? And what is the relationship (if, indeed, there is one) between such impairment and suicide? The fact that these questions and others are continuously begged simply reiterates an earlier point: that Durkheim's macro-sociological explanations all presuppose some social-psychological theory, whose precise nature is never made explicit (Lukes, 1972, pp. 213–22).

Even *The Elementary Forms* – Durkheim's greatest work – is not without flaws; indeed, it contains most of the problems discussed earlier, and a few others besides. In sharp contrast to Max Weber, for example, Durkheim largely ignores the role of individual religious leaders, as well as the way religion functions in social conflict and asymmetrical relations of power. The "collective effervescence" stimulated by religious assemblies presumes a social psychology never made explicit, and Durkheim's account of how such gatherings generate totemic symbols is dubious, to say the least. His definition of religion, preceded by an extended argument by elimination and containing a massive *petitio principii*, bears little relation to anything that the central Australians themselves understand by their beliefs and behavior; and students of aboriginal religion like W. E. H. Stanner have spent months looking for instances of the sacred–profane dichotomy, even to the point of questioning their own competence, before admitting that the Australian facts simply do not fit (Stanner, 1967, p. 229).

If there is a single feature of the work more disturbing than any other, it is Durkheim's treatment of the ethnographic evidence. The choice of the "single case" of central Australia has an intrinsic appeal to anyone familiar with the "scissors and paste" method of comparative religion epitomized in *The Golden Bough*; but in practice this focus led Durkheim to ignore counter-instances among the neighboring Australian tribes, or to interpret them arbitrarily according to some *ad hoc*, evolutionary speculations, or to "correct" them in light of the more advanced, and hence allegedly more edifying, American tribes. In fact, there is no evidence that Australian totemism is the earliest totemism, let alone the earliest religion; and, though technically less advanced than the North American Indians, the Australians have a kinship system which is far more complex. But then, *pace* Durkheim, there is no necessary relationship between the "simplicity" of a society (however that is defined) and that of its religious beliefs and practices; nor, for that matter, is there any necessary relationship between religion and totemism generally (*wakan* and *mana* have no discernible relationship to the "totemic principle"). Even if we limit ourselves to Australian tribes, we find that the central tribes are atypical; that the major cohesive force among aborigines is the tribe rather than the clan; that there are clans without totems (and totems without clans); and that most totems are not represented by the carvings and inscriptions on which Durkheim placed so much weight. Finally, we may choose to circumvent the details of Durkheim's interpretation of the ethnographic literature altogether, observing that its *raison d'être* – the notion that the "essence" of religion itself may be found among the Arunta – is, in Clifford Geertz's (1973, p. 22) words, "palpable nonsense." What one finds among the Arunta are the beliefs and practices of the Arunta, and even to call these "religious" is to impose the conventions of one's own culture and historical period.

Criticisms such as these have led some scholars to suggest that the Australian data were introduced simply to illustrate Durkheim's theories, rather than the theories being constructed or adopted to account for the data. But this suggestion requires at least one major qualification in the light of what we know about the historical development of Durkheim's ideas on religion. The rather formal, simplistic conception of religion characteristic of Durkheim's early work, for example, persisted at least until the appearance of Baldwin Spencer and F. J. Gillen's *Native Tribes of Central Australia* (1899); and it was the largely psychologistic and utilitarian interpretation of these ethnographic data proposed by Frazer (and endorsed by Spencer himself) which led Durkheim back to the more determinedly sociological (even mystical) views of Robertson Smith, and to the contrived and even grotesque evolutionary interpretation of these data found in "Sur le totémisme" (1902). If the theories of *The Elementary Forms* do not "explain the facts" of Australian ethnography, therefore, it is because so much of their original purpose was to explain them away (see Jones, 1985).

The most ambitious claim of *The Elementary Forms*, of course, is that the most basic categories of human thought have their origin in social experience; but this claim, Steven Lukes has argued, is not one but six quite different claims which Durkheim did not consistently and clearly distinguish: the *heuristic* claim that concepts (including the categories) are collective representations; the *causal* claim that society produces these concepts; the *structuralist* claim that these concepts are modeled upon, and are thus similar to, the structures of society; the *functionalist* claim that logical conformity is necessary to social stability; the *cosmological* claim that religious myth provided the earliest systems of classification; and the *evolutionary* claim that the most fundamental notions of modern science have primitive religious origins. The structuralist, cosmological, and evolutionary claims, Lukes observed, have been both challenging and influential. But the heuristic claim, by conflating the categories with concepts in general, confuses a capacity of mind with what is better described as its content. In so far as society is literally defined in terms of collective representations (as the later Durkheim increasingly did), both the causal and the functionalist claims seem simply to restate the heuristic claim, and are vulnerable to the same objection; but, in so far as society is construed in structural terms (as in *The Division of Labor*), the causal claim in particular is open to serious objections. The very relations proposed between the structures of primitive societies and their conceptual apparatus, for example, would seem to presuppose the primitives' possession of precisely those concepts. Finally, Durkheim's sociology of knowledge seems susceptible to at least as many empirical objections as his sociology of religion (Needham, 1963, pp. vii–xlviii).

CONCLUSION

At the outset, I suggested that we think of social theories as "languages" or "vocabularies" – ways of thinking or speaking about social phenomena – that are cobbled together by theorists to serve their own, quite concrete, interests and purposes. As we have seen, Durkheim's interests and purposes were intertwined with those of the Third French Republic, with producing the kind of citizen who would not simply obey its laws, but would also respect and revere its institutions. For this purpose, he found the traditional vocabulary of Cartesian rationalism – with its emphasis on "clear and distinct ideas" – utterly inadequate. For he was convinced that the notion of society as an "idea" would always remain insufficient to guarantee the veneration of future citizens of the Republic. Instead, relying heavily on writers like Boutroux, Fustel, Espinas, Schäffle, Wundt, Montesquieu, and especially Rousseau, Durkheim constructed the vocabulary of "social realism" – with its insistence that social facts are complex and concrete *things* – and then demonstrated its utility in the study of social differentiation, morality, education, crime, suicide, religion, knowledge, and science. Like all vocabularies, Durkheim's was limited in its capacity to deal with certain kinds of questions; but unlike its seventeenth-century antecedent, it has proved extremely powerful for the kinds of things that twentieth-century people want to do.

Bibliography

Writings of Émile Durkheim

Gumplowicz, Ludwig, *Grundriss der Soziologie*. 1885. *Revue Philosophique*, 20, 627–34.

La Science positive de la morale en Allemagne. 1887. *Revue Philosophique*, 24, 33–58, 113–42, 275–84.

Course in Sociology: Opening Lecture. 1888. In Mark Traugott (ed.), *Émile Durkheim on Institutional Analysis*. Chicago: University of Chicago Press (1978), pp. 43–70.

Individualism and the Intellectuals. 1898. In Robert N. Bellah (ed.), *Émile Durkheim on Morality and Society*. Chicago: University of Chicago Press (1973), pp. 43–57.

Concerning the Definition of Religious Phenomena. 1899. In W. S. F. Pickering (ed.), *Durkheim on Religion: a Selection of Readings with Bibliographies*. London and Boston: Routledge & Kegan Paul, pp. 74–99.

On Totemism. 1902. *History of Sociology*, 5 (1985), 79–121.

Sur la séparation des églises et de l'état. 1905. *Libres entretiens*, 1ère série, 369–71, 496–500.

The Determination of Moral Facts. 1906. In Émile Durkheim (ed.), *Sociology and Philosophy*. New York: Macmillan (1974), pp. 35–62.

Lettres au Directeur de la *Revue Néo-Scholastique*. 1907. *Revue Néo-Scholastique*, 14, 606–7, 612–14.

Value Judgments and Judgments of Reality. 1911. In Émile Durkheim (ed.), *Sociology and Philosophy*. New York: Macmillan (1974).

The Elementary Forms of the Religious Life, translated by Joseph Ward Swain. 1915. New York and London: Free Press.

Suicide: a Study in Sociology, translated by John A. Spaulding and George Simpson. 1951. Glencoe, IL: Free Press of Glencoe.

Rousseau's Social Contract. 1960. In Émile Durkheim (ed.), *Montesquieu and Rousseau: Forerunners of Sociology*. Ann Arbor, Michigan: University of Michigan Press, pp. 65–138.

Moral Education: a Study in the Theory and Application of the Sociology of Education, translated by Everett K. Wilson and Herman Schnurer. 1961. New York: Free Press of Glencoe.

Primitive Classification, translated by Edward Sagarin. 1963. Chicago: University of Chicago Press.

Individual and Collective Representations. 1974. In *Sociology and Philosophy*. New York: Macmillan, pp. 1–34.

The Evolution of Educational Thought: Lectures on the Formation and Development of Secondary Education in France. 1977. London and Boston: Routledge & Kegan Paul.

Rousseau on Educational Theory. 1979. In W. S. F. Pickering (ed), *Durkheim: Essays on Morals and Education*. London and Boston: Routledge & Kegan Paul, pp. 162–94.

The Rules of Sociological Method. 1982. In Steven Lukes (ed.), *The Rules of Sociological Method and Selected Texts on Sociology and Its Method*. London and Basingstoke: Macmillan, pp. 29–163.

Pragmatism and Sociology, translated by J. C. Whitehouse. 1983. Cambridge: Cambridge University Press.

The Division of Labor in Society, translated by W. D. Halls. 1984. New York: Free Press.

Quid Secondatus Politicae Scientiae Instituendae Contulerit (Montesquieu's Contribution to the Rise of Social Science), translated by W. Watts Miller and Emma Griffiths. 1997. Oxford: Durkheim Press.

Further reading

Alexander, Jeffrey C. (1983) *Theoretical Logic in Sociology, Volume 2. The Antinomies of Classical Thought: Marx and Durkheim*. Berkeley and Los Angeles: University of California Press.

Alexander, Jeffrey C. (ed.) (1988) *Durkheimian Sociology: Cultural Studies*. Cambridge: Cambridge University Press.

Bellah, Robert N. (ed.) (1973) *Émile Durkheim: On Morality and Society*, translated by Mark Traugott. Chicago and London: University of Chicago Press.

Berger, Peter (1967) *The Sacred Canopy*. New York: Doubleday.

Berger, Peter and Luckman, Thomas (1967) *The Social Construction of Reality*. New York: Doubleday.

Besnard, Philippe (ed.) (1983) *The Sociological Domain: the Durkheimians and the Founding of French Sociology*. Cambridge: Cambridge University Press.

Black, Donald (1976) *The Behavior of Law*. New York: Academic Press.

Bloor, David (1982) Durkheim and Mauss Revisited: Classification and the Sociology of Knowledge. *Studies in the History and Philosophy of Science*, 13, 267–97.

Bourdieu, Pierre (1989) *La Noblesse d'État: Grands Corps et Grandes Écoles*. Paris: Minuit.

Bourdieu, Pierre and Wacquant, Loïc J. D. (1992) *An Invitation to Reflexive Sociology*. Chicago: University of Chicago Press.

Boutroux, Émile (1895) *Natural Law in Science and Philosophy*, translated by Fred Rothwell. London: D. Nutt (1914).

Boutroux, Émile (1916) *The Contingency of the Laws of Nature*, translated by Fred Rothwell. Chicago and London: Open Court.

Braudel, F. (1949) *The Mediterranean and the Mediterranean World in the Age of Philip II*. Glasgow: Collins (1966).

Bury, J. P. T. (1985) *France, 1814–1940*. London: Methuen.

Cladis, Mark S. (1992) *A Communitarian Defense of Liberalism: Émile Durkheim and Contemporary Social Theory*. Stanford, CA: Stanford University Press.

Clark, T. N. (1973) *Prophets and Patrons: the French University and the Emergence of the Social Sciences*. Cambridge, MA: Harvard University Press.

Collins, Randall (1985) *Three Sociological Traditions*. New York and Oxford: Oxford University Press.

Coser, Lewis A. (1971) *Masters of Sociological Thought*. New York: Macmillan.

Douglas, Mary (1966) *Purity and Danger: an Analysis of Concepts of Pollution and Taboo*. London: Routledge Kegan Paul.

Douglas, Mary (1973) *Natural Symbols: Explorations in Cosmology*. London: Barrie and Rockcliff.

Erikson, Kai (1966) *Wayward Puritans: a Study in the Sociology of Deviance*. New York: Wiley.

Fenton, S. (1984) *Durkheim and Modern Sociology*. Cambridge: Cambridge University Press.

Frazer, James (1890) *The Golden Bough*. New York: Macmillan.

Frazer, James (1899) The Origin of Totemism. *Fortnightly Review*, 68, 657–65, 835–52.

Gane, Mike (1988) *On Durkheim's Rules of Sociological Method*. London: Routledge & Kegan Paul.

Geertz, Clifford (1973) Thick Description: toward an Interpretive Theory of Culture. In *The Interpretation of Cultures*. New York: Basic Books, pp. 3–30.

James, William (1902) *The Varieties of Religious Experience*. Harmondsworth: Penguin (1983).

Jones, Robert Alun (1985) Durkheim, Totemism and the Intichiuma. *History of Sociology: an International Review*, 5(2), 79–121.

Jones, Robert Alun (1986) *Émile Durkheim. An Introduction to Four Major Works*. Beverly Hills, CA and London: Sage.

LaCapra, D. (1972) *Émile Durkheim: Sociologist and Philosopher*. Ithaca, NY and London: Cornell University Press.

Lehmann, Jennifer M. (1994) *Durkheim and Women*. Lincoln and London: University of Nebraska Press.

Lévi-Strauss, Claude (1955) *Tristes Tropiques*. Paris: Librarie Plon.

Lukes, Steven (1972) *Émile Durkheim: His Life and Work. A Historical and Critical Study*. New York: Harper & Row.

Lukes, Steven (1982) Introduction. In Steven Lukes (ed.), *Durkheim: the Rules of Socio-logical Method and Selected Texts on Sociology and Its Method*. New York: Macmillan, pp. 1–27.

Lukes, S. and Scull, A. (eds) (1983) *Durkheim and the Law*. Oxford: St Martin's Press.

McManners, John (1972) *Church and State in France, 1871–1914*. London: Church Historical Society.

Malinowski, Bronislaw (1922) *Argonauts of the Western Pacific*. London: Routledge & Kegan Paul.

Mauss, Marcel (1925) *The Gift*. New York: Free Press (1954).

Mayeur, Jean-Marie and Rebérieux, Madeleine (1984) *The Third Republic from Its Origins to the Great War, 1871–1914*. Cambridge: Cambridge University Press.

Merton, R. K. (1949) *Social Theory and Social Structure*. New York: Free Press; revised edition, 1957; enlarged and revised edition, 1968.

Needham, Rodney (1963) Introduction. In Rodney Needham (ed.), *Primitive Classification*. Chicago: University of Chicago Press, pp. vii–xlviii.

Parsons, Talcott (1937) *The Structure of Social Action*. New York: Free Press.

Pickering, W. S. F. (1984) *Durkheim's Sociology of Religion: Themes and Theories*. London, Boston and Melbourne: Routledge & Kegan Paul.

Pickering, W. S. F. and Martins, H. (eds) (1994) *Debating Durkheim*. London and New York: Routledge.

Pope, Whitney (1976) *Durkheim's Suicide: a Classic Analyzed*. Chicago and London: University of Chicago Press.

Ritzer, George (1992) *Sociological Theory*. New York: McGraw-Hill.

Robertson, Smith, William (1889) *The Religion of the Semites*. 2nd edn 1894. New York: Schocken (1972).

Schmaus, Warren (1994) *Durkheim's Philosophy of Science and the Sociology of Knowledge: Creating an Intellectual Niche*. Chicago and London: University of Chicago Press.

Spencer, Baldwin and Gillen, F. J. (1899) *The Native Tribes of Central Australia*. London: Macmillan.

Stanner, W. E. H. (1967) Reflections on Durkheim and Aboriginal Religion. In M. Freedman (ed.), *Social Organization: Essays Presented to Raymond Firth*. Chicago: Aldine, pp. 217–40.

Swanson, Guy (1960) *The Birth of the Gods: the Origin of Primitive Beliefs*. Ann Arbor: University of Michigan Press.

Thompson, Kenneth (1982) *Émile Durkheim*. London and New York: Tavistock/Routledge.

Traugott, Mark (ed. and trans.) (1978) *Émile Durkheim on Institutional Analysis*. Chicago: University of Chicago Press.

Wallwork, Ernest (1972) *Durkheim, Morality and Milieu*. Cambridge, MA: Harvard University Press.

Zola, Émile (1892) *La Débâcle*. Chester Springs, PA: Dufour (1969).

7

Georg Simmel

Lawrence A. Scaff

Life, Work and Orientation

As one of the most important modern social theorists, Georg Simmel has always presented an impressive yet ambiguous face to the world. A prescient and brilliant diagnostician of our times, as Habermas has acknowledged, he has also been seen as more interested in the suggestive *aperçu* than in systematic science (Habermas, 1991, p. 158). Simmel was a key founder of sociology in Germany, and his essays received international recognition during his lifetime, but his work as a whole has nevertheless been treated as an ambivalent "experiment" with "impressionist" leanings (Lukács, 1918, cited in Gassen and Landmann, 1993, p. 175; Frisby, 1992). Conflicting judgments about Simmel should not be surprising, however, considering the task that he set for himself to write as both a philosopher and sociologist, ignoring the usual disciplinary fetters, while probing the dynamics of modern social and individual experience in all of its aspects, from economics to art, with an uncompromising earnestness and originality. Much of what remains engaging and instructive in Simmel's work has to do with the reach, depth and risks of his intellectual journey. In an ironic twist that Simmel would have appreciated, the very marginality of his daring seems to have ensured his centrality in our own times.

Simmel was an intellectual of the *fin de siècle*. Born in the very heart of old Berlin in 1858, he lived in the city nearly all his life, experiencing its rise from a modest and sleepy provincial capital to a teeming, industrialized metropolis and center of world power. Only in 1914 did he move to a chair in philosophy at Strasbourg, Alsace, dying of liver cancer in that disputed city four years later as the Great War ground to a halt outside its gates. The intellectual, cultural, and political life of Berlin was essential for Simmel. He was a man of the city, a close observer of its dynamic social life, and a devotee of its varied sociocultural milieu. In one of his rare autobiographical statements, he commented that "Berlin's development from a city to a metropolis in the years around and after the turn of the century coincides with my own strongest and extensive development" (quoted in Frisby, 1992, p. 19).

That personal development took place most importantly within the Philosophical Faculty of the Humboldt University, where Simmel was a student and lecturer for nearly forty years, though never gaining a regular professorial appointment – a source of bitter disappointment. The problems, topics, and themes of his many writings over these decades breathe the spirit of this most urban of universities and its powerful intellectual traditions and profoundly unsettled environment of sublime spectacle and dynamic pace. Contemporaries understood this fact. As the philosopher Karl Joël observed in reviewing *The Philosophy of Money*, the work some regard as Simmel's major achievement, it could only have been "written in these times and in Berlin" (Frisby, 1992, pp. 11, 19). It was in this urban center also that Simmel moved from philosophy to sociology, delivering the first lectures on sociological subjects in a German university in 1893–4. His sociological commitments were underscored later when, with Max Weber and Ferdinand Tönnies, he founded the German Sociological Society, inaugurating its first meeting in 1910 with his important paper on "sociability."

Georg Simmel was the youngest of seven children in a family of Jewish heritage from Silesia, now in southern Poland. Both parents had converted to Christianity, his mother to Protestantism as a teenager, and his father to Catholicism during a business trip to Paris. The son followed his mother's example, though he never entirely lost his Jewish identity and thus felt the sting of antisemitism. Simmel's father, Edward, a successful businessman and founder of the firm "Felix and Sarotti" (later the well known chocolate company), died when young Georg was sixteen, leaving him in the care of a family friend, Julius Friedländer. This tragic event proved fortuitous, however, as Friedländer had successfully established the "Edition Peters" music publishing firm, and the generous inheritance he left Simmel allowed the promising young scholar to pursue an academic career, despite years spent without a regular salaried position. Simmel's life path thus paralleled those of others in his generation, such as Weber, Sombart, or slightly later Robert Michels, in which the sons fled the comfortable confines of the *Besitzbürgertum*, the wealthy upper middle class, for the speculative fields of science – a flight made possible in part by inherited wealth or the condition Weber ironically labeled his "miserable *rentier* existence."

One of the most significant aspects of Simmel's upbringing and university years was his introduction not simply to philosophy and social theory, but also to artistic circles in Berlin. Supported by Friedländer, Simmel continued a musical education begun in his youth, studying both piano and violin. But even more importantly he became acquainted with the Graef family, home of the famous painter, and through the members of the family came into contact with artistic circles, the figures of the Berlin *Secession*, and eventually the symbolist poet Stefan George and his circle. It was also through the daughter, Sabine, that he met his future wife, Gertrud Kinel, who with Sabine had studied painting at the celebrated *Académie Julien* in Paris.

By the 1880s and 1890s the interest in these circles in the inner life, emotions, the psyche, and artistic expression had congealed in a new aesthetic "culture of feeling" in urban centers like Berlin, Vienna, and Paris – a cultural movement, as historians have pointed out, that was sharply set off from the dominant liberal, politically oriented, moralizing, and philosophical culture of the era. Simmel was immersed in both cultures, associating with the poets attracted to Stefan George and composing experimental verse and prose for the art nouveau journal *Jugend*. Yet he was also dedicated to the rigors of Kantian philosophy, while publishing in Karl Kautsky's socialist publication, *Die neue Zeit,* and also becoming active in the politically engaged Social Science Students Association (the *Sozialwissenschaftliche Studentenvereinigung*). He thus bridged the great cultural divisions of his times, showing an inclination to multiple perspectives and group affiliations. His work can be seen as an effort to understand the different and opposed sides of these divisions, to rethink the problems of each through the new science of "sociology" and the modes of inquiry characteristic of "philosophical culture," as he titled one of his most important collections of essays.

Critical synthesis of contradictory viewpoints, system building, or reconciliation between opposing forces in the world was not Simmel's ambition, however. For again and again he presents himself to us as a man of ideas having an uncommon will to originality, adopting an "experimental" stance, a mode of writing, and a "style" that reveals the unique grammar of his thinking. His emphasis is on maintaining the dualisms, the dyadic tensions, rather than imposing a new synthesis or schematic "master narrative." Today some would call such a view "postmodern," though for Simmel himself it was merely "modern." If as a modernist he singled out a particular moral-political problem, then it had to do with individuality: how can our individuality be preserved in the face of the dominating forces external to us? Or, as he notes in the idiom of *The Philosophy of Money*, it is "the discrepant relationship between objective and subjective culture, which forms our specific problem" (Simmel, 1990, p. 450). Simmel's social theory and sociology represent an effort to address this assertion.

YOUNG SIMMEL: THE EARLY WRITINGS

"I began with epistemological and Kantian studies, which went hand in hand with historical and social scientific studies," wrote Simmel about his own starting points (Gassen and Landmann, 1993, p. 9). This self-appraisal referred quite obviously to the neo-Kantian movements of the time, represented in Berlin by Wilhelm Dilthey, and also to Simmel's participation in lectures and seminars offered by famous historians like Theodor Mommsen and Heinrich von Treitschke. But the "social scientific" reference is more obscure. In part because of the detailed recent work of Klaus Köhnke (1996), we now know considerably more about this aspect of the intellectual point of departure and its significance for Simmel's mature work.

As a budding social scientist in his early twenties, Simmel in his earliest written work actually dealt with a field of social psychology known as *Völkerpsychologie* or ethnopsychology, founded by one of his most important teachers, Moritz Lazarus. His first effort at a dissertation, subsequently rejected by his committee, bore the striking title "Psychological and Ethnographic Studies on the Origins of Music," and incorporated an evolutionary perspective informed generally by Spencer and Darwin. Indeed, Dilthey himself later commented appropriately on the early Simmel that his "standpoint is Spencer's evolutionary theory" (Köhnke, 1996, pp. 65, 77; Gassen and Landmann, 1993, p. 22). The reason for this assessment had to do with an effort to postulate mechanisms and stages of evolutionary change with regard to the production of human culture – in this case, musicality. But Simmel was also fascinated by problems in the less controversial field of Kantian philosophy, where much of his early work was centered. Kant was the subject of his successfully defended dissertation of 1881, and problems in Kantian ethics and logic formed the subject matter for his habilitation four years later. When he began lecturing at the University of Berlin in 1885 the subjects revolved around philosophical and ethnopsychological problems: ethics, Kant, and the significance of Darwinism.

It took Simmel a decade to shift "from ethnopsychology to sociology," as he noted himself – a transition that went hand-in-hand with the gradual substitution of evolutionary theory by a more "formal" approach. When the transition was completed he began offering the first sociology lectures in a German university. So whereas his good friend Max Weber came to sociology by way of political economy, Simmel developed his perspective through engagement with ethnography, psychology, and philosophy. This particular intellectual path had important implications for the form and content of the Simmelian sociological field, in contrast to what has come to be called a "Weberian" perspective.

We see something of Simmel's developing intellectual perspective in the highly varied work leading up to the *Philosophy of Money* (1900). Many of Simmel's lifelong themes are evident in essays and lectures on: epistemological problems; the philosophy of history; pessimism and culture; the nature of sociology; the psychology and social position of women; the problem of style and fashion; the sociology of the family; and the contributions and significance of major figures like Goethe, Nietzsche, Michelangelo, and Rembrandt. But the major dimensions of his social theory are announced in two studies: *On Social Differentiation: Sociological and Psychological Investigations* (1890), and the weighty two-volume opus, *Introduction to the Moral Sciences: a Critique of Basic Ethical Concepts*. Notwithstanding Simmel's mature criticism of the latter as a "youthful sin," these studies are important for showing the formulation of his central questions and the emergence of his sociology from evolutionary and developmental problematics. The text on social differentiation establishes a fundamental truth that Simmel carries with him the rest of his life, namely, what he calls "the unity of society as reciprocal interaction of its parts." The key concept of "interaction" or *Wechselwirkung*, with its connotations of reciprocal (macro) causes and effects brought about by exchanges among individual (micro) units, is already well defined in this work and later becomes a highly nuanced element in Simmel's methodology. It is used in this early context to articulate a theory of social differentiation reminiscent of Durkheim's in *The Division of Labor in Society*, though the Durkheimian evolutionary framework is replaced by autonomous processes of differentiation within and among social groups, operating analogously to the principle of the "conservation of energy." Moreover, Simmel's most urgent problem is not the Durkheimian treatment of social facts as "things," *sui generis*, but rather the protection of individuality, a core value he establishes in this text that is itself a product of social interaction.

The eclecticism and experimentalism of the *Introduction to the Moral Sciences* has tended to diminish its importance. It is fair to say that it has "no recognizable thesis" and offers an "undisciplined reflection on the social" (Köhnke, 1996, pp. 167–8). But it is nevertheless the key early work, for it focuses Simmel's life work and theme around a "double relationship" expressed in the following way: "On the one hand the individual belongs to a whole and is a part of it, while on the other hand s/he is independent and stands opposed to it" (Simmel, 1989, volume 3, p. 178). The overriding concern of the *Introduction* involves answering the questions: how is this double relationship possible, and what are the categories for its analysis? As for J. S. Mill, Simmel's version of the moral sciences encompasses that branch of practical philosophy dealing with ethics and customs or mores; thus, much of his effort leads the reader on a tour through the standard categories: the ought, egoism, altruism, duty, happiness, freedom. But along the way Simmel begins to introduce sociological considerations bearing on the traditional problems of practical philosophy. "With Simmel the formation of *sociological* concepts begins within the framework and thus with the medium of ethics," as Köhnke maintains (1996, p. 397). The basic concepts of social life then start to take shape – individual, group, family, estate, or status order (*Stand*) – as do, most importantly, the forms of interaction and sociation – competition, opposition, super- and subordination, emulation, and the like.

It is with the insertion of this new conceptual language that the venerable "moral sciences" of the nineteenth century give way to the new sociology of the twentieth. In Germany Simmel was the key figure in leading this transformation, as was Durkheim in France. And across the Atlantic it was this Simmelian "interactionist" social perspective that so strongly influenced his American student, Robert Park, and through him led to the formation of the "Chicago School" of American sociology.

SIMMEL'S SOCIAL THEORY: THE PHILOSOPHY OF MONEY

At the time Simmel was working through issues in ethics and the epistemology of the human sciences, he also began to engage with topics in political economy and models of *Homo economicus*. A paper on the "psychology of money," first delivered in Gustav Schmoller's economics seminar in Berlin, appeared in 1889, and it was followed by brief studies on the role of money in modern culture and in the relationship between the sexes. This work culminated in the seminal volume published in 1900, *The Philosophy of Money.*

Simmel's striking *fin de siècle* title concealed a number of important lines of thought. As "philosophy" his inquiry raised a question about the meaning of "money" as commodity, value, and symbol for the quality of human life. Simmel remarked that he was interested not only in the conditions that produce a money economy, but also in the effects of money and its exchange and use values "upon the inner world – upon the vitality of individuals, upon the linking of their fates, upon culture in general" (Simmel, 1990, p. 54). Such a question cannot be given an exact answer, to be sure, but instead presupposes a method that Simmel referred to as "hypothetical interpretation and artistic reconstruction." In this sense philosophy remains a special form of questioning, whose subject matter is always the "totality of being." Interestingly, however, Simmel's version of philo-sophical inquiry does not proclaim such a totality. Instead, it proceeds at the level of phenomena that are specific, concrete, limited, and finite. Its investiga-tions are justified by the possibility "of finding in each of life's details the totality of its meaning" (Simmel, 1990, p. 55) – a quintessential Simmelian statement of purpose.

Methodologically, then, for Simmel the "philosophy" of money is distinct from the political economy of the modern capitalist economy, as practiced by Marx and his followers, for

> The attempt is made to construct a new storey beneath historical materialism such that the explanatory value of the incorporation of economic life into the causes of intellectual culture is preserved, while these economic forms themselves are recog-nized as the result of more profound valuations and currents of psychological or even metaphysical pre-conditions. (Simmel, 1990, p. 56)

In other words, Simmel hopes to uncover the psychological premises upon which modern economic forms must rest. These premises are worked out in terms of the inner valuation of money and the reaction to it as an abstract, impersonal power. The preconditions for the modern economy are found in the depersonalizing norms of calculation and efficiency that encourage us to view the world simply as an "arithmetical problem" having definite solutions. Employing architectonic imagery, Simmel has thus chosen to reinterpret Marx's materialist foundational-ism through the medium of a psychologically attuned critique of the modern age. Alternatively, we might say that those aspects of the individual's orientation toward life that Max Weber spoke of as a "spirit" or an "ethos," Simmel tends to treat at the ground level of "psychological preconditions." For Simmel, how-ever, the outcome of such an ordering of relations must be not so much a clearer view of history, but rather a nuanced understanding of the clash between sub-jective and objective moments in the total life of our evolving civilization.

To reach this understanding and accomplish its purpose *The Philosophy of Money* uses a distinctive perspective informed by juxtaposing "objective" and "subjective" realms of experience, a distinction that becomes central for Sim-mel's entire theory of culture. In this text the objective forms of the money economy are considered not in order to lay bare the economic substructure of society, but in order to probe what might be called their subjective consequences for the make-up of individuals and the content of social life. The problem is this: there is a contradiction that becomes increasingly evident in the modern age between the simultaneous "increase" in objective (or material) culture and the "decrease" in subjective (or individual) culture. Whereas the former becomes more and more refined, complex, sophisticated, expansive, comprehensive, and domineering, the latter in relation to it becomes cruder, simpler, more trivial, limiting, fragmentary, and anarchic:

> Just as our everyday life is surrounded more and more by objects of which we cannot conceive how much intellectual effort is expended in their production, so our mental and social communication is filled with symbolic terms, in which a comprehensive intellectuality is accumulated, but of which the individual mind need make only minimal use.... Every day and from all sides, the wealth of objective culture increases, but the individual mind can enrich the forms and contents of its own development only by distancing itself still further from that culture and developing its own at a much slower pace. (Simmel, 1990, p. 449)

In the face of such a dynamic tendency Simmel then speaks of "the fragmentary life-contents of individuals" and "the insignificance or irrationality of the individual's share" of objective culture. Stated somewhat differently, the material artifacts and technologies we have created are set against ourselves and against human purposes. We lose control of our objective culture, are assaulted and overwhelmed by it, and begin to respond to it in different and opposed ways: with passivity or aggression, fascination or repulsion, immersion or escape. This initial insight into the duality of our experience presents Simmel with his philo-sophical *and* sociological problem: how is an opposition possible between ourselves and the contents of the world we have created? And what can it mean for the forms of sociation, of individual action in society?

Turning to the first question, the sociology of cultural contradictions is not difficult to conceive: objectification has its root causes in such solid facts as the division of labor; that is, the differentiation of functions and specialization of tasks in the economic order. Indeed, Simmel has already established differentia-tion as an irreducible general phenomenon and category of social life, whose true home is found in the increasingly complex money economy. But differentiation soon spreads everywhere and "brings about a growing estrangement between the subject and its products," which then "invades even the more intimate aspects of our daily life" (Simmel, 1990, p. 459). While gaining a hold over the life-world through differentiation, the money economy also prepares the way for the subversion of this world, just as it creates the conditions for our self-estrangement. In addition, the fetishism of objects is aligned with the fixation of a psychological dependence upon a quality Simmel refers to as *die Mode* – namely, style or fashion. That which is newly "fashionable" and *au courant* reveals itself in the commanding power of style. The problematic features of economic life are defined not merely by a separation between purportedly "natural" subjects and the material means of production or products of labor, but by the psychological transformation of external forms into a *reified* content. What Simmel thought of as "technological progress" is thus accompanied at the level of individual consciousness by a new interiority or *subjectivism* that renders the ephemeral continuous and the marginal central.

Now the primacy of style, characterized by Simmel at a key juncture in his reasoning as "one of the most significant instances of distancing" (Simmel, 1990, p. 473), is most importantly an indication of the increasingly uneasy awareness of a growing tension within the economy of the ego, or an increasing gulf between the self and objects, the self and others, all of which result from the individual's absorption into the entirely fluid realm of psychological experience. But distancing is also a precondition for sociation and group life. It gives us a starting point for addressing Simmel's second question about the forms of sociation.

One of the great achievements of *The Philosophy of Money* is the way it sets forth a phenomenology of our efforts to cope with the "social-technological mechanism" of the "objective" world, a line of thinking on a par with Freud's later attempt in *Civilization and Its Discontents*. What Simmel is able to do is demonstrate both the opportunities for freedom of the personality on the one hand, and the alternatives for mastery of the world on the other. In the third chapter the *types* of alternatives become quite explicit, and they are subsequently elaborated in some of Simmel's finest essays, such as those on "fashion" and the "metropolis," as well as in his last chapters on sociological topics in the *Fundamental Problems of Sociology* [*Grundfragen der Soziologie*] (see Simmel, 1917, chapter 3; 1971, pp. 294–339): greed or avarice, a life of extravagance, ascetic poverty, cynicism, the blasé attitude or position of complete indifference, reserve, or aversion, the appropriation of "style" in the name of "being different," even conviviality as the "play form" of social interaction – all represent the choice of an ethos, a way of life, occasioned by the intensification and heightening of experience in our material world. In Milan Kundera's language, they are ways of making this "lightness" bearable, of staking out a ground for freedom and personal choice.

For Simmel these psychological alternatives are manifested in two interesting and contrasting ways. First, they are self-referential and reflexive, and they provide a powerful commentary on Simmel's own unique cast of mind and stylistic peculiarities as a "theorist." Second, they recombine in the social types of his sociological analysis and occasional essays: the stranger, adventurer, miser, spendthrift, dandy, coquette, lover, aesthete, and so forth. These figures and the social roles they play signify *possible* responses to the dynamic forces unleashed in the money economy. But there are other responses as well, potentially an even infinite variation. (Parenthetically, Simmel once complained that what counts as sexuality is too limited, a situation modern society may seem determined to remedy!) In one of his last statements on the subject, he gave the idea the following form:

> I should like to think that the efforts of mankind will produce ever more numerous
> and varied forms for the human personality to affirm itself and to demonstrate the

value of its existence. In fortunate periods, these varied forms may order themselves into harmonious wholes. In doing so, their contradictions and conflicts will cease to be mere obstacles to mankind's efforts: they will also stimulate new demonstrations of the strength of these efforts and lead them to new creations. (Simmel, 1917, p. 103; 1950, p. 84)

Moreover, Simmel tends to view the ideological manifestations of political activity and social movements, such as socialism and feminism, in a similar light. That is, they too arise as a response to the impersonal, disintegrating effects of "money" on associational life.

When precisely a social movement arises, or why one type or direction is chosen over another, are the historical causal questions that Simmel sets off to one side. That is the weakness of his brilliant, process-oriented intellectual tour de force. But the strength of his unconventional analysis is that a "new storey beneath historical materialism" has been constructed and prepared for its new occupant: a general and a formal sociology.

Sociology: interaction and experience

Simmel's main contributions to systematic sociology are found in two texts, the so-called "major" and the "minor" sociologies: that is, the essays begun in the 1890s and supplemented with later material in the thousand-page opus of 1908, *Sociology: Investigations of the Forms of Sociation*; and the four brief essays penned toward the end of his life and published in 1917 as *Fundamental Problems of Sociology: Individual and Society*. The latter provides a kind of overview of the path Simmel had followed, and in it he distinguishes among three kinds of sociology: general, pure or formal, and philosophical. The distinction can be described in terms of three kinds of problem areas: inquiry into the relationship between individual and society, viewed from the standpoint of the individual or the social; inquiry into the *forms* of interaction among individuals, the reciprocal relations that make up what we call society; and inquiry into the modes and presuppositions of knowledge suggested by the sociological point of view.

These problem areas of the discipline share a number of features. First, they adhere to a conception of society emphasizing its dynamic and process-oriented qualities: "Society exists where a number of individuals enter into interaction [*Wechselwirkung*]," Simmel writes, noting that "interaction always arises on the basis of certain drives or for the sake of certain purposes" (Simmel, 1971, p. 23; 1992, pp. 17–18). Indeed, he argues, "one should properly speak, not of society, but of sociation [*Vergesellschaftung*]. Society merely is the name for a number of individuals, connected by interaction" (Simmel, 1917, p. 14; 1950, p. 10). Society is thus not a reified whole or an observable object that exists *sui generis*, as Durkheim claimed, but a fluid reality composed of willing, acting, conscious individuals who impose a scheme of interpretation on their actions and engagements. It can be viewed as a kind of *a priori*, but only because we are social animals given to sociation and sociability, not because it exists independent of us.

A second commonality is a conception of sociology that "asks what happens to people and by what rules they act, not insofar as they develop comprehensible individual existences in their totality, but insofar as they form groups through interaction and are determined by this group existence" (Simmel, 1917, p. 15; 1950, p. 11, translation altered), a formulation taken up by Louis Wirth and others in the "Chicago School." As the specialized science of society, this sociology therefore "must exclusively investigate these interactions, these kinds and forms of sociation" (Simmel, 1971, p. 25; 1992, p. 19). That is sociology's central task, and it is one Simmel pursued for three decades with perspicacity and seemingly inexhaustible energy in a stream of essays, chapters, and occasional writings. His statement of the task also helps to demarcate the contested boundary between sociology and psychology, an important distinction because of the charges of "psychologism" that have burdened these Simmelian formulations. Whereas sociology's domain is sociation, psychology's is the structure of personality, or the quality Simmel called the irreducible "core of individuality" that makes each person unique.

Third, they share a basic assumption about methodology, namely, the view that sociological inquiry proceeds according to its own canons of knowledge, not according to the nomothetic intentions of the physical sciences. Sociology is essentially a reflexive science, aware of the way knowledge is conditioned by the knowledge-seeker, emphasizing in all domains of life what Simmel calls the "universality of sociation," and using an inductive method. To study sociation is to adopt "a methodology which is wholly different from that for the question of how nature is possible" (Simmel, 1971, p. 8; 1992, p. 45), as Simmel states the case. In contrast to Durkheim's conceptual realism, Simmel thus advocates a thoroughgoing philosophical nominalism that underscores the constructed and purposeful aspects to knowledge in the human sciences.

The chapters of the major or "*grosse*" *Sociology*, as it has been called, are often regarded as the *locus classicus* of Simmel's substantive contribution. They bring together the main outlines of both a general and a pure or formal sociology that proceeds with Euclidean precision from the most elemental of units (the hypothesis of the autonomous individual); to complex interactive units (dyads, triads, groups, organizations, bureaucracy, state); to complex social relationships (subordination, conflict, secrecy, trust), abstract ordering principles ("spatial" relationships), and particular social types (the stranger). Some of Simmel's most insightful studies are found in these investigations of the formal, abstract properties of, say, the "eternal triad" in human relationships, the unusual dynamics of the conspiratorial clique, or the positive functions of intense conflict for group solidarity. Every one of these studies is directed toward advancing our understanding of sociation processes and their typical forms, and all are rich with suggestions for investigating specific actual instances of social life.

Throughout these multifaceted studies it is clear that the most obvious underpinning of Simmel's scientific questioning in the *Sociology* and the *Fundamental Problems of Sociology* is the concept of "interaction," or, as the German word *Wechselwirkung* implies, action that has "reciprocal effects." It is a relational concept that is designed to get at the "objective" aspects of social life which exist outside of any particular individual and are then located between individuals. To speak of an interaction is to characterize a relation between a subject and an object (both of which may be human individuals). The appropriate images for this characterization are spatial, directional, and three-dimensional: movement to and fro, repetitious circular motion, the sweep of a curve, or (one of Simmel's favorites) the spiral movement from one "level" to another. The dynamics of rhythm, pace, and tempo are a part of this Simmelian language, as are the possibilities for either progression or regression, development or implosion, sympathy or antagonism, forming connections or breaking apart, certainty or ambivalence. Ironically, the very range and undecidability of these opposed categories has led critics, starting with Georg Lukács, to place this analysis itself in the "ambivalent" category – a charge that a Simmelian sociologist would say misses the point of Simmel's scientific intentions and ignores the ambivalence inherent in social life.

Summing up, we can say that interaction involves processes like objectification, differentiation and distanciation. Interaction also creates social "forms" – roles, institutions, social structures – and produces social effects, such as integration or marginalization. But this is not the entire story, for it is equally important to recognize, as Nedelmann (1990) has suggested, that Simmel's sociology actually proceeds from a double perspective: on the one side the focus of attention is interaction, and on the other it is "lived experience" or *Erleben*. The potential for this second perspective is already present in the *Philosophy of Money*, where Simmel expresses his interest in understanding the "inner world" and "vitality" of individuals. Then, in his mature sociology, such as the remarkable essay on the metropolis (Simmel, 1971, pp. 324–39), this interest is translated into an effort to grasp the effect of institutional forms produced by interaction on the *Geistesleben* – that is, on the mental, spiritual, and intellectual life of the individual. It is not the structure of the personality, the province of psychology, after all, that is at stake in this perspective, but rather the effort of individuals to integrate the "forms" of the social world, of which they are a part, into their own mental life. It is a matter of developing or choosing one's self, an act that is not merely personal, but social. Along with objectification, therefore, comes the reverse process of internalization of roles, norms, social attitudes, and behaviors – in a word, the process of socialization.

Simmel's sociology thus leaves us with a unique perspective on the fully "socialized" individual as both a cause and an effect: as the agent of interaction, as well as the resultant of the social structure and institutions produced by interaction. The circularity of this account would not have bothered Simmel, for it gave his analysis a secure way to understand sociology's perennial conundrum: the relationship between agency and structure.

The theory of culture

In his sociology Simmel tends to think of interaction in terms of the "forms" it produces. But he also begins to introduce a vitalistic concept into his thinking, as did contemporaries like Henri Bergson: "Life" expresses itself through interaction, and out of life certain forms emerge that make life itself possible – predictable, secure, bearable, pleasurable, and creative. The difficulty, as Simmel begins to see, is that these forms tend to congeal and rigidify, a concern voiced later by Charles Cooley also. The forms become a constraining "culture" opposed to life, and then set off the eternal struggle between "life" and "form." This insight leads Simmel in the direction of a theory of culture as powerful as that developed by Freud.

The logical dualisms that serve as building blocks for a theory of culture become implicit by the time Simmel writes his last chapter to *The Philosophy of Money*, for in that text two of his most important notions are present: the "objectification of mind," and the growing tension in modernity between "material" and "individual" culture. But it is not until completing some of his last essays, especially "The Concept and Tragedy of Culture" (1911) and "The Conflict in Modern Culture" (1918), that Simmel successfully elaborates the assumptions, arguments, and details of this aspect of his work.

Simmel actually selects a twofold dualism for his point of departure: the Kantian opposition between subject and object, but also the opposition between self-consciousness and the "natural" world without consciousness of itself. "Humans, unlike the animals," he writes in "The Concept and Tragedy of Culture,"

> do not allow themselves simply to be absorbed by the naturally given order of the world. Instead, they tear themselves loose from it, place themselves in opposition to it, making demands of it, overpowering it, then overpowered by it. From this first great dualism springs the never-ending contest between subject and object, which finds its second tribunal within the realm of spirit [*Geist*] itself. (Simmel, 1968, p. 27)

Or as he says later in "The Conflict in Modern Culture": "Whenever life progresses beyond the animal level to that of the spirit, and spirit progresses to the level of culture, an internal contradiction appears. The whole history of culture is the working out of this contradiction" (Simmel, 1971, p. 234). The contradiction between the vital forces of "life" and the timeless forms of "culture" presupposes a process of objectification, which Simmel describes in terms of human mind or spirit projected outside itself, creating "structures" that exist independently of the creative subject, and becoming an autonomous force opposed to that subject. The subject thus becomes "objectified" in this process, which results in a radical and permanent tension – a *Formgegensatz* in Simmel's terminology – between vital, finite life and the fixed, timeless forms it is destined to create as a precondition for its own expression and survival. While the former seem transient, finite, fluctuating, relative to subjects, inward, and immediately experienced, the latter appear to be permanent, timeless, static, objectively valid, external, and mediated by distance. Simmel then announces his major insight: "The idea of culture dwells in the middle of this dualism."

Essentially two senses of the concept of culture seem to follow from this theoretical perspective. The first elaborates the metaphor of culture "as the path of the soul to itself," a formulation that could be read as a comment on an ascetic stance toward life that one also finds discussed in Nietzsche and Freud. Yet against the one-sided criticism of asceticism as repressive, Simmel's idea of culture suggests expression, development, and fulfillment of that which is essentially human: Culture can become

> the completion of the soul . . . in which it takes the detour through the formations of the intellectual-historical work of the species: the cultural path of the subjective spirit traverses science and the forms of life, art and state, vocation and knowledge of the world – the path on which it now returns to itself as higher and perfected spirit.

Thus, from this perspective "life" must also be something formed, and the activity of culture can offer it what Simmel calls a "unity of the soul"; that is, the enticing prospect of a "solution to the subject–object dualism" through the promise of setting the preconditions for the pursuit of what could be designated self-development and the cultivation of personality.

In Simmel's view we appear to consist of a bundle of directions for self-development, all having varied potentialities. However, it is also the case that as cultural beings our choices are not arbitrary, but are instead governed by our culturally derived sense of "personal unity." Using Simmel's own peculiar language, we see that "Culture is the way that leads from closed unity through unfolding multiplicity to unfolding unity" (Simmel, 1968, p. 29). Or in more direct phrasing,

> culture exists only if man draws into his development *something that is external to him* . . . the perfection of the individual is routed through real and ideal spheres outside of the self. The perfection does not remain a purely immanent process, but is consummated in a unique adjustment and teleological interweaving of subject and object. (Simmel, 1971, p. 230)

Thus, we can say that culture is necessarily dualistic, necessarily objective and subjective, and it makes possible the *process* of forming the self, an "unfolding unity," through reciprocal action between the objective and the subjective.

This conception of culture is rich with paradox, for on the one hand culture requires the perpetuation of an unresolved dualism, while on the other it is thought of as mediating or synthesizing the dialectically separated poles of our existence. Stated somewhat differently, whereas on one level it assumes unresolved difference, on another it urges development through mediative inclusion of the "other." Subjective life, driven toward perfection of its identity, "cannot by itself reach the perfection of culture," yet culture "is always a synthesis" of subjective life and the contents of life that "presupposes the divisibility of elements as an antecedent." Today it is especially modernity that accounts for such otherwise incomprehensible tension and potential confusion, for as Simmel maintains: "Only in an analytically inclined age like the modern could one find in synthesis the deepest, the one and only relationship of form between spirit and world" (Simmel, 1968, pp. 30, 35). We should accurately speak of a *longing* for synthesis and wholeness as most characteristic of the modern.

The clearest depiction of a second sense to the concept of culture comes at the end of Simmel's thinking on the subject in "The Conflict of Modern Culture," where he decides to speak of culture not so much whenever it functions through mediation, but rather

> whenever life produces certain forms in which it expresses and realizes itself: works of art, religions, sciences, technologies, laws, and innumerable others. These forms encompass the flow of life and provide it with content and form, room for play and for order. But although these forms arise out of the life process, because of their unique constellation they do not share the restless rhythm of life, its ascent and descent, its constant renewal, its incessant divisions and reunifications. These forms are cages for the creative life which, however, soon transcends them. They should also house the imitative life, for which, in the final analysis, there is no space left. They acquire fixed identities, a logic and lawfulness of their own [*eigene Logik und Gesetzlichkeit*]; this new rigidity inevitably places them at a distance from the spiritual dynamic which created them and which makes them independent. (Simmel, 1971, p. 375 translation modified)

For Simmel, not capitalism, vocational specialization, or instrumental rationality, but rational culture itself becomes the new "iron cage," employing Weber's well known metaphor from *The Protestant Ethic and the Spirit of Capitalism*. Moreover, this culture also possesses an "internal and lawful autonomy" of the kind Weber assigned to the different life-orders and value-spheres of the world. As a distinctive supralife form, culture is in this way of thinking set squarely against the forces of (creative) life. Culture is not merely the path to self-recognition, but also the dwelling place of repressive order. In one sense culture suggests movement and possibility, in another rigidity and limitation.

Simmel's theory raises this quality of culture that he refers to variously in his later essays as a paradox, crisis, conflict, or tragedy to the conscious level, not in order to abolish or transcend it, as some have supposed, for that would destroy culture and its sources in life, but in order to view cultural paradox as a moment in its own development. Like all of human life, culture has a history too, which shows that in the modern present "we are experiencing a new phase of the old struggle," in Simmel's words; it is "no longer a struggle of a contemporary form, filled with life, against an old, lifeless one, but a struggle of life against form as such, against the principle of form" (Simmel, 1968, p. 12). The peculiar and increasing "formlessness" of modern life is the hallmark of the present, and in agreement with Weber, Simmel believes it has been accompanied by numerous exaggerated expressions of life: endless searches in the avant-garde for originality and heightened experience, strivings for a "new ethic" or a "new religiosity," attempts to sanctify the soul in blasé and cynical personal styles. "Thus arises the typical problematic situation of modern man," Simmel maintains:

his feeling of being surrounded by an innumerable number of cultural elements which are neither meaningless to him nor, in the final analysis, meaningful. In their mass they depress him, since he is incapable of assimilating them all, nor can he simply reject them, since after all, they do belong potentially within the sphere of his cultural development. (Simmel, 1968, p. 44)

However, in Simmel's view it was not always so, for in a rare historical detour he suggests that at the very center of culture, from antiquity to modernity, has been a movement from an assumed "unity of being" (Greek philosophy), to "god" (Christianity), "nature" (the Renaissance), the "self" (the Enlightenment), "society" (the nineteenth century), and finally "life" (modernity), a schematic developmental process that has parallels in Weber's well known and concise critique of the illusory meanings Western culture has assigned to science and the search for knowledge. Just as Weber's modern science has now become disenchanted, or disabused of its innocent pretense, so Simmel's modern culture has surrendered the delusion of unitary meaning. For Western thought to move from Kant's critique of pure reason to Simmel's critique of culture has meant precisely to replace the universal individuality of a transcendental ego, situated in a single and generalizable world of mechanistic properties, with the unique individuality of a determinate subject, dispersed into multiple and particularizing worlds of qualitative variation. Furthermore, Simmel's historic diagnosis of modern culture's paradoxes and tragedies is given an immediacy it would otherwise lack because now our experience has driven the tension between "life" and its "forms" (most importantly including science and knowledge among them) to the greatest extreme yet attained.

In his scientific work Simmel responds in three important ways to the contemporary state of affairs outlined in his theory of culture. In the first place he is intrigued by the many social forces, organized groups, interactions or processes of sociation, sociability, and conviviality (*Geselligkeit*) that aim, as he remarks in his essay on Rodin, "to subordinate the whole of life to a meaningful order" which will serve "that deepest longing of the soul to mould everything that is given in its own image" (quoted in Böhringer and Gründer, 1976, pp. 234–5). This perspective and attendant subject matter can be understood as focused on the attempts in the modern age to recover a lost unity to culture, to find a way of overcoming the paradoxical juxtaposition of life and form. Even the unique concept of "conviviality," as Tönnies noted, was for Simmel precisely the "play form" of reciprocal action or interaction that created a space for "the sense of liberation and relief" indispensable for coping with the conditions of culture (quoted in Coser, 1965, p. 52). But in evaluating the modern search for meaningful order, a healthy metaphysical skepticism often prevents Simmel from doing more than honoring such attempts as humanly understandable and significant efforts from within culture to "solve" the crisis the tension between objective and subjective culture has produced. Genuine solutions lie in the unforeseen future, at the "end" of our history, so to speak. According to Simmel's theory of culture attempts aimed in this direction will lead to further fragmentation and differentiation, to a continuing

proliferation of cultural forms, to further tensions between objective and subjective culture.

   A second response becomes apparent in the realm of aesthetics, through the
quest for "salvation through art" and the experience of conducting one's life as a
"work of art." Certainly Simmel's writing on art and artists, such as Rembrandt,
Goethe, Rodin, and George, his own authorial experimentation with poetry, and
the essay form *sub specie aeternitatis* in the modernist journal of art nouveau,
Jugend, are inclined in this direction. In addition, so is the aesthetic dimension
implicit in the concept of "lived experience" or *Erleben* in his sociology. Indeed,
some of Simmel's most provocative formulations appear in connection with the
aesthetic dimension of *individual* experience, as distinct from social interaction:

> The problem that afflicts us in all areas, namely, how purely individual existence
> can be unified, how one can reject consideration of general norms...without
> descending into anarchy and rootless caprice – this problem has been solved by
> Rodin's art as art always solves spiritual problems: not in principle, but in indi-
> vidual perceptions [*Anschauungen*]. (Böhringer and Gründer, 1976, p. 233)

Similarly, the closest Simmel ever came to a personal answer to the problem of
culture was in his own "individual perceptions," not in a definitive, principled
"solution" to the conflict and "tragedy" of culture his analysis disclosed. No such
solution existed, for to say that the widespread cultural problem can only be
resolved aesthetically is to say that it can and must remain unresolved.

   But if Simmel was attracted to the light of aesthetic judgment as a source of
illumination, as he most certainly was, then he was also pulled in the direction of
the clear air of reflection – caught, as it were, between the imperatives of Kant's
first and third critiques. Like Weber and Freud, Simmel also chose to bind
himself to the vocation of science, to choose intellect over latent possibility.
This was his third response to the ultimate conflicts and tragedy of culture. In
one of his very last comments, for instance, he reasoned,

> It is a philistine prejudice that all conflicts and problems are dreamt up merely for
> the sake of their solution. Both in fact have additional tasks in the economy and
> history of life, tasks which they fulfill independently of their own solutions. Thus
> they exist in their own right, even if the future does not replace conflicts with their
> resolutions, but only replaces their forms and contents with others. In short, the
> present is too full of contradictions to stand still. This itself is a more fundamental
> change than the reformations of times past. The bridge between the past and the
> future of cultural forms seems to be demolished; we gaze into an abyss of unformed
> life beneath our feet. But perhaps this formlessness is itself the appropriate form for
> contemporary life. Thus the blueprint of life is obliquely fulfilled. Life is a struggle
> in the absolute sense of the term which encompasses the relative contrast between
> war and peace: the absolute peace which might encompass this contrast remains an
> eternal secret to us. (Simmel, 1971, p. 393)

To speak of the breakdown of cultural tradition and continuity is to return to the
paradoxical idea of form's absence as itself a form. This striking version of our

acceptance of a formless present and our muted curiosity in the face of mystery may vouchsafe the interpretation of Simmel as a "tragic" and "ambivalent" thinker, trapped by the modern cultural dynamic and unable to penetrate those "eternal secrets" that might lead us into another world. Perhaps in this respect Simmel remained a cultural being, his imagination attuned solely to the rhythms of his own time.

However, in Simmel's defense one should say that the barrier to affirming definitive solutions and a new world, when it arose, was not inability but unwillingness: the other worlds, the alternatives made available in culture, were still for Simmel a part of that unprecedented modern culture he had so carefully dissected in all of its complexity and contradiction. In his critical judgment of those alternatives Simmel surely shed that alleged "ambivalence" that has haunted his reputation as sociologist and philosopher. With good reason he reserved the right, recalling Wittgenstein's well known epigram, to pass over the evaluation of any number of proposed solutions in silence.

The essential achievement of Simmel's theory is to emphasize the dialectical interplay that gives substance, direction, and shape to culture – especially now a modern culture delineated, so to speak, by the struggle between life and form. Simmel is convincing in maintaining that this struggle, considered in the abstract, is inevitable and necessary as a presupposition for culture – a position that separates his analysis from any dialectical syntheses, or the variations on Marx's historical materialism. Yet we can say that it is the very search for resolution and transformation of the dialectical aporia, for reconciliation of life with form, that is most characteristic of the sociology of associative activity in specifically modern culture. Simmel understands this insight, and therefore defends an "empirical" cultural sociology that rests upon his claims about culture's paradoxes. The subject matter for this sociology, in other words, is established by the great refusals to accept the essential opposition between external, material forms and humanity's subjective strivings. We can achieve some measure of judgment, Simmel tells us, by viewing such refusals from a distance, honoring their necessity, but also declining to enlist under the banner of their hopes for reconciling the dualisms of the culture we call our own.

Woman and female culture

One of the most remarkable and prescient of Simmel's contributions to cultural sociology was his work on woman, gender, and difference. In Germany in the 1890s the women's movement began to gain a following in socialist and liberal circles, with growing numbers of women taking on public roles, participating in organizational activity, entering the universities, and preparing for the professions. As a close observer of social change, Simmel responded with a series of essays that staked out a theoretical position based on his overarching views about society and culture.

Discussion of the "woman question" in the philosophical traditions before Simmel had generally followed one of two possible patterns of thought: either woman was treated as "similar" to man because of a shared basic nature, as argued by Plato; or woman was considered "different" by virtue of differences in biology, psyche, being, or some other factor, as claimed by both Kant and Hegel. Occasionally a writer would articulate a position that combined elements of both views, as did J. S. Mill in "The Subjection of Women." Regardless of the particular orientation, in all of these discussions the major questions were always: similar or different with respect to what goods or values in social life; and what is the relevance of any claimed similarities or differences for social life?   Simmel's approach is a striking instance of the argument from "difference," similar to that of the developmental psychologist Carol Gilligan today. That is, he essentially adopts the view that woman is different in socially important ways, such as having a special relationship to the contents of culture, or having a different "sense of justice." Consider his most comprehensive statement on the issues in "Female Culture" (1911), for instance:

> Frequently the "legal antipathy" of women is stressed: their opposition to legal norms and judgments. However there is no sense in which this necessarily implies an animus against the law itself; instead, it is only against *male* law, which is the only law we have, and for this reason seems to us to be the law as such. In the same way, our historically defined morality, individualized by considerations of both time and place, seems to us to fulfill the conditions of the concept of morality in general. The female "sense of justice," which differs from the male in many respects, would create a different law as well. (Simmel, 1984, p. 68)

However, this "difference" is not understood as a basis for subordination. It is seen instead as an opportunity for developing multiplicity and cultural variation, as a possibility for promoting the emergence of new cultural forms. The reason for this radical perspective is grounded in the logic of Simmel's theory of culture.

Starting from his fundamental distinction between "objective" and "subjective" culture, Simmel links the difference between male and female experience to the process of objectification. The aspects of life that he calls the "cultural capital" of an era are found in its objective culture, and this culture, "with the exception of a very few areas . . . is thoroughly male" (Simmel, 1984, pp. 65, 67). The dichotomy between objective and subjective is then restated in numerous ways in Simmel's writing, but its basic alignment is with a view of woman's difference having to do with notions of differentiation and totality. As Simmel records the idea in one summation, "If there is any sense in which the distinctive psychic quality of woman's nature can be expressed symbolically, it is this: Its periphery is more closely connected with its center and its aspects are more completely integrated into the whole than holds true for the male nature" (Simmel, 1984, p. 73). Now it is not always clear what Simmel wants to infer or conclude from this kind of assertion, or even if he is fully committed to it. There is an experimental quality to such thoughts that may defy our normal expectations for clear and distinct reasoning. But such an experimental claim poses the obvious questions: What social changes occur when women move into the domains of objective culture? If women also create objective culture, is it then a qualitatively different *kind* of culture? Is there, or can there be, such a thing as *female* culture, and if so, what would it be like?

Bearing these qualifications in mind, Simmel nevertheless forges ahead and proposes a number of hypothetical answers to his questions, perhaps surprising to us for their contemporaneity. For instance, he suggests that woman accomplishes something in objective culture men cannot achieve, because of her capacity for empathy, using the example of diagnosis and care in medicine. Or he suggests that woman's unique character and ability can lead to newer forms of knowledge, alluding to the importance of "understanding" in writing history. However, for a contemporary feminist like Marianne Weber, writing a reply to Simmel in the journal *Logos* ("Woman and Objective Culture," 1913), these hypotheses sounded far-fetched, perhaps merely a projection of male needs and a romanticization of woman's difference. Moreover, they still failed to distinguish unambiguously between nature and nurture, between all that is naturally endowed and everything that is socioculturally determined.

Despite these difficulties, Simmel's last word poses an interesting challenge. For in his formulation culture itself is two-sided: it assumes a difference that is gender-specific; its subject is "man" and his choices. But culture also develops through mediative inclusion of the other, of "woman" and her being. This formulation, however, is set forth from within the perspective of objective (male) culture. Is there any other (female) perspective that can be stated in a different language? Consider Simmel's speculative conclusion to "Female Culture," a rare paragraph in which he seems to anticipate the course of the most radical directions of thought in the late twentieth century, especially those challenges to so-called "phallogocentrism" associated with postmodern critics:

> From the standpoint of cultural history, consider the extreme point that the ideal of the independence and equality of women seems to be capable of reaching: an objective female culture parallel to the male and thereby annulling its brutal historical idealization.... Under these circumstances, the male monopolization of objective culture would persist, but with justification. This is because objective culture as a formal principle would qualify as a one-sided male principle. Juxtaposed to it, the female form of existence would present itself as a different form, autonomous on the basis of its ultimate essence, incommensurable on the basis of the standard of the male principle, and with contents that are not formed in the same way. Thus its meaning would no longer turn on an equivalence *within* the general form of objective culture but rather on an equivalence between two modes of existence that have a completely different rhythm. One [male culture] is dualistic, oriented to becoming, knowledge, and volition. As a result, it objectifies the contents of its life out of the process of life in the form of a cultural world. The other [female culture] lies beyond this subjectively constituted and objectively developed dichotomy. For this reason, the contents of its life are not experienced in a form that is external to them. On the contrary, it must search out a perfection that is immanent to them. (Simmel, 1984, pp. 100–1)

Simmel, like modern feminism, does not know what this "immanent perfection" might look like, or what kind of "world" it might create. But the insight of his commentary is to foresee the trajectory of the line of thinking that the argument from *difference* must follow. The world, as he says, is "a form of the contents of consciousness." In this view the argument from difference is all about forming and raising consciousness; once that has taken place, the social world will not be far behind.

Religion and art

Simmel's writings in the sociology and psychology of religion spanned two decades, from "A Contribution to the Sociology of Religion" of 1898, to the concluding section in "The Conflict of Modern Culture" of 1918. Among this work it was the lengthy essay, *Religion* (1906; 2nd edn 1912), published in Martin Buber's popular multi-volume series on different aspects of modern society, *Die Gesellschaft*, that provided the most sustained discussion of his views.

The subject matter in these writings is not simply the sociology of religion as a field for observing interaction, but more particularly the "lived experience" of the religious person. In contrast to Max Weber's well known essays in the sociology of religion, Simmel's work thus tends to play down comparative historical or institutional questions, while instead investigating the inward and personal aspects of religiosity or "religiousness" – the side of his sociology concerned with "experience." As Phillip Hammond has suggested, in contrast to Weber's "religiously unmusical" self-description we seem in this body of work to be confronted with the "religiously musical" side of Simmel's perceptions (Simmel, 1997, p. vii).

Following the tradition of thought that is also exemplified in William James's *The Varieties of Religious Experience*, Simmel distinguishes between religion as a doctrine or "set of claims," and religion as a "form of life" or a "state of being," agreeing with James that the latter is his primary concern. Both might be said to explore the meaning of Kant's notion that religion is "an attitude of the soul." But unlike James, Simmel explicitly repudiates the mechanistic psychology that views religiosity as a mental entity, instead proposing to see it as "a form according to which the human soul experiences life and comprehends its existence" (Simmel, 1997, pp. 5, 50). "All religiosity," he asserts,

> contains a peculiar admixture of unselfish surrender and fervent desire, of humility and exaltation, of sensual concreteness and spiritual abstraction; this occasions a certain degree of emotional tension, a specific ardor and certainty of the subjective conditions, an inclusion of the subject in a higher order – an order which, at the same time, is felt to be something inward and personal. (Simmel, 1997, p. 104)

Religiosity is thus a type of affective relationship, an aspect of the dialectical struggle between "life" and "form" that Simmel places at the center of his theory of culture. Religion in this sense is not life itself, but a form that emerges out of life and makes an important aspect of our experience possible. For Simmel life's rebellion against form guarantees the renewal of religious experience and the emergence of new forms of the religious life. Religiosity thus provides the essential dynamic of religion as a set of claims. In his important summation,

"Just as cognition does not create causality, but instead causality creates cognition, so religion does not create religiosity, but religiosity creates religion" (ibid., p. 150). Or as Simmel expresses the idea in another passage, the logical sequence the observer must follow is from religiosity to "social phenomena" to "objective religion" (ibid., p. 211).

As in other parts of his thought, one important problem Simmel confronts is framed by the advance of the scientific outlook and the powers of technological civilization: what can be the meaning and experience of religiosity in the modern age, he wants to ask, when we are faced with a withdrawal of the "content" of religion, while the "religious need" – that is, the form called religiousness – remains with us? How are we to understand the reality of a religiosity that exists *independent* of any content, that can be transformed, so to speak, from "a transitive to an intransitive activity" (ibid., p. 23)? Simmel's answer requires that he propose a conjecture:

> The real gravity of the current situation is that not this or that particular dogma but the object of transcendent faith per se is characterized as illusory. What survives is no longer the form of transcendence seeking new fulfillment but something more profound and more desperate: it is a *yearning*, once fulfilled by the idea of transcendence, and now – although it is a concrete reality within the soul – paralyzed by the withdrawal of the content of faith and as if cut off from the path to its own life. (ibid., p. 9)

This observation is congruent with Freud's later theme in *The Future of an Illusion* (1927), and it allows us to understand the modern penchant for experimentation with religiosity. In "The Conflict in Modern Culture," Simmel argues that the modern turn to mysticism and its various forms (such as Zen Buddhism or "New Age" spirituality today) represents an attempt to find a way out of the dilemma. No doubt there are others, though they all may in the last analysis "become equally entangled in contradictions," as Simmel (1997, p. 23) notes.

But there is a second problem for Simmel in this part of his work, for he wants to assess the connection between religiosity and social phenomena. Can there be instructive parallels or analogies between religious conduct and social interaction? Simmel's complex responses take different forms themselves. But in general his reflections on art, subjectivity, inwardness, or reconciliation trace the engagement of the self – especially the contested modern self – with religiosity. Moreover, especially in the longest text, *Religion*, his point is that religiosity is itself a *social* form, observable within other non-religious relationships, serving as a template for appropriate interactions, triggering the search for social unity in a "higher order," or modeling the relationship of the individual to the group. Such passages show Simmel at his best, revealing for him the problems a sociology of religion should pursue:

> We can see, for example, that many human relationships harbor a religious element. The relationship of a devoted child to his parent, of an enthusiastic patriot to his country, of the fervent cosmopolite to humanity; the relationship of the worker

to his insurgent class or of the proud feudal lord to his fellow nobles; the relationship of the subject to his ruler or of the true soldier to his army – all these
relationships, with their infinite variety of content, can be seen to share a psychological form. This form has a common tone that can be described only as religious.
(Ibid., p. 104)

The interaction between the human being and his God thus encompasses the whole
range of possible relationships, both sequentially and simultaneously. In doing so it
unmistakably reiterates the behavioral patterns that exist between the individual
and his social group. Here we see the same phenomenon of an individual subjected
to a supreme power yet permitted a degree of freedom; passive reception that still
allows room for a responsive reaction; the self-surrender that does not exclude
rebellion; the mixture of reward and punishment; the relationship of a single
member to the whole, even though that single member still desires to be a whole
himself. One feature of religion in particular can be transposed to the relationship
of the individual to the group: that is the humility with which the pious person
attributes everything he is and has to God's generosity and sees in divine power the
source of his being and strength. For man is not absolutely nothing in relation to
God: though only a grain of dust, he is not an utterly insignificant force but is at
least a receptacle ready to receive its contents. Thus there are strong similarities
between the religious and the sociological forms of existence. (Ibid., p. 157)

In this view not only are there parallels between religious activity and social
activity, but the element of religiosity is contained within other, non-religious
relationships. By understanding religiosity, we can also grasp the nature of social
interactions.

Moreover, for Simmel there is a strong affinity between religion and art, or
between the religious life and the artistic life, which then accounts for their
historic attraction and repulsion in the great world religions. On the one hand,
then, he can envisage an "essential similarity between the form of the religious
life and that of art" and postulate "the ultimate similarity of form through which
religion always anticipates art and art always stimulates religious sentiment"
(ibid., p. 67). The most important reason for this similarity has to do with the
process of distanciation at work in both the artistic and religious realms. For
both art and religion project their objects into a world "beyond" the empirical
here-and-now, Simmel argues, but only in order to draw these objects into the
close and immediate orbit of our consciousness. Paradoxically, the distance
created between the self and its objects of perception makes possible the subjective possession of these objects and the complete and apparently unmediated
identification with them. Of course, in actuality there is a source of mediation in
social interaction and group life. Thus, if Rembrandt can be seen as the "painter
of the soul," offering a vision of reconciliation for the inner life, as Simmel holds,
then it is because these notions of soul, reconciliation, and inner life have
meaning and value for us as social beings.

On the other hand art proclaims its autonomy and competition with the
religious life: "*l'art pour l'art*" in the rallying cry of the *fin de siècle*. The
significance of this challenge for Simmel becomes marked in the essays on art

forms and major artists, where in historical and comparative perspective he explores the great dualisms of nature and spirit, content and form, our existence in the life world and the contrasting reality of the work of art. The attraction of *modern* art especially lies in its ability to work through and heighten these age-old dualisms in such a way as to present art as "salvation" from the everyday. Toward the end of his essay on Rodin, for example, Simmel comments,

> Ancient sculpture sought the logic of the body, so to speak, whereas Rodin seeks its psychology. For the essence of modernity as such is psychologism, the lived experience and interpretation of the world in terms of the reactions of our inner life and actually as an inner world, the dissolution of the fixed contents in the fluid elements of the soul, from which all substance has been removed, and whose forms are only forms of motion. Thus the really modern art is music, the most moving of the arts. Thus it was lyric poetry based upon music which most satisfied the longing of the times. Thus landscape painting is the specifically modern achievement of painting, for it is an *état d'âme* and its use of color and composition dispenses with logical structure more than the body and figural composition. (Simmel, 1983, p. 152)

So whereas art in antiquity achieved its goal by freeing us from discontent through a perfection of style that negated the flux of life, Simmel contends, modern art rescues us by grasping the truth of the fluidity, motion, and dissolution of form that we experience. Art is capable of validating our lived experience, a powerful argument for substituting the aesthetic for the religious life, and for Simmel one of the important tendencies at work in modernity.

Problems in Simmel's Thought

The identification and elaboration of important dynamic, dualistic tensions in our experience is one of the most striking aspects of Simmel's thought. His treatment of the category of "life" held in creative tension with "form" is only the most abstract of these dualisms. Surely among the most striking is his exploration of the ways in which individual autonomy and freedom are both opposed to social formations and constraints, but then also authorized and made possible by such formations and constraints. One of the most consequential for modern life is the dynamic interplay between our subjective historical identities and the objectified social-technological forces that challenge those identities, both canceling and reinforcing or reshaping them.

The complexity in this dynamic mode of thinking is one source of the fascination with Simmel. But it is also a contributing source for the questioning of his general approach, method of inquiry, and overall contribution to social theory. This questioning can be reduced to four problem domains: subjectivism, aestheticism, formalism, and ambivalence.

Subjectivism. One of the earliest criticisms of Simmel focused attention on the speculative quality of his thinking. To be sure, Simmel was not an "empiricist" in the usual sense of the word, nor did he want to be one. However, neither was he a system-builder whose edifice of thought rested on metaphysical foundations. Avoiding either of these polarities, did he nevertheless have a method of inquiry that could give "systematic coherence" to his approach? Did he provide any guidance at the level of, say, Durkheim in *The Rules of Sociological Method*? For Simmel the answer to such challenges is difficult to formulate, and that difficulty has fed the suspicion among critics that methodological rigor is not among the scientific values promoted in Simmel's work.

Aestheticism. Closely related to the charge of subjectivism is the concern that Simmel's distinctive style or manner of thinking – his *Denkart* – is driven and characterized by aesthetic considerations. From this point of view, for example, his version of "political economy" in the *Philosophy of Money* is highly individualized, and notwithstanding an array of brilliant constructions, it lacks the clear conceptual underpinnings and critical edge of Marx's *Capital*, or the explicit analytic categories and systematic intentions of Weber's *Economy and Society*. Instead of merely writing a text, it is as if Simmel wants to compose a dense texture of images that will convey, like a canvass or a score, the essential experience of a phenomenon – in this case "money" as metaphysical power. According to this critical view such results are like a work of art in the hands of a master: admirable for their perfection, originality, and singularity, but not in principle "falsifiable" according to the canons of science.

Formalism. Of course, Simmel was also an acknowledged master of "formal" analysis of social interaction. But the difficulty is that such analysis can appear unhistorical and untested by rigorous, substantive comparative applications. It tends to stress only formal properties, rather than investigating historical patterns or developmental logics. Thus, unlike Marx and Weber, Simmel cannot be said to have a comparative historical sociology, or a structural analysis of stratification systems, or a developmental sociology of the modern state. His formal sociology might be viewed as a suggestive heuristic for understanding historical and structural dimensions of a given society, but it is not in itself an analysis, for example, of actual structures or historical patterns of domination.

Ambivalence. While often viewed as a diagnostician of the *Zeitgeist*, Simmel has also been accused of reveling in that diagnosis at the expense of developing an unambiguous political position, or making a clear choice about the most desirable path toward a rational future. Simmel's thought is never short on critical perspectives, but in this view those perspectives remain as equally valued possibilities, rather than temporary and questionable positions that must be overcome. His mature thinking thus never connects with transformative action projects, but leaves us instead merely reflecting on the "tragedy" or "fate" or "possibilities" of our times.

Now these four problem areas speak to the provocative and unique character of Simmel's voluminous writings. Better brilliant errors than dull correctness, as Weber once remarked. But in partial defense of Simmel it must be said that many of the charges against him misunderstand or misdirect the tasks he set for himself. Unwilling to pose as a utopian or futurologist, Simmel was content to dissect social life to expose the sinews that made sociability, individuation, and differentiation possible. Content to leave historical and structural problematics to others, he concentrated his efforts on a *general* level of analysis about history, society, economy, or religion *as such*. Not particular histories or particular religions were Simmel's concern, but rather the writing of what we call "history" as an idea and creative act, or the formation of what we call "religion" out of the quality of experience identified as religiosity. For Simmel, then, the loss in specificity of subject matter can be compensated by an unexpected turn, an experimental line of inquiry, a unique depth of understanding. In the last analysis he wanted surprise and experimentation, and it is these qualities that challenge the most earnest criticism.

SIMMEL'S POSITION IN MODERN SOCIAL THEORY

Returning to Simmel's intellectual and social world of the *fin de siècle*, there was a legendary quality to his public presence in the prewar Berlin of his time. Not many sociologists or philosophers receive the garland of poetic declamation from their students. Simmel was one of the few who did:

> The differences are illusionary;
> Is the flamingo nobler than the stork?
> I sink into my seat painfully
> For the great analyst Geork.
> There I sit in my brown vest,
> And the army of objects envelop me.
> Oh, will the problems never rest,
> The walled-in smoke of indifference encircles me.
> What is the meaning of life? This question
> Is foolish, but it exists nevertheless,
> It needles me for seven thousand days of vexation:
> I sit there in agony, ill-fated, helpless.

So wrote Kurt Hiller in 1911 in the avant-garde expressionist journal, *Die Aktion*, commemorating in doggerel the spell Simmel cast over audiences that included Georg Lukács, Ernst Bloch, and Robert Park. The long shadow of this influence can be seen in their quite varied later work, even in the famous insights about "alienation" and "reification" in Lukács's essays in *History and Class Consciousness* (1922), or the "cultural criticism" advanced by Siegfried Kracauer and members of the early Frankfurt School, as well as the "interactionist" perspectives of the Chicago School of American sociology.

But Simmel never intended to be a founder of a school or movement, in contrast to Durkheim or Marx, and many of those who explicitly borrowed his name, such as Hiller, were marginal figures and outsiders to the academy and the major social and political movements of the time. For the main orthodoxies in social theory and philosophy Simmel seemed to remain a brilliant essayist and wide-ranging intellect, a master of the insightful *aperçu* and the ambiguities of modern life, but a thinker without a philosophical system or a unified, marketable sociological doctrine. It is an interesting comment on the peculiarities of our times to note that it is precisely these alleged deficiencies that have once again made Simmel an engaging presence, even for some an insightful "postmodernist" *avant la lettre*. Simmel, of course, thought he was merely "modern."

With neo-Kantian theory in eclipse during the twentieth century, Simmel's profile in philosophy has retreated into the shadows. But the legacy of his thought has remained strong in several major fields of sociology, where it first attracted attention, especially in the United States, perhaps because the traditions stemming from George Herbert Mead or Robert E. Park bear a certain family resemblance to Simmel's work. Most obviously symbolic interactionism, formal sociology, and conflict sociology all owe a major debt to the Simmelian analysis of interaction processes and patterns of sociation. Indeed, these subject matters and areas of inquiry, represented, for example, by the work of Lewis Coser in conflict theory, are at the core of what was seen for decades as Simmel's unique contribution.

Today, however, a new Simmel has taken the stage. The renaissance of interest in Simmel and his work, some eighty years after his death, is explained by several considerations: renewed interest in cultural theory and analysis, a spate of writings on modernity and its discontents, concern with substantive topics (such as the sociology of emotions, feminism and gender, or the sociology of fashion and art) that Simmel cultivated almost alone, dissatisfaction with orthodox sociological empiricism, and the energizing disarray in social theory generally. Among the "classics" Simmel can seem to offer the most sustained, varied, and intriguing discussions of a full range of problems and topics, some of them quite exemplary, that touch on these thematic interests of the present. Apart from the self-sustaining project of pursuing "science for science's sake," as a good Simmelian might put it, what we can hope to find in Simmel's work is an orientation, a series of insights, even a kind of deep programmatic understanding about what is significant in social life that will satisfy our need for clarity about our own situation in the modern world and in sociology. Some have gone even further to find in his work a "research program" for comprehending the "historical anthropology of the modern" (Nolte, 1998). Whether in its weak or strong form, ultimately these orientations are the grounds on which the interest in Simmel's work will be sustained for the foreseeable future.

Simmel was a great raconteur, often lacing lectures and essays with illustrative fables and anecdotes. One of his favorites told the story of the farmer who on his death bed advised his children to search for a treasure he had buried in the fields. They diligently followed his directions, plowing hard and deep, but found no buried treasure. However, the following year the land yielded a three-fold harvest. Like these heirs, we won't find the treasure, Simmel announced, but the world we have cultivated in looking for it will prove many times more fruitful, because such cultivation is the necessary condition for our imagination, intellect, and spirit. And so it is with the promise of Simmel's work. The fable aptly captures the last important legacy of his sociological and philosophical investigations, and suggests the importance of our relation to his science and to him as a cultivator of the intellect and enthusiast for the life of the mind.

Acknowledgment

The author is indebted to Leon Warshay for his critical comments and helpful suggestions for this essay.

Bibliography

Writings of Georg Simmel

Grundfragen der Soziologie (Individuum und Gesellschaft). 1917. Berlin: Göschen.

The Sociology of Georg Simmel (translated and edited by K. Wolff). 1950. New York: Free Press.

Conflict and the Web of Group-affiliations (translated by K. Wolff and R. Bendix). 1955. New York: Free Press.

Georg Simmel 1858–1918 (edited by K. Wolff). 1959. Columbus: Ohio State University Press.

Essays on Sociology, Philosophy and Aesthetics by Georg Simmel (edited by K. Wolff). 1959. Columbus: Ohio State University Press.

The Conflict in Modern Culture and Other Essays (translated by P. Etzkorn). 1968. New York: Columbia Teachers College Press.

Georg Simmel on Individuality and Social Forms: Selected Writings (edited by D. Levine). 1971. Chicago: University of Chicago Press.

The Problems of the Philosophy of History (translated by G. Oakes). New York: Free Press.

Philosophische Kultur: Gesammelte Essais. 1983. Berlin: Wagenbach.

Georg Simmel: on Women, Sexuality, and Love (translated by G. Oakes). 1984. New Haven, CT: Yale University Press.

Schopenhauer and Nietzsche (translated by H. Loiskandl et al.). 1986. Amherst: University of Massachusetts Press.

Einleitung in die Moralwissenschaft: Eine Kritik der ethischen Grundbegriffe. Georg Simmel Gesamtausgabe, volumes 3 and 4. 1989. Frankfurt: Suhrkamp.

The Philosophy of Money (edited and translated by D. Frisby and T. Bottomore). 1990. London: Routledge, 2nd edn.

Soziologie: Untersuchungen über die Formen der Vergesellschaftung. Georg Simmel Gesamtausgabe, volume 11. 1992. Frankfurt: Suhrkamp.

Essays on Religion (edited and translated by H. J. Helle and L. Nieder). 1997. New Haven, CT: Yale University Press.

Further reading

Böhringer, H. and Gründer, K. (1976) *Ästhetik und Soziologie um die Jahrhundertwende: Georg Simmel*. Frankfurt: Klostermann.

Coser, L. (ed.) (1965) *Georg Simmel*. Englewood Cliffs, NJ: Prentice Hall.

Frisby, D. (1992) *Sociological Impressionism: A Reassessment of Georg Simmel's Social Theory*, 2nd edn. London: Routledge.

Freud, Sigmund (1927) *The Future of an Illusion*. London: Hogarth Press.

Gassen, K. and Landmann, M. (1993) *Buch des Dankes an Georg Simmel*, 2nd edn. Berlin: Duncker & Humblot.

Habermas, J. (1991) *Texte und Kontexte*. Frankfurt: Suhrkamp.

Isaksen, L. and Waerness, M. (eds) (1993) *Individuality and Modernity: Georg Simmel and Modern Culture*. Bergen: Sociology Press.

Jaworski, G. (1997) *Georg Simmel and the American Prospect*. Albany: SUNY Press.

Kaern, M., Phillips, B. and Cohen, R. (eds) (1990) *Georg Simmel and Contemporary Sociology*. Dordrecht: Kluwer.

Köhnke, K. C. (1996) *Der Junge Simmel in Theoriebeziehungen und sozialen Bewegungen*. Frankfurt: Suhrkamp.

Leck, R. (2000) *Georg Simmel and Avant-garde Sociology: the Birth of Modernity, 1880-2000*. Amherst: Humanity.

Lukács, Georg (1971) *History and Class Consciousness* (translated by R. Livingstone). London: Merlin Press.

Nedelmann, B. (1990) On the Concept of "Erleben" in Georg Simmel's Sociology. In M. Kaern et al. (eds), *Georg Simmel and Contemporary Sociology*. Dordrecht: Kluwer, pp. 225–41.

Nolte, P. (1998) Georg Simmels Historische Anthropologie der Moderne: Rekonstruktion eines Forschungsprogramms. *Geschichte und Gesellschaft*, 24, 225–47.

Weinstein, D. and Weinstein, M. (1993) *Postmodern(ized) Simmel*. New York: Routledge.

8

Charlotte Perkins Gilman

CHARLES LEMERT

More than any sociologist of her day, perhaps more than any since, Charlotte Perkins Gilman fearlessly abridged the artificial divide between fact and fiction. Herein lies her abiding witness to all women and men who live their lives between doubt and hope, wherein the disciplined practice of social theory begins. Without fiction, there is no imagination; without imagination, no dreams; without dreams, facts hardly matter. Theories are the ways people use their imagination to talk about the factual realities that hedge their social dreams.

Strictly speaking, a fiction is a fashioning, an imitating, of things the truth of which is not merely, or presently, factual. There would be no progress, not even scientific progress, without these imaginative fashionings after the real. Hence the disputatious role of theory in both practical and scientific life. Many people, ordinary ones and scientists alike, hate theory. Yet they could not live without it. When all is said and done, theory is the more or less disciplined talk by which people make what sense they can of their social worlds. Theory, thus, does its work in the always unsettled space between doubt and promise. Theory seeks, thereby, to describe the possible in order to capture the imagination of others. Whether it tells stories or explains data sets, theory is the work of telling others what one holds to be true about the world. Its hope is to convince others to see things as one sees them, even to invite their participation. This is true, surely, of the most formal scientific theory. But it is pointedly true of theories, like social theories, which cannot help but depend on fiction to find and describe their facts.

Charlotte Perkins Gilman very well understood this perplexingly simple first condition of her craft, which ultimately is the craft of anyone who aims to be socially engaged. Gilman's social theories of the man-made world have endured over time because she seemed to understand without instruction on the subject that, in her day, the factual state of women in the world economy could only be described from some distant standpoint of the social imagination. The arrangements that consign many women to the bourgeois family and the commandments of men were as arbitrary then as they are now. But then there were no theoretical or sociological languages sufficient to their description. Far from being stranger than fiction, the strangeness of the factual is that, in many times and places, reality's finest expressions can only be rendered as fiction.

Among feminist social theorists at the start of the twentieth century, Charlotte Perkins Gilman had no peer because no one saw and spoke with such convincing imagination of the ways Gilded Age capitalism arrogantly structured the lives of women and men. Gilman was a sociologist and a disciplined social thinker. She was not, however, an academic (though she did occasionally write for academic journals like *The American Journal of Sociology*). Her social theory took the form of social criticism of the prevailing foundations of bourgeois social life and its economic arrangements. In books like *Women and Economics* (1898) and *The Home* (1903) – just two of the countless essays, lectures, and books of this kind – she shook the gendered foundations of modern life. In her day, only W. E. B. Du Bois among social critics we read today rivaled Gilman's popularity as a writer. No academic sociologist in the United States came close.

Just the same, to have been a woman in that day, even an intellectual one, meant that if one were to move and shake the public sphere dominated by white males one had to discover some indirect path to the popular imagination. At the end of the nineteenth century, one of the most popular forms of entertainment was the magazine that arrived, usually weekly, at the door of women at homes. This is why the art of fiction was so important to Gilman and other socially conscious women of the time, notably her distant, older relative, Harriet Beecher Stowe – both of them published their best known work in the periodic press. It is, in fact, not entirely implausible to suggest that Gilman's "The Yellow Wallpaper" (1892) did for the social criticism of gender relations what *Uncle Tom's Cabin* had done forty years earlier for race relations. Gilman's disturbing short story of a woman driven mad by the man-made world did not start a war as Abraham Lincoln famously said of Beecher's book in relation to the American Civil War. But for much of the century since its publication in 1892, "The Yellow Wallpaper" did give vent to the outrage of women trapped in a system that exploited their domestic services. Gilman's short fiction was the opening shot of her war of words against the (to use her word) androcentric biases of the world capitalism system. For a full quarter century from this opening blast to the surprising, otherworldly ideas in her feminist utopia, *Herland*, in 1915, Gilman wrote widely read works of fiction. Yet Gilman's fiction always expressed the more studied values of her critical social theory. At every turn, her work gives off, still today, the sweet scent of the long-feared, always inviting, intercourse between the real and the imaginary.

It would be a long time after Gilman quit her public life and work during the First World War before C. Wright Mills, in 1959, would coin the phrase "the sociological imagination." But not even Mills understood what Gilman did about the importance of imagination to social thought. For Mills, the sociological imagination was more a rhetorical hammer used to loosen the grip of academic sociology's empirically narrow and theoretically abstract methods. Mills, of course, urged upon us the notion that sociology always begins in the needs of ordinary people who suffer personal troubles for want of the ability to imagine the larger social structures that are, in most instances, the deeper cause of their sufferings. Mills was one of the first to plant the seeds of formal sociology in the concerns of practical life. But he was not *the* first. More than sixty years before Mills, Gilman saw that social thought was always the imaginative work of bringing into public view the force of social structures in the fate of the troubled individual. Granted, she did not put the idea as succinctly as did Mills. But he, by contrast, never came close to her in plumbing the depths of imagination itself. Gilman's "The Yellow Wallpaper" set a new standard for the use of fiction to tell the truth of the emotional consequences of social and economic structures, much as *Herland* opens possibilities for feminist social criticism that nonfiction writing can never achieve.

THE PERSON

Imagine, if you will, an educated woman of the working or middle classes – any woman who comes to mind. She is, more often than not, white. She is educated, married with children, well sheltered, with all the necessary provisions and many of the desirable unnecessary ones. Her duty in the social contract with her husband and his world is to care for the children and manage the household. In return, she is offered the honor of being considered a good woman, one who by her domestic labor and sound moral values fulfills the social ideal expected of such a woman. She receives no direct financial compensation. She is left in the home for long hours, sometimes days, with little or no help. The husband, by contrast, enjoys life at work in the wider world. She accompanies him rarely, but entertains his work acquaintances frequently. She is permitted no vocation of her own outside the family circle, save for activities that advance the good name of the householder himself. She feels confined. She very often falls into depression, for which she takes to her room on doctor's orders.

Today it is relatively easy to image such a woman. Many of our mothers or grandmothers experienced just this and knew what it meant to be thus confined. Even though today's economy has put such a life well beyond the expectations of all but a small number of generally quite wealthy families, it is not too difficult for us today to imagine the suffering of the women for whom Charlotte Gilman wrote. They are the paradigm of what is wrong with the so-called traditional family. These are the women who suffered "the problem that has no name" that Betty Friedan would describe for a later generation of women in *The Feminine Mystique* (1963). Gilman was among the first to speak to and for these women. The woman in question was the subject of "The Yellow Wallpaper" – a woman driven to illness, not by the abuse of the man in her life, but by the man-made world. The yellow wallpaper is the nightmarish entanglements of a woman trapped in a system that demands her obedience and denies her participation.

In the 1880s Charlotte Perkins Gilman lived what Betty Friedan would describe in the 1960s for a later generation of women. She was herself a victim of the problem with no name. But Gilman (at the time, Charlotte Stetson) would not succumb to her personal troubles. She had married Walter Stetson, an artist, and a good man, in 1884. Their only child, Katherine, was born the following year. Neither brought wealth to the marriage. Walter respected Charlotte's creative gifts, but his career came first. He was the breadwinner. Her work had to be set aside. The first signs of her depression appeared soon after childbirth. Somehow, even as Charlotte lay ill in 1887, a young woman confined to her own room, Charlotte knew – she just knew – that her illness was not of her own doing. She understood very well that Walter and her physician (the same physician who a generation earlier had been called to the bedside of Harriet Beecher Stowe, for the same "female" illness) were kindly men. The fault was not theirs any more than hers. They too were caught up in the structured relations of bourgeois life in early capitalist America. Though Charlotte Stetson would not find the formal language to describe the system until her first great work of social theory in 1898, *Women and Economics* were already the key words in her personal vocabulary. By courage and personal force, she exercised the sociological imagination to know that what was at stake in a bourgeois woman's life was ultimately an issue of economic structures. Gilman was the sort of person who trusted her feelings long enough to find the words that shaped the intellect that eventually described the structured reality for others. Few social theorists live in such a way that the qualities of their personal lives lead to robust theories of worlds we all inhabit. Gilman did.

The circumstances of Gilman's family of birth were, almost certainly, the source of her feminist sensibilities. She was born on her father's side into one of the nineteenth century's most famously unconventional families. Charlotte's father, Frederick Beecher Perkins, was kin by marriage to the family of Lyman Beecher and his remarkable children. Henry Ward Beecher, the abolitionist; Catharine Beecher, the feminist; Isabella Beecher Hooker, the suffragist; and Harriet Beecher Stowe, the writer – all carried forth their father's reformist values. From childhood, Charlotte witnessed firsthand the worldly work of the Beecher women. Yet what influenced her more was not so much her proximity to the famous family as her painful distance from its, to her, most important member – her father.

Frederick Perkins left his wife, Mary Prescott Perkins, and their two small children in 1869. Charlotte was but nine years old. His abandonment put her, her mother, and her brother at incessant risk of financial ruin. Though Frederick clearly inherited the learning and independence of the Beechers, he utterly lacked the family's deeper sense of personal responsibility. Perkins attended Yale, but dropped out. He studied law, but never practiced it. Eventually, he settled into a stable career as a librarian – first at the Boston Public Library, then (in 1880) as Director of the San Francisco Public Library. He supported the family erratically. He sent money and affection as it pleased him. The economic disaster of the abandonment was severe enough. But its emotional consequences were far the worse. Through her adolescence, Charlotte seized every opportunity to maintain relations with her father, who, true to form, resisted – most hurtfully on one occasion by cutting off her tender affections toward him in an abrupt and cruel letter of rejection.

Only a man damaged by some larger force could behave as harshly as Frederick Perkins did toward his wife and children. And the damage did not end with him. It seldom does in families. Charlotte, like many abandoned children, never stopped longing for her father's affections. It was no accident then that when she in her turn abandoned Walter in 1888 she moved with Katherine (then three) to California – first to Pasadena, then to Oakland, across the Bay from her father. Still, though he was nearby, he kept his distance. Most appalling of all, her father refused to visit his wife, Mary, as she was dying in the late winter of 1893. As she had before, Charlotte covered her pain at this insult added to injury. Her journal entry of March 7, 1898 was stark and false to the events of the day:

> Mother died this morning at 2.10. I lie down at 5.20 & rise at seven – I could not sleep. Get the breakfast and then go to the city, stopping at Dr. Kellogs, an undertakers, & the [San Francisco] Enquirer's Office. Go to father. To Mr. Worcester, lunch at Mrs. Morses, father again, and home.... Father over in the afternoon. (*Diaries*, p. 520)

With rare exceptions, this was a typical journal entry – plain, strict to the facts, devoid of feeling. Though the author of "The Yellow Wallpaper" was a woman of powerful feelings when it came to literary expression, her private journal expunged the emotions she could not bear to embrace directly – and for good reason.

Charlotte had been emotionally starved by *both* parents, though for different reasons. Her mother Mary, in part because of her husband's abandonment, forced herself never to embrace Charlotte. In her personal memoir, *The Living of Charlotte Perkins Gilman*, written late in life, Charlotte recalls her sad search as a child for her mother's love:

> Having suffered so deeply in her own list of early love affairs, and still suffering for lack of a husband's love, [my mother] heroically determined that her baby daughter should not so suffer if she could help it. Her method was to deny the child all expression of affection.... She would not let me caress her, and would not caress, unless I was asleep. This I discovered at last, and then did my best to keep awake till she came to bed, even using pins to prevent dropping off, and sometimes succeeding. Then how rapturously I enjoyed being gathered into her arms, held close and kissed. (Gilman, 1935, pp. 10–11)

Those who have never experienced the effects of emotional deprivation in childhood may find it difficult to believe that the loss of parental affections can have lifelong effects. But clinical records are filled with cases of children thus deprived who never truly give up the search for parental love lost in the earliest years. The brave ones are those who satisfy their desires through good work and positive relations in adult life. Charlotte was brave. Here were the feelings that gave rise to her ideas.

Still, it would be wrong to shrink the whole of Charlotte Gilman's life into the events of early childhood. Her life story turns on any number of contradictions that defy simple explanation. For one thing, "The Yellow Wallpaper" would never have been possible had not Charlotte trained herself, even in childhood, to look hard at the world about her. At the same time, the looking and longing could well have been the cause of the mental illness that struck her down in 1887 and continued to haunt her after. But, also, though Charlotte was intermittently depressed throughout life, she always managed to recoup her energies. Once she had fled her own room of the yellow wallpaper, she was rarely immobilized by the depression. She began her public career in 1888 shortly after leaving Walter for California and her confinement. From then until retirement she worked so productively as to put her more canonical contemporaries, Max Weber and Émile Durkheim, to the test. (And, recall, Weber too suffered a breakdown, but unlike Gilman, his kept him from work for a number of years.)

Over a full quarter century, Charlotte Gilman wrote seven substantial works of social theory, at least four novels, plus countless essays, poems, and short stories. At the height of her powers, Gilman single-handedly wrote and published her own monthly magazine. From 1909 to 1916, *The Forerunner* was an exclusive forum for her ideas. She wrote *every* word of it – all the articles, including some of her best fiction and social criticism, and every jot of copy. For seven years it sold briskly, and helped make Gilman the literary force she was in the years before the First World War.

Yet when she retired *Forerunner* in 1916, the year after she finished *Herland,* she too began to retire. Though she published a few books after, this was the effective end of her life's work. Perhaps something about the Great War depressed her own sense of hope, as it had that of so many other moderns. The political collapse in Europe led to a train of debilitating events from which the world did not recover until well after the Second World War. The twentieth century is often said to have been the most violent in human history because war led to economic failure, which led again to war, then war again and again. Throughout the century that began in such high hopes for human progress, liberal political ideals were never able for more than a few years in the 1920s and then again in the 1950s to sustain the peace upon which the good society depends. This is surely why the First World War dealt such a deadly blow to radical reformers in the United States.

Gilman's own ideals were clearly influenced, as was the thinking of most left liberals at the end of the nineteenth century, by the reformist spirit of the socialist utopians. Edward Bellamy, who wrote *Looking Backward* (1888), was by all odds the most important. (Gilman's own socialist utopia, *Herland,* bears Bellamy's influence.) But there were many other social visionaries, including the social gospel movement with which Anna Julia Cooper and other settlement workers were loosely affiliated. Even the W. E. B. Du Bois of *Souls of Black Folk* (1903) – though true only to his own values – was under the sway of liberal hope that dominated in the first decade or so of the twentieth century. The war brought all this to an end. Gilman was far from alone in losing her way because of the devastating effects of the Great War of 1914.

Still, as significant as world events were to Gilman's early retirement from public work, her ever-complicated story turns again back to the importance of the personal. For her, the personal and the social were never far from each other. So it is also likely that she retired during the years of the First World War in order to enjoy the pleasures of married life to George Houghton Gilman, with whom she left New York after 1922 for the seclusion of his family home in Norwich, Connecticut. But the retirement came only after two decades of worldly success made possible by her second husband's financial and personal security.

Her long and successful marriage to Gilman gave Charlotte much more than the name by which she is known. The second marriage gave her the enduring domestic peace necessary for creative work. She had begun *Women and Economics* in the late summer days of 1897. These were the fresh early days of her romance with Houghton. She married her distant cousin in June 1900. They settled in New York City, there to renew regular relations with her now teenage daughter who had been living with her father. Ironically, she settled comfortably into the very sort of married life she had left in 1888 as a younger woman. In her memoir (Gilman, 1935, p. 381), Charlotte says of her second marriage: "We were married – and lived happily every after. If this were a novel now, here's a happy ending."

Today, it is well understood that the living of a life necessarily includes the retelling of its story and that the retelling cannot be done without a healthy dose of fiction. Few of us, if any, have more than a passing direct recollection of the events of our pasts. If we are to have a life's story to tell our friends and lovers and children we must rely on the stories told us by others. All the stories that compose our life stories cannot help but take poetic liberties with facts no one truly remembers. Charlotte's own life story does indeed read like a novel, which is why her own *The Living of Charlotte Perkins Gilman* very nearly ends with the account of her marriage to Houghton. In a book of twenty-one chapters, she has very little to say of her life after the marriage in 1900. Only four scant chapters account for the thirty-five years she lived after 1900. Indeed, all of the prodigious work of the New York years before the War are reduced to these few, haphazard chapters.

In Charlotte's artful fiction of her life, the drama is condensed into the deprivations of childhood, the depression and the first marriage, the flight for freedom in California, the years of growth and eventual fame. When Houghton enters at the end of the century, Charlotte's life comes to its "happy ending," as she put it – just more than halfway through her seventy-six years. It did not occur to her to finish *The Living of Charlotte Perkins Gilman* until 1935, on the eve of her death, nearly ten years after the first, incomplete draft was written. After Houghton died in 1934, Charlotte (well aware that she too was near death) moved back to California to be with her daughter Kate. Then, insisting on control of death as of her life's story, she took her life on August 17, 1935, preferring, as she said, "chloroform to cancer."

She had found happiness with a man. This charming oddity of her life's story could only be because she found in Houghton what she had lost in childhood. He provided, one might suppose, the loving embraces her parents had withheld. But the path to this man was anything but direct. In her love letters during their courtship, Charlotte's feelings of love for him are referred not to the losses of her childhood, but to the terrible loss of her young womanhood. Still, again, her story turns in a surprising direction. In a letter of Thursday, September 2, 1897, after a long day of work on *Women and Economics*, Charlotte wrote to Houghton: "I think I am taking more comfort with you than I have since the days of Martha Luther – my girl friend of '77–'81" (Hill, 1995, p. 93).

Charlotte's friendship with Martha Luther during late adolescence in Providence, Rhode Island, was the first openly passionate relationship of her life. In *Charlotte Perkins Gilman: the Making of a Radical Feminist: 1860–1896*, Mary A. Hill, Gilman's most accomplished biographer, interprets Charlotte's passion for Martha as a significant passage from the disappointments of childhood to the boldness of her adult feminism:

> Defiance, anger, crying spells – all reflected the intensity of family battle. After all, her self-sacrificing, domestic, and emotionally dependent mother had clashed irreconcilably with her cool, ambitious, independent father. Now these mother–father conflicts erupted once again, this time in herself. To some extent, Martha provided a "lofty" isolated refuge, but the real peace-keeping maneuver, Charlotte decided would be to strengthen her "self" and kill off the inclinations to remain "merely" a woman or to become a mother and a wife. (Hill, 1990, p. 74)

Just how important was the youthful relationship to Martha? And how did it figure, if at all, in her feminism, and especially in the striking platonic lesbianism of *Herland*?

It is not, of course, uncommon for a young woman to hold fast to other women in the developmental search for an independent self. But Charlotte clung to Martha ferociously. Not even Carroll Smith-Rosenberg's (1975) well known argument that nineteenth-century women often petted, kissed, and slept with each other without heteronormal embarrassment quite accounts for Charlotte's devotion to Martha Luther.

Charlotte's matter-of-fact journal entries for the last weeks of October 1881 betray (as in the case of her mother's death) a studied attempt to control otherwise uncontrollable feelings. Late October 1881 brought the end to Martha's passions for Charlotte. Martha accepted Charles Lane's proposal of marriage. Charlotte's diary records the surface of daily life, thus signaling her deeper emotions. The entry for October 17, 1881, is poignant: "Go to Miss Diman's. Miss Alden sick. I tell stories to Louise, who has an ulcerated throat. Home & get work. Go to Martha's all alone. Stay till almost 8. Nice talk. ('*No!*') Draw letter for guttersnipe. Sew" (*Diaries*, p. 86). "Nice talk" ? – ("*No!*") Of course not. And who exactly is the guttersnipe? Martha? Her fiance? Gilman, distraught, relaxes her guard in these sharp contradictions to the facts of the day. Then, resorting to form, she takes up work, "Sew." Entries for the two weeks following the 17th make only passing references to her dear friend – with the pointed exception of Thursday, October 27: "Martha there. We take walks & converse. Verily I love the damsel" (*Diaries*, p. 87). Then, on the Tuesday following, November 1, Charlotte writes: "No Abby owing to rain. Study and darn. Martha over. She hath a ring. I have a pain. Give her my blessing. Write to Sam and tell him all about it. Post the same. Note to Abigail. Sew" (*Diaries*, p. 88) Martha hath a ring; Charlotte hath a pain! Though they would continue their now deeply altered friendship for many years, only Charlotte seems to have kept its special importance.

In the chapter of her memoir devoted to her first marriage to Walter in 1884, Charlotte begins with reference to the relationship with Martha:

> Looking back on my uncuddled childhood it seems to me a sad mistake of my heroic mother to withhold from me the petting I so craved, the sufficing comfort of maternal caresses. Denied that natural expression, my first memory of loving any one – not to mention [she names several childhood friends; then continues – CL]. Immeasurably the dearest, was Martha. Martha stayed. We were closely together, increasingly happy together, four of those long years of girlhood. She was nearer and dearer than any one up to that time. This was love, but not sex. (Gilman, 1935, p. 78)

These words were written in 1925, thirty-four years after Martha left her. Still she adds: "This was love, but not sex." Though some speculate that Martha may have been a first lover, it is unlikely that we will ever know. But the speculation is encouraged by the evidence of the years after the break-up of her first marriage – the early California years.

In 1891 Charlotte met and by all reckoning fell in love with Delle Knapp, with whom she lived in Oakland in two rooms of a boarding house, along with Kate and Mary Prescott, who was gravely ill. Charlotte's journals are now filled with references like "Delle spent the night," and her memoir comments on the loss of still another love. "My last love proves even as others" (Gilman, 1935, p. 141). Clearly she loved Delle as she had Martha. But how, and to what effect?

Whether or not Charlotte Gilman enjoyed sexual relations with Martha and Delle, it is clear that they and other women were absolutely central to her efforts to establish an independent and feminist self-understanding. Late in life in her memoir Charlotte was notably defensive about the possibility of a sexual relationship with Martha and oddly silent about the affair with Delle. Why? Why would a woman who could be so shockingly honest about her mental illness, and so sharply disdainful of the marital conventions of the day, wish to cover the sexual feelings of those affairs? Just as the perverse matter-of-factness of her journals belies her true feelings, so the denial of sexual activity at a time in life when it would have made little difference to anyone (certainly not her husband) reveals something unsettled about Gilman's early attractions to women. What?

It may well be that nineteenth-century women, as Carroll Smith-Rosenberg explains, enjoyed physical contact with each other not so much for sexual pleasure as for nurturing shelter from the androcentric world. But this alone does not fully account for the fact that, as in Charlotte's case, there could have been erotic passion in these relationships even when they were not consummated. Then as now, sexual pleasure is polymorphous. And sex is more than pleasure. Sex is a social thing regulated by the needs and purposes of the whole wide social world.

Social historians of sex and sexuality in the Victorian era – notably John D'Emilio, Michel Foucault, and Steven Seidman – explain how industrial capitalism intruded upon mundane patterns of sexuality in order to shape the bourgeois family as the social unit in which labor is reproduced. Control sex; control the family. As Seidman notes in *Romantic Longings* (1991), in the Victorian era the contrast between normal heterosexuality and deviant homosexuality did not exist as we know it today. The control of sexuality was exercised according to a different social ideal of the productive, and reproductive, family. (This, not at all coincidentally, was precisely the defining moment for the bourgeois family Gilman worked to unmask and reform.) In the Victorian Age, says Seidman, sexualities were distinguished by a different social formula: between sex in the family and *all* other forms of sex. The perceived need was to regulate sexual practices in the service of industrial capitalism. Homosexuality was not talked about then as it is today. Homosexuality simply was not the issue. Disciplined families were. Thus, the very sexual practices that in our day would be viewed as homosexual were not, in Gilman's youth, fraught with social trouble as they are now. This may well explain why, when Gilman wrote in 1925 about her youthful affair in 1881, she *did* feel a need to explain the erotic away. Times had changed. Gilman lived on both sides of the historical divide after which homosexuality was born to American political consciousness.

This does not mean, however, that Charlotte's youthful desire for the love of women was any less significant to her feminist consciousness. Surely, as she says, the affair with Martha – like her love for Delle (and others about whom we know even less) – was a "refuge" (her word) that allowed her to work through the emotional deprivations of childhood which led to the fated marriage to Walter. Surely, in our day, we would think of them as lesbian or bisexual relations of one or another kind. But, whatever their sexual nature, these relations gave her courage to brave the losses of childhood and to live on her own in the California years, and thus to prepare for the enduring refuge provided by her marriage to Houghton. Gilman's story is perfect proof of the wisdom of Adrienne Rich's famous 1980 essay. In "Compulsory Heterosexuality and Lesbian Experience," Rich distinguished the *lesbian experience*, which includes the practice of homosexual relations, from the *lesbian continuum*, which includes all "woman identified experience" whether sexual or not. Nearly a full century after Charlotte's painful break-up with Martha, Adrienne Rich described the lesbian continuum as the encompassing possibility that it is (but for which the nineteenth century lacked a social vocabulary). The power available to women in their relations with each other, said Rich (1993, p. 239), "comprises both the breaking of a taboo and the rejection of a compulsory way of life." For Charlotte the lesbian continuum included both those relations that *might* have been sexual and those that clearly were not. Those of the latter kind were, if less acute at the time, more enduring over the years – most specially, her long friendships with Jane Addams, with whom she lived for a while at Hull House, and with Grace Channing, who after the divorce married Walter and helped raise Charlotte's daughter Kate. Without her relations along the lesbian continuum, Charlotte Gilman would not have become the most important feminist social theorist of her day.

In her public life, Gilman worked tirelessly, by writing and lecturing, to accomplish two social goals: get women out of the family into the economy; restructure the bourgeois family itself. Both have come to pass in ways Gilman could not have anticipated. Contrary to Gilman's expectations, we know from writings like Arlie Hochschild's *Second Shift* (1989) that women who attempt simultaneously to maintain career and family suffer impossible burdens. Today, the bourgeois family is much transformed by a rapacious global economy that has drawn most women out of the household to struggle, with or without a domestic partner, just to keep family life afloat. At the same time, as we know from works like Judith Stacey's *Brave New Families* (1990), women are indeed restructuring the traditional family. Women in families they chose (as Kath Weston has put it) are freer and more equal, though more burdened, than in Gilman's time.

After the First World War, Gilman fell out of favor – so completely so that Connecticut College, a leading school for women but a few miles from her home in Norwich, ignored one of the century's most important feminists as though she had never existed. Still, as feminism was reborn after the 1960s, Gilman regained the place of recognition she had earned. It is possible that this great visionary also envisaged the renewal of her ideas. Near the end of her life, Gilman wrote: "This is the woman's century, the first chance for the mother of the world to rise to her full place, her transcendent power to remake humanity, to rebuild the suffering world – and the world waits while she powders her nose..." (Gilman, 1935, p. 331). With a wink at the degrading expectations of the man-made world, Gilman leaves the future open, the sentence dangling on an ellipsis. In much the same way, her public life came to an open end. We know, if she did not, that her ideas anticipated the important outlines of feminist social theory at the end of the twentieth century.

THE THEORY

It may be for fear of embarrassment that so few theorists comment on the original meaning of the word "theory." According to the *Oxford English Dictionary*, the word derives from the Greek *theoros*: "one who travels in order to see things." Thus, another of the original meanings is, simply, "a spectacle." In our scientific age, these definitions of a very high-minded activity are surprising. They would not have been to Gilman. She was, if not a tourist, certainly a pilgrim who walked her way through her own inner space to get to a fresh view of the spectacle of industrial capitalism and its effects on women. It was not a pretty picture.

Today those with eyes to see can see what Gilman saw behind the debris of a family system crushed, in our time, by a capitalism more cruel than even in Gilman's time – or Marx's for that matter. For those more accustomed to a socialism derived from Marx's painstaking analysis of the evils of the capitalist mode of production, Gilman's progressive socialism might well seem a faint copy of the original. American socialists of the end of the nineteenth century – writers like Henry George, Edward Bellamy, and Gilman herself – understood something of European socialism after Marx. But, for the most part, they developed their ideas in quite independent ways. Perhaps it was the American pragmatism in them that caused these early radicals to attack the selfishness of the industrial bosses with a comparably positive, even evolutionary, principle of human progress. One of the ironies of the Gilded Age is that nearly everyone from the bosses of industry to their radical opponents was caught up in the innocent hopefulness of the new industrial world.

Thus it was that even those, like Gilman, who self-consciously represented social groups oppressed by the dominant social order were alive with hope. W. E. B. Du Bois and Anna Julia Cooper are two of the more astonishing examples. They spoke for the American Negro oppressed by Jim Crow laws in the South and social segregation in the North. Still, in their writings of the last decade of the nineteenth century, both Du Bois and Cooper wrote with surprising confidence in the future of American society. Du Bois, in the most famous chapter of *Souls of Black Folk*, looked to a day when the Negro would be a "coworker in the kingdom of culture." Similarly, Cooper, in *A Voice From the South*, ordained black women who experienced the cruel injustices of the American South as the moral leaders of the day – of a progressive era with "such new and alluring vistas ... opening out before us."

Gilman, likewise, concluded *Women and Economics* with a word of hope: "When the mother of the race is free, we shall have a better world, by the easy right of birth and by the calm, slow, friendly forces of social evolution" (Gilman, 1898, p. 340). This after 340 pages of relentless criticism of the evil she called the "sexuo-economic relation" at the heart of capitalism. Today readers will not be enchanted by the optimistic coda. Still, like other classic ideas, Gilman's basic feminist principles outlive the cocoon in which they developed.

One of the arguments among feminists at the end of the twentieth century is over the uncertain identity of women caught between family and the workplace. Though the debate has taken many different turns in the last generation, it always returns to the dilemma Gilman tried to resolve by her social criticism of the sexuo-economic relation. She meant, in effect, to complicate the idea of sex – or, in our term, gender. A woman's gender circumstance is always, and necessarily, determined by, but not reducible to, her economic situation. Gilman never thought of Woman in the abstract. For the most part, she resisted the inviting danger of feminist essentialism.

Essentialism abstracts an important feature into a definition. Women are different from men. But their difference in fact may or may not be a difference in kind. Feminist essentialisms tend, one way or another, to claim that a woman's unique nature is a stable, immutable property of her gender. The allure of the essentialist move is the gain of a critical tool made powerful by isolating analytic qualities which may be turned back against arbitrary social arrangements that put those qualities at risk. While meant to sharpen racial, sexual, or gender differences, the problem with essentialisms of all kinds (even strategic ones) is that they don't speak very subtly to the lived reality of women's lives – or for that matter to the lives of those excluded because of their sexual orientation or their race. Essentialisms may be necessary to the polarizing purposes of certain political moments, or the analytic work of theorists, but they are not practical to the experience of real people they are meant to represent. In the vocabulary of our time, Gilman was more interested in the situated knowledge of women's lives. She was a writer and a social critic, a public speaker and an organizer. Her work was with those who do not tolerate abstractions well. In the one surprising instance toward the end of her career where she lapsed into a kind of inadvertent essentialism, she did so almost by the accident of her political and literary purposes. Even then, there was no doctrinal conviction. Gilman wrote about women's lives, as lived.

People live in families, or the hope of families – or, at least, of other forms of intimate association. Yet for their domestic arrangements to survive economically, they must work. Most women (and some men) who live in a world dominated by capitalist greed live with uncertainty doubled. For them the search for intimate association and viable work is hard work and neither can be had without the other. Gilman saw, early in the evolution of modern industrial society, that women had been assigned twice the responsibility for half the pay (if that). This is the sexuo-economic relation. Women must produce and reproduce the family association without which society would fail; and they must do this while held in servile relation to the man-made world.

"Economic progress is almost exclusively male" (Gilman, 1898, p. 8). This is Gilman's opening shot in *Women and Economics*. Among animals, she believed, only the human is so dominated by the male. There is some truth in this. "Queen bee" is a gender slur because it is a biological reality. In her day the continuing backwash of social Darwinianism encouraged the sociobiological gesture in Gilman's early writings. (Lester Ward, the academic sociologist who most influenced her thinking, encouraged Gilman along this line.) Still, Gilman's argument survives her questionable biological claims, which, even today, retain a certain rhetorical force. Gilman equated the female human being with the work horse. Both are servile to a master. "Their labor is the property of another: they work under another will; and what they receive depends not on their labor, but on the power and will of the other" (Gilman, 1898, p. 7).

True to her poetic gifts, Gilman uses a strong comparative figure, but she does not lose sight of the broader economic idea. She aims to show that the relations of men to women are entirely arbitrary to economic convenience. "The labor of women in the house, certainly enables men to produce more wealth than they otherwise could; and in this way women are economic factors in society. But so are horses" (Gilman, 1898, p. 13). The opening allusion to the human female as the work horse of the species sets up the argument that follows. Step by step, with compelling logic, Gilman dismantles each of the then prevailing moral sentiments that served once (and still do in many places) to justify the domestic confinement of bourgeois women. Does not the human female's sexual beauty gain her the natural happiness of marriage? Is it not her nature to sacrifice independence for the sake of home and children? Is she not paid in kind by the support of the breadwinner husband? Do not the children require her attentions? Is not the home the hearth of civilization? The book is a careful exposition of the stupidity of the assumptions that, in her day, would have tempted many to say, in reply to each question: "Well, yes, of course." Gilman's sustained rebuttal of the true womanhood ideal is one of the earliest and still most persuasive exposés of the naturalistic sex role theories that came to dominate social science after the Second World War.

Still, Gilman's thinking was itself a kind of crypto-functionalism. Though her biological figures of speech are a bit heavy-handed for our day, her underlying social theory makes complete sense if we accept that, in the end, Gilman was more a social reformer than a devotee of the principle of social evolution. Her argument is that the fate of the female is necessarily bound to that of the male, as in turn his is to hers. It is not men who are selfish, but the system that makes them so. Greed is at the heart of the economy. "Social life tends to reduce this [self-ishness], which is but a belated individualism; but the sexuo-economic relation fosters and develops it" (Gilman, 1898, p. 338). Here is the sociological imagina-tion at its best. In the normal course of daily life, Gilman is saying, a woman may suffer, but she does not actually see the selfishness of the world behind the men who make her the work horse. The true nature of the relation between the sexes can only be seen in structural perspective. This steady attention to the economic realities is what saves Gilman's ideas from the more naive functionalist thinking that, years later, Talcott Parsons made prominent in American sociology.

Gilman was first and foremost a socialist utopian. Her theories of social evolution served a political ethic more than a scientific concern. Had she been more the Marxist, she might have called for a reversal of the gender relations. But her radicalism was of another kind. She, like Du Bois and Bellamy, Cooper and George, looked to historical progress, not revolution, for a better society. At the end of the twentieth century very few people of certifiable common sense would trust the future for assurance of a better life. Hope, today, is all too realistically hedged by the stark economic realities that have so assaulted family life. Only the most fortunate few enjoy the security of breadwinning, productive labor. For most, the sexuo-economic relation persists, worse perhaps than even Gilman might have imagined.

Still, Gilman's ideas bear consideration because they navigate the waters between gender relations and economic reality with such a keen eye. She had lived at economic risk as a child, and had suffered firsthand the effects of the sexuo-economic relation on her family. Her ideas were always grounded in these experiences. As a result, she looked to a possible future more to understand the present than to predict a necessary outcome. And, just as she held out for the unrequited affections of her despicable father, so she could, at one and the same time, forcefully attack the men who made the androcentric world *and* feel compassion for them.

So we may trace from the sexuo-economic relation of our species not only definite evils in psychic development, bred severally in men and women, and transmitted indifferently to their offspring, but the innate perversion of character resultant from the moral miscegenation of two so diverse souls, – the unfailing shadow and distortion which has darkened and twisted the spirit of man from the beginnings. We have been injured in body and in mind by the two dissimilar traits inherited from our widely separated parents, but nowhere is the injury more apparent than its ill effects upon the moral nature of the race. (Gilman, 1898, p. 339)

She pulls no punches. Nor does she fail to understand that it is the structure of things that causes social evil. If women suffer more acutely, they do not suffer alone. Their men and their children are subject to the same ill moral effects.

When all is said and done, Gilman was a hard-headed realist about the practical consequences of the sexuo-economic relation. It is a curious thing that her phrase has not been reclaimed in this day, when it would seem so apt to the debates over the relative merits of identity and socialist politics. Today, through the contributions of thinkers like Judith Butler and Nancy Fraser, we know that women are not alone in the struggle to find a satisfactory recognition for their social identity, on the one hand, and to gain access to a fair share of economic wealth necessary for a decent life, on the other hand. Men as well as women, people of color as well as whites, heterosexuals as well as homosexuals, struggle with this dilemma. Far from being a postmodern oddity, this is, in many ways, the fundamental dilemma of modern life. Gilman, who lacked all the fancy terms we have today, understood this fundamental fact of life. Men as well as women would benefit from a wholesale transformation of the sexuo-economic relation. Even when she was writing her fiction, or concentrating on specific social issues like the quality of life in the bourgeois home, Gilman understood this. "A home life with a dependent mother, a servant-wife, is not an ennobling influence" (Gilman, 1898, pp. 262–3). When the woman is diminished, so is the man. A good decade before writing this, Charlotte grasped the principle perfectly well in her own life, even in the earliest of her fiction writings, well before she had worked out the theory.

"The Yellow Wallpaper," written six years before *Women and Economics*, remains today her most commanding, and disturbing, picture of the spectacle of the bourgeois family. The story begins innocently enough. The scene is a rented summer cottage, but it was a "cottage" in the grand bourgeois sense of turn-of-the-century retreats that became in our day wealthy suburbs like Newton, Massachusetts, or Greenwich, Connecticut. "Cottage" already signals just what sort of family story this is.

The man in the story condenses the two separate characters of Charlotte's own experience. John is made to be both husband and physician. The unnamed wife is attended by a woman, John's sister – a "perfect and enthusiastic housekeeper" who "hopes for no better profession" (p. 7). There are children. But it is the man – John, the physician husband – who figures as the looming object of the narrator's attentions.

Then, even as the idyllic scene is set, we are warned of something "queer" about the house itself.

It is very seldom that ordinary people like John and myself secure ancestral halls for
the summer.

A colonial mansion, a hereditary estate, I would say a haunted house, and reach
the height of romantic felicity – but that would be asking too much of fate!

Still I would probably declare that there is something queer about it.

Else, why should it be let so cheaply? And why have stood so long untenanted?
John laughs at me, of course, but one expects that in marriage. (Gilman, 1892, p. 1)

Gilman the author is playing with the incongruity between the outside and inside
of things. She uses the excess of the cottage, and its long vacancy, to invite the
story's narrative line – that what is off is that this ideal little family will not
achieve the felicity of a summer's retreat. The reader's eye is drawn to John by a
gentle note of complaint. A woman expects a man to laugh at her. Is male
dismissal of female sensibility the queer structure of the arrangement? Does
Gilman ask us to think of the house as an icon for the whole of the bourgeois
domestic scene – even, perhaps, for the whole of the economic structure that is so
delicately hinted at by the pretense of the ironic "cottage"?

The poetic power of a short fiction is that it depends so weightily on the
reader's imagination. So few words to say so much. Here the reader is invited by
the queer exterior of the cottage to imagine the impending trouble. It is a
"beautiful place" with a "delicious garden . . . never such a garden" (p. 2). But
the central figure of the story is the room with ghastly yellow wallpaper:

dull enough to confuse the eye in following, pronounced enough to constantly
irritate and provoke study and when you follow the lame uncertain curves for a
little distance they suddenly commit suicide – plunge off at outrageous angles,
destroy themselves in unheard of contradictions. (p. 4)

On the exterior, all is delicious. Inside, all is confusing, suicidal, and contradictory.

The deadly interior of the house is, of course, the metonym of the bourgeois
woman's confinement. Though the facts of Charlotte's own confinement in 1887
are absent in the fiction, the yellow wallpaper expresses the woman's nightmare.
Her own physician, Dr S. Weir Mitchell, was the leading medical specialist in
women's illnesses, as they were called. His treatment was the same rest cure
which he had earlier prescribed for Harriet Beecher Stowe. The treatment,
intended as a relieving ministry, was in fact a harsh imposition the man cannot
understand. The woman must refrain from all labor – bed rest, an occasional
visit from the children, and, in Charlotte's case, no reading or writing. The rest
cure, thus, by depriving her of what she needs most, is bound to fail for most –
certainly so for Charlotte.

The woman confined to this absurd contradiction is drawn into the wallpaper
itself. The yellow wallpaper – "not arranged on any laws" (p. 3) – comes alive as
the emblem of world's work on women.

Behind that outside pattern the dim shapes get clear, clearer every day.
It is always the same shape, only very numerous.

And it is like a woman stooping down and creeping about behind that pattern. I don't like it one bit. (p. 10)

The woman sees herself in the suicide patterns of the wall. She and contradiction become insanely one and the same. She is one with other women. "Sometimes I think there are a great many women behind [the moving patterns of the wall-paper], and sometimes only one" (p. 15).

It would be easy to miss the importance of what happens next. The woman is driven mad: by the wallpaper; by the domestic arrangement; by the world. But she attacks in self-defense by stripping the paper away sheet by sheet. This cannot be. The man, John, intervenes. But the woman overcomes. The story ends:

"I've got to get out at last," said I, "in spite of you and Jane. And I've pulled off most of the paper, so you can't put me back!"

Now why should that man have fainted? But he did, and right across my path by the wall, so that I had to creep over him every time! (p. 20)

The man faints. The woman escapes. But who is Jane? She is never introduced. Could she be John's sister, the perfect housewife who aspires to nothing more – the true woman, that is, that Charlotte could never be? Or, could Jane be the disturbed self of the woman who must always face her confinement? Is it possible that by this accidental woman Gilman is telling us that women, even when they escape the nightmarish world of the family, must in effect leave behind their very own selves – or, if not their selfhood, the ideal self that the world would impose? At the least, the woman who escapes must leave behind the true woman who remains with John (see Knight, 1992). And, in the image of the swooning husband (a reversal of the hysterical woman image), are we to think that even if she flees, then he is left in the garish room?

The queer house with its deadly room is the problem – not the woman, not even the man. Women, thus, are faced with an impossible choice. If they conform to the gentle absurdity of the man-made world, they are drawn into that world's selfish madness. If they rebel they must leave themselves behind as Charlotte did when she left Walter in order to reinvent herself. Fiction very often leaves the important questions unanswered. But in Gilman's case, Charlotte explains herself by what she became in real life, and by what she wrote in so many words in subsequent writings that made her social program completely obvious.

Woman alone cannot reform herself. Her freedom is freedom for all, even her man, especially her children. "The largest and most radical effect of restoring women to economic independence will be in its result in clarifying and harmonizing the human soul" (Gilman, 1898, pp. 331–2). The human soul demands a structural change in the sexuo-economic relation.

Gilman would play this theme again and again. In *The Home* (1903) she wrote more bitterly of the "domestic mythology," attacking in plain language the pieties of the American home. As to the virtues of home-cooking, for one example, she asks, in effect: but have you ever actually tasted it?

"Home-cooking" is an alluring phrase, but lay aside the allurement... [and ask] whose home-cooking are we praising? Our own, of course. Which means nothing but that the stomach adapts itself to what it has to live on – unless it is too poisonous.... The long-suffering human system (perhaps toughened by ages of home-cooking) – will adapt itself even to slow death. (Gilman, 1903, pp. 124–5)

Here is but a taste of Gilman's radical, practical socialism at its most cynical best. Why not, she asks, encourage a system in which those expert in tasteful, nutritional cooking prepare the food for the community? Would not all be healthier and happier under such a system?

The Home holds up very well today for its relentless practical sneering at the absurd practices of the bourgeois family. The book offers what might be called a countercultural course in home economics. After a brief history of the family, Gilman unmasks the domestic mythology, just as, in *Women and Economics*, she attacked the ideal of true womanhood. "Let us begin," she says (pp. 38–9), starting with the highest of American values about the home, "with that fondly cherished popular idea – 'the privacy of the home.' " No one has privacy at home, least of all the mother. "The mother – poor invaded soul – finds even the bathroom door no bar to hammering little hands" (p. 40). The chapters following continue in this vein, exposing such myths as the home as the housewife's workshop, the lady of the house, and domestic arts, as well as home-cooking.

The more general analytic themes of *Women and Economics* are reconsidered in the closing chapters of *The Home*. As the woman suffers, so too do the boy and girl children – and the men! In passages that anticipate Nancy Chodorow's criticism of sex-role theory in *Reproduction of Mothering* (1978), Gilman unmasks the damage done by the sexuo-economic relation in the home:

The home teaches the boy that women were made for service, domestic service, that the principal cares and labours of life are those which concern the boy, and that his own particular tastes and preferences are of enormous importance. As fast as he gets out of the home and into the school he learns quite other things, getting his exaggerated infant egotism knocked out of him very suddenly, and, as he gets out of school and into business, also into politics, he learns still further the conditions of life. (p. 273)

Though shorn of the theoretical sophistication of Chodorow's book (and perhaps a little too forgiving of the male ego), Gilman brings home the idea that gender differences are produced (and reproduced) in the arbitrary confines of the bourgeois home. Girls become wives and mothers after the example of the mother. Boys become men, full of their own importance, in reaction to the example of the servile mother.

Gilman never turned away from her socialist values. But neither did she come close to a systematic analysis of the capitalist mode of production. She was always clear that the problem at the heart of the sexuo-economic relation was that women were excluded from productive labor. Liberate women, therefore, and you will liberate the world, as she argued in a later work of social criticism,

The Man-made World: "The scope of purpose of human life is entirely above and beyond the sex relationship.... To develop human life in its true powers we need full equal citizenship for women.... An economic democracy must rest on free womanhood; and a free womanhood inevitably leads to an economic democracy" (Gilman, 1911, p. 260). Gilman's last major work of fiction, *Herland*, provides the graphic details of her dream of an economic democracy. Like Bellamy's *Looking Backward*, Gilman's utopia is set stark against the evils of capitalist individualism. Yet, unlike other socialist programs of her day, and unlike her own earlier writings, *Herland* takes a surprising step toward what amounts to a feminist essentialism. Only a world of women, from which all men from the outer world of economic competition are excluded, can be a true economic democracy.

Curiously, unlike "The Yellow Wallpaper" in which the narrator is the suffering woman, the *Herland* story is told in the voice of one Vandyck Jennings, who, more curious still, is a sociologist. Jennings and two male companions from the real world come upon a lost colony of women. The women of Herland are descendants of a small band of female ancestors who, two thousand years before, survived a series of wars and natural disasters. Facing the destruction of the world as it was (by implication, as it still is!), the ancestral mothers rose up against the men who would have kept them as slaves. These women were expressly "white" (p. 56) and otherwise, we are led to believe, remarkably endowed. In particular, they are able to reproduce themselves without benefit of the male sex. Over the centuries the saving remnant of women developed a most peaceful society with a prosperous economy. In Herland social control is exercised by force of personal will, not violence; the needs of all are produced in common, without competition; love (though a markedly sexless love) is shared out of respect, without domination. In a departure from her earlier concepts of sexual equality, Gilman seems to say that only women can bring about this socialist utopia.

The story itself is predictable. The three male visitors are discovered, overcome, and held. Their female captors possess a mystical power over the three men. It is clear that the ability of Herland women to control others by civilized force, not violence, is somehow key to the many virtues of their society. Childcare is shared and thoughtful, education is liberal to the individual's need, economics is practical to the requirements of all. Nothing is out of order in this world without evil.

Nothing, that is, until the men arrive. *Herland*'s dramatic interest is sustained by the tantalizing possibility that the men from the outer society will reintroduce the long-lost sexuo-economic ethic. The men themselves are portrayed so as to represent the full range of appalling male habits: sexual appetite, competitiveness, boastful pride. Of the three, only the narrator-sociologist, Vandyck Jennings (despite his name, a caricature of bourgeois idiocy), turns out to be half-plausible as a mate for one of the Herland women. The story comes to its resolution just as Jennings is on the verge of enticing his love to leave Herland, to return with him to the outer world. Then tragic recognition dawns. The risk of discovery and pollution by the world's sexuo-economic values is too great.

The relationship is forbidden. The men are expelled on the not entirely believable trust that they will never betray the way back to Herland. The novel ends, thus, on a tease. Will the corrupt world of poverty, war, and human greed find its way back to Herland, where social evil has been overcome? Will the dream survive?

Just as important as the novel's literary tease is its philosophical tease. Did Gilman change her mind in the end? Is it only women who can maintain an economic democracy? Was she, for all those years, really a closet essentialist? There is no way to know. It is possible that she was led to the appearance of an exaggerated feminist standpoint position by the demands of her genre. A feminist utopia does, after all, require a strong feminist socialism. The free rein of the literary imagination induces a more relaxed attitude toward theoretical principle. On the other hand, by the time Gilman published *Herland* in 1915 she had devoted nearly a quarter century to life and work as a feminist social critic. She knew what she thought. There are few indications in her nonfiction social criticism that she was edging toward a change of heart. *The Man-made World*, written just a few years before *Herland*, held firm to the practical feminist and socialist ideals that had governed Gilman's life work. It is possible she changed her mind; but unlikely. It makes most sense to leave the question open.

One of the considerable strengths of Gilman as a social critic is that she was willing to rethink just about everything. It is, therefore, entirely possible that toward the end she wanted to push her radical ideas to their extreme, not to make a point of principle, but in order to explore still another facet of the troubles women face in the sexuo-economic relation. She had lived as a woman who herself had struggled to escape the compulsory heterosexuality of that relation. Though she remained a woman who loved a man, she very well understood the need women have to escape the man-made world. Her final fiction was, perhaps, a final study of the prospects, if not the realities, of a woman's freedom from that world. *Herland* is not in the end an attack on men. Vandyck Jennings was a plausible partner, just as Walter had been to Charlotte in her youth. The problem the novel, and Gilman's work as whole, seeks to solve is that of the structured relationship between the genders designed by a coercive economic system. She had no settled judgment on this. Nor do we today.

ASSESSMENT

In her day, Gilman's ideas were quite out of the ordinary. Where the bourgeois values of the Progressive Era coveted capital gain from the rising fortunes of industrial America, Gilman challenged the complicity of capitalist America. Where other white feminists of her own and earlier generations (including her Beecher relatives) narrowed their struggle for women's rights to the right to vote, Gilman identified the suffering of women with the structured whole of societies shaped by the capitalist world system. Where many early feminists like Ellen Key and Margaret Sanger were willing to use the term "feminist" (which came into the culture first in 1910) to further the separate but equal status of women, Gilman challenged the very idea of the women's sphere and called for a complete transformation in gender relations. Where bourgeois people of all kinds held the family as a sacred sphere for women's work, Gilman attacked the bourgeois family as a ridiculous pretense and unmitigated disaster for everyone – men as well as women.

Though not by any means alone in her views, Charlotte Gilman was strikingly the odd woman out of context, even among radicals. Perhaps it was the sharpness of her views that made her the most influential feminist social theorist in the two decades on either side of the end of the nineteenth century. Nancy Cott, in *The Grounding of Modern Feminism* (1987, p. 41), has written:

> Since the 1890s, from California to the East Coast, as a soul stirring speaker and a prolific writer, Gilman had been conveying her critique of the "sexuo-economic" relation that she saw binding women to men, molding women to exaggerate sex-specific characteristics and to rely on men as economic providers. Gilman elevated into a theory of social evolution the changes that perspicacious women saw happening around them; she urged women to move in the direction already pointed out, by leaving their ancient unspecialized home occupation, following the path marked by modern industry and professions, and exercising their full human capabilities in useful work of all sorts.

This was indeed the program that made her famous. Carl Degler thus began his 1956 essay, a foundational study in modern Gilman studies, with the following assessment:

> When Charlotte Perkins Gilman published *Women and Economics* in 1898, the feminist movement in America gained an advocate of uncommon intellectual power and insight. Quickly acclaimed on both sides of the Atlantic [by *Nation* magazine and *The London Chronicle*] for having written "the most significant utterance" on the women's question since Mill, she became the idol of radical feminists and was later judged [by Carrie Chapman Catt] "the most original and challenging mind which the woman movement produced." (Degler 1989, p. 11)

With more reserve, Mari Jo Buhle (1992, p. 270) assesses Gilman's place in history as that of "an analytic bridge between the views of the nineteenth century's woman's movement and the 'scientific' socialist conceptions of woman's advance common to the early twentieth century." Gilman's thinking was, indeed, a bridge to twentieth-century feminism – but it was hardly a scientific socialism. When, after the 1960s, feminism emerged as a force in American, and world, politics, Gilman's ideas returned to favor, but not because of their scientific value.

There are, of course, many ways in which Gilman's thinking is impossible for today's situation. The most prominent of these was her utter blindness to race; not to mention her relative innocence as to the difference made by poverty. She wrote for white, middle-class women – for those, like herself, who bore the brunt of the true womanhood ideal behind the late nineteenth-century bourgeois family. She did not, perhaps could not, see that African-American women, and their families, are differently situated in their domestic lives because the sexuo-economic relation affects them differently (Lanser, 1989). And, even with her impassioned hostility to the capitalist system, she does not seem to have recognized that poverty affects women and their families more harshly than even bourgeois confinement. In these ways, Gilman's thinking is limited.

In other ways, Gilman was way ahead of her times and perfectly suited for today's thinking. Her idea of what later came to be called the sociological imagination still serves well because, as noted, it breaks down abstractions at every turn. She avoided essentialisms, where she did, because she was politically and ethically committed to resolving the troubles women experienced in a family arrangement defined by a false and arbitrary value system. She pursued her work open to all available methods and thus, today, instructs the academically cautious. Because she had lived what she thought, Gilman very well understood the barriers with which social sciences protect themselves from the creative indefiniteness of the literary imagination. Few social critics have written as much good fiction as they have nonfiction and done so with such fine regard for the larger critical issues of the day.

Some may find her fiction too determined by her social values. Others may find her social ideas too indefinite for today's theoretical sophistication. And anyone with sensitivity to the realities of social differences will find her indifference to race a disturbing error of judgment. How could a daughter by marriage of one of the nation's great abolitionist families not imagine that women of color suffered the sexuo-economic relation differently and more severely than white women? Gilman's passions ran deep. Her socialist values were firm. She had a keen eye for political principle and for social theory. Yet she could not see the difference that many, even in her day, realized was the difference at the heart of America's moral sickness. Gilman simply could not entertain thoughts as dark as these. The ones she could were, however, good enough for a lifetime's work, and good enough for us today to appreciate that, whatever the dangers, feminist promises are worth imagining and keeping.

Bibliography

Writings of Charlotte Perkins Gilman

The Yellow Wallpaper [1892] and Other Writings (edited by Lynne Sharon Schwartz). New York: Bantam Books (1989).

Women and Economics: a Study of the Economic Relations between Men and Women as a Factor in Social Evolution. 1898. Boston: Small, Maynard & Co. (reprinted New York: Source Book Press, 1970).

The Home: Its Work and Influence. 1903. New York: McClure, Phillips & Co. (reprinted Urbana: University of Illinois Press, 1972).

Human Work. 1904. New York: McClure, Phillips & Co.

The Man-made World or, Our Androcentric Culture. 1911. New York: Charlton Company (reprinted Johnson Reprint Corporation, 1971).

The Living of Charlotte Perkins Gilman. 1935. New York: Appleton-Crofts Co. (reprinted Madison: University of Wisconsin Press, 1990).
Herland [1915] *and Selected Writings by Charlotte Perkins Gilman* (edited by Barbara Solomon). 1992. New York: Signet.
The Diaries of Charlotte Perkins Gilman (edited by Denise Knight), 2 volumes. 1994. Charlottesville: University of Virginia Press.

Further reading

Bellamy, Edward (1888) *Looking Backward.* New York: Penguin (1960).
Buhle, Mari Jo (1992) Charlotte Perkins Gilman. In Mari Jo Buhle, Paul Buhle, and Dan Georgakas (eds), *Encyclopedia of the American Left.* Urbana: University of Illinois Press, pp. 270–1.
Chodorow, Nancy (1978) *Reproduction of Mothering: Psychoanalysis and the Socialization of Gender.* Berkeley: University of California Press.
Cott, Nancy F. (1987) *The Grounding of Modern Feminism.* New Haven: Yale University Press.
Degler, Carl (1956) Charlotte Perkins Gilman and the Theory and Practice of Feminism. *American Quarterly,* 8, 21–9. Reprinted in Sheryl L. Meyering (ed.), *Charlotte Perkins Gilman: the Woman and Her Work.* Ann Arbor: University of Michigan Research Press (1989), pp. 11–29.
Du Bois, W. E. B. (1903) *Souls of Black Folk.* Chicago: A. C. McClurg (reprinted New York: Bantam, 1989).
Friedan, Betty (1963) *The Feminine Mystique.* New York: W. W. Norton.
Hill, Mary A. (1990) *Charlotte Perkins Gilman: the Making of a Radical Feminist, 1860–1896.* Philadelphia: Temple University Press.
Hill, Mary A. (ed.) (1995) *A Journey Within: the Love Letters of Charlotte Perkins Gilman, 1897–1900.* Lewisburg: Bucknell University Press.
Hochschild, Arlie (1989) *Second Shift.* New York: Avon Books.
Knight, Denise D. (1992) The Reincarnation of Jane: "Through This" – Gilman's Companion to "The Yellow Wallpaper." *Feminist Studies,* 20, 287–302.
Lanser, Susan S. (1989) Feminist Criticism, "The Yellow Wallpaper," and the Politics of Color in America. *Feminist Studies,* 15, 415–41.
Rich, Adrienne (1980) Compulsory Heterosexuality and Lesbian Experience. In Henry Abelove, Michele Aina Barale, and David M. Halperin (eds), *The Lesbian and Gay Studies Reader.* New York: Routledge (1993), pp. 227–54.
Seidman, Steve (1991) *Romantic Longings: Love in America, 1830–1980.* New York: Routledge.
Smith-Rosenberg, Caroll (1975) The Female World of Love and Ritual: Relations between Women in Nineteenth Century America. *Signs,* 1(1).
Stacey, Judith (1990) *Brave New Families.* New York: Basic Books.

9

George Herbert Mead

Dmitri N. Shalin

Introduction

George Herbert Mead was trained as a philosopher, taught in a philosophy department, and published primarily in philosophy journals, but his lasting impact was in the field of sociology. The fact that the science of society was still young at the time helps to explain this anomaly. The borderline separating the fledgling discipline from its academic neighbors was still unclear: sociologists did not have much academic turf to protect and felt free to borrow their insights from neighboring fields. The peculiar blend of Romantic idealism and pragmatic activism accomplished by Mead also had something to do with his popularity among social scientists, who found in his life work a model for balancing scholarship and advocacy at a time when America was awash in reform. Finally, it was the bold manner in which Mead married philosophical and sociological idioms that inspired his contemporaries. Mead labored hard to spell out the sociological significance of contemporary philosophical currents and, along with John Dewey, brought a radically sociological imagination to philosophical discourse. While his role in social science is well recognized, Mead's original contribution to philosophy has only recently begun to be fully appreciated (Habermas, 1984; Joas, 1985; Aboulafia, 1986, 1991).

This chapter explores the interfaces between Mead's philosophical and sociological thought, his effort to combine academic pursuits with political engagement, and the impact his work has had on social theory. The discussion draws on Mead's publications, as well as his unpublished papers and correspondence gathered in the Joseph Regenstein Library, University of Chicago (the Mead Papers gathered in this collection are abbreviated below as MP). In his lifetime, Mead published several dozen professional articles and book reviews; they were partially reprinted in 1956 under the title *George Herbert Mead on Social*

Psychology (abbreviated thereafter as GHM) and in a 1964 collection *Selected Writings* (SW). Most of Mead's professional writings appeared in print after his death. His lectures on social psychology were published in 1934 as *Mind, Self, and Society* (MSS). More notes on the subject were brought out in 1982 under the heading *The Individual and the Social Self* (TIS). Mead's philosophical writings were collected in the 1938 volume *The Philosophy of the Act* (PA), the 1936 book *Movements of Thought in the Nineteenth Century* (MT), and the 1932 publication *Philosophy of the Present* (PP), based on the lecture series Mead delivered at Berkeley one year before his death.

Mead's life and theoretical corpus have been the subject of several studies which variously inform present discussion (Natanson, 1956; Barry, 1968; Miller, 1973; Joas, 1985; Baldwin, 1986; Shalin, 1984, 1988). Without attempting to do full justice to his numerous contributions, this survey sketches Mead's social theory and places it in historical context. The chapter starts with Mead's biography and intellectual sources, moves on to his social and political theory, and concludes with reflections on Mead's relevance to contemporary social thought.

THE BIOGRAPHICAL CONTEXT

Mead was born in 1863, at South Hadley, Massachusetts, into a family distinguished by its long roots in New England Puritanism and passionate commitment to Christian values. His father, Hiram Mead, served as a pastor at various South Hadley congregations. In 1869, Hiram moved to Oberlin College, where he was offered a chair in Sacred Rhetoric and Pastoral Theology at the newly established theological seminary. When he died in 1881, at the age of 54, the obituary noted "the quiet, aggressive energy of our brother," his "positiveness of conviction and of self-reliance . . . modified by delicacy of feeling and gentleness of manner" (*The Oberlin Review*, May 28, 1881, pp. 212–13). Many poor students, the obituary went on, would have had a hard time completing their college work were it not for Hiram Mead's generous help.

Mead's mother, Elizabeth Storrs Billings, a woman noted for her learning and piety, also taught at Oberlin College, and before that, served as a top administrator at Mount Holyoke College. She personally saw to it that the young George would go through his daily regimen of prayer, study, and good works. It was her desire to see her son follow in his father's steps that stirred Mead toward the Christian ministry. Even after Mead began to waver in his faith, he continued to push himself along this path for his mother's sake. "My mother lives in me," Mead wrote to Henry Castle, his college buddy and soul mate, on March 30, 1885 (MP, box 1, folder 1). "Her happiness is bound up in me. I sometimes wonder if it is not my duty to profess Christianity just for the infinite satisfaction it would give her." Shy, studious, and deferential to his parents, Mead seemed perfectly suited to continue the tradition that featured several generations of clergymen on both sides of the family. This must have been his main option when he enroled at Oberlin College, where he took up the classics, rhetoric, and moral philosophy, interlaced with mandatory prayer meetings. But the Christianity Mead imbibed in his formative years was now undergoing rapid changes, struggling to meet the challenges of the late nineteenth century.

German historical criticism, which made its way into the USA midway through the century, raised doubts about the historical veracity of the Bible. These doubts were reinforced by Darwinism, which offered a radically different perspective on the origins of humankind. The downturn in the economic cycle further undermined the appeal of mainstream Protestantism. With rising unemployment and labor unrest, it was harder to sustain its individualistic tenets that predicated personal success on the individual's moral fiber. The mounting economic woes opened the door to socialist doctrine. Throughout the rest of the century, socialism steadily won recruits on US campuses, pushing evangelical Christianity to the left. While mainstream Evangelicals tended to moralize socio-economic problems by blaming them on assorted personal vices, the Social Gospel movement placed moral issues into a social context and scolded society for its failure to furnish conditions under which every one of its members could thrive. Shaping the human being in the image of God, according to the new evangelicals, meant more than cleansing his soul by prayer; it also required changing the social and economic conditions that corrupted his spirit. "Christian socialists should teach by fact and not by sentiments," explained the Reverend W. D. P. Bliss (quoted in Shalin, 1988, p. 915), "by fact about city gas works, not mere talk about city brotherhood."

These momentous currents intersected at Oberlin College, a Congregationalist institution renowned for its piety and abolitionist sentiments and proud of its place in the forefront of the movement toward socially minded Christianity. *The Oberlin Review*, the campus publication that Mead coedited in his senior year, was among the first in the nation to open its pages to the new teachings. It debated the pros and cons of entering the ministry, pondered the impact of Darwinism on the church doctrine, and urged its readers to take up the Social Gospel, an increasingly influential creed that spurred municipal reform, immigrant surveys, and the social settlement movement.

The new spirit planted the seeds of doubt in Mead's mind about ministry as a vocation. He began to drift away from church teachings, though the process was slow and painful. As late as 1884, Mead confessed to Henry Castle, "I believe Christianity is the only power capable of grappling with evil as it exists now. There can be no doubt of the efficacy of Christ as a remedial agent and so I can speak of him as such. . . . I cannot go out with the world and not work for men. The spirit of a minister is strong with me and I come fairly by it" (MP, April 23 and March 16, 1884, box 1, folder 1). The decision to shun the priesthood was further complicated by his father's untimely death. This tragic occasion placed Mead's family in a precarious financial situation, forcing him to wait on tables in the campus dining hall and sell books door-to-door as a way to offset his tuition costs. Thoughts about the heartache his decision to pursue a secular career might cause his mother terrified the young man. Still, Mead found traditional faith increasingly untenable on intellectual grounds and unappealing as a profession. Indeed, the latter offered less prestige than it once did, as well as fewer financial rewards. Should I choose ministry, explained Mead to his friend (MP, letters to

Henry Castle, March 16 and February 23, 1884, box 1, folder 1), "I shall have to let persons understand that I have some belief in Christianity and my praying be interpreted as a belief in God, whereas I have no doubt that now the most reasonable system of the universe can be formed to myself without a God."

The June 23, 1883, issue of *The Oberlin Review* contained a brief entry on George Mead, who was about to leave Oberlin: "Mead, G. H., Oberlin. Phi Kappa. Essayist at oratorical contest. Has supported himself in part. After graduation will make money, then? Born Feb. 1863." His acutely felt need to support his family led Mead to try his hand as a land surveyor for the Wisconsin Central Railroad Company. This was the first time Mead ventured far beyond the genteel environs of his alma mater and got to see up close the people whom he hoped to teach Christianity. The experience proved unsettling. Mead liked the job, the opportunity to work outdoors, the chance to learn practical skills, but the contacts with the workers on his team left him confused. He was distressed by their callous ways and the little interest they showed in spiritual matters. "The engineer has been drunk off and on and mostly on for the last week," complained Mead to Henry (MP, March 30, 1885, box 1, folder 1), "and between his quarrels with his wife and quarrels with his [fore]man and quarrels with his boarders he has kept himself and the camp in an uproar and has so sickened me that I have about lost my interest in him and creatures of his species.... A drunken man howling right outside your tent would destroy the concentration of Socrates and hideousness of the scene seems to slowly close in upon your soul ... and yet I ought to find my work and real life interest in working for such men."

Mead also tried to work as a tutor, but the rewards turned out to be equally meager. His charges did not care much for scholastic exercises, and neither did their parents, who were more concerned with the kids helping on the farm than with their progress at school. Mead's failure as a tutor deepened his depression, renewed the doubt about his calling. "I am discouraged Henry. I seem so far off from anything worth living for and I do not see that I gain strength at all by which I can reach anything. My life is spasmodical uneven without purpose. ... Even Christianity looks dreary to me now. I have nothing to offer any woman that would give love an opportunity [to] envigorate my life. It is a sapless dying" (MP, February 8, 1885, box 1, folder 3).

The turning point came in 1887 when Mead joined his friend Henry Castle at Harvard and resumed his secular education. Since his early college years Mead relished philosophical speculations, but he did not see therein any realistic prospects for a career. For one thing, teaching metaphysics was not a common occupation at the time. Also, it appeared to be removed from the burning issues of the day, not a field for someone anxious to serve humanity. But as Mead discovered at Harvard, the academic field was changing fast, drawing its members into a politically charged discourse and publicly minded activism. He could see this in Josiah Royce, perhaps the most influential teacher in Mead's student career, as well as in William James, a highly visible Harvard psychologist and philosopher. The spirit of reform that permeated the country in the 1890s made it respectable for the professorate to engage in social advocacy. Quite a few academics found themselves involved in local and national politics; some toyed with socialism and supported radical reforms.

Mead's decision to pursue an academic career was reinforced by his experience in Germany, where he went in 1888 after winning a prestigious Harvard scholarship that allowed him to pursue doctoral studies abroad. He appeared to have had some help from William James, who took a keen interest in Mead's career, corresponded with Mead's mother, wrote reference letters on Mead's behalf, and was so impressed with the earnest, studious lad that he asked Mead to tutor his children. In Germany, Mead was struck by the active role professors played in public policy debates and the respectability socialism commanded in academic circles. His letters home are brimming with enthusiasm for reforms. He wonders how they could be transplanted to the States, talks about "opening toward everything that is uplifting and satisfying in socialism," urges his friend "to get a hold upon the socialistic literature – and the position of socialism here – in Europe," and deplores in the most sweeping terms American politics: "American political life is horribly idealess.... Our government in ideas and methods belongs so to the past.... We had never had a national legislature in which corrupt motives in the most pecuniary form could be more shamelessly used than in the present" (MP, August 1890, October 21 and 19, 1890, box 1, folder 3). At one point, Mead appeared to be ready to jump into politics himself: "Life looks like such an insignificant affair that two or three or more years of utterly unsuccessful work would not seem to me in the slightest dampening, and the subjective satisfaction of actually doing what my nature asked for of infinitely more importance than anything else.... I mean that I am willing to go into a reform movement which to my eyes may be a failure after all; simply for the sake of the work" (MP, October 19, 1890, box 1, folder 3).

With his political imagination running wild, Mead was neglecting his academic studies. An ambitious thesis on the perception of space and time that he intended to write would never be completed. In 1891, Mead returned to the States, without a degree but with an offer from the University of Michigan to become an instructor in philosophy and physiological psychology. He also brought with him to Ann Arbor his newly wedded wife, Helen Castle, the sister of his dear friend Henry Castle, and the future heiress of the Dole Pineapple fortune. The move to Michigan proved auspicious in one more respect, for there Mead met his lifelong colleague and friend, John Dewey. Already a well established academic, Dewey shared with Mead a puritanic upbringing, a strong desire to do good (his mother used to ask John, "Are you right by Jesus?"), and a passion for social democracy and philosophical discourse. Dewey's encounter with socialism came at about the same time as Mead's. In 1888, Dewey (1969, p. 246) speculated about the "tendency of democracy toward socialism, if not communism" and opined that "there is no need to beat about the bush in saying that democracy is not in reality what it is in name until it is industrial, as well as civil and political . . . a democracy of wealth is a necessity." The foremost public intellectual of his generation, Dewey would become a role model for Mead, who was struggling to reconcile his secular career with his spiritual longings. That Mead's thinking was still utopian and religiously colored at the time can be gleaned from a rambling letter he wrote in June of 1892 to his parents-in-law: "[I] have been able to follow the connection that has gradually been established between abstract philosophy and daily life. I have learned to see that society advances – men get closer and closer to each other and the Kingdom of Heaven is established on the earth, so far as man becomes more and more organically connected with nature.... [I]t seems to me clearer every day that the telegraph and locomotive are the great spiritual [engines?] of society because they bind man and man so close together, that the interest of the individual must be more completely the interest of all day by day. And America is pushing this spiritualizing of nature [and] is doing more than all in bringing the day when every man will be my neighbor and all life shall be saturated with the divine life" (MP, box 1, folder 3).

Around the time this letter was penned, the University of Chicago invited John Dewey to chair its Philosophy Department. Dewey accepted the offer on the condition that he could bring along his junior colleague. This gave Mead an opportunity to join a premier university in a city famous for its social experimentation. From the fall of 1893 until his death in April of 1931, Mead remained active in city politics. He served as a treasurer for the University of Chicago settlement, helped arbitrate the labor–management dispute in the Chicago garment district strike, and headed the Chicago Educational Association and the Immigrants Protective League of Chicago. In 1918, he was elected president of the City Club, a reform-minded organization of professionals and business people, a high honor that confirmed Mead's standing in the community and sealed his reputation as a public intellectual.

On the academic front, Mead's career was less spectacular. He did not publish enough to reach the top of the academic pecking order. In fact, he did not publish a book during his lifetime. Reasons for this are many. Mead found academic writing to be a painful exercise, so much so that the struggle to commit his ideas to paper would sometimes leave him on the verge of tears. Although Mead generated enough material to fill several volumes, he rarely felt satisfied with what he wrote, continuously reworking his ideas and putting off publication dates. The insights he was trying to communicate required a new theoretical framework, a language that was yet to be invented. "As I look back," Dewey observed on Mead's death (PP, pp. xxxvii, xxxix–xl), "I can see that a great deal of the seeming obscurity of Mr. Mead's expression was due to the fact that he saw something as a problem which had not presented itself at all to other minds. There was no common language because there was no common object of reference.... He was talking about something that the rest of us did not see.... The loss which American philosophy has suffered by Mead's untimely death is increased by the fact that there is every reason to think that he was beginning to get a command of his ideas which made communication to others easier and more effective."

Another trait distinguishing Mead and explaining his relative obscurity was "the combination of great originality and unusual deference to others which marked his personality.... While he was an original thinker, he had no sense of being original. Or if he had such a feeling, he kept it under. Instead of bringing to the front as novelties the problems which were occupying his mind (which they were even as problems), he chose to link them to ideas and movements already current" (Dewey, in PP, p. xxxvi). Indeed, Mead often credited others with insights that were largely his own. His style, deceptively exegetic at times, made many colleagues miss the originality of his thoughts, which came across in Mead's conversations more clearly than in his writing. It was during his lectures on ethics, logic, philosophy, and social psychology that Mead articulated his path-breaking ideas. Soft-spoken, somewhat retiring, but friendly in his demeanor, Mead evoked warm feelings in those who were privileged to know him personally, even though he tended to speak in monotone in the classroom, sometimes repeated himself during lectures, and felt ill at ease with questions in the classroom. Students flocked to his classes. His course on social psychology in particular attracted attention at the university, drawing students from different departments and establishing his reputation as an innovative thinker. At some point, students hired a stenographer to capture his continuously evolving thought. We owe them a debt of gratitude for preserving Mead's ideas for posterity.

THE INTELLECTUAL SOURCES

Even after Mead embarked on an academic career, he continued to wonder about his true calling and search for discursive props that could satisfy his longing for spiritually meaningful existence. Several intellectual currents making the rounds in his days imprinted themselves on Mead's mind. One was Darwinism, which placed human agency in a broad evolutionary context and demystified reason as a natural phenomenon that belongs to a wide behavioral continuum stretching from the lowest biological forms to the highest ones. John Watson, Mead's colleague at the University of Chicago, radicalized Darwin's premises, vowing to purge psychology from the remnants of spiritualism and to turn it into an exact science of human behavior reducible in its entirety to environmental pressures. Early in the twentieth century, Albert Einstein formulated his relativist physics, which impressed Mead deeply and caused him to rethink his social theory. Important though these developments were in shaping his imagination, they came to Mead filtered through the dual prism of German idealism and American pragmatism – the two intellectual currents that aggressively tackled social issues and passionately advocated responsible being in the world.

Transcendental – or as Mead calls it "Romantic" – idealism is a philosophy that sets itself against dualism and tries to bridge the gap between mind and matter, subject and object, freedom and responsibility. The reality is objective because there are subjects who turn it into an object of their activity – mental activity, that is, for idealists understood reason as primarily an affair of the mind. In and of itself, reality is meaningless, indeterminate; an *a priori* scheme must be imposed on it before it begins to make sense, an *a priori* scheme inherent in the mind. Thus, the subject plays a constitutive role in generating reality. Yet it is only dimly aware of this role, of the fact that reason continuously constructs reality as an objective and meaningful whole. Romantic idealists sought to rectify this situation; they set out to illuminate the transcendental categories humans use to construct their universe, and in the process make humanity realize its responsibility for the world they inhabit.

What Mead found so intriguing about this metaphysics is its sociological underpinnings. "In a very definite sense," he wrote, "we can speak of this philosophy as one which is social in its character" (MT, p. 147). We can see this already in Kant (1951, p. 137), who stipulated that every time the individual makes a generalization, "he disregards the subjective private conditions of his own judgment and reflects upon it from a *universal standpoint* (which he can only determine by placing himself at the standpoint of others)." The rational individual raises a claim on behalf of the entire community whenever he judges something to be the fact. Reason is not idiosyncratic, nor is it compelled by things themselves; it is guided by the spirit of the community, whose logic reason imposes on the outside world. Notice the peculiarly interactionist locution Kant uses to explicate the public nature of reasoning – placing oneself at the standpoint of the other. It thematizes the self which, according to Kant, is the mark of a genuinely human being: "That I am conscious of myself is a thought that already contains a twofold self, the I as subject and the I as object. How it might be possible for the I that I think to be an object...is absolutely impossible to explain, even though it is an indubitable fact; it indicates, however, a capacity so highly elevated above sensuous intuition that...it has the effect of separating us from all animals, to which we have no reason to attribute the ability to say I to themselves" (Kant, 1983, p. 73). What makes humans unique is that they can grasp themselves as objects without ceasing to be subjects, and they can do so by recourse to *a priori* categories, or, which is the same thing, by assuming the standpoint of the community. Yes, the self as an objective phenomenon is socially constituted. A moral being is a self that places itself in the shoes of other people and follows the golden rule: "Do unto others as you would like others to do unto you." Kant generalized this old biblical injunction into the theory of "categorical imperative," which bids us to do what stands to reason. Act in such a way that the principle underlying your conduct could serve as a law for the entire community, urged Kant, and the community in question would be rational and just. This precept is not only profoundly social, it is also radically democratic in its premise that every individual is a rational being entitled to speak on behalf of the whole community.

To be sure, Kant's thinking was sociological only in its implications. It is the humans' transcendental abilities that constitute society, Kant thought, and not the other way around. The *a priori* categories are universal, unalterable, and inherent in each individual mind; they represent not a particular group or society but the widest possible community – humanity as a whole. Still, the sociological dimension implicit in this philosophy was undeniable, and it came clearly to the fore in Kant's successors. Reality is constructed, Hegel agreed with Kant; things themselves are grasped objectively when they become objects for the mind; but the mind in question is not individual, nor are its *a priori* categories eternal. The flesh and blood person is the mind's immediate locus, but its *a priori* categories are historically emergent and socially derived. This is particularly evident in the case of self, which cannot grasp itself through immediate introspection and which implies a community: "The self perceives itself at the same time that it is perceived by others," contended Hegel (1967, pp. 661, 229). "Self-consciousness exists in itself and for itself . . . by the very fact that it exists for another self-consciousness; that is to say, it is only by being acknowledged or 'recognized'.'" As seen from the Hegelian perspective, human history is an ongoing process that gradually brings humanity to self-consciousness, compels it to take stock of its taken-for-granted beliefs, and allows reason to reshape the objective world according to its own consciously chosen rationales.

Romantic idealists made an important discovery: something at the very core of consciousness must remain unconscious if consciousness is to do its job of apprehending objective reality. This unconscious transcendental hideaway is socially and historically emergent. For as long as individuals remain oblivious to the constitutive nature of their *a priori* judgments, the objective world they generate persists in its unyielding thingness. When they stop taking for granted their *a priori* categories and subject them to self-conscious critique, they are bound to disrupt the old structures and, to the extent that new *a priori* beliefs take hold of their minds, bring about a new reality.

These romantic ideas would reverberate throughout the human sciences, engendering new strategies for conceptualizing the bio-psycho-social processes. These strategies aimed at overcoming the dualism and bringing the macro-world directly in touch with the micro-world. The key metaphor of this era was the microcosm recapitulating the macrocosm. It is present in the psychologists' concern for the unconscious, the biologists' discovery of the genetical code, the linguists' preoccupation with the universal grammar, anthropologists' interest in cultural values – everywhere the search was on for an equivalent of the transcendental *a priori* enciphering the larger whole. Romantic idealism left its mark on sociology as well. Feuerbach, Marx, Stirner, Coleridge, Emerson, and other late Romantic thinkers would translate its message into the notions like "species being," "social being," "the self," and kindred concepts undermining the dichotomy of personality and society and re-establishing humans as masters over their fate. "Above all we must avoid postulating 'Society' again as an abstraction vis-a-vis the individual. The individual is *the social being*," wrote Marx (1964, pp. 137–8). "Just as society itself produces *man as man*, so is society *produced* by him. Activity and mind, both in their content and in *their mode of existence*, are social: *social* activity and *social* mind. . . . Man, much as he may therefore be a *particular* individual . . . is just as much the totality – the ideal totality – the subjective existence of thought and experienced society for itself."

In Europe, the transcendentalist strategy crystallized into interpretive sociology, with its constructionist agenda and signature attempt to telescope macro-structural phenomena into individual action. "Such concepts as 'state,' 'association,' 'feudalism,' and the like," maintained Weber (1946, p. 55), "designate certain categories of human interaction. Hence it is the task of sociology to reduce those concepts to 'understandable' action, that is, without exception to the actions of participating individual men." The same strategy was realized in Simmel, who linked his famous question "How is society possible?" to the Kantian one, "How is nature possible?" His answer mirrors the transcendentalist logic: "The unity of society is directly realized by its own elements because these elements are themselves conscious and synthesizing units.... The large systems and the super-individual organizations that customarily come to mind when we think of society are nothing but immediate interactions that occur among men constantly, every minute, but that have crystallized as permanent fields, as autonomous phenomena" (Simmel, 1971, p. 7; 1950, p. 10).

A similar strategy was at work in the United States, where Josiah Royce, James Baldwin, Charles Cooley, George Mead, and other minds laboring at the turn of the century sought to appropriate the Romantic legacy. They tackled the problem from a different angle, however. Whereas European sociologists focused on the *a priori* beliefs that motivate conduct and bind together individuals into a social whole, American philosophers and social scientists centered on self-consciousness as a locus of social control and societal change. As Mead (MT, p. 125) put it, "The Romantic philosophy pointed out that the self, while it arises in the human experience, also carries with it the very unity that makes society possible." The *Identitätsphilosophie* (yet another name for transcendental idealism) was interpreted here to mean that reality has to be processed through self-consciousness to emerge as an objective and meaningful whole. Whatever can be said about nature, the famous idealist principle "no object without a subject" sounds almost like a truism when applied to society: the self must identify with a social role before the latter comes to be an objective fact. There would be neither slaves nor masters without individuals acting the part. The structure of social roles found in any given group is inseparable from the structure of selves discernible in its members. The romantic intertwining of self and society had an added appeal to reform-minded Americans because it implied that human agency matters, that the self critically reflecting on its own taken-for-granted beliefs can bring about a more rational society. This activist creed, originally formulated in the aftermath of the French Revolution, fitted well with the Progressive spirit of the time: "When the Revolution came, many institutions which long seemed to be things in themselves, showed that they were nothing but phenomena. And when new constitutions and social orders had to be planned, the spirit of the age emphasized the fact that, at least in the social world, it is the office of human intelligence to impose its own forms upon the phenomena, and to accept no authority but that of the rational self" (Royce, 1919, p. 277).

The last statement belongs to Josiah Royce, the Harvard professor who, in a series of articles published in the 1890s, laid out an agenda that had much to do with Mead's research program. Two of these articles are particularly noteworthy as precursors of Meadian thought, one titled "The External World and the Social Consciousness" (Royce, 1894) and the other "Self-consciousness, Social Consciousness, and Nature" (Royce, 1895). What Royce (1894, p. 531) proposed here was that "neither vividness, nor intrusive resistance to our will, nor peculiarly insistent relation to our muscular experience, nor regular recurrence, suffice to define the notes of externality as we now define them. It is social community that is the true *differentia* of our external world." As an object in our experience, Royce argued, the self submits to this principle as well, for it is social in its origin and substance. Royce credited Romantic idealists in general and Hegel in particular for articulating this insight: "Self-consciousness, as Hegel loved to point out, is, in fact, a mutual affair. . . . I am dependent on my fellows, not only physically, but to the very core of my conscious self-hood, not only for what, physically speaking, I am, but for what I take myself to be. Take away the conscious Alter, and the conscious Ego, so far as in this world we know it, languishes, and languishing dies" (Royce, 1894, p. 532; 1895, p. 468). Along with James Baldwin (1897), Royce speculated about role-playing among children as a mechanism for appropriating self-identity, the relationship between self-consciousness and mental illness, the self's responsibility for its community, and similar subjects that pointed to a fruitful line of inquiry. Mead took it over and pushed it further along than any other scholar of his generation. Much as he was indebted to this tradition, however, Mead transcended it in at least one crucial way: unlike Royce, Mead looked at the dynamics of mind, self, and society not from the idealist but from the pragmatist standpoint. Along with Peirce, James, and Dewey, Mead fastened his intellectual enterprise to "the assumption of the pragmatist that the individual only thinks in order that he may continue an uninterrupted action, that the criterion of the correctness of his thinking is found in his ability to carry on, and that the significant goal of his thinking or research is found not in the ordered presentation of the subject matter but in the uses to which it may be put" (PA, p. 97).

That pragmatism and transcendental idealism are kindred currents goes without saying. The continuity between the two was acknowledged by all principal players in the American pragmatist movement: Charles Peirce, William James, John Dewey, and George Mead. In the words of James (1970, p. 133), pragmatism represents "a new *Identitätsphilosophie* in pluralistic form." Both pragmatists and Romantics stressed agency, responsibility, and the constructed nature of reality, often making it hard to say where romanticism ends and pragmatism begins. There is, of course, one crucial difference, and it has to do with the way each philosophy conceives of human agency. Romantic idealists equate agency with conceptual reasoning continuously perfecting itself throughout the spiritual evolution; pragmatists define reason in post-Darwinian terms as an embodied conduct evolving through biosocial evolution. For Romantic idealists, the transcendental *a priori* is the domain of abstract thought and values; pragmatists transform it into an emotionally charged, biologically grounded, socially informed *a priori* that stands for habit or routine action in which humans are implicated before they can grasp it conceptually. Pragmatists endeavored to reclaim "the universe of nonreflectional experience of our doings, sufferings, enjoyments of the world and of one another" (Dewey, 1916, p. 9). They keep reminding us that "mental processes imply not only mind but that somebody is minding" (PA, p. 69). "The mother minds her baby; she cares for it with affection. Mind is care in the sense of solicitude, anxiety, as well as of active looking after things that need to be tended" (Dewey, 1958, p. 263). Once the cognitive abilities were reconnected to the body, reason lost some of its luster. "Reason, anyway, is a faculty of secondary rank," observed Peirce (1976, p. xxi). "Cognition is but the superficial film of the soul, while sentiment penetrates its substance."

This momentous shift in perspective marked a turning point in the evolution of pragmatism. First articulated by Charles Peirce, pragmatism found a new life in James's *Principles of Psychology* (1890), a widely read volume which tied mental processes to action and brought into wide circulation the concept of social self. Mead and Dewey worked out a similar version of pragmatism in the 1890s, through intense discussions about the nature of the psychical that went back to their Michigan years. Like many of their colleagues at the time, Dewey and Mead sought to find answers to intractable metaphysical problems with the help of psychology, a fledgling discipline that broke away from philosophical discourse while retaining some of its concerns. It was during his preparation for the college course on physiological psychology that Mead realized that "the body and soul are but two sides of the same thing," that "our psychical life can all be read in the functions of our bodies," that "it is not the brain that thinks but our organs insofar as they act together in the processes of life" (MP, letter to the Castle family, June 1892, box 1, folder 3). Dewey came to see mind as minding via his critique of the stimulus–response schema. Of particular interest in this respect is his influential article "The Reflex Arc Concept in Psychology" (Dewey, 1972, volume 5, pp. 100, 106), in which he demolished the notion that stimulus precedes conduct: "In any case, what precedes the 'stimulus' is the whole act, a sensori-motor co-ordination. What is more to the point, the 'stimulus' emerges out of this co-ordination.... *Now the response is not only uncertain, but the stimulus is equally uncertain; one is uncertain only in so far as the other is.* The real problem may be equally well stated as either to discover the right stimulus, to constitute the stimulus, or to discover, to constitute, the response." As the last statement shows, pragmatists were fighting their battle on two fronts: they sought to break with the idealist propensity to intellectualize human agency and, at the same time, tried to avoid the reductionist tendency inherent in behaviorism and positivism. The label "physiological psychology" under which pragmatists packaged their discoveries should not mislead us, for this was a nonreductionist, philosophically sophisticated, and, above all, social psychology that they strove to articulate.

Pragmatists were aided in their efforts to steer away from reductionism by the insight into the intimate relationship between reason and community. "The unit of existence is an act," postulated Mead (PA, p. 65), "the act stretches from the stimulus to response," but the act in question, Mead would hasten to add, is itself a part of a larger social undertaking: "What I have attempted to do is to bring rationality back to a certain type of conduct, the type of conduct in which the individual puts himself in the attitude of the whole community to which he belongs. This implies that the whole group is involved in some organized activity and that in this organized activity the action of one calls for the action of the other organisms involved. What we term 'reason' arises when one of the organisms takes into its own response the attitude of the other organisms involved.... When it does so, it is what we term 'a rational being'" (Mead, MSS, p. 334). Dewey took a similar sociological turn. "[M]an is essentially a social being," he claimed from the outset (1969, volume 1, p. 232), "the nonsocial individual is an abstraction arrived at by imagining what man would be if all his human qualities were taken away." To establish human agency as social to the core was important to pragmatists because this placed humans on the same level with society and accorded it a status befitting a truly democratic society. In such a society, individual actions count, each human being is a society in miniature, and the fate of the whole is intertwined with the fate of its individual parts. Here, again, pragmatists revealed their debt to romanticism and its favorite metaphor of man-the-microcosm, which resonated with the progressive creed: "If then, society and the individual are really organic to each other, then the individual is society concentrated... the localized manifestation of its life... its vital embodiment. And this is the theory, often crudely expressed, but none the less true in substance, that every citizen is a sovereign, the American theory, a doctrine ...that every man is a priest of God. In conception, at least, democracy approaches most nearly the ideal of all social organization; that in which the individual and society are organic to each other (Dewey, 1969, volume 1, p. 237).

As time wore on, Mead and Dewey would increasingly shun Protestant rhetoric and Romantic shibboleth. In one of his last articles, titled "Royce, James, and Dewey in Their American Setting," Mead distanced himself from his Harvard teachers, whose lofty idealism, he charged, was alien to the pragmatic spirit of America (SW, p. 391). Alas, he overstated his case. Mead and his colleagues owed more to their Romantic predecessors than they were willing to concede. Blended with Protestant yearnings and thoroughly Darwinized, Romantic teaching foreshadowed a theory that sought to explain America to itself and guide the changes ravaging society on the eve of the twentieth century. Pragmatism was the name of this theory, and it found in George Mead "a seminal mind of the very first order" (Dewey, in PP, p. xl), one of its most original interpreters.

THE THEORETICAL CORPUS

Any attempt to reconstruct Mead's theory faces hurdles. His publications, lecture notes, written fragments, and correspondence give us a good idea about the evolution of his thoughts, but they do not convey a developed theoretical system. It is up to the interpreter to trace the missing links, to recover the systemic features binding together Mead's theoretical corpus.

We also need to bear in mind that Mead was not a professional sociologist. A philosopher by training, he dabbled in physiology, psychology, pedagogy, political theory, and theoretical sociology. His thinking transgressed interdisciplinary boundaries, and this became a handicap once the rationalization process in academia began to favor autonomous disciplines whose practitioners looked askance at their colleagues venturing too far into neighboring fields. If an interest in Mead is now growing, it is in part because the boundaries separating rival academic fields have grown porous and tolerance for alternative research styles is on the rise.

Another problem in reading Mead is his propensity to mingle analytical perspectives. It is one thing to explicate self in the evolutionary perspective, i.e. philogenetically, where any reference to "other selves" is illegitimate, and another to explain how children acquire selves ontogenetically, with a developed human society already in place and other selves lending themselves as the back-drop for conceptualizing the socialization process. A still different approach is called for when behavior is explained *in situ* or sitogenetically, when the researcher confronts fully minded individuals juggling their identities and tran-scending established norms. Mead often shifts gears, moving briskly between phylogeny, ontogeny, and sitogeny, and in the process confuses his interpreters.

One last difficulty to be mentioned is the unconventional nature of Mead's theory, especially as it evolved in the last two decades of his life, when Mead endeavored to revamp his thoughts in line with the developments in nonclassical physics. This new tack brought Mead into an uncharted territory where he struggled to find language adequate to his insights and to formulate a pragmatist cosmology built on the notion of pansociality. Reconstructing this phase of Mead's thinking is all the more important, given the attention social theorists now pay to neighboring fields and nonclassical perspectives.

While it can hardly do justice to Mead's theory in all its richness and complex-ity, the following sketch highlights the sociological imagination that distin-guishes American pragmatism and its contribution to our understanding of what it means to be human in this world.

Evolution, relativity, and sociality

Modern evolutionary theory has painted natural history as a process evolving in stages from inchoate blobs of matter to complex mechanical systems to element-ary biological forms to higher primates, and then all the way to humans with their self-conscious conduct and rational organizational forms. Social scientists traditionally focus on the tail end of this evolutionary process and model their insights on those of natural science. Mead pretty much stood this approach on its head when he looked at naturalists' discoveries through the social scientist's eye. "The difficulty is found in the fact that the physical scientists present a situation out of which the human animal and his society arose," observed Mead (PA, p. 606). "It has indeed been the procedure of science to explain society in terms of things which are independent of social characters and to represent the social situation as one that has been fortuitous and utterly unessential to its existence of that out of which it has arisen. [Our] undertaking is to work back from the accepted organization of human perspectives in society to the organization of perspectives in the physical world."

What set Mead's imagination off and led him into uncharted waters was the theory of relativity. Its author, Albert Einstein, displayed an uncommon curiosity about the way things appear when sampled from different perspectives. He used to imagine how passing objects would appear to people inside the train and to those gathered on the train station; or else, he would place himself on the edge of a light beam and try to figure out whether the observer stationed on the nearby planet would experience the passing event in the same fashion as the one riding the light beam. Such practice, Mead realized, is a kind of role-taking that marks an intelligent creature simultaneously inhabiting several reference frames: "the relativist is able to hold on to two or more mutually exclusive systems within which the same object appears, by passing from one to the other... as a minded organism he can be in both" (PP, p. 81). This ability to be in several places at once engenders the possibility of different yet equally objective measurements for the same event. Whether light signals emanating from two distant objects were emitted simultaneously cannot be ascertained without the observer being positioned somewhere between the two sources of light. When observers change their positions, the objective reality as measured by the instrument will change as well. The moving body has as many objective readings for its mass, length, and momentum as there are inertial systems in which it is registered.

Relativist phenomena point to the vaguely social manner in which physical things interact with each other. Physical relativity reveals "sociality in nature which has been generally confined to thought," "the social" in its most primitive form (PP, p. 63). Sociality signifies the simultaneous presence in more than one reference frame that alters the character of the event. "Relativity reveals a situation within which the object must be contemporaneously in different systems to be what it is in either.... It is this which I have called the sociality of the present.... Sociality is the capacity to be several things at once" (PP, pp. 63, 49). The fact that a body can have one mass in one inertial system and a different mass in another points to a protosocial situation in which an object enjoys multiple memberships in several systems exerting a cross-pressure on the thing. "I have referred to the increase in mass of a moving body as an extreme case of sociality," wrote Mead (PP, pp. 52–3). A quality that a moving body acquires as a result of its multiple memberships is called "emergent" and the process that brings it into existence "emergence," which Mead defined as "the presence of things in two or more different systems, in such a fashion that its presence in a latter system changes its character in the earlier system or systems to which it belongs" (PP, p. 69). Mead understood that relativist physics appeared to have boosted idealism, but he declined to endorse its subjectivist implications. Neither emergence nor relativity implies subjectivity, he contended; both are natural phenomena requiring no subject; reference frames belong to nature, not consciousness, which appears on the scene belatedly as a by-product of the increasingly more complex relativist phenomena.

The body traversing the mechanical universe does not "choose" among the possibilities it faces, though there is a measure of uncertainty as to where its trajectory will bring it in the end. Nor does it feel pleasure or pain while suffering through its permutations. It is not until the evolutionary process reaches the next stage that the physical body begins to feel its immediate surroundings. The ability to sense one's way around turns the mechanical body into a biological organism, elevates mechanical motion to the level of purposeful conduct, and transforms physical matter into organized environment inhabited by sentient creatures. This crucial step in evolution signifies the beginning of life, which Mead (PP, p. 69) explicated as "a process in which the individual by its action tends to maintain this process both in itself and in later generations, and one which extends beyond what is going on in the organism out into the surrounding world and defines so much of the world as is found in the sweep of these activities as the environment of the individual." Environment is always someone's environment, whether it is a particular individual or the entire species, and when different species appear on the scene, they bring with them an altered environment. There is "a relativity of the organism and its environment, both as to form and content. . . . Emergent life changes the character of the world just as emergent velocities change the characters of masses" (PA, p. 178; PP, p. 65). As a food object, grass comes into being with certain kinds of animals, while the organism's digestive tract adjusts to the changes in its environment. The important point that sets Mead's approach to evolution apart from Spencer's is that the organism does not simply adapt itself to external stimuli – it picks its stimuli through its sensitivity and action, such as food foraging, nest-building, mating behavior, and similar practices, and through its agency displays a rudimentary intelligence. "Stimuli are means, but the tendency, the impulse, is essential for anything to be a stimulus. This tendency is what marks intelligence. We find it in all stages, perhaps even below life, in crystals. . . . Intelligence is the selection by the organism of stimuli that will set free and maintain life and aid in rebuilding the form" (TIS, p. 109). Life is relativity brought to a higher level; it signifies a more advanced form of sociality that brings choice into the universe, allows selection between alternative reference frames. It also brings a temporal spread within the organism's purview, which spans the duration of the ongoing act and reflects the organism's ability to foresee the outcome of one's action. A sentient organism favors some reference frames over others, evading those threatening its existence and searching for the ones beneficial to its survival. "Each organism puts its frame of reference on the world" (TIS, p. 115), and in doing so, it maintains, expands, and transforms its environment.

The natural selection process changes its character with the onset of life. Now it features a conflict between competing reference frames favored by species striving to maintain their habitat. A reference frame that organism imposes on the world is called "perspective" – the term Mead borrowed from Alfred Whitehead to describe emergent characteristics that organisms confer on the world through their action and the adaptive changes that the organism undergoes in the process. "The perspective is the world in its relationship to the individual and the individual in his relationship to the world" (PA, p. 115). As species evolve, they bring into the world new perspectives, and as the range of their activity increases, so does their ability to control their environment. This control reaches a qualitatively new stage when the individual succeeds in "getting oneself into the field of one's action," when it emerges as an object within its own field of experience, when it becomes a "self" (TIS, p. 123).

Before the self takes its rightful place as the latest evolutionary emergent alongside mechanism and organism, the living creature must catch its own reflection in other reference frames. Some of this proto-reflexive conduct is already apparent in lower biological forms endowed with senses, yet the animal is unable to switch perspectives or take up a different role at will, nor does it go about its role-playing in a systematic fashion. The animal cannot be another to itself because its biological, physiological, and psychological limitations do not allow it to move in and out of its reference frame. "A perspective can be recognized as such only when lying in the field within which it is no longer a perspective" (PA, p. 607). The ability to leave one's perspective at will and consciously take the role of the other transcends the biological organization of perspectives rooted in heredity. The perspectives must be organized socially for the human being to engage in interaction with oneself, to bring one's action under symbolic control. This breakthrough signifies that the organism has brought within its purview the social process as a whole: "The social organization of perspectives arises through the individual taking the role of the other within a social act whose various phases are in some sense present in his organism. . . . [B]y the social mechanism of thought and reflection, the individual transfers himself to another object and organizes the environment from the standpoint of the co-ordinates of that center, he selects another family of duration, another space-time" (PA, p. 610).

Individuals mastering this feat are conscious *and* self-conscious at the same time. They now have what is commonly referred to as mental life, the ability to move freely from one reference frame to another: "It is here that mental life arises – with this continual passing from one system to another, with the occupation of both in passage and with the systematic structure that each involves. It is the realm of continual emergence" (PP, p. 85). This transition presupposes the sociological organization of perspectives, and it signifies the arrival on the evolutionary scene of "minded organisms." In Mead's vocabulary, the term "mind" designates the ability to place oneself in different perspectives in a systematic fashion, to survey oneself from the standpoint of other individuals, to direct one's actions with reference to the social act, and ultimately, to criticize and reconstruct this social act as a whole. "Mind is coterminous with a group. [It] is that part of experience in which the individual becomes an object to itself in the presentation of possible lines of conduct" (TIS, pp. 162, 177). The emergence of mind signifies a new stage in the evolutionary process "when the process of evolution has passed under the control of social reason. . . . Men in human society have come into some degree of control of the process of evolution out of which they arose" (PA, pp. 508, 511).

To sum up, Mead proposed a cosmology that took the category of the "social" as its fundamental principle. He recast evolution as a process that is accompanied by the growth in sociality, by the ability to occupy more than one reference frame or perspective at the same time. He envisioned physical relativity as a primordial form of sociality and conceived of self-consciousness as the highest known evolutionary form of relativity. In this pansocial reckoning, mind and matter are not juxtaposed to each other: the two are perennially evolving sides of the ongoing process of natural evolution: "mind as it appears in the mechanism of social conduct is the organization of perspectives in nature and at least a phase of the creative advance of nature. Nature in its relationship to the organism, and including the organism, is a perspective that is there. A state of mind of the organism is the establishment of simultaneity between the organism and a group of events" (SW, p. 316). This theory suggests "a universe consisting of perspectives. In such a conception the reference of any perspective, as a perspective, is not to an absolute behind the scenes but from one perspective to another" (PA, p. 119). With this daring discursive turn, Mead raised a host of fresh issues and suggested new ways of conceptualizing problems that traditionally occupied social scientists. The new social theory, which Herbert Blumer would later label "symbolic interactionism," brought into one continuum mind, self, and society as three aspects of the same process that calls for a thoroughly sociological treatment and that must be examined in concrete situations.

Mind, self, and society

Mechanism, organism, and the self are the key evolutionary emergents representing three stages in the development of relativity-cum-sociality. Each stage is ushered in by a set of agents who bring their own perspectives to bear on the world, turning it into an environment or a field of objects peculiar to themselves. "A social organism – that is, a social group of individual organisms – constitutes objects not constituted before.... Wealth, beauty, prestige and various other objects appear in this environment because of its determination by the human social individual, and these are the springs of conduct. The same may, of course, be said of the environment of the biological form. Food, danger, sex, and parenthood are all springs of action and are such because these objects are determined as such by the susceptibilities of the animal forms. Finally, physical objects are at rest or are in motion because of their determination of the here and the there of the percipient event" (PA, p. 201 and MSS, pp. 130). Central among the objects comprising the human environment is the "self" – an emergent property of the human body transformed by social interactions to a point where it grows conscious of its multiple presence in different systems and uses this awareness to conduct itself intelligently. As a minded organism, the self simultaneously inhabits mechanical, biological, and symbolic worlds. While all three are relatively autonomous from each other, they are tied together through multiple feedbacks. Intelligent behavior feeds back into the biological organism: it reshapes its central nervous system, rewires neural connections in the brain, alters the structure of affect. Germs, earthquakes, and interstellar calamities, in turn, remind the minded agents who pride themselves on being the evolution's pinnacle that they are very much a part of the physical and biological realms. All evolutionary domains are tied together by the bonds of sociality. Strictly speaking, there is no reality that is asocial and no minded existence unburdened by the flesh.

Such is the logic underlying Mead's general enterprise. It has several implications for social theory, none more important than this: social theory has to integrate self-conscious humanity with biological corporeality and mechanical physicality in an ecologically sensitive framework that leaves ample room for qualitatively different evolutionary spheres. What are the other features distinguishing this pragmatist approach? It must be *dialectical, decentered, emergent, interactionist* and *process-oriented.*

Like all pragmatists, Mead avoids the dichotomies commonly found in social theory, such as nature and culture, behavior and institution, self and society. He adopts a dialectical strategy that places polar terms on equal footing and renders both contingent on each other. This essentially Romantic strategy makes superfluous questions like "What comes first, self or society?" Each is an abstraction representing a measured linguistic take on the unfractured process: "Human society as we know it could not exist without minds and selves, since all its most characteristic features presuppose the possession of minds and selves by its individual members; but its individual members would not possess minds and selves if these had not arisen within or emerged out of the human social process.... The organization and unification of a social group is identical with the organization and unification of any one of the selves arising within the social process in which that group is engaged" (MSS, pp. 227, 144). Mead follows a similar strategy when he talks about social institutions. He declines to elevate them into a separate realm of social facts. Dialectically understood, an institution is "nothing but an organization of attitudes which we all carry in us.... It makes no difference, over against a person who is stealing your property, whether it is Tom, Dick or Harry. There is an identical response on the part of the whole community under these conditions. We call that the formation of the institution" (MSS, pp. 211, 167). The circle involved in this reasoning is called "hermeneutical." Polar sociological terms are explicated in this circle as flip sides of an ongoing process in which the individual is reproduced as a self-conscious whole while society is generated as a concrete totality of individual perspectives: "The organization of social perspectives in human society takes place through the self, for it is only the organization of a group as the attitude of the individual organism toward itself which gives rise to the self, and it is the activity of the self, so constituted toward and in the group, that is responsible for the peculiar organization of a human community" (PA, p. 625).

The dialectical strategy deployed by Mead results in a characteristically decentered view of consciousness, vaguely reminiscent of Hegel's *Phenomenology of Mind.* Whereas traditional theory locates subjectivity within the organism and juxtaposes to it objective reality on the outside, pragmatist theory disperses consciousness widely and treats mind as a property of social structure. "The locus of mind is not in the individual. Mental processes are fragments of the complex conduct of the individual in and on his environment.... If mind is socially constituted, then the field or locus of any given indivdiual mind must extend as far as the social activity or apparatus of social relations which constitutes it extends; and hence that field cannot be bounded by the skin of the individual organism to which it belongs" (PA, p. 372; MSS, p. 223). Individual mind is not a mental event; it is practical minding in the course of which the individual comes to terms with a larger social act. When the agent places itself in the group perspective and successfully completes a social act, it proves itself to be a mindful, conscious being. When individuals fail in their concerted effort to mesh their action with that of a social group, they open themselves to charges of being mindless or subjective: "The subjectivity does not consist in the experience having the metaphysical nature of consciousness but in its failure to agree with a dominant common perspective which claims the individual.... The objectivity of the perspective of the individual lies in its being a phase of the larger act. It remains subjective in so far as it cannot fall into the larger social perspective" (PA, pp. 610, 548). This is not to suggest that disagreement with the dominant perspective automatically renders the act asocial and the individual involved mindless. The mind embodies group spirit, particularly during the individual's early stages of growth, but if its growth is healthy, mind evolves into a critical, reflective, and reconstructive agency that makes personal experience available to others and compels the group to look at the world in a new way. The affairs of the mind, therefore, are not inherently subjective; mind transcends the individual, it can take up a new perspective at any time. Self-conscious mind is society unto itself in its concrete historical manifestation, and this is precisely why the mind's activity has such a pervasive impact on society. "[T]he whole nature of intelligence is social to the very core," urges Mead (MSS, 141); its immediate locus may be individual, but it reaches as far as society ever extends. Mind's *raison d'être* is to embrace what it is not, which is why it remains open to novelty and serendipity. A decentered mind changes the world by changing itself, by revamping the familiar structure of worn-out perspectives that no longer allow the world to test its potentialities.

Pragmatist social theory zeroes in onto the world's emergent properties. Reality evolves, pragmatists contend, and it never ceases to do so, even at the rudimentary stages of physical evolution: "Things emerge, and emerge in the mechanical order of things, which could not be predicted from what has happened before" (MSS, p. 88). Unsuspected objects appear on the evolutionary scene whenever a new agent is powerful enough to impose on the world its own reference frame. While major evolutionary events are recorded in the annals of science as epoch-making breakthroughs, minor metamorphoses or emergent transformations abound in any given era. This is most notable in the environment populated by self-conscious creatures who are endowed with the extraordinary capacity to change their perspective at will. "The self by its reflexive form announces itself as a conscious organism which is what it is only in so far as it can pass from its own system into those of others, and can thus, in passing, occupy both its own system and that into which it is passing" (PP, p. 82). The self is always on the move, reaching beyond itself, turning into another. At any given moment it is poised to take a quantum leap from one perspective to another and thereby cause an instantaneous – emergent – evolution in its environment. Objective world is the world full of objects brought into existence by self-conscious agency. "There is no self before there is a world, and no world before the self" (TIS, p. 156). This Romantic locution is meant not to mystify but to assert that multiple realities are normal, that ours is the world in the making, that we dwell in what James called "the pluralistic universe" or the universe contingent on our ability to identify with many a universal. A social universal is real when enough individuals generalize their actions in its terms. The new terms bring about a new reality and a new present. "Reality exists in a present" (PP, p. 32), says Mead. An indefinite article in this statement reminds us that there is no absolute time frame to measure the simultaneity of events in nature. With each emergent transformation, a different time structure appears that binds together those involved by a shared sense of the past, with the past understood as "a working hypothesis that has validity in the present within which it works" (PA, p. 96). According to Mead, the past is as hypothetical as the future; it changes with the perspective, with the practical task at hand. "Now the past that is thus constituted is a perspective, and what will be seen in that perspective, and what will be relations between the elements, depends upon the point of reference. There are an infinite number of possible perspectives, each of which will give a different definition to the parts and reveal different relations between them" (PA, p. 99). As the situation runs its course, so does its time structure. A situation has a duration, it endures as long as the agents involved in it keep joining perspectives, sharing a past, and working for a common future. Once the engaged selves assume different guises and adopt alternative time lines, the situation mutates, and so does the reality it engenders. Outside of the time-bound situation, reality remains indeterminate. It takes a quantum of action to salvage it from its indeterminate state, to frame it in definite terms, something that can happen only in the here and the now and that can be grasped only *in situ* and *in actu.*

The pragmatist emphasis on emergent transformations does not imply that pragmatist theory is indifferent to the world's structural properties. Society is very much a structure, according to Mead, and so is the "self as a certain sort of structural process" (MSS, p. 165). Society is comprised of groups, organizations, institutions, and suchlike historical formations that constrain individual action. Each such structural formation revolves around a bundle of privileged perspectives sustained by a power arrangement that reproduces an institutional past in the present and extends the status quo into the future. Recalcitrant individuals unwilling or unable to abide by the existing structure of perspectives will be punished. Yet all these social entities are interactional emergents rather than impenetrable castes. These are emergent universals that have to be brought into being anew with every situational encounter. Individuals are the ones who will ultimately have to choose a perspective and subsume themselves under a social universal. The self's capacity to leap from one universal to another renders social universals fuzzy, makes them appear less as solid "bodies" and more like overlapping "fields." The last term surfaces in Mead's writings, as it does in James and Dewey, who often speculate about "fields of interaction" and "relatively closed fields," and alert us to the changes a thing undergoes "according to the field it enters" (quoted in Shalin, 1986a, pp. 16–17). This is indeed an apt metaphor for the interactionist outlook on social structure. It bids us to look at society as a vast sea of intermeshed fields populated by conscious selves ever ready to make a quantum leap from one symbolic reference frame to another. It is this incessant coming and going, entering and departing, identifying with and dumping the role that is at the heart of social dynamics, as seen from the pragmatist viewpoint. "Membership," correlatively, is more of an achievement than it is an ascription in this pragmatist universe, an on-again/off-again affair, or an "actual occasion" (Alfred Whitehead). Social structure makes itself felt as an ongoing process which ebbs and flows, as group members wander through perspectives and juggle their identities. While the social universe comprised of perspectives is undeniably real, it derives its reality from the particulars who must unlock these perspectives and situate themselves in its time horizons. A towering presence in every individual's experience, society is but a structure of competing time-lines and emerging identities. All power in society is ultimately dependent on the power to universalize the particular and to particularize the universal.

To sum up, Mead's pragmatist theory invites us to look at society as a pluralistic universe at the core of which are perspectives managed by self-conscious individuals. These perspectives are structured, but the structures in question are in flux – they never cease to emerge in the here and now of situational encounters during which humans haggle over the past, present, and future. In this quantum-like world, structure is a processed time or time processing. "You cannot have a process without some sort of a structure, and yet structure is simply something that expresses this process as it takes place" (MT, p.164). Social structure manifests itself in a regime of simultaneities that gives disparate individuals a past to share, a present to grapple with, and a future to strive for. An emergent community thus formed persists as long as a sense of it continues to nourish its members. Intermittent and elusive as this structural process must be, it is the primary focus of interactionist sociology.

Intelligence, conversation of gestures, and significant symbol

Now we turn to evolutionary social psychology, an important part of Mead's theoretical corpus in which he traces consciousness, language, and self-regarding conduct to their evolutionary precursors. We saw earlier how Mead tackled the problem philosophically by hitching consciousness to relativity: "If we accept those two concepts of emergence and relativity, all I want to point out is that they do answer to what we term 'consciousness,' namely, a certain environment that exists in its relationship to the organism, and in which new characters can arise by virtue of the organism" (MSS, pp. 141, 330). This philosophical insight was fleshed out further, with the substantive input coming from physiology and psychology. One scientific current exerted an especially strong influence over Mead's research agenda: "behaviorism," a radical teaching championed by John Watson, who favored behavior-oriented inquiry over the more traditional, intro-spection-based psychological research. Mead accepted the notion that psychology must approach its subject from the standpoint of behavior, yet he rejected the reductionist strictures prohibiting references to consciousness. In particular, Mead parted company with behaviorists on what qualifies as "stimulus." For Watson, stimulus was an event existing prior to and independent from the response it elicits. Mead cast stimulus as a by-product of an ongoing action, as a phase in the larger act in which the actor selects among many possible perspectives those best answering its current agenda. What is or is not a stimulus cannot be decreed by an outside observer, but must be determined *in situ* and *in actu*, in light of the actor's changing agenda and, in the case of humans, in the broader context of collective behavior. Our social psychology "is behavioristic," explained Mead (MSS, p. 8), "but unlike Watsonian behaviorism it recognizes the parts of the act which do not come to external observation, and it emphasizes the act of the human individual in its natural social situation." In keeping with the behaviorist agenda, however, Mead sought to trace consciousness to animal conduct in its advanced social forms.

Several conditions must be met before instinctive behavior evolves into mindful conduct and the organism seizes itself as an object in its own experience. First of all, a highly sophisticated physiological apparatus has to be in place that enables the organism to delay its immediate response. Second, the cooperation between individual members of the species must reach a high degree of organization, with every member assigned a place in its group and compelled to carry out a part in the larger social act. Third, a prolonged period of infancy is required, during which youngsters practice role-taking, build their sense of self, and learn to measure their conduct by a collective yardstick. Fourth, self-consciousness calls for the forms of communication based on the language of significant symbols. And, fifth, a new regime of managing perspectives has to emerge that separates the sociological principle of organization from the biological one.

Already in graduate school Mead took a keen interest in the physiology of social conduct. He closely followed the developments in brain research and was fascinated with the workings of the central nervous system, in which he saw a biological network uniquely suited for mapping social relations. Its sociological import, Mead surmised, is to be found in the progressively expanding neuron paths that enable the organism to anticipate the future course of action and control its conduct. "[I]t is the function of the central nervous system in the higher forms to connect every response potentially with every other response in the organism.... The central nervous system, in short, enables the individual to exercise conscious control over his behavior. It is the possibility of delayed response which principally differentiates reflective conduct from nonreflective conduct" (PP, p. 125; MSS, p. 117).

Another biological factor favoring humans in their evolutionary ascent is the hand. The versatility that manipulation added to behavior gave humans an edge in the animal kingdom. Along with the hand came tool-making. "Man is essentially a tool-using animal," stressed Mead, "man's hand provides an intermediate contact that is vastly richer in content than that of the jaws or the animal paws.... Man's implements are elaborations and extensions of his hands" (PA, p. 471; MSS, 363). As tool-makers, humans expand their ability to reshape their environment, and to the extent that they master the ultimate tool – symbolic language – they gain control over their own species and affect the direction of evolution itself. "The human hand, backed up, of course, by the indefinite number of actions which the central nervous system makes possible, is of critical importance in the development of human intelligence.... Man's hands have served greatly to break up fixed instincts.... Speech and the hand go along together in the development of the social human being" (MSS, pp. 249, 363, 237). This last point needs to be elaborated further.

Humans are not the only intelligent creatures in the universe. Intelligent behavior is widespread among animals. However, intelligence on the subhuman level differs from what Mead variously calls "social intelligence," "rational intelligence," or "reasoning conduct" found among tool-making animals. At the level of rational intelligence, action is differentiated into several increasingly autonomous phases: "impulse," "perception," "manipulation," and "consummation." Impulse begets image, manipulation tests the percept, purposeful conduct consummates action and satisfies the original drive. It is an impulse – hunger, danger, sexual arousal, or any other drive – that sets the act in motion and makes an object appear in experience. "The starting point of the act is the impulse and not the stimulus" (TIS, p. 114). Impulse converts random events into a definite "situation," turns chaotic reality into "a world in which objects are plans of action" (SW, p. 276). A situation registers in the actor's experience as an "image," "percept," or "perceptual object" that invites "manipulation" – testing of experienced objects via direct contact. Tactile experience either reaffirms the reality of a distant perception or calls it into question, suggesting new perceptual hypotheses. The action's final phase is "consummation" – behavior that appropriates the thing and satisfies the organism's original impulse. "We see what we can reach, what we can manipulate, and then deal with it as we come in contact with it. [The animal's] act is quickly carried to its consummation. The human animal, however, has this implemental stage that comes between the actual consummation and the beginning of the act" (MSS, p, 248). What makes tool-aided behavior so important in the history of intelligence is that it enriches the range of perceptual objects in experience, adds ideas to our mental repertoire, expands time horizons open to the individual, and broadens the spatial properties of the environment within which humans can act: "Ideation extends spatially and temporally the field within which activity takes place" (PP, p. 88). Ideational processes free conduct from its blind reliance on biological drives. The organism that delays its impulsive response and methodically tests its percepts takes a giant step toward rational intelligence. "[R]easoning conduct appears where impulsive conduct breaks down. When the act fails to realize its function, when the impulsive effort to get food does not bring the food, where conflicting impulses thwart each other – here reasoning may come in with a new procedure that is not at the disposal of the biological individual" (MSS, p. 348).

The final step on the road to rational intelligence requires the introduction of symbolic tools into the behavioral repertoire, something that happens to primates involved in complex social interactions. Mead takes great pain to emphasize that this advance implies group behavior. Reason originates in collective behavior implicating the entire community, where every member has a role to play, all roles are potentially interchangeable, and each bit player can, in principle, substitute for the other. On that definition, elaborate social organizations found in insect societies do not qualify as rational. Individual members in such communities are biologically programmed to do their parts – they are physiologically unable to exchange their roles. A honey bee genetically fit to scout a field for pollen cannot collect it, the one that brings it back to the beehive does not know how to process it, the honey-producing specimen would not bear offspring, the queen bee is incapable of defending itself, and the fighting bee can do little more than sting, after which it may die. Mead calls this pole of social differentiation "individual or physiological," and contrasts it with the "person-ality" or "institutional pole," which presupposes the basic physiological identity of individual members and the fundamental interchangeability of social roles (MSS, pp. 227–34). The latter organizational principle can be traced to collective behavior "in which one organism, in a group of organisms, by its conduct stimulates another to carry out its part in a composite co-operative act.... the individual act [is] a part of the larger social whole to which it in fact belongs, and from which, in a definite sense, it gets its meaning" (PA, p. 189; MSS, p. 8). The various strands of individual conduct implicated in this communal act are, in Mead's vocabulary, "social roles," while the individuals who weave their actions into the tapestry of a group exercise are "personalities" or "social actors." "A person is a personality because he belongs to a community, because he takes over the institutions of that community into his own conduct" (MSS, p. 162). Mindful conduct, then, consists in acting according to a collective script, with every player ready to step in and take the role of other actors in a group: "The evolutionary appearance of the mind and intelligence takes place when the whole social process of experience and behavior is brought within the experience of any one of the separate individuals implicated therein, and when the indi-vidual's adjustment to the process is modified and refined by the awareness or consciousness which he thus has of it" (PA, p. 189; MSS, pp. 8, 134).

What makes mind different from other brands of intelligence is that it is mediated by symbolic tools. These tools immensely expand time horizons, give symbol makers a grip on their selves, and turn language users into responsible moral creatures. No matter how smart animals might be, they do not have reason or rational intelligence. Only symbolically mediated conduct can pro-perly be called rational: "Reason is the reference to the relations of things by means of symbols. When we are able to indicate these relations by means of these symbols, we get control of them and can isolate the universal characters of things, and the symbols become significant. No individual or form which has not come into the use of such symbols is rational" (PA, p. 518). Philogenetically, symbolic communication grows from a nonsymbolic one, which Mead charac-terizes as "the non-significant conversation of gestures." Each participant engaged in this conversation keeps a close watch on everyone else's movement, posturing, facial expression, and other body language signs communicating behavioral attitudes. "Gesture" is the term Mead adopted from the psychologist William Wundt to designate a behavioral act in its early stages, "which serve as the cues or stimuli for the appropriate responses of the other forms involved in the whole social act" (PA, p. 448). Whatever the gesture's social significance, it is not initially available to the actor (the point on which Mead parted company with Wundt). It is only when gestures become transparent to actors themselves that they can be termed "conscious," the conduct involved "rational," and the communication accomplished "conscious conversation of gestures." Mead calls gestures purposefully used to communicate and identical in meaning to all parties involved "significant symbols." The totality of symbols mediating interactions in a society at any given historical stretch is "language." Mead is quick to point out that, from the evolutionary-behavioristic standpoint, meaning is not a subjective event but a social relationship between various components of group behavior: "Meaning is thus a development of something objectively there as a relation between certain phases of the social act; it is not a psychical addition to that act and it is not an 'idea' as traditionally conceived. A gesture by one organism, the resultant of the social act in which the gesture is an early phase, and the response of another organism to the gesture, are the relata in a triple or threefold relationship [that] constitutes the matrix within which the meaning arises, or which develops into the field of meaning.... Language is ultimately a form of behavior and calls for the rationally organized society in which it can properly function" (MSS, p. 76). For all its behavioral grounding, significant symbol is a qualitatively new stage in the evolution of intelligence that coincides with the emergence of thinking and that makes the social organization of perspectives possible. Symbols transformed intelligent behavior peculiar to animals into rational, self-conscious conduct separating human beings from their most developed ancestors.

To summarize, Mead traces rational intelligence and consciousness to the changing physiology, hand manipulation, tool-making, and role-playing that bring into experience a wide array of new perceptual objects with which humans can experiment in a systematic fashion. The most consequential tool that appears along this evolutionary path – significant symbol – weakens the organism's dependence on its biological drives and opens the door to self-conscious social control. A system of significant symbols is language, and "language [is] a principle of social organization that has made the distinctly human society possible" (MSS, p. 260). Symbolic communications bring rationality into the world and turn members of a community into moral creatures responsible for their conduct. "It is as social beings that we are moral beings" (MSS, p. 385). Community-minded, language-mediated, self-referential conduct is socially rational, and society it engenders is rational – human – society.

Play, game, and the generalized other

Mead is perhaps best known for his theory of the self. His writings on its genesis, structure, and function shift analytical focus from the phylogenetic inquiry to the ontogenetic one, which no longer prohibits references to consciousness, language, and social institutions. Ontogeny deals with children growing up among adult members of their species. While most of what Mead has to say on the subject falls within this theoretical perspective, we should bear in mind how such sociopsychological concepts as "role-taking" and "generalized other" fit into his pragmatist cosmology.

The self is a special case of relativity designating an organism that is aware of its multiple relationships with other things in the pluralistic universe. The body that has reached this evolutionary stage dwells in its multiple perspectives consciously, chooses among affiliations at will, and knows beforehand the role it takes. From the cosmological standpoint, "generalized other [is] the object as

expression of the whole complex of things that make up the environment....The generalized attitude of the other is an assumption of a space that
is absolute over against the relativity of individual organisms" (PA, pp. 193,
310). The generalized other is a totality of perspectives constituting the situation
in someone's experience at any given moment, and role-taking is the mechanism
that allows the individual to explore the otherness of the world by assuming
emotionally charged attitudes and becoming another to oneself. We can see this
most vividly in children engaged in play-acting. The individual takes the role of a
mother, of a dog, of a train; one child claimed to be scrambled eggs! No object is
immune from being enacted by a human fledgling exploring the meaning of
things in their relationship to the self and the self in its relationship to the world.
In infancy and early childhood, all things appear alive in experience; it is only
later that children learn to differentiate between physical and social objects and
reserve role-playing for expressly social occasions: "The physical object is an
abstraction which we make from the social response to nature. We talk to
nature; we address the clouds, the sea, the tree, and objects about us. We later
abstract from that type of response because of what we come to know of such
objects. [Nature] acts as it is expected to act. We are taking the attitude of the
physical things about us, and when we change the situation nature responds in a
different way" (MSS, p. 184). The whole universe arising in experience is, thus,
social through and through. It is in this world that the child "is gradually
building up a definite self which becomes the most important object in his
world" (MSS, p. 369). Unlike objects experienced by intelligent animals, the
self belongs to the realm of signification and implies an elaborate group life in
which the individual takes active part. The following statement captures the
thrust of Mead's theory: "The individual experiences himself as such, not
directly, but only indirectly, from the particular standpoints of other individual
members of the same social group, or from the generalized standpoint of the
social group as a whole to which he belongs. For he enters his own experience as
a self or individual, not directly or immediately, not by becoming a subject to
himself, but only in so far as he first becomes an object to himself just as other
individuals are objects to him or in his experience; and he becomes an object to
himself only by taking the attitudes of other individuals toward himself within a
social environment or context of experience and behavior in which both he and
they are involved" (MSS, p. 138).

Play-acting is the form in which the self grows in ontogenesis. Children
engaged in role-taking accomplish several things. They explore the social structure, find their place in a group, master rule-bound conduct, face punishment for
rule-breaking, learn to negotiate conflicting identities, and discover the meaning
of creativity. Mead singles out two critical stages in this process: "play" and
"game." At the play stage, children act in a way resembling things and people
immediately surrounding them. No partners are necessary for such an exercise,
for all the parts are played by the same person. "The child becomes a generalized
actor-manager, directing, applauding, and criticizing his own roles as well as
those of others" (PA, p. 374). The youngsters commonly address themselves in
the third person or invent "the invisible, imaginary companion which a good

many children produce in their own experience" (MSS, p. 150). At this early stage, the child's sense of self is quite rudimentary, reflecting more or less superficial characteristics of those who stimulate the child's imagination the most. With time, this self begins to exhibit a greater coherence, as the child connects several disparate parts and navigates between them with confidence. "In the play period the child utilizes his own responses to these stimuli which he makes use of in building a self. The response which he has a tendency to make to these stimuli organizes them. He plays that he is, for instance, offering himself something, and he buys it; he gives a letter to himself and takes it away; he addresses himself as a parent, as a teacher; he arrests himself as a policeman" (MSS, pp. 150–1).

The situation changes when imaginary companions are replaced with real partners who interact with a child according to the rules of the game. The self corresponding to this stage is more coherent, internally differentiated, and it is increasingly generalized to reflect the social act as a whole. Playing at being someone does not require a clear-cut time perspective; the past and future are here ill-defined. The game, on the other hand, brings into experience a bigger chunk of environment and offers a far more elaborate time frame where the legitimate past and possible future outcomes are spelled out in vivid details. "The child is one thing at one time and another at another, and what he is at one moment does not determine what he is at another," articulates Mead on the transition from play to game. "He is not organized into a whole. The child has no definite character, no definite personality. . . . But in a game where a number of individuals are involved, then the child taking one role must be ready to take the role of everyone else. . . . The nature of the game is such that every act in the game is determined and qualified by all the other acts. This is expressed by the rules of the game, and implies in each individual a generalized player that is present in every part that is taken" (MSS, pp. 159, 151; PA, p. 374). Game is no longer a childish matter; it is a serious learning exercise modeling responsible conduct in the adult world. The child engaged in game activity "is becoming an organic member of society. He is taking over the morale of that society and is becoming an essential member of it" (MSS, p. 159). A society, after all, is but a series of games adults play, games governed by certain rules, offering tangible stakes, punishing the losers and showering benefits on the winners. To play these high-stake games, humans must learn how to speak the right language, sign themselves in proper terms: "The alley gang has its vocabulary, and so does the club" (TIS, p. 151). Participants in the game also need to know how to juggle identities competing for their attention, to negotiate their membership in various interactional fields, to integrate their disparate selves into a more or less coherent whole, and to bring their action into line with the generalized perspective of the entire community.

"Concrete other," "specific other," "organized other," "generalized other" – these are the terms Mead uses to describe the range of individual and collective others whom we encounter on the road to a full-grown selfhood. The expression "significant other," widely used today, was coined by Harry Stack Sullivan, but it goes back to Mead's concept of a person on whom we model our conduct. The term "generalized other" designates a play team or community of indefinite size whose perspectives have been incorporated into the individual's self. "The organized community or social group which gives to the individual his unity of self may be called 'the generalized other.' The attitude of the generalized other is the attitude of the whole community. . . . It is in the form of the generalized other that the community exercises control over the conduct of its individual members; for it is in this form that the social process or community enters as a determining factor into the individual's thinking" (MSS, p. 154–5). The self fashioned after the generalized other and guided by the group rules is an instrument of social control. By providing its members with selves and minds, society equips them with an ability to criticize their own conduct and to correct their actions accordingly. Self-regarding conduct is by its nature self-critical, the person possessing self-consciousness has a critical attitude built into his or her conduct. "Thus he becomes not only self-conscious but also self-critical; and thus, through self-criticism, social control over individual behavior or conduct operates by virtue of the social origin and basis of such criticism. That is to say, self-criticism is essentially social criticism, and behavior controlled by self-criticism is essentially behavior controlled socially" (MSS, p. 255).

It would be wrong to infer from the above that selfhood turns humans into social robots forever chained to their predetermined identities. Those partaking in numerous symbolic fields are bound to experience a cross-pressure on their identities, which routinely bump against each other and force on the actor tough choices. The conflict is endemic to the social process, and this conflict is inscribed in the selves that emerge in its course. "A highly developed and organized human society is one in which the individual members are interrelated in a multiplicity of different intricate and complicated ways whereby they all share a number of common social interests, yet, on the other hand, are more or less in conflict relative to numerous other interests. . . . Thus, within such a society conflicts arise between different aspects or phases of the same individual self,. . . as well as between different individual selves" (MSS, p. 307). Which particular interest or affiliation wins in any given encounter is problematic; not even the self-conscious individual can be entirely sure how the situation will break out in the end. Self-regarding behavior is creative, either by serendipity or by design. It is also critical and reconstructive; to the extent that self-conscious actions jolt the situation from its original course, they serve not only as an instrument of social control but also as a springboard for social change: "Human society, we have insisted, does not merely stamp the pattern of its organized social behavior upon any one of its individual members, so that this pattern becomes likewise the pattern of the individual's self; it also at the same time, gives him a mind, [and] his mind enables him in turn to stamp the pattern of his further developing self (further developing through his mental activity) upon the structure or organization of human society, and thus in a degree to reconstruct or modify in terms of his self the general pattern of social or group behavior in terms of which his self was originally constituted" (MSS, p. 263).

To conclude, the self is a social structure that appears on the evolutionary scene alongside rational intelligence and symbolic communication. It evolves in stages, beginning with the play stage during which the child tests the otherness of the world by assuming emotionally charged attitudes and imitating animate and inanimate objects, followed by the game stage where the self begins to exhibit a structure reflecting a set of rules. "The game, in other words, requires a whole self, whereas play requires only pieces of the self" (TIS, p. 145). A mature self takes the attitude of the generalized other – a set of privileged perspectives binding together group members. To those who measure their actions by the same generalized other and feel bound by the same reference frame, the emerging structure might appear absolute. Yet this generalized perspective, institutionally privileged though it might be, is relevant only in a given situation and to the present set of participants. The game goes on as long as people keep on playing by its rules; the situation is restructured when those involved take on different disguises and switch to other symbolic fields. While it comes into being within a particular society, the self is not fettered by its symbolic confines. Self-conscious agents criticize the existing perspectives, dump the familiar guises, and conceive new communities endowed with alternative structures of past, present, and future. To understand these dynamics, we need to move beyond phylogeny and ontogeny and immerse ourselves in sitogeny – a theoretical perspective that examines embodied selfhood and the emergent evolution of human society.

Self, biological individual, and the "I"–"me" dialectics

We saw earlier how human agency gradually emancipates itself from its physical limitations by substituting the social organization of perspectives for the biological one, rational action for impulsive reaction, nonsignificant conversation of gestures for significant communication, and time-conscious conduct for behavior with undifferentiated time-structure. The term "supplementing" is, actually, more appropriate here than "substituting," for the sociological organization of perspectives does not cancel the patterns of sociality found in philogenetically more primitive forms. Although the evolutionary process gives humans the hitherto unknown measure of control over their destiny, it does not turn them into disembodied creatures subsisting in purely symbolic space. The human being is very much a body weighed down by its physical, biological, physiological, and psychological characteristics, all of which exert a continuous influence over individuality and critical reflexivity.

"The line of demarcation between the self and the body is found, then, first of all in the social organization of the act within which the self arises, in its contrast with the physiological organism," maintains Mead (PA, p. 446). Yet he is quick to point out that "the self does not consist simply in the bare organization of social attitudes," that it "is a social entity that must be related to the entire body," that "Walking, writing, and talking are there as physiological processes as well as actions of the self," and that, consequently, it "would be a mistake to assume that a man is a biologic individual plus a reason, if we mean by this definition that he leads two separable lives, one of impulse or instinct, and another of reason" (TIS, p. 148; MSS, pp. 173, 347). Society blends together mechanism, organism, and the self in a complex system of feedbacks that tie together the organizational principles governing perspectives in each evolutionary domain. The question that particularly interested Mead was how the body responds to its selfhood and how the self manages its body. The Freudian solution to the self–body problem gave primacy to unconscious instincts over self-consciousness. Mead, who was very much aware of this solution, rejected it on the ground that Freud underestimated the extent to which the social forces transform our impulsive life. Reason is not just a cipher for immutable drives, a rationalization disguising primordial impulses, nor is society merely a censor reigning in the recalcitrant soma. The societal influence goes far deeper. Society remodels the body's circuits, reshapes the structure of affect, and supplies human agents with symbolic tools that help them mobilize bodily resources for the public good. At the same time, society never obliterates impulses and stamps out emotions. The body or biological individual is a vital link in sociological dynamics.

The biological individual, according to Mead, is the organized group of drives, impulses, and habits that we carry within ourselves and that are variously molded by our group life. Humans excelling in social etiquette have to master the complex machinery of the body to dramatize their social identities. The self abiding by social norms, however, "is very different from the passionate assertive biological individual, that loves and hates and embraces and strikes. *He* is never an object; *his* is a life of direct suffering and action" (MSS, p. 370). It is not that this passionate beast is closed to self-consciousness, although our impulses and gestures are more transparent to outside observers than to ourselves. The point is that impulses and habits are informed by social processes as much as they inform them. The fact that they are amenable to social control does not mean that they can be readily accessed by self-consciousness. "The sets of habits which we have of this sort mean nothing to us; we do not hear the intonations of our speech that others hear unless we are paying particular attention to them. The habits of emotional expression which belong to our speech are of the same sort. We may know that we have expressed ourselves in a joyous fashion but the detailed process is one which does not come back to our conscious selves. There are whole bundles of such habits which do not enter into a conscious self, but which help to make up what is termed the unconscious self" (MSS, p. 163). The biological individual is a creature of impulses and habits, a body unconscious of itself. While the body can exist without a self, the self is fundamentally an embodied experience, an agency that situates itself in the world by mobilizing the organism's semiotic resources. As it signs itself in the flesh, the self gives the body its marching orders, molds it according to a script, and in the process, transforms an indeterminate situation onto an acting stage with distinct spatio-temporal characteristics. An embodied self has a past to claim and the future to strive for, though each is real only in the present where social actors situate themselves with respect to particular reference frames. Once the time structure binding disparate agents into a group has dissipated, the self recedes into the background, the body slips into unconsciousness, and the biological individual takes over. "The biological individual lives in an undifferentiated now; the social reflective individual takes this up into a flow of experience within which stands a fixed past and a more or less uncertain future.... The subject is the biologic individual – never on the scene, and this self adjusted to its social environment, and through this to the world at large, is the object.... Thus the biological individual becomes essentially interrelated with the self, and the two go to make up the personality" (MSS, p. 351, 372–3).

It might seem odd that a theorist who cast the self as a rational process would talk about the "unconscious self." To understand this conceptual twist, we need to remind ourselves that Mead sought to bridge the gap between various evolutionary forms of sociality, that he was a biosocial theorist who took a keen interest in Freud. Mead's views on the subject should also be judged in light of his interest in Romanticism and the subject–object dialectics. We find the direct counterpart to idealism in the theory of "I" and "me," which recast the idealist *a priori* in quasi-naturalistic terms. The transcendental ego, a mysterious realm of paradigmatic preconceptions informing our judgment, turns up in Mead as the unconscious self, biological individual, or "I" – the domain of habituated drives and semi-socialized impulses. What the Romantics called phenomenal self appears in Mead's theory as the conscious self or "me." "The 'I' is the transcendental self of Kant," Mead tells us. "The self-conscious, actual self in social intercourse is the objective 'me' or 'me's'" (SW, p. 141).

The distinction between "I" and "me" serves several strategic functions in the Meadian discourse. It helps square off sociological theory with the notion of indeterminacy, with the fact that our calculated actions routinely produce unanticipated consequences: "However carefully we plan the future it always is different from that which we can previse. [The individual] is never sure about himself, and he astonishes himself by his conduct as much as he astonishes other people" (MSS, pp. 203–4). This distinction biologizes the transcendental *a priori*, which Mead reinterprets as a domain of embodied values and creative drives: "The possibilities of the 'I' belong to that which is actually going on, taking place, and it is in some sense the most fascinating part of our experience. It is there that novelty arises and it is there that our most important values are located" (MSS, p. 204). "Me," by contrast, "is a conventional, habitual individual who is always there. It has to have those habits, those responses that everybody has" (MSS, p. 197). From the sociological standpoint, "me" is an actor obeying common rules. Our "me's" are modeled after conventional roles and historical identities waiting to be claimed as our own. "We are individuals born into a certain nationality, located at a certain spot geographically, and such and such political relations. All of these represent a certain situation which constitutes 'me'; but this necessarily involves a continued action of the organism toward the 'me' in the process within which that lies" (MSS, p. 182). While the "me" is socially scripted, the "I" is not; it represents an improvised response of the body to whatever the situation demands. The resultant self-framing does not always fall within a conventional perspective, though; it can break the established time frame and turn the situation into a stage with action props and time horizons all its own. Whether they stumble on new reference frames or consciously look for alternatives, agents do more than replicate old meanings in the course of interactions. They also express their individuality and imaginatively reconstruct the present situation. Social creativity, according to Mead, flows from "those values which attach particularly to the 'I' rather than to the 'me,' those values which are found in the immediate attitude of the artist, the inventor, the scientist in his discovery, in general in the action of the 'I' which cannot be calculated and which involves a reconstruction of the society, and so of the 'me' which belongs to that society.... To the degree that we make the community in which we live different we all have what is essential to genius, and which becomes genius when the effects are profound" (MSS, pp. 214, 218).

Now, we can see how the "I–me" dialectics advances the Meadian enterprise as a whole. It does so by making make room for the primitive forms of relativity in the world transformed by reason. There is the perennial tension between the biological and sociological imperatives, between the impulsive "I" and the rational "me." For society to maintain its current structure, the "me" has to get a hold of the "I": "The relation between the rational or primarily social side of the self and its impulsive or emotional or primarily anti-social and individual side is such that the latter is, for the most part, controlled with respect to its behavioristic expressions by the former" (MSS, p. 230). Social control works its magic by colonizing the body, compelling it to hide itself under familiar guises, transforming primeval urges into socially acceptable conduct. Self-consciousness is a process that situates the body within its environment by harnessing impulses and mobilizing emotions for public display. Looked at in this perspective, emotions are early warning signals that the body sends to itself as it symbolically traverses numerous references frames, relates itself to others, and evaluates prospective selves. Temporal spread is crucial to understanding human emotions. The more complex the spatio-temporal structure, the richer the organism's emotional life. Intelligence is an emotionally charged agency evaluating its spatio-temporal options in the pluralistic universe.

This is not to say that the rational self always keeps the biological vessel in check. The self weaves its texture from an unyielding stuff, which makes the fit between the body and the self problematic. Having failed to follow the script, the body finds itself in an unfamiliar self, surrounded by an unknown universe, generalizing the other in as yet uncertified fashion. Such experiences are at first accessible to the individual only, but they become part of the public agenda as individual experiences are isolated through symbolic media and incorporated into the communal reality: "This common world is continually breaking down. Problems rise in it and demand solutions. They appear as the exceptions... in the experience of individuals and while they have the form of common experiences they run counter to the structure of the common world. The experience of the individuals is precious because it preserves these exceptions. But the individual preserves them in such form that others can experience them, that they may become common experiences" (SW, p. 341).

To recapitulate, Mead undertook a sitogenetic inquiry into the relationship between the body and the self. The question he raised was how the biological organism maintains its selfhood and the conscious self manages its biological agency. His answer to this question was that selfhood is an embodied experience marshaling the semiotic resources of the body with the help of the symbolic stock of society. Whatever feats we accomplish as self-conscious, creative beings, we accomplish because we have bodies, for "only insofar as the self is related to the body is it related to the environment" (TIS, p. 148). The embodied self is a self-conscious body, an organism referenced in a particular perspective, an emotionally engaged subject situated in time and space. Mead distinguished between the "I" and "me" phases of the self, the former representing impulsive, unconscious parts of ourselves, and the latter the rational, self-conscious parts. "Taken together they constitute a personality as it appears in social experience. The self is essentially the social process going on with these two distinguishable phases" (MSS, p. 178). The "I–me" dialectics brings into sociological focus human agency and places embodied subjectivity in its sociohistorical context. It also raises critical questions about the relationship between personal freedom and public necessity and the historical transformation of the pluralistic universe. The last section of this chapter is devoted to these issues.

Democracy, progressivism, and social reconstruction

Picture a game in which everyone takes part freely, all players follow the generalized other, and no one is barred from trying a particular role. Add to this a provision for revising the rules and inventing new games, and you will get the Meadian blueprint for a humane, democratic community permeated with team spirit and open to continuous improvement. Whatever part the individual plays is illuminated here by the sense of shared purpose and the enjoyment of common products, the sentiments equally prized in a fair game and just society. "It is this that gives joy to creation and belongs to the work of the artist, the research scientist, and the skilled artisan who can follow his article through to its completion. It belongs to co-ordinated efforts of many, when the role of the other in the production is aroused in each worker at the common task, when the sense of team play, *esprit de crops*, inspires interrelated activities. In these situations something of the delight of consummation can crown all intermediate processes. It is unfortunately absent from most labor in modern competitive industrial society" (PA, p. 457).

This statement captures the ambivalence that Mead shared with many contemporaries whose belief in the perfectability of human society was tempered by the keen awareness of its multiple failures. Indeed, Mead's pragmatist cosmology was tailor-made for the Progressive era. It envisioned the pluralistic universe whose inhabitants incessantly multiply perspectives, reinvent their selves, and reconstruct their community for the common good. No society embodies this ideal better than democracy. At its heart is a universal discourse or system of symbols binding individuals into a social whole and transparent to "every citizen of the universe of discourse" (PA, p. 375). Democratic society never stops restructuring its perspectives and broadening its horizons of universality – "'universal' discourse to be universal has to be continuously revised" (MSS, p. 269). Democracy makes its symbolic and material resources available to all its members – it is "responsible for the ordering of its process and structure so that what are common goods in their very nature should be accessible to common enjoyment" (SW, p. 407). Democratic society teaches its members to place themselves in each other's shoes. More than that, it gives everyone a practical chance to experiment with new roles and selves. When it lives up to its promise, democracy approximates what Mead calls "a universal society in which the interests of each would be the interests of all" (PA, p. 466).

The above description should not be taken to mean that the pluralistic universe is devoid of tension, that everything in it hangs together. Local lingos and competing agendas find their place in a democratic society alongside overarching cultural symbols. If attitudes we carry in ourselves clash, it is because institutions of society operate at cross purpose: "Each social institution with the good that it subtends asserts and maintains itself but finds itself in this assertion in conflict with other institutions and their goods" (PA, p. 498). Far from being a threat to the democratic discourse, conflict is its lifeblood. Democratic society does not merely tolerate competing discourses – it encourages and protects them. What makes the tension between perspectives vying for attention in a democratic society constructive is the fact that they are open to criticism. Democratic society teaches its members to use their mind critically, it makes its symbolic resources available to all its members, and it systematically lowers the barriers separating classes and impeding communication across group boundaries. By contrast, nondemocratic societies limit their members' participation in common discourse and zealously police the selves they can rightfully call their own. Castes, estates, classes, cliques – human history abounds in exclusive interactional fields formed around privileged perspectives designed to keep nonmembers at bay. The most insidious in this respect are social configurations based on caste. Superficially, they resemble insect communities whose members are stuck with their parts because they are physiologically outfitted to play them. Ideology that goes with such a society often blames biological differences for the fact that some of its members are barred from particular roles. In reality, social conventions backed by power are primarily responsible for the rigid pattern of role-taking in closed societies. "The development of democratic community implies the removal of castes as essential to the personality of the individual; the individual is not to be what he is in his specific caste or group set over against other groups, but his distinctions are to be distinctions of functional difference which put him in relationship with others instead of separating him" (MSS, p. 318). Like every game, democratic society calls for a division of labor, which poses no immediate threat to social intelligence. As long as every role is there for the taking and no one is shut out of the game, there is ample room for our universal nature to play itself out. Needless to say, American society in the late nineteenth and early twentieth centuries fell short of this democratic ideal.

Mead hammered away at the last point in his political writings. He decried the fact that symbolic means for self-realization were distributed unequally among American citizens. He urged the lowering of economic barriers hampering the disadvantaged. He personally participated in the Chicago immigrants' surveys, documenting their living conditions and educational needs. Immigrants who flooded the country at the turn of the century and supplied much of its labor power, Mead pointed out, were often shortchanged by a system that favored industrial education for future laborers and liberal arts education for well-to-do classes. Mead singled out the factory system for his criticism, charging that the assembly-line technology threatened to reduce universal beings to an appendage in a mechanical process whose overall purpose and ultimate products eluded a machine operator: "The man who tends one of these machines becomes a part of the machine, and when the machine is thrown away the man is thrown away, for he has fitted himself into the machine until he has become nothing but a cog" (quoted in Shalin, 1988, p. 928). Tearing down class barriers, eliminating artificial restrictions, revamping dehumanizing social technologies – such were the causes to which Mead dedicated himself in his political life. Progressivism meant for him a commitment to "the 'democratic ideal' of removing such restrictions," of getting on with social reconstruction and advancing democratic reforms (SW, p. 406). How can the democratic changes be effected? Mead sought the answer to this question in the temporal dynamics of social inter-actions.

Social change in the pluralistic universe is inextricably linked to its spatio-temporal structure and heavily relies on our ability to fashion disparate actions into a meaningful whole via the continually renewed sense of shared past and future. Each society has its own time horizons, its own unique history that its members recount to themselves and their offspring. When the historical narrat-ive changes, the pluralistic universe slips off its symbolic moorings and expands its familiar confines. "The past that is there for us, as the present is there, stands on the same basis as the world about us that is there. . . . The histories that have most fastened upon men's minds have been political and cultural propaganda, and every great social movement has flashed back its light to discover a new past" (PA, pp. 94–7). We can pull off this remarkable feat of rediscovering – reinventing – our pasts because society provided us with minds whose locus is not in the head but in the situation implicating the entire group and the general-ized other. It is this decentered, time-conscious mind that "frees us from bondage to past or future. We are neither creatures of the necessity of an irrevocable past, nor of any vision given on the Mount" (PP, p. 90). Thanks to its special brand of relativity, rational intelligence not only cushions the effect of biological drives but also delivers humans from the dictate of implacable social norms. Our minds allow us to revise our past, set up a hypothetical future, select suitable means, and appropriate the self that ties all the elements of the situation together in a continual passage from the past to the present and into an indefinite future. The pluralistic universe owes its spatio-temporal structure to self-referential conduct. When the latter undergoes restructuring, the former changes as well: "The relations between social reconstruction and self or personality reconstruction are reciprocal and internal or organic. . . . In both types of reconstruction the same fundamental material of organized social relations among human indi-viduals is involved, and is simply treated in different ways, or from different angles or points of view, in the two cases, respectively; or in short, social reconstruction and self or personality reconstruction are the two sides of a single process – the process of human social evolution" (MSS, p. 309).

It would be a mistake to conclude from the above that Mead saw reconstruc-tion in society as a purely cognitive affair. Social institutions are ingrained in our emotional habits as much as in logical thinking, which is why social change has to engage both "me" and "I," with the rational "me" pointing the way and the unconscious "I" realizing the imagined future. It takes time for the biological individual to slip into the new self, to change the habits of the heart, which resist the coercion. The new discourse must be backed up by the adjustments in the entire body where our values are sedimented into habits. To achieve its goal, social reconstruction has to mobilize the embodied self, "the individual as embodying the values in himself. . . . We want a full life expressed in our instincts, our natures. Reflective thinking enables us to bring these different values into the realm of possibility" (PA, pp. 625, 463–4). Social reconstruction feeds on emotional substance, it is literally "bodied forth" by the agent redeeming its claim to selfhood in the flesh. Social changes that result in lowering social barriers release emotions conducive to democratic discourse and bring about selves conversant with wider ranging communities: "The breakdown of barriers is something that arouses a flood of emotions, because it sets free an indefinite number of possible contacts to other people which have been checked, held repressed. [The] person does get out of himself, and by doing so makes himself a definite member of a larger community than that to which he previously belonged" (MSS, p. 219).

Despite the confident outlook Mead shared with other progressives, he stayed away from optimistic predictions about the future of democracy; nor did he put a seal of approval on specific forms it ought to take. Such predictions ran contrary to his pragmatist spirit that favored experimentation over doctrinaire social engineering. The future is uncertain, Mead said repeatedly, "there are no fixed or determined ends or goals toward which social progress necessarily moves; and such progress is hence genuinely creative and would not otherwise be progress. . . . The moral question is not the one of setting up a right value against a wrong value; it is a question of finding the possibility of acting so as to take into account as far as possible all the values involved" (MSS, p. 294; PA, p. 465). Still, we can glean the broad outlines of a democratic society he favored from praises he sang to "team work," "universal discourse," "international mindedness," and "the community values of friendship, of passion, of parenthood, of amusement, of beauty, of social solidarity in its unnumbered forms" (SW, p. 311). Whatever helps make the universe of discourse more inclusive is progress. Whoever incorporates the experience of the other into one's own and guides one's actions accordingly is a moral being. Whichever value finds its embodied expression in a democratic community is a concrete universal.

Mead's pragmatic optimism was tempered by the realization that no society can assure the individual a happy life. Meaningful, yes, but not necessarily a happy one. Because the pluralistic universe is forever changing, humans are never completely at home in it: "Human society is not at home in the world because it is trying to change that world and change itself; and, so long as it has failed to so change itself and change its world, it is not at home in it as the physiological and physical mechanism is" (PA, p. 476). What this statement implies is that we cannot lead an authentic life in society as long as we are not trying to change it, yet our concerted efforts to transcend the existing order turn us into spiritual nomads unable to identify completely with any given self. There is no such thing as an authentic self in Mead's social cosmology. Every self we claim as our own will have to be shed, however snugly we might be wrapped into our conventional "me's." The biological individual disguised under a historical mask will sooner or later turn into a corpse, but our dramatic personae will go on, re-enacted by numerous others, eager to step into our shoes: "There is a need for salvation – not the salvation of the individual but the salvation of the self as a social being" (PA, p. 476).

In sum, Mead's social theory called for a continually expanding social universe in which no perspective is foreclosed to its inhabitants, all symbolic resources are distributed equally among its members, and everyone can – and ought to – be an agent of social change. The political system that best approximates this blueprint is democracy. For all its failures, democracy comes closest to realizing the universality of human nature and the creativity of social intelligence. To live up to its promise, democratic society has to keep reinventing itself, and that means re-examining its past, reconstructing its present, and reimagining its future. Social change has a temporal dimension, predicated on the fact that social structure is rooted in a past continually recycled by skilled narrators. When the old historical narrative is revised and the new one finds its way into public discourse, individuals discover a new past, which turns out to be as emergent as the future. "The past is a working hypothesis that has validity in the present within which it works but has no other validity" (PA, p. 96). Social change has a somatic dimension. It requires an alignment between the biological resources of the "I" and the discursive skills of the "me." Social reconstruction is not a teleological process gravitating to some predestined goal; it is an open-ended process whose time horizons are revised by successive generations. The social change that brings down class barriers, levels economic disparities, spreads around symbolic resources, and increases team spirit is progressive. For all the good change brings to society, it does not guarantee happiness and fulfilled selfhood. For transcendence is a distinctly human mode of being in the world and the ultimate form of authenticity available to humanity.

CONCLUSION

I have pieced together disparate strands of Mead's thought and tried to show them as parts of a vast, unfinished project that will continue to nourish our sociological imagination well into the future. In my closing remarks, I would like to bring into sharper relief a few key insights and unresolved issues in his pragmatist cosmology.

Central to the pragmatist project is the problem of historically situated agency. There are two radical solutions to this problem that Romantic idealists bequeathed to modern social thought. One equates human agency with reason, grammar, norm, or a similar structural principle that disembodies subjectivity and drains agency of its emotional substance. Another approach tends to naturalize and deracinate human agency, reducing the transcendental *a priori* to more or less immutable drives, impulses, and behavioral dispositions. Pragmatists refuse to linguistify or biologize agency. Steering between these two extremes, they conceptualize human agency as a historically situated, fully embodied, emotionally grounded selfhood. Mead acknowledges that the individual is born into a symbolic universe that is already there, but he declines either to dissolve agency into symbolic forms or to reduce it to behavioral drives. There is more to personhood than its symbolic hulk; we are vested in the world with our entire bodies, which are as much a product of society as our beliefs and values. Sociality shapes our neural circuits and affective responses, but our emotional habits and behavioral proclivities feed right back into social structure. Sociological analysis is impoverished when it is preoccupied exclusively with the normative/structural/discursive or the impulsive/affective/behavioral side of the social processes. That is what social pragmatists mean when they say that culture is embodied and body is uncultured – the two must be studied jointly in the context of human society.

While Mead brought into focus the relationship between the biological individual and the self, he might have drawn too sharp a line between conscious and unconscious procesess, between the rational self and the biological individual. This can be gleaned from his belief that animals have no selves, that they know neither past nor future, and that, consequently, "animals have no rights" and "there is no wrong committed when an animal life's is taken away" (MSS, p. 183). An argument can be made that for all their inferior instrumental and symbolic skills, animals are not as different from humans as Mead contended. Since we think not just with our heads but with our entire bodies, rational thinking and emotional intelligence may share considerable evolutionary grounds. Pragmatist sociologists should take a closer look at the continuity of animal and human intelligence. They might want to juxtapose Mead and Freud and reconceptualize the unconscious as historicized, fleshed out, habitualized agency. They also need to re-examine the "I– me" dialectics, and particularly the manner in which the self cares for its body in different cultural settings. The sitogenetic analysis of self–body interactions is a promising line of inquiry that Mead's followers should take seriously.

Mead's social cosmology offers a fresh look at social structure as an emergent event predicated on its members' ability to manage perspectives and process time. This view breaks with the classical theory that casts social structure as something akin to an immovable ether subsisting in absolute space and time and informing individual conduct without being informed by it. In the pragmatist reckoning, social structure is an event unfolding *in situ* where its strategic properties are determined by conscious agents situating themselves across space and time. The self is perceived here as a nonclassically propertied object, a social particle quantum leaping from one interactional field to another. Every time agents assume new disguises and lend emotional substance to their selves, they affect the group's status as a universal, objective, and meaningful whole. This relativist approach renders social structure contingent on the quantum of objectivity supplied to it by self-conscious individuals. The structure of the self evolving in the individual's experience reflects the structure of the community to which this individual belongs, and vice versa, the group structure is encoded in the self-identities of its individual members. Society as a whole transpires here as an emergent system of generalized perspectives held in common by individuals inhabiting the same symbolic niche or environment endowed with emergent spatio-temporal properties by self-conscious agents.

This innovative approach raises questions regarding the relationship between the micro and macro levels of sociological analysis, questions that Mead has not answered adequately. His theory may be seen as positing an over-emergent view of social order that does not do justice to recurrent patterns in social interactions and overarching time sequences. It is true that group perspectives owe their objectivity to self-conscious agents, but the degrees of freedom with which individuals may choose a particular perspective as the basis for self identification vary greatly from one interactional field to another. Societies tend to privilege some perspectives and discourage their members from taking others. Social control mechanisms determine who can raise specific self-claims, under what circumstances, and how such claims can be redeemed and validated. Mead showed that the emergent evolution is built into human agency as it manifests itself on the micro level in concrete situational encounters. He did not explain why certain families of duration become privileged. Neither did he outline the logic that governs the historical evolution of macrostructural patterns. More conceptual work has to be done here. Interactionists need to demonstrate how the emergent time-processing generates relatively stable societal patterns. The gap between macrostructural dynamics and emergent transformations on the micro level is yet to be bridged in interactionist sociology.

The pragmatist emphasis on corporeal selfhood adds a potentially valuable dimension to the theory of social and political institutions. The latter are generally equated with a symbolic code or a normative grammar enciphering relations between individuals in a given organization. The Meadian approach draws attention to the corporeal dimension of social institutions and invites an inquiry into authoritarian emotions, aristocratic demeanor, and the body language of democracy. Indeed, polity affects our entire body. Democracy, in this sense, is an embodied institution. There is more to it than a constitutional system of checks and balances and a list of civil rights. It is also a demeanor, the practical care we take of our own and other people's bodies and selves. The body politic is the politics of the body. The strength of democracy is in civility, which cannot be legislated any more than it can be reduced to a biological drive. Democracy communicates in the flesh; it is a conversation that blends nonsignificant and significant gestures, with each set codifying democratic politics in its own special way. Body language speaks volumes about the body politic and measurably affects the quality of life.

The problem with Mead's political theory is that it does not confront head on the issue of power. Mead tends to blur the distinction between symbolic and economic resources, understates the barriers that market economy places on equitable distribution of resources, and underestimates the extent to which economic, cultural, racial, ethnic, and other divisions subvert the universal nature of intelligence. While he acknowledged the role conflict plays in the pluralistic universe, Mead believed that the cooperation between individuals, groups, and nations is the order of the day, that "revolutions might be carried out by methods which would be strictly constitutional and legal" (SW, pp. 150–1). Alas, Mead might have overdosed on the Progressive era's optimism about the plasticity of human nature and the perfectability of society. His enthusiasm for democracy is infectious, but his take on American political institutions and their democratic promise needs to be complemented by a closer analysis of power, class, and privilege. The pragmatist challenge is to conceptualize the obdurate realities of power that delimit our freedom to assume roles and devise new perspectives.

Finally, I want to single out the ecological dimension of the pragmatist social cosmology. Mead places humans at the pinnacle of evolution and treats self-consciousness as the highest known form of relativity. At the same time, he considers human agency to be an extension of natural phenomena, an emergent product of natural evolution. Although self-referential conduct dramatically alters the way living beings exist in the world, social intelligence does not exempt humans from mechanical laws, nor does it insulate them from biological limitations. For all our fabled reflexivity, we are still suffering, mortal beings. Physical, biological, physiological, psychological, spiritual, and sociological perspectives intersect in our existence, determining our unique mode of being in the world. Selfhood simply designates a new mode of integration of these qualitatively different forms of relativity. Divested from its corporeal substance, the self is just a linguistic fiction, an unsubstantiated discursive claim. By the same token, agents outside their self-conscious reference frames are nothing more than biological entities devoid of rationality and unable to feel oneness with the rest of the world. Our ability to empathize with all creatures, large and small, to place ourselves in the shoes of any other thing, is, indeed, unique. "Is it necessary that that feeling of unity or solidarity should go beyond the society itself to the physical universe which seems to support it?" asks Mead (PA, p. 478). He hesitates to answer this question in the affirmative. As a lapsed Protestant, he probably did not want to be accused of anything like spiritualism and religious exaltation. But our ecological awareness might cause us to reconsider this question and ponder the spiritual implications of Mead's social cosmology.

Bibliography

Writings of George Herbert Mead

Philosophy of the Present. 1932. Chicago: University of Chicago Press.
Mind, Self, and Society. 1934. Chicago: University of Chicago Press.
Movements of Thought in the Nineteenth Century. 1936. Chicago: University of Chicago Press.
The Philosophy of the Act. 1938. Chicago: University of Chicago Press.
George Herbert Mead on Social Psychology (edited by Anselm Strauss). 1956. Chicago: University of Chicago Press.
Selected Writings: George Herbert Mead (edited by A. J. Reck). 1964. New York: Bobbs-Merrill.

The Individual and the Social Self. Unpublished Work of George Herbert Mead (edited by David L. Miller). 1982. Chicago: University of Chicago Press.

Further reading

Aboulafia, Mitchell (1986) *The Mediating Self: Mead, Sartre, and Self-determination.* New Haven, CT: Yale University Press.

Aboulafia, Mitchell (1991) *Philosophy, Social Theory, and the Thought of George Herbert Mead.* Albany: State University of New York Press.

Baldwin, James M. (1897) *Social and Ethical Interpretation in Mental Development.* New York: Macmillan.

Baldwin, John (1986) *George Herbert Mead: a Unifying Theory of Sociology.* Beverly Hills, CA: Sage Publications.

Barry, Robert M. (1968) A Man and a City: George Herbert Mead in Chicago. In M. Novak (ed.), *American Philosophy and the Future: Essays for the New Generation.* New York: Charles Scribner's Sons, pp. 173–92.

Dewey, John (1916) *Essays in Experimental Logic.* New York: Dover.

Dewey, John (1934) *Art and Experience.* New York: G. P. Putnam's Sons (1958).

Dewey, John (1969–72) *John Dewey: the Early Works, volumes 1–5.* Carbondale: Southern Illinois University Press.

Dewey, John (1986) Pragmatism and Social Interactionism. *American Sociological Review,* 51, 9–29.

Diner, S. J. (1980) *A City and Its Universities: Public Policy in Chicago, 1892–1919.* Chapel Hill: University of North Carolina Press.

Habermas, Jürgen (1981) *The Theory of Communicative Action. Volume 1, Reason and the Realization of Society.* Boston: Beacon Press (1984).

Hegel, G. W. F. (1967) *The Phenomenology of Mind.* New York: Harper and Row (1967).

James, William (1890) *Principles of Philosophy.* New York: Dover.

James, William (1909) *Essays in Radical Empiricism and Pluralistic Universe.* Gloucester: David McKay (1967).

James, William (1909) *The Meaning of Truth.* Ann Arbor: University of Michigan Press (1970).

Joas, Hans (1985) *G. H. Mead: a Contemporary Reexamination of His Thought.* Cambridge: Polity Press.

Kant, Immanuel (1804) *What Real Progress Has Metaphysics Made in Germany since the Time of Leibniz and Wolf.* New York: Abaris Books Inc. (1983).

Kant, Immanuel (1790) *Critique of Judgment.* New York: Bobbs-Merrill (1951).

Marx, Karl (1844) *The Economic and Philosophic Manuscripts of 1844.* New York: International (1964).

Miller, David L. (1973) *George Herbert Mead: Self, Language and the World.* Austin: University of Texas Press.

Natanson, Maurice (1956) *The Social Dynamics of George H. Mead.* Washington, DC: Public Affairs Press.

Peirce, Charles (1976) *The New Elements of Mathematics.* Atlantic Highlands, NJ: Humanities Press.

Royce, Josiah (1894) The External World and the Social Consciousness. *Philosophical Review,* 3, 513–45.

Royce, Josiah (1895) Self-consciousness, Social Consciousness, and Nature. *Philosophical Review,* 4, 465–85.

Royce, Josiah (1919) *Lectures on Modern Idealism*. New Haven, CT: Yale University Press.

Shalin, Dmitri N. (1984) The Romantic Antecedents of Meadian Social Psychology. *Symbolic Interaction*, 7, 43–65.

Shalin, Dmitri N. (1986a) Pragmatism and Social Interactionism. *American Sociological Review*, 51, 9–29.

Shalin, Dmitri N. (1986b) Romanticism and the Rise of Sociological Hermeneutics. *Social Research*, 53, 77–123.

Shalin, Dmitri N. (1988) Mead, Socialism, and the Progressive Agenda. *American Journal of Sociology*, 93, 913–51.

Simmel, Georg (1908) *George Simmel on Individuality and Social Forms*, edited by D. N. Levine. Chicago: University of Chicago Press (1971).

Simmel, Georg (1950) *The Sociology of Georg Simmel*, translated and edited by K. Wolff. New York: Free Press.

Weber, Max (1926) *From Max Weber: Essays in Sociology*. New York: Oxford University Press (1946).

10

W. E. B. Du Bois

Charles Lemert

I once had dinner alone in a hotel restaurant in provincial South Korea. After ordering, I left the dining room for a moment. Upon returning, I thought it necessary to explain that I had already been seated. Before I could, the *maître de* said, "Your meal is waiting for you, sir." How could he have known who I was amid so many in a very large restaurant? It took a while before I figured it out. The answer, of course, was that I was the one and only white person in the place. I was easy to spot, perhaps even interesting to follow, as I moved irregularly in violation of local prejudices.

When, just about a century ago, W. E. B. Du Bois wrote so memorably of the color line, he meant to evoke experiences of this kind, though ones very different in their occurrence and meaning. On my side of the color line, such a prejudice is a curiosity. On the side Du Bois had in mind, it is the fundamental fact of life. This is why Du Bois began his most famous book, *The Souls of Black Folk* (1903), as he did:

> Herein lie buried many things which if read with patience may show the strange meaning of being black here at the dawning of the Twentieth Century. This meaning is not without interest to you, Gentle Reader, for the problem of the Twentieth Century is the problem of the color line. I pray you, then, receive my little book in all charity, studying my words with me, forgiving mistake and foible for sake of the faith and passion that is within me, seeking the grain of truth hidden there. (Du Bois, 1903, p. xxxi)

Du Bois wrote in a voice attuned to his purpose. Whites were principal among the gentle readers to whom he had addressed his book, so lovingly composed, but far from gentle in its adventures across the color line. A few paragraphs beyond, he left no doubt which side he was on. "Need I add that I who speak here am bone of the bone and flesh of the flesh of them that live within the Veil?" (p. xxxi). He may have supposed that this coming out was required by the book's declaration of purpose: "Leaving, then, the white world, I have stepped within the Veil, raising it that you may view faintly its deeper recess" (p. xxxi).

Du Bois was thirty-five years old when *The Souls of Black Folk* astonished the world. His education at Fisk, Harvard, and Berlin was behind him. His Harvard doctoral thesis had created a stir of recognition among historians. His now classic urban ethnography, *The Philadelphia Negro* (1899), had also been well received. Du Bois had, thus, given public notice of his intention to write the scientific record of the Negro community in America. At the end of the nineteenth century, most black Americans had been born to mothers or fathers who had been slaves. In those few years of emancipation, other leaders of the race had begun to set the record straight. But none was so supremely qualified as Du Bois to make the facts known. He was, then and ever, the sociologist using science in the service of his politics.

But he was much more than an engaged social scientist. Through the better part of the twentieth century, Du Bois was never far from the center of the politics that shaped the history of the American Negro. In 1998, thirty-five years after Du Bois's death in 1963, Julian Bond was elected chairman of the board of the National Association for the Advancement of Colored People (NAACP). As he took over the leadership of the organization Du Bois helped to found in 1909, Bond recalled a family photograph showing him as a small boy holding the hand of the great man: "I think for people of my age and generation, this was a normal experience – not to have Du Bois in your home, but to have his name in your home, to know about him in your home, to have grown up in this movement. This was table conversation for us" (*The New York Times*, February 28, 1998, p. A1). In the years after its publication in 1903, *Souls* brought Du Bois's name into the homes of black people across the world. He passed quickly beyond mere fame to the higher status Bond describes. For many, he became an icon of racial possibility. There had been moral leaders, poets, race men, political organizers, and intellectuals before him. But no one before had so perfectly combined all these qualities.

For better or worse, Du Bois was well aware of his moral position among American Negroes (the name he fought to dignify by the capital N). He was, perhaps, too insistent upon his moral position. He identified himself with the history of his race by the subtitle he chose for one of four memoirs, *Dusk of Dawn: an Essay toward an Autobiography of a Race Concept* (1940). Today Du Bois is honored as much by criticism of his shortcomings (notably, Reed, 1997; Carby, 1998) as by praise of his genius. In retrospect, it seems odd that anyone could be put forth, or put himself forth, as the embodiment of a people's hopes. That the idea was once entirely reasonable, and is still plausible to many, is measure of the man's stature and accomplishments.

Du Bois must be on the shortlist of men and women of the twentieth century whose influence spread without ceasing as the many years of their lives passed by. Picasso and Borges might head such a list. Joyce just misses. He died relatively young, as did Franklin Roosevelt and Babe Ruth. The list is not long.

Du Bois lived long, and worked hard. He was more famous at the end of life in 1963 than he was at the century's start. In the first decade of the century, Du Bois defied Booker T. Washington's concessions to white power. In the second decade, he became the NAACP's principal spokesman. In the 1920s, he was a leader of the Harlem Renaissance. In the 1930s, he wrote *Black Reconstruction*, still another classic work of scholarship. In the 1940s, after forty years' work in the Pan-African movement, he was recognized as the spiritual leader of blacks the world over. In the 1950s, he defied the American government's indictment of communist conspiracy. In the early 1960s, he traveled the world, quit America altogether, and settled in Ghana to begin work on his life's dream of an *Encyclopedia Africana*. He was 95 when he died, still working. He died, as icons often do, at precisely the right moment – on the eve of the 1963 March on Washington. From the death of Frederick Douglass in 1895 to Martin Luther King Jr's coronation the day after Du Bois's death, no other person of African descent was as conspicuous in the worldwide work of contesting the color line.

Du Bois may well have been a genius. But his accomplishments were born of his work ethic. Most days, for nearly eighty years, Du Bois began his work precisely on schedule at seven-thirty in the morning. Each hour, thereafter, was parsed for a specific task until bed around ten at night. He attributed his longevity to moderation in food and drink, daily exercise, and eight full hours of sleep. Personal discipline was the means to his many accomplishments. He wrote twenty-three books of fiction and nonfiction, of which many endure – three as classics. His articles, essays, and letters are too many to count. Still, his literary work never interfered with his politics. He founded the Niagara Movement, which led to the NAACP, not long after he began organizing the international Pan-African movement. He established and edited three magazines, including *Phylon* and *The Crisis*. He traveled, lectured, while always, somehow, answering his mail. In first six decades of the twentieth century, in the politics of race, there was no debate in which he did not figure.

Du Bois's genius is evident less in the bulk of his work than in its style. Though in person he could be arrogant and difficult, in writing he was refined. It takes a while for some readers of *Souls of Black Folk* to realize the full meaning of the plural *Souls*. Even today, when the famous double consciousness passage trips from every tongue, the subtlety of its underlying idea is easy to miss.

> After the Egyptian and Indian, the Greek and the Roman, the Teuton and Mongolian, the Negro is a sort of seventh son, born within the veil, and gifted with second-sight in this American world – a world which yields him no true self-consciousness, but only lets him see himself through the revelation of the other world. It is a peculiar sensation, this double-consciousness, the sense of always looking at one's self through the eyes of others, of measuring one's soul by the tape of a world that looks on in amused contempt and pity. One ever feels his twoness, – an American, a Negro; two souls, two thoughts, two unreconciled strivings; two warring ideals in one dark body, whose dogged strength alone keeps it from being torn asunder. (Du Bois, 1903, pp. 2–3)

This is no mere social psychology of the racial double bind. The American Negro is caught, yes. But by "dogged strength" he overcomes what he "ever feels." He is two at once, always unreconciled. He is, yes, at war within because of the war without. But the struggle is his strength. The "peculiar sensation of always looking at one's self by the tape of the world that looks on in amused contempt and pity" gives the American Negro the "gift of second-sight."

And there is more to this gift than meets the analytic remove of the white eye. The Veil works mysteriously – one might even say, spiritually – on the two souls beyond it, as it does on the white soul before. This is why, in beginning the book, Du Bois offered to lift the Veil for whites, while warning them that, if they go with him who is flesh of the flesh with them within, they will see what they cannot fully understand. The line and the Veil – Du Bois returned again and again to these figures. But he never allowed them to relax into analytic calm. Analysis is for the scientist that Du Bois was. But science moved just one of his souls. His spiritual being energized the other. The two souls, together, made him self-consciously who he was. The color line is the stark exterior of the American Negro's experience. Though a figure of speech, the color line remains an analytic tool, a category serving to divide, classify, and segregate. By contrast, the Veil lends moral uncertainty to the analytic expression. In the early pages of *Souls* the two figures of speech appear side-by-side as if to allow the Veil to unsettle the analytic police work of the color line. From behind the Veil, the Negro ridicules the white world that "looks on in amused contempt and pity" – those, that is, who deploy their pitiful powers to measure the souls of others. The measure taken is nothing beyond its cruel effects, for which, ironically, whites are disadvantaged. They suffer in ignorance. Their color line segregates the terrifying object of white desire. But the line they draw turns out to be a Veil with the reciprocal effect of imposing the blindness upon which their civilization depends. In attempting to cover their eyes, whites are doubly crippled. They are mute as well as blind, even though, everyone knows, we talk all the time about that which we do not wish to see. Whether sexual or economic, white consciousness in the late nineteenth century was wide awake to the facts of life. Burgeoning industrial America could not live without the Negro's laboring powers – powers that exceed field and forge, thus locking imposer and imposed in a darkness only one understood. Thus, the unspeakable corollary to the Negro's gift of second-sight – that moral consciousness encouraged by the secreting Veil – is the apartheid that organizes the singular soul of white folk.

Du Bois, the scientist, respected the mysteries of race. In 1940, nearly forty years after *Souls*, Du Bois wrote in *The Dusk of Dawn* of the white world. As he had done in *Souls*, he wrote here of the mysteries of the color line:

> With the best will the factual outline of a life misses the essence of its spirit. Thus in my life the chief fact has been race – not so much scientific race, as that deep conviction of myriads of men that congenital differences among the main masses of human beings absolutely condition the individual destiny of every member of a group. (Du Bois, 1940, p. 139)

The doubling of consciousness works both ways – to obverse but comparable effect. In weakening the exterior, it strengthens the interior life of black folk. In protecting the fragile culture of white folks, it weakens their souls. On both sides, the Veil determines the destiny of all.

THE PERSON AND THE CONTEXT

More than any of the great social thinkers who were on stage as the nineteenth century ended, Du Bois was a mover in the global politics of his days. As prominent as Durkheim was to Third Republic French politics, or Weber to late Weimar Germany, or Gilman to American socialism – none so stirred the history of his times as did Du Bois. Few of the others even survived the First World War, which, in its way, killed Durkheim and Weber, while sending Gilman into retirement. Only Freud and Du Bois among this remarkable group survived to expand their work after the Great War.

The First World War changed everything for the hopeful bourgeois peoples who prevailed near the beginning of the twentieth century. In *All Quiet on the Western Front*, the greatest of all novels about that war, Erich Maria Remarque puts these words into the mouth of the generation that had suffered through it: "We will become superfluous even to ourselves, we will grow older, a few will adapt themselves, some others will merely submit, and most will be bewildered; – the years will pass by and in the end we shall fall into ruin." And so, for many, it was. It would be a good quarter century before calm would settle in the West, then only if one ignores the wars throughout its decolonizing empire – Africa, Korea, Vietnam, and Afghanistan; then Africa again and still. Raymond Mon was not far wrong. The twentieth was the "century of total war." Among the rising middle classes, especially in America, the last glimmers of nineteenth-century optimism faded in the shadows. Not even the short run of the 1920s with its white flappers and New Black renaissance in the urban North could revive the simple innocence that had prevailed before the Great War.

Only those social thinkers attuned to the darker, less conscious forces of social evil were able to flourish after the war. Freud and Du Bois were chief among these few – Freud because he believed in the deeper drive toward evil; Du Bois because he knew just how the destiny of the American Negro was necessarily at odds with that of white folk. He knew very well that this war meant opportunity for blacks. It meant the end of the hordes of European immigrant workers coming to serve American industry, which nudged ajar the door of economic opportunity to blacks. Thus began the great wave of migrations to the industrial North. Thereafter, Negro politics and culture were decisively more urban and Northern than rural and Southern. Though the feudal relations of racial production would remain in force in the South until the 1960s, the urban and industrial migrations brought with them a new cultural awareness that would eventually destroy the racial caste system from which so many had fled. For one, the renaissances in South Side Chicago and Harlem, in particular, marked the coming out of black culture into the consciousness of whites. For another, they meant that blacks came to understand their side of the Veil better, and differently. Du Bois's own struggle with these social forces approximated what they meant to the millions who had already come to look to him for guidance.

In 1915, after the Great War had begun, but before the United States had entered it, W. E. B. Du Bois's "leadership position towered above all" (Lewis, 1993, p. 513). In *Souls*, Du Bois had begun the move toward leadership with an essay, "Of Mr. Booker T. Washington and Others," a revision of an earlier, shorter comment on the Principal of the Tuskegee Institute and the leading race man at the turn of the century. The essay was respectful but firm. Du Bois knew what he was doing by placing it third among the essays in *Souls*. Though his words would not immediately provoke his public rivalry with Washington, the battle began at that moment. The struggle between Du Bois and Washington in the first decade of the twentieth century was, in effect, the beginning of the transformation of a racial politics rooted in the traditions of the feudal South into a politics of the urban and urbane North.

Washington had been born in slavery and educated at the all-Negro Hampton Institute. He directed Tuskegee as the institutional emblem of his famous compromise with white power. Du Bois had been born free in the North and went to Harvard. He became the intellectual emblem of those devoted to the unique moral and cultural contributions of the Negro to American society. The rivalry between Washington and Du Bois is often viewed as one over principles. Indeed it was. But there would have been no philosophical differences had there not been, deeper still, economic realities by which the color line took on its urgency. Hence, the First World War changed things for whites in one way; for blacks in another. Washington's politics were rooted in the convenience of the whites who profited from the feudal traditions of the South. Du Bois's rose on the surge of industrialization in which feudal domination was refracted in the still cruel, but more rational, capitalist world system. Washington dominated Negro politics at the end of the nineteenth century by force of his ability to control. He was as adroit at pulling the strings of black submission as Du Bois was at inspiring resistance to oppression. This difference was Washington's weak hand when faced with Du Bois's more spiritual challenges – and the Great War was the political and economic divide between the two.

To understand the importance of the war to Du Bois's leadership after 1915, one must compare his situation to the conditions of Washington's leadership some twenty years before. Booker T. Washington rose to prominence on the wings of Northern white relief at his 1895 Atlanta Compromise: "that in all things purely social we can be as separate as the fingers, yet one as the hand in all things essential to our mutual progress." Washington's memorable figure of the hand and fingers was for whites balm spread upon the sores of racial trouble. The year after, in 1896, *Plessy* v. *Ferguson* gave legal sanction to the restoration of racial apartheid in the American South. Washington's compromise was a double assurance to whites who feared the freedoms that permitted the social contact attendant upon the practical necessities of their economic contract with black labor. Washington's Tuskegee Institute was flush with white philanthropic payback for the Principal's single-minded devotion to the industrial education of blacks.

In "Of Mr. Booker T. Washington and Others," Du Bois summarized the political and social effects of Washington's 1895 speech: "It startled the nation to hear a Negro advocating such a programme after many decades of bitter complaint; it startled and won the applause of the South, it interested and won the admiration of the North; and after a confused murmur of protest, it silenced if it did not convert the Negroes themselves" (Du Bois, 1903, p. 31). Then, on the point of his differences with Washington, Du Bois continued:

> Mr. Washington distinctly asks that black people give up, at least for the present, three things,–
>
>   First, political power,
>   Second, insistence on civil rights,
>   Third, higher education of Negro youth,–
>
> And concentrate all their energies on industrial education, and accumulation of wealth, and the conciliation of the South. The policy has been courageously and insistently advocated for over fifteen years, and has been triumphant for perhaps ten years. As a result of this tender palm-branch, what has been the return? In these years, there have occurred:
>
>   1. The disfranchisement of the Negro.
>   2. The legal creation of a distinct status of civil inferiority for the Negro.
>   3. The steady withdrawal of aid from institutions for the higher training of the Negro. (Du Bois, 1903, p. 37)

Du Bois was still young when he wrote these words, green to the world of racial politics. Though respectful, he was tough – tough enough to reveal the lie in oversimplifying his doctrine of the talented tenth. Du Bois's commitment to higher education was far more than an elitist ideology of the supremacy of culture over economics. Though it is true that Du Bois felt that the poor must be led by the educated, it is not true that his politics were a mere culturalist reflex to Washington's crude economism.

When it came to racial politics Du Bois understood very well that the color line is always drawn in the factual sands of civil rights, political power, and false economic hopes. He spoke to the terrible misery visited upon the black poor, rejected forever from real economic progress – and rejected as much by Washington's smarmy compromise as by the feudal lords of Jim Crow. That he had staked his position in the cultural politics of racial difference (as Cornel West has put it) does not mean Du Bois had no feel for economic or political justice. Adolph Reed (1997) may think that culture is the realm of elite compromise. But those who share his tiresome view of politics may never have contemplated the contradiction between Du Bois and Washington. The latter was the proponent of the real politics of compromise and economic uplift, and it was Washington who lived the life of luxury as the private cars of Northern philanthropists eased onto the private rail link that led to his mansion at Tuskegee. It was Du Bois, the Northern freeman, who grew up poor (as had Washington); and Du Bois who remained, if not poor, always on the margins of economic security. He lived with the poor, in practice as in the imagination, in a way that the Washington of the

Atlanta Compromise did not. Du Bois's talented tenth doctrine, so often the object of orthodox sneer, was a doctrine of cultural politics founded in fine awareness of the suffering brought down by the political economy of Negro life.

It is true that Booker T. Washington had been born of slavery and that his labor on behalf of poor Negroes in the South was based on his own firm principles. To have built Tuskegee, as he did, is to set one's hands to the hard hewn tools of field and factory. And it is also true that Du Bois, though he never enjoyed the resplendent comforts of Washington's later years, took advantage of a privileged education at Harvard and Berlin. His cultural advantage, more than once, gained him the generosity of white friends who protected him in trouble and sent him to travel abroad. Still, Du Bois never compromised. He died in Ghana and is buried alongside the continuing economic misery of sub-Saharan Africa. The one, Washington, aligned himself with the poor in a racial politics that served the interests of the white and well off. The other, Du Bois, walked and talked with the well off; yet, in the end, it was his photograph that hung in the homes of the poorest blacks. Du Bois earned the respect of the poor because he spoke, and wrote, with feeling for their condition. In his personal style, he could indeed be a mannered snob. But his words, and actions, rang with feeling for the poor with whom he took his stand.

Du Bois's feeling for the poorest of those within the Veil was born less of his own childhood poverty than of the accident of years he spent in adolescence in Tennessee. At the end of high school in 1884, Du Bois had hoped to go straight to Harvard. But for a number of reasons, not excluding race, Du Bois was not admitted on first application. So, in 1885, he began three years of study in the South, at Fisk University in Nashville. Then, for the first time, he experienced life lived fully within the Veil:

> Consider how miraculous it all was to a boy of seventeen, just escaped from a narrow valley: I will and lo! my people come dancing about me, – riotous in color, gay in laughter, full of sympathy, need and pleading; darkly delicious girls – 'colored girls' – sat beside me and actually talked to me while I gazed in tongue-tied silence or babbled in boastful dreams. (Du Bois, 1920, p. 14)

This is how Du Bois remembered those adolescent pleasures many years later. His feelings for those youthful years in black Nashville were undiminished when, even later, he was in his nineties: "Into this world I leapt with enthusiasm. A new loyalty and allegiance replaced my Americanism: hence forward I was a Negro" (Du Bois, 1968, p. 108). To the end of life, he held the Tennessee years as the source of his racial pride – and as the antidote to the first rude, boyhood shock of racial difference.

More important even than the Negro world of Fisk and Nashville was a small village in the far eastern mountains of Tennessee where Du Bois spent the summers of 1886 and 1887 teaching school among the poorest of rural black folk. In his *Autobiography*, written some seventy years after those two college summers, he wrote of this impossibly remote village as though it were still his own:

I have called my community a world, and so its isolation made it. There was among us a but half-awakened common consciousness, sprung from common joy and grief, at burial, birth or wedding; from a common hardship in poverty, poor land and low wages; and, above all, from the sight of the Veil that hung between us and Opportunity. (Du Bois, 1968, p. 120)

These are virtually the same words he had used when he first wrote of this village in *Souls* (p. 48). When he repeated them at the end of life, Du Bois had long been assured of his place in the wider world. The repetition was, thus, a way of giving account of his life's work – a way of saying that, though he had traveled the globe, his life remained in community with the most poor and forgotten.

From those summer days of college in 1886 and 1887, Alexandria, Tennessee, was his spiritual community. Thereafter, Du Bois kept Alexandria, far forgotten by the world, dear among his most special memories of youth. As other stories of the early years faded, those of this one place seemed as special to him at the end of life as at the beginning. Alexandria was, perhaps, an antidote for the lingering poison from his earlier childhood in Massachusetts. Though Great Barrington gave him his start, and was relatively free of racial ugliness, it was also where the sad losses of his life returned. Great Barrington is where his mother endured the miseries of poverty, abandonment, and early death. There, too, he had laid to rest his dear son, Burghardt, dead in infancy because the white hospitals of Atlanta refused him treatment.

But, most of all, this northern, free village was where a white girl's rude dismissal of his party card first taught him the truth of racial differences. It was there, or so he says at the beginning of *Souls* (p. 2), "in the early days of rollicking boyhood that the revelation first bursts upon one, all in a day, as it were." He had done nothing more than join the fun and games of mixed company, when his ease with white children was broken by "one girl, a tall newcomer" unacquainted with local customs. "Then it dawned upon me with a certain suddenness that I was different from the others; or like, mayhap, in heart and life and longing, but shut out from their world by a vast veil" (p. 2). From that moment in childhood, he resolved to live, as he said, "beyond" the Veil. He disdained that little white girl's rejection, just as much as he relished the late adolescent reverie of the "darkly delicious girls" of Nashville.

Why the two types of girls: one white and removed; the others darkly delicious? Hazel Carby (1998, chapter 1) somewhat plausibly suggests that Du Bois may have been like other race men in imagining his adult masculinity as beyond, not just the Veil, but even the frivolity of girlish adolescence. If so, his fully adult recollection of the pleasures of the racial community (written more than thirty years after the first days in Nashville) was also a completely serious adult meditation on the origins of his life work. In his poetic imagination, the two types of girl were, assuredly, figures of the mysterious sexual play at work in racial differences. They were nameless. But a third would appear, fully named and human, as the one most dear to his understanding of the political situation.

The early chapters of *Souls* are, in effect, the manifesto of Du Bois's racial politics. Though *Souls* is a collection of essays, many previously published, they

are ordered with purpose. The first four chapters, especially, declare the foundational principles of his vocation. In the first chapter, "Of Our Spiritual Strivings," he announces the double consciousness principle, stated lyrically against
the historical fugue of Negro life in America. In the second, "Of the Dawn of
Freedom," he scores the facts of life for the Negro American from the hope of
Emancipation in 1865, through the rise of Reconstruction and the Freedman's
Bureau, and their abandonment in the 1870s, to the beginnings of Jim Crow. In
the third chapter, "Of Mr. Booker T. Washington and Others," he joins the
philosophical to the political, against the facts of the previous chapter. His
argument with Washington was not a matter of personal preference but of
historical necessity. Then comes the story of his community. In the fourth
chapter, "On the Meaning of Progress," Du Bois completes his manifesto. His
criticism of Washington is framed by the historical record – the failure of
Reconstruction, and the restoration apartheid in the South – by, as he puts it
(p. 49), "the barriers of caste" which Washington had so easily disregarded. Here
is Du Bois resetting the clock of racial history in America. Washington's compromise would never do because the backward conditions of Negro life are
insufficient by standards ever more rigorous than even those of the feudal South.

Of these opening chapters of *Souls*, none is more poignant, and important,
than the fourth. "Of the Meaning of Progress" is surely one of Du Bois's most
inventive literary moments. Here he means to call into question the most
cherished value of the very Western culture that formed the one of his two
souls. Here is the "beyond" of the Veil addressed to his gentle white readers.
Here is one of his most elegant theoretical claims posed, not as insistence, but in
the surprise of simple stories told of his relationship to poor, isolated Alexandria.

"Of the Meaning of Progress" is irony that sneaks upon the reader. Here, he
makes no mention of the easy frivolity of Fisk and Nashville. Du Bois leaps
directly to the rural hills where he tells the story of Josie Dowell, the third of the
figurative girls in his early life. When he first meets Josie, she is still a child, but
"the center of the family: always busy at service, or at home, or berry picking; a
little nervous and inclined to scold, like her mother, yet faithful, too, like her
father" (p. 45). At first, Josie might seem to be poor kin to the darkly delicious
girls he knew in Nashville – perhaps the more bracing antidote to the rejecting
white girl of Great Barrington. Yet Du Bois switches the figure of speech. "She
had about her a certain fineness, the shadow of an unconscious moral heroism
that would willingly give all of life to make life broader, deeper, and fuller for her
and hers" (p. 45). Josie, the nervous scold, is in fact the "shadow" of moral
heroism. She is double consciousness. She, and her family, "knew that it was a
hard thing to dig a living out of a rocky side-hill" (p. 45). Their hardship
"awakened common consciousness [of] the Veil that hung between us and
Opportunity" (p. 48).

The story breaks off, abruptly. Then it is picked up again, ten years later when
Du Bois returns to Alexandria. The Fisk years are long past. Harvard and Berlin
are too. His life's work has begun. Every possibility lies ahead. He visits his
community, his spiritual home where the gentle reader might reasonably expect
some good word of Josie's progress in life. But "Josie was dead, and the gray-

haired mother said simply, 'We've had a heap of trouble since you've been away'" (p. 49). Like Josie, his emblem of the Veil's terrible effects, the community Du Bois had taken as his own has disappeared. "My log schoolhouse was gone. In its place stood Progress; and Progress, I understand, is necessarily ugly" (p. 50). The third figurative girl of his childhood had become the measure of liberal culture. But was she, as Carby (1998, p. 20) proposes, the sign of its failure – that is, a play on feminine frailty? Or, was she the beyond in which lay the uncertain hope for racial progress? Carby is too sure of herself. It seems more probable that Du Bois left both possibilities open to the work that lay ahead.

In those ten years much had come to pass. The return visit to Alexandria may have been as early as 1896, the year after Washington's Atlanta Compromise and the year of *Plessy* v. *Ferguson*. If it was 1896, then it was also the year when Du Bois was formulating his theory of the double consciousness (which was first published in 1897). He had returned to "his" community when his own spiritual striving hung in the balance between the formidable possibilities gained by the highest education the world could offer *and* his moral commitment to those whose meager training was the condition of their suffering. The passage of the return was more, much more than mere nostalgia for the terrible intrusion of Progress upon his community. As the coming urban culture advanced on the hillsides from which Josie's family dug out a living, Du Bois turned away from the feelings for those he had lost. He felt sorrow at Josie's death and Alexandria's passing. But he did not give in to sentiment. He asked instead the hard question of the very idea of Progress that lay at the heart of the European civilization that so enriched his other soul.

> My journey was done, and behind me lay hill and dale, and Life and Death. How shall man measure Progress there where the dark-faced Josie lies? How many heartfuls of sorrow shall balance a bushel of wheat? How hard a thing is life to the lowly, and yet how human and real! *And all this life and love and strife and failure, –is it the twilight of the nightfall or the flush of some faint-dawning day?*
>
> Thus sadly musing, I rode to Nashville in the Jim Crow car. (p. 52, emphasis added)

The train from the Cumberland Plateau down to Nashville heads West. In the late afternoon, riders may face the setting sun. Yet, as anyone who has lived in the humid summer heat of the American South knows, the afternoon light can be a deception and a relief. The midday heat lingers, but the thick air sometimes stirs. The light can change tone, breaking bright through the branches. Hence the illusion of which Du Bois wrote. The light could just as well appear to be a dawning as a setting. "Is it," indeed, "the twilight of nightfall or the flush of some faint-dawning day?" The question rose on the beginning of a new century, double-sided and unsure like all else for those then within the Veil. What, then, is the meaning of liberal Progress when measured against the death of Josie – against the passing of the "shadow of moral heroism?"

Nearly forty years later, in the *Dusk of Dawn* (1940), Du Bois would return to this image of the uncertain meaning of the shadows. In the intervening four decades after his sad ride west in the Jim Crow car, Du Bois himself had traveled east to Atlanta, then to New York City, then again to Atlanta, and Europe, and Africa. In 1940 the light, while dusky still, promised a new day. The dusk had become a dawn.

> I have essayed in a half-century three sets of thought centering around the hurts and hesitancies that hem the black man in America. The first of these, "Souls of Black Folk," written thirty-seven years ago, was a cry at midnight thick within the veil, when none rightly knew the coming day. The second, "Darkwater," now twenty years old, was an exposition and militant challenge, defiant with dogged hope. This the third book started to record dimly but consciously that subtle sense of coming day which one feels of early mornings when mist and murk hang low. (Du Bois, 1940, p. xxiv)

Why the switch from dusk to dawn? He wrote in 1940 as the cloud of another war hung over the world, a world still suffering the after-effects of the Great Depression. How could that have been a coming day? Again, the answer lies in the differential consequences of the First World War, which dashed the progressive innocence of whites, while opening – however, slightly – industrial opportunity in the north to blacks.

In 1903, when Du Bois could not yet see the new day, the American Negro suffered the still feudal South and economic margins of the North. Booker T. Washington was the man in charge. Jobs in the industrial North belonged to white immigrants from Europe. In 1914, a million and a quarter Europeans came to America; by 1917, barely a hundred thousand came (Lewis, 1979, p. 21). In that necessary lapse arose an economic opportunity for millions of blacks in America – for, that is, the men and women who would have been the generation of Josie's unborn children. Though it would be years more until Franklin Roosevelt would begin truly to desegregate war mobilization industries during the Second World War, jobs were open to a whole generation as never before. Southern blacks rode the Jim Crows north to work in Chicago, Cincinnati, New York, Philadelphia. Booker T. Washington would die in the first full year of the great migration. His Tuskegee home lay in the lowland just south of the mountains. Tuskegee draws its water from the Tennessee hills of Josie's village as, no doubt, it drew its students from those few of Josie's generation who escaped the hills for the faint promise of a better life at skilled labor. Tuskegee is not far from Montgomery, Alabama, where, on a cold December day forty years after Mr Washington's death, Rosa Parks would lead Martin Luther King Jr, a still very young son of Atlanta's talented tenth, back from his northern education into the rural South of the Civil Rights Movement.

The War of 1914 opened the way for Du Bois and those of his cultured advantages to measure both the facts and the spiritual truths of brothers and sisters like Josie. The valued life would be slow in coming, impossibly far off even today for millions, but the spiritual striving of which Du Bois wrote in 1903 would come to good effect. The color line would ride north on the migrations. When, in the first words of Souls, he proclaimed it the problem of the twentieth century, Du Bois was looking far ahead beyond the misery of Josie's sad death, beyond the dusk of his youth, beyond the regional effects of the Veil. He looked to the possible dawn, for him and millions of others – for those especially who gathered in Washington the day after his death in 1963 to dream, not just of interracial hand holding, but of the recognition that the color line was structured deep in the nation, and the world, as a whole. Josie, for him, was not so much a local failure as the emblem of the realities and the promises known only to those with the gift of second sight.

THE PERSON AND HIS IDEAS

All great thinkers come to their ideas in relation to those who went before. Weber makes no sense without Kant, nor Marx without Hegel, nor Durkheim without Montesquieu, nor Gilman without Bellamy. Yet each is more than the sum of the borrowings. So it is with Du Bois – with one difference. He was, if not superior to his contemporaries, much more *sui generis*. He owed his debts, to be sure. But somehow, Du Bois always (perhaps even perversely on occasion) turned his borrowings to his own purposes.

When on rare occasion Du Bois encountered an intellectual peer at close hand, as he did Max Weber in the summer of 1904, it was the other who took the intellectual initiative. The following March, Weber wrote Du Bois, praising *Souls*, offering to take care of a German translation, and seeking his advice (Weber to Du Bois, letter of 30 March 1905, in Du Bois, 1973, pp. 106–7). Du Bois, it seems, did not pursue the translation invitation, just as he seldom acknowledged the influence Weber must have had on him since his student days in Germany. This surely was in part due to Du Bois's isolation and his relative inability to broker comparable deals for those better established in the white world. But it was also his nature to think as he acted – in terms he alone would fashion.

Du Bois's three greatest works all bear the stamp of a thinker who turned the relative isolation of his working conditions to his advantage. His *Philadelphia Negro*, the first great work of American urban ethnography, is often said to be a methodological copy of Charles Booth's earlier classic, *Life and Labour of the People of London* (1889–91). But David Levering Lewis, reading behind the empirical mass of the work, observes (Lewis, 1993, p. 190) that Du Bois thoroughly and remarkably "refined and applied what he borrowed." Hence, Du Bois's most distinctive theoretical conviction: that race never stands alone, apart from the economic realities. *The Philadelphia Negro* appeared fours years before *Souls*, which is itself the work of a man who, apart from the summers in Tennessee, had spent more than a year living among the poor he interviewed in Philadelphia's all black Seventh Ward.

Even today some have trouble seeing what Du Bois saw pretty much on his own. Race makes little sense apart from class. Though, as time went by, Du Bois reformulated this thinking, race for him was always in part a class effect. Later in life, well after the First World War had cleansed nearly everyone of unfettered faith in Progress, he became more the Marxist. To some, *Black Reconstruction* (1935) might appear to be an exercise in class analysis. It was, to be sure, but it was more than that. *Black Reconstruction* endures because no other work of its day, and not many since, examines the facts of economic history in terms of the relations of *racial* production (Roediger, 1991, pp. 11–13).

Not only was he his own man in the way he thought, but Du Bois adapted his thinking to the changing facts of racial politics. At no other point is this more evident than, as always, in the unusual use to which he put his most memorable concept. Where did he get the double consciousness idea at the start of *Souls*? To think about Du Bois is, eventually, to consider this question, for which there is a long list of likely sources: Goethe, Emerson, Herder, Sojourner Truth, William James (see, among others, Gates, 1989, pp. xviii–xxii; Rampersad, 1990, pp. 74–5; Early, 1993, pp. xvii–xxii; Lewis, 1993, pp. 282–3; Lemert, 1994, p. 389; Zamir, 1995). All are possible. Yet, in the end, it hardly makes a difference which might have been uppermost in Du Bois's mind. He thought as few others did, turning everything to his own ends.

Double consciousness is at once borrowed and invented to contain no fewer than three themes at once. As Paul Gilroy rather awkwardly puts it:

> Double consciousness emerges from the unhappy symbiosis between three modes of thinking, being, and seeing. The first is racially particularistic, the second nationalistic in that it derives from the nation state in which the ex-slaves but not-yet-citizens find themselves, rather than from their aspiration towards a nation state of their own. The third is diasporic or hemispheric, sometimes global and occasionally univeralistic. This trio was woven into some unlikely but exquisite patterns in Du Bois's thinking. Things become still more complicated because he self-consciously incorporated his own journeying both inside and outside the veiled world of black America into a narrative structure of the text and the political and cultural critique of the West which it constructed through an extended survey of the post-Civil War history of the American South. (Gilroy, 1993, p. 127)

Du Bois would have sooner not had Gilroy's compliment, with all its unforgiving jargon, had it not been for its basic truth. His thinking was "unlikely but exquisite" – and it was because Du Bois thought from the three points of view at once.

Race, nation, and Africa were always on his mind, from the earliest days. If Africa was not so explicit in the better known early writings, it was there in his 1896 Harvard doctoral thesis on the suppression of the African slave trade (Du Bois, 1898), as it was in the meditations on Alexander Crummel and the sorrow songs at the end of *Souls*. It is all too easy to hear, in the double consciousness lyrics, nothing but the play of race and nation. But Africa too is there, behind the origins of the distinctive black soul, behind the economic hardships that gave voice to the sorrow songs.

It is a long journey, for Du Bois, from birth in 1868 in Great Barrington, Massachusetts, to death and burial in 1963 in Accra, Ghana. At his state funeral in Accra, President Kwame Nkrumah began, "We mourn the death of

Dr. William Edward Burghardt Du Bois, a great son of Africa" (Du Bois, 1970, p. 327). Just a few years before, during a world tour in the year of his ninetieth birthday, he had been celebrated in the capitals of Europe, the Soviet Union, and China. After this he quit all civil relations with the United States and went to Africa. He died a citizen of Ghana – truly a revered son of Africa. But why had he traveled so far? In the answer lies the code to his life's work, and to his social theory.

In 1920, Du Bois published his second intellectual memoir, *Darkwater*. The Great War had ended, leaving the world uncertain. He was fifty-two, and in charge of his own destiny. In the years since *Souls*, Du Bois had helped found the NAACP. He became its most famous spokesman as editor of *Crisis* magazine, which he founded. In 1914, *Crisis* had 33,000 subscribers (Lewis, 1993, p. 474) – not to mention the thousands more to whom the magazine was passed from hand to hand. The number of American Negroes who regularly read the editor's views on every important issue of the day is impossible to know. He was also much in demand as a speaker (and claims to have spoken to 18,000 "human souls" in 1913 alone). Du Bois wrote and spoke less as the scholar, more as the political actor. Mr Washington was gone. If there was a spokesman in the war years, it was Dr Du Bois – who, of course, offered the whites in charge none of the easy comforts of compromise.

But the war years were troubling to Du Bois's own early racial philosophy. By 1920 he, and his many followers, understood that the ideals of the double consciousness – "this longing to attain self-conscious manhood, to merge his double self into a better and truer self" (Du Bois, 1903, p. 3) – would have to be reconsidered. Though thousands of Negroes had joined Du Bois in supporting Woodrow Wilson in 1912, and, after 1914, millions more had served well in industrial work (and many later still in the war effort), little was returned that would promise an end to the longing for "manhood." Thus, as he would say in *Dusk of Dawn* (p. xxiv; quoted above), the memoir of 1920, *Darkwater*, was a "militant challenge, defiant with dogged hope." He took the color line ever more seriously. This is when Africa begins to figure more urgently, if not yet saliently, in Du Bois's thinking. He had long worked with Africa in mind. In 1900 he had participated prominently in the first Pan-African meetings held in Europe. By 1919, as the war was ending, and the first truly international Pan African Congress was convened, Du Bois was a leader among those seeking to unite representatives of the African diaspora. Thereafter, Du Bois thought more and more of Africa.

Gilroy (1993) is surely right to say that Du Bois continued to think from three angles at once. But, just as in *Souls* race and nation were the more prominent of his points of view, then, beginning with *Darkwater* in 1920, Africa came clear in his picture of the racial situation as his American nationalism began to fade.

What, then, is this dark world thinking? It is thinking that as wild and awful as this shameful war was, *it is nothing to compare with that fight for freedom which black and brown and yellow men must and will make unless their oppression and humiliation and insult at the hands of the White World cease. The Dark World is going to submit to its present treatment just as long as it must and not one moment longer.* (Du Bois, 1920, p. 49, original emphasis)

This defiance stands in a bitter essay, sarcastically titled "The Souls of White Folk." He is thinking of race now in relation to the colonized world, and Africa. He speaks less of the "American Negro."

Twenty years later still, in *Dusk of Dawn* (1940), the most upbeat of his first three memoirs, all is clear. His thinking has changed. America is more an object of disappointment than of hope. Where race had been joined to nation, now race was joined to class and the world. Africa had become a way of thinking about the economic misery of blacks in global perspective. Between 1920 and 1940, there were three paths, each importantly connected to the other: culture, Africa, and economics.

> After the [First World War], with most Americans, I was seeking to return to normalcy. I tried three paths, one of which represented an old ideal and ambition, the development of literature and art among Negroes through my own writing and the encouragement of others. The second path was new and had arisen out of war; and that was the development of the idea back of the Pan African Congress. The third idea was quite new, and proved in a way of greater importance in my thinking than the other two; and that was the economic rehabilitation and defense of the American Negro after the change and dislocation of war. (Du Bois, 1940, p. 268)

The defiance is more focused now. These words appear in an essay titled "Revolution."

Du Bois's first path was, of course, that of his important work in the Harlem Renaissance. As editor of *Crisis* he was able to publish Claude McKay, Langston Hughes, Jean Toomer, Countee Cullen, and Jessie Fauset, among others. Though the cultural works of the Renaissance would endure to advance the nation's debt to American Negro culture, both Harlem and *Crisis* would decline with the economic collapse of 1929. As subscriptions to *Crisis* fell below the break-even point, Du Bois lost his hold on power within the NAACP (Marable, 1986, chapters 6 and 7). By 1934, after 24 years, he was terminated from the organization he helped to found. At age 65, he returned to Atlanta University to resume a career as teacher and scholar. The year following, he published what may well be his most important work of empirical scholarship, *Black Reconstruction*, in which the theme was that Reconstruction had failed not because of the cultural unreadiness of the newly freed slaves, but because of economic realities. *Black Reconstruction* was a political economy of race relations. Du Bois's idea of culture, though European in content, was always bound politically to the cultural uplift of the American Negro (tied, that is, to his youthful nationalism). It is not surprising, therefore, that the other two of his interwar years paths converged upon each other. The turn to class and economic realities, encouraged surely by the bitter effects of depression upon his cultural work, led away from the nation to the world – and of course to Africa.

Dusk of Dawn is of course a continuing play of light against the darkness introduced in the story of Josie in *Souls*. Nowhere, however, does the figure play with such personal force as it does in his recollection, in *Dusk of Dawn*, of his first sight of Africa:

> When shall I forget the night I first set foot on African soil? I am the sixth generation in descent from forefathers who left this land. The moon was at the full and theaters of the Atlantic lay like a lake. All the long slow afternoon as the sun robed herself in her western scarlet with veils of misty cloud, I had seen Africa afar. Cape Mount – that mighty headland with its twin curves, northern sentinel of the realm of Liberia – gathered itself out of the cloud at half past three and then darkened and grew clear. On beyond flowed the dark low undulating land quaint with palm and breaking sea. The world grew black. Africa faded away, the stars stood forth curiously twisted – Orion in the zenith – the Little Bear asleep and the Southern Cross rising behind the horizon. Then afar, ahead, a lone light shone, straight at the ship's fore. Twinkling lights appear below, around, and rising shadows. "Monrovia," said the Captain. (Du Bois, 1940, pp. 117–18)

Light against the dark, from the beginning – the Veil, the blue sky above the color line, Josie's twilight, darkwater, the dusk of dawn, and now "the world grew black, . . . the twinkling lights appear below, around, and rising shadows." Here at long last is the true reversal of the figure. Here is the true dawn, found in the dusk of Africa, which after 1940 became the measure of the light, white, colonizing world.

Africa dawned for Du Bois in the setting sun of what was left of his liberal nationalism. His faith in America, always drawn in against the color line, eventually disappeared. Neither the advantages of the Great War for the American Negro nor the successes of the Harlem Renaissance were enough to overcome the brutal reality of a world economic system that had dominated since the nineteenth century. He was, perhaps, a little chagrined at his own naive hope that the system could work for good. "It was not until the twentieth century that the industrial situation called not only for understanding but action" (Du Bois, 1940, p. 289). The action had already begun. Apart from his cultural work in the 1920s, Du Bois devoted more energy to the organizational work of four Pan-African congresses: 1919 in Paris; 1921 in London, Brussels, and Paris; 1923 in London, Paris, and Lisbon; and 1927 in New York. But in 1935, *Black Reconstruction* was to be his last great work of science. His turn to action meant Africa.

"I think it was in Africa that I came more clearly to see the close connection between race and wealth" (Du Bois, 1940, p. 129). Race, nation, and Africa were, as Gilroy says, the three structural elements of his thinking – or his soul, really. But Gilroy's scheme (1993, pp. 126–7) does not account for the growing force of Du Bois's spiritual journey to Africa. He gave up on nation, because, in the experience of his life time (which had nearly spanned the three-quarters of a century since Emancipation), the nation had in effect given up on him, on his race (see Roediger, 1991, pp. 111–13). To embrace Africa required him to let go of America, which had promised what it did not deliver.

Though Marx had figured in Du Bois's later thinking, it was just as clear that Marx's own limited ability to envisage the precise global terms of class struggle would in turn limit his appeal to Du Bois. Marx understood that capitalism was a world enterprise, and he understood something about the colonial situation, but he recognized little at all about the racial foundations of the colonial system. Though others would later describe these global relations of racial production, Du Bois was one of the first of the great decolonizing thinkers. When race is considered an economic, as well as a social, thing it must be thought also as a global thing. Hence Africa in the shifting balance of Du Bois's intellectual categories. His Marxism, such as it was, was always something more. That more was not so much Afrocentric as Pan-African. He avoided all essentializing categories. He was thinking, now, of race as a global and economic problem that required action. He was, that is, already a harbinger of the decolonizing thinkers to come (see James, 1998, p. 423).

> Looking at this whole matter of the white race as it confronts the world today, what can be done to make its attitudes rational and consistent and calculated to advance the best interests of the whole world of men? The first point of attack is undoubtedly the economic. The progress of the white world must cease to rest upon the poverty and the ignorance of its own proletariat and of the colored world. (Du Bois, 1940, p. 171)

How, then, did he journey from white New England to Africa? It is plain that he traveled spiritually through Alexandria, Tennessee. "How shall we measure Progress," he asked in his youth, "there where the dark-faced Josie lies?" He had no choice, its seems, but eventually to go to Africa. His own struggle against the color line led him, as it would lead others who came after him, through the dusk of America's oddly confused brand of race-based colonialism to the world, where there where fewer moral deceptions. In Africa, a colony was just that, a colony where few could mistake the true intentions of the whites in charge. Josie came to be the measure of much more than the liberal idealism of Progress. She was, for him, the measure of the structured injustice of the world system itself. She was just that important because whatever else she meant to him in the summer of 1886, she grew, as mythic figures often do, into the archetype of racial suffering. Whatever dawn there would be would be the dawn that rose on the dark-faced Josie. Though he first wrote of Josie at about the same time he wrote *Souls*, it can be said that the famous double-consciousness ideal was already up against the deeper economic realities that would surface over the years. This is why Du Bois repeated the story of Josie so many times, even in his last years of life. She had taught him, in the deeper workings of his spiritual life, that the American Negro could not for long measure his soul "by the tape of a world that looked on in amused contempt" (Du Bois, 1903, p. 3). By the end, the hard realities of the world economy had made Africa, and the rest of the decolonizing world, the true measure of the failures of white world.

In the end, Du Bois was no longer an American Negro, any more than he was African-American except by spiritual kinship with his fathers and their fathers. He was African and socialist. He called for economic action, for a revolution in the colonial system. As ever, he expressed himself in the idiom of religion, now joined to revolutionary politics (Du Bois, 1968, p. 404):

Awake, awake, put on thy strength, O Zion; reject the meekness of missionaries
who teach neither love nor brotherhood, but emphasize the virtues of private profit
from capital, stolen from your land and labor. African awake, put on the beautiful
robes of Pan-African socialism.

You have nothing to lose but your chains!

You have a continent to regain!

You have human freedom and human dignity to attain!

When Du Bois died in 1963, the great first wave of postcolonial poets and
activists were already known around the world: Gandhi, Fanon, Memmi,
Cesaire. The wars of colonial liberation were well along. The once hard-
sealed global grip of White Progress was slipping, never again to be what it
once was.

ASSESSMENT

Du Bois had his blind spots to be sure. Given his magnificent training in
economic and social history, one might say that he was a bit slow in coming to
recognize that race was at the foundations of the colonial system, hence at the
heart of capitalism and class oppression. But how does one fault someone when
he came to the issue well before others? Aimé Cesaire's *Discourse on Colonialism* (1955) and Albert Memmi's *The Colonizer and the Colonized* (1959) would
not appear for a good fifteen years and more after Du Bois's first systematic
meditations on the colonial system in *Dusk of Dawn*. It would be still another
two decades before the first social scientific studies of the capitalist world system
appeared, in works like Immanuel Wallerstein's *The Modern World System*
(1974, volume 1).

It might be said, too, that Du Bois never touched upon the psychological
effects of the colonial experience that so defined Frantz Fanon's *Black Skin,
White Masks* (1952) and *The Wretched of the Earth* (1961). That the former
student of William James who had proven himself such a fine intuitive psychologist in *Souls of Black Folk* never seems to have thought about Freud, who
conceived of the Unconscious as a dark continent, is, simply, a bafflement. Still,
criticisms of the sins of omission measure the work against an impossible
standard. The fairer question is always: what endures as valuable, hence truly
classical, in its own right? Here there can hardly be any question that, apart from
the exceptional qualities and ambitions of his life and politics, Du Bois stands
alone in two important respects. Better than any other work since, his *Black
Reconstruction* uses empirical evidence to demonstrate that, insofar as race is a
social construct, it is constructed of economic blocks. While works like David
Roediger's *The Wages of Whiteness* begin to take up the empirical demonstration of Du Bois's line, none comes close to the systematic analysis of *Black
Reconstruction*. And, though there are important and provocative theoretical
discussions of race as a social and economic formation, not even such prominent
works as Michael Omi and Howard Winant's *Racial Formation in the United*

States (1994) match up against Du Bois's patient teasing of the theory from the historical record.

It is one thing to say that race and class must always be thought in their relationship. It is another actually to do it. Today, we know very well from the important advances of especially queer theory and its affines that, in so far as analytic work demands an artificial setting apart from the empirical contents, analysis itself is a dubious, if necessary, activity. Du Bois, of course, had little patience for the fine points of metatheory. His politics required too much for that. But it also forced him to change his mind, which he did several times through the years.

Yet there is little reason to suppose that the younger Du Bois was of a markedly different intellectual disposition than Du Bois the elder, as (for example) the Durkheim of *Elementary Forms of the Religious Life* (1912) was so beyond himself as to be a virtual stranger to the Durkheim of *Suicide* (1897). The outlines of the economic themes of *Black Reconstruction* were already present in his youth in *Philadelphia Negro* and *Souls*, not to mention his doctoral thesis (1898/1965). It was not just that he changed his mind over the years, which he did, but that he understood from the first, as Gilroy sees, that race, nation, and Africa (plus class, which Gilroy sees less sharply) were part and parcel. Those inclined to say that we today have begun to solve the problem of analytic categories and their relations have only to reflect on the furor attending to each new book of William Julius Wilson, since at least The *Declining Significance of Race* (1987). Wilson insists, as did Du Bois, that race can never stand on its own when the ravages of class disadvantage are as severe as they are today and were in Du Bois's lifetime. All of Du Bois's major works bear examination today – as models of just how courage and steadiness of purpose can produce, over a life's work, the careful explanation of just what the constant shifting of analytic categories against each other looks like.

Beyond the tributes that still can be paid him, the complaint that stands to scrutiny is that Du Bois never even began to see that race and class, even Africa and the world, present themselves differently to men and women. Hazel Carby is absolutely right on this score. But, even she, usually the more astute social theorist, does not quite get to the heart of this problem (probably because she limits herself to *Souls*). Still, Carby gives a good account of the way Du Bois used gender unconsciously "to mediate the relation between his concept of race and his concept of nation" (Carby, 1998, p. 30). She has in mind, to be sure, the figure of Josie but also the grand way he spoke of racial uplift as the work of manhood. She shrewdly describes the way that, for Du Bois, racial manhood was the beyond of feminine sufferings and strivings – as in his subtextual references to Mr Washington "as analogous to his anonymous black mother" (Carby, 1998, pp. 38–9).

It is true that Du Bois, who enjoyed respectful, if also lustful, relations with many women throughout his life, did not think of gender as one of the differentiating conditions of black experience. Yet he would have hardly have survived the political wars in the NAACP without the ministrations of Mary White Ovington, to mention just one of the women with whom he enjoyed tender *and* respectful relations. There were others, of course: his own mother (anything but anonymous) and his dutiful first wife of fifty years, Nina – for whom, both, the gender difference meant confinement to the homes they provided for the boy and the great man. Yet he was blind to gender. Why? Was it only because he was through and through the Victorian gentleman? Or was it that – unlike race and class, even Africa – it was much more difficult for him (for any man?) to think gender seriously in the absence of a feminist culture? To think with these powerful analytic terms is to live with them.

On the other hand, Du Bois might never have so fully thought through the experiences of race and class that made him *the* race man of his times without the real and figurative effects of the experience with Josie. So, here again, one must pause before condemning. Feminist thought, from which has come today's understanding of gender, has itself been troubled, as Judith Butler puts it in *Gender Trouble* (1990). Among much else, gender is about sex, and sex is about the play of differences that no one of right mind – save those stuck in the missionary position – would think to categorize. One of the unexplored curiosities of Du Bois's spiritual infatuation with Josie is his confession late in life that his own first sexual experience was with not one of the darkly delicious girls of Fisk, but Josie's mother (Lewis, 1993, p. 71). Those sad words he took with him in the Jim Crow car back to Nashville and life itself were, thus, the words of innocence lost many times over.

It is possible, of course, to say, as Carby does, that Du Bois's all-too-male attitude toward gender was nothing more than the arrogance of the race man. Or it is possible to say that Josie had such power over him because she, and his experience with her and her family, so powerfully brought home to him all the realities of black experience. He had as little to say about the sexual as about gender differences. But are the silences the same? Or do they make a difference in how one thinks about these things? Here is a dusk, the dawn of which Du Bois did not think through. Yet, one supposes, since they were there below the surface of his recollections of Josie, had he lived in our time, he might have.

Bibliography

Writings of W. E. B. Du Bois

The Suppression of the African Slave Trade to the United States of America, 1638–1870. 1898. New York: Longmans, Green (reprinted New York: Russell & Russell, 1965).

The Philadelphia Negro. 1899. Philadelphia: University of Pennsylvania (reprinted New York: Schocken, 1967).

The Souls of Black Folk. 1903. Chicago: A. C. McClurg (reprinted New York: Bantam, 1989).

Darkwater: Voices within the Veil. 1920. New York: Harcourt, Brace (reprinted New York: AMS Press, 1969).

Black Reconstruction in America, 1860–1880. 1935. New York: Harcourt, Brace (reprinted New York: Atheneum, 1992).

The Dusk of Dawn: an Essay toward an Autobiography of a Race Concept. 1940. New York: Harcourt, Brace (reprinted New Brunswick, NJ: Transaction, 1984).

Color and Democracy: Colonies and Peace. 1945. New York: Harcourt, Brace.

The World and Africa. 1947. New York: Viking (reprinted New York: International Publishers, 1965).

The Autobiography of W. E. B. Du Bois. 1968. New York: International Publishers.

W. E. B. Du Bois Speaks. Speeches and Addresses, 1920–1963 (edited by Philip S. Foner). 1970. New York: Pathfinder.

The Correspondence of W. E. B. Du Bois/Selections, 1977–1934, volume I (edited by Herbert Aptheker). 1973. Amherst: University of Massachusetts Press.

Further reading

Butler, Judith (1990) *Gender Trouble: Feminism and the Subversion of Identity.* New York: Routledge.

Carby, Hazel (1998) *Race Men.* Cambridge, MA: Harvard University Press.

Early, Gerald (1993) *Lure and Loathing.* New York: Penguin.

Gilroy, Paul (1993) *Black Atlantic.* Cambridge, MA: Harvard University Press.

Gates, Henry Louis (1989) Darkly, As through a Veil. Introduction to *Souls of Black Folk*, pp. vii–xxix.

James, C. L. R. (1998) Black Power and Stokely. in Charles Lemert (ed.), *Social Theory.* Boulder, CO: Westview Press, pp. 419–28.

Lemert, Charles (1994) A Classic from the Other Side of the Veil: Du Bois's *Souls of Black Folk. Sociological Quarterly*, 35, 385–96.

Lewis, David Levering (1979) *When Harlem Was in Vogue.* New York: Oxford University Press.

Lewis, David Levering (1993) *W. E. B. Du Bois. Biography of a Race*, 1868–1919. New York: Henry Holt. Volume 2 forthcoming.

Marable, Manning (1986) *W. E. B. Du Bois: Black Radical Democrat.* Boston: G. K. Hall.

Omi, Michael and Winant, Howard (1994) *Racial Formation in the United States.* New York: Routledge.

Rampersad, Arnold (1990) *The Art and Imagination of W. E. B. Du Bois.* New York: Schocken.

Reed, Adolph L. Jr (1997) *W. E. B. Du Bois and American Political Thought.* New York: Oxford University Press.

Roediger, David (1991) *The Wages of Whiteness.* London: Verso.

Shamoon, Zamir (1995) *Dark Voices. W. E. B. Du Bois and American Thought*, 1888–1903. Chicago: University of Chicago Press.

Wallerstein, Immanuel (1974) *The Modern World System.* New York: Academic Press.

West, Cornel (1993) The New Cultural Politics of Difference. In *Keeping Faith. Philosophy and Race in America.* New York: Routledge, pp. 3–32.

Wilson, William Julius (1987) *The Declining Significance of Race.* New York: Knopf.

11

Alfred Schutz

Mary Rogers

Maurice Natanson (1973, p. 166), first a student and later a colleague and friend of Alfred Schutz (1899–1959), wrote of Edmund Husserl what might also be said of Schutz, namely that his work put him "in the company of those who labor at foundations." Schutz's focus was the "primordial foundation...that makes all understanding possible" (in Grathoff, 1989, p. 212), namely the life-world (*Lebenswelt*) or the world of everyday life. He aimed to show what makes the everyday world possible at all and how it in turn makes understanding possible, including scientific understanding.

Schutz's theorizing goes to the roots of social reality where consciousness moves beyond its own duration and naively grasps its world. For him, that world can be had only in and through mutuality; it is inescapably intersubjective. The world given to consciousness as a taken-for-granted certainty is also marked by multiplicity – its multiplicity of forms and structures, its multiplicity of worlds of experience, its multiplicity of members spanning the past (predecessors), the present (anonymous contemporaries and interacting consociates), and the future (successors). Finally, Schutz shows that to have a world means to make meanings, both the subjective meanings individuals constitute in grasping their own acts and the objective meanings they constitute in interpreting others' subjectively meaningful acts.

Around these core concerns Schutz built up a descriptive framework that delineates the presuppositions not only of members' shared world but also of individuals' biographical situations. He thus took upon himself the goal of philosophically illuminating the coterminous grounds of sociality and individuality. By focusing on the essential connections between social structure and personhood, he carved out theoretical space for illuminating lived experiences of intersubjectivity. Within that space his virtual conversations with Husserl, Max Weber, Max Scheler, Henri Bergson, William James, George Herbert Mead,

Charles Horton Cooley, Talcott Parsons, and other intellectual predecessors and contemporaries gave way to a framework whose analytical power is far-reaching as well as foundational.

THE PERSON: A MULTIPLICITY OF ROLES

Before we look at some of the notions anchoring Schutz's framework, let us get a preliminary sense of the person who masterminded it. For getting acquainted with Schutz the person, there may be no more instructive source than his correspondence with Aron Gurwitsch (Grathoff, 1989), which spans 1939 to 1959. Schutz, like Gurwitsch, talks about being Jewish, being an immigrant, working in a language that feels alien, finding venues for his essays, and negotiating a career in academic institutions where pecking orders, interpersonal networks, and disciplinary boundaries weigh heavily. Like Gurwitsch, Schutz enjoyed the benefit of a non-employed spouse who typed his manuscripts and also, in his case, letters that he dictated onto tapes. Domestic and international travel pervaded Schutz's life, typically for business but sometimes for vacations and respite.

Schutz mentions 15- and 16-hour days working on various of his papers, particularly on weekends when he found release from the daytime/nighttime bifurcation that marked his weekdays. Nearly all his life Schutz held a full-time position with a banking firm that intensified the challenges of his scholarly work. As early as 1940 Schutz wrote to Gurwitsch, "by night I am a phenomenologist, but by day an executive. At the moment my day life is taking over my night life" (p. 26), a circumstance accounting for letters written at three or so in the morning. In his letters Schutz worries about his son George's eyesight after a horrible accident and about his daughter's and his son's schooling; he mourns the death of his father; he worries at times about his wife Ilse's health and well-being. Schutz also worries about his friend Gurwitsch's job prospects and publishing options. At the same time he delights in and draws sustenance from their friendship.

During the early years of their correspondence these "philosophers in exile" address one another, "Dear Friend Schutz" and "Dear Friend Gurwitsch." For some years they stick with the formal *Sie* before abandoning it for the more personal *Du*. Schutz (p. 119) took the initiative: "Why do we still say '*Sie*' to one another? I won't go along with this nonsense any longer!" Several times Schutz (pp. 45, 123, 119) expresses longing for a "heart-to-heart talk" with his friend, whom he describes as his "ideal reader." At one point Schutz's salutation is to "My dear friend and robber of my sleep!" (p. 153). Another salutation finds Schutz addressing Gurwitsch as his "Select and inestimable friend!" (p. 273). In no way did Schutz's ardor preclude wittiness. He closed one letter, "With intersubjective love, your primordi(n)al and egological Alfred" (p. 263). Nor did Schutz's ardor preclude modesty: "You have no idea how much I learn from you, even when you talk about things I am very familiar with" (p. 293).

Unafraid to say in writing what they meant to one another, Schutz and Gurwitsch also confide to one another what they think of other people's work. A spacious seminar room of great minds is gathered together in these letters – Kant, Scheler, Leibniz, Mead, Dewey, James, Sartre, and Husserl, the founder of phenomenology, whose thinking animates both correspondents. Schutz had never formally studied with Husserl any more than with Weber or Bergson, two other major influences on his thinking. As Helmut Wagner (1983, pp. 46–7) describes it, at the behest of his friend Felix Kaufmann and his wife Ilse, Schutz sent Husserl a copy of his *Phenomenology of the Social World* (1932). Kaufmann, who was acquainted with Husserl, suggested that Schutz go to Freiburg to meet him. Schutz went, and he visited Husserl a number of other times before the latter's death in 1938. Husserl's daughter Elizabeth described their bond as "a deep human tie."

Also showing up in these letters are individuals such as sociologist Lewis Coser (a colleague of Gurwitsch at Brandeis University) and philosophers Hannah Arendt, Dorion Cairns, and Marvin Farber. Philosophers of science such as Carl Hempel and Ernest Nagel also make appearances. In these letters one also sees the close bond between Schutz and Natanson taking shape. Schutz comments on the dissertation about Mead's work that earned Natanson a *summa cum laude* and, later, on how he has begun sending his former student manuscripts to edit. One also learns that Schutz and Natanson had even translated Husserl's *Ideas I* and *II* together, though their translation was never published (p. 221).

What these letters disclose is magnanimous spirit, dogged determination, and astonishing stamina (despite worsening health conditions that ended Schutz's life in 1959). Schutz had, to say the least, an enormous appetite for life. For him, that meant multiple roles and responsibilities as well as abiding mutualities. It also meant a habitual inclination to look for "common bases of mutual understanding rather than merely to criticize" (Schutz, in Grathoff, 1978, p. 96).

MULTIPLICITY AND MUTUALITY

Schutz (1964, p. 137) theorizes a social world that includes not only mundane fare but also "death and dream, vision and art, prophecy and science." Yet he emphasizes that in the "natural attitude" people routinely move from one type of situation to the next with the undisturbed sense that *the* one world is just there as the ever-present stage for their projects. In the world of everyday life the world "out there" is nothing less than certain.

It is also nothing less than replete with multiplicity. People's bodies guarantee the multiplicity of zones wherein they can more or less readily manipulate some part of the social world. Commonsense individuals take for granted, for instance, that some people and things are within reach, others are, for the time being, beyond ready reach, and others remain stubbornly beyond reach for as far ahead as they can see. They also take for granted that some individuals who shaped their world – ancestors, inventors, revolutionaries, prophets, and others – are long since gone from it; that many who will inherit their world are not yet on the scene; that some with whom they share the planet or make their society are entirely unknown to them and others (their consociates) are known in varying degrees of intimacy, anonymity, and intensity.

People in everyday life often leave it for a multiplicity of purposes shaped by the system of relevances currently active within their biographical situation. They step into the world of the theater or religion or dreams or science, and they know how to step back into the world of everyday life when desire or necessity moves them. Commonsense individuals thus move among multiple realities or worlds, typically without undue anxiety or upset. All the while, their lived experiences continuously seal their sense that they inhabit but one world whose certainty lies beyond question and whose reality is straightforward. As Schutz (1967, p. 75) puts it, "instead of discrete experiences, we have every-where continuity, with horizons opening equally into the past and the future. However diverse the lived experiences may be, they are bound together by the fact that they are *mine*." Schutz calls this experiential continuity a "primal unity." It eventuates alongside the equally essential, double-sided unity of human consciousness and social reality. Bluntly put, Schutz allows no theoretical room for *human* consciousness that is not also *social* consciousness.

Schutz calls the specifically social aspect of our consciousness its Thou-orientation. Without that orientation neither a world nor a self is possible. The *Thou-orientation* involves recognizing another human being as having a life and a consciousness fundamentally like my own. In our actual experiences the Thou-orientation entails more or less recognition of that primal sort, and it may or may not be reciprocated in the face-to-face situation which it presupposes (Schutz, 1967, pp. 163–4). Schutz (1962, p. 57) puts the Thou-orientation at the heart of social reality as well as human consciousness: "since human beings are born of mothers and not concocted in retorts, the experience of the existence of other human beings and of the meaning of their actions is certainly the first and most original empirical observation [a human being] makes."

Out of that observation – the direct, indeed sensuous, observation of social reality – grows a multiplicity of social relationships, both direct and indirect as well as more or less intimate or anonymous. Direct connections with other human beings have, in principle, the form of the *We-relationship* involving not only reciprocal Thou-orientations but also "sympathetic sharing" of one another's lives for however long a time is desirable and possible (Schutz, 1967, p. 164). "In such a relationship," says Schutz (1962, p. 17), "fugitive and super-ficial as it may be, the Other is grasped as a unique individuality...in its unique biographical situation (although revealed merely fragmentarily)."

The lived We-relationship entails stunning possibilities. It means that I can "keep pace with each moment of [my partner's] stream of consciousness as it transpires," thus making me "better attuned to him [or her] than I am to myself"; it means that whether we join hands or not, we do join glances, eventuating in an "interlocking of glances" and a "thousand-faceted mirroring of each other"; it means that we "witness the literal coming-to-birth of each other's experiences" (Schutz, 1967, pp. 169, 170, 179). In one of my favorite passages Schutz (1967,

p. 178) sketches such possibilities from the standpoint of a partner in a "We" remembering the Other's "you of yesterday":

> When I have a recollection of you,... I remember you as you were in the concrete We-relationship with me. I remember you as a unique person in a concrete situation, as one who interacted with me in the mode of "mutual mirroring" described above. I remember you as a person vividly present to me with a maximum of symptoms of inner life, as one whose experiences I witnessed in the actual process of formation. I remember you as one whom I was for a time coming to know better and better. I remember you as one whose conscious life flowed in one stream with my own. I remember you as one whose consciousness was continuously changing in content.

Such memories are contingent. Every lived We also allows for failures to connect or even hurtful disconnection, whether gradual or abrupt. Emphasizing that actual We-relationships *more* or *less* fulfill the possibilities of that social form, Schutz points toward the missteps and lapses that often infiltrate lived We-relationships. He notes, for instance, how people can become more concerned with the We-relationship than with its other participant(s). To that extent they diminish their involvement and become less "genuinely related" to their partners, tending in the extreme to render them "object[s] of thought." By failing to get more and more attuned to their partners, they miss the "higher level of the We-experience" where they can "enrich" their understanding not only of their partners but also of other people (Schutz, 1967, pp. 167, 171). More generally, Schutz illuminates the discontinuous, challenging character of any real-life We:

> In actual life,... a marriage or a friendship is made up of many separate events occurring over a long period of time. Some of these events involve face-to-face situations, in others the partners simply exist side by side as contemporaries. To call such social relationships "continuous" is erroneous in the extreme, since discontinuity and repeatability are included in their very definition.

For Schutz, the everyday world rests on and takes shape around the primordial, though often problematic, mutuality of the We-relationship. Common-sense actors routinely and prereflectively live in the "vivid simultaneity of the 'We'." They grasp the Other in the immediacy of his or her current stream of consciousness. To grasp oneself, however, requires retrospective glances at past or just-past experiences. One cannot, in other words, both live within and reflect on one's own experiences. Therefore, Schutz (1962, pp. 174–5) emphasizes,

> In so far as each of us can experience the Other's thoughts and acts in the vivid present whereas either can grasp his [or her] own only as a past by way of reflection, I know more of the Other and [the Other] knows more of me than either of us knows of his own stream of consciousness. This present, common to both of us, is the pure sphere of the "We."

In Schutz's judgment this circumstance regarding knowledge of self and Other offers "a sufficient frame of reference for the foundation of empirical psychology and the social sciences. For all our knowledge of the social world, even of its most anonymous and remote phenomena and of the most diverse types of social communities, is based upon the possibility of experiencing an alter ego in vivid presence" (Schutz, 1962, p. 175). This socially and methodologically consequential circumstance boils down to a foundational mutuality constituted in every We as each participant grasps the Other's Now. Schutz puts it this way: "The alter ego . . . is that stream of consciousness whose activities I can seize in their present by my own simultaneous activities." In such mutual seizing, whatever its culturally and biographically specific shape, lie the roots of social life and social structure. As Schutz (1967, p. 171) writes,

> The world of the We is not private to either of us, but is our world, the one common intersubjective world which is right there in front of us. It is only from the face-to-face relationships, from the common lived experience of the world in the We, that the intersubjective world can be constituted.

Thus, the primordial mutuality of the We signals the possibility of roles and statuses, of institutions and various forms of resistance to them, and of socialization and resocialization. Overall, says Schutz, we are joined together by "common influence and work." From such bonds, which vary in intensity and intimacy as well as immediacy, comes all the multiplicity of social reality. Schutz (1962, p. 53) defines *social reality* as

> the sum total of objects and occurrences . . . experienced by the common-sense thinking of [people] living their daily lives among their [other people], connected with them in manifold relations of inter-action. It is the world of cultural objects and social institutions into which we are all born, within which we have to find our bearings, and with which we have to come to terms.

Schutz delineates in great detail the thick folds of social reality. He describes how our experiences of other people get more remote and anonymous as we turn toward our mere contemporaries with whom we have no face-to-face contact. Schutz (1967, p. 181) says that such turning entails "pass[age] through one region after another" (eight in all), beginning with our consociates and ending with cultural artifacts that implicitly attest to the subjective meanings of persons unknown to us. Put differently, the world of our mere contemporaries is a web of ideal types, which Schutz (1967, pp. 176ff.) delineates in the only of his books published during his lifetime, namely *The Phenomenology of the Social World*.

To account for our anonymous, mediated connections with all living individuals beyond our consociates, Schutz (1967, p. 177) lays out theoretical scaffolding that describes the "gradual progression from the world of immediately experienced social reality to the world of contemporaries." His concept of *They-orientation* concerns our consciousness of contemporaries; it parallels the Thou-orientation involved in direct, unmediated social relationships (Schutz, 1967, p. 183). Characterizing knowledge of one's contemporaries as "inferential and discursive," Schutz (1967, p. 184) also characterizes it as ideal-typical; that is, made up of "interpretive schemes for the social world *in general*" (p. 185, emphasis added). Impersonal and anonymous, They-relationships among contemporaries have ideal types as their bedrock:

> Whenever we come upon any ordering of past experience under interpretive schemes, any act of abstraction, generalization, formalization, or idealization, whatever the object involved, there we shall find this process in which a moment of living experience is lifted out of its setting and then, through a synthesis of recognition, frozen into a hard and fast "ideal type." (Schutz, 1967, p. 187)

Overall, Schutz (1967, p. 9) emphasizes that "Living in the world, we live with others and for others, orienting our lives to them." Throughout his work he shows that the "social world is by no means homogeneous but exhibits a multiform structure" (Schutz, 1967, p. 139). That structure conditions the meanings members constitute: "Each of [the social world's] spheres or regions is both a way of perceiving and a way of understanding the subjective experiences of others." Selfhood and sociality are thus conjoined in a "dialectic of intersubjectivity" (Schutz, 1964, p. 145), which takes shape from They-relationships as well as We-relationships. In the end Schutz's corpus shows how thoroughly "They" and "We" are implicated with one another.

MEANING AND MUTUALITY

Within Schutz's framework making sense means, at root, naming the objects of one's experiences. Such naming involves *typification*, which carries several meanings in Schutz's work. It refers, first, to the application of relevant types to the objects of one's experiences. Such application entails consciousness of similarities between what one has more recently experienced and what one previously experienced, whether firsthand or vicariously. To be conscious of *this* object, one must have already been conscious of objects like it in one or more ways. Those previous objects of one's experiencing thus serve as reference points. Sedimented from one's past experiences, these retentions (expectations built up from one's prior experiences) are themselves typified, or named as this or that type of person or thing.

Language is the storehouse of types and thus the root system of the meanings people constitute. Schutz was passionate about language's role in sense-making. Himself a wielder of English as a second language, Austrian-born Schutz knew, for instance, that "In order to command a language freely as a scheme of expression, one must have written love letters in it; one has to know how to pray and curse in it and how to say things with every shade appropriate to the addressee and the situation" (Schutz, 1964, p. 101). So, too, he understood that "The fringes [of words and sentences] are the stuff poetry is made of; they are capable of being set to music but they are not translatable" (ibid.). Making meaning is thus infinitely more comfortable and certain when one can use the "mother tongue"; that is, when one is linguistically at home. Schutz implies that making sense becomes more difficult the more constrained our vocabularies, the more uncertain our semantics, the more insecure our literacy.

Second, typification concerns the abstractive character of intentionality (or consciousness-of). Schutz and Luckmann (1973, p. 241) stress that the "praxis of everyday life" generally revolves around the "typical repeatability" of objects of experience, not their uniqueness. Thus, individuals abstract from an object those features or characteristics it appears to have in common with objects named in the same way. To that extent they make the object more or less anonymous by suppressing its uniqueness in favor of its commonalities with other objects. Typification thus dovetails with anonymity, which we will consider before long.

Finally, typification refers not only to a process but also to its results. Typifications are categories of typicality that individuals build up, both individually and collectively, as they go about the business of "construct[ing] . . . complex world[s] of experience" (Schutz, 1967, p. 13) for themselves. Schutz (1967, p. 81) emphasized the resourcefulness of sense-makers in the everyday world. He noted that "ordinary" people

> in every moment of [their] lived experience light upon past experiences in the storehouse of [their] consciousness. [They] know about the world and . . . know what to expect. . . . The [person] in the natural attitude "has" . . . a stock of knowledge of physical things and fellow creatures, of social collectives and of artifacts, including cultural objects. He [or she] likewise "has" syntheses of inner experience. Among these are to be found judgment contents (or propositional contents) which are the result of . . . previous acts of judgment. Here also are to be found all products of the activity of the mind and will.

Schutz thus credits the individual's experiences a great deal.

At the same time he points to the stock of knowledge that language undergirds and gives rise to – the lore, guidelines, parables, principles, doctrines, findings, news, and all else that makes up the "cookbook knowledge" whereby we make our way in the world of everyday life. For the most part, Schutz characterizes the individual's stock of knowledge at hand as a hodgepodge. Built up unsystematically, shaped by pragmatic motives, and reflective of the individual's shifting system of relevances, the stock of knowledge at hand is nevertheless generally effective. It lets us get on with our daily affairs without undue puzzlement or upset. It serves our practical purposes, and it promotes taken for grantedness where otherwise there would be distractions from the purposes at hand. Typically, then, our stock of knowledge at hand ensures us a soundly familiar world.

An individual's stock of knowledge at hand takes biographically specific shape, to be sure, but it is also thoroughly social. It is a collective as well as an individual achievement that reflects the intersections of social structure with the individual's life course. Schutz (1964, pp. 120ff.) emphasized that the social stock of knowledge is nonrandomly distributed so as to constitute the broad categories of expert, well informed citizen, and layperson. Knowledge is, then, socially stratified and specialized. Its social shape follows the lines of the various *finite provinces of meaning* Schutz theorized.

Reshaping and extending William James's notion of sub-universes of reality, Schutz devoted considerable theoretical attention to the overlapping but distinct worlds of meaning-compatible experiences. In the course of a day or even an hour people experience any number of these worlds. In fact, Schutz (1970, p. 15) stressed that we actually live simultaneously in several worlds by virtue of how our relevances interplay and overlap. The worlds of dreams, of religion, of theory, of science, of the theater, and so forth each elicit a distinctive "cognitive style." We know by virtue of some sort of "shock" or "leap" – some sort of transitional experience, so to speak – when we are crossing the experiential boundary roughly dividing one finite province of meaning from another. After having seen an engaging film in a theater, for instance, our passage up the aisle and into the lobby represents such a shock. It has gotten dark and begun to rain. These are the first signals that "the" world has gone on without us and has been there all the while we were "away." As we re-enter the world of everyday life, which Schutz deemed the "paramount reality" due to its sheer certitude and overarching givenness, we sustain a measure, however briefly, of strangeness or shock.

Each finite province of meaning entails a distinctive "tension of consciousness" as well as distinctive ways of experiencing time, self, and others. All these aspects of cognitive style involve distinctive typifications, with each province thus ordered by a characteristic vocabulary that enables us to grasp its objects – daydreams, theatrical roles, theorems, heresies, and such – and make sense of our experiences of them. Each province of meaning thus has linguistic boundaries that dovetail with their experiential boundaries. Moving from one to another finite province of meaning means shifting vocabularies as well as making some sort of leap. The two are coterminous experiences.

SUBJECTIVITY AND INTERSUBJECTIVITY

That finite provinces of meaning are rooted in language means that the world of everyday life remains our home base among them. *Its* commonplace words infiltrate and ultimately anchor other finite provinces of meaning. Their linguistic roots also guarantee finite provinces of meaning an intersubjective dimension. Natanson (in Webb, 1992, p. 284) says that Schutz "was trying to understand how individuals are able to comprehend one another," which made "the problem of intersubjectivity...the central issue of the everyday world" for Schutz. Helmut R. Wagner (1970, p. 30), another of Schutz's students, describes Schutz's theoretical focus this way: "living in the world of everyday life, in general, means living in an interactional involvement with many persons.... The phenomenologically most basic problem here is that of intersubjectivity."

For Schutz (1966, p. 82), "intersubjectivity is not a problem of constitution...but is rather a datum (*Gegebenheit*) of the life-world. It is the fundamental ontological category of human existence." Thus, Schutz set about the task of showing how other people's "interpretations of my situation and mine of theirs codetermine the meaning this situation has for me" (Schutz, 1964, p. 196).

As I make sense of my own experiences, I can never cut myself off from the meanings sedimented in my stock of knowledge, which essentially includes a multiplicity of meanings established by predecessors, mere contemporaries, and consociates as well as by myself. More fundamentally, I cannot forswear language. I cannot, then, leave others behind as I reflect on this or that of my experiences. Schutz (1967, p. 32) was emphatic on this score: "every act of mine through which I endow the world with meaning refers back to some meaning-endowing act...of yours with respect to the same world. Meaning is thus constituted as an intersubjective phenomenon." Each of us inescapably lives in "a shared world of interpretation which carries with it a horizon of expectancies and demands" (Natanson, 1970, p. 40) woven from the stuff of social life as well as the threads of my own experiences.

Yet subjectivity does have an existence resolutely its own. It needs no liberation from the "inter." Instead, implies Schutz, subjectivity always has two sides – the singular and the plural, the unique and the shared, the solitary and the collective. As Natanson (1970, p. 56) reminds us, *subjectivity* means subject-bound. When it is subjects-bound, it amounts to intersubjectivity, which takes shape around the prospect, however fulfilled or not, of two or more subjects coming to terms with and gearing into the world together. It takes shape as two or more persons come to sense that they understand one another enough that they can generally take their mutual understanding for granted.

All the while, Schutz (1967, p. 32) emphasizes that "an action has only one subjective meaning: that of the actor" whose action it is. In the face of wide-spread attempts – Freudian and otherwise – to inform people about what their actions *really* mean, Schutz aligned himself with interpretive sociology as Weber shaped it. He leaves no theoretical space for "subjective meaning" to denote anything other than whatever meaning subjects assign to their own actions. My experiences remain pre-eminently *mine*, then. The only subjective meaning they can possibly have is what I give them.

Yet Schutz (1964, p. 9) equally emphasizes that "My experience of the world justifies and corrects itself by the experience of the others with whom I am interrelated by common knowledge, common work, and common suffering." The meanings I make grow out of knowledge, work, and suffering that are simultaneously mine alone and ours together. No other human being knows precisely what I know, nor is there anyone whose projects and actions match mine or whose trials and tribulations are identical to my own. Yet I know that great multitudes of people know much of what I know and gear themselves into the world much as I do and feel pain much the way I do. In short, I take for granted that I am far from alone in "the" world or even in "my" world.

At the same time I take for granted that I am capable of understanding the people around me. Schutz (1962, p. 27) reminds us, however, that there is no more than "a mere chance, although a chance sufficient for many practical purposes, that the observer in daily life can grasp the subjective meaning of the actor's acts." The odds may favor us more or less, but we live with no guarantee that we can come to understand what this or that person's action meant. The challenge at hand, after all, is to enter the Other's situation and adopt his or her perspective on or account of the action (Natanson, 1970, p. 100). All the while, though, I have only my own experiences as a point of access to another's experiences. As Schutz (1967, p. 106) puts it, *"everything I know about your conscious life is really based on my knowledge of my own lived experiences,"* including my experiences of your actions.

Schutz (1964, p. 13) theorizes that in the world of everyday life "I am able to understand other people's acts only if I can imagine that I myself would perform analogous acts if I were in the same situation, directed by the same because motives, or oriented by the same in-order-to motives." Thus, understanding others' actions means understanding their situations from retrospective and prospective viewpoints. Such understanding means, then, grasping the background circumstances or antecedent conditions (because motives) or the anticipated outcomes (in-order-to motives) associated with an individual's acts. Understanding another's action thus necessitates what Mead called "taking the role of the other." It requires what Schutz (1962, pp. 11–12) called a *reciprocity of perspectives* whereby, first, I assume that Other and I have interchangeable standpoints in the sense that if we swapped physical places, we would each see things "with the same typicality" that the other had previously experienced; and, second, that despite our different biographical situations Other and I have purposes and relevances that are the same or substantially similar for all practical purposes. Schutz says the reciprocity of perspectives in everyday life revolves around the "structural socialization of knowledge." That knowledge involves familiarity with people's typical purposes in typical situations such as funerals, breakfast buffets, or homeless shelters. Thus what each of us seeks in a typical situation overlaps considerably with what others seek; our *in-order-to motives* dovetail. Our *because motives*, the circumstances we see as having shaped our past actions, are also typically similar by virtue of the social stock of knowledge, including language, that we use to account for those actions.

Schutz (1964, p. 15) thus theorizes that in everyday life

> More or less naively I presuppose the existence of a common scheme of reference for both my own acts and the acts of others. I am interested above all . . . in [others'] intentions, and that means in the in-order-to motives for the sake of which, and in the because motives based on which, they act as they do.

Schutz goes on:

> Convinced that they want to express something by their act or that their act has a specific position within the common frame of reference, I try to catch the meaning which the act in question has, particularly for my co-actors in the social world, and, until presented with counter-evidence, I presume that this meaning for them, the actors, corresponds to the meaning their act has for me.

Such presumption sometimes falters. Commonsense individuals know from their own experiences that the Other sometimes surprises them with "strange" or unfamiliar purposes and relevances. Usually, however, the typicality delineated in and reinforced by the social stock of knowledge prevails, and life proceeds along its well traveled pathways. Although Schutz's theorizing emphasizes this latter state of affairs, he does map out the contours of misunderstanding in everyday life. That theoretical mapping brings us back to the matter of anonymity.

Schutz (1962, p. 27) noted that the more standardized and anonymous an action is, the greater one's chances are of grasping its subjective meaning. Imagine, for instance, a Roman Catholic couple touring a French city on a Sunday morning and passing by a cathedral as parishioners are celebrating Mass together. Even though these tourists are unfamiliar with this specific church and these specific parishioners, they nonetheless recognize the liturgy whereby participants sit, stand, and kneel together at standard junctures, and they deem it not at all strange that the key celebrant is wearing an unusual costume for a contemporary Western man. The passers-by adequately grasp the meaning of what they are seeing; they experience no perplexity.

That scenario contrasts with one involving an intimate We-relationship of some duration. Imagine one partner announcing, "I think we should talk about spending less time with one another. I need more space." Psychobabble aside, such an announcement disrupts the mirroring typical of close, face-to-face relationships. It is likely to leave the listener at least momentarily dumbfounded or at a loss to understand the partner's motives. The more attuned we are to the biographically situated person rather than a *type* of person, the harder it can be to grasp the subjective meaning of his or her actions when they depart from what is typical and familiar in the world we have made together.

As we have seen, alongside lived We-relationships of more or less intimacy or anonymity lie They-relationships with anonymous contemporaries like the people attending Mass in the cathedral. Schutz (1967, p. 185) theorized that "when I am They-oriented, I have 'types' for partners." In general, it is easier to understand types than individuals. Schutz goes on to say why: namely, they are "part of our stock of knowledge" about the social world. We-relationships, however, modify those types and leave us with more singularity and less anonymity to grasp. With more than a little theoretical acumen, Schutz (1967, p. 186) literally underscored that "*The typical and only the typical is homogeneous*, and it is always so. In the typifying synthesis of recognition . . . I abstract the lived experience from its setting . . . and thereby render it impersonal" and anonymous.

Schutz (1962, p. 29) emphasized that

> the general thesis of the reciprocity of perspectives . . . presupposes that both the observed and the observer are sharing a system of relevances sufficiently homogeneous in structure and content for the practical purpose involved. If this is not the case, then a course of action which is perfectly rational from the point of view of the actor may appear as non-rational to the partner or observer and vice versa.

An utterance that momentarily upsets or disorients a partner in a close We-relationship typically reflects at least a short-term disjuncture between the relevances of the speaker and those of the listener. Beyond such relationships the failure to understand – that is, the failure to grasp the subjective meaning of an Other's action – points to a standing divergence between Ego's and Other's systems of relevance. In order to understand the Other, Ego must temporarily set aside his or her own relevances enough to adopt the Other's point of view and thus grasp what she or he meant by a given action or course of action. This challenge of grasping the subjective meanings of people's actions lies at the heart of interpretive sociology and poses methodological challenges in all the social sciences. Schutz addressed this aspect of social-scientific methodology in considerable detail.

INTERPRETIVE SOCIOLOGY AND CONTEMPORARY SOCIAL THEORY

After serving in the First World War, Schutz studied at the University of Vienna (1918–1921), where he earned his law degree. Thereafter he joined the banking house Reitler & Company as a legal consultant. He worked full-time with that firm nearly the rest of his life – first in Vienna and later in New York after he, Ilse, and their two children escaped the Holocaust and settled there in 1939. By that time Schutz's *Phenomenology of the Social World* had been on scholars' bookshelves for seven years.

That volume grew out of Schutz's postgraduate fascination with Weber's sociology. As Wagner (1983, pp. 14–15) describes it, Schutz was particularly taken with the opening chapter of Weber's *Wirtschaft und Gesellschaft*, which had appeared in 1922. He accepted Weber's "fundamental approach and the core of his methodology" and soon began the project of philosophically undergirding and augmenting Weber's stance. The first chapter of Schutz's book is "The Statement of Our Problem: Max Weber's Basic Methodological Concepts"; its last is "Some Basic Problems of Interpretive Sociology." By elaborating the philosophical foundations of Weber's work, Schutz contributed a great deal to the logic of social inquiry, particularly qualitative methodology.

In all likelihood his teaching let Schutz enlarge those contributions beyond what they would otherwise have been. In the spring of 1943, Schutz offered the first of his courses as a member of the Graduate Faculty of the New School for Social Research, "Introduction to Sociological Theory." That fall he taught the "Theory of Social Action," and the spring of 1944 found him co-teaching a seminar on Mead with Albert Salomon. During the fall of 1944 Schutz taught "Social Groups and Problems of Adjustment," followed in the spring by "Problems of a Sociology of Knowledge." Over the years to come Schutz also offered seminars on "Self and Society," "Problems of a Sociology of Language," and "Methodology of the Social Sciences" (Wagner, 1983, pp. 87–8, 91). These graduate seminars gave him hard-won occasions for interacting with individuals whose systems of relevance revolved around philosophy, social science, and academic We-relationships. His part-time academic work facilitated Schutz's contact with academic contemporaries such as Talcott Parsons and Robert MacIver and connected him with such promising students as Peter L. Berger and Thomas Luckmann as well as Natanson and Wagner. Through it all he managed to complete a number of important papers, many of which extended the social theorizing begun in his 1932 book.

One such paper is pivotal. First published in *Social Research* (summer 1960), "The Social World and the Theory of Social Action" lambasts objectivist, particularly behavioristic, social science. Schutz (1964, p. 3) begins,

> At first sight it is not easily understandable why the subjective point of view should be preferred in the social sciences. Why address ourselves to this mysterious and not too interesting tyrant of the social sciences, called the subjectivity of the actor? Why not honestly describe in honestly objective terms what really happens, and that means speaking our own language, the language of qualified and scientifically trained observers of the social world? And if it be objected that these terms are but artificial conventions..., we could answer that it is precisely this building up of a system of conventions and an honest description of the world which *is* and is alone the task of scientific thought.

Schutz goes on to argue against displacing social reality with a "fictional world" based on scientific methods that illuminate some matters but fail when it comes to intersubjectivity. More generally, Schutz is impatient with social science that revolves around "skillfully and expediently chosen idealizations and formalizations of the social world which are not repugnant to its facts" but do not capture its texture of mutuality and its fabric of meanings.

Such social science ignores "the actor in the social world whose doing and feeling lie at the bottom of the whole system" (Schutz, 1962, p. 6). It thus abandons the *lived* character of social reality. Although he conceded that they have some role to play, Schutz largely inveighed against research methods narrowly concerned with statistical correlations, formal models, and social trends. For him, the most urgent questions in the social sciences center on actors' subjective meanings. Schutz (1964, p. 8) believed that "safeguarding...the subjective point of view is the only but sufficient guarantee that the world of social reality will not be replaced by a fictional non-existing world constructed by the scientific observer."

In one fashion or other such fictional worlds typically fill the pages of journals like the *American Sociological Review* and the *American Political Science Review*. The fare in such journals is far from a balanced mix. Instead, the articles routinely ignore people's lived experiences and subjective meanings. If issues of meaning get raised at all, they most often center on the meaning of this or that blip on the statistical horizon. By contrast, Schutz (1964, p. 13) argued that "social things are only understandable if they can be reduced to human activities; and human activities are only made understandable by showing their in-order-to and because motives." Thus, he insisted that the chief aim of the social sciences is to clarify "what is thought about the social world by those living in it" (Schutz, 1967, p. 222).

With these prognostications Schutz points to a huge methodological paradox, namely that social scientists must act substantially like commonsense actors in order to do their work well. To understand social reality they must, like com-monsense members, try to understand the people who constitute it together through their meaningful activities and relationships. If social scientists fail to do that – that is, fail to illuminate sense-making activities in the everyday world – they simultaneously fail to unearth the grounds of their own activities, which always come down to making sense by some means or other. The result is a naive social science that takes for granted what it ought to be analyzing. Schutz sought to defamiliarize such social science by depicting it as a dead-ended pathway into social reality. His theorizing repositions social scientists by revealing their close kinship with common-sense observers. As we will see, ethnomethodologists deploy Schutz's insights along these lines and are among his most significant successors.

Schutz (1967, p. 141) asserted that "the *starting point* of social science is to be found in ordinary social life." In no way did Schutz equate common-sense and scientific sorts of understanding, but he did insist that "the two spheres overlap." The terms of that overlap are types; the bridge between the two spheres is thus typification. In everyday life, says Schutz (1967, p. 187), people typify both people and actions. Their stock of knowledge at hand comprises, in other terms, *personal ideal types* such as childcare worker, golfer, minister, and neighbor intertwined with *course-of-action types* such as tending children, playing golf, preaching, and neighboring. The former category typifies the people who do this, that, or the other thing(s), especially their in-order-to and because motives; the latter typifies their projects and actions.

From these types that pervade the world of everyday life Schutz sees only a short, though significant, step to the types used in the worlds of theory and of social science. He points out, for instance, that common-sense interpretations using course-of-action and personal ideal types have social-scientific parallels not only in role theory but also in the distinction between subjective and objective meanings (Schutz, 1962, p. 149). Like other scientists, social scientists seek the latter type of meanings. What distinguishes their fields of study is that they ultimately seek objective interpretations of subjective meanings.

This definitive circumstance means social scientists need to remain vividly aware of how the meaning of any action necessarily differs for the actor, for the actor's partner in a We-relationship, and for the observer who is not a particip-ant in that relationship (Schutz, 1962, p. 24). We have already seen that lived We-relationships vary enormously in immediacy, intimacy, and intensity so that the "outside" observer and the "inside" participant are more or less dissimilar in their points of view. They cannot make precisely the same objective sense of the actor's subjective meaning. Their respective positions entitle them to differing degrees of familiarity with and knowledge of the actor's relevances, biographical situation, and typical in-order-to and because motives.

To some significant extent social scientists must remain Outsiders, then. No matter how much participant observation, direct observation, ethnographic labor, or other methodical work they do, they cannot become full-fledged members of an Other world, which its members are continuously making together and which links their biographical situations together in multiple ways. Social scientists will always remain, at least in part, the Observer (except when lying about or covering up their main in-order-to motive). Participants in their research will use that sort of personal ideal type to typify the social scientist. To some extent they will rely on the course-of-action type "doing research" to account for his or her behavior.

In large measure the social scientist is thus fated to be a perennial outsider. All the while, though, social scientists also remain insiders unable to extricate themselves from the ties of the life-world. Experiencing some familiarity, sharing the language, recognizing some (if not all) of the types of people and action constituting the world of his or her observations, the social scientist draws on the very resources that social science research should illuminate. As Schutz (1967, p. 10) put it, social scientists' data

> are the already constituted meanings of active participants in the social world. It is to these already meaningful data that [their] scientific concepts must ultimately refer: to the meaningful acts of individual men and women, to their everyday experience of one another, to their understanding of one another's meanings, and to their initiation of new meaningful behavior of their own. [Social scientists] will be concerned, furthermore, with the concepts people have of the meaning of their own and others' behavior and the concepts they have of the meaning of artifacts of all kinds. So we see that the data of the social sciences have, while still in the prescientific state, those elements of meaning and intelligible structure which later appear in more or less explicit form with a claim to categorial validity in the interpretive science itself.

In a nutshell, then, insider/outsider social scientists face the standing challenge of developing "methodological devices for attaining objective and verifiable knowledge of a subjective meaning structure" (Schutz, 1962, p. 36). Negotiating the experiential borderland they inhabit as both insiders and outsiders, social scientists intent on representing nonfictional worlds must put into play a logic of inquiry that respects their paradoxical positioning.

Schutz (1967, p. 15) felt that "the man whose thought has penetrated most deeply into the structure of the social world" was Max Weber. In Schutz's (1982, pp. 42–3) judgment the Thou

> stands in the center of Weber's considerations. He intends to comprehend the Thou and his meaning scientifically....However, this Thou is different from all other objects of experience in that it can be understood. Therefore, his comprehension demands a particular method. To exactly formulate this method is the purpose of the main part of this study.

For Schutz (1962, pp. 24–5), that method has its origins in the world of everyday life. Specifically, he theorizes that "the postulate of the 'subjective interpretation of meaning,' as the unfortunate term goes, is not a particularity of Weber's sociology or of the methodology of the social sciences in general but a principle of constructing course-of-action types in common-sense experience." Social scientists *reflectively* pursue what is typically prereflective among common-sense actors, and that difference is significant. Still, though, the two types of actors engage in typifying other actors along the same broad channels. In the end, for example, social scientists can only grasp people in the everyday world as personal ideal types, not as living individuals in their uniqueness, much as common-sense actors can only grasp their mere contemporaries as types who lack unique biographical situations and one-of-a-kind bodies.

Inevitably, such typification does carry the risk of fictionalizing Others and their world. For social scientists committed to minimizing that risk, Schutz (1962, pp. 43–4) laid out three postulates. The *postulate of logical consistency* requires compatibility of one's findings with the principles of formal logic and thus applies to social-scientific findings a criterion that has little applicability to common-sense knowledge. The *postulate of subjective interpretation* requires that social scientists explore the kind of consciousness, including its typical contents, that one must presuppose in order to account for observed actions. The *postulate of adequacy* requires that scientific models of action be formulated so as to make sense to the actors themselves and their consociates "in terms of common-sense interpretation of everyday life." This last postulate ensures close attention to individuals' subjective meanings and others' common-sense interpretations of those meanings by requiring that scientific models of action be comprehensible to those whose actions they are supposed to represent. This postulate also stands to make (or keep) social scientists aware of how their own typifications of social reality revolve around "constructs of the second degree" (Schutz, 1962, p. 59) or "second-order constructs" that build on the first-order or common-sense constructs operative in everyday life.

Schutz thus theorized a logic of inquiry capable of lending strength to any methodology that departs from the hegemony of measurement and statistics in the social sciences. In particular, Schutz's stance resonates not only with ethnomethodology but also with other varieties of social theory that have emerged over the past thirty or so years – feminist theory, queer theory, and multicultural social theory in all its far-reaching richness. Let me offer two examples. The first is Dorothy Smith's social theorizing.

Smith (1990, p. 2) observes that "Sociology created . . . a construct of society that is specifically discontinuous with the world known, lived, experienced, and acted in." Taking off from Schutz's notions about the fictional worlds that social scientists routinely construct, Smith (1990, p. 3) lays out a logic of inquiry that "relies on the insider's knowledge of how the social relations and organization in which she participates work, how they are put together." Smith helped to establish *standpoint theory*, which emphasizes the distinctive slant on a social world that any given social positioning necessarily entails. Smith typically emphasizes women's standpoints as an antidote to the fictionalizing – that is, false universalizing – common among social scientists who often take only men's viewpoints into account.

Renato Rosaldo's theorizing also illuminates the diffuse reach of Schutz's thinking. Trained in anthropology and pursuing work in Chicano/a studies as well, Rosaldo (1993, pp. 169ff.) also emphasizes standpoint as a theoretical line of access to nonfictionalizing methodologies. He cites Schutz as a "key antecedent" to the notions of "subject position" or "positioned subject," which refers to the social location of the experiencing person (Rosaldo, 1993, p. 227). His methodology explicitly problematizes the notion of culture by centering on cultural border zones and implicitly problematizes "home" as much contemporary social theorizing does.

Between the lines of much feminist, queer, and multicultural social theory lie tales about the difficulty many people face making a home for themselves. Much of that theorizing illuminates domestic violence against women and children and elderly men, familial rejection of lesbian daughters and gay sons, hate crimes, and institutionalized biases that systematically deprive racial, sexual, ethnic, and other minorities of the resources necessary to speak with powerful voices in today's postindustrial societies. Schutz wrote rather little about such injustices, though he did write a major paper on "Equality and the Meaning Structure of the Social World" (Schutz, 1964, pp. 226ff.) Schutz (1982, p. 212) had also outlined work on race and sex differentiation, among other things. Yet two of Schutz's essays offer stunning grounds for theorizing about home and thus are key resources for many social theorists today.

"The Stranger: an Essay in Social Psychology" and "The Homecomer" both appeared in the *American Journal of Sociology* (1944 and 1945, respectively). "The Stranger" implies what it means to have a home – to be "accepted or at least tolerated," to feel centered rather than at a loss in one's environment, to experience typicality as "an unquestioned matter of course" and thus as a shelter of taken-for-granted meaning, to know one belongs (Schutz, 1962, pp. 91, 99, 102, 104). "The Homecomer" more explicitly addresses the matter. Home, says Schutz (1962, p. 108), means

> father-house and mother-tongue, the family, the sweetheart, the friends; it means a beloved landscape, "songs my mother taught me," food prepared in a particular way, familiar things for daily use, folkways, and personal habits – briefly, a peculiar way of life composed of small and important elements, likewise cherished.

Schutz goes on to observe that the phrase "to feel at home" expresses "the highest degree of familiarity and intimacy." With such formulations as these Schutz provides theoretical leverage for many of the issues drawing contemporary theorists toward horizons with a multicultural and often postmodernist cast.

A similar generalization might be proffered about Schutz's attention to the body. With renewed and imaginative theorizing about the body in the humanities as well as the social sciences today, Schutz's treatment of the body sets him apart from many of his philosophical and sociological contemporaries. Schutz (1962, p. 148) theorized the body of the Other as an "expressional field" whereby we glean the thoughts, feelings, and motives currently informing the Other's stream of experience. Ego's body is equally central. My body is at the center of my physical world; it is the material basis for "gear[ing] into the outer world" through my work (Schutz, 1962, p. 227). It is also the basis for my "feeling of life," which is what Schutz (1982, p. 77) calls each person's awareness of his or her own body. Schutz (1982, p. 102) also spoke of the "privileged position" somatic experiences occupy and about how touch evokes awareness of the body's boundaries. As with his theorizing about home, Schutz's theorizing about the body gives his work a contemporary feel and, more importantly, substantial relevance today.

ASSESSMENT

Assessing Schutz's thought seems easy enough until one takes stock of its impact. Except for a few key instances, Schutz's impact has been substantially indirect but dramatically diffuse. His work directly affected Natanson's corpus, which is a stunning achievement bringing together phenomenology, the philosophy of the social sciences, sociology, and much else under the aegis of human experiencing. Schutz's work also shaped the landmark study of Peter Berger and Thomas Luckmann, namely *The Social Construction of Reality: a Treatise on the Sociology of Knowledge* (1967). Berger and Luckmann's masterpiece, itself widely influential, draws on the insights of Weber, Marx, and Durkheim, as well as those of Schutz. To my way of thinking, though, the Schutzian character of this study outweighs its Weberian or other intellectual dimensions. From beginning to end Berger and Luckmann concern themselves with the very questions lending coherence to Schutz's framework. They want to know, for instance, what people's faces *mean* during face-to-face interaction and how two people (A and B) could conceivably launch a sociohistorical world together.

Schutz also directly, though less heavily, influenced Harold Garfinkel, who during the 1960s established ethnomethodology as a major force in the social sciences and beyond. Schutz and Garfinkel corresponded briefly as well as met one another, and the latter's doctoral dissertation (completed under the tutelage of Parsons) incorporates some of Schutz's ideas. Schutz's ideas had a comparable impact on some of Goffman's later work, especially *Frame Analysis: an Essay on the Organization of Experience* (1974). Goffman's twenty-page introduction to this opus revolves around his exploration of James's and Schutz's thinking about experience, meaning, and multiplicity. Goffman's remaining 500-plus pages can be read as a detailed delineation of Schutz's ideas about the social stock of knowledge and, to a lesser extent, any given individual's stock of knowledge at hand. As we saw, Schutz also influenced Dorothy Smith's theorizing. Overall, then, his direct impact on social theorists would seem concentrated in the realms of phenomenology, ethnomethodology, social dramaturgy, and feminist standpoint theory along the lines developed by Natanson, Garfinkel, Goffman, and Smith, respectively.

Yet Schutz's ideas show up across a much wider range of social theory than that, as Rosaldo's work illustrates. For the most part, in fact, it seems that Schutz's influence has been unusually diffuse. Wherever qualitative methodologies are taken seriously, for instance, his ideas have a sound chance of being heard, if only indirectly. For the most part quantitative methods show *how much* is going on in some social world. Quantitative researchers are also good at showing how much one aspect of social reality correlates with other aspects.

All the while quantitative approaches do little to illuminate *what* is going on in a social world. That task is implicitly left to qualitative inquiries, and Schutz's ideas are capable of establishing the root systems of such approaches. Theorizing about human consciousness, experiencing, knowledge, action, taken for grantedness, and intersubjectivity guarantee his relevance to those pursuing qualitative methods. Rosaldo (1993, p. 207) writes that

> the fiction of the uniformly shared culture increasingly seems more tenuous than useful. Although most metropolitan typifications continue to suppress border zones, human cultures are neither necessarily coherent nor always homogeneous. More often than we usually care to think, our everyday lives are crisscrossed by border zones, pockets, and eruptions of all kinds.

I can hear Schutz applauding that formulation. His ideas are as much at work in Rosaldo's volume as anyone else's that Rosaldo invokes. Yet Schutz's name has no place in Rosaldo's index, and he may well have gotten no more than the one citation I have already mentioned.

Overall, then, Schutz's legacy seems to be that of diffuse impact. He launched no identifiable school of thought, and he gathered around him no clear-cut band of disciples. Yet his work gets cited time and time again as social theorists grapple anew with the stubborn question of what it means to share a world while living a life that no one else can have. As social theorists focus their attention on texts and language, discourse and narratives, home and its challenges, bodies and somatic experiences, and much else that Schutz addressed, his impact may well concentrate itself along more decided channels. All the while one does well to bear in mind that impact is a secondary measure of quality. As Schutz himself recognized, connections, contacts, and networks interplay with organizational affiliation as major influences on how much attention and what kind of reception a scholar's ideas get. By and large, those circumstances disadvantaged Schutz.

Until the last several years of his life, Schutz worked only part-time in academe. His part-time affiliation was not with an Ivy League institution, nor was it with the University of Chicago or any of the other centers of lively philosophizing and theorizing. Schutz had no mentor promoting his career, promulgating his ideas, helping him get published, or showing him the ropes of the American academic system. Moreover, Schutz worked in areas of social theory that are hard to define, if only because of their transdisciplinary reach. Nevertheless, he established a name for himself by dint of the powerful framework he built up. Put differently, Schutz's ideas are the main reason he is widely known. His is not a reputation resting to any discernible degree on the advantages common among widely known twentieth-century social theorists.

Bibliography

Writings of Alfred Schutz

Collected Papers I: The Problem of Social Reality (edited by Maurice Natanson). 1962. The Hague: Martinus Nijhoff.

Collected Papers II: Studies in Social Theory (edited by Arvid Brodersen). 1964. The Hague: Martinus Nijhoff.

Collected Papers III: Studies in Phenomenological Philosophy (edited by Ilse Schutz). 1966. The Hague: Martinus Nijhoff.

The Phenomenology of the Social World (translated by George Walsh and Frederick Lehnert). 1967. Evanston, IL: Northwestern University Press.

Reflections on the Problem of Relevance (edited by Richard M. Zaner). 1970. New Haven, CT: Yale University Press.

The Structures of the Life-World (with Thomas Luckmann, translated by Richard M. Zaner and H. Tristram Engelhardt Jr). 1973. Evanston, IL: Northwestern University Press.

Husserl and His Influence on Me. 1977. In Don Ihde and Richard M. Zaner (eds), *Interdisciplinary Phenomenology*. The Hague: Martinus Nijhoff, pp. 124–9.

Life Forms and Meaning Structure (translated and edited by Helmut R. Wagner). 1982. London: Routledge & Kegan Paul.

Further reading

Berger, Peter and Luckmann, Thomas (1967) *The Social Construction of Reality*. New York: Doubleday.

Goffman, Erving (1974) *Frame Analysis: an Essay on the Organization of Experience*. New York: Harper and Row.

Grathoff, Richard (1978) *The Theory of Social Action: the Correspondence of Alfred Schutz and Talcott Parsons*. Bloomington: Indiana University Press.

Grathoff, Richard (1989) *Philosophers in Exile: the Correspondence of Alfred Schutz and Aron Gurwitsch, 1939–1959*. Bloomington: Indiana University Press.

Natanson, Maurice (1970) *The Journeying Self: a Study in Philosophy and Social Role*. Reading, MA: Addison-Wesley.

Natanson, Maurice (1973) *Edmund Husserl: Philosopher of Infinite Tasks*. Evanston, IL: Northwestern University Press.

Natanson, Maurice (1986) *Anonymity: a Study in the Philosophy of Alfred Schutz*. Bloomington: Indiana University Press.

Rosaldo, Renato (1993) *Culture and Truth: the Remaking of Social Analysis*. Boston: Beacon Press.

Smith, Dorothy E. (1990) *Texts, Facts, and Femininity: Exploring the Relations of Ruling*. New York: Routledge.

Wagner, Helmut R. (1970) Introduction. In Helmut Wagner (ed.), *Alfred Schutz on Phenomenology and Social Relations*. Chicago: University of Chicago Press, pp. 1–50.

Wagner, Helmut R. (1983) *Alfred Schutz: an Intellectual Biography*. Chicago: University of Chicago Press.

Webb, Rodman B. (1992) The Life and Work of Alfred Schutz: a Conversation with Maurice Natanson. *Qualitative Studies in Education*, 5(4), 283–94.

12

Talcott Parsons

Victor Lidz

Introduction

Talcott Parsons (1902–79) was, and remains, the pre-eminent American sociologist, noted primarily for the broad scope and analytic depth of his theory of human social action. The trends of thought that brought him to leadership in sociological theory were established in his first articles and sustained, through many modifications and elaborations, over fifty years of publication. He published more than ten books, including several with collaborators, seven volumes of collected essays, three edited books, and perhaps as many as 100 additional essays. Several of his major writings – *The Structure of Social Action* of 1937, *The Social System* of 1951, *Economy and Society* (with Neil J. Smelser) of 1956, and "On the Concept of Political Power" of 1962 (in Parsons, 1969) – are landmarks in the development of sociological theory. The central force in shaping curricula in sociology at Harvard University from the late 1920s to the mid 1960s, he was the most influential teacher of sociologists in his generation (Fox, 1997). From the 1930s to the early 1970s, he was a mentor to scores of graduate students who later became creative social scientists.

Parsons's main concern was to develop a coherent conceptual scheme for sociology that would be applicable in all times and places, would address all aspects of human social organization, and would be open to progressive refinement as the advancing discipline gained in ability to relate theory to empirical knowledge. This concern remained constant throughout his career and provides the unity to theoretical and empirical writings that are otherwise extraordinarily diverse in sources of ideas, topics addressed, and levels of technical elaboration. Parsons's expansive understanding of the mandate for theory in intellectually disciplined or 'scientific' sociology was based on a sophisticated methodology, rooted in his undergraduate and graduate studies of Kant, but modified under the influence of A. N. Whitehead's philosophy of science.

Parsons is often compared to such builders of comprehensive theories as Comte and Spencer, but this mischaracterizes his undertaking. His efforts were focused on developing conceptual schemes or frames of reference to facilitate empirical investigation. Following Whitehead, he viewed establishing frames of reference as logically preliminary to empirical research, including the phase of empirical research that involves generating hypotheses to be tested. He thus regarded his own distinctive contribution as clarifying frames of reference and their consequences for empirical hypotheses and propositional theories (Lidz, in Klausner and Lidz, 1986, chapter 6). He understood that empirical feedback, primarily from the research findings of others, was essential for assessing the value of his conceptual and propositional work. Although most of his conceptual work was highly abstract, and some of it became very complicated, it never had the character of a closed system (Lidz and Bershady, 2000).

A strong commitment to progressive development of his ideas was a striking characteristic of Parsons's manner of work. He was an astute and persistent critic of his own writings. Never complacent about what he had accomplished, he rarely remained satisfied with particular formulations for more than a brief time. Whenever he returned to a specific topic, even in lectures to undergraduate classes, he endeavored to advance new considerations and new formulations. (He apparently prepared fresh notes for every class and every public presentation.) He undertook new books or major articles with the expectation of developing significantly new theoretical ideas. In second drafts of writings, he typically made major revisions and extensions of ideas he had thought his creative best only weeks or months before.

The strength of Parsons's drive for innovation creates difficulties for scholars who wish to understand and critique his theories. While there are fundamental continuities across his writings, he changed important formulations at several points. Subordinate formulations were changed frequently. Writings that introduced changes, especially of technical details, frequently omitted frank justifications for the changes. Interpreting the evolution of Parsons's theory thus requires not only mastery of many difficult writings, but also careful attention to changing conceptual frameworks and shifting details.

THE PERSON

Early life and studies

Talcott Parsons was born on December 13, 1902 in Colorado Springs, Colorado, where his father, a Congregational minister by training, served as Professor of English and later Dean of the Faculty at Colorado College. Parsons's parents maintained the ascetic Protestant culture associated with their New England heritage. However, Edward Parsons combined a conservative and disciplined personal manner – he and his wife maintained a teetotaling household – with liberalism on social issues. He held a strong interest in the Social Gospel move-ment and in intellectual matters. Talcott Parsons came to identify with his family connection to the eighteenth-century theologian, Jonathan Edwards, and as an adult also combined an ascetic modesty in personal manners (but not teetotal-ing) with a liberalism on social issues and interpersonal generosity to colleagues and students.

In 1917, Edward Parsons was forced out of Colorado College by trustees who were displeased with his role in reporting improper conduct on the part of the college president. He later became president of Marietta College in Ohio. In the short term, however, he moved his family to New York City, where Talcott Parsons prepared for college at the progressive Horace Mann School. He then attended Amherst College, where his exceptional academic promise became apparent. At Amherst, initially planning to follow an older brother into medi-cine, he studied biology and gained a broad overview of evolutionary theory, comparative anatomy, and physiology that later supported his turn to functional theory in sociology. However, course work in economics resonated with his strong concern for social reform and social justice. Economics at Amherst was dominated by the institutional school, and Parsons gained exposure, through Walton Hamilton, to its latest trends of thought. Parsons studied figures such as Veblen, Commons, Sumner, and Cooley, whose writings addressed the social and institutional aspects of the economy. He also read various American and English economic historians who described the institutional growth of the industrial economy and the many social problems it engendered. He gained sufficient perspective on the institutional school to appreciate that it was largely an out-growth of the German school of historical economics. A course on Kant's *Critique of Pure Reason* with George Brown, a Scottish trained philosopher who emphasized disciplined and critical reading of master texts, influenced Parsons's later tendency to study and restudy selected works by major authors.

After graduating from Amherst in 1924, Parsons matriculated at the London School of Economics (LSE). For a young scholar of economic institutions with sympathy for socialist ideals, the LSE was then a major academic center, and Parsons enrolled with high expectations. Through classes and personal encoun-ters, he came to know several of the LSE luminaries: R. H. Tawney, Morris Ginsberg, Bronislaw Malinowski, and Harold Laski (Parsons, 1977, chapter 1). His participation in Malinowski's seminar left the most favorable impression as well as lasting friendships with E. E. Evans-Pritchard, Meyer Fortes, and Raymond Firth, later major figures in British social anthropology, who also took the seminar. Ginsberg's teaching in sociology was encyclopedic in scope, but made a poor impression. It reified utilitarian concepts and lacked close engagement with specific materials. When an opportunity arose to spend a year in Germany on a fellowship, Parsons gladly accepted the chance to study the German historical school of economics.

Parsons often commented that his assignment to the University of Heidelberg and involvement with the scholarship of Max Weber was serendipitous. He had scarcely known Weber's name. His placement at Heidelberg in 1925 was a chance decision by administrators of the fellowship program. Arriving in

Heidelberg five years after Weber's death, he found that Weber's "ghost" still dominated local social science. Weber's contributions were emphasized in lectures and in informal contacts with faculty. Parsons soon studied *The Protestant Ethic and the Spirit of Capitalism* and was deeply moved by Weber's understanding and analysis of the heritage in which he had been raised (Parsons, 1977, chapter 1). He quickly became immersed in the larger body of Weber's writings, including the comparative studies of religious ethics and civilization, the theoretical schemes of *Economy and Society*, and the methodological essays. He then studied other bodies of scholarship that were essential background to Weber, namely, Rickert and the neo-Kantian movement in historical and social scientific methodology; other key figures in the German historical school of economics, especially Schmoller, Sombart, Below, and Brentano; Mengel and the Austrian marginalist school; and Karl Marx. Methodologically, he was strongly influenced by Weber's writings, the broader neo-Kantian movement, and a second thorough reading of Kant in Karl Jaspers's seminar.

During the 1925–6 academic year, Parsons learned that he could earn a doctorate at Heidelberg without unduly extending his stay in Germany. He focused his studies on the theoretical understanding of the first emergence of modern capitalism and planned a dissertation on the conceptual frameworks needed to interpret and analyze the historical materials. From the outset, the works of Max Weber were to be the centerpiece of his discussion. At the suggestion of his dissertation supervisor, the economic historian and social scientist Edgar Salin, he confined his dissertation to leading figures in the German literature, concentrating on Weber and Sombart.

After his year in Heidelberg, Parsons, extensive notes on his German readings in hand, returned to Amherst to serve as Instructor in Economics for the academic year 1926–7 while writing his doctoral dissertation. He taught a course on sociology as well as courses in economics. In the spring of 1927, he received an appointment as Instructor in the Department of Economics at Harvard for the next fall. His appointment at Harvard brought sufficient economic security that he could marry Helen Walker, whom he had met at LSE. They remained happily married until his death. They had three children, all born in the 1930s: Anne, who became an anthropologist whose interests overlapped with her father's, but whose contributions were cut off by depression and suicide in 1964; Charles, who has become a distinguished philosopher and logician, now professor at Harvard University; and Susan, who has become a bank attorney.

In the summer of 1927, Parsons submitted his doctoral dissertation to Heidelberg. Its German title, according to official records, corresponded to *The Spirit of Capitalism in Weber and Sombart*. He successfully defended the dissertation before a committee of Jaspers, Alfred Weber, and Salin. His doctorate was awarded in 1929 after publication of his two articles on "'Capitalism' in Recent German Literature: Sombart and Weber" (Parsons, 1991), meeting the requirement of German universities that dissertations be published.

Parsons's appointment at Harvard rested largely on his ability to represent German historical economics. He later said that he regarded himself as a sort of advanced graduate student even though he held faculty title because his German degree had been gained with far less study than was required for American doctorates. He accordingly sat in on the seminars in economic theory of such senior colleagues as Taussig and Schumpeter, and actively exchanged ideas with several junior faculty colleagues (Parsons, 1977, chapter 1). He was aware that his training in German historical economics seemed overly specialized in American settings. To compensate, he studied the rapidly developing American neoclassical economics, its background in Marshall and the British marginalists, and Pareto. He also began to reframe his ongoing research in the terms of American economics, where a synthesis of the institutional and neoclassical approaches would be a significant topic (Camic, Introduction to Parsons, 1991). However, his interests were also open toward sociology. He taught in the undergraduate program on social ethics along with other faculty members who held broad interests in social science and advocated the founding of a sociology department.

Political values and interests

When Parsons arrived at LSE, his political views were sympathetic to democratic socialism and optimistic that future economic systems could reduce the inequality and oppressive work conditions of major capitalist systems. However, his intellectual interests were stronger than his ideological tendencies. After a year of study at the LSE, he was disappointed by the lack of intellectual imagination and discipline he had found in the social and economic thought of the British left. In Heidelberg, he encountered in Max Weber's writings the stimulating imagination and uncompromising conceptual rigor he had sought. His later political and economic views were likely influenced by Weber's scorn for every strain of utopianism in modern thought. But he did not assimilate the conservatism that predominated in the German academic world.

In his early years at Harvard, if not before, Parsons's residual commitment to socialism gave way to a growing appreciation that markets are needed to institutionalize economic efficiency. He recognized that socialist planning could not substitute for markets without great losses in efficiency and the creation of wealth. This view was strengthened after the Second World War, when studies of the Soviet industrial system demonstrated the inefficiencies of planned economies. By the early 1930s, Parsons looked to better regulation of capitalist production as a more promising path to social improvement than socialism. During the Great Depression, he became a firm supporter of Roosevelt's New Deal, with its emphasis on overcoming the deprivations of poverty and ethnic or racial discrimination. For the rest of his life, he was an adherent of the liberal wing of the Democratic Party and, as an academic, was particularly committed to the freedoms of conscience, speech, publication, and association. He tended to look to expansion of a prosperous middle class as the most effective way to pursue values of social equality. From the mid-1950s to the end of his life, he identified himself as a "Stevenson Democrat" or "academic liberal." Yet he retained a sympathy for the ideals of democratic socialism and opposed the left only when he sensed that it had become authoritarian or radically utopian. His wife Helen's sympathies remained more to the left and more quickly sensitive to new movements, such as the opposition to the Vietnam War.

THE THEORY

The Department of Sociology and *The Structure of Social Action*

In 1930, the Russian émigré sociologist, Pitirim Sorokin, who had served in the Kerensky government and later taught at the University of Minnesota, arrived at Harvard to chair a new Department of Sociology. Parsons transferred to the new department expecting a better fit for his long-term interests. However, he soon found himself in frequent conflict with Sorokin, who disparaged his work and obstructed his promotion. He remained an Instructor until 1934 and did not become a tenured associate professor until after *The Structure of Social Action* (*SSA*) had appeared in 1937 and he had been offered a full professorship by the University of Wisconsin. Even then, his promotion occurred only after the intercession of Lawrence J. Henderson, the renowned physiologist who had developed an interest in sociology, taught in the new department, and appreciated Parsons's contributions. Nevertheless, the new departmental setting appears to have liberated Parsons's thought by legitimating his broad interests and shift to conceptual frameworks beyond both neoclassical and institutional economics.

By the mid-1930s, Parsons's main concerns encompassed the relationships between economic and all other social institutions, with a focus on the conceptual and theoretical tools needed to understand this large empirical field. He had translated Weber's *Protestant Ethic and the Spirit of Capitalism* (1930) and focused his scholarship increasingly on Weber rather than other figures in the German school. He had studied the theoretical systems of Alfred Marshall and Vilfredo Pareto and published important articles on their works (Parsons, 1991, chapters 8 and 15). The article on Marshall long remained widely read among economists. He had also begun serious study of the works of Émile Durkheim, whose critique of utilitarian thought provided a key reference point for his own conceptual efforts.

Harvard's new Department of Sociology attracted an exceptionally talented group of graduate students and Parsons soon emerged as its most influential teacher. Within a decade, he had established himself as sociology's most important cultivator of student talent and had placed capable and productive students in leading departments across the country. His postwar status as the central figure in American sociology followed the maturation of his early students' careers when they returned to the universities after military or government service.

The flowering of Parsons's thought in the setting of the new department also involved a significant turn toward the empirical materials of sociology. He initiated a course on comparative institutions, which he then taught many times down to the end of his career. The course was framed in terms of the full scope of Weber's empirical writings. Parsons taught the theory needed for comparative institutional analysis, but during the 1930s and 1940s invited distinguished specialists in many civilizations and historical epochs to teach the empirical materials. He forged intellectual relationships with many of these scholars and studied their writings and other works they cited. His own conceptual schema was affected in its many phases by engagement with empirical materials covered in this course. His writings on the German class structure and the rise of Nazism, the expanding role of professions in American society, the nature of medieval European civilization, or the civilizations of Antiquity were all influenced by the materials of his course on comparative institutional analysis.

Parsons began to formulate the foundations of his own theory in a series of essays that appeared in the early and middle 1930s. These included the essays on Marshall and Pareto, but also three essays that addressed in general terms the sociological elements embedded in economic theory. A 1935 essay entitled "The Place of Ultimate Values in Sociological Theory" was significant in three respects: it was the first major publication in which he addressed sociological theory rather than economic theory as his central topic, thus signaling a shift in his professional identity; it was the first essay to present aspects of the conceptual scheme that later became the core of *SSA*; and it outlined a shrewd and bold argument about the importance of values as structural determinants of social action, staking out a position that Parsons continued to refine throughout his career (Parsons, 1991, chapter 18).

The conceptual scheme to which these essays pointed was presented comprehensively and in greater depth in *SSA* (Parsons, 1937). In *SSA*, Parsons proposed a comprehensive and well integrated frame of reference that departed radically from the empiricism and positivism that were then dominant orientations in American sociology. His conceptual scheme was based initially on a probing evaluation of leading European economists and sociologists of the late nineteenth and early twentieth centuries, particularly Weber, Durkheim, Pareto, and Marshall. The action frame of reference, as Parsons called it, was a careful synthesis of a small number of premises and categories that, he claimed, are fundamental to all sociological understanding. Parsons did not present his frame of reference as a complete or precise theory, but as a thoroughly justified, well balanced set of basic concepts essential to the development of more technical theory (Lidz and Bershady, 2000). He supported his claims for the action frame of reference empirically with a critical review of the evidence amassed in Weber's comparative studies and in Durkheim's major writings.

As presented in *SSA*, the action frame of reference centers on the notion of the "unit act," a hypothetical entity representing any and all instances of meaningful human social behavior. Parsons specified four essential elements of the unit act: ends, means, norms, and conditions. These four categories of elements (and, in some statements, a category of effort) are essential in the sense that no social action can exist without the presence of at least one instance of each. Every instance of social action, regardless of time, place, or cultural context, necessarily contains exemplars of each category. In developing the idea of the unit act,

Parsons emphasized that the normative elements of social action have the same status as the more familiar elements of ends and means. An emphasis on studying the normative elements of social action, and on understanding the ways in which values and norms, when institutionalized, become structural to society, remained central to Parsons's writings throughout his career.

Parsons limited the scheme of *SSA* to basic concepts in order to concentrate on justifying its premises and essential elements. The justification entailed thorough critiques of the works of Marshall, Pareto, Durkheim, and Weber, but with a focus on the implications for basic premises and concepts. Parsons claimed that his critiques of these four major figures demonstrated that, despite the differences in their intellectual backgrounds, they had "converged" in emphasizing common concepts, which amounted in essence to the action frame of reference. Over the years, his argument has met with much skepticism by scholars who have documented many differences among the works of these theorists, especially Durkheim and Weber. For Parsons's purpose, however, convergence meant principally that the four theorists had agreed that social scientific frames of reference must include normative elements as well as means, ends, and conditions.

Despite the controversies over convergence, Parsons's treatments of all four figures became touchstones for critical evaluations of theoretical works in the social sciences. More than sixty years later, they remain key starting points for critical assessments of the theorists addressed. Due to their rigor, the treatments of Weber and Durkheim remain especially influential, even though a great deal more is now known about the biographies, connections to other scholars, and practical-ideological outlooks of all four figures. Down to the 1960s, *SSA* was the most influential single work in defining the core of the sociological tradition. Yet its aims were concerned less with assessing the writings of other scholars than with establishing the elementary and universal importance of the action frame of reference as a foundation for sociological understanding.

As compared with earlier American theories, Parsons's framework was distinctive in the extent of its emphasis on normative phenomena. Parsons argued that normative elements are necessary for any ongoing social relationships to maintain a degree of social order. In so far as the events of social life exhibit institutional continuity or coherence, the workings of normative elements, e.g. social values (ideals for relationships and institutions) and norms (rules of conduct), are necessary objects of sociological study. The normative components of a social system can be shared by its many participants, and accordingly their goals, and the means they select to pursue their goals, can be regulated by the same standards of conduct. Values and norms constrain or limit actors in their choices of ends or means, and hence are *regulative* in a manner not true of ends or means. Actors who share normative standards are able to develop reciprocal expectations of one another. Concrete expectations often differ according to specialized social roles, but actors in different roles and pursuing different ends may yet agree on the expectations appropriate to each of the parties engaged in common relationships. By focusing on the shared elements of normative order and common grounds of expectation, Parsons was able to analyze the *integration* of social action in a way that is not possible for utilitarian theorists, behaviorists, or other positivists whose theories focus on ends, means, and/or situational conditions as determinants of human behavior.

The methodological foundations of *SSA* are important not only for understanding that work, but because with little change they shaped Parsons's later work as well. Parsons's methodological ideas had sources going back to his early studies of Kant (Bershady, 1973), but were influenced by two senior scholars at Harvard in the 1930s: the physiologist, L. J. Henderson and the philosopher, A. N. Whitehead, whose *Science and the Modern World* and *Process and Reality* impressed Parsons (Lidz, in Klausner and Lidz, 1986, chapter 6). For Parsons, Henderson's "approximate definition of fact" as "an empirically verifiable statement about experience" (Parsons often Kantianized the definition by saying "phenomena") "in terms of a conceptual scheme" made an essential point. A fact does not inhere in a phenomenon itself. An event or phenomenon cannot, as Parsons often said, "speak for itself." A fact is a *statement* about a phenomenon. It must be formulated by a person who conceptualizes his or her cognition of the event or phenomenon. Stable statements of facts are not possible without a well ordered conceptual element. To generate and organize many facts about complex events, a carefully framed scheme of concepts is needed.

Whitehead emphasized that all elements of scientific knowledge are, by logical necessity, abstract in some degree. He called the empiricist failure to recognize elements of abstraction in all kinds of scientific constructs, even direct statements of fact, the "fallacy of misplaced concreteness." In his view, the relations of scientific knowledge to empirical reality cannot be understood with precision unless the underlying abstractions are clear. He used the term frames of reference to designate the carefully designed modes of abstraction that have guided the most important innovations in science. In *Science and the Modern World* (1925), he demonstrated that the crucial contributions of Galileo, Newton, Lavoisier, Darwin, and others (what we now call the great scientific revolutions) depended on revisions in basic frames of reference. This perspective is in a sense the keystone in the arch of *SSA*'s argument. Parsons was setting out to create a scientific revolution. He sought to establish a frame of reference that would enable sociology to extend and deepen its understanding of social facts. All his major writings are efforts to develop, elaborate, and clarify a central frame of reference for sociology and related disciplines.

After *The Structure of Social Action*

As Parsons completed *SSA*, he followed the advice of senior colleagues that his next project should be empirical and planned a participant-observer study of medical practice. His underlying interest was in the professional type of role relations. With the debates of the Great Depression years over economic systems as background, Parsons suggested that professional role-relationships are structured in a way that falls between the principle of self-interest in capitalism and the principle of collective interest in socialism (Parsons, 1949, chapter VIII). The professional is expected to act in the interest of the client rather than out of self-interest. Pay for professional services is limited by ethical standards, and was then often modified on a "sliding scale" by what clients could afford, not set at whatever price an openly competitive market would bear. (Today, health insurance rather than the practitioner's sliding scale protects covered patients from overwhelming medical costs.) Parsons in fact spent substantial time over more than a year observing several medical practitioners in their work at Harvard Medical School hospitals. As became typical of his later empirical studies, however, the main results were empirically informed theoretical essays. His interests encompassed resolution of theoretical problems with practical and empirical implications, but did not extend to careful reporting of empirical observations and findings.

In the late 1930s, Parsons became a leader among Harvard faculty who organized public opposition to Nazism in Germany and *Bund* activities in America (Gerhardt, 1993). He outspokenly opposed Nazi violations of academic freedom in the German universities and their attacks on many elements of German high culture. Later, he was active in opposing German militarism and expansionism, and became an early proponent of support for Great Britain and preparing the USA for war. His opposition to Nazism remained free of anti-Germanism, however, and he continued in the 1930s and 1940s to acknowledge his intellectual debt to the Kantian and liberal traditions of German culture. During the war years, he wrote a series of notable papers on the causes of Nazism in nineteenth- and twentieth-century German social structure (in Gerhardt, 1993).

Too old for military service during the Second World War, Parsons remained at Harvard, teaching and continuing his research. From 1943 to the end of the war, he taught in a Harvard program to prepare military, intelligence, and diplomatic officers to operate governments in occupied territories, including Germany and Japan. He also consulted with government agencies about matters of wartime policy, but did not become deeply engaged in the war effort as did some of his close Harvard associates. After the war, Parsons worked to promote permanent government funding for the social sciences. The Social Sciences Research Council asked him to prepare a document for use in lobbying Congress to include the social sciences in the mandate of the National Science Foundation. The model was to be the report prepared by Vannevar Bush that had persuaded the Truman administration and the Congress that the nation should continue the public investments in science that had been initiated during the war. Parsons's knowledge, interests, and professional connections seemed to make him an ideal advocate for the social sciences, but his report (in Klausner and Lidz, 1986, chapter 2) was too long, too theoretical, and too turgid for use in lobbying. Viewed as an academic report, however, it discussed an extraordinary range of the applied social science that had been conducted as part of the war effort and outlined a numbers of imaginative proposals about how further development of the same social scientific techniques could benefit the nation in peacetime.

During the postwar period, Parsons became increasingly active in the American Sociological Association (then the Society). He attended meetings, served on committees, and on several occasions gave well attended and influential talks. In 1949–50, he served as President and later as Secretary. Giving particular attention to opportunities to promote sociological research, he sought out government and foundation support, including for types of large-scale data collection and archiving he did not personally conduct. Developing networks of communication with scholars in Europe, Asia, and elsewhere was another longstanding professional priority. With the first warming of the Cold War in the mid-1960s, he cultivated ties with Soviet, Hungarian, Czechoslovak, and Polish social scientists. He was pleased to learn that informal translations of chapters of *The Social System* circulated underground in the Soviet Union, where means of duplicating texts were strictly controlled.

During the Cold War years, Parsons served on the board of Harvard's Russian Research Center (RRC). He took part in the Harvard administration's early discussions with the Carnegie Foundation and the Department of State to plan the RRC and was later involved in decisions about its initial staffing. At the start, the RRC was directed by the anthropologist, Clyde Kluckhohn on the basis of his wartime experience in studying closed societies at a distance. Parsons was strongly committed to the idea that, under Cold War conditions, the USA sorely needed more scholarly knowledge of the Soviet Union. He remained on the RRC board until the mid-1960s when his wife, Helen, retired from her long-term role as administrative assistant to the Director.

Parsons's major organizational venture in the postwar period was establishing Harvard's interdisciplinary Department of Social Relations (Nichols, 1998). The department originated in a collaboration among Clyde Kluckhohn in anthropology, Henry A. Murray and Gordon Allport in psychology, and Parsons in sociology. The myth of the department's founding is that each of the principals was hated by his chairman (Sorokin in Parsons's case) and believed his professional advancement was being improperly blocked. Founding a new department was a political coup that created new opportunities for each, especially Parsons, who became the first chairman. (But in fact Parsons had succeeded Sorokin as chair of sociology in 1944.) All of sociology moved into the new department along with the social and cultural anthropologists and the clinical and social psychologists. A curriculum was developed that combined training in each of the several disciplines with interdisciplinary proseminars and requirements that each student take courses in at least one field outside his or her own discipline. Although the department's founding myth captured some truth of the academic politics, the formation of the department was part of a broader interdisciplinary trend in that period. Talented students flocked to the new department and the special opportunities it offered. For more than a decade, the new curriculum was taught with élan and accepted by most students with enthusiasm. The later work of such early Social Relations students as James Olds, Renee Fox, Robert Bellah, Clifford Geertz, and Neil Smelser shows that the interdisciplinary curriculum had important and enduring effects. Due largely to Parsons's commitment, the benefits were more consistent among sociologists than among anthropologists and particularly psychologists.

Toward a General Theory of Action and *The Social System*

Just as the founding of the Sociology Department had enabled Parsons to write *SSA*, the founding of the Department of Social Relations initiated the period of Parsons's greatest and most self-confident creativity. The new department convened a faculty seminar (including as Visiting Professors Edward A. Shils from the University of Chicago and the psychologist Edward Tolman from the University of California at Berkeley) to develop a manifesto on the importance of interdisciplinary thought to sociology, psychology, and anthropology. The work was published as *Toward a General Theory of Action* (Parsons and Shils, 1951). It included a collaborative statement signed by most of the seminar participants and then their separate contributions. Parsons's contribution, in collaboration with Shils, was a long, dense essay entitled "Values, Motives and the Theory of Action."

This essay presented two cross-cutting dimensions for analyzing differentiation among processes of social action, still defined basically in the sense of *SSA*. One dimension pertains to the tendency of ongoing systems of meaningful action to differentiate into three independent but interdependent subsystems: culture, social systems, and personality. This conception of the threefold differentiation of action systems became one of the most famous themes in Parsons's work. The second dimension concerns the differentiation of elements of action into moral-normative, cathectic-affective, and cognitive gradients. The authors argued that cultural, social, and personality systems all differentiate along these three gradients and, indeed, connect with one another independently along each gradient. The conception of this second dimension of differentiation also became a famous theme in Parsons's work. He had used essentially the same triad of concepts, with slightly different terms, in an unpublished working paper prepared in the late 1930s. The earlier document indicates that the triad derived from parallel ideas in Kant, a source not acknowledged in the 1951 publication. The new scheme's emphasis on culture, social system, and personality was widely interpreted as referring, at least approximately, to the domains of anthropology, sociology, and psychology, and thus as legitimating the new department's commitment to interdisciplinary collaboration. The essay's thorough exploration of the connections between the two dimensions of differentiation produced a far more detailed analytical scheme than Parsons had put forward in *SSA*. The new scheme reached a level of analytical detail that made it more useful for empirical research.

"Values, Motives, and Systems of Action" was quickly followed by *The Social System* (Parsons, 1951), a major work that explored the sociological aspects of the same analytical scheme. Older manuscripts make clear that a work entitled "The Social System" had been in preparation since the early war years. After years of slow progress and dissatisfaction with the results, Parsons rapidly revised and expanded his manuscript after the conceptual scheme of "Values, Motives, and Systems of Action" had crystallized. *The Social System* addressed basic issues of definition and conceptual clarification of the social system and introduced a focused approach to functional analysis of social systems. In chapters that proved highly influential, it discussed processes of socialization and personality development, the classic problems of deviance and social control, and the relations between social systems and cultural belief systems. A particularly successful chapter combined themes from Parsons's earlier observational study of medical practice with his new conception of the social system to discuss the doctor–patient relationship. The resulting discussion became a charter for the early development of medical sociology as a specialty.

The key conceptual-theoretical innovation was a shift in analytical focus from the "unit act" of *SSA* to the "social system." Parsons defined social systems as consisting of interactive *relationships* among individuals. The conceptual framework for sociology was thus based on abstracting the dynamics of interaction from the more comprehensive processes of meaningful human conduct. Sociology became the study of factors of interaction that keep relationships in stable states (equilibria) or force relationships to change. Parsons again identified shared normative standards as a principal basis of stability and continuity in social relationships. However, his normative emphasis was reformulated in more dynamic terms. He now accentuated normative *expectations* that specify general norms (or rules) to particular role relationships and situations of interaction. Individuals who interact hold expectations of one another based on the specific social roles they occupy. Each actor supports his or her expectations of others by using a variety of tactics to sanction the others. The sanctioning tactics may include offering rewards for compliance with expectations and threatening, or actually imposing, punishments for noncompliance. Actual sequences of interaction are outcomes of the expectations and sanctions introduced by each party. Parsons noted that a "double contingency" applies to even the most elementary relationships because decision-making by each party is independent.

One feature of Parsons's conception of social systems runs sharply counter to common intuition. In Parsons's definition, the personalities of individual social actors are not parts of social systems or even societies as large-scale social systems. Rather, personalities are outside social systems because they constitute another class of system of action. Parsons therefore took up the question of how social systems and personality systems relate to one another in the ongoing processes of social action. With his characteristic emphasis on normative elements, he focused on a linkage between the institutional norms of a society and the superegos of individual personalities. He argued that the normative structures of a society and the superegos of its individual actors constitute the *same* moral-normative cultural content, but differently incorporated in the two kinds of system. The normative content is internalized in personalities and institutionalized in social systems. This formulation opened up a way of understanding the relationships between 'social structure' and 'personality' by incorporating dynamic ideas from psychology and psychoanalysis, as well as sociology. Yet it avoided the strong temptation to confound social dynamics with personality dynamics. This was a temptation to which many other theorists, from Malinowksi to Erich Fromm to Abraham Kardiner to Theodor Adorno, had succumbed in one respect or another. Parsons also highlighted a theme of the "institutional integration of motivation," stating that the motivational systems of individual personalities can be coherent and directed to specific goals only in so far as they are supported by social institutions and relationships. Reciprocally, social institutions require concertedly motivated individuals if the responsibilities associated with their constituent social roles are to be fulfilled.

The Social System also introduced new formulations in functional analysis. Parsons hypothesized that all social systems, whether mere dyads or entire societies, must manage problems of resource allocation and social integration. Resource allocation involves processes to ensure that role incumbents can command the means necessary to attain expected ends. The nature of the resources in question varies immensely by the type of social relationship in question. Particular kinds of tools, personnel trained in special skills, and financial means are frequently crucial types of resources. Economic markets are the most efficient mechanisms for allocating resources in response to the diverse needs of many units of a society. The need for integration is in the long run as urgent for social systems as the need for resources. Mechanisms of social control are needed to ensure that actors respond to one another's expectations and fulfill role obligations in reciprocal, mutually reinforcing ways. Large-scale social systems require formal methods of social control and dispute resolution, such as courts, legal procedure, and mechanisms of law enforcement. Parsons recognized that processes of resource allocation and processes of social integration often operate in tension or conflict with each other. Resource allocations that support efficiency in the early stages of industrialization, for example, may engender conflicts among social classes that threaten integration of the society. In many societies, the solidarity of traditional family and kin groups has required distribution of financial resources that disperses business capital and undermines family-based enterprise.

Both "Values, Motives, and Systems of Action" and *The Social System* addressed problems of classifying components of action systems, whether motivational patterns of personalities, social relationships, or cultural beliefs. Parsons had long been unsatisfied with the global terms used by sociologists to classify relationships and institutions, especially Ferdinand Tönnies's famous contrast between *Gemeinschaft* (person-to-person community) and *Gesellschaft* (impersonal society). He therefore proposed a multidimensional scheme for classifying relationships, which he termed the pattern variables or, occasionally, pattern alternatives. Five dichotomous pattern variables were presented. Two of the variables define choices in actors' orientations or general attitudes to objects in a situation of action. The first is affectivity versus affective neutrality, and defines whether an actor will seek direct gratification or adopt a stance of renunciation toward the object. The second pattern variable is universalism versus particularism, and defines the kind of value-standard to be engaged in the situation. A universalistic standard evaluates an open set of objects in terms of the same criteria, as when a teacher uses the same criteria to grade all students in a class. A particularistic standard invokes different criteria for each kind of relationship between actor and object, e.g. between father and son, or between fellow citizens of a town (versus outsiders). The third and forth pattern variables concern modalities or characteristics of objects that an actor selects as significant for his conduct in a situation. The third pattern variable is ascription versus achievement (later stated as quality versus performance), and defines whether the object is significant for what or who it is or for what it does or can do. A person who obtains a job as a member of the employing family gets it by ascription, while a person who obtains it by prior training and experience gets it by achievement. The fourth pattern variable is specificity versus diffuseness, and defines the scope of the object's significance for the actor. Does an actor relate to another only as a fellow employee, for example, or also as a close friend or family member whose overall well-being is of concern? The fifth pattern variable is self-orientation versus collectivity-orientation, and defines whether the actor pursues his or her personal ends or the ends of a collectivity (e.g. a sports team, research group, or nation) in relating to objects.

All five pattern variables were presented as phenomenological dichotomies. At a given choice-point in a process of action, one term in a pattern variable must be chosen and the other rejected. Together, the five pattern variables were claimed to provide an exhaustive definition of basic alternatives for social action. Few critics have agreed with this claim, although most have agreed that the pattern variables capture basic options facing social actors. As a set, the pattern variables offer a conceptually powerful and elegant alternative to the *Gemeinschaft–Gesellschaft* dichotomy. The combination of affectivity, collectivity-orientation, particularism, ascription, and diffuseness is a multidimensional characterization of *Gemeinschaft*, while the combination of affective neutrality, self-orientation, universalism, achievement, and specificity is a multidimensional characterization of *Gesellschaft*. Parsons, however, noted the importance of various other pattern variable combinations as well. He maintained that a number of combinations are helpful in characterizing the functional significance of various institutions within larger systems. The pattern variables have been used in many studies in sociology and political science, and the results confirm their ability to discriminate types of functional significance.

At publication, Parsons presented *The Social System* as an authoritative and carefully considered successor to SSA. In fact, it was creative and filled with suggestive leads for further investigation, but many of its formulations were still provisional. Only months after it appeared, Parsons started work on a new foundation for functional theory, which he called the "four function paradigm." He then used the new functional concepts to reorganize practically the entire theory of social action. Because of the status originally claimed for *The Social System*, however, many sociologists who had been interested in Parsons's earlier work failed to follow the subsequent evolution of his theory. Many sociologists who did encounter parts of his later writing failed to grasp their significance because they continued to rely on *The Social System* for an overview of his theory. When telling critiques of *The Social System* were published, often focusing on its weak chapter on social change, its brilliant but flawed discussion of deviance and social control, or its inadequate presentation of functional analysis, many in the profession at large were not aware that Parsons's thought had already moved far beyond the criticized formulations.

The emergence of the four function paradigm

After writing *The Social System*, Parsons's major interest was to refine the concept of *function* in social systems. Building on the notions of allocation and integration, he strove to develop an abstract, generalized, and multidimensional scheme to address basic issues of how social systems are organized. His effort began to bear fruit with *Working Papers in the Theory of Action* (Parsons et al., 1953), which introduced the so-called four function paradigm.

The four function scheme originated in Parsons's collaboration with Robert F. Bales. Bales had conducted laboratory studies of interaction in small groups assigned specific tasks for discussion. To examine issues of leadership, authority, conflict, maintenance of task-focus, and group solidarity, Bales had devised a scheme of sixteen categories to describe types of contribution to group process. He had shown that he could observe groups, record the predominant category of contribution made by each act of a group member, and later analyze the shifting emphases, or "phase movements", among the sixteen categories of group interaction (Bales, 1950). Bales argued that over time phase movements enable the interaction of group members to address various "needs" of task-oriented groups, e.g. the need for clear coordination to attain specific goals or the need for mutual positive feeling among members. Working together, Parsons and Bales grouped the sixteen categories of interaction process into four more general categories that appeared to represent fundamental "needs" of the groups.

In their initial formulation, the four "functional" categories were stated as results of empirical generalization about the needs of groups. They were presented basically as an outcome of empirical studies of a particular kind of group. The four categories were said to demarcate the dimensions of social "space" within which "phase movements" occur. They were designated 'functions' because the phase movements were thought to respond to enduring needs of groups.

A bolder formulation emerged later in *The Working Papers*: namely, that any and every social system needs to handle the same four general "system problems" in order to function. Parsons and colleagues argued that social relationships and institutions – or, more precisely, *aspects* of them – can be classified by how they contribute to managing one or more of the four "system problems." Parsons soon referred to the system problems as "functions." By the 1960s, the notion of function was presented less as a system problem than as an abstract *dimension* of social organization. The resulting "four function paradigm" became an explicit or implicit theoretical frame for practically everything Parsons wrote after the mid-1950s. With the four function paradigm, he approached more closely the goal set early in his career of developing an abstract, formal, and universal ground for sociological analysis and explanation.

The four system problems or functions are:

- *Adaptation*, the processes of gaining generalized control over conditions in the environment of the action system. Often, these processes involve generating new resources or allocating available resources more efficiently among units of the system in order to gain new capabilities for future action.

- *Goal attainment*, the processes of organizing the activities of social units into a concerted effort to achieve a desired change in the system's relationship to its environment. Other collectivities or societies may be principal factors in the environment and predominating over their interests may be a chief goal.
- *Integration*, the processes of adjustment to one another by units of the system. The processes may promote long-term attachment to the system and/or mutual dependence among autonomous units.
- *Pattern maintenance*, the processes of generating long-term commitment to shared values and other principles of action that distinguish the system of reference from other systems.

Particular processes of action may be located on all four dimensions, but generally they are able to specialize on any one dimension only at the expense of capabilities on the other three dimensions. Moreover, strength on one dimension during one phase of action typically requires an ongoing system to develop compensatory strengths on other dimensions during later phases. A system that emphasizes adaptation in one phase might generate strains that require greater emphasis on the integrative dimension soon afterward.

Because the four function paradigm was so abstract, many years of work were needed before Parsons's earlier formulations could be thoroughly assimilated to it. It can be argued that Parsons never completed this task despite a great deal of recasting of earlier ideas. However, the strengths and attractions of the four function paradigm were fundamental. Early "functionalist" theories, including formulations in *The Social System*, were open to the basic criticism that the number of functions was indefinite and empirical analyses often resulted in hypotheses about new functions. Early functional analysis therefore had an *ad hoc* quality that reduced its appeal as a strategy for theory construction. By contrast, the theory of four system problems constituted a definite and *a priori* list of basic functions. The four function paradigm also led to interesting hypotheses about patterns of organization that obtain among social institutions differentiated in terms of function. These hypotheses were gradually clarified as Parsons applied the paradigm to wider ranges of empirical materials.

In its last chapter, the *Working Papers* proposed that the four functions might be used to represent major dimensions of structural differentiation in society as a whole. This speculative idea forecast much of Parsons's theoretical work over the next two decades. Through that work, a theory of four functionally specialized *subsystems* of society gradually took shape. Each of the four subsystems was treated as a complex set of dynamically interdependent institutions that could in turn be analyzed along the same four functional dimensions. The new theory of societal subsystems (and *sub*subsystems) presented an approach to macrosocial analysis that, although never completely worked out, remains even today more comprehensive and analytically incisive than any alternative scheme.

In outline, the four subsystems of society, as they came to be identified, are:

- The *economy* is the subsystem specialized about the development and allocation of basic resources for use by individuals and collective units of the society. It consists of such institutions as markets for labor and capital, entrepreneurial roles, the legal complexes of property, contract, credit, and employment, and the organizational structure of business firms.
- The *polity* is the subsystem of society specialized about coordination of the pursuit of collective goals. Governmental agencies at all levels, including the administrative, executive, legislative, and judicial arms of public authority, are the primary institutional components of the polity, although Parsons also emphasized various nonpublic organizations and the role of the citizen.
- The *societal community* is the subsystem specialized about the integration of society. Social classes, status groups, ethnic groups, groups that share elements of 'lifestyle', and other groups that maintain diffuse and enduring ties of solidarity contribute to a society's manner of social integration. The dynamically interrelated phenomena of integration and conflict are shaped largely by institutions of class structure, status order, and 'primordial' solidary ties, but also by common law and the informal normative orders of custom or community mores.
- The *fiduciary system* is the subsystem specialized about the transmission (or reproduction), maintenance, and development of a society's enduring values and shared culture. The institutions of religion, family and kinship, and socialization and education are major constituents of the fiduciary system. Following the lead of Max Weber, Parsons emphasized that change in fiduciary systems, notably in religious ethics, have historically been the greatest forces toward long-term and large-scale social change.

The theory of societal subsystems retained Parsons's earlier emphasis on normative order. However, it achieved a new level of analysis of the forms that normative structures assume and the functions they serve in different institutional settings, such as economic exchange, relationships of political authority, solidarity ties among members of a status group, or processes of socialization in family life. Parsons thus opened up a new approach to analyzing modes of articulation between normative orders and practical institutions of societal functioning, e.g. economic markets, political bureaucracies, class structures, or families. His new synthesis transcended in principle (not always in specific empirical discussions) the nineteenth-century dichotomies between normative and interest-driven or ideal and material factors in social causation. Parsons argued that *every* effective social institution embodies an *integration* of normative and interest-driven, ideal and material factors. To be sure, the two dimensions can under practical circumstances be stripped apart. Relationships must then be formed on either ideal or contrary material grounds, and the pursuit of self-interest may become possible *only* through violation of normative rules. Such situations typically arise during periods of rapid social change and frequent conflict. However, the effective long-term functioning of social institutions depends on a normative regulation of material, interest-driven factors. Under such conditions, the pursuit of self-interest reinforces the controlling normative institutions, as when the ordinary conduct of business requires reliance upon the institutions of property, contract, and employment.

The Marshall Lectures and Economy and Society

Parsons spent the academic year of 1953–4 at the University of Cambridge in England, where he was invited to deliver the first Marshall Lectures. He knew when he accepted a visiting professorship that Cambridge had not yet made a place for sociology on its faculty, but was considering whether to do so. The social science faculty was dominated by a strong group of economists and economic historians who were skeptical of sociology. Parsons hoped to advance sociology's cause at Cambridge by demonstrating in a new way that the discipline could make significant contributions to economic understanding. The core of this demonstration was to use the four function scheme of the subsystems of society to analyze the relations between economic institutions and other major institutional structures of society.

The Marshall Lectures (Parsons, 1986) started with the idea that Keynes's treatment of the twofold exchange between the aggregate of business firms and the aggregate of households (wages for labor; goods and services for consumer spending) could be treated as a boundary relation between the adaptive and pattern maintenance subsystems of society. Parsons then suggested that each of the four classic factors of economic production, labor, capital, organization, and land, could be treated as an input to the economy from an extra-economic source. Just as labor (meaning a trained and socialized capability to perform economically valuable work) was an input from the pattern maintenance system, so capital (the financial means of controlling and allocating "real" economic resources) was an input from the polity, and organization (the capability to develop innovative relations of production) was an input from the system of social integration. All three of these factors – not only labor – entered the economy through twofold exchange relationships, which Parsons began to call "double interchanges." When viewed in disaggregation, the double interchanges were clearly mediated by complicated, highly differentiated markets. The factor of land Parsons treated as a special case. He used the term "land" to refer to the commitment of resources to economic production rather than to other possible uses, e.g. political or cultural. Land thus represented a factor generated through the specification of general cultural values to the legitimation of economic institutions, activities, and use of resources.

A related conceptual innovation in the Marshall Lectures was to use the four function theory to analyze the economy itself into subsystems (and later sub-subsystems). Parsons aligned the double interchanges with the resulting scheme of subsystems of the economy: the labor for wages, goods and services for consumer spending interchange was treated as the boundary relationship of the economy's goal attainment subsystem; the interchanges centering on capital markets were identified as the boundary relationship of the adaptive subsystem; the input of the factor of organization was placed at the economy's integrative subsystem; and markets involving "land" were treated as part of the economy's pattern maintenance function.

An implication of Parsons's treatment of the economy's boundary relationships is that the four subsystems of society are joined together through six double interchanges, each of which is a dynamic mechanism enabling two subsystems to adjust to each other's ongoing operational needs. In addition, each subsystem is regulated internally by a factor that, like "land" in the economy, represents the commitment of resources to a broad type of social process. In sum, by combining the four function theory with the theory of double interchanges, Parsons had developed a model for analyzing the ways in which functionally differentiated institutions adjust to one another's changing operations and requirements. Parsons later suggested that the general equilibrium of a society could be analyzed in these terms. This vision of how social process might be analyzed in relation to institutional structure guided a great deal of Parsons's later work.

While writing the Marshall Lectures, Parsons began a correspondence on many of the key ideas with Neil J. Smelser. Smelser had studied with Parsons as an undergraduate and was then taking courses in economics at Oxford. He was able to relate many of Parsons's Marshallian formulations to then current trends of Keynesian economics. When Smelser returned to Harvard for graduate studies, he collaborated with Parsons in expanding the Marshall Lectures into *Economy and Society* (Parsons and Smelser, 1956). *Economy and Society* achieved greater analytical detail in its use of the four function and double interchange schemes than any of Parsons's other works. It discussed the specific institutions that regulate each kind of market involved in the many boundary processes of the economy and its subsystems. *Economy and Society* thus presents the most thorough demonstration of Parsons's emphasis on the institutional regulation of social process. Smelser (1959) later examined the historical conflicts involved in the growth of the double interchange relationship between businesses and households in eighteenth- and nineteenth-century England.

Family and socialization

While working on *Economy and Society*, Parsons also continued to collaborate with Bales. *Family, Socialization and Interaction Process* (Parsons and Bales, 1955) discussed the American middle-class family of the postwar era as a social institution. It emphasized the emergence of the "nuclear" family made up of husband, wife, and children as the typical household unit, and as autonomous from extended kinship units in terms of organization and budget. It examined role structures within the family, noting the importance of both gender and generational axes of role differentiation. The core of the book analyzed the structure of the parent–child role relationship as it evolves during the lengthy process of socialization of children. Socialization was presented as a multistaged, highly dynamic process of engaging children in more inclusive social relationships, starting with the mother–baby dyad, then progressing to inclusion of the father, then perhaps other children, then relatives, peers, and eventually others in the local community, and beyond. At the same time, children engage these relationships increasingly at the level of symbolic communication and in terms of affective investment as well as bodily drives and needs. Parental control of the process (the generational axis of role differentiation) is essential to children's internalization of moral-normative standards of conduct as an integral part of their growing reliance on symbolic communication. Parsons argued that parental control requires maintaining a mutually supportive coalition between mother and father and consistency in normative standards when interacting with children.

Family...is the most thoroughly developed of Parsons's contributions to the integration of sociological and psychodynamic theory. The work addresses, perhaps more insightfully than any recent study, the profoundly affectual and emotional make-up of relationships in the modern nuclear family, with an erotically based love relationship between parents, the non-erotic love of parents for children, and the love of children for parents that gradually transcends childhood eroticism in favor of more stable affective ties. The emotional intensity of familial relationships often places them under great stress and leaves them highly vulnerable if normative discipline is transgressed or compromised. The family is also portrayed in thoroughly dynamic terms, with emphasis on the rapid change in its role-relationships as children mature, parents grow older, and relations evolve with such entities as business firms, schools, and voluntary associations in the broader community. As a consequence of this broad analysis, Parsons and Bales viewed contemporary American family relationships as highly susceptible to failure, both in terms of divorce and in terms of disturbances in the socialization of children. Their discussion included a number of hypotheses about how disturbed relationships between parents and children might result in emotional illness for the children. *Family*..., along with sections of *The Social System* and his collection of papers, *Social Structure and Personality* (1964), show that Parsons was also among the most creative psychoanalytic theorists of the 1950s and 1960s.

Parsons has been criticized by feminists for his treatment of gender differentiation in the role structure of the family. There is little doubt that he reified the gender roles of the 1950s and did not anticipate later changes. But it should be remembered that when he wrote gender relations were very different from those of today. He did not have the intent of restricting women's roles that his discussion might imply today. His characterization of the emotional and dynamic qualities of family life should not be rejected along with his reification of older gender relationships. As Miriam M. Johnson (1988) has argued, his abstract notion of differentiation in gender roles and in gender-related styles of interaction continues to hold importance for studies of family and gender.

American society

From the early 1950s, Parsons held the ambition of writing a work on American society that would combine four function macrosocial analysis with an overview of current social scientific knowledge and an interpretation of the society's principal features. In the late 1950s, he wrote several lengthy working papers to try out his ideas. In 1960, he invited Winston White, a student who had just finished his doctorate and whose main interest was the interpretation of American society, to collaborate. Together, Parsons and White drafted several chapters, then reorganized their chapter outline and wrote seven or eight new chapters totaling over six hundred pages. At that point, White left the profession of sociology and Parsons set the project aside without publishing any of their writings on American society. The result has been to leave a large gap in the record of his developing thought.

With the emergence of the four function theory, Parsons had sharpened a theme in his writing that predated even *SSA*. This theme, rooted in Max Weber's comparative studies of civilization, is that shared value orientations are a controlling factor among the many elements that make up institutional orders. Parsons had proposed that social structures can be analyzed into four kinds of elements, values (ideals), norms (rules), collectivities, and roles, that respectively serve pattern maintenance, integrative, goal attainment, and adaptive functions. He also suggested that these elements of structure form what he called a cybernetic hierarchy, a concept he derived from Norbert Wiener (1948). For Wiener, a cybernetic relation involves a well designed regulator guiding a more powerful mechanism, as when a thermostat controls a furnace or a steering wheel guides a car. Parsons noted that Freud made a similar point when he compared the ego's relation to the id with a rider's relation to a horse. Yet Freud had noted that riders can lose control and the horse can become a runaway. Control relationships can break down and the more forceful mechanism can run free, but at the cost of losing guidance. What Parsons proposed is that the relationships among values, norms, collectivities, and roles (or among ideals, practical interests, and material conditions) constitute a series of cybernetic relationships, though ones in which control may be placed at risk under conditions of stress.

The manuscripts on American society emphasize the importance of a value system as a set of cybernetic controls guiding the long-term evolution and general characteristics of a society. Parsons had pronounced his emphasis on values in a number of essays, but had left it to his book on American society to argue the claim in detail. The draft materials address this issue far more thoroughly than any of his published writings. In particular, they spell out the concept of a value system in greater detail. Parsons had in mind a complex system of many factors, themselves hierarchically organized. They extend from abstract religious premises, to religious ethics in Weber's sense, to generalized secular moral beliefs (in American culture, the "law of nature" and "universal human rights"), to ideals of social organization, to more specific values that legitimate the "land" factors in the economy and similar complexes in the other subsystems of society. Parsons argued that the most general elements of a value system tend to be highly stable even over centuries of social change, whereas the more specific elements change under the pressures of social movements or advances in institutional differentiation.

The manuscript portrayed a unity of American values that derives from generalized religious premises he characterized as "instrumental activism."

These premises were rooted in the Puritan heritage of early colonial settlers. Instrumental activism is the belief that everything in the human condition should be mastered by human will and energies and perfected to the extent possible. Its religious dimension is the effort to build "the kingdom of God on earth." Yet many secular strivings derive meaning from the same premises of mastery. Athletes who train prodigiously, scholars who study intensely, and entrepreneurs who cultivate new methods of production may all be responding to instrumental activism's mandate for self-perfection. At the level of collectivities, business firms, universities, and voluntary associations may all follow the same ideals of mastery and progressive perfection, yet be active in different domains of society and guided by different specific values of achievement. In this manner, Parsons accounted for functional, social class, ethnic, and regional variation in specific value orientations, while also arguing that American society showed a strong consensus around underlying principles of instrumental activism, and had done so since early in its history.

The polity, power, and symbolic media of interchange

After publishing *Economy and Society*, Parsons wrote a number of essays in the late 1950s and early 1960s that together conceptualize the political subsystem of society (or polity) in terms parallel to his four function analysis of the economy. A notable essay (Parsons, 1969, chapter 9) reinterpreted the findings of then recent survey research on voters and the electoral system in terms of a double interchange between the polity and the integrative subsystem of society. A later essay (Parsons, 1969, chapter 13) presented a four function analysis of the primary subsystems of the polity. The most important essay, "On the Concept of Political Power" (Parsons, 1969, chapter 14), gave a stronger formulation of the double interchange between the polity and the integrative subsystem, presented a radically new concept of power, and opened a new dimension to Parsons's treatment of social process. The essay argued that public politics in modern democracies involve interchanges of both factors of further process and products of process between the polity and the integrative subsystem. The polity receives the factor of "interest demands," or expressions of opinion about needed changes in public policy, from the organized citizenry as a sector of the integrative system. The integrative system receives "policy decisions" as a factor for adjusting the lives of citizens to changing social circumstances. The polity also receives "political support" in the form of votes that, as aggregated under the electoral laws, determine holders of office in a formally binding way. The integrative system then receives "leadership responsibility" as assurance that the well-being of the citizenry will be addressed through political process.

This double interchange shares certain characteristics with the double interchange between business firms and households. As an equilibrium process, it contains significant capabilities to absorb and adjust to social change. It also has capabilities for growth and expansion, as when new types of interest-demands enter the political arena and become sources of more effective political action. Parsons suggested that a well ordered polity is capable of long-term expansion similar to the growth of modern economies. Expansion should benefit the citizenry through increased levels of attainment of the society's collective goals. However, Parsons also noted that polities can experience contractions that reduce the level of effective political activity and harm the collective well-being. He suggested that contractions in public trust can restrict the scope of interest-demands acceptable in the polity and/or of leadership responsibility acceptable among the citizenry, thus precipitating a sort of political depression. He cited McCarthyism as an example of a deflationary force in American politics of the 1950s.

In demonstrating the possibilities for political expansion and contraction, Parsons raised the question of whether political life involves a mediator of process similar to money's role in the general equilibrium of the economy. Keynes had shown imbalances in the circulation of money as wages and as consumer spending to be sources of depression. Parsons hypothesized that political process must have an analogue of money. He therefore proposed that power is a circulating medium for political relationships and a measure of political efficacy, much as money is both a medium of economic exchange and a measure of economic value. If power is viewed as a capacity to make formally binding decisions on behalf of a collectivity, it can be seen as something expended with every political decision, just as money is expended with every purchase. In expending power, officials must anticipate ways of gaining renewed power. Parsons argued that binding decisions issued by public authorities amount to a form of calculated investment designed to attract new power through future electoral support.

The new conception of power departed from ideas long established in political science. In the conventional view, an authority exercises power *over* others and often as means of frustrating their pursuit of individual goals. Power relationships are regarded as zero-sum, such that power of one person is held at the expense of others. Power has also typically been portrayed as a diffuse resource, as in the idea that *any* means of attaining ends over the wishes of others is power. Parsons noted that figures from Machiavelli to Weber to a number of influential contemporaries favored the conventional view. He argued, however, that power is a *specialized* resource that enables duly authorized officers to make binding decisions on behalf of a collectivity, whether the nation, a state, a city, or a private agency or firm. The binding quality of power distinguishes it from other means of pursuing ends, such as expenditures of money or personal influence. Parsons acknowledged that power can be exercised *over* others, as in a binding court decision or military order, but also noted that it is often used impersonally and in some circumstances becomes binding only by aggregation, as when the votes of a majority elect an official. He also argued that power, when properly regulated, can serve the public benefit and bring advantages, including greater power, to the citizenry as well as public officials. Power should not be viewed as intrinsically zero-sum, but as zero-sum only in certain limited circumstances, such as political competition. Finally, Parsons suggested that power, like circulating currency, is a symbolic entity. Previous literature had linked power closely with force, but Parsons argued that actors generally resort to force when their power has been challenged and their ability to command is uncertain (Parsons, 1967, chapter 9). Power is a quality of commands that renders them duly authorized and likely to be obeyed. It is linked to the situated procedures through which it is issued, and its symbolism, as in the forms of court orders, military commands, or legislative enactments, is intrinsic to its efficacy. In this respect, it is like legitimate currency, which derives its value from its precise printed form and the situations of its use.

Parsons's conception of power as a circulating medium overturns a number of long respected but empirically limited preconceptions. It also led him to the more general insight that money is not the only circulating symbolic medium, but one of a class of media. He soon argued that each of the primary subsystems of society must have its own circulating medium. An essay on influence soon followed (Parsons, 1969, chapter 15), treating it as the capacity to persuade and as the circulating medium of the integrative system. Although unsatisfactory in certain respects, the essay capitalized on the body of research on personal influence and reference group relationships by Paul Lazarsfeld, Robert K. Merton, and their colleagues. A few years later, Parsons completed his scheme of media circulating in society with an essay on value-commitments as the medium of the fiduciary system (Parsons, 1969, chapter 16). Although this essay is persuasive in its general argument, it lacked significant bodies of previous empirical research to build upon and accomplished less than the essays on power and influence in guiding future research.

A source of confusion about Parsons's writings on power, influence, and value commitments has been that these media obviously do not circulate in definite quantities in the manner of money. We each have money in our wallets and bank accounts, and can calculate precise quantities of our money, even if its real purchasing power changes over time. Goods and services we buy have definite prices or quantities of money needed for their purchase. Power, influence, and value commitments do not share this precise quantitative form. Public policies are not promulgated by expending specific amounts of "power chits," nor are there definite "power prices" for resolving particular policy issues on behalf of the public. But we do commonly view power, influence, and commitments in quantitative terms. We speak of high officials as exercising a great deal of power, of leaders in a profession as highly influential, or of a person who has taken on too many responsibilities as overcommitted. We understand that systems of authority are built on methodical allocations of power among officials, and we know that a new office, such as an Independent Counsel investigating the conduct of a president, can affect an entire structure of powers. We expect high officials to have greater power than their formal subordinates. Parsons also seems correct by common intuition when he argues that a public official who expends power to promulgate a major policy is risking his or her future command of power. If the policy proves successful and popular, the official may acquire greater power, but if it fails, he or she will likely lose power.

Parsons believed that differences in quantitative form are functionally related to the kinds of social resources or capacities that the media represent. While power, influence, and commitments have quantitative aspects, their uses would be compromised if, like money, they circulated in definite quantities. We can understand this point easily with respect to commitments. Commitments circulate in the form of promises to undertake courses of action that others can rely upon in planning their own related activities. However, the amount of effort needed to fulfill a commitment often changes with unanticipated circumstances. An actor may know that he or she has made a large commitment, but not know the extent of the effort that will be required to fulfill it. Yet the commitment would be valueless to others if they could not count upon its fulfillment despite changed circumstances. The theory of generalized symbolic media has been reviewed and partially reframed in Lidz (2001).

The theory of social evolution

In early 1963, Alex Inkeles, then a departmental colleague, asked Parsons to contribute to a new textbook series. Inkeles suggested that Parsons might update *The Social System* in terms of such ideas as the four function paradigm, the double interchanges, and the societal media. Parsons, however, chose to address materials he had been teaching in his course on comparative institutional analysis. He had radically revised the course two years earlier to emphasize a perspective of social evolution. In the proposed book, he planned to analyze a number of historical societies that differed in institutional complexity and in basic cultural pattern. He also hoped to develop a theory of social change that would place the understanding of societies and institutions on the basis of a universal dynamic, comparable to Darwin's theory of natural selection.

Parsons did not complete the social evolution project until after 1970. By then he had written two books, *Societies: Evolutionary and Comparative Perspectives* (1966) and *The System of Modern Societies* (1971). The first book presented a broad typology of primitive, archaic, historic, and "seed bed" societies. The chapter on so-called primitive (nonliterate) societies drew upon a wide range of anthropological materials on Australian, African, South American, and Asian "tribal" peoples. It discussed the religious, kinship, political, and economic institutions of several societies and clarified the general idea of different levels of institutional complexity among nonliterate societies. However, Parsons's discussion of how simpler societies may have evolved into more complex ones did not successfully integrate theoretical analysis with empirical materials.

Parsons presented the archaic type of society by comparing the Egyptian and Mesopotamian civilizations of antiquity. The type is defined in terms of a number of interdependent criteria: craft literacy, central cults where priests monopolize the rituals and interpretation of religious beliefs and mythology, written codes of law, a class system secured by legally codified discriminations among aristocrats, commoners, and slaves, a central administrative apparatus, consolidation of authority around an institution of kingship, intensive agriculture, storehouses for essential goods, local markets for craft and agricultural produce, and concentration of the non-agricultural population in towns. Egyptian and Mesopotamian civilizations both included all of these elements, yet differed in basic ways. Egyptian society emphasized the pattern maintenance and political functions and assimilated religious and political institutions closely to one another in the cult of the divine pharaoh. By contrast, Mesopotamian societies emphasized adaptive and integrative institutions. They gave greater autonomy to extended household units for agricultural and craft production. Their legal systems were more highly developed, their social class systems more flexible, and trade among city-states was more active. Egypt established one unified society that dominated a largely stable territory over thousands of years. Mesopotamian civilization spawned many independent states, endemic rivalry and warfare, mixing of populations through trade and conquest, and repeated rise and fall of empires.

Parsons's discussion of "historic" civilizations covered the classical Chinese, Indian, Islamic, and Roman Empires. All these civilizations extended over vast domains and included populations of many ethnicities. Their cultural foundations rested on religio-philosophical belief systems with transcendental conceptions of sources of value and legitimation for social institutions. Their class systems included honored status groups for the primary interpreters and proponents of the religio-philosophical traditions. Following Max Weber, Parsons carefully analyzed the social make-up and privileged ways of life of these key status groups. The contrasts between the Confucian literati and mandarins in China and the Brahmin priesthood in the Indian caste system, for example, highlight differences between the two civilizations affecting practically every social institution. The Confucians sought worldly honor by cultivating genteel ways of life, participating in the affairs of the patrimonial state, gaining wealth from land rents, and leadership of their extended families. The Brahmins sought to flee everything that represented worldly attachment. In terms of the so-called 'caste system' (a Western term), the Brahmin order was constituted of many independent kinship-based groups that were essentially local in importance, but shared the prestige of priesthood. They typically lived off fees for performing rituals for many other 'caste' groups, and sometimes off land rents or service as literate advisors to ruling households as well. Their positions in the 'caste system' prevented them from participating directly in major economic or political roles and from accumulating wealth or power. Their prestige rested on a monopoly of priestly "magic" and mastery of classic religious writings.

Parsons analyzed each of the major "historic" civilizations in terms of a common set of concepts derived from the four function paradigm. He thus attended to economic production through the organization of agriculture, the crafts, and trade, to political life through institutions of patrimonial authority, administration, territorial control, and military organization, to integrative institutions through class systems, status groups, inter-ethnic relations, and institutions of law, and to religious traditions and cult practices. By using a common scheme to analyze the several "historic" civilizations with their radical differences, Parsons made a significant contribution despite the brevity of his discussion.

Parsons called ancient Greece and Israel the "seed bed" societies because they were not important for their size, wealth, or power, but for effects of their religious and philosophical cultures on later civilizations in a number of epochs. Greek philosophy was the ultimate source of ideals of objective reason that became essential to early Christian theology, Medieval theology, Renaissance philosophy, and Enlightenment rationalism. Greek ideals of the *polis* or autonomous, politically organized city-state, mediated by the Roman republican tradition, became the primary cultural source of late Medieval and Renaissance political ideals and later of modern republican traditions. The Israelite conception of a transcendent, but personal and jealous, God who enters history to reward and punish peoples for their human achievements and failings became the primary source of Christian theodicy and religious ethics. Hebrew sacred writings have become sources of ethical renewal for Western civilization in a number of periods, but especially during the Reformation. The biblical figures of the later prophets, notably Isaiah, have been particularly important. For sociology, the interesting problem is to understand the mechanisms of social change that enabled elements of ancient cultures to affect basic cultural and institutional patterns over millennia down to our time.

The System of Modern Societies had the primary goal of presenting modern society as a distinctive evolutionary type that first emerged in Western civilization but has grown to have worldwide impact. Parsons first tried to systematize the explanation of why modern society *originated* only in Western civilization. He started by emphasizing that a distinctively dynamic civilization had emerged in the West several centuries before modern institutions. This development began with the fragmentation of Western Roman authority and the emergence of many small, overlapping, yet competing societies, often both tribal and feudal. Medieval civilization then developed through a number of consolidating forces: the Christian religion with a partly universalistic priesthood and church hierarchy; the heritage of Roman *imperium*, with ideals of effective law and authority; a class system centering on an "international" feudal-military nobility; political authority based in fortified manors, but aggregated into hierarchies, albeit unstably, through personalistic feudal ties; agricultural production based in peasant villages; and active commerce and craft production centered in towns and cities.

As early as the eleventh and twelfth centuries, a new European civilization had been created through growth of the monastic orders, literacy, scholarship, systematic theology, and "bureaucratic" organization of the Church; consolidation of large political domains in France, England, Spain, and the Holy Roman Empire; the extension of trade across the continent and to the Near East and Asia; the independence of cities and their cultivation of republican traditions dating from antiquity; and the rapid evolution of craft production and organized guilds. Through these changes, the European peoples consolidated a civilization distinct in its institutional elements from antiquity, bounded (except for Spain) against Islamic Asia, Africa, and the Near East, and growing in cultural and technical sophistication. This civilization was then transformed by the cultural movements of the Renaissance, with its elaboration of secular culture in the arts, technology, and moral belief, and the Reformation, with its redirection of fundamental religious beliefs and ethics.

Following Weber, Parsons emphasized that the Calvinist ethic of inner-worldly asceticism provided, against a background of other movements in the Reformation, a special impetus to break with traditional institutions and devise new ones. The two centuries following the Reformation were a period of intense social conflict and repeated efforts to create new social foundations. The societies where ascetic Protestant sects came to predominate, e.g. Geneva, Holland, England, and the North American colonies, established stringent religious ethics and disciplined social orders. By the eighteenth century, ascetic Protestantism began to accommodate secular as well as religious ethical reasoning. Instead of its original opposition to all worldly activities, it gave rise to recognizably modern elements of what Weber called the "Spirit of Capitalism." A new emphasis was placed on creative entrepreneurship and on efficient use of secular talents, energies, and resources, including financial credit. The economic forces that created the Industrial Revolution were set loose first in England, then in the Low Countries and the USA, and eventually throughout the North and West of Europe. Within decades, the Industrial Revolution produced a growing, and increasingly self-confident "middle class," generating pressures toward democratizing political change and the overturn of aristocracies. Starting with the American and French Revolutions, and proceeding through the nineteenth century, but with a different history in each nation, electoral institutions that enfranchised common citizens and promoted competition among political parties took power away from privileged groups and placed it in the hands of the people's elected representatives.

The USA institutionalized a *combination* of the Industrial and Democratic Revolutions more rapidly and thoroughly than any other society. It also proceeded the most radically in placing a middle class without ascriptive privileges in a prominent position in the class system. Its legal system firmly but flexibly protected new forms of property, contract, and employment. By the first decades of the twentieth century, American society had developed the largest-scale and most efficient industrial system supported by the most highly differentiated occupational structure. These changes were soon complemented by what Parsons called the Educational Revolution, a radical upgrading of popular education. After the mid-twentieth century, a large majority of each population cohort in the USA was completing secondary education and more than half of each cohort was receiving some higher education. At the same time, university-based research and advanced training of personnel in the sciences and other technical fields were transforming the workforce and the economy's capacity for innovation.

In his chapter on American society, Parsons argued that its institutionalization of the Industrial, Democratic, and Educational Revolutions had created a new evolutionary type of society during the nineteenth and twentieth centuries. In the remainder of the book, he discussed the different patterns of institutionalization of such "modernity" among the European nations, the Soviet Union, and Japan, and examined the prospects for its spread, in partial or complete forms, to other societies. In this discussion, Parsons predicted, still early in the Brezhnev regime, that the Soviet Union could not sustain its authoritarian political system in a world where democracies predominate, and hence would give way to more democratic institutions.

Parsons's two small books provide a powerful introduction to comparative and historical analysis in sociology. The evolutionary types of society are presented in comprehensive terms, yet with sharp delineation of their chief institutional elements. The discussions of institutional change, both emergence of more highly developed types and processes of decline of civilizations, are well integrated with the four function paradigm. In these respects, the books importantly advanced the theory of social change. Despite his ambition of outlining a theory of social evolution similar in status to Darwin's theory of evolution, however, Parsons did not develop a concept truly analogous to natural selection, and hence did not create an authentic theory of social evolution. Moreover, he did not really prove that historical change in society is susceptible to analysis in terms of evolution. A view that history is the general category of change for human social action and that evolution involves dynamics that apply only to biological systems (including the human species) is more consistent with the theory of social action.

The general action system

In a long essay (Parsons, 1970), Parsons used the four function paradigm to reanalyze social action into primary subsystems. The previous classification of culture, social system, and personality was replaced with a scheme that emphasized differentiation and functional alignment among four subsystems. Culture was treated as pattern maintaining due to the effects of core beliefs and values in establishing principles for the entire action system. The social system was treated as integrative owing to the effects of normatively established intersubjective reality and actual interpersonal attachments, among actors who participate in common relationships and milieux. The personality was treated as goal attaining due to the effects of motivational structures in developing *agency* to implement action. Parsons introduced the concept of behavioral organism to stand for the adaptive subsystem. The behavioral organism consists, in this treatment, of the aspects of the individual actor as organism that facilitate physical implementation of action. The senses, the ability to speak, the capacity for coordination of fingers and hands, and the intelligent capabilities of the brain are necessary facilities for human social action.

With the new functional subsystems identified, Parsons proposed a more radical innovation: to treat the four subsystems of action as dynamically related to each other through interchange processes. He identified a symbolic medium for each of the four subsystems: definition of the situation for cultural systems, affect for social systems, performance capacity for personality, and intelligence for the behavioral organism. He justified briefly the proposition that each of the six interfaces between pairs of the subsystems should be viewed as subject to the double contingencies of interchange. He then proposed two pairs of input and output categories for each of the six interchanges. He made clear that his proposals regarding media and interchange categories were tentative and subject to change following critical evaluation.

The essay is one of the boldest of Parsons's technical writings, although its new formulations in fact built upon ideas that he had been developing for a decade in working papers and discussions with research assistants. As the paper's technical appendix notes, some of the formulations were published despite strong arguments in favor of alternatives. The paper also left ambiguous the empirical relationship between processes of the general action system and processes within social systems (including the societal interchange processes) and the other subsystems of action. Parsons continued active discussion of alternative formulations for the general action system down to just weeks before his death.

The American societal community

Throughout the 1970s, Parsons worked intermittently on a lengthy book on the integrative subsystem of American society. His plan for the book had two sources. One was his old commitment to write an interpretive work on American society. The other was a realization that his concepts for analysis of societal integration were comparatively undeveloped, even though he had identified the societal community as the central subject matter of sociology. He accordingly planned a last major book as both a case study of the American societal community and a presentation of concepts for analyzing social integration. After some seven or eight years of intermittent work, Parsons finished a draft of the book, more than 800 typescript pages, the day before leaving on the trip to Germany, during which he died. The manuscript is a rough draft that Parsons would have revised in fundamental ways had he lived. As he left it, it is an unusual combination of abstract theory, general discussion of problems of social integration, summary of historical information, review of data from other sociological studies, and personal reflection.

The general theoretical framework of the manuscript is presented in a chapter on the relations between the societal community and its major environments, including the other three subsystems of society, the societal communities of other nations, and the three nonsocial subsystems of action. Parsons then discussed features of historical experience that have affected the specific institutional patterns of the American societal community: the activistic value system, the multiethnic composition of the population, the traditions of individualism, and the prevailing culturally grounded discomfort with ascriptive class hierarchies. Subsequent chapters address the ethnic and primordial ties of solidarity, the specific forms of class solidarity and cleavage, the principal institutions, such as the law, that protect impersonal, *Gesellschaft*-type relationships, the social foundations for collective action in the relationship between the societal community and polity, and the distinctive protections for individuality and individualism in American society. The final chapter, on individualism, addressing in part themes suggested by Franois Bourricauld (1981), is a fine summary of Parsons's basic lifelong perspective on American society.

The human condition

Parsons retired from active teaching at Harvard after the spring semester of 1973. In the following academic year, he began to teach courses at the University of Pennsylvania in collaboration with several members of the department who shared his interests. He also joined an informal faculty seminar to discuss new developments in the theory of action. The discussions started with consideration of Parsons's response, in a brief memorandum, to questions that Charles Lidz and the present author had raised about the conception of the behavioral organism as the adaptive subsystem of action. Lidz and Lidz (1976) had argued that the notion of behavioral organism violates the idea of a system *constituted* entirely of meaningful action because it is made up of aspects of the human organism. They had proposed the concept of a behavioral system, constituted by cognitive schemas in the sense of Jean Piaget, as a stronger formulation of the adaptive subsystem of action. Today, they would use the term "mind," in a sense deriving from George Herbert Mead, for the system of cognitive schemas. In his memorandum, Parsons accepted the new proposal, but argued for a need to examine how systems of social action are related to environing systems. Discussion of the memorandum, its implications, and succeeding formulations continued in the faculty seminar for several years. The outcome of these deliberations was Parsons's long essay, "A Paradigm of the Human Condition" (Parsons, 1978, chapter 15). In brief, Parsons argued that the human condition as experienced by actors involves relationships between the system of action and three other systems. In four function terms, systems of action serve the integrative function of the human condition as system. They are placed in three orders of environment: namely, physico-chemical environment (adaptive), the human organic and ecological environment (goal attaining), and a telic or transcendental environment (pattern maintaining). With these system identifications worked out, Parsons suggested tentative terms for subsystems, media, and interchange categories.

The idea of a telic system has been controversial. However, Parsons was not positing that a God or Divine Principle sets the most general pattern or direction for human action, but rather that all systems of action are intrinsically open with respect to ultimate principles. Any given system of action – at the most inclusive level, a civilization – follows specific ultimate principles of action. Its characteristic principles are not the only possible principles, however. In times of cultural stress, as in the Reformation, pressures arise to change them. Yet, Parsons argued, there are limited possibilities for changes of principle. He proposed that Weber's concepts of inner-worldly and other-wordly, mysticism and asceticism, demarcate the dimensions of transcendental possibilities for principles of action. The telic order thus presents the limited possibilities for ultimate principles of action.

Parsons treated action systems as integrative to the human condition because particular systems of action serve to interrelate elements of all three environments (physico-chemical, organic-ecological, and telic) in terms of their own characteristic meaning-patterns. A system of action thus provides the anthropocentric basis of the integration of the human condition, which is different, as Parsons often said, from the fish condition (or horse and ape conditions). Moreover, the human condition has different experiential meaning for Americans, ancient Greeks, premodern Chinese, etc., and for various status groups within any of these societies.

The essay on the human condition was Parsons's last major publication. Commentators have noted that its broad scope and philosophic quality make it a suitable final statement. The essay is also representative of Parsons's work in opening large issues, proposing insightful and suggestive answers, yet leaving significant problems unresolved, some of them affecting basic formulations. Like so much else that Parsons wrote, it leaves a great deal for other social scientists to do.

Applied writings

Although the distinctive importance of Parsons's work derives from the conceptual schemes he developed, he also wrote many essays on specific empirical problems and matters of social policy. The secondary literature, following the subtitle of his first collection of essays (Parsons, 1949), conventionally divides his writings between contributions to "pure" theory and "applied" essays. But there is actually no sharp division in his thought. Addressing applied problems was for Parsons a way of evaluating the insights produced by his general theory and often resulted in redirection of his theoretical efforts in order to strengthen empirical understanding. Several of his empirical studies animated formulations that he later presented at the level of "pure" theory. Some of the key innovations of *The Social System* grew out of empirical inquiries into processes of socialization and social control and the institutions of medical practice.

Some critics have argued that it was inconsistent for Parsons to write essays on questions of social policy if he prized the objectivity of his theory. Parsons, however, adhered to Max Weber's position that every authentic contribution to empirical knowledge *combines* the pursuit of objectivity with an effort to capture relevance to contemporary practical values (Parsons, 1967, chapter 3). The scientist or scholar seeks to meet the standards of objectivity (in logic and statistical inference, for example) established in his or her discipline when making an argument or demonstration. Yet choices of subject matter and decisions about what problems are important to address necessarily fall back on extra-scientific standards. Such standards are often provided by the political and ideological discourses of the era. Parsons often indicated that the intended value-relevance of his applied writings was grounded in "academic liberalism." He was particularly concerned with the First Amendment freedoms, civil rights, academic freedom, democratic sharing of power, and maintaining world peace. The following discussion addresses only portions of Parsons's applied writings, focusing on essays that convey his social and political views.

In the late 1930s and early 1940s, Parsons wrote several essays that sought to explain the rise of Nazism in Germany (collected in Gerhardt, 1993). His analysis focused on the late but rapid industrialization of Germany and the many social strains its generated, the comparatively late political unification of the nation, the pressures placed on enduring institutions of local *Gemeinschaft*, and the particularly bitter conflicts in the class structure. Unlike most Americans writing on Germany in that era, Parsons expressed his distaste for Nazism without generalizing it to anti-Germanism. He explicitly maintained his respect for German traditions of high culture and scholarship.

At the University of Cambridge in 1953, Parsons found that many English intellectuals believed Joseph McCarthy to be emerging as the "American Hitler." They talked of preparing Europe for the USA's decline into fascism. Parsons wrote an essay entitled "Social Strains in America" (Parsons, 1969, chapter 7) to demonstrate that McCarthyism was a limited political movement with poor prospects for gaining control of the nation. He argued that the social base for McCarthyism was largely in the small towns and in proprietors of small businesses. Groups that had suffered economic decline during the rise of large industry and big government were the base of the movement. They saw trends in the larger society as false to their ways of life and were receptive to McCarthy's extravagant allegations that traitors were common among leaders of big government. Writing before the Senate hearings in which Joseph Welch successfully confronted McCarthy, Parsons argued that the McCarthy movement was a classic "bubble" phenomenon and would disappear rapidly after McCarthy was challenged directly.

At the peak of the Cold War, Parsons wrote essays on American foreign policy in relation to the system of international relations (Parsons, 1967, chapter 14; 1969, chapter 12). At the time, many scholars as well as political leaders advocated uncompromising prosecution of Cold War policies to gain every possible advantage over the Soviet Union as bitter adversary. Parsons, however, argued that the USA and the Soviet Union shared strong interests in limiting conflict to protect against a nuclear "hot war." He emphasized the American interest in developing greater confidence in the international order on the part of the Soviet Union. The constraints imposed on the pursuit of national aims by international institutions might provide important protections against war.

Parsons later participated in the early Pugwash Conferences, where scientists from the USA and Soviet Union started discussions on shared control and destruction of nuclear weapons. In the mid-1960s, with the first thawing of the Cold War, he made contacts with Soviet sociologists at international meetings, visited the Soviet Union to promote professional relationships, and invited Soviet scholars to the USA and Harvard.

With the rise of the Civil Rights movement, Parsons sought to contribute to its cause by clarifying in sociological terms its importance to the nation. His essay "Full Citizenship for the Negro American?" (Parsons, 1969, chapter 11) started with the theoretical question of what part civil rights play in the integrative institutions of modern societies. Parsons also addressed the question historically by examining major stages in the development of Anglo-American institutions of civil rights. He distinguished three separate complexes of citizenship rights: the legal, involving autonomous courts and equal protection of the laws; the political, involving the franchise and the ability to exercise influence in the political process; and the welfare, involving health, education, and welfare policies to ensure that citizens have the capability to participate effectively in the competitive modern economy.

Parsons also reviewed the historical processes by which various religious, ethnic, and racial groups have gained more complete citizenship rights following earlier exclusion from full community membership. Down to the immigration of Irish Catholics escaping famine, the USA had been overwhelmingly Protestant and, aside from slaves and small numbers of freed Blacks, white and Anglo-Saxon. From the 1840s to the 1920s, the population became much more diverse with large-scale immigration from Ireland, Central Europe, Scandinavia, Eastern Europe, and Italy. Negative feelings toward new ethnic and religious groups were often strong. Catholics and Jews especially were in many respects excluded from the communities of American life. Parsons traced the social changes that led to the inclusion of these groups on an equal (or nearly equal) basis, often after decades of discrimination and deprivation. He proposed that these processes of inclusion provided in key respects a model for the inclusion of African Americans. He also noted that full inclusion under the protections of legal rights, a process advanced by *Brown* v. *Board of Education* (and after Parsons wrote by the 1960s Civil Rights Acts), created abilities for African Americans to press for recognition of other rights in court. He was optimistic that establishing voting rights for African Americans throughout the country would produce favorable political changes. Political leaders would then have political needs of their own to respond to the interests of African Americans. Parsons predicted that more complicated struggles would follow before African Americans would attain equal status with respect to welfare rights. He doubted that African Americans would achieve complete equality as citizens until they had benefited for a substantial period of time from equal educational opportunities, equal health care, and equal welfare support. Today, his predictions appear largely correct, although the struggle for sufficient welfare rights faces still greater political obstacles than he had anticipated.

In the late 1960s, Parsons collaborated with Gerald M. Platt on an empirical study of faculty roles in colleges and universities. When the student demonstrations of that time created a crisis in the universities, Parsons and Platt redirected their research into a broad analysis of academic institutions. The resulting book, *The American University* (Parsons and Platt, 1973), is a comprehensive analysis of research universities emphasizing their specialization around producing, preserving, and transmitting intellectually disciplined knowledge. Contrary to common perceptions, Parsons and Platt argued that undergraduate as well as graduate education had been strengthened in scope and quality by the growth of research activities. However, they discussed undergraduate education as a dynamic process involving important elements of personal change. The modern university is ideally a stimulating yet supportive environment that frees students to explore new intellectual and personal interests. Aside from curricular challenges, students often encounter new extracurricular opportunities in the arts, in politics, in moral and religious subcultures, and in community service. Students often enter friendships with people from religious, ethnic, racial, or social class backgrounds different from their own.

Parsons and Platt noted that college students often undergo a great deal of stress when new types of experience challenge their former life-orientations. The stress tends to be especially great for students whose families have not previously experienced higher education, and hence might not understand or support new decisions regarding fields of study, extracurricular interests, political causes, friendships, or future careers. A generation of rapid expansion in higher education had greatly increased the numbers of students who were the first in their families to attend college, and thus probably increased student stress. The expansion of the universities also produced significant institutional dislocations. With larger student bodies, student–faculty relationships had become less personal. The formation of student friendships had become more complicated as student bodies grew more diverse in regional, ethnic, racial, social class, and cultural backgrounds. With larger academic departments, relationships among faculty colleagues also had become more impersonal and often more competitive. The vast growth in administrative structures created difficulties in dealing with students in nonbureaucratic ways, a problem symbolized in the 1960s by student ID numbers and computerization of academic records. The crisis of the 1960s and 1970s had thus been precipitated by rapid change, weakened social integration of university life, and resulting stresses on students.

In response to student demands for change, Parsons and Platt recommended a number of reforms, but warned that the system of higher education should protect its many gains of the postwar years. If the benefits of the Educational Revolution were to be fully preserved, the special institutional make-up of research universities had to be protected. Recalling the damage done to the University of California by state officials reacting to student demands and demonstrations, they noted the dangers to carrying out reforms in a way that might politicize the universities. In terms of both academic freedoms and commitments of public resources, reaction from the right posed a greater threat to the universities than student activism.

Some of the reforms proposed by Parsons and Platt were: to increase the "relevance" of curricula by modestly expanding programs in the arts and in the applied social sciences; to improve university officials' communication with student leaders; to strengthen informal relations between faculty members and students; to add student members to some university committees to ensure attention to student views; and to improve the quality of administrative services for students. However, Parsons and Platt did not expect such changes to have large or rapid consequences. They maintained that the life-stage of "studentry" was intrinsically a time of personal change and stress. During periods of national political turmoil, the stress on students was simply prone to creating problems for universities. Parsons and Platt were confident that over some years the turmoil would abate and university life would be normalized. In the meantime, the principal duty of educators was to protect the freedoms of thought, speech, and association that are essential to academic life.

CRITIQUES OF PARSONS'S THEORY

From publication of *SSA* to the end of his life, Parsons was a controversial figure who faced substantial professional criticism. The content of the criticism has changed over time, as new perspectives have emerged and often defined their intellectual positions in part by their stances toward Parsons. It would be impossible to review all the significant controversies here, but it is appropriate to comment on several well known ones.

In 1940, Alfred Schutz sent Parsons a laudatory but critical essay he had written on *SSA* (Grathoff, 1978). Parsons must have been pleased by the respectful discussion of his work, even though some of Schutz's views were in fact quite different from his own. However, Schutz put Parsons in a difficult position by saying that he would publish his essay only if Parsons agreed "in principle" with his criticisms. The difficulty for Parsons was that he could not agree with Schutz's key points. Schutz proposed that the methodology concerning frames of reference and categories of analysis should be presented in the terms of a philosophical epistemology, not as a nonphilosophical, social scientific methodology. He also proposed to revise basic concepts, including subject of action, object of action, rational action, and normative orientation, in terms of his own phenomenological theory. In doing so, he focused almost entirely on face-to-face and person-to-person relationships, leaving aside the institutional and macrosocial analyses that were fundamental to Parsons. The divide between Parsons and Schutz was too wide to be readily bridged, and their correspondence ended in mutual discomfort. However, an impression has lasted in sectors of the profession, unfairly, I believe, that Parsons prevented Schutz from publishing a stringent critique.

In the late 1940s, Robert K. Merton developed the view that theory construction in sociology in its then current condition should concentrate on problems of the "middle range." The middle range was set off against atheoretical descriptive studies of particular settings and against Parsons's research program, which was characterized as "Grand Theory." Merton's account of the value of such middle range concepts as reference groups or the two stage flow of influence was persuasive. He established the scientific validity of his approach, and most sociologists ever since have been more comfortable with a middle range methodology. However, Merton mischaracterized Parsons's approach. Parsons's primary goal was not to develop macroscopic causal generalizations about large-scale institutions or society as a whole (Grand Theory), but to clarify basic premises and categories as antecedents to precise analysis at any level of social organization (Parsons, 1953, chapter 17). Questions of the appropriate frame of reference for sociology, as articulated in *SSA*, were the distinctive focus of Parsons's methodology. His empirical studies, e.g. discussions of the professions, social control, the family, or processes of socialization, were in actuality middle range as often as macrosocial. In later years, Parsons argued that his debate with Merton had created a false opposition. There had been no need for sociologists to choose between the two approaches. Both he and Merton had made large contributions despite their methodological differences.

In the 1950s and 1960s, Ralf Dahrendorf (1959), Louis Coser (1956), and then others developed the criticism that Parsons's theory could not deal with phenomena of social conflict. They argued that Parsons's focus on systems, functional "contribution" to systems, and the integration of systems obscured the social reality of conflict in a haze of emphasis on social harmony. They proposed that "system theory" requires a complementary "conflict theory" in order to capture the full range of social phenomena. As a corollary of this criticism, they argued that, lacking a theory of conflict, a systems theory could also not come to terms with social change. A complementary conflict theory would thus open systems theory to the analysis of social change as well. However, Parsons's writings exhibit a great deal of attention to empirical conflict and change. Both conflict and change are treated at length in *SSA*, especially in the discussions of Weber's and Pareto's work. Parsons's essays on Germany and the rise of Nazism also deal extensively with conflict and change.

Although Dahrendorf and Coser were particularly critical of *The Social System*, that work, too, treats phenomena of conflict, but primarily in terms of stress or strain in relationships or institutions. The difference is less in perception of conflict than in the ways conflict is conceptualized and linked to change. Dahrendorf and to a degree Coser failed to recognize conflict and change in *The Social System* because of the terms used. Dahrendorf was looking for a Marxian analysis with a focus on conflict among social classes and a direct tie between class conflict and social change. Coser, too, was in part misguided by Marxian preconceptions, but was also disturbed by Parsons's neglect of Simmel's treatment of conflict as a basic social form. Parsons sought to maintain Weber's multidimensional analysis of change in terms of religious ethics, routinization of charisma, rationalization, and bureaucratization as well as conflict among classes and estates. For Parsons, the task was to synthesize these elements of a theory of change in terms of a theory of system dynamics, including strain in relationships and institutions. To accept a bifurcation between system theory and conflict theory would, for Parsons, have been to betray a commitment to developing a unified frame of reference.

During the ideological turmoil of the late 1960s and the 1970s, a number of figures associated with the New Left broadened the conflict theory criticism of Parsons, while also turning it into an ideological attack. In the New Left view, Parsons ignored conflict and change while extolling an ideal of perfect system integration and social harmony because he was a spokesman for the Establishment. The methodology of "value-freedom" was interpreted as a smokescreen to hide blatant partisanship on behalf of the dominant classes and social order. Parsons's status as a senior professor at Harvard was at times cited as sufficient proof of his role as Establishment spokesman. In an influential version of this argument, Alvin Gouldner (1970) stressed the conservatism of L. J. Henderson and the "Pareto Circle" at Harvard as evidence of Parsons's politics. Gouldner's account of Parsons's theoretical work, however, was little more than a caricature. As we have seen, Parsons's political outlook was more ambivalent to the social order of his times and based on specific value-judgments, hardly on a general social harmonism. In a later work, William Buxton (1985) interpreted Parsons's *corpus* as a defense of the "capitalist nation-state." Although Buxton's interpretation is more nuanced than Gouldner's, it overemphasizes the institutional forms of nation-state and capitalism, about which Parsons was in key respects ambivalent. Buxton underemphasizes the institutions of universalistic law, citizen's rights, representative democracy, and competitive elections, which were more important to Parsons's attachment to the American political system.

A thoughtful and penetrating criticism of Parsons's theory of action was developed in the 1950s and 1960s by his former student, Harold Garfinkel. The criticism pertains to the understanding of how normative order regulates the conduct of individual actors. Garfinkel (1967) argued that Parsons greatly underestimated the complexity of subjective processes involved in an actor's judgment regarding how to interpret and whether to observe normative rules. The applicability of specific norms to an actor's conduct in a given social situation rests on many implicit typifications that serve to define the situations – typifications of the social setting, characteristics of the actors, their interests and intentions, their previous experience, and expectable events – all of which Parsons had not explored. To be sure, Parsons himself argued that norms are not self-actualizing. He understood that a set of norms requires the actors in a situation to communicate their expectations to one another, and frequently threats of sanctions as well. Only with the support of give and take regarding expectations and sanctions is a normative order able to regulate actual conduct in the situation. Although Parsons saw the "double contingency" in the normative guidance of actors' conduct, Garfinkel contributed a deeper understanding of the intricate judgment that each actor must use to define the situation and clarify the applicability of norms to his or her own conduct. Parsons himself never grasped Garfinkel's critique or its importance, but a number of his protégés have accepted the need to reconstruct the understanding of how normative orders are actually implemented in interaction.

As we have seen, Parsons consistently maintained that theoretical propositions in sociology must be analytical in form and deal with abstractly conceived aspects or qualities of social objects, not concrete objects. A criticism that Parsons lodged against Weber was that the ideal type method stood halfway between concrete and fully analytic theory. Consistent with his methodology, Parsons built his later theory of subsystems of society in terms of abstract propositions about analytically defined aspects of institutions and relationships. Reinhard Bendix (Bendix and Roth, 1971) criticized Parsons's foundation for system theory by arguing that Weber's ideal type methodology is sharply at odds with Durkheim's functionalism, the precursor of system theory. Bendix had conducted a number of important historical and comparative studies using a modification of Weber's ideal type scheme. He expressed skepticism that analytical schemes based on system theory could be as insightful as an ideal type methodology. Indeed, abstract system theory is difficult to use for original comparative-historical research. Parsons's studies of German social history predate his formal system theory and are basically ideal-typical. His late comparative and historical writings were largely syntheses of evidence developed in previous studies. They used the system theory mainly as an analytical framework for integrating the works of other scholars. Sociologists such as Robert N. Bellah (1957), Neil J. Smelser (1959), S. N. Eistenstadt (1963), and Mark Gould (1987) have successfully used analytic systems theory for historical research, but the respects in which their studies actually transcend ideal type analysis in organizing empirical evidence has perhaps not been fully assessed. Ideal type analysis may be regarded as a proven empirical method in historical sociology, and the intellectually conservative critic may be skeptical of Parsons's claim for the empirical superiority of analytic system theory.

A related consideration pertains to Parsons's stance toward the methods of analysis developed by the German idealist-historicist school. Parsons accepted the method of interpretive understanding or *Verstehen* as it figured in Weber's methodological and empirical writings. He understood that a theory of meaningful social action requires a method of *Verstehen* as its empirical complement. However, he did not perceive the procedures by which historical knowledge is developed to be closely related to theoretical issues in sociology and did not seek himself to advance the methodology of *Verstehen*. He also distanced himself from the German historicists who provided the chief background to Weber's writings on *Verstehen* in a mistaken belief that they had generally insisted on the need for different categories and procedures of understanding for each historical epoch, thereby undermining all grounds for comparative analysis and generalization. On this basis, he failed to build on such contributions as Dilthey's and Simmel's writings on interpretation and historical knowledge. A result is that Parsons tended to invoke knowledge of historical figures without carefully evaluating the formal procedures by which historians had synthesized knowledge of them.

In the 1980s, Parsons's *corpus* received major scholarly evaluations by Jürgen Habermas and Jeffrey Alexander. Habermas (1987) portrayed Parsons's work as the one theoretical system of recent sociology that constitutes essential background to any future general theory. His critical assessment focuses on aspects of the theory of action that are directly relevant to his own theory of communicative action. Of particular interest to Habermas are, first, the conception of social action as a situated process engaging particular actors and, second, the formal system theory. The crux of Habermas's argument is that, contrary to Parsons's claim, these two perspectives were not adequately integrated. Habermas maintains that the two are in fact independent frames of reference, and he appears to argue that in principle the two cannot be authentically integrated. He reviews elements of both formulations in considerable and technical detail, but concentrates on the conception of social action and its relations to his own theory of communicative action. The system theory, especially its four function version, appears of less value to Habermas, a judgment likely related to his longstanding rejection of German system theory. The present author finds it unfortunate that Habermas focused so much of a frequently penetrating and insightful discussion on one sweeping, and largely forced, conclusion.

Alexander (1983) presents Parsons's work as a culmination of the classical tradition and the pre-eminent contribution since Durkheim and Weber. Alexander provides the most comprehensive and detailed review of Parsons's formulations available in one publication, and thus his study is an indispensable source. He follows the evolution of Parsons's thought through its early, middle, and late stages, and outlines the major late-stage formulations, including the four function paradigm, the double interchanges, and the symbolic media. His discussion focuses particularly on inconsistencies among different presentations of the late system theory and often alleges confusion when the actuality is that Parsons revised or supplemented formulations. He rejects the use of the four function interchange models for systems of action other than social systems, although he does not fully explicate the grounds for doing so. As an overall criticism, he alleges that Parsons's basic formulations overemphasize ideal factors in social organization and underemphasize material factors. This point can be conceded for many – but hardly all – of Parsons's empirical writings, but Alexander does not demonstrate that the criticism applies to the basic frame of reference or chief theoretical propositions. More recently, Alexander has led a "neofunctionalist" movement that strives to build upon the basic thrust of Parsons's functionalism without becoming entangled in its complicated formulations.

Parsons's Intellectual Legacy

In May 1979, Parsons traveled to Heidelberg for a celebration of the fiftieth anniversary of his doctoral degree. The occasion was a success. He enjoyed the papers presented by a distinguished group of German scholars and his own talk was well received. He and his wife Helen then went to Munich. In an active day at the university, he made two presentations, one a seminar talk and the other a public lecture, both of which were again well received. That evening, he suffered a massive stroke and was suddenly dead. To have died after a day on which he had lectured twice and engaged students and colleagues in the excitement of recent ideas was a fitting end for the 76-year-old sociologist.

Parsons's legacy can be summarized at three levels. At a first level, his methodology of seeking a scientific revolution by concentrating on the essential ideas of a frame of reference is his most important contribution. His commitment to critical study of frames of reference was complemented by a dedication to establishing technical standards for the evaluation of theoretical work. Despite the volumes that have been written about Parsons's intellectual biases, the chief characteristic of his thought is actually a determination to follow logic and evidence wherever they may lead in refining sociological concepts, ideological attachments and previous theoretical formulations aside. The frequency with which new research persuaded him to overturn previous ideas is a clear index of his attachment to reason. The intensity of Parsons's commitment to fundamental theoretical issues provides a weighty model for future sociologists, particularly in the USA, where empiricist styles of scientific work predominate. The model is all the more powerful because it strikes out against the cultural grain and, in America, will be followed by only a handful of sociologists in any generation. Parsons himself realized that his personal commitment to theoretical work was built on unusual speculative abilities, a dispassionate (affectively neutral) manner of critiquing and evaluating ideas, and the patience to examine and re-examine ideas over years and decades. He understood that only a few could work creatively in this manner.

At a second level, Parsons's legacy consists of major concepts and themes that appear to be enduring contributions: the action frame of reference, the limits of economic theory, normative order and social control, the concept of social system, the idea of functional analysis, the conception of social institutions, the institutional integration of motivation, the professional role relationship, and the basic notion of generalized symbolic media of interchange. These are all fundamental ideas that social scientists today and for the foreseeable future can adopt and modify for their own studies. Many of these ideas are so fundamental to sociological analysis that it is hard to conceive of a sociology that does not make routine use of them. It is also hard to envision a future sociology that will not be strengthened by study of Parsons's writings to learn how he used these ideas and what insights he brought out of them.

At a third level is the Parsonian theory of action as a formally integrated theoretical system. Here we are in the domain of the formal action frame of reference; system theory; the four function paradigm; the primary subsystems of society and their constituent sectors; the symbolic media, double interchanges, and the interchange categories; and the analysis of social institutions as structural elements of society. This theory was projected in bold and methodical terms, albeit with lacunae, oversights, conflicting formulations, and simple mistakes. Despite the many gaps in its presentation, it is a uniquely powerful theory. No other theorist has had Parsons's level of commitment to developing a technically refined theory. No figure since Weber and Durkheim has had his courage to exploit fundamental sociological insights so thoroughly and boldly. The result is that the theory of social action, despite its lacunae, partial formulations, and errors, presents uniquely rich opportunities for scholars who will address its difficulties and undertake its further development.

Bibliography

Writings of Talcott Parsons

The Structure of Social Action. 1937. New York: McGraw-Hill.
Essays in Sociological Theory: Pure and Applied. 1949. Glencoe, IL: Free Press.
The Social System. 1951. Glencoe, IL: Free Press.
Essays in Sociological Theory, revised edition. 1953. Glencoe, IL: Free Press.
Social Structure and Personality. 1964. New York: Free Press.
Societies: Evolutionary and Comparative Perspectives. 1966. Englewood Cliffs, NJ: Prentice Hall.
Sociological Theory and Modern Society. 1967. New York: Free Press.

Politics and Social Structure. 1969. New York: Free Press.

Some Problems of General Theory in Sociology. 1970. In J. C. McKinney and E. A. Tiryakian (eds), *Theoretical Sociology: Perspectives and Developments*. New York: Appleton-Century-Crofts.

The System of Modern Societies. 1971. Englewood Cliffs, NJ: Prentice Hall.

Social Systems and the Evolution of Action Theory. 1977. New York: Free Press.

Action Theory and the Human Condition. 1978. New York: Free Press.

The Marshall Lectures (edited by R. Swedberg). 1986. Uppsala: Research Reports from the Department of Sociology, Uppsala University.

The Early Essays (edited by C. Camic). 1991. Chicago: University of Chicago Press.

Family, Socialization and Interaction Process (with R. F. Bales). 1955. Glencoe, IL: Free Press.

Working Papers in the Theory of Action (with R. F. Bales and E. A. Shils). 1953. Glencoe, IL: Free Press.

The American University (with G. M. Platt). 1973. Cambridge, MA: Harvard University Press.

Toward a General Theory of Action (edited with E. A. Shils). 1951. Cambridge, MA: Harvard University Press.

Economy and Society (with N. J. Smelser). 1956. Glencoe, IL: Free Press.

The Protestant Ethic and the Spirit of Capitalism, by Max Weber, translated by Talcott Parsons from the original German of 1903–4. 1930. New York: Scribner's.

Further reading

Alexander, J. C. (1983) *Theoretical Logic in Sociology. Volume 4, The Modern Reconstruction of Classical Thought: Talcott Parsons*. Berkeley, CA: University of California Press.

Bales, R. F. (1950) *Interaction Process Analysis: a Method for the Study of Small Groups*. Cambridge, MA: Addison-Wesley.

Bellah, R. N. (1957) *Tokugawa Religion*. Glencoe, IL: Free Press.

Bendix, R. and Roth, G. (1971) *Scholarship and Partisanship; Essays on Max Weber*. Berkeley, CA: University of California Press.

Bershady, H. J. (1973) *Ideology and Social Knowledge*. Oxford: Basil Blackwell.

Bourricaud, F. (1981) *The Sociology of Talcott Parsons*. Chicago: University of Chicago Press (original French edition 1977).

Buxton, W. (1985) *Talcott Parsons and the Capitalist Nation-state*. Toronto: University of Toronto Press.

Coser, L. A. (1956) *The Functions of Social Conflict*. Glencoe, IL: Free Press.

Dahrendorf, R. (1959) *Class and Class Conflict in Industrial Society*. Stanford, CA: Stanford University Press.

Eisenstadt, S. N. (1963) *The Political Systems of Empires*. New York: Free Press.

Fox, R. (1997) Talcott Parsons, My Teacher. *The American Scholar*, 66, 395–410.

Garfinkel, H. (1967) *Studies in Ethnomethodology*. Englewood Cliffs, NJ: Prentice-Hall.

Gerhardt, U. (ed.) (1993) *Talcott Parsons on National Socialism*. New York: Aldine DeGruyter.

Gould, M. (1987) *Revolution in the Development of Capitalism: the Coming of the English Revolution*. Berkeley: University of California Press.

Gouldner, A. W. (1970) *The Coming Crisis of Western Sociology*. New York: Basic Books.

Grathoff, R. (1978) *The Theory of Social Action: the Correspondence of Alfred Schutz and Talcott Parsons*. Bloomington: University of Indiana Press.

Habermas, J. (1987) *The Theory of Communicative Action. Volume 2, Lifeworld and System: a Critique of Functionalist Reason*. Boston: Beacon Press (originally published in German, 1981).

Johnson, M. M. (1988) *Strong Mothers, Weak Wives: the Search for Gender Equality*. Berkeley: University of California Press.

Klausner, S. Z. and Lidz, V. (1986) *The Nationalization of the Social Sciences*. Philadelphia: University of Pennsylvania Press.

Lidz, V. (2001) Language and the "Family" of Generalized Symbolic Media. In A. J. Trevino (ed.) *Talcott Parsons Today: his Theory and Legacy in Contemporary Sociology*. Lenham, MD: Rowman and Littlefield.

Lidz, V. a;nd Bershady, H. J. (2000) Convergence on Method in Theory Construction. *Oesterreichische Zeitschrift für Soziologie*, special issue, 45–106.

Lidz, C. W. and Lidz, V. (1976) Piaget's Psychology of Intelligence and the Theory of Action. In J. Loubser, R. C. Baum, A. Effrat, and V. Lidz (eds), *Explorations in General Theory in Social Science*, 2 volumes. New York: Free Press, pp. 195–239.

Nichols, L. T. (1998) Social Relations Undone: Disciplinary Divergence and Departmental Politics at Harvard 1946–1970. *The American Sociologist*, 29, 83–107.

Smelser, N. J. (1959) *Social Change in the Industrial Revolution*. Chicago: University of Chicago Press.

Whitehead, A. N. (1925) *Science and the Modern World*. New York: Macmillan.

Wiener, N. (1948) *Cybernetics: Or Control and Communication in the Animal and the Machine*. New York: Wiley.

Index